Professional Chef

Level 3 S/NVQ

   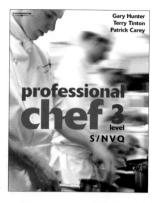

GARY HUNTER, TERRY TINTON,
and PATRICK CAREY

Professional Chef

Level 3 S/NVQ

DELMAR
CENGAGE Learning

Australia • Brazil • Japan • Korea • Mexico • Singapore • Spain • United Kingdom • United States

DELMAR
CENGAGE Learning

Professional Chef: Level 3 S/NVQ
Gary Hunter, Terry Tinton, and Patrick Carey

Publishing Director: John Yates

Publisher: Melody Daves

Development Editor: Lizzie Catford

Content Project Editor: Lucy Mills

Manufacturing Manager: Helen Mason

Production Controller: Maeve Healy

Marketing Manager: Jason Bennett

Typesetter: Book Now Ltd, London, UK

Cover design: hctcreative

Text design: Design Deluxe Ltd, Bath, UK

For product information and technology assistance,
contact **emea.info@cengage.com**.

For permission to use material from this text or product,
and for permission queries, email **clsuk.permissions@cengage.com**

British Library Cataloguing-in-Publication Data
A catalogue record for this book is available from the British Library.

ISBN: 978-1-84480-531-0

Cengage Learning EMEA
High Holborn House, 50-51 Bedford Row
London WC1R 4LR

Cengage Learning products are represented in Canada by Nelson Education Ltd.

For your lifelong learning solutions, visit
www.cengage.co.uk
and **www.delmar.cengage.com**

Printed by C&C Offset, China
2 3 4 5 6 7 8 9 10 – 10 09 08

Brief contents

CONTENTS

About the authors

GARY HUNTER

Head of Culinary Arts at Westminster Kingsway College, Gary has 14 years' experience of teaching within further, higher and vocational education and has been awarded the City & Guilds Medal for Excellence in recognition of his exceptional work and personal dedication to delivering a continuing high standard of education and training to students and trainees for the catering industry. He has travelled the world as a consultant for Barry Callebaut giving seminars on chocolate and cuisine. He is also an experienced international culinary competition judge. As a leading Chef Patissier in the UK, he has won numerous awards and competition medals and has worked with and trained many of today's successful chefs. Gary has recently helped to write the diploma in professional cookery qualification at levels 1, 2 and 3.

TERRY TINTON

A Chef Lecturer and Professional Chef Diploma Course Coordinator in Culinary Arts at Westminster Kingsway College, Terry is a strong and confident chef with many awards spanning a hugely successful career. He has held a senior chef position at the House of Commons and worked extensively across Switzerland and Germany. He holds the Advanced Hygiene Award and is the driving force for developing first-year students at the college.

PATRICK CAREY

Senior Lecturer at Westminster Kingsway College, Patrick is a qualified lecturer with 12 years' experience in vocational education. An exceptionally experienced international chef with a vast knowledge of classical and present day cookery techniques. He was the winner of the Senior Toque d'Or Competition, gaining distinctions across the board in the 706/3 examination.

Acknowledgements

Personal Acknowledgements

Sarah-Jane Hunter
Phillip Hunter

Charlotte Hunter
Paul Hunter

Estelle Hunter
Patricia Long

Hilary Hunter
John Long

Margaret Tinton
Yvonne Hall
Rosaleen Lane

Lewis Tinton
Terence Tinton
Andy Tinton

Sharon Carey
Kate Tinton
Paul Lane

Aoife Carey
Liam Lane

Neil Rippington, the author of the Level 1 book in this series, for all his contributions throughout the project
Richard Hughes

College Acknowledgements

Andy Wilson
Jose Souto
Chris Loder
Terry Shoesmith

Geoff Booth
Simon Stocker
Barry Jones
Clare Mannall

Ian Wild
Bob Brown
Alexandra Roberts

Allan Drummond
Javier Mercado
Vince Cottam

Students

Kyle Mcgrady
Luke Fouracre
Robert Hall
Kirstie McIntyre

Tony Hayes
Maxium Shearer
Robert Boer
Leon Coultress

Heather Gil-Abillera
Lucien Bintcliffe
Luca Boccia
Selin Kiazin

Samantha Doorgachurn
Andrew Giles
Luke Monaghan
Ben Arnold

Reviewers

Anita Tull, Kensington
and Chelsea College

Tony Taylor of Bournemouth
and Poole College

Iain Baillie of South Downs College

Sponsors

Russums Catering
Suppliers

Furi Knives

Barry Callebaut
Chocolate

Steelite Catering Crockery

Chef Contributors

Gordon Ramsay
Angela Hartnett
Paul Gayler
Beverley Dunkley

Shane Osborn
David Cavalier
Thierry Dumouchel
Javier Mercado

Martyn Nail
Mark Askew
William Curley
Nick Patterson

Paul Rankin
Andre Garrett
Tony Hoyle

Photography and Resources

William 'Bill' Hull, Professional Photography

Billingsgate Fish Market
Westminster Kingsway
College
Susie Mitchell,
photographer

Smithfield's Meat Market
Barchester Healthcare
Think Vegetables
Seafish, the Sea Fish
Industry Authority

New Covent Garden
Russums
Eureka

Compass UK
Electrolux
The Ritz Hotel

Quality Meat Scotland (QMS) represents the Scottish red meat industry and promotes Scotch Beef, Scotch Lamb and Specially Selected Pork to a national and international audience. Our activities range from helping the industry improve their methods of production and quality of products to increasing customer awareness and preference for Scotch product. QMS also helps in the development of new markets in the UK and around the world. For additional information: www.qmsscotland.co.uk and www.chefsguidetoscotchbeef.org.

Foreword

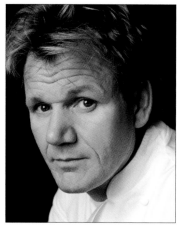

As a friend of Westminster Kingsway College I have been fortunate to have benefited from the enormous experience of the UK's first and most prestigious professional chef school by receiving some of their graduates into my restaurants. It is with genuine excitement that I write this foreword for this modern, progressive, culinary book written by Gary Hunter and his dedicated team from the College.

As we prepare our students, trainees and apprentices for the rigours of being a chef, we use many tools to ensure a quality educational and training experience. These tools are similar to the instruments of a great rock band or classic orchestra, working together to create exceptional music. One of the most important instruments is this *Professional Chef* book. It provides you with the essential elements, expertise and knowledge of this wonderful vocation and contains the collective wisdom of talented professional chefs dedicated to the world of gastronomy.

When you become a chef of a restaurant or even run your own business as I have, I ask that you absorb its contents, analyse its information, and learn from the chefs who have given their time and support for this book and practice its concise instructions.

With the up-to-date knowledge and fundamental skills learned from this book you will gain a strong foundation to form the basis to become a capable and endowed chef. I am sure that every college will be using this book as the new standard in catering education.

Gordon Ramsay

A quick reference guide to the qualification

NVQ/SVQs (National/Scottish Vocational Qualifications) are recognised nationally and follow a common structure and design across all vocational subjects. To be awarded an NVQ/SVQ demonstrates that you have the competence (having sufficient skill and knowledge) to perform a job at a certain level. *Assessment* will take place once you and your assessor consider you to be competent.

Each NVQ/SVQ is divided into *units*. The unit relates to a specific task or skill area of work. The *elements* that make up a unit describe in detail the *skill and knowledge* components of the unit. To pass a particular unit you will need to accomplish various tasks.

- What you must do – gives information on the actions to be undertaken to pass each element within a unit.
- What you must cover – gives a range of situations, recipes, commodities and tasks for you to cover.
- What you must know – this is the underpinning knowledge or theory section that proves you understand the subject covered in the element.
- Evidence requirement – this addresses how much you need to cover by assessment using observation and alternative methods of assessment.

To achieve an NVQ/SVQ there will be a set of specific tasks and processes to go through.

1   At the commencement of any programme of study you should receive an *induction* which will give you a detailed explanation of the qualification and the support that is available for you to use.

2   An *initial assessment* should be undertaken to assess your current degree of understanding and skills level for the qualification and to set out an action plan of the particular units you will undertake to complete the NVQ/SVQ. This assessment system will also identify specific areas of training and teaching that you will require.

3   Your competence and ability to carry out a task will be *assessed* by your assessor when both you and they consider you to be ready. Your assessor will regularly observe the tasks that you are carrying out, the outcomes of which will be recorded into your *portfolio of evidence*.

4   Your understanding and the background knowledge of the unit subject is also measured through questions asked by your assessor. The questions are usually required to be answered in a written format or verbally and then recorded in your portfolio of evidence. This is known as *underpinning knowledge*. The activities and theory covered in this book will provide you with plenty of examples, knowledge and practice to help with these.

5   The portfolio of evidence will be eventually completed by you and your assessor. It is designed to help you demonstrate your competence at a particular level. At this stage and usually during the process of training and assessment an *internal verifier* will check the consistency of the assessor's work.

6   Finally, the *awarding body* (the body responsible for checking the qualification and awarding you the certificate) will appoint an *external moderator* to carry out final checks before certification.

This book will cover the expanse of knowledge and complex skills necessary to meet the qualification requirements at NVQ/SVQ Level 3. Moreover it will give you the opportunity to enhance your knowledge of the industry with modern up-to-date techniques alongside classical skills that are the fundamentals of a good chef.

The Performance Criteria

What You Must Do

The performance criteria of an NVQ/SVQ will list the required actions that you must achieve to complete the task in a competent manner. This means demonstrating the practical skill in an adequate, professional and safe way to your assessor. In all NVQ/SVQ portfolios this is now stated in the form of 'what you must do'.

As an example, the 'what you must do' criteria for unit *3FP1 Prepare fish for complex dishes* states that to achieve the national standard the candidate must:

1 Select the type and quantity of fish needed for the dish.

2 Check the fish to make sure it meets quality standards.

3 Select and use the tools and equipment correctly.

4 Prepare the fish to maintain its quality and meet the requirements of the dish.

5 Safely store any prepared fish not for immediate use.

All of these criteria must be adequately assessed against the next stage, called 'what you must cover'.

What You Must Cover

This next section clearly states exactly what skills should be covered on a range of different types of fish using a variety of different cooking techniques. As an example, the 3FP1 unit covers the following:

1 Fish
   a. White fish – round
   b. White fish – flat
   c. Oily fish
   d. Exotic fish

2 Prepare by
   a. Gutting
   b. Filleting
   c. Cutting:
      i.   Darne
      ii. Goujons

iii. Plait

iv. Paupiette

v. Suprême

vi. Tronçon

d. trimming

e. skinning

f. marinading

g. portioning

h. cold smoking

i. coating

j. topping

k. covering

It is important to understand that all fish types and preparation techniques have to be assessed in order to pass the element. The NVQ/SVQ portfolio will normally state the minimum requirements needed to pass the unit through observation of the physical task and how the rest of the assessments can be covered, usually by professional witness statements or questioning.

What You Must Know

Further assessment of a candidate's knowledge and understanding of the skills relating to the unit may be assessed through theoretical tasks such as questions or assignments. This stage is known as the 'what you must know' section. Any questioning should be performed under certain conditions that have been set by the Sector Skills Council (People 1st). It must be:

■ in an environment where the candidate feels comfortable to take the assessment,

■ supervised to ensure the assessment is authentic,

■ conducted in line with the appropriate Awarding Body guidelines.

Assignments can also be used under the assessment strategy. The strategy allows centres to use materials that have been developed, and the use of assignments is an option within this.

A centre wishing to use an assignment will need to get the Awarding Body's approval before using the assignment. Assignments will also need to be administered within controlled conditions by the centre or college.

Introduction

The purpose of this book is to direct and introduce you to the techniques and advanced knowledge necessary for you to develop into a master chef in the hospitality and catering industry.

By following instruction from an experienced professional mentor or tutor and committing yourself daily to attention to culinary detail with dexterity and discipline, you will begin to understand the dedication required to be a master chef.

During my time as a chef in this industry I have always striven to learn each day and to ask important questions, not only about the development of my skills and knowledge but also of myself and my gastronomic values. I have continuously been inspired by the many great chefs and individuals I have worked with. Some have become my mentors and invaluable resources for my own progression and search for culinary achievement.

Many books have also inspired me to learn and to challenge concepts in cookery. Some of these I still refer to for guidance and inspiration today. An inspirational book or a precise recipe is as valuable as your armoury of chef knives. And it is with this in mind that you should use this book; as an encouraging and instructional resource to place alongside your battery of knives, kitchen equipment and collected recipes.

This book features some of the top chefs in this country, whose talent, dedication and energy have helped them inspire many chefs today. They share their philosophies, recipes and experience for you to learn from. This will also provide you with an important reference point to attain the advanced professional skills and knowledge needed in today's modern and challenging world of cuisine.

Enjoy learning and enjoy cooking!

Gary Hunter

About the book

Mapped to the qualification
Each chapter addresses a specific unit of the Level 3 Professional Cookery S/NVQ qualification.

16
Breads and doughs

3FPC4 Prepare, cook and finish complex bread and dough products

LEARNING OBJECTIVES

The aim of this chapter is to enable you to develop skills and implement knowledge in the bakery principles of producing a range of complex breads and dough products. This will also include information on materials, ingredients and equipment.

At the end of this chapter you will be able to:

■ Identify the main methods of production for fermented dough products
■ Identify each type of complex fermented dough and finished bread product
■ Understand the use of enriching ingredients in bakery
■ State the quality points of various complex dough products
■ Prepare, bake and present each type of complex dough product
■ Identify the storage procedures of fermented dough products
■ Identify the correct tools and equipment used in the production of fermented dough products

Learning objectives at the start of each chapter explain the skills and knowledge you need to be proficient in and understand by the end of the chapter.

Preparation of a parfait

Sautéing onions and herbs

Combining minced meat with onions and beating together

Adding eggs and cream to the base mixture

Blending in a food processor to a course mixture

Seasoning the pâté mixture

Covering the mixture with streaky bacon and plastic film

Step-by-step sequences
illustrate each process and provide an easy-to-follow guide.

Assessment of knowledge and understanding

You have now learned about the health and safety responsibilities for everyone in the workplace. This will enable you to ensure your own actions reduce risks to health and safety.

To test your level of knowledge and understanding, answer the following short questions. These will help to prepare you for your summative (final) assessment.

Health and safety law

1 Discuss the various reasons why health and safety laws exist and the benefits that enforcing these provide.

2 Give three examples of implications of not conforming to health and safety laws.
i) _____ ii) _____
iii) _____

3 State who the Health and Safety at Work Act 1974 covers and why is it in place.

4 Explain why it is important to keep yourself up to date with current health and safety legislation.

Assessment of knowledge and understanding
at the end of each chapter contains questions, so you can test your learning.

PURCHASING SPECIFICATION

■ Cauliflowers should have tight and firm flower heads that are white in colour.
■ Other brassicas should also have tight heads and bright colouring.
■ They should not feel limp and the stems should be strong.

Purchasing Specifications
provide helpful advice for buying commodities.

Recipes Modern and traditional recipes for each commodity.

CHEF'S PROFILE

Name: ANGELA HARTNETT

Position: Chef Patron at Angela Hartnett at the Connaught

Establishment: The Connaught Hotel

Current job role and main responsibilities: I oversee all the food and beverage operations at the hotel:
- breakfast
- afternoon tea
- room service
- restaurant (one Michelin star).
Currently employ 110 staff.

When did you realise that you wanted to pursue a career in the catering and hospitality industry?
I always wanted to run my own restaurant from an early age. My grandparents owed a fish and chip shop.

Experience:
1 Midsummer House, Cambridge
2 Gordon Ramsay, Aubergine
3 Marcus Wareing, Petrus
4 Gordon Ramsay Holdings

What do you find rewarding about your job?
I love teaching young cooks and get pleasure from seeing the customers when they have enjoyed dining with us.

What do you find the most challenging about the job?
Finding good staff and retaining them.

What advice would you give to students just beginning their career?
Choose a path you enjoy and are passionate about.

Who is your mentor or main inspiration?
My family and their love of food. Also Gordon Ramsay and Nadia Santini.

What traits do you consider essential for anyone entering a career as a chef?
- Understanding the source of your produce
- People management skills
- Common sense
- Organisation

A brief personal profile:
- Chef de Partie, Aubergine
- Sous Chef, Petrus Restaurant
- Executive Chef, Hilton Creek Dubai
- Chef Patron, Connaught Hotel
- Won Hotel Restaurant of the Year
- Won BMW Newcomer of the Year

Can you give one essential kitchen tip or technique that you use as a chef?
Taste everything.

Ricotta and wild sorrel tortellini with a pistachio pesto and garlic foam

INGREDIENTS	10 PORTIONS	4 PORTIONS
Plain pasta dough	1kg	400g
Ricotta cheese	500g	200g
Pistachio nuts	125g	50g
Parmesan cheese	125g	50g
Olive oil	175ml	70ml
Basil leaves	½ bunch	¼ bunch
Wild sorrel	175g	70g
Garlic	10 cloves	4 cloves
Fresh full fat milk	125ml	50ml
Good-quality salt and white pepper	To taste	To taste

Method of work
1 Mix the ricotta with the chopped blanched sorrel leaves, season well.
2 Roll out the pasta into thin sheets and cut out into circles approximately 5cm in diameter.
3 Brush the pasta circles with water and spoon the ricotta into the middle.
4 Fold the pasta over and pinch the points together (see making tortellini, page 170).
5 Make the pesto using half the oil, lightly toasted pistachios, basil and Parmesan by placing all the ingredients in a liquidiser and pulsing until almost smooth (the consistency should be slightly thicker than a sauce).
6 Blanch the garlic in boiling water for 2 minutes, place the garlic into the milk and bring to the boil; remove the pan from the heat and liquidise.
7 Blanch the pasta in boiling salted water, drain and mix in a bowl with the pesto.
8 Pulse the garlic mixture until a foam appears, spoon over the tortellini and serve.

 **CHEF'S TIP**

When rolling and storing pasta, use semolina and not flour to prevent it sticking together; this will ensure the strands or sheets are separate and prevent the cooking liquid becoming cloudy and thick with gluten.

Chef's Profiles provide advice from leading industry figures and an insight into what motivated them during their training.

Health and safety boxes draw your attention to important health and safety information.

HEALTH & SAFETY

Fire exit doors must be clearly marked, remain unlocked during working hours and be free from obstruction. Fire extinguishers should be available and ready for use in every kitchen.

Scrambled eggs

INGREDIENTS	4 PORTIONS	10 PORTIONS
Medium eggs	4–8	10–20
Butter	80g	200g
Cream	40–80ml	100–200ml
Good-quality salt and pepper	To taste	To taste

Method of work
1 Melt the butter in a thick-bottomed sauté pan.
2 Beat the eggs in a basin and season.
3 Add to the pan and cook very gently.
4 When they begin to set, add the cream, remove from the heat and continue to stir until lightly set (baveuse).
5 Serve immediately.

 HEALTH & SAFETY

Use unsalted butter and low sodium salt.

 VIDEO CLIP
Scrambling eggs

Video Clip If your college adopts the virtual kitchen at this level (www.virtualkitchen/level3.co.uk) you will be able to view a video demonstration online.

 CHEF'S TIP

Experiment using other marinades, such as tikka or garlic and chilli. Pigeon is a strongly flavoured bird and this will come through even when other strong flavours are used.

QUALITY POINTS

- Cock birds have a tendency to be drier and tougher than hens
- Bronze birds can have residual dark feather stubs; these can be removed with duck tweezers
- The flesh should be dry to the touch and without excess blemishes
- If the windpipe is still intact, it should be pliable and not rigid
- The breast should be plump in intensively reared birds and slightly leaner in the rarer organic varieties

Quality Points provide information to help you assess the freshness of products.

Chef's tip boxes share the authors' experiences of the catering industry, with helpful suggestions for how you can improve your skills.

1

Maintain the health, hygiene, safety and security of the working environment

LEARNING OBJECTIVES

The aim of this chapter is to enable you to acquire expertise and put into practice in the workplace, a knowledge of the health and hygiene practices. It discusses the health and hygiene requirements and policies that you will need to know about if you are to work safely and hygienically in the kitchen. This will also include information on the resources at the disposal of the chef to implement regulations to prepare, cook and hold food safely.

At the end of this chapter you will be able to:

■ Identify and understand prevailing legal requirements of health and safety

■ Understand and appreciate the importance of personal responsibility in the workplace

■ Carry out an effective and efficient risk assessment process

■ Identify the correct attire for the chef in the workplace

■ Be aware of your responsibility for personal cleanliness during food preparation and cooking in the workplace and unsafe behaviour

1

HEALTH & SAFETY

Always take time to familiarise yourself with your company's health and safety procedures. This may seem like a time-consuming process, but it is not only for the benefit the employer. It will also hopefully ensure that you are able to prevent yourself and others from encountering health and safety issues within the workplace.

HEALTH & SAFETY

It is advisable to regularly check the Internet, especially government websites, for health and safety updates or amendments, and to make your employer aware if you believe these are not being adhered to. Employees can be just as liable for negligence as employers.

Health and safety should be discussed with all employees upon appointment and further detailed in any contract of employment. The contract could give full details of procedures, advise of any staff handbook that may be available or give contact details of a relevant manager to contact for further health and safety information.

It is the responsibility of an employer to ensure that all new staff are fully trained in health and safety. The employer must also maintain ongoing training for existing members of staff so that everyone is up to date with procedures and understands the correct operation and maintenance of equipment and the emergency plan to follow, in line with current legislation.

Given the enhanced vulnerability of those who work within a kitchen, there are four main areas that require particular attention when assessing health and safety:

- The safe and hygienic handling, storage and usage of food
- The personal hygiene, cleanliness and appearance of employees
- The provision of safe premises and the correct training for safe use and storage of equipment
- The correct labelling, notification, training, handling and storage of hazardous substances

LEGAL REQUIREMENTS FOR HEALTH AND SAFETY AT WORK

Many new health and safety regulations have been implemented over the years, and existing legislation is regularly updated to cater for ever expanding technology, changing working methods and increased numbers of employees within the workplace.

The main pieces of legislation that need to be addressed, implemented and adhered to by an employer in an establishment, by law, are laid out in the following sections.

The Health and Safety at Work Act 1974

This Act is in place to cover employees, employers, the self-employed, customers and visitors. It lays down the minimum standards of health, safety and welfare required within each area of the workplace. As with all health and safety provisions, it is an employer's legal responsibility to ensure that the Act is fully implemented and that as far as reasonably practicable the health and safety of all those they are responsible for is correctly managed.

The Health and Safety Information for Employees Regulations 1989

Current regulations require that an employer must provide employees with health and safety information in the form of notices, leaflets and posters, all of which are available through the Health and Safety Executive (HSE). Where an employer has more than five employees, a written health and safety policy must be in place for the establishment. This should be issued to every employee, clearly outlining their personal health and safety responsibilities to the employer, to other staff and to customers, visitors and the public.

The Workplace (Health, Safety and Welfare) Regulations 1992

The key message within these regulations is to ensure that those working in the hospitality and catering industries maintain a safe and healthy working environment. The regulations set out the legal requirements for those in a working environment, such as indoor temperature, lighting, ventilation and staff facilities.

The Food Hygiene (England) Regulations 2006

These regulations provide the framework for the enforcement of EU legislation in England. There are similar regulations in Wales, Scotland and Northern Ireland. The Food Safety (General Food Hygiene) Regulations 1995 and the Food Safety (Temperature Control) Regulations 1995 no longer apply. Many of the requirements of these regulations are included in new EU legislation, so what businesses need to do from day to day has not changed very much. The main new requirement is to have 'food safety management procedures' and to keep up-to-date records of these.

The Manual Handling Operations Regulations 1992

These regulations provide employers and employees with guidelines on how to protect oneself when lifting heavy objects. A risk assessment must be carried out for all activities that involve manual lifting, and employees must be trained how to correctly handle heavy items and, if applicable, how to use any equipment for this purpose.

The Control of Substances Hazardous to Health (COSHH) Regulations 1999

The COSHH regulations were put in place to ensure the correct storage, handling, use and disposal of hazardous substances and are relevant to everyday working practices.

HEALTH & SAFETY

- First aid should only be given by a qualified first-aider.
- A first aid certificate is only valid for three years. After this period, it must be renewed with additional first aid training.
- Know what action you can take within your responsibility in the event of an accident occurring.
- An accident report book should be available to record details of any incident that has occurred.

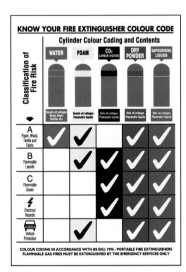

Most hazardous substances are identified through the use of specific symbols, which should be clearly shown and recognisable on items.

COSHH regulations were recently consolidated (2002) and employers are now held responsible for assessing the risks from hazardous substances and for controlling exposure to them to prevent ill health. Any hazardous substances identified should be formally recorded in writing and given a risk rating. Safety precaution procedures should then be implemented and training given to employees to ensure that the procedures are understood and will be followed correctly.

The Electricity at Work Regulations 1989

These regulations are very important for kitchens. The frequent use of electrical equipment means that electrical items will be prone to maintenance issues and will therefore require regular checking. The regulations state that every item of electrical equipment within the workplace must be tested every twelve months by a qualified electrician.

In addition, a trained member of staff should regularly check all electrical equipment for safety. It is recommended that this is carried out at least every three months, but most employers undertake this annually.

The Fire Precautions Act 1971

This Act states that all staff must be aware of and trained in fire and emergency evacuation procedures for their workplace.

The emergency exit route must be the easiest route by which all staff, customers and visitors can leave the building safely. Fire action plans showing the emergency exit route should be prominently displayed throughout the premises.

Where there are more than twenty employees, it is a compulsory requirement of the Act that a fire certificate is obtained. This further applies where there are ten or more employees on different floors at any one time.

The Fire Precautions (Workplace) Regulations 1997

These require that every employer must carry out a risk assessment for their premises under the Management of Health and Safety Regulations.

- Any obstacles that may hinder fire evacuation should be identified as a hazard and dealt with.
- Suitable fire detection equipment should be in place.
- All escape routes should be clearly marked and free from obstacles.
- Fire alarm systems should be tested on a weekly basis to ensure they are in full operational condition.

HEALTH & SAFETY

Fire exit doors must be clearly marked, remain unlocked during working hours and be free from obstruction. Fire extinguishers should be available and ready for use in every kitchen.

HEALTH & SAFETY

BCF (vaporising liquid) fire extinguishers emit vapours that starve fires of oxygen. They are dangerous when used in confined spaces.

Reporting of Injuries, Diseases and Dangerous Occurrences Regulations (RIDDOR) 1995

All injuries must be reported to the member of staff responsible for health and safety: this includes injuries involving guests, visitors and staff. The kitchen accident report book must be completed with basic personal details of the person or persons involved, together with a detailed description of the incident. Each accident report book should comply with the Data Protection Act 2003. An injury may lead to legal consequences, therefore all witnesses must provide a clear and accurate statement of events.

RIDDOR's key message is that you must report any:

■ Fatal accidents

■ Work-related diseases

■ Major injuries sustained while at work

■ Potentially dangerous event that takes place at work

■ Accidents causing more than three days' absence from work.

The Government regularly reviews, updates and implements new health and safety legislation. It is therefore important to ensure that this is closely monitored so that any necessary changes can be made. Employers should be provided with regular updates as and when necessary. However, it is a good idea to monitor these personally to ensure that there is plenty of time to comply with any changes in legislation.

HEALTH & SAFETY

It is wise to have relevant inoculations, including those against tetanus and hepatitis, to protect against ill health.

HSE Inspectors and local authority Environmental Health Officers can carry out spot checks at premises at any time. Strict penalties can be imposed on anyone who does not comply with legal requirements. These officials can issue prohibition notices and improvement notices, and they have the power to prosecute and can seize, render harmless or destroy anything deemed to be of imminent danger.

In addition to ensuring that health and safety law and the legal guidelines are complied with, it must be remembered that if the working duties of staff change or the premises are adapted in any way – whether this be structurally or in terms of business methods – then additional health and safety procedures may have to be considered and implemented.

It is a legal requirement that all health and safety procedures in place must also be clearly set out in report form, in case it should be required by other parties, such as the employer, employee or an enforcement officer. This report will contain a risk assessment, the procedures in place to minimise, reduce or abolish any risks, the procedures for making all persons aware of the policy and the procedures for recording information, such as any accidents that may occur.

HEALTH & SAFETY

Wash your hands with a liquid gel from a sealed dispenser. Soap should be discouraged because bar soap can accumulate germs when passed from hand to hand. Disposable paper towels or warm-air hand dryers should be used.

HEALTH & SAFETY

Cuts and abrasions on hands should be covered with a clean, waterproof, blue-coloured dressing to minimise the risk of secondary infection. Disposable gloves may be worn for additional protection.

HEALTH & SAFETY

Always ensure that the accident report book is in an accessible place for everyone to use and that everybody is trained in the documentation of accidents. It is important that the report book is monitored for regular occurrences.

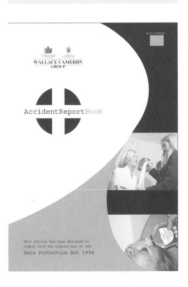

An accident report book

YOUR RESPONSIBILITY IN THE WORKPLACE

Although employers have a legal obligation to ensure health, safety and security within the workplace, employees, colleagues and other persons are also responsible for taking these issues in hand.

You should ensure that you are aware of all health, safety, hygiene and security procedures and regulations that are in place and abide by these as far as possible at all times, being clear as to what applies to your area of work. Further, it is helpful to monitor colleagues within your own particular area of work to ensure continuity. You should also make sure you know who is responsible for health and safety within the company so that you may direct any questions or concerns or report any incidents to them.

If you are aware of any member of staff who is not working in accordance with relevant procedures, your employer or line manager should be notified immediately. If your employer is in breach of procedures, you should notify the HSE or an Environmental Health Officer as soon as possible. When other people break health and safety law, it is not just you that is put at risk but also work colleagues and possibly the public and visitors.

Any personal responsibility for health and safety within your area will usually mean that you are responsible for the health and safety of others within this area. As well as monitoring staff to ensure that all procedures are being adhered to, regular checks should be carried out, for example on equipment, to minimise any safety hazards.

Any health, safety, hygiene or security issue, such as a burnt hand or a case of food poisoning, must be reported immediately to the line manager or other designated member of staff. The issue must be recorded appropriately, stating the following:

- Date and time of incident
- Name of person(s) involved
- What happened
- Where it happened
- Who else was present
- Why it is believed to have happened
- Any remedial action that is required.

Professional chefs and all food preparation employees must be conscientious concerning health and hygiene matters in every aspect of their job role and set tasks. An unbearable sight is that of a chef with a dirty uniform and no hat, standing outside the back door of a restaurant, smoking. Not only does it give the public a poor opinion of a noble profession, it is also illegal and could lead to sanction from the local authority.

The chef must be particularly conscious of the need for hygiene because many commodities have to be handled and prepared for customers without any type of heat treatment. High standards of hygiene are essential to prevent food poisoning, food spoilage, loss of productivity or pest infestation, any of which could lead to criminal prosecution for malpractice.

Food hygiene covers more than just the sanitation of work areas; it includes all practices, precautions and legal responsibilities involved in the following:

■ Protecting food from risk of contamination

■ Preventing organisms from multiplying to an extent which would pose a health risk to customers and employees

■ Destroying any harmful bacteria in food by thorough heat treatment or other techniques.

PERSONAL HYGIENE

Good hygiene systems must be followed by all food handlers. Regular hand washing is a requirement of the chef, and in all aspects of a chefs' working day. The following procedure should be followed:

1 Use an approved hand washing detergent, which should be provided by the employer, preferably in liquid form and from a dispenser

2 Use hot water and an approved drying system

3 Apply an alcohol-based hand disinfectant for maximum disinfection.

Hand washing must be undertaken:

■ Before commencing work (to wash away general bacteria)

■ After using the toilet or contact with faeces

■ After breaks

■ Between touching raw food and cooked food

■ Before handling raw food

■ After disposing of waste

■ After cleaning the workspace

■ After any first aid or dressing changes

■ After touching face, nose, mouth or blowing your nose

■ Hand washing and sanitation should take place at every possible opportunity

Tasting food whilst cooking

Whilst it is good practice for a chef to constantly taste food during cooking, you must use a spoon that is washed between tastings. A disposable plastic spoon that is discarded after tasting is best practice. The practice of tasting

HEALTH & SAFETY

When handling or preparing food, blue plasters should be used so that they are easily identifiable when lost. These dressings can feature an internal metal strip that allows them to be detected by electromagnetic equipment and metal detectors in large food production units.

Two students fully dressed in chef's uniforms

HEALTH & SAFETY

Plastic disposable spoons should be used to taste food during preparation and cooking and then disposed of immediately. Use a new spoon for each tasting.

A chef tasting food with a plastic spoon

IMAGES COURTESY OF RUSSUMS.CO.UK

Hair tied back with a hairnet and hat

Chef with short hair and a chef hat

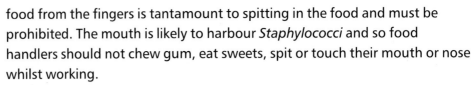

A skullcap

A chef hat

A chef jacket

Non-slip safety shoes

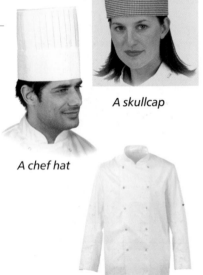

An apron

food from the fingers is tantamount to spitting in the food and must be prohibited. The mouth is likely to harbour *Staphylococci* and so food handlers should not chew gum, eat sweets, spit or touch their mouth or nose whilst working.

Hair

Hair should be washed regularly and kept covered. It should be tied up if shoulder length and placed inside a hairnet. To maintain food hygiene standards many types of hat are now available from suppliers, most of which are disposable. They also present a professional image in serving and kitchen areas that are visible to the public and customers.

Cuts, boils and septic wounds

Food handlers should always cover cuts, grazes, boils and septic wounds with the appropriate dressing or with brightly coloured blue waterproof plasters. Cuts on fingers may need extra protection with waterproof fingerstalls or latex disposable gloves.

Smoking

This is prohibited where food is being prepared because:

■ There is a danger of contaminating food with *Staphylococci* from the fingers which may have touched the lips and the saliva on the cigarette end.

■ It encourages coughing.

Jewellery and cosmetics

Food handlers and chefs should not wear watches, rings, earrings or other piercings because they can harbour dirt and bacteria. Plain wedding bands are permitted, but these can still harbour significant levels of bacteria. Strong-smelling perfume may cause food to be tainted and make-up should be used minimally.

Protective clothing

Every person handling food must wear protective clothing. It should be lightweight, washable and strong. White clothing has the advantage of showing up dirt easily. It is important that chefs wear the following protective garments in the kitchen environment:

1 Chef hat or skullcap
2 Chef jacket – double breasted
3 Apron – long and made from heavy cotton
4 Non-slip safety shoes

5 Trousers – comfortable fit and preferably cotton

6 Chef neckerchief – coloured appropriately (if required).

Protective clothing is worn to protect the food from risk of contamination and to help protect the chef from spillages of any kind. Protective clothing should not be worn outside of food premises, including travelling to and from work.

Chef neckerchief

Chef trousers

POTENTIAL HAZARDS

Hazardous substances

An employer or colleague in charge of stock delivery should ensure that all hazardous items are clearly labelled. All staff should be trained in the correct procedures for how to deal with these.

If you are ever unsure of the origin or type of a substance, do not ignite a flame or switch on gas or electricity or go near, touch, inhale or move the substance. Report the substance immediately to your line manager, warning other members of staff to stay away from it until the hazard has been dealt with in the appropriate manner.

Manual handling

Employers must ensure that they have trained each member of staff in the correct handling of large, heavy or awkward items to prevent as far as possible any accident or injury.

Make sure you are aware of how to handle objects in the correct manner. If you are unsure of how to deal with any item, ask a colleague or your line manager for advice and/or assistance.

Fire drills

Make sure you are aware of who the designated fire warden on the premises is. Take time to familiarise yourself with the premises' fire action plan, noting where emergency exits are located and where the safe meeting point is.

HEALTH & SAFETY

All hazardous substances must be identified when completing the risk assessment. This includes cleaning agents and some preservatives. Where possible, high-risk products should be replaced with lower-risk products. The COSHH assessment should be reviewed on a regular basis and updated with any new products.

HEALTH & SAFETY

If a fire alarm occurs, never use a lift to leave the building. Fire can quickly get out of control and the lift shaft could act as an oxygen source when used.

HAZARD ANALYSIS AND RISK ASSESSMENT PROCESS

Regular health and safety checks should be made to ensure that safe practices are being used. The Health and Safety at Work Act 1974 covers all full-time and part-time employees and unpaid workers (such as work placements for students). Everyone needs to be aware of their legal duties for health and safety in the workplace as required by the Act.

VIDEO CLIP Effective cleaning and organisation

The Health and Safety Executive (HSE) is the body appointed to support and enforce health and safety in the workplace. The HSE has defined the two concepts for hazards and risk:

■ A *hazard* is something with the potential to cause harm

■ A *risk* is the likelihood of the hazard's potential being realised.

A hazard has the potential to cause harm and everyone must identify working practices within the kitchen environment which could harm people. All staff are required to make sure that the kitchen equipment and the workplace in general are well-maintained and safe to use.

Two examples of this are:

■ A light bulb that requires replacing is a hazard. If it is one out of several it presents a very small risk, but if it is the only light within a walk-in refrigerator it poses a high risk.

■ A pot of boiling hot oil on a trolley top is a potential hazard. It can fall off, causing spillage onto clothes, causing burns and creating a slippery floor surface unless cleared away immediately. Therefore it is high risk.

VIDEO CLIP
Using kitchen equipment correctly

As soon as any hazard is observed, it must be reported to the designated authority or line manager so that the problem can be rectified. Hazards can include:

■ Obstructions to corridors, stairways and fire exits

■ Spillages and breakages

■ Faulty electrical machinery.

The hazard and risk assessment table opposite gives an overview of how to spot and deal with potential risks and hazards.

Potential hazards and risks can be found in all areas of a kitchen. They will affect every aspect of the kitchen, from the receiving of goods to the preparing of food, and from the building itself to the equipment within each area. Therefore, checks have to be made by all staff and at regular intervals. If these are not made then individuals and groups may be responsible, and in turn liable, for injuries or health risks to themselves and others, which can carry fines and heavy penalties. This applies to all staff, regardless of whether they are part-time or full-time.

Signage and information should be readily available for all staff or members within an establishment.

Within catering establishments, extra or special attention is required in four main areas:

■ Safe storage of chemicals

■ Safe work and customer areas

■ Safe and hygienic food preparation and service areas

■ Safe customer and staff equipment areas and storage.

HAZARD	POTENTIAL RISK	ACTION REQUIRED
Wet floors or walkways	Slips, trips or falls	Signage to warn customers and employees Cleaning of area Reporting of risk Reporting of any maintenance that may be needed, e.g. a leaking roof or sink
Kitchen machinery	Cuts, burns, scalds, electric shock, alien bodies in food products	Maintenance reports Regular servicing Staff training
Lifting of heavy items, e.g. boxes, saucepans, equipment	Strains and sprains, slipped disks, cuts, bruises	Staff training on manual handling Re-arrangement of area so items do not have to be lifted so high or far Purchase of lifting equipment if required
Cleaning chemicals	Chemical burns, contamination to food and food handlers, slips and falls, inhalation of fumes	Staff training Readily available information sheets for each chemical Storage away from food in a separate lockable cupboard
Cross-contamination	Food poisoning, spoiling of food, illness, sickness	Staff training Correct storage containers Colour coding of kitchen utensils and equipment Food labelling Regular kitchen checks Availability of sanitisers

The following simple flowchart can be used when assessing situations and areas where risks and hazards can occur and determining how to prioritise and deal with those issues in an appropriate manner.

Assess the potential risk or hazard and if appropriate remove the problem

Reduce or minimise the risk once it has been identified

Assess which risks are of immediate priority or critical and deal with those safely and correctly

Implement a control system

HAZARD ANALYSIS CRITICAL CONTROL POINTS

Hazard Analysis Critical Control Points (HACCP) is an internationally recognised and recommended system of food safety management. It focuses on identifying the critical points in a process where food safety problems (or 'hazards') could arise and putting steps in place to prevent things going wrong. This is sometimes referred to as 'controlling hazards'. Keeping records is also an important part of HACCP systems.

HACCP involves the following seven steps:

1 Identify what could go wrong (the hazards)
2 Identify the most important points where things can go wrong (the critical control points – CCPs)
3 Set critical limits at each CCP (e.g. cooking temperature or time)
4 Set up checks at CCPs to prevent problems occurring (monitoring)
5 Decide what to do if something goes wrong (corrective action)
6 Prove that your HACCP plan is working (verification)
7 Keep records of all of the above (documentation).

Your HACCP plan must be kept up to date. You will need to review it from time to time, especially whenever something in your food operation changes. You may also wish to ask your local Environmental Health Officer for advice. Remember that, even with a HACCP plan in place, you must comply with all of the requirements of current food safety legislation.

Disposal of waste is another HACCP matter, as bacteria and other pathogens can multiply at an alarming rate in waste disposal areas. In ideal circumstances, the areas for cleaning crockery and pots should be separate from each other and from the food preparation area.

Waste bins in the kitchen should be emptied at regular and short intervals and be kept clean. Food waste can be safely disposed of in a waste disposal unit. Oil can only be disposed of by a specialist oil disposal company and must not be placed in a sink or waste disposal unit.

THE REPORTING OF MAINTENANCE ISSUES

The preparation of food for cookery must take place on surfaces that are hygienic and suitable for use. Work surfaces, walls and floors can become damaged, and they too can be a source of contamination and danger to customers and staff alike. This should be reported to your line manager.

A maintenance reporting system can easily be designed to suit each establishment and each section in that kitchen. Good practice is to carry out a weekly maintenance check and to have a set procedure for repairing or replacing equipment. This can lead to a more economical maintenance programme. It is much cheaper to repair little and often than to wait until equipment is dangerous and perhaps risk injury or litigation. Areas for attention are:

■ Cracks in walls

■ Damage to tables and work benches

■ Cooking equipment such as pots, pans and utensils

■ Windows, sanitary systems and lights

■ Flooring and any other structural issues

■ Electrical equipment relating to that particular operation.

MAINTENANCE REPORT FORM				Date:	
AREA	ITEM	PROBLEM	ACTION TAKEN	DATE JOB COMPLETED	SIGNATURE
Larder	Fridge	Seal gone around the door	Reported it to maintenance 5/06/06	10/06/06	

Example of a maintenance report form

SECURITY IN THE WORKPLACE

This topic can cover a range of different issues. But in every instance a risk assessment will have to be implemented in order to assess any immediate dangers or threats that are apparent within an establishment. The hotel and catering industry can be an area of high risk due to the many different areas it encompasses, and the risks do not just affect customers but also staff and the establishment itself.

The main security issues within the catering industry are:

■ Theft

■ Fraud

■ Assault

■ Terrorism

■ Vandalism.

Theft

Theft can cover a range of offences, including such things as the dishonest and unlawful taking of food and drink (by staff as well as by customers), equipment, furniture or furnishings, as well as taking as souvenirs or keepsakes items that are of value.

All items that are unlawfully taken from a premises will have to be replaced, either at the company's expense or your own. All property is at risk, regardless of whether it is the customer's, the employee's or the employer's. Theft usually involves the taking of money, which is why many venues have strict measures in place to minimise the amount of money or merchandise on the premises at any one time.

Aggravated theft or robbery, where the use of violent or aggressive behaviour can lead to assault in addition to theft, has to be assessed as a security risk.

Fraud

This is an ever increasing security issue due to the way that technology and the electronic world have evolved and continue to change. More and more customers and businesses are using credit cards to pay for goods and items, often via means such as the Internet or card machines. This can make it easy for computer-based fraudsters to access credit card and bank account details.

All employees and employers should be extra vigilant for counterfeit credit cards and currency. Due to modern advances in technology, such items are becoming increasingly harder to spot.

Another growing area of concern is that of false claims for expenses and damages. These can range from dry cleaning bills to personal injury claims. Keeping full and accurate documentation of incidents and occurrences can save companies thousands of pounds a year by preventing fraudulent claims.

HEALTH & SAFETY

Train staff on customer care, and on how to defuse potentially volatile situations.

Assault

An assault on a staff member or a customer, whether within an establishment or outside, is a very serious security matter. All assaults, physical and verbal, should be dealt with and treated with the utmost importance.

Strict security codes and procedures should be in place to protect everyone at the premises. Staff should be trained on how to correctly manage unexpected situations, both how to deal with an incident and how to recognise and hopefully diffuse any situation before it reaches a critical point – foresight can be a very good deterrent and helpful aid to all.

Terrorism

This has become a threat that customers and staff are very aware of and should be taken very seriously. All threats of this nature, such as telephone calls and suspect packages, should be dealt with very carefully. Any incidents should be dealt with in the same way as a fire action plan: assess the situation, seek appropriate action or help and then evacuate the area in a calm manner.

Vandalism

Vandalism, the malicious damage of property by customers, staff or outside influences, can be costly and time-consuming to rectify. It covers a range of security risks, from direct physical damage to property, graffiti and arson, to internal or external damage to the premises. All areas of vandalism need to be considered.

Managing security

Companies, employers and establishments should do all they can to reduce security risks and hazards. In a lot of cases simple procedures, such as taking and logging the contact details of all staff and customers, will not only prove helpful in the event of an incident but can also help to prevent an incident taking place. Deterrents such as signage stating that no valuables or large amounts of money are kept on the premises can deter opportunists or petty criminals from attempting to gain access.

Having effective monitoring procedures for such things as stock rotation and levels and keeping up-to-date records of what has come in and gone out of the premises will help reveal any major discrepancies. If staff and customer records are also held, this should mean that any issues can be thoroughly checked and resolved.

The main areas of premises that require security are the front and back entrances. At the front entrance there should be some sort of reception desk or a person to meet and greet both customers and staff so that information and details can be thoroughly checked. All visitors should sign in and out and be given some form of identification, such as a visitor's pass, to carry when on the premises. Staff should be trained fully, and if at any time they see anyone or anything suspicious or irregular then they should phone or notify the correct person/manager or the police immediately.

At the back door, anyone making a delivery should be expected to have identification. Deliveries should only be accepted from reputable companies that have already been nominated or screened for security. All maintenance personnel should have an appointment or a person or point of contact and be booked in on arrival. If necessary, telephone the visitor's employer to verify their details.

Closed-circuit television (CCTV) can be very useful as a security measure, and signage stating that the premises has CCTV is another good deterrent. Unfortunately CCTV is costly and it can be off-putting to customers and staff. Very discrete camera devices are now available, which can blend in with the surroundings very well.

If this type of system is to be used, there should be procedures in place for monitoring and recording the images. The time, date and area should be

HEALTH & SAFETY

Give all staff a contact list of emergency numbers, or make sure a list is easily accessible, in case of any unexpected situations.

noted on all recordings so they can be easily listed and checked. This will also help to ensure that the recording media are re-used on a rotation basis. Video monitoring systems for CCTV should be kept in a secured area or office, with limited access by a minimal number of employees, whose names should be recorded.

The amount of cash in an establishment can be of major concern as this can encourage not just petty theft but also organised crime. If it is known that cash is kept on the premises then this can be a serious security risk. Staff should be trained in handling cash and there should be procedures in place so that takings and payments are cashed up at the end of each shift. A safe should be used, or if possible money taken to the bank to avoid large amounts being available.

Businesses can encourage customers to pay by credit or debit cards to help reduce the amount of available cash. This can, however, lead to the risk of credit card fraud, a common scam that is becoming ever more present in all industries. Staff should be trained to check for signatures and name details with all card or cheque transactions. They should also be taught how to check for counterfeit notes and coins.

HEALTH & SAFETY

When looking to implement security or work procedures, visit well established venues and assess what they do and use that as a guide. If they are well established then they must have very good policies.

General security measures that are effective are good lighting and clear areas around and close by the premises. These allow customers and staff to see clearly anything suspicious or any potential danger. Leaving lights on or on timers can help to deter potential problems as it can give the impression that someone is present in the building. Doors, windows and access gates must all be locked when leaving a premises after close of business.

Within any establishment, all systems that are in place – whether for food ordering or for security – have to be maintained and managed. Policies or systems have to be introduced to cover the range of potential risks identified in a hazard analysis. Therefore, all staff will have to be trained on all these elements – from security threats to bomb alerts to customer or employee theft. Make sure these policies are strict and are adhered to at all times. Ongoing checks and assessments are needed to monitor present security risks and to identify new ones. Resources should be set aside to cover the cost of security. In the long run this can prove very cost effective. This could be internally by the company or from an external source.

Having an understanding of the relevant legislation means that the establishment and its employees will know their rights and the boundaries of what they are legally required to do. Security and safety go hand in hand. However, they are two separate issues. They need to be managed separately, but co-ordinated so that a balance between safety and security can be achieved.

Assessment of knowledge and understanding

You have now learned about the health and safety responsibilities for everyone in the workplace. This will enable you to ensure your own actions reduce risks to health and safety.

To test your level of knowledge and understanding, answer the following short questions. These will help to prepare you for your summative (final) assessment.

Health and safety law

1 Give three examples of implications of not conforming to health and safety laws.

i) _____   ii) _____

iii) _____

2 State who the Health and Safety at Work Act 1974 covers and why it is in place.

_____
_____

3 Explain why it is important to keep yourself up to date with current health and safety legislation.

_____
_____

Personal responsibility in the workplace

1 List five points that need to be covered when reporting incidents that occur within the kitchen.

i) _____   ii) _____

iii) _____   iv) _____

v) _____

2 Give four examples of health and safety that you are personally responsible for in your own area of the kitchen.

i) _____   ii) _____

iii) _____   iv) _____

Security within the workplace

1 Explain why and how customer and employee fraud is a concern for businesses and what measures can be taken to limit it.

_____
_____

2 Discuss the importance of addressing and implementing security measures within the workplace, detailing how this can benefit the employer, employees and customers/the public.

_____
_____

Research Task

Design and draw your own kitchen, based on a medium-sized premises with approximately twenty kitchen staff. Then, detail a health and safety risk assessment and necessary health and safety action plan to implement.

You should ensure that the premises, equipment, food, storage (of equipment and chemicals), room size and space, and number of staff are all taken into consideration.

2

Maintain food safety when storing, preparing and cooking food

2GEN3.1 **Keep yourself clean and hygienic**

2GEN3.2 **Keep your working area clean and hygienic**

2GEN3.3 **Store food safely**

2GEN3.4 **Prepare, cook and hold food safely**

LEARNING OBJECTIVES

The aim of this chapter is to enable the candidate to acquire expertise and put into practice their knowledge of the health and hygienic practices within the workplace. It discusses the health and hygiene requirements and policies that you will need to know about if you are to work safely and hygienically in the kitchen. This will also include information on the resources at the disposal of the chef to implement regulations to prepare, cook and hold food safely.

At the end of this chapter you will be able to:

■ Be aware of your responsibility for personal cleanliness during food preparation and cooking in the workplace and for unsafe behaviour

■ Maintain clean and hygienic work surfaces and equipment

■ Check food into the premises and identify specific labels

- Understand the correct use of storage control, the stock rotation system and keeping records
- Know how to safely defrost food and thoroughly wash food
- Know the regulations for the safe cooking, the safe holding and the safe reheating of food
- Chill and freeze cooked food that is not for immediate consumption
- Identify food bacteria and other organisms and food hazards in the workplace

INTRODUCTION

The chef must be particularly conscious of the need for hygiene: many commodities have to be handled and prepared for the customer without any type of heat treatment. High standards of hygiene are essential to prevent food poisoning, food spoilage, loss of productivity, pest infestation and potential criminal prosecution for malpractice.

Food hygiene implies more than just the sanitation of work areas. It includes all practices, precautions and legal responsibilities involved in the following:

1 Protecting food from risk of contamination
2 Preventing organisms from multiplying to an extent which would pose a health risk to customers and employees
3 Destroying any harmful bacteria in food by thorough heat treatment or other techniques.

PERSONAL HYGIENE

It is a requirement that good hygiene systems are followed by all food handlers. Chapter 1 covers personal hygiene in depth.

A CLEAN AND HYGIENIC WORK AREA

The use of premises which are clean and can be correctly maintained is essential for the preparation, cooking and service of food. Cross-contamination risks should be minimised by the provision of separate preparation areas for the various raw and cooked foods. The table describes the various fittings and fixtures that need to be considered in a kitchen before the main equipment is planned:

FIXTURES AND FITTINGS	RECOMMENDATIONS
Ceilings	White in colour to reflect the light. Smooth-textured, without cracks or peeled paint/plaster. Usually panelled to hide the ventilation system.
Floors	Should have a durable, non-slip and non-permeable material. They can be tiled but polyurethane screeds are now used extensively in food processing areas. This type of screed is fast to install, offers good levels of chemical resistance even to the most aggressive acids and fats, and can be installed to withstand steam cleaning. It is a slip-resistant surface (equally important), designed to give a textured finish.
Lighting	Good lighting is essential to avoid eye strain. Natural light is best but where artificial lighting is used some thought should be given to the type used.
Ventilation	The requirements of a high-performance kitchen ventilation system for the modern kitchen. The extracted air should be free from grease and odours, and be discharged up single or multiple chimney stacks. A canopy system should be built around the existing structure of the kitchen to cover at least all cookery areas. The incorporation of a balancing system to ensure equal extract along the whole cook line is very important.

Replacement air is introduced into the kitchen through low-velocity diffusers mounted in the front face of the canopy and spot cooling nozzles can also provide a cooler air temperature in the kitchen. These are a potential source of dirt, grease and dust and should be cleaned on a very regular basis. |
| Walls | Ceramic wall tiles were considered the best surface for areas where liquids splash a wall surface, potentially overcoming a damp or hygiene problem. Many such areas still exist in industrial and commercial hygiene-sensitive areas. Their durability, long-term appearance and cost of maintenance can be questionable and today there is a viable alternative to consider. Modern alternatives to ceramic wall tiles include PVC wall cladding systems, resin wall coatings and screed mortars. They offer a hygienic finish capable of withstanding heavy-impact use. |

EQUIPMENT

Work surfaces and equipment for the preparation, cooking and service of food should be impervious and easy to clean. Equipment should be constructed from materials which are non-toxic, corrosion resistant, smooth and free from cracks. Apparatus such as a **bain-marie** should be able to store hot food for up to two hours at an ambient temperature of 63°C and regular temperature checks should be taken. The surfaces should be easy to clean even when hot and should allow the food to be presented in an attractive manner.

Worktops and chopping boards

It is very important to keep all worktops and chopping boards clean because they touch the food your customers are going to eat. If they are not properly clean, bacteria could spread to food and make your customers ill.

- Always wash worktops before you start preparing food.
- Wipe up any spilt food immediately.
- Always wash worktops thoroughly after they have been touched by raw meat, including poultry, or raw eggs.
- Never put ready-to-eat food, such as tomatoes or fruit, on a worktop or chopping board that has been touched by raw meat, unless you have washed it thoroughly first.

If you have a dishwasher, this is a very effective way to clean plastic chopping boards. Dishwashers can wash at a very high temperature, which kills bacteria. Otherwise, wash chopping boards thoroughly with hot water and detergent. Sanitise boards on a regular basis using an appropriate sanitising substance.

Ideally, it is standard practice to have separate chopping boards for raw meat and for other foods. A standardised system of coloured boards and knife handles which help to minimise cross-contamination are widely available. They should be as follows:

- Red   – raw meat and poultry
- Yellow – cooked meat and poultry
- Blue   – raw fish (in this book, white and wooden backgrounds may be used for photographic purposes)
- Brown – vegetables
- Green – fruit and salads
- White – dairy and pastry items.

Coloured high-density chopping boards

IMAGE COURTESY OF RUSSUMS.CO.UK

These boards must be cleaned between use, ideally with sanitiser and clean cotton, non-woven fabric or specialised paper cleaning cloths. They should be soaked over night in a sterilising solution on a regular basis. The boards are stored in racks and should not be touching each other.

If boards become damaged they should be discarded. Bacteria can multiply in cracks and blemishes, and be the cause of contamination.

Kitchen cloths

Dirty, damp cloths are the perfect breeding ground for bacteria. It is very important to wash kitchen cloths and other cleaning cloths, sponges and abrasive materials regularly and leave them to dry before using them again.

Ideally, try to keep different cloths for different jobs. For example, use one cloth to wipe worktops and another to wash dishes. This helps to stop bacteria spreading.

The safest option is the use of disposable kitchen towels to wipe worktops and chopping boards. This is because you throw the kitchen towel away after using it once, so it is less likely to spread bacteria than cloths you use again.

Tea towels can also spread bacteria, so it's important to wash them regularly and be careful how you use them. Remember, if you wipe your hands on a tea towel

CHEF'S TIP

As a result of changes in European food hygiene regulations on 1 January 2006, the Food Standards Agency has issued new guidance on temperature control legislation in England, Wales and Northern Ireland. The guidance contains advice on the types of foods that are required to be held under temperature control and on the circumstances in which some flexibility from the temperature control requirements is allowed. The guidance is intended to complement best practices in the food industry, which might involve, for example, keeping foods at chill temperatures below the legal maximum and thereby providing additional assurances of food safety.

VIDEO CLIP
Receipt and storage of produce

after you have touched raw meat, this will spread bacteria to the towel. Then, if you use the tea towel to dry a plate, the bacteria will spread to the plate.

Knives, spoons and other utensils

It is important to keep knives, wooden spoons, spatulas, tongs and other utensils clean to help stop bacteria spreading to food. It is especially important to wash them thoroughly after using them with raw meat, otherwise they can spread bacteria to other food.

Once again, a dishwasher is a very effective way to clean knives and other utensils because dishwashers can wash at a very high temperature, which kills bacteria. Otherwise, wash them thoroughly with hot water and detergents.

SAFE FOOD STORAGE

An HACCP food management system will also examine the point of food storage. It should cover the receiving of goods where the core temperatures and condition of the delivery is thoroughly checked. Fresh meat that has been delivered should have a core temperature of a maximum of 8°C. All fresh produce should be delivered in unbroken, clean packaging and in clean delivery vehicles that are refrigerated. If you suspect a delivery has not met the requirements of your HACCP it should be refused and returned immediately to the supplier. A goods inwards sheet showing the company, invoice number, core temperature, any problems and how they were dealt with allows received goods to be monitored.

An example of a Goods Received Checklist.

Chef's name _____

Production area _____

Goods Received Checklist

Date	Time	Supplier	Order correct	Delivery note/ Invoice number	Fault (Identify product)	Action	Temperature reading	Signature

After the commodity has been received it needs to be correctly stored. Raw meat and fish should be stored and covered in separate refrigerators at 4°C. If there is not enough capacity for two separate refrigeration systems, *cooked products must be stored above fresh meat*. Fish should be stored as low in the refrigerator as possible. This is the coldest part of the refrigerator and a layer of crushed ice will help to keep the temperature down. This method eliminates cross-contamination from storage and optimises quality. All foods should be labelled with the date of delivery/production, a description of the contents and the recommended use by date.

HEALTH & SAFETY

When unpacking a delivery, always ensure the product packaging is undamaged to avoid possible personal injury from broken goods.

A well laid-out store room

TYPES OF BACTERIA THAT CAUSE FOOD POISONING

Salmonella

There are approximately over 2000 types of Salmonella; the most common varieties are *Salmonella enteriditis* and *Salmonella typhimurium*. These organisms survive in the intestine and can cause food poisoning by releasing a toxin on the death of the cell. The primary source of salmonella is the intestinal tract of animals and poultry. It will therefore be found in:

- Human and animal excreta
- Excreta from rats, mice, flies and cockroaches
- Raw meat and poultry
- Some animal feed.

Food storage label

Staphylococcus aureus

About 40–50 per cent of adults carry this organism in their nose, mouth, throat, ears and hands. If present in food, *Staphylococcus aureus* will produce a toxin which may survive boiling for 30 minutes or more. The majority of outbreaks are caused by poor hygiene practices which result in direct contamination of the food from sneezing or uncovered septic cuts and abrasions. Frequently, the cooked food has been handled whilst still slightly warm, and these storage conditions have encouraged the organism to produce its toxin.

VIDEO CLIP
Control of pests and infestations

Clostridium perfringens

This is commonly found in human and animal faeces and is present in raw meat and poultry. This organism forms spores which may survive boiling temperatures for several hours. Outbreaks can involve stews and large joints of meat which have been allowed to cool down slowly in a warm kitchen and either eaten cold or inadequately reheated the following day.

Bacillus cereus

This is a spore-forming organism. The spores survive normal cooking and rapid growth will occur if the food has not been cooled quickly and refrigerated. This bacteria will induce nausea and vomiting within five hours of ingestion.

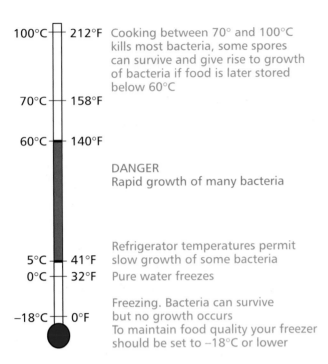

100°C ┤├ 212°F Cooking between 70° and 100°C
kills most bacteria, some spores
can survive and give rise to growth
of bacteria if food is later stored
below 60°C

70°C ┤├ 158°F

60°C ┤├ 140°F

DANGER
Rapid growth of many bacteria

5°C ┤├ 41°F Refrigerator temperatures permit
slow growth of some bacteria
0°C ┤├ 32°F Pure water freezes

Freezing. Bacteria can survive
but no growth occurs
−18°C ┤├ 0°F To maintain food quality your freezer
should be set to −18°C or lower

Food temperature safety guide

Food allergies and intolerances

It is critical to be aware of the issues of food allergies and intolerance when preparing, cooking and serving certain foods:

■ An allergy to food is the hypersensitivity of food constituents. The immune system reacts to a particular food, believing it is not safe to eat. In severe circumstances this can cause a life-threatening reaction.

■ An intolerance to food does not involve the immune system and is generally not life threatening. However, it can still make people ill and it may affect their long-term health.

The following are examples that the chef needs to be aware of:

■ *Lactose intolerance* – a condition in which the body lacks the enzyme lactase and so cannot process lactose. Lactose is present in milk and dairy products.

■ *Coeliac disease* – an intolerance to gluten, a protein substance present in wheat, rye, barley and oat products.

■ *Peanuts and tree nuts* – peanuts in particular can cause extreme reactions and even death. It is impossible for the chef to guarantee a nut-free diet to the guest.

■ *Eggs* – intolerance to the proteins in egg whites or yolks, or sometimes both.

■ *Fish* – fish allergies are more common in children than adults; even the smell can bring on a reaction in a sensitive person. Common fish known to cause symptoms are cod, salmon, trout, herring, bass, swordfish, halibut and tuna.

■ *Shellfish* – reactions to the ingestion of shellfish can be severe, even at the level of inhalation of cooking vapours. Great care should be taken to avoid cross-contamination between shellfish products and all other foodstuffs that might be in contact with the diner. Shellfish commonly known to cause allergic reactions include shrimp, crab, crayfish, lobster, oysters, clams, scallops, mussels, squid and snails. People allergic to shrimp often suffer from respiratory allergy. Crab is also a potent allergen. Shrimp, lobster and crawfish contain common major allergens, making cross-reactivity between shrimp and crab, and lobster and crawfish possible.

Food storage and temperatures

Raw meat, poultry and game and charcuterie – 4°C or below. Store away from cooked meat and cooked meat products to avoid any risk of cross-contamination.

Cooked meat – 4°C or below. Keep away from raw meat and meat products.

Uncooked fish – 4°C or below. Keep in separate compartments or in plastic fish trays with lids if possible, and away from other foods which may become tainted.

Frozen food – –18°C or below. Thaw only immediately prior to using the commodity.

Fish (smoked or cured) – 8°C. Keep in chilled storage away from other foods, which may become tainted.

Fruit (fresh and dried). Store in a cool, dry, well-ventilated area, away from other food, at least 15cm from the ground. Discard at the first sign of mould growth. Do not overstock.

Pasta, rice and cereals – Store in self-closing tightly lidded containers in dry cool storeroom or cupboard.

Eggs – Refrigerate at 8°C or below. Use strictly in rotation and ensure the shells are clean.

Fats, butter, dairy and non-dairy spreads – 8°C or below. Keep covered and away from highly flavoured food, which may taint.

Milk and cream – 8°C or below. In a separate dairy refrigerator that is used for no other purpose and in strict rotation.

Canned and bottled goods – Cool, dry, well-ventilated storage area. Blown, rusty or split tins must not be used.

Root vegetables – Store in sacks or nets as delivered in cool, well-ventilated area.

Leaf and green vegetables – 8°C. Use on day of delivery.

Glass fronted fridge

Freezers, whether upright or chest freezers, should be maintained at a maximum temperature of –18°C. All food should be covered to prevent **freezer burn** and labelled with the date of production and a use by date.

Ambient stores should be clean and well ventilated, with mesh over windows and doors to help with pest control. All foodstuffs must be stored away from the floor and be rotated on a first in and first out basis.

PREPARING, COOKING AND STORING FOOD SAFELY

Frozen food should be defrosted in a refrigerator and treated as fresh food with the same use by date. All root vegetables must be washed prior to peeling and then rewashed after peeling. Leaf vegetables such as cabbage and spinach should be washed in several changes of cold water to allow soil and grit to go to the bottom of the sink. Ideally a separate preparation area should be facilitated to help prevent cross-contamination.

Chilling food not for immediate use should ideally be achieved in blast chillers where the core temperature is brought down from 70°C to 4°C in 90 minutes or less. With these temperature ranges both pathogenic and bacterial growth is inhibited although not completely stopped.

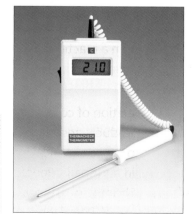

Digital food thermometer

If food that has been cooked is not for immediate consumption, or is to be frozen, it should be well covered with cling film or ideally vacuum packed to create an airtight barrier and prevent freezer burn. Storage should be within manufacturer's guidelines and the foods must be clearly labelled as previously mentioned.

 CHEF'S TIP

The correct measurement of temperature should be monitored by the use of an accurate digital food thermometer. The probe is inserted into the centre of meat joints or placed onto the surface of other ingredients to give a temperature reading within a few seconds. Alcohol-based sanitiser wipes should be used to clean the stainless steel probe after every use to prevent cross-contamination.

AREAS WHERE HAZARDS MIGHT OCCUR

STEP	HAZARD	CONTROL
Receipt of goods	■ Contaminated high-risk foods ■ Damaged or decomposed goods ■ Incorrect specifications ■ Growth of pathogens between the time of receipt and storage	■ All deliveries inspected and checked by a staff member ■ Appropriate labelling ■ Prompt and correct storage
Storage	■ Contamination of high-risk foods ■ Contamination through poor handling ■ Contamination by pests ■ Spoilage of food by decomposition	■ Correct usage of refrigeration regimes ■ Foods must be suitably stored in the correct packaging or receptacles ■ Materials that are in direct contact with food must be of food-grade quality ■ A contract for a pest control service must be in place ■ Correct stock rotation ■ Out of date and unfit food stuffs must be segregated from other foods and removed from the premises
Preparation	■ Contamination of high-risk foods ■ Contamination through poor handling ■ Growth of pathogens and toxins	■ Keep raw and cooked foods separate ■ Use pasteurised eggs for raw and lightly cooked egg dishes ■ All food contact surfaces must be fit for purpose ■ Food handlers must be trained in hygienic food handling techniques ■ Keep the exposure of fresh foods at ambient temperatures to a minimum ■ Label all food that is to be used more than one day in advance of production with its description and use by date
Cooking	■ Survival of pathogens and spores	■ Cook all foods to the minimum recommended temperature
Chilling	■ Growth of pathogens, spores = toxin production ■ Contamination	■ Cool foods as quickly as possible, to 8°C in 90 minutes ■ Keep food that is chilling loosely covered ■ Use only clean equipment

STEP	HAZARD	CONTROL
Hot hold	■ Growth of pathogens and toxin production ■ Contamination by staff and customers, especially in self-service operations	■ Maintain food at 63°C and discard after 2 hours ■ Keep containers covered when not in service ■ Use sneeze screens ■ Supervise self-service
Cold hold	■ Growth of pathogens and toxin production ■ Contamination by staff and customers especially in self-service operations	■ Keep food at 5°C and discard after 4 hours ■ Keep containers covered when not in service ■ Use sneeze screens ■ Supervise self-service

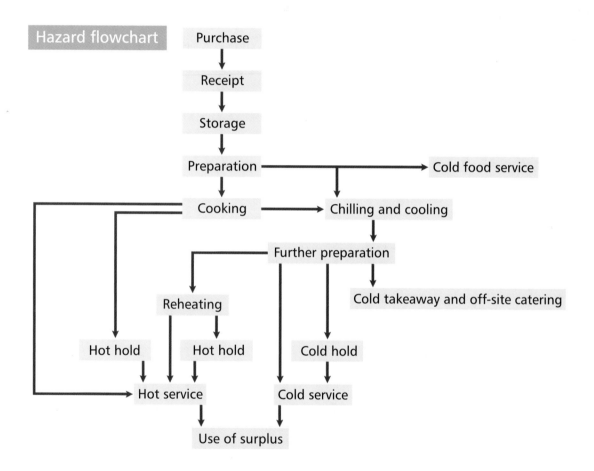

Hazard flowchart

General hazard controls to consider

■ Regular servicing of equipment

■ Use of a temperature probe to check on stored food

■ Use of a temperature probe to check on food storage equipment

■ Investigation of all complaints of suspected food-borne illnesses

■ Regular inspections by a health and safety officer

■ Frequent self inspections

■ Comprehensive cleaning programmes

■ Adequate staff training in food handling and hygiene practices.

In every professional kitchen, a working system that controls the purchase and use of all ingredients needs to be maintained. It should detail the work flow to prevent hazards from occurring during the storage, preparation, cooking and service of food.

Assessment of knowledge and understanding

You have now learned about the health and hygiene responsibilities of everyone in the workplace. This will enable you to ensure your own work areas, food preparation, cookery and service actions reduce risks in health.

To test your level of knowledge and understanding, answer the following short questions. These will help to prepare you for your summative (final) assessment.

1 State the food safety hazards that wearing jewellery can cause.

_____

2 Identify who health hazards are reported to.

_____

3 Identify the importance of reporting illnesses quickly and the significance of stomach illnesses.

_____

4 State three reasons why work surfaces and chopping boards should be clean and hygienic.

i) _____ ii) _____

iii) _____

5 Explain the reason for regular maintenance checks.

_____

6 Explain the importance of storing food at the correct temperature.

_____

7 Describe the term 'stock rotation'.

_____

Research Task A

Carry out a HACCP assessment on the following products. Consider the hazard, the critical control point and the action to be taken.

(a) Fresh raw poultry _____

(b) Fresh fruit and vegetables _____

3

Ensure appropriate food safety practices are followed whilst food is prepared, cooked and served

3GEN1 Ensure appropriate food safety practices are followed whilst food is prepared, cooked and served

LEARNING OBJECTIVES

The aim of this chapter is to enable the candidate to develop skills and implement knowledge which will ensure food safety practices are followed during food production.

At the end of this chapter you will be able to:

- Identify which legislation a chef is responsible for
- Understand the use of control measures
- State the causes of food safety hazards
- Understand how to control food safety hazards
- Identify biological, chemical and physical hazards
- Implement food safety procedures
- Understand the importance of due diligence

THE CHEF'S RESPONSIBILITIES FOR FOOD SAFETY

The professional chef is responsible for ensuring that food safety and the legislation that surrounds are strictly enforced at all times.

A chef's role in the kitchen is not only to produce high quality food but also to ensure that the customer is kept happy and safe. Food safety is defined as the safeguarding of food from 'farm to fork'. This means ensuring that the produce is fit to eat, that it is stored, prepared and cooked to a constant high level; and that the administrative tasks are completed as required, such as keeping fridge temperature records.

One of the most important skills a chef can acquire in the kitchen is organisation; this will facilitate cleaning, cooking, storage and record-taking. This skill will be developed with experience and will ensure that a highly motivated, professional kitchen is maintained at all times.

Daily activities that need to be completed are:

- Fridge and freezer temperature monitoring
- Received food temperature monitoring
- Cold and hot hold temperature monitoring
- Core temperature monitoring
- Disinfection of all contact areas.

Weekly activities that need to be completed are:

- Deep cleaning of the kitchen
- Checking, signing and collation of all records
- Updating of record files (files are to be kept for a minimum of three months).

It has been shown that an organised, clean and safe working environment will produce higher quality produce and make for a happier environment to work in. An enjoyable working environment will also help to reduce staff absence and reinforce team spirit.

CHEF'S TIP

A laminated chart situated in the kitchen listing routine tasks such as fridge temperature monitoring is a simple way to ensure the tasks are completed.

LEGISLATION AFFECTING ALL FOOD HANDLERS

The law

The law states that all catering businesses are required to produce food that is safe to eat, and that proprietors must be able to demonstrate what they have done to ensure they are serving safe food – and have this written down.

The law explained

Due diligence is the main legal defence endorsed by the Food Safety Act 1990. It provides the best protection to companies that need to demonstrate in court that all reasonable precautions have been taken to avoid the sale of unsafe food.

The first step for food manufacturers developing a HACCP system is to set up a team, whose members must be adequately trained in HACCP principles and their application. This team will also decide who should be responsible for implementing the system.

The next stage is to carefully identify each step in the preparation of each dish, starting with the purchase of the ingredients and ending with sale to the customer, and to formulate these steps into a flowchart, such as that below. Each element of the flowchart would then need to be broken down and additional detail added, such as transport in a clean vehicle with temperature controls.

Each step then needs to be carefully analysed to identify what could go wrong and result in a safety hazard to the customer. Such hazards include bacteria, foreign bodies and chemical contaminants.

In addition, where vegetarian, vegan or allergen-free food is prepared alongside other food, it is important to undertake a risk assessment to identify, segregate or manage any allergens or ingredients that could cause harm or discomfort to customers.

The next stage is to identify what can be done to control potential hazards.

 CHEF'S TIP

The HACCP system relies on staff adhering to the rules and regulations. Ensure that all staff are aware of their responsibility at all times.

Transportation from supplier

Food received, checked, decanted, temperature controlled, stored

Food sent to the kitchen, decanted, washed, prepared and temperature monitored

Food cooked, temperature checked

Food served to customer

Controls may include:

■ Separation of raw and cooked foods to avoid cross-contamination

■ Personal hygiene rules to avoid contamination by bacteria

■ Correct cooking times and temperatures to destroy harmful bacteria.

For every step where a potential hazard has been identified, it will be necessary to consider whether or not the customer will be harmed if nothing is done. That will dictate which steps are critical control points.

The next stage is to set standards, or critical limits, for the controls. These will specify the conditions that must be met to ensure that the food will be safe. Checks should be carried out at predetermined times and records kept to show that the controls are working.

If monitoring shows that critical limits are not being met, a designated person must take corrective action. They must also record what action has been taken.

Whenever a recipe is altered, a new dish added to the menu, a new activity introduced or the structure of the kitchen changed, the HACCP system must be reviewed. But even if no changes take place in the kitchen, the HACCP system should be reviewed at least once a year.

HAZARDS

The following two diagrams outline the different types of hazards and the consequences associated with them.

CHEF'S TIP

Any produce that may cause an allergic reaction should be stored in a sealed container and only used as required.

VIDEO CLIP
An EHO visit to a professional kitchen

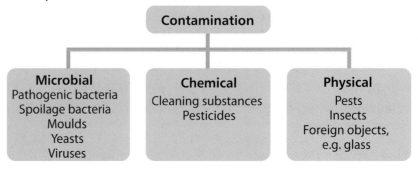

Contamination

Microbial
Pathogenic bacteria
Spoilage bacteria
Moulds
Yeasts
Viruses

Chemical
Cleaning substances
Pesticides

Physical
Pests
Insects
Foreign objects,
e.g. glass

The factors which can cause food poisoning include:

- Biological contamination
- Physical contamination
- Chemical contamination.

Biological contamination is caused when ideal conditions, such as warmth, food, moisture and time, are afforded to pathogens. Poor personal hygiene practices, cross-contamination, storage, chilling and cooking can all lead to food poisoning. Food poisoning is caused when pathogenic micro-organisms, bacteria in particular, are present in sufficient amounts to make the body ill. Different pathogens affect the body in different ways, and the end result can be diarrhoea, vomiting, dehydration and even death.

Physical contamination is caused when an objectionable substance is present in food, such as glass found in a beef stew. Physical contamination can produce symptoms in the same way as bacterial poisoning.

Chemical contamination occurs when a chemical such as sanitiser, bleach or washing-up liquid comes into contact with food and is ingested by a person. The usual reaction is vomiting, which should be avoided if possible because any injury received during swallowing may be worsened by vomiting.

CHEF'S TIP

Charts allow people to absorb information quickly and easily. When displayed in appropriate areas of a kitchen they help to ensure that best practices are used.

VIDEO CLIP
Core temperatures

VIDEO CLIP
Colour coded chopping boards

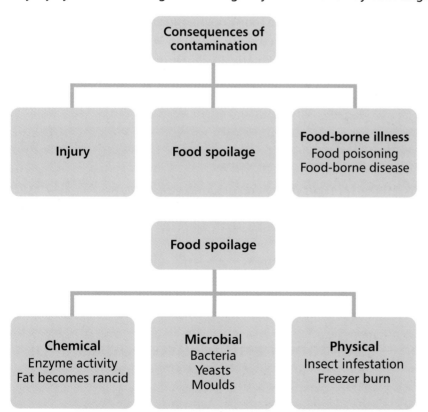

Food-borne illness is mainly associated with poor handling of foodstuffs. This is why chefs and food handlers undergo such thorough training.

Food poisoning and food-borne disease are separate hazards and there are various differences between the two.

Food-borne diseases:

- Incubate for a longer period of time
- Require a smaller amount to make somebody ill
- Are transported on food but do not use it to multiply
- Can be spread by items other than food
- Can enter the bloodstream
- Symptoms may or may not include vomiting or diarrhoea.

CONTROLS

Food safety needs to be addressed by ensuring that adequate controls are in place. Controls range from those which require regular adjustment to those which cannot be altered, such as design and construction of premises. All control measures should be built into the organisation's framework and continually monitored by the senior personnel responsible for their implementation.

Controls come in many forms, from spot checks of staff uniforms to advanced training and HACCP.

Staff should be regularly tested on their knowledge and on the effectiveness of the monitoring systems used in the organisation. A kitchen is only as effective as its weakest member of staff; if a chef is unable to take temperatures, cook correctly or follow standard hygiene practices then an incident is likely to occur.

 CHEF'S TIP

A monthly test of all staff (which is then recorded) will give reassurance to the chefs, management and Environmental Health Officer that every effort is being made to ensure that best practices are used and that a due diligence defence is being built should the need arise.

Assessment of knowledge and understanding

You have now learned about the responsibilities for food safety and working effectively as a team member to maintain high levels of food hygiene. This will enable you to ensure your own positive actions contribute effectively towards controlling the working environment in the safety of handling food from delivery to presentation to the customer.

To test your level of knowledge and understanding, answer the following short questions. These will help to prepare you for your summative (final) assessment.

Identify which legislation a chef/food handler is responsible for

1 List the four pieces of legislation that a chef/food handler is responsible for.

    i) _____   ii) _____

    iii)_____   iv) _____

2 Briefly describe the legislation in relation to your work and how it may affect you.

    _____

    _____

Understand the use of control measures

1 Describe how using control measures may reduce the risk of a food poisoning incident.

2 State why control measures are used within a kitchen environment.

State the causes of food safety hazards

1 Describe the three main groups of food safety hazard.

i) _____ ii) _____

iii) _____

2 List at least two hazards associated with each group.

Understand how to control food safety hazards

1 Describe how each group of hazards can be controlled within a kitchen environment.

2 State who is responsible for each control.

3 Explain why controls are used and what effect there could be if controls were not implemented.

Understand the importance of due diligence

1 Briefly describe due diligence and why it is so important for a professional chef.

Research Task

Using your knowledge of a professional kitchen, whether a school, college, restaurant, hotel, etc., devise a simple HACCP chart. The chart should refer to:

■ Meat

■ Fish

■ Dairy

Identify any problems in the existing system and offer possible solutions.

4

Establish and develop positive working relationships in hospitality

HS2 Establish and develop positive working relationships in hospitality

LEARNING OBJECTIVES

The aim of this chapter is to enable you to develop competence and put into practice positive working relationships and contribute to an efficient hospitality team. It discusses the importance of communication, working relationships and behaviour issues. This will also include information on how to improve yourself and your own skills and knowledge.

At the end of this chapter you will be able to:

■ Understand the importance of clear communication in the workplace

■ Understand equal opportunities and employment law

■ Comprehend recognising and valuing diversity

■ Realise the importance of meeting the special needs of colleagues and customers

INTRODUCTION

Hospitality is an industry that revolves around the needs of people. Positive working relationships – between staff and colleagues and between staff and customers (individuals, internal departments and other organisations) – are an essential part of making the business work.

Anything that does not reflect a positive working relationship will inevitably cause staff dissatisfaction, customer dissatisfaction or poor teamwork. These can damage your organisation's effectiveness and its vital relationship with the customer. You will be in the front line of this process every day, acting as a crucial link between the business and other people. You will also be the first point of contact for both the customers and management.

To work in this industry, you have to be good with people: the people you work for, the people you work with and the people you provide services for. These skills can be taught, but they require a degree of effort and willingness to succeed. An enthusiastic person with few skills is better than a highly trained one with an uncaring attitude.

Communication is the fundamental building block for an organisation's success and growth; without it, business will perish. Chefs will have to converse with other chefs, and with waiters, managers and customers, and each is as vital as the next.

The main aim is to satisfy, or indeed exceed, the customers' expectations, and this can only be done by the individuals in the organisation working as a coherent team. The customers are always at the top of the tree as they pay the bills; they create the cash that will allow the staff to earn a wage and which increases the business's success.

COMMUNICATION

Body language is a technique that allows professionals to express themselves without words. This technique can be used in conjunction with verbal communication to great effect. Body language can take many forms:

- *Facial expression* – shows emotion and provides feedback
- *Touch* – shaking hands, greetings, apologies
- *Posture* – sitting, standing, leaning
- *Proximity* – the distance between people
- *Appearance* – dress, clothes, hair
- *Eye contact* – indicating apathy, interest or boredom
- *Hand gestures* – disagreement, anger, welcome

Essential elements of communication are asking questions and making points; these take confidence and practice. Questions should be asked in a way that will produce the most informative answer; using inappropriate phrasing or body language may result in an incomplete or unhelpful reply.

 CHEF'S TIP

The first impression always counts.

 **VIDEO CLIP**
Team meetings

 CHEF'S TIP

There are no individuals in the kitchen – teamwork is the only way to succeed

 CHEF'S TIP

Body language is used by everyone on a daily basis; the skill comes in knowing when you can use body language to your advantage and to create an atmosphere/environment which suits you.

VIDEO CLIP
Briefing the front of house prior to service

VIDEO CLIP
A chef masterclass

CHEF'S TIP

Any segregation of employees will cause the working environment to become strained. Kitchens are hard, heated and unsociable places which require a strong sense of teamwork – any segregation will make this impossible.

During a discussion you should remember the following key points:

◼ Once a speaker has finished express your appreciation.

◼ Use a brief summary of the speaker's points to show you have listened and grasped the concept of the discussion.

◼ Ensure you have your say but in a controlled professional manner. If you need to, write your question down and read it out using a calm, clear voice. Always avoid aggression as this will prevent any worthwhile feedback.

Listening skills are of paramount importance in communication and teamwork. They help us to understand what information or support other people need and ensure we can work cohesively as a group.

EQUAL OPPORTUNITIES

It is the right of every person to be able to seek employment regardless of their race, creed, disability, sex or any other distinguishing feature. The law enforces this right to allow people to work and to prevent them from being segregated or victimised.

Everyone comes into the workplace with different skills. It is the job of senior personnel to utilise those skills and help all staff develop into well-rounded employees. Staff should not be chosen because they are black, Asian, white, small or tall, but because they have what it takes to succeed, both individually and for the company.

What is equal opportunities?

The policy of equal opportunities aims to effect positive behaviour through legislation so that discrimination is prohibited. It is established on moral and ethical influence and is concerned with promoting the rights of all members in our society.

Equal opportunities focuses on assuring the equality of different groups, particularly minorities. It seeks to lessen any disadvantages that can be experienced by being in a minority group. Legislation is supported by practical procedures to assist under-represented groups in the workforce. Programmes are designed to help ensure that training opportunities and funded projects are open to the wider community and those groups who have been traditionally under-represented. For example, health and safety training being delivered in the native language rather than in English.

What is diversity?

Diversity concentrates on the difference of individuals. Managing diversity is based on an economic case for appreciating and valuing difference, rather than the moral case for treating people equally. Equal treatment offers benefits and advantages to employers to invest in ensuring that everyone in the workplace is valued and given the opportunity to develop their potential, which in turn will develop the potential of the business.

By integrating equal opportunities into your programme structure and embracing diversity you will add value to the work you do and help create a strong team. The employer can demonstrate a commitment to equality in a number of ways, including:

- Development of an equal opportunities policy
- Implementation of a policy statement
- Monitor and evaluate the policy with members of staff.

By ensuring these points are understood and made available to all staff, equal opportunities and diversity will be widely acknowledged.

As chefs, we embrace diversity as food has no limitations, and the larger our ethnic background, the more information, techniques and products we can source and learn from.

CHEF'S TIP

Key points of legislation need to be made available to all staff. It is advisable that a laminated copy is placed in the kitchen to aid staff's understanding and knowledge.

Equal opportunities and related legislation in the UK

- Disability Discrimination Act 1995
- Employment Equality (Age) Regulations 2006
- Employment Rights Act 1996
- Health and Safety at Work Act 1974
- Management of Health and Safety at Work Regulations 1999
- Part-time Workers Regulations 2000
- Race Relations Act 1976
- Sex Discrimination Act 1975

- Employment Act 1989
- Employment Relations Act 1999
- Equal Pay Act 1970
- Human Rights Act 1998
- Maternity and Parental Leave etc Regulations 1999
- National Minimum Wage Regulations 1999
- Protection from Harassment Act 1997
- Rehabilitation of Offenders Act 1974
- Working Time Regulations 1998

This list covers the legislation associated with the hospitality industry, but it is by no means exhaustive. The legislation must be followed and adhered to at all times; the relevant information and requirements are usually collated and enforced by a team of trained personnel (usually a Human Resources department).

MEETING EXPECTATIONS

These are a few points that will assist in meeting and exceeding expectations, both internal (staff) and external (customers). It is the responsibility of all staff to strive for perfection and create a welcoming and professional place for customers to visit.

VIDEO CLIP
Customers' special requirements

Assessment of knowledge and understanding

You have now learned about the responsibilities you have to develop positive working relationships. This will enable you to ensure your own positive actions contribute effectively towards the whole team.

To test your level of knowledge and understanding, answer the following short questions. These will help to prepare you for your summative (final) assessment.

Understand the importance of clear communication in the workplace

1 State three reasons why communication is important within the workplace.

i) _____ ii) _____

iii) _____

2 Describe the difference between verbal and physical communication.

_____

Understand equal opportunities and employment law

1 List five Acts relating to equal opportunities.

i) _____ ii) _____

iii) _____ iv) _____

v) _____

2 State how they are relevant to a busy kitchen environment.

_____

Comprehend recognising and valuing diversity

1 State how diversity within a kitchen can be of benefit.

_____

2 Describe briefly how diversity can be achieved within the hospitality industry.

_____

Realise the importance of meeting the special needs of colleagues and customers

1 Describe what is meant by the phrase 'exceeding customer expectations'.

_____

2 State why it is important to understand the needs of customers.

_____

Research Task

Communication is important when working in a busy environment like a kitchen. State five things you can do to ensure the kitchen operation works smoothly on a daily basis.

5

Contribute to the control of resources

LEARNING OBJECTIVES

The aim of this chapter is to give you an understanding of the contribution of resources within a kitchen and to encourage you to develop skills and implement knowledge for controlling resources, including assessment and understanding of the importance of equipment, colleagues and suppliers as resources.

At the end of this chapter you will be able to:

- Identify and understand the importance of equipment, colleagues and suppliers

- Understand time management skills

- Identify the correct way to monitor costs

- Utilise information systems in the workplace

- Have a competent knowledge of health and safety requirements

EQUIPMENT, COLLEAGUES AND SUPPLIERS

The importance of the kitchen within a business is obvious and tangible. However, it is only by the chef making sure that all colleagues are fully aware of business issues that a kitchen can function to its full potential.

All members of a team employed in a kitchen and all suppliers used to resource the kitchen should establish solid working relationships, with communication skills being the key to achieving this.

Equipment as an important resource

Without the correct equipment in a kitchen, the production of a menu would not be possible and cost effectiveness would be greatly reduced. Generally speaking, good-quality equipment items – whether ovens, stoves or a chef's personal knives – will last longer and perform the required job much better than their cheaper counterparts, so long as regular maintenance is carried out.

The word 'equipment' encompasses all tools used within a kitchen, which typically fall into three categories:

- *Large equipment* – such as steamers, sinks, tables and oven ranges
- *Mechanical equipment* – such as food blenders, electric mixers and slicing machines
- *Utensils and small equipment* – such as bowls, spoons, pots, whisks and pans.

All equipment within a workplace must conform to the EU Safety Directive. In January 1995, British Standards combined with European Standards to create a legal requirement that all equipment must carry the CE mark. The initials CE do not stand for any specific words, but the mark indicates that the required safety standards are met. CE marking is a declaration by a manufacturer that their product meets all the appropriate provisions of the relevant legislation. It gives companies easier access into the European market to sell their products without the need for adaptation or rechecking.

Not all equipment will have a CE mark, especially equipment imported from the USA and other non-EU countries. Not only is such equipment likely to require modification to work on AC current (necessitating the use of an electric transformer), it is also unlikely to have a comprehensive warranty. This may mean that any breakdowns or maintenance will have to be dealt with by the manufacturer in the country of origin (unless they have an office in the country of purchase). Although they will have their own safety standards, they may not be the same standard as the CE mark.

All staff should be fully trained and competent in the use of all equipment in the workplace. Everyone must be aware of the safety measures that are in

CHEF'S TIP

All equipment within the kitchen, whether large, mechanical or a utensil, should be correctly maintained and checked at regular intervals to ensure safe use.

VIDEO CLIP
Use of portable equipment

CHEF'S TIP

Never assume that all kitchen staff are aware of correct maintenance and cleaning procedures for equipment. All new staff members should be shown the procedures that must be followed to ensure safety.

place and the correct course of action to take in the event of any accidents. Further, it is advisable that all staff are aware of how to properly clean and maintain all equipment. If equipment is not properly cleaned and stored hygienically, the risk of contaminating foods is significantly increased.

Electrical equipment should be checked and maintained on a regular basis to ensure the safety of staff, which is paramount (see Chapter 1). However, equipment that is well-maintained and looked after also lasts longer and so does not have to be replaced as frequently, helping to keep equipment costs low.

Colleagues as an important resource

The importance of your staff and colleagues within the kitchen is fundamental. Generally, good communication skills, understanding, flexibility, adaptability, teamwork and patience will allow colleagues to work well and function as a team.

Creating a contented working environment and a team that is flexible and with good morale will make staff more productive. It will also lower staff turnover and reduce sick leave, and so reduce recruitment costs and help prevent staff shortages.

Regular training and staff development schemes will give employees the opportunity to perfect existing skills and learn new skills, and are viewed positively as evidence that a company is investing in its employees. They are also a break from the working day; it is refreshing for staff to do something a little different from the normal routine. Make sure that all staff are aware of any new or ongoing training schemes, and that sufficient cover will be available if they are away from the kitchen.

Appraisal or progress reviews, where one member of staff looks at the way another employee/member of staff is performing in their job role, are an important method of communication. It is usual for an employee to receive an appraisal from their line manager.

Appraisals provide an opportunity to review an individual's performance against set targets. Each team member has their own strengths and weaknesses. It is important to utilise those strengths and to improve areas of weakness through setting appropriate personal goals and an action plan.

Performance appraisals will identify:

- Results achieved against preset targets
- Any additional accomplishments and contributions.

This may seem overwhelming, but it is an important and useful process. To make sure that you get the most out of appraisals:

- Identify with your line manager the tasks that you see need to be accomplished, and how these will be met

CHEF'S TIP

It is a good idea to note in a diary, on a calendar or on the computer when electrical equipment is due for a safety check to ensure that it does not get overlooked.

An aluminium case for storage of knives

CHEF'S TIP

Make sure that all staff know where all equipment is stored within the kitchen. A lot of precious time can be lost trying to locate items.

CHEF'S TIP

Be proactive within the workplace by regularly taking time to review courses that are available or of interest to you. Most employers will actively encourage their staff to further their skills for the benefit of the workplace.

CHEF'S TIP

Team-building exercises, both inside and outside of the workplace, are a good way of getting to know your colleagues better and of learning improved ways of working together.

■ Identify your training need; training will provide you with a greater range of skills and expertise, which will ultimately improve your opportunities for promotion, giving you increased responsibilities

■ Identify any obstructions which are affecting your progress

■ Identify any changes to your current job role

■ Identify what additional responsibilities you would like

■ Identify and focus on your achievements to date against the targets set

■ Update your action plan, which will help you achieve your targets.

If personal targets are not being met, it is important to identify the reasons why. New performance targets can then be put in place to resolve any difficulties. At the following appraisal, the agreed objectives and targets set for the previous period will be reviewed.

In order to develop personally and to improve your skills professionally, it is important to have personal targets against which you can measure your achievement. If these are confidential, the workplace policy on confidentiality should be observed. All targets set should be SMART.

SMART TARGETS	
Specific	Specific targets outline exactly what the employee aims to do, rather than expressing vague general aims.
Measurable	Outlining how the employee will know they have met the targets and what evidence will show this.
Achievable	Challenging for the employee, but not too difficult.
Realistic	The opportunities and resources should be available.
Time-bound	There should be both interim and final deadlines.
Targets can be even **SMARTER**. They can be:	
Enjoyable	
Rewarding	

It is important to your employer that you are consistent. You must always perform your skills to the highest standard and present and promote a positive image of the industry and the business you represent. Entering culinary competitions, where you will have the chance meet and compete against other chefs, will give you the opportunity to see new techniques and exchange ideas and develop your skills. This is an intense learning strategy and will also create a positive reputation for you and your place of work. There are many different competitions both on a local and national basis with categories for both junior and senior chefs.

Chefs can also learn and develop through the membership of professional associations. Developing a network of associates, friends and peers is very important for business and learning. Chefs, employers, suppliers, training providers and managers are able to exchange ideas and to discuss ways to help meet industry targets, such as training, profitability and links to other industries across the world.

The continuation of learning is essential for success in this industry, and the prospect of continuing to acquire knowledge and further develop skills to advance one's career is a great incentive. Colleges have diverse courses of study to help match your development plan: they also assess the skills that the industry will require in the future for your job to be carried out effectively and for you to progress in your profession.

Suppliers as an important resource

Finding suitable suppliers of produce can be a very challenging and lengthy process. It is therefore vital for the running of a kitchen that solid working relationships are established with suppliers.

Suppliers must be able to provide good-quality produce on a regular basis at a reasonable price, and finding good ones can be very difficult. Most chefs and businesses source their produce from wholesalers, with those that supply specialist commodities usually being recommended by word-of-mouth from other kitchens. A good reputation will indicate a good supplier, one who may be invaluable for obtaining your required produce.

There are two main buying methods, commonly referred to as 'informal' and 'formal'. Informal buying means that an agreement between supplier and purchaser will be verbal, and formal buying means that a written agreement will be put in place, usually by means of a computerised ordering system.

When considering which supplier to employ, you should take the following factors into account:

■ *Quality* – Never instruct a supplier before sampling the produce they have to offer, especially when dealing with a large wholesaler as you may have to sign a contract agreeing to purchase goods for a minimum period of time or with a minimum delivery cost. You should always establish work principles and delivery times with the supplier. It is a standard practice to request a visit to a supplier's establishment to assess their workplace and code of work.

Food produce should always be fresh, clearly labelled, properly packaged and stored within health and safety regulations, and the supplier should be aware of the origin of their produce and have the relative paperwork available.

■ *Quantity* – You will need to establish the volume of goods that your suppliers regularly have available, especially with smaller suppliers. If this is not determined first, you may run the risk of not being able to obtain stock when specifically required. With equipment items, if the supplier does not have a good stock you run the risk that they will not be able to replace goods within a reasonable timescale.

VIDEO CLIP
Online ordering systems in the kitchen and restaurant

CHEF'S TIP

Never feel pressurised by a supplier to use their produce. You set the standard, and you will have to accept the consequences if the produce is not of a good quality.

CHEF'S TIP

It is good practice to appoint 'secondary' staff to deal with ordering goods in the absence of the usual designated person so that at all times there is someone in the kitchen who is aware of the ordering procedure and the suppliers used.

■ *Cost* – A supplier's cost must be calculated carefully prior to instruction/agreement. Check that any carriage charges are made clear, whether VAT is included in the prices or must be added, if any ordering charge or minimum order amount applies and if there are any other additional costs that you may be unaware of.

■ *Reliability* – It is very important that suppliers are reliable. If they are not able to deliver produce to you as regularly as you require and in a correct state, the kitchen will not be able to run smoothly. You could be left without goods and unable to prepare a menu or certain dishes. When purchasing electrical items, ask about customer aftercare as there may be additional maintenance, servicing or repair costs that need to be taken into consideration. Check the timescales for emergency call-outs.

If using a supplier on a regular basis, it is a good idea to negotiate over prices, especially for large orders of non-specialist items. You can both benefit through the cost efficiencies of regular large orders.

MATCHING RESOURCES TO TARGETS

Work targets will be set for each individual, who will have a personal and team obligation to meet them. When presented with work targets, it is a good idea to go through them thoroughly to establish any points that you may have queries on or are not happy with. Once you are happy with what is required and when it is required by, you can use your knowledge of your team and their various strengths to allocate the required tasks. You should then brief the individuals and the team in a brief meeting.

The ability to set shared targets and make plans is essential for successful teamwork. If chefs do not know what they are aiming to achieve, they cannot determine what has been achieved. If there is no real planning, progression cannot be properly monitored to review how well things are going and to learn from the experience. It is during these stages that team members can support each other and provide help where necessary to achieve the end result.

When preparing a menu it is essential that all foods required are obtained in plenty of time, along with any specialist or additional equipment that may be needed. It is bad practice to fall behind with targets due to poor preparation, lack of foresight or a negative attitude towards the workplace. Time management is an important skill for chefs working in the hospitality industry. In order to manage your time most effectively, you must have a realistic assessment of all the tasks required and then plan the workload accordingly.

The keys to matching suitable resources to work targets:

■ *Ascertain* – Look at and listen to what is being required of you or your team.

■ *Ask* – If you are uncertain of any points, do not be afraid to ask, otherwise errors could occur that you will be responsible for.

- *Assess* – Establish everything that will be required to carry out the task, such as food produce, equipment and staff, and whether anyone will need any special briefing.
- *Action* – Order anything that is required, brief yourself and your colleagues before beginning the task.
- *Monitor* – Once everything is in place, ensure that it is monitored continually. Do not assume that everything will run according to plan.
- *Review* – It is only by reviewing how a task has been carried out and whether a target has been successfully achieved that you can make constructive criticism. This will enable you to improve your skills in order to achieve targets.

Setting personal targets enables you to monitor your own progression and understanding in this area, and may highlight any areas in which you require further training.

TIME MANAGEMENT

Within the kitchen and serving areas it is important to have a good comprehension of both your personal time management and that of your colleagues. By establishing these you will be able to ensure that you work well as a team, and that each process is carried out in as little time as possible and will fall in line with the role that each member of staff performs. The result will be a smooth running and efficient workplace.

As in any workplace, the ability to prioritise is an important skill. Establishing which processes take longest and which require the most attention and keeping strictly to deadlines will enable you to complete tasks in plenty of time and to a high standard.

Starting each working shift with a team meeting will enable colleagues to discuss the schedule of events and any issues or concerns that they may have with regard to pre-planning, communication, time-setting and special arrangements. It is also good practice to have a daily table of events, detailing what each member of the team will be doing and approximate times that they should complete their tasks by. Any special events, changes to a menu or produce to be worked with that requires extra attention should be discussed thoroughly with individuals well in advance.

Besides being provided with either a verbal or written timetable of events, each individual member of staff should monitor their own time management. Not everyone is good at managing their time, but there are now a variety of courses available to employees that can help provide individuals with positive methods and tips on how to improve their time management.

Each member of the team performs a valuable role in the workplace. Team members rely on each other being alert and punctual so that colleagues are not left at a disadvantage due to someone else's poor timekeeping, time allocation or not being alert and awake.

 CHEF'S TIP

Constructive team and personal criticism is just as helpful as praise. It will help you to perform better within the workplace, giving you realistic targets to build on and achieve.

 CHEF'S TIP

Ensure you arrive in plenty of time before your shift starts so that you are able to review and assess the timetable of events for the shift and manage your time around this.

COST CONTROL

Cost control is essential in the running and maintaining of any business, with the aim being to retain as much money as possible by paying out as little as possible in costs. The costs of employing staff, purchasing food produce, purchase, repair or replacement of equipment, and even the rent on a building, must be closely monitored at all times.

First and foremost, any business will need to devise a budget. This will give approximate guidelines for how much money can be allocated (usually on a company financial year basis) to the running of each contributory sector of the business, such as how much money can be spent on staff wages, supplies and equipment.

Based on this budget, a target profit figure will be set. The target profit will take costs into consideration, and will usually consist of a gross figure (all monies received) and a net figure (minus any expenses paid out).

Knowing the exact cost of each process and every item that is produced allows you to monitor profits made by each division based on the cost of each meal produced. Furthermore, it makes it possible to see where changes may be needed, such as to prevent over-ordering (wastage of goods), and where any economising strategies could be put into place. You can also use costing knowledge to estimate other costs, so that you can quote for catering for any special functions, such as weddings or corporate events.

Cost will generally fall under one of three headings:

■ *Food or material costs* – The cost of buying these items is variable as several contributory factors will affect it, such as the volume of business, ordering of speciality goods, catering for any functions, any temporary staff that may be required and, worst-case scenario, spoiled goods.

■ *Labour* – Labour costs are split into two sub-elements:
  – *Direct labour*: wages for staff directly working in or with the kitchen, such as chefs, housekeepers, waiters, bar staff and any other kitchen workers
  – *Indirect labour*: wages to all other staff involved indirectly in the running of the kitchen, such as managers, maintenance personnel and general office staff.

The income within a kitchen will pay all direct labour costs and indirect labour costs will be covered by income from the departments that these employees work for.

■ *Overheads* – These costs include expenses such as utility bills, purchase of equipment and rental of premises.

Further to the above, cleaning materials will have to be accounted for. These are considered as overheads. It is easy to forget that everything within a kitchen needs to be cleaned regularly and so there must be sufficient

CHEF'S TIP

When given team financial targets, aim to exceed expectations by setting a new target higher than the actual target. You will not only feel personal satisfaction but will achieve good results for the business, which will be gratefully recognised by any employer.

Staff wages are one of the costs of running a business

cleaning equipment at all times. Therefore, any budget will need to ensure enough money is allocated for cleaning items, such as dish cloths, towels, brooms and cleaning fluids.

Profit

■ *Gross profit* – the monetary difference between the cost of the food used to create a dish and the selling price of the dish as purchased by a customer is referred to as 'gross' or 'kitchen' profit.

SALE PRICE – FOOD COST = GROSS PROFIT (KITCHEN PROFIT)

■ *Net profit* – the monetary difference between the selling price of the food to a customer and the total cost incurred to create the dish, including labour, food and overheads, is referred to as 'net' profit.

SALE PRICE – TOTAL COST = NET PROFIT

The cost of each dish is calculated then the total costs worked out per day, per week, per month and per year.

Any profit made is always shown or referred to as a percentage of the selling price. This is calculated as follows:

GROSS PROFIT
GROSS PROFIT (£) × 100 ÷ SELLING PRICE (£) = GROSS PROFIT (%)

NET PROFIT
NET PROFIT (£) x 100 ÷ SELLING PRICE (£) = NET PROFIT (%)

When calculating the cost of a dish, the actual cost price of ingredients needs to be determined. This is achieved by totalling the costs of all ingredients used to create a dish and then dividing this by the number of portions you will be able to make from all the ingredients. The table below gives an example of how food costs and production costs, such as labour and overheads, relate to the selling price of a dish.

PRICE AND COSTS FOR COQ AU VIN	
Selling price	£17.50
Food cost	£9.00
Labour and overheads	£4.50
Total cost	£13.50
GROSS PROFIT	£8.50
NET PROFIT	£4.00

In this example, the gross profit is 49 per cent and the net profit is 23 per cent.

A simple rule that can be used to calculate the selling price of a dish is that the food cost of the dish should equal 45 per cent of the selling price. The selling price of the dish can then be calculated as follows:

Food cost of coq au vin = £9.00

$$\text{Selling price} = \frac{£9.00 \times 100}{45} = £20.00$$

Selling the coq au vin at £20.00 therefore makes a gross profit of 55 per cent.

A general example of how this works over a working week is as follows:

WEEKLY PROFITS	
Food sales for one week	£32,000
Food cost for one week	£15,000
Labour and overheads for one week	£11,500
Total costs for one week	£26,500
GROSS PROFIT	£17,000
NET PROFIT	£ 5,500

This works out as 53 per cent gross profit and 17 per cent net profit for the week.

Accurate monitoring and controlling of the food cost of certain items makes it much easier to meet a budget and to monitor, and in turn to control, where any profits and losses are made.

It is very difficult to save money on costs and to meet a budget within the catering industry as most resources have variable prices. Buying items in bulk and taking advantage of special offers/rates and the seasonality of foods can all contribute toward making savings.

As a guideline, the following points should be considered when monitoring cost control:

- *Quality of produce at a fair price* – it is generally best not to select 'cheaper' alternatives for most items as the quality does not tend to be as good; having to repair or replace broken equipment or replace poor-quality foods will cost more in the long term, and not just in terms of money but also labour and other resources.
- *Portion control* – ensure that all staff are aware of portion sizes to be served for each dish to limit wastage.
- *Waste control* – regularly check rubbish bins to ensure that only waste is being disposed of, and not quality items or produce that could otherwise be utilised.

- *Theft* – to prevent any items leaving the premises 'through the back door', any bags, coats or purses belonging to staff should be stored securely out of the kitchen area and regular stocktakes should be completed; all doors to the premises other than main entrances should be alarmed so that managers will be aware if anyone is entering or leaving the building by these routes.
- *Weekly stocktake* – stock should be checked on a weekly basis, and it is easier to do this if it is split into the main food categories, i.e. fish, meat, vegetables, fruit, dairy and other, and equipment; if costs dramatically increase, the stocktake will give an insight as to where it has increased.
- *Ensure prices are correct* – when pricing dishes, at least a 40–50 per cent dish cost should be incorporated as you will not only have to cover the cost of the specific food product(s) but you will also have to cover other items such as condiments; inflation also needs to be taken into consideration as this will increase yearly and prices will need to cater for this.

INFORMATION SYSTEMS

An information system is simply a means of communicating various pieces of information to those working within an establishment. Several different information systems will exist within the kitchen area and all staff should be aware of how these work.

VIDEO CLIP
Use of computers

An electronic point of sales system (EPOS), such as MICROS, can be used to improve control over the restaurant or kitchen. Such systems offer the most integrated restaurant-operation applications available to the chef. Applications are built for individual businesses, providing the tools to potentially increase profitability. Up-to-the-minute information is always available, and reports on labour management, equipment inventory, food costs and guest loyalty programmes can be easily generated. Such systems allow detailed financial reporting and analysis and streamline ordering and recipe management.

Installing technology in the kitchen will help to improve time management and so allow you to spend time planning for the future.

Ensuring the retention and growth of the customer base are vital for any business, but especially so within the hospitality industry. Consumers in this day and age expect to be served with efficiency, professionalism and politeness. Installing an EPOS system in your area can allow you to reach higher levels of customer service by having all the information you need on a database.

An EPOS system will allow you to maintain real-time information on your stock inventory levels and recipe ingredients and costs, as well as competitive supplier quotes. You will have a record of what was ordered and when, and even which member of the team communicated with which supplier.

Suppliers can now usually accept orders electronically via email

Assessment of knowledge and understanding

You have now learned about the importance of equipment, colleagues and suppliers as valuable resources within the kitchen. You will have gained an understanding of the importance and need for time management, information systems, cost control, matching resources to work targets and health and safety within this workplace. This will enable you to effectively recognise, assess and implement the skills required to carry out these tasks.

To test your level of knowledge and understanding, answer the following short questions. These will help to prepare you for your summative (final) assessment.

Equipment, colleagues and suppliers as important resources

1 Discuss the benefits of creating a team that works well together and the importance of communication in the workplace.

Time management and cost control

1 Detail the importance of cost control and how this relates to a budget.

Work targets and information systems

1 Discuss the benefits of setting personal targets.

Research Task

You now have an understanding of cost control and how to cost dishes on a menu.

Complete the table below and cost a starter, main and dessert using the information provided, taking the following assumptions into account:

■ The cost of labour and overheads are 55 per cent of the food cost per portion

■ The food cost is 45 per cent and the selling price is fixed at 100 per cent.

	STARTER	MAIN	DESSERT
Selling cost of dish	£	£	£
Bulk food cost	£36.75	£69.75	£26.25
Portions provided	15	15	15
Food cost per portion	£	£	£
Cost of labour and overheads	£	£	£
Total cost	£	£	£
GROSS PROFIT	£	£	£
NET PROFIT	£	£	£
GROSS PROFIT	%	%	%
NET PROFIT	%	%	%

6

Developing recipes and menus

HS9 Contribute to the development and introduction of recipes and menus

LEARNING OBJECTIVES

The aim of this chapter is to enable you to develop competence and put into practice the relevant skills associated with menu planning. It discusses the importance of understanding issues associated with menu planning, and includes information on how to improve yourself and your skills and knowledge regarding this topic.

At the end of this chapter you will be able to:

- Develop new recipe ideas
- Recognise dietary requirements
- Write an informative and balanced menu
- Understand how to market your menu
- Support the implementation of the menu

INTRODUCTION

As a chef becomes secure with the pace and structure of an existing menu, it is natural to want to improve or change its content, structure or design. To be able to do this, a thorough understanding of menu planning and implementation is imperative. There will be very few menus created in a chef's life that can be labelled 'perfect'.

Input from third parties will allow a menu to be developed that suits the needs of both the business and the customers. When developing new ideas for a menu, certain considerations should be taken into account:

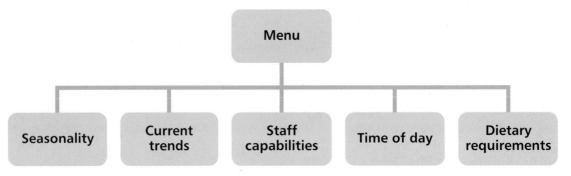

Factors affecting menu design

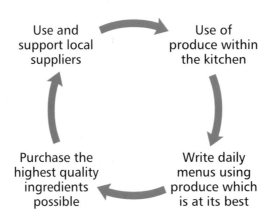

Menu consideration cycle

SEASONALITY

Many foods are seasonal, such as fruits, vegetables, game, fish and certain meats.

■ *Fruit and vegetables* can generally be purchased throughout the year; if they are not in season in this country they will be in season somewhere in the world and can be transported quickly by air. However, locally sourced foods are generally cheaper, more environmentally friendly and more flavoursome than commodities sourced from overseas.

- *Fish* that are about to breed and are full of eggs (roe) will not only have less flavour but also a lower flesh yield than fish that are in season. This will obviously affect portion control and costs for the dish overall.
- *Game* can only be killed when not breeding or raising young; each game animal has an allocated season. At the very start of a game season the flavour of the flesh can be a little characterless.
- *Meat* seasonality is usually restricted to lamb. Spring lamb is very tender, but it is also quite expensive; the development of the menu should take this into consideration.

The choice and convenience offered by the all year round availability of a full range of food produce from all over the world has allowed chefs to produce eclectic menus. However, there are many benefits to a return to following the seasonal cycles of nature, and of buying fresh, seasonal produce from local suppliers.

The increasing awareness of health-related issues and concerns about the quality, sources and types of food we consume are increasingly influencing consumers' opinions. The environmental impacts of excessive 'food miles' – the transporting of food produce long distances – and the 'traceability' of food are also key factors that influence consumers' buying behaviour.

Food miles are a measure of how far ingredients have travelled, from the farmer who produces it to the consumer who eats it. The concept is sometimes known as 'farm to fork'. The total distance includes the journey from farm to processor, then from processor to retailer and finally from retailer to consumer. It includes travel within the UK as well as between countries. Generally, the further food has to travel, the longer it spends in transit. That means that vital vitamin content can be lost and the nutritional value of fresh foods will inevitably decline. Transporting food over long distances will also consume a lot of fuel, whether it travels by road or air. This inevitably increases carbon dioxide emissions and contributes to global warming.

CURRENT TRENDS

Chefs should always be totally aware of what competitors and trends are doing. Studying the reviews of top chefs' restaurants and reading the media's commentaries on the attitudes of customers to the new food trends is important research for writing your new menu. Speak to your customers, suppliers and team when creating new dishes, and consider what will both meet the needs of your existing customers and attract new ones.

VIDEO CLIP
The future chef

TYPE OF MENU

- À la carte – items on the menu are individually priced and are cooked or finished to order; this allows the guest to construct their own menu.

Wednesday 23rd May 2007

Consommé Celestine £3.50

Baby Vegetable and Tomato Terrine with Fig Salad £4.50

Sardine Niçoise Salad £4.75

Duck & Chicken Liver Ravioli with Wild Mushroom & Madeira Jus £5.00

Poached Egg on a Toasted Muffin with Smoked Salmon,
Asparagus Spears and Dill Hollandaise £5.25

Smoked Venison, Pomegranate, Cherry, Watercress &
Mixed Bead Salad £5.25

Classic Fish Pie with Tossed Green Vegetables £7.50

Délice of Lemon Sole with a Crab Mousse, Vegetable Spaghetti, Parsley Potatoes
and Glazed White Wine Sauce with Chilled Grapes £8.75

Grilled Red Snapper with Spinach & Garlic Tagliatelle, Mediteranean Vegetables
and a Basil Pesto £9.25

Veal Goulash with Wild Mushrooms and Parsley Gnocchi £8.50

Braised Pork Belly, Sage Derby Mash, Wilted Spinach, Broad Beans
and Cider Rosemary Jus £9.25

Duck Leg Confit with Cretan Potato, Spring Greens and Orange Jus £10.25

Pea and Mint Risotto with Feta Cheese, Pea & Mint Salad £7.75

Pan-fried Sunblushed Tomato & Basil Polenta with Sunblushed Tomato,
Olive & Pine Nut Salad £7.75

Roast Chicken, Game Chips, Watercress Bread Sauce, Jus, Lemon & Thyme Seasoning,
Roast Potatoes, Mixed Green Vegetables (from the Carving Trolley) £9.50

Mango and Lychee Brochette with Coconut Sorbet and Banana Tuille £4.50

Pear Tatin Coupe £4.50

Strawberry and Cream Berlingot £4.50

Orange and Poppy Seed Cake with Melon Sorbet and
Sweet Ginger Prada £4.50

Coffee from £1.50

An à la carte menu

■ **Table d'hôte** – a set menu, with a set price. Table d'hôte menus usually have only limited choices, such as a meat, fish or vegetarian option, and an option for people with special dietary needs.
Menus can range from a single course to a nine- or ten-course 'grazing menu'. The portion sizes should reflect the size of the menu; for a

Selection of canapés with Champagne

Veal Kidney, Veal Liver, Veal Sweetbread and foie gras terrine
with a little set Port Jelly, with grain mustard sauce, salad leaf
garnish and a taco biscuit

Lobster, Mussel, Monkfish and Scallop in a Shortcrust,
herb and saffron tartlet with a shellfish essence sauce

Trio of Lamb
Shepherds Pie, Offal Faggot, petite cannon of lamb,
Cretan Potato, medley of beans, red wine jus

Stilton and quince jelly Brulee in a shot glass with a peppercorn
and poppy seed spoon shaped Tuille type biscuit

Passion fruit mousse with a dried pineapple crisp,
and a Campari sorbet

Coffee and Infusions

A function menu

single-course menu the portion size should satisfy the appetite, and with a multi-course menu the entire menu should satisfy the appetite without making guests feel too full or unable to finish their meal.

Banquet and function menus are usually table d'hôte menus, carefully designed with the needs of the customer in mind. Care should be taken not to include dishes that take a long time to assemble or contain food that will deteriorate quickly and so will not hold for service.

■ *Cyclical* – menus which are designed to be repeated at given intervals; usually on a weekly, monthly or seasonal basis. Cyclical menus are usually used in canteens and educational institutions and in facilities that have groups of people for set periods of time, such as training centres. In canteens and staff restaurants, where the customers eat every day, the cycle should be longer and start on different days of the week so that the customers will not feel bored by the repetition of the food on offer.

MENU

22 May 2007

****

Chilled fresh cherry tomato soup with a Langoustine cocktail

Pan-fried breast of Quail with a blood orange and chicory salad

Smoked mushroom Parfait served with a Gravadlax of field
mushrooms and wet garlic, lemon zested crisp bread

****

Fillet of beef with a herb crust, Pressed Breast of Veal on a Rosti
potato served with broccoli and glazed carrots, Red Wine jus

Sweet Potato Gnocchi with a sauté of Plantain
and a Pepperonata sauce

Pan-fried Grey Mullet with a trout and dill Boudin on Macaire
potatoes, buttered runner beans and caramelised button onions,
Soubise foam

****

A table d'hôte menu from a small hotel

Stock control will be more efficient with cyclical menus: the stock
requirements will be known well in advance and therefore stock levels can
be kept low. In large operations, long-term agreements or forward
purchasing can lead to further discounts with suppliers.

■ *Breakfast* – an extremely important part of a hotel's repertoire of food
service. Generally, the last impression a guest receives of a hotel's food is
the breakfast service. Breakfast menus can be à la carte, buffet style or
continental. The offer can include a selection of the following:

- Cereals, porridge and yoghurts
- Fruit juices, fresh and preserved fruit
- Fried meats, such as sausage, bacon,
  black pudding, kidney dishes
- Selection of breads and morning
  goods, such as croissants

- Egg dishes
- Smoked fish
- Cold meats
- Sautéed potatoes
- Preserves
- Tea, coffee, chocolate

DIETARY REQUIREMENTS

Understanding the various requirements of people who have special dietary needs is a requirement of the modern chef.

- *Coeliac* –No gluten is allowed in the diet (e.g. breads and biscuits; any foods that contain wheat flour). Soya flour, which does not contain gluten, can be used as a substitute to wheat flour in most cases.

- *Diabetic* –Avoid foods that contain sugar or glucose, show the sugar content of dishes, or provide alternative courses that allow the guest to choose dishes that are high or low on the glycaemic index. Most diabetics can moderate their medication to suit menus as long as they know the menu in advance.

- *Nut allergic* –Some people have an extreme intolerance to nuts; they can go into anaphylactic shock after consuming even the slightest trace of nuts, which will require immediate medical help. Menus should indicate clearly whether nut products have been used.

- *Shellfish allergic* –Sufferers may experience a range of symptoms, from a slight rash to extreme anaphylactic shock.

- *Dairy intolerance* –Soya-based products can be used to replace dairy products in cooking.

- *Vegan* –Vegan diets contain no animal products at all.

- *Vegetarian* –Vegetarian diets include no meat or fish products.

- *Ovo-lactarian* –Vegetarian diet that includes eggs and dairy products.

- *Lactarian* – Vegetarian diet that includes dairy products but not eggs.

Hospital patients

Any menu in a hospital should be written by both the chef and a dietician. The dietary requirements of the patients are of paramount importance in hospital catering.

Schoolchildren

There is a renaissance in the desire to provide schoolchildren with a healthy diet; one which is free from excess fatty and processed foods. The budgetary constraints placed upon school caterers can be very restrictive in the production of these menus.

College/university students

Similar to schools, the menus on offer should be healthy but substantial to allow for the higher metabolic rates of this group. Menus should reflect a diversity of styles and ethnic cuisines.

People at work

Consideration should be given to the occupation of the recipients of the food. Soldiers in training and manual workers from a building site, for example, will require a lot of calories, but office workers use fewer calories and may desire a more healthy diet. Chefs working in the financial and corporate business sector may receive requests such as a "lunch requirement to help secure a big deal". A substantial contract may be at stake, so the menu should be discussed carefully with the client or principal butler to ascertain the client's requirements.

WRITING AN INFORMATIVE AND BALANCED MENU

When writing a menu consider the following points:

- *Avoid jargon* – do not use unnecessary jargon that might intimidate the guest, and do not over-embellish the description of each dish.
- *Use local and understandable language* – certain words will not translate into English from a menu planning point of view, such as mayonnaise or sauerkraut. These are words that have over time become part of the English language. If foreign language is used, sometimes it is best to state a simple explanation in English underneath or to ensure the food service team can translate the menu perfectly for the customer.
- *Keep it simple* – use menu descriptions that are simple to understand, and avoid including too many dishes as the customer will have difficulty in choosing.

VIDEO CLIP
Menu production, using fridges and storing stock

DEVELOPMENT OF THE MENU

Menus must evolve with the needs of the customer and the business, and for most chefs, change is important: it keeps interest and ambition alive. But changes to menus should be structured to allow for smooth transitions.

Before making any changes, critically evaluate the menu. Check the sales mix of each dish and then write recipes that fit in with the structure of the existing menu and complement dishes that you intend to keep. The recipes should be costed to fit into the business plan and achieve the required profit margins.

VIDEO CLIP
Producing a balanced menu

Implementing menu changes

1   When designing recipes, take into account all previously mentioned factors and ensure that food costings are correct.

VIDEO CLIP
How to cost recipes

2 Produce an accurate specification sheet for each dish.

DISH SPECIFICATION SHEET

Chef: Date:

Name of Dish:

[Photograph of dish]

Ingredients required

Quantity	Ingredient	Quantity	Ingredient

Equipment required

Method of work

Appropriate sauces, garnishes, glazes and accompaniments for the dish

Quality points for the main ingredients

Potential food allergies related to the dish

Measure to be taken to prevent life-threatening reactions to allergens

Head chef with a new dish

3 Test cook each dish.

4 Taste test each dish.

5 Discuss the merits of each dish and make any changes that are deemed necessary.

6 If a dish is approved, present it to the service team to sample and describe the dish to them exactly. It is important that the service staff have an understanding of every new dish as their recommendations can lead to the dish being a success.

Service staff being briefed on new dishes

7 Meet with some of the customers who have tried the new menu and get their feedback. This has the advantage of making the clientele feel included and builds a rapport with them.

MARKETING THE MENU

Menu changes can work in favour of a business if the new menu is marketed well. When devising a marketing strategy, you should consider how best to reach your customers and what you can do to generate interest in your offering:

Assessment of knowledge and understanding

You have now learned about the development and introduction of recipes and menus. This will enable you to make a positive contribution in their implementation.

To test your level of knowledge and understanding, answer the following short questions. These will help to prepare you for your summative (final) assessment.

Developing new recipe ideas

1 State three stages in the development of new recipes.

i) _____ ii) _____

iii)_____

2 Explain why it is important to give an in-depth briefing to service staff when introducing new menu items.

_____

3 Explain why it is important to consider the customers' needs when developing new recipes.

_____

Costing recipes

1 What are the financial advantages of a cyclical menu?

_____

_____

2 Explain the term 'gross profit'.

_____

_____

Recognising dietary requirements

1 Name two allergies the can bring on anaphylactic shock.

i) _____ ii) _____

2 Who should compile menus for hospitals?

_____

_____

3 Explain two factors to consider when planning dishes for school children.

i) _____ ii) _____

Writing an informative and balanced menu and marketing the menu

1 Explain why it is important not to have too many dishes on the menu.

_____

_____

2 List two methods of marketing a menu.

i) _____ ii) _____

Support the implementation of the menu

1 List the stages that should be followed when testing a recipe.

_____

_____

Research Task

Using your knowledge of a professional kitchen, devise a simple menu for use in each of the following places (one menu for each):

■ School

■ College

■ Restaurant

■ Hotel

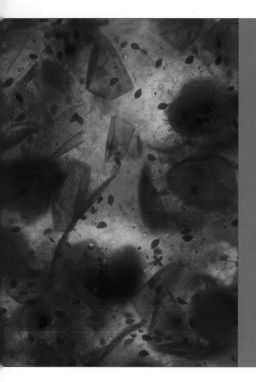

7

Stocks and sauces

3FPC1 Prepare, cook and finish complex hot sauces

3FPC11 Prepare, cook and finish dressings and cold sauces

LEARNING OBJECTIVES

The aim of this chapter is to enable you to develop skills and implement knowledge in the preparation and cookery principles of hot and cold sauces, stocks and dressings. This will also include materials, ingredients and equipment.

At the end of this chapter you will be able to:

- Identify each sauce, stock and dressing variety and finished product
- Understand the use of relative ingredients in stock, sauce and dressing cookery
- State the quality points of various stock, sauce and dressing commodities and end products
- Prepare and cook each type of stock, sauce and dressing variety
- Identify the storage procedures of stocks, sauces and dressings
- Be competent at preparing and cooking a range of stocks, sauces and dressings

INTRODUCTION

Sauces

A sauce is most accurately described as a flavoured liquid, which in essence is a base that has been thickened. A **stock** is generally regarded as the base for many sauces and is an extremely important component.

The thickenings used for sauces vary greatly, depending on the base ingredient.

For instance, hollandaise is thickened by adding **clarified butter** to egg yolks, mayonnaise by adding oil to egg yolks, **beurre blanc** with whisked butter, and cream sauces are reduced with double cream.

Modern sauces are lightened by using less fat to take into account society's healthier lifestyles. However, **cream**, **jus** and butter are still used to complement many dishes.

A sauce performs an important role in a dish: it complements, enhances and creates an attractive finish to the dish. The sauce's appearance should be glossy and its consistency correct, and it should have a defined flavour but never overpower the flavour of the main ingredient of the dish. The potential of a sauce to highlight a dish is often overlooked, and the seasoning will perform a pivotal role: a bland sauce will ruin a perfectly cooked meal.

There are several basic techniques for making sauces.

HEALTH & SAFETY

Many sauces contain dairy produce and so the base ingredients should be kept below 8°C (4°C is best practice) until required.

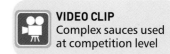

VIDEO CLIP
Complex sauces used at competition level

Deglazing

This is the process of allowing the caramelised pan or tray juices and sediment to be released into added liquid, which may be water, stock, wine or other liquid-based commodities.

Any excess fat is drained off first, then the liquid is added while stirring rigorously over a hot stove. The liquid is reduced and a good jus or stock added. A small amount of butter can also be added to finish the sauce. The liquid is then passed through muslin cloth and a fine **chinois** to create a smooth consistency.

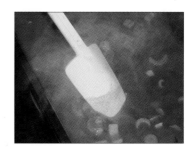

Deglazing a pan

Skimming

This process is one of the most important a chef must master. A well skimmed sauce or stock will have clarity and clear flavour, which will be ruined if left unattended. The use of a perforated spoon or small ladle to remove the scum and foam that develops at the surface of a cooking liquid will prevent the stock or sauce from becoming cloudy and bitter.

Any excess traces of fat or oil can be removed by dragging dish papers across the top of the liquid until it is crystal clear. A brown stock can be chilled until it gelatinises and the fat can then be removed from the surface before using.

It is important to skim stock

Passing a stock

Reducing a liquid

Whisking butter into a sauce

Straining and passing

Forcing a liquid or **purée** through a drum sieve, conical strainer, chinois or muslin cloth will ensure the finished sauce is smooth and emulsified. The use of muslin cloth when passing a jus is essential to remove excess sediment (this process is generally repeated at least twice to ensure a crystal-clear finish).

Reducing

By reducing a liquid over a fierce heat a more intensified flavour is achieved. However, the volume of liquid is reduced, which must be taken into account when preparing a dish and for portion control. Over reducing a liquid can result in the appearance of a bitter flavour.

Whisking and blending

These processes rely on rapid movement to **emulsify** products such as creams, eggs and purées, giving them a light, smooth and delicate flavour and appearance. This is caused by the increased aeration within the sauce.

Egg-yolk based emulsified sauces, such as hollandaise sauce, require the eggs to be beaten over a bain marie, which cooks the egg yolks but prevents them from curdling. The vigorous whisking during the cooking process increases the volume of the sauce.

THICKENING SAUCES

Roux

The most well-known of all thickening agents in the kitchen, the basic **roux** is a combination of equal quantities of melted butter and flour mixed together over heat until the mixture comes away from the sides of the pan.

Three types of roux are generally used in professional cookery. A white roux is generally used with the addition of boiled milk to achieve a béchamel sauce. A blond roux is achieved by cooking the mixture for slightly longer until a light sandy colour develops. White stock is then added to create a **velouté** sauce. The last is a brown roux, which uses flour browned in the oven. Brown stock (estouffade) can then be added to make a brown sauce (**espagnole**).

Beurre manié

Beurre manié is a combination of equal quantities of flour and butter made into a paste. This cold uncooked mix is whisked into hot liquid and cooked out until the desired thickness is achieved.

Breadcrumbs/rice

These are used in a raw state and added to a hot sauce. The cooking process makes their starch molecules burst and the starch content will then thicken the liquid.

Butter

Whisking or hand blending small cubes of chilled unsalted butter into a hot sauce will give a glossy rich texture. However, the sauce must not be reboiled as the butter within the sauce will split from the water content.

Powdered starch thickening agents

These come in numerous forms, such as cornflour, arrowroot and fecule. To use these products a little powder should be mixed with cold liquid until a paste is formed, this mix is then whisked into hot liquid which will instantly thicken. The paste must be smooth and gradually added otherwise lumps will form in the sauce.

Arrowroot becomes transparent once added to sauce and is therefore used when thickening hot fruit sauces when clarity is required.

Egg yolks and cream (liaison)

This mixture is achieved by whisking the egg yolks and cream with a small quantity of a hot sauce. It is then added to the remaining hot sauce. The resultant sauce must not be allowed to boil again as it will curdle. This sauce thickening agent is classically used when using velouté sauces; it will enrich the sauce and will only thicken it slightly.

EMULSIFIED SAUCES

This area of sauce-making requires the most skill. The keys to a good emulsified sauce are the order in which ingredients are added, the temperature, and the speed at which the ingredients are blended.

Emulsified sauces are produced by dispersing fats as small droplets in liquids they would not otherwise mix with. Various proteins are used to stabilise the emulsion formed by mixing the two principal ingredients. The most common emulsified sauces are mayonnaise, hollandaise and beurre blanc. However, many other water-based solutions can be emulsified with fats by using egg yolks, powdered lecithin, gelatine or agar-agar as a stabiliser. When egg yolk is used it is the lecithin protein it contains that acts as the stabiliser.

The fat is slowly added to the liquid (e.g. water, vinegar or lemon juice) and this is slowly whisked to form an emulsion. The two liquids will combine with the stabiliser, and if the conditions are right (correct temperature and constant manipulation) they will coagulate and form an emulsion.

All emulsified sauces are unstable and will separate if stored for too long or at the wrong temperature. There are methods to rescue a separated emulsification: putting a few drops of hot water in a bowl and whisking the curdled mix into it slowly can sometimes remedy the problem.

Temperature control can be a problem for hollandaise sauce. A mix that has separated due to being too cool can be brought back by whisking it into a little boiling water. A hot mix can be remedied in a similar fashion but instead using iced water.

BUTTER SAUCES

Three main types of butter sauce are used in the kitchen:

Hot butter sauces

■ **Beurre noisette** – nut-brown butter, classically served with fish

■ **Beurre noir** – black butter, classically served with skate wings or veal brains

Warm butter sauces

■ *Beurre blanc* – white butter, classically served with vegetables, fish or white meats

■ *Hollandaise* – classically served with grilled meats, or made into a derivative such as mousseline or moutarde

■ *Béarnaise* – similar to hollandaise, but a reduction of shallots, pepper and tarragon is used to create the flavour of the sauce

Cold butter sauces

■ *Café de Paris butter* – contains a mix of fresh herbs and spices. Other condiments such as marjoram, mustard, dill, rosemary, tarragon, paprika, capers, chives, a little curry powder, parsley, shallots, garlic, anchovies and Worcestershire sauce is beaten into unsalted butter. The resulting compound butter is shaped into a cylinder and chilled. When served, a piece is sliced off and allowed to melt on top of, for example, grilled **entrecôte** steaks.

■ *Parsley butter* – softened unsalted butter has a little lemon juice and chopped fresh parsley beaten into it. Seasoning and a little cayenne pepper are added and then chilled before use. This butter is sometimes also known as beurre Maître d'Hotel.

VELOUTÉ SAUCE

The velouté sauce is made in the same way as a béchamel sauce except that stock replaces the milk content and no clouté is used. A liaison is added to finish the sauce.

Variations of velouté are:

■ *aurore* – addition of fresh tomato sauce

■ *curry* – addition of curry paste

■ *estragon* – addition of tarragon

HEALTH & SAFETY

Warm sauces fall into the temperature danger zone and must be carefully controlled to prevent bacterial growth.

VIDEO CLIP
Tomato and basil beurre blanc

BROWN SAUCE (ESPAGNOLE)

Classically, a brown sauce is made by taking a brown roux and adding brown stock. This can then be mixed with the same quantity of brown stock and reduced by half to create a **demi glace**.

In modern professional cookery, a brown sauce or jus is made by browning meat trimmings and some aromatic vegetables before **deglazing** with wine and adding brown stock. This is then reduced, passed and seasoned, and the consistency checked before using.

Variations of brown sauce are:

- *bordelaise* – addition of red wine and bone marrow
- *chasseur* – addition of mushrooms, white wine, shallots, fresh tarragon and tomato **concassé**
- *diable* – addition of chopped shallots, vinegar, Worcester sauce, cayenne pepper and peppercorns

PURÉED AND BLENDED VEGETABLE SAUCES

These sauces are the most versatile as they can be used on all types of meat, fish, poultry, game and vegetarian dishes. The sauce base is made by puréeing or blending a cooked main ingredient (e.g. garlic, roasted red peppers) and then a stock, cream or butter is added to obtain a smooth, well-flavoured sauce. These sauces can be served hot, warm or cold.

FOAMS

This type of sauce has recently transformed modern high-class restaurant dishes. The base liquid, which may be cold or hot, is aerated by whisking, blending or by using a gas-charged siphon to create a frothy texture. The foam is then spooned onto the dish; but it should only be added at the last minute to ensure that the air remains in the sauce for the duration of the customer's eating experience. A heavy, well-flavoured sauce can be used to create a light delicate accompaniment that still keeps the taste required. Foams best suit cream, vegetable or fruit sauces as it is difficult to keep denser sauces aerated.

VIDEO CLIP Producing foams using a bamix and espuma

When aerating a sauce, the size of the container needs to be double the volume of sauce being used. If a blender is used, it should be positioned so that its blades skim the surface of the sauce, which causes the bubbles/froth to develop. A siphon will inject gas directly into the liquid, and will expel the foam directly into the bowl, glass or plate being used to serve the dish.

A gelatinisation agent, such as gelatine or agar-agar, is sometimes used to stabilise the foam and create a stronger, foamier texture.

Olive oil flavoured with herbs and chillis

FLAVOURED OILS

The idea of using flavoured oils in sauces is being explored more and more. There are many different oils and flavours available, which makes them extremely versatile. They may be used sparingly to complement sauces and dishes, adding colour and texture, or they may be a main component.

Spices lend themselves exceptionally well to oil flavouring; they are first dry roasted and then added to good-quality oil, which is then allowed to **simmer** for at least an hour. Herbs can be finely chopped or puréed into oil, which allows the natural chlorophyll to turn the oil a green colour.

Oils such as white and black truffle are expensive and very pungent; a few drops added to dishes such as risottos are extremely effective. Flavoured oils can be stored for long periods of time if kept in airtight containers in cool, dry conditions.

COULIS

A **coulis** is made by very slowly warming through ingredients, such as plum tomatoes, shallots, oil, fresh basil and garlic, and then liquidising them into a fine sauce. The base ingredients form an emulsion, in which the oil is blended into the sauce. Because of the emulsification, this kind of sauce cannot be served hot and must be carefully monitored.

Fruit coulis are generally puréed fruits that have been combined with sugar in the form of stock syrup to adjust the consistency. A little lemon juice can be added to enhance the natural flavours of the fresh fruits.

VINAIGRETTES

Classically, a vinaigrette is an emulsion of three parts oil and one part vinegar, with the addition of a little mustard and various flavourings and seasonings. It is considered to be a typically French dressing, and is used mostly for salads and **hors d'oeuvres**.

Modern vinaigrettes use the lightest oils, flavoured vinegars and subtle mustards to complement each dish as required. They can be served cold or warm.

Split dressings

These dressings are technically vinaigrettes as they contain the same ingredients, however due to the fact that emulsification has not taken place they belong to their own classification.

MAYONNAISE

HEALTH & SAFETY

When making mayonnaise, use only pasteurised egg. This will reduce the risk of salmonella.

This is an emulsion of egg yolks, oil, mustard, vinegar and lemon juice. The egg yolks form the main structure as the lecithin protein they contain prevents the sauce from splitting. Mayonnaise is the basis of many classical dressings and sauces for the larder section.

Some derivatives of mayonnaise are:

- Tartare sauce
- Remoulade
- Aïoli.

CREAM-BASED SAUCES

There are two main types of cream-based sauce:

■ Cooked   ■ Uncooked.

The cooked versions are mentioned earlier; for example fish cream sauce, which is a reduction of fish stock, white wine, shallots and cream, reduced to a coating consistency. Other types of cream sauces can be produced from a basic velouté base by adding cream to the final stages of cooking.

Cold cream sauces can be whipped, thickened, flavoured or poured, and can be served as accompaniments with salads, cold meats and starters. Different types of cream base can be used, such as crème fraîche, soured cream, whipping cream and natural yoghurt.

PESTO

This is an Italian sauce that originates from Genoa but is today widely used throughout cuisine. The basic ingredients for pesto are a good-quality virgin olive oil, garlic, pine nuts, parmesan cheese and fresh basil. Sun-dried peppers and tomatoes can be added for a twist on this classic sauce.

PURÉE-BASED SAUCES

Purée-based sauces are usually cooked recipes containing vegetables or fruits and are blended and passed through a chinois. To produce a coarse purée, the main raw ingredient is blended and not passed.

SALSA

Salsa simply means 'sauce' in Spanish. Salsas can be served either warm or cold and are used either to add spice to a dish or to balance an already heavily spiced dish and 'cool' it down. They can be produced from fruit or vegetables, or a mix of both. Salsas are regarded more as a cross between a salad and a dressing, rather than strictly as a sauce.

REDUCED VINEGARS

Vinegars such as balsamic, cider or red wine reduce well and form a syrup-like consistency. Reduced vinegars can be presented onto a plate to give a sweet, slightly thick and syrupy appearance. They are used generally to add colour and decoration to a plate, in collaboration with other dressings and sauces.

STORAGE OF COLD SAUCES AND DRESSINGS

Sauces and dressings should be made on a daily basis to get the freshest flavour possible. If they need to be stored, they should be kept chilled and must be correctly labelled and dated during storage.

Some dressings and sauces are, however, better left to mature, such as Cumberland sauce. These should be kept chilled in a covered container.

Dressings that use oil as a main ingredient will begin to solidify when chilled. It will be necessary to allow such dressings to warm up to room temperature before use; this allows the dressing to become fluid again.

An alternative method of storage is to vacuum pack sauces into various sized portions. Some sauces can also be frozen and defrosted as required.

RECIPES

Hollandaise sauce

INGREDIENTS	10 PORTIONS
White wine vinegar	2tbsp
Water	2tbsp
Crushed peppercorns	1tsp
Egg yolks	4
Clarified unsalted butter	250g
Lemon juice	½ lemon
Good-quality salt and ground white pepper	To taste

Method of work

1 Place the vinegar, water and peppercorns into a saucepan and place onto a medium heat. Reduce by one-third.

2 Strain the liquid through a fine chinois and allow to cool slightly.

3 Mix the egg yolks with the liquid and **whisk** over a bain marie until the ribbon stage is achieved.

4 Slowly trickle the warm clarified butter into the egg mixture, whisking constantly until the sauce has emulsified into a thick and glossy consistency.

5 Add the lemon juice and **correct** the seasoning. Keep warm until required for service.

 CHEF'S TIP

Temperature is very important when making hollandaise sauce: if the liquid is too hot the egg will scramble, and if the butter is too hot or too cold the sauce will split.

Whisking the egg yolks and liquid over a bain marie

Drizzling the butter into the egg mix while whisking

Beurre blanc

INGREDIENTS	10 PORTIONS
Shallots, chopped	2 each
White wine vinegar	3tbsp
White wine	4tbsp
Water	2tbsp
Diced unsalted butter	200g
Lemon juice	½ lemon
Good-quality salt and white pepper	To taste

Method of work

1 Place the shallots, white wine vinegar, white wine and water in a pan and reduce by half.

2 Remove from the heat. Whisk in the **diced** cold butter until emulsified and the sauce thickens to the correct consistency.

3 Season well and add a little lemon juice.

 CHEF'S TIP

This sauce works well if fish, chicken or vegetable stock is used instead of water. Ensure the butter is diced small and is cold before whisking in as this helps emulsification.

Béarnaise Sauce

INGREDIENTS	10 PORTIONS
White wine vinegar	2tbsp
Water	2tbsp
Fresh tarragon	2tsp
Crushed peppercorns	1tsp
Egg yolks	4
Clarified unsalted butter	250g
Lemon juice	½ lemon
Fresh chopped tarragon	2tsp
Fresh chopped chervil	2tsp
Good-quality salt and ground white pepper	To taste

Method of work

1 Place the vinegar, water, tarragon and peppercorns in a saucepan and reduce by one-third.

2 Strain the liquid and allow to cool slightly.

3 Mix the egg yolks with the reduced tarragon liquid and whisk over a bain marie until the ribbon stage is achieved.

4 Slowly pour the warm clarified butter into egg mix, whisking constantly until the sauce is thick and glossy.

5 Add the lemon juice and season.

6 Add the chopped chervil and tarragon to the sauce. Keep warm until required for service.

 CHEF'S TIP

Keep the sauce warm by placing near a heat lamp or hotplate, but ensure the container sits on a cloth and the top is covered to prevent splitting.

Velouté sauce (modern version)

 CHEF'S TIP

This sauce relies on the ingredients for its distinctive delicate flavour, so only use good quality wine and stock

INGREDIENTS	10 PORTIONS
Parsley stalks	4tsp
Shallots, chopped	4 small
Unsalted butter	75g
White wine	100ml
White stock	350ml
Double cream	350ml
Good-quality salt and white pepper	To taste

Method of work

1   Sweat off the parsley stalks and shallots in the butter without any colour. Add the white wine and reduce by two-thirds.

2   Add the stock and reduce by a further two-thirds.

3   Add the double cream and simmer until reduced by half and the desired consistency has been achieved.

4   Pass through a fine chinois and correct the seasoning.

Veal Jus

 CHEF'S TIP

Good flavour and colour are achieved by browning the meat and vegetables: too little and the sauce will be too light, too much and the sauce will taste burnt.

INGREDIENTS	10 PORTIONS
Brown veal stock	900ml
Beef trimmings	200g
Garlic	1 clove
Fresh thyme	3tsp
Red wine	200ml
Mirepoix of vegetables (carrots, celery, onion and leek)	100g
Tomato purée	25g
Good-quality salt and white pepper	To taste

Method of work

1   Brown the beef trimmings with the garlic and thyme in a saucepan or in a roasting tray in the oven at a high temperature.

2   Add the mirepoix of vegetables and tomato purée and brown again.

3   Deglaze the pan with the red wine and remove all sediment from the bottom.

4   Add the stock and reduce by half. Skim continuously to remove the scum.

5   Pass through a chinois, correct the consistency and the seasoning.

Light chicken jus

INGREDIENTS	10 PORTIONS
Brown chicken stock	750ml
Chicken carcasses	400g
Shallots	5
Mushroom trimmings	10
Garlic	½ bulb
Bay leaf	1
White wine	200ml
Tomato purée	25g
Good-quality salt and white pepper	To taste

CHEF'S TIP

Remove as much fat from the chicken carcasses as possible. This will reduce the amount of fat released into the sauce and will cut down on skimming.

Method of work

1   Chop the chicken carcasses into small pieces. Colour in a hot pan with a little oil until golden brown in colour.
2   Add the chopped shallots, mushroom trimmings, garlic, bay leaf and tomato purée and continue to colour all the ingredients.
3   Add the wine and reduce until only a little liquid is remaining.
4   Add the stock and reduce by half, skimming continuously.
5   Pass through a chinois and muslin cloth, then thicken as required and correct the seasoning.

Bordelaise sauce

INGREDIENTS	10 PORTIONS
Veal jus/demi glace	450ml
Shallots	4
Vegetable oil	45ml
Red wine	200ml
Crushed peppercorns	1tsp
Bay leaf	1
Bone marrow	60g
Unsalted butter	40g
Good-quality salt and white pepper	To taste

CHEF'S TIP

The marrow can be kept frozen until required and then soaked. This will defrost the marrow and remove any unwanted blood deposits.

Method of work

1   Finely chop the shallots. Sweat in the oil with the peppercorns and bay leaf.
2   Add the red wine and reduce by half.
3   Add the jus. Bring to the boil and simmer, skimming occasionally.
4   Soak the beef bone marrow for 20 minutes in cold water, then clean and slice.
5   Add a knob of the butter to the jus and whisk in to give a good glaze.
6   Add the marrow to the sauce to warm through and serve.

Fresh tomato sauce

INGREDIENTS	10 PORTIONS
Unsalted butter	100g
Shallots, finely chopped	4
Fresh chopped thyme	1tsp
Bay leaf	1
Chopped garlic	4 cloves
Ripe plum tomatoes, chopped	800g
Tomato purée	25g
Caster sugar	75g
Tomato juice	150ml
Fresh basil stalks	3tsp
Good-quality salt and white pepper	To taste

CHEF'S TIP

This sauce is vibrant in colour and flavoursome. As an alternative, the tomatoes can be cut into concassé and the purée omitted. The same cooking procedure applies except do not blend to leave the chunky texture.

Method of work

1 Sweat the shallots, thyme, bay leaf, and garlic in butter.
2 Add the chopped plum tomatoes, purée, caster sugar, tomato juice and basil stalks.
3 Simmer for 45 minutes.
4 Blend in a liquidiser until smooth and pass through a chinois.
5 Correct the seasoning and serve.

Court bouillon

INGREDIENTS	10 PORTIONS
Leeks	10
Celery	5 sticks
Carrot	5
Onion	5
Shallots	10
Fennel	2½
Garlic	2 cloves
Fresh bay leaf	1 leaf
Fresh parsley	Sprig
Peppercorns	12 each
Juice and zest of lemons	5 lemons
White wine	60ml

CHEF'S TIP

This stock is essential for fish cookery and can be made in advance, but it should not be kept for longer than four days.

Method of work

1 Chop all vegetables and place in a saucepan with the herbs, cover with cold water and bring to the boil.
2 Add the remaining ingredients and simmer for 30 minutes.
3 Chill and store in a sealed container in a refrigerator until required.

Roasted yellow pepper sauce

INGREDIENTS	10 PORTIONS
Yellow peppers	400g
Olive oil	30ml
Chopped garlic	2 cloves
Chopped onion	80g
Vegetable stock	250ml
Double cream	75ml
Good-quality salt and white pepper	To taste

Method of work

1 Pre-heat an oven to 180°C.
2 Deseed and chop the peppers roughly. Place in a bowl with the olive oil, chopped onions, chopped garlic and season well with salt and pepper.
3 Place onto a tray and roast for 20 minutes.
4 Remove the roasted vegetables from the oven and liquidise in a food blender, slowly adding the stock.
5 Pour into a saucepan and bring to the boil, add the cream and cook to the required consistency.
6 Pass through a chinois, correct the seasoning and serve.

 CHEF'S TIP

This sauce works with red or green peppers or tomatoes. For a more subtle taste, the vegetables can be blanched in vegetable stock instead of being roasted.

Champagne and dill cream foam

INGREDIENTS	10 PORTIONS
Shellfish sauce (see recipe on p. 78)	250ml
Champagne	100ml
Fresh chopped dill	3tsp
Full fat milk	75ml

Method of work

1 Bring the sauce to the boil and add the champagne, milk and dill.
2 Place a small amount into a tall jug or container. Using a hand blender, aerate until foam begins to appear.*
3 Spoon the foam over a finished dish at the last minute of service.

*Alternatively, place into a siphon and charge with a gas cartridge. Keep the siphon warm in a bain marie of hot water at 80°C for service. Shoot the foam through the siphon when required and serve.

 CHEF'S TIP

Foams are excellent for giving flavour but with a very light taste. The key to a good foam is milk, which allows the sauce to froth and hold volume for long enough to serve.

Milk and chopped dill added to the sauce

Aerating using a hand blender

Shellfish sauce

CHEF'S TIP

Ensure the alcohol is burned away completely or the finished sauce will have a bitter flavour.

INGREDIENTS	10 PORTIONS
Lobster/crab/langoustine shells	450g
Garlic	3 cloves
Mirepoix of vegetables (carrots, onions, leek and celery)	100g
Tomato concassé	150g
Brandy	125ml
Fish stock	250ml
Double cream	150ml
White wine	100ml
Diced butter	50g
Fresh dill	2tsp
Fresh tarragon	1tsp
Good-quality salt and white pepper	To taste

Method of work

1 Roast the seafood shells with the garlic and mirepoix of vegetables until golden brown in colour.
2 Deglaze the pan with brandy and flambé.
3 Add the tomato concassé and fish stock and bring to the boil.
4 Skim constantly and simmer for 40 minutes until reduced by half.
5 Add the double cream and continue to reduce.
6 Pass the sauce through a chinois into a clean saucepan. Bring the sauce to the boil to reduce again and adjust the seasoning.
7 Add the wine. Add the cubes of butter, whisking continuously.
8 Add chopped fresh herbs to finish.

Roasting the shells

Vegetable nage

CHEF'S TIP

This stock really needs 24 hours to sit, to allow the vegetables to infuse the liquor. There is no quick way of making this; but the end product is worth the effort.

INGREDIENTS	10 PORTIONS
Onions	80g
Carrots	80g
Celery	50g
Leek	50g
Garlic	3 cloves
Lemon juice	½ lemon
White peppercorns	¼tsp
Star anise	1
Water	500ml
White wine	50ml
Fresh tarragon, basil, coriander, thyme and parsley	Sprig of each

Method of work

1 Slice all the vegetables and place into a saucepan with the lemon juice, garlic, peppercorns, star anise and water.
2 Bring to the boil and simmer for 10 minutes.
3 Remove from heat. Add the wine with all the fresh herbs.
4 Cool and refrigerate for a minimum of 24 hours before using as required.

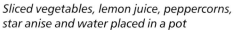

Sliced vegetables, lemon juice, peppercorns, star anise and water placed in a pot

Adding the wine and all the herbs

Sweet curry sauce

INGREDIENTS	10 PORTIONS
Unsalted butter	30g
Diced onion	40g
Diced pineapple	400g
Diced banana	50g
Diced apple	50g
White flour	30g
Madras curry paste	30g
Grated coconut	1tbsp
Chicken stock	500ml
Bouquet garni	1 small

CHEF'S TIP

If possible, use fresh coconut and add some of the milk to the sauce to give a really authentic taste.

Method of work

1 Sweat the onions in the butter, stir in fruit and cook for approximately 5 minutes.

2 Add in the flour, curry paste and coconut. Cook out for 5 minutes, stirring continuously to prevent burning. Add the chicken stock and bouquet garni.

3 Bring to the boil and simmer for 45 minutes. Check the seasoning and serve.

Sprinkling in the flour, curry paste and coconut

Mussel stock

INGREDIENTS	10 PORTIONS
Fresh cleaned mussels	750g
Water	300ml
White wine	100ml
Shallots	50g
Celery	40g
Fresh parsley and thyme	Sprig of each

Method of work

1 Place the water, white wine, chopped shallots, sliced celery, parsley and thyme into a saucepan and bring to the boil.

2 Add the mussels, cover with a lid and boil for 3–4 minutes.

3 Remove the mussels and use if required for another dish.

4 Leave the stock to stand for 5 minutes to let any grit sink to the bottom. Strain through muslin cloth. Use as required.

CHEF'S TIP

This is more of a liquor than a stock, however the flavour that can be produced is excellent and will make a real difference in many dishes.

Savoury sabayon

INGREDIENTS	10 PORTIONS
Egg yolks	6
Warm water	4tbsp
Lemon juice	2 lemons
Salt	4g
White wine	240ml
Chives, chopped	4tsp

Method of work

1 Whisk the egg yolks and water over a bain marie until the ribbon stage is achieved.
2 Slowly add the lemon juice and warmed white wine.
3 Continue to aerate until the mixture doubles in size.
4 Season well and add the chopped chives.
5 This sauce can be used as a glaze under or over meat, fish or poultry dishes.

Saffron fish sauce

INGREDIENTS	10 PORTIONS
Fish stock	500ml
White wine	250ml
Noilly Prat	200ml
Finely chopped shallots	100g
Double cream	400ml
Saffron	1tsp
Diced unsalted butter	70g

Method of work

1 Bring the stock, white wine, chopped shallots and Noilly Prat to the boil and reduce by half.
2 Add the cream and bring back to the boil. Reduce until the sauce has thickened to the required consistency.
3 Remove from the heat and add the saffron, allowing 5 minutes to infuse into the sauce.
4 While the sauce is still warm, whisk in the butter a little at a time on the side of the stove.
5 Strain the sauce through a fine chinois. Reheat without boiling and serve as required.

Reducing stock with white wine, shallots and Noilly Prat

Adding the cream

Adding the saffron

Assessment of knowledge and understanding

You have now learned about the use of the different types of dressings and sauces and how to produce a variety of them utilising an array of commodities and cooking techniques.

To test your level of knowledge and understanding, answer the following short questions. These will help to prepare you for your summative (final) assessment.

Quality identifications

1 Explain the importance of using fresh vegetables when making stocks and sauces.

2 Describe why is it important to use only good-quality bones when making stocks.

Materials and storage

1 Explain why sauces should be kept hot in a bain marie and not on the stove top.

2 State why aluminium pans should be avoided when making a stock.

Preparation

1 Explain how a curdled hollandaise sauce can be corrected.

2 Explain three ways of removing oil from a stock or sauce.
   i) _____ ii) _____
   iii)_____

Cooking

1 Explain why skimming sauces is important.

2 List four ways to thicken a sauce.
   i) _____ ii) _____
   iii)_____ iv)_____

3 Explain what happens if the sabayon overheats when making a hollandaise sauce.

Health and safety

1 Where and how should warm butter sauces be kept for service?

2 Stocks should be chilled as quickly as possible: state how long they should be blast chilled and to what temperature.

CHEF'S PROFILE

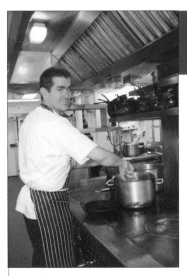

Name: SHANE OSBORN

Position: Chef/Co-owner

Establishment: Pied à Terre

Current job role and main responsibilities: Cooking hands-on at Pied à Terre.

When did you realise that you wanted to pursue a career in the catering and hospitality industry?
I started in catering when I was 13 as my mother was a caterer. It was my first part-time job.

Training: I started a four-year apprenticeship in 1985 at the age of 15.

Experience:
- Le Bateau Ivre in France (two Michelin stars)
- L' Oranger
- The Square
- Pied à Terre, under Tom Aikens.

What do you find rewarding about your job?
Every day is a school day. Working with people who are passionate about their job.

What advice would you give to students just beginning their career?
Aim for the top. Always try to do better the next day, and don't ever give in.

Who is your mentor or main inspiration?
I thrive on the need to improve myself – to better myself and the food I cook every day.

What traits do you consider essential for anyone entering a career as a chef?
Stamina and determination.

Can you give one essential kitchen tip or technique that you use as a chef?
Learn how to season!

8

Cold starters, salads and canapés

3FPC9 Prepare, cook and present complex cold products

LEARNING OBJECTIVES

The aim of this chapter is to enable you to develop skills and implement gathered knowledge in the preparation, cookery and presentation principles of different cold starters, salads and canapés. This will also include the appropriate use of materials, ingredients and equipment.

At the end of this chapter you will be able to:

- Identify a range of commodities and their uses in cold larder work
- Understand the use of relative ingredients, selecting and stating the quality points of various commodities and cold dishes
- Prepare, cook and present a range of cold dishes
- Identify the correct storage procedures and holding temperatures of canapés, salads and cold starters
- Select the required tools and equipment for preparing and cooking cold dishes

VIDEO CLIP
Canapés: prawn with lemon dressing and pâté en croute

CHEF'S TIP

Always try to keep dishes simple when using top-quality fresh ingredients. Using a maximum of five different food components will prevent the dish from becoming too complicated.

INTRODUCTION TO THE CHEF GARDE MANGER

The **chef de garde manger** is a mixed position within the professional kitchen. *Garde manger* is a French term which translates as 'keeping to eat'. Historically, the title was given to a chef whose job was to take charge of raw food and keep it fit to eat. This chef had to be skilled in the science of food preservation and preparation and in the art of food presentation.

The role of the modern chef garde manger, or larder chef, has evolved in response to changes in dining trends and in technology in the kitchen. This chef is still responsible for the production and preservation of cold soups, salads, **canapés, charcuterie** products, cheeses, condiments and **buffets**, but now they are also likely to present centrepieces in fat, carved fruits and vegetables and create ornate decorative dishes using poultry, game, fish, shellfish and meat.

THE BEGINNING OF A MEAL

Certain words have been used to describe an element, dish or type of course in the culinary arts. Every once in a while, words used to describe a course or dish can mislead the customer. This can be the case with **amuse bouches**, appetisers and hors d'oeuvres. Each term is associated with small, delicate portions of food and so it can easily be assumed that they are all the same type of dish.

■ *Amuse bouches* (sometimes called amuse gueules) – these are little savoury nibbles, to be eaten within two bites and offered just for fun as 'mouth amusements' before the starter course is served. They can be presented hot or cold.

■ *Appetisers* – these are small portions of food that are the first food to be served at the table. They are part of the planned menu, served before the starter or a main course. Some chefs use this small appetiser as something to titillate the appetite. Pre-dessert appetisers are even served in many high-class modern restaurants.

■ *Hors d'oeuvres* – this term, which translates literally as 'outside the works', was borrowed by French chefs to refer to delicate, small portions of food served separately (or apart) from the main meal. Usually served as a starter on its own.

Many different terms are used internationally for starters or hors d'oeuvres, and most countries have some form of starter course or small presentation of food to indulge the appetite. The following are examples of various countries' approaches to small food dishes, either to be served at the beginning of a meal or as the meal itself:

- *Antipasti* (Italy) – small salads, cooked vegetables, fungi, fish dishes, eggs or cured meats, simply decorated
- *Antojitos* (Mexico) – small servings of spiced vegetables and pulses with tortilla bases, such as tacos, quesadillas and enchiladas
- *Chat* (India) – small portions of food eaten at all times of the day
- *Dim sum* (China) – meaning 'touch the heart', dim sum was originally a Cantonese custom linked to the Chinese tradition of yum cha (drinking tea); served in traditional Chinese tea houses
- *Meze* (Greece) – can be as simple as a small bowl of olives, or more complicated, such as stuffed marinated vine leaves; served with a pre-dinner drink
- *Tapas* (Spain) – the tradition of tapas was to serve a slice of ham, cheese or bread over a glass of sherry at roadside inns, and because this custom spurred the sales of alcoholic beverages, tapas became well established; there are many different varieties, with every region having its own speciality tapas.

Meze

Tapas

HORS D'OEUVRES

When choosing the menu, the hors d'oeuvres are carefully selected to complement the following courses. The selection of hors d'oeuvres on a menu needs to offer a complete range to cater for all diets (e.g. vegetarian or vegan diets or religious restrictions).

Hors d'oeuvres can be served as a starter or as a main course. An extended selection can be served as a buffet. This is similar to the Russian zakuskis, which are usually a collection of small hors d'oeuvres presented on a separate table for guests to help themselves to before the main meal commences.

A single hors d'oeuvre is a simple cold dish with one main ingredient and an accompanying garnish. Hors d'oeuvre varies contain a selection of main ingredients; each will contain small quantities of a range of products. The idea for plated combinations of themed ingredients, or assiettes, originated from this.

There are three main types of hors d'oeuvres:

- *Hors d'oeuvre* chaud – hot items, can be vegetable-based, meat, game, fish, egg, dairy, soufflé or tartlet
- *Hors d'oeuvre singular* – single-food items, served only with certain dressings and in one piece or one portion, for example avocado pears, caviar, stuffed eggs, langoustine, melon, pâté or diverse fruit cocktails
- *Hors d'oeuvre variés* – selection of items consisting of multiple ingredients. They can be cut into small dice, strips, cubes or pieces, include pickled, marinated or seasoned ingredients and be served with additional fresh herbs, dressings, vinaigrettes or mayonnaise-based sauces.

CHEF'S TIP

The chef garde manger requires many specialised pieces of equipment and tools to complete this diverse work. The main tools and equipment that will be used are:

- Canale knife

- Turning knife

- Tomato knife

- Small and medium palette knives

- Parisienne cutters (large and small)

CHEF'S TIP

Other specialist equipment includes:

- **Terrine** moulds, in a range of sizes
- Digital thermometer, to gauge internal cooking temperatures
- Corer or set of specialist knives, to sculpt vegetables
- Small glazing brush.

VIDEO CLIP
Marinated red meat on crispy leaf salad

VIDEO CLIP
Marinated white meats with walnut and apple salad

HEALTH & SAFETY

Regular checks should be carried out on all items of electrical equipment to ensure that they work properly and conform to all relevant safety regulations.

CHEF'S TIP

If you do not have a steady hand, squeezable plastic bottles are good way to apply sauces and dressings to plates.

VIDEO CLIP
Using poultry: lemon chicken and turkey salad

COMMODITIES

Cold red and white meat products

All cuts of meat should be purchased as fresh as possible, and chefs should receive each product and evaluate its quality before using. The chef garde manger should be capable of noting the warning signs when meat is lacking in quality; such as excessive odour, slimy to the touch, incorrect weight, incorrect delivery temperature, dull rather than bright colouring, poor marbling in certain cuts and tough texture.

Storage and hygiene must be thoroughly considered when preparing and cooking meat products. Being high in protein, meats carry a considerable risk of bacterial cross-contamination. Care must be taken to ensure meats are not served undercooked.

The cold state of prepared and cooked meat should be monitored carefully. Red meats have a high fat content, which may begin to solidify and congeal within the presented dish after a period of time.

Pork has a number of uses within the garde manger. Its high fat content makes it a good source of moisture within pâtés, terrines and stuffing or farce.

Veal is a very lean meat, similar to beef, and so is lacking in natural fats. Veal tends to be mixed with pork when making terrines, pâtés or raised pies so that the fat from the pork will keep the dish moist.

Cold poultry products

Poultry is the most versatile of all the meats within the garde manger. It is an easy commodity to work with and there is little wastage; all parts of a bird can be used to make items such as mousses, ballotines and galantines. The winglets can be turned into small canapé items, such as chicken cherries. It is an inexpensive commodity and can be very cost effective to serve.

Foie gras is a commodity much prized by chefs throughout the world and is considered a universal delicacy. It is the enlarged liver from a goose or duck that has been force fed and fattened for a period of up to five months. These speciality poultry do not exercise and are overfed, which results in a substantial fatty liver. The following quality checks should be carried out when purchasing foie gras:

- A light yellow to amber colour
- Firm to the touch, but should give slightly under thumb pressure and the mark should remain visible
- The fewer blemishes apparent, the higher the grade.

When preparing foie gras for cold dishes (such as for mousses, terrines, parfaits and forcemeats) the liver must be cleaned and have all the veins removed before cooking. As little damage as possible should be done to the liver during preparation.

Cold game products

Most game items have a prominent flavour and are relatively simple to use within the garde manger. The flavour and tenderness of game begins to improve as it ages. The technique of aging game is to hang the carcass for between 7 and 14 days (depending on the type of game) at a temperature of 1–3°C. This allows the enzymes in the meat to break down the complex proteins in the carcass.

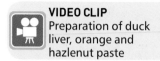

VIDEO CLIP
Preparation of duck liver, orange and hazlenut paste

After the aging process the flavour and tenderness can be further enhanced by marinating. This should, however, never be done to mask or overpower the natural flavours of the meat. The acids contained in a marinade, such as vinegar, citric juices and alcohol, will break down proteins in the meat, making it tenderer. However, the meat should not stay in a marinade for too long. The most common dishes for game products are game pies, terrines and pâtés.

Cured and smoked meats

Curing is the addition of salt, sugar or nitrate to any protein to preserve, flavour and colour the meat. The salt penetrates the flesh and dehydrates the meat by a process called osmosis. This results in a lower moisture content, which inhibits the growth and reproduction of bacteria.

The basic curing methods can be applied to meat products in many different ways:

Cured meats and dried sausages hanging for purchase

- ■ *Dry curing* – the curing ingredients are applied directly onto the meat. This is the slowest method, and is used in curing hams, bacon, salt beef and other small cuts of meat.

- ■ *Dry sugar curing* – sugar and nitrate are added to salt, which is then directly applied to the surface of the meat. The meat is always cured in a refrigerator. This method can be used for poultry, game and smaller cuts of meat.

- ■ *Brine curing (pickling)* – the meat is cured with a brine made from salt and nitrate, and sometimes sugar. The meat is soaked for a specific time in a refrigerator. Large cuts of meat are cured in this way, such as ham and turkey.

Smoking is another method of preserving meats. It also adds flavour and colour to the meat, and can be used for other commodities such as fish. The process for smoking meats is the same as for curing, followed by washing and smoking.

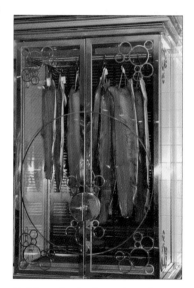

Cold smoked salmon hanging for purchase

There are two methods of smoking food, cold and hot smoking:

- ■ *Cold smoking* – a controlled flow of smoke at about 35°C is blown over the commodity for about 5–6 hours. This creates a lightly smoked and slightly drier product.

■ *Hot smoking* – the smoking temperature is higher at 70–80°C and the heat of the smoke will cook the product as it is being smoked. This usually produces a stronger, smokier flavour.

Smoking times will vary for different types of produce, being anything from 20 minutes to several days. The most commonly used woods for smoking are beech, oak and chestnut, with additional flavours such as juniper, sage and rosemary used for aromatic flavourings. Further flavours that can be used include hickory, scented teas (such as jasmine), fir wood and pine needles.

Technique for hot smoking

Placing tea leaves into the bottom of a tray

Placing a cooling rack over the tray

Laying the food items to be smoked onto the rack

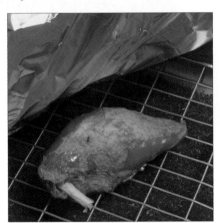

Covering with foil and placing onto a stove top

Lifting the foil to reveal the item being smoked

Vegetables and fruit

A fruit and vegetable stall at a local market

These are widely used within the garde manger due to the variety of different methods in which they can be cooked and presented.

A wide range of salad greens are available for use in the kitchen and freshness is the key when purchasing. A good salad green is one that has retained its moisture, crispness and colour and is free of bruising.

Good quality bulbs, roots, tubers and young vegetables are easier than ever to source and are increasingly popular for use in simple salads. Baby fruits and vegetables are visually appealing food items and require little preparation.

Eggs

The common hen's egg is not the only type of egg to be used in the preparation of salads and cold dishes. Many menus opt for duck or quail eggs, which can transform a simple salad into a diverse culinary experience.

Eggs can be served boiled or poached to accompany salads and cold dishes, and are a valuable source of protein and vital nutrients.

Farinaceous products

Farinaceous ingredients – starchy products high in carbohydrate, such as polenta, couscous, noodles, bulgur wheat, pearl barley and pastas – are ideal ingredients for salads.

Chefs are rediscovering traditional recipes from around the world, such as tabbouleh and Moroccan couscous.

Fish

Fish is a diverse commodity, and it is generally a light and flavoursome option within a menu. Smoked salmon, fish terrines and gravadlax are standard starter dish concepts.

The same health and safety precautions that apply to meat also apply to fish. Fish should not be stored for longer than three days and smoked products and raw products should be kept in separate refrigerators.

Dairy-based products

Dairy products, such as fresh milk, different creams, crème fraîche, fromage frais, yoghurt and cheeses, are important commodities in the garde manger. The use of cheese as a course on a menu is increasing in popularity.

When creating a cheese selection for a menu, at least three types of cheese should be offered: a hard cheese, a blue-veined cheese and a soft cheese, either with a downy rind or with a washed rind. (A washed rind cheese is one that has had its rind soaked or rubbed with brine or alcohol, whereas a downy rind cheese has been left to ripen and develop a white dappled rind.)

To prevent cheeses from drying out they should be wrapped in cheesecloth or waxed paper, depending on the variety, which allow the cheese to 'breath'. All types should be stored in a refrigerator, ideally being removed approximately one hour prior to serving. By serving cheese at ambient temperature, the customer will be able to fully appreciate the texture, flavour and smell of each cheese.

Fungi

Mushrooms have a broad range of characteristics and different flavours. Although they have a high water content, their nutritional content is greater than that of green vegetables, although not as high as root vegetables.

CHEF'S TIP

When sourcing eggs be sure to pick those with a Red Lion stamp. This means that the farm where the egg was produced has been inspected and the eggs are protected against infection from Salmonella.

Quail's eggs

VIDEO CLIP
Using fish: mixed fish salad with crispy croutons

Smoked mackerel

CHEF'S TIP

If choosing a selection of cheeses for a board to present to customers, the chef should consider:
- whether the cheeses are in season, because they will then be at their finest
- how long they have been matured; the more mature, the stronger and more prominent the taste
- the use of cheeses produced locally by a farmers or artisan cheese makers.

British and continental cheeses

Varieties of mushrooms

The three main mushroom classifications are:

■ Field or wild mushrooms

■ Cultivated mushrooms

■ Exotic mushrooms.

Fresh hand-picked wild mushrooms are expensive, which will immediately add to the selling price of a dish. Prices for hand-picked mushrooms will also fluctuate due to their availability and seasonality.

One of the most popular ingredients with chefs is the truffle. Prices for both black and white truffles can be very high, with white truffle prices reaching high into the thousands of pounds per kilogram at certain times of the year. Usually originating in Italy, white truffles are used to favour oils or are used in cooking a range of dishes, such as risottos.

Rice

Rice is a versatile product to cook and present, and is used as a starchy carbohydrate accompaniment to a number of meat, poultry and fish dishes.

Sushi is essentially cold cooked rice dressed with vinegar, shaped into bite-sized portions, decorated with raw or cooked fish, egg or vegetables and wrapped in seaweed. The vinegar rice used in sushi is slightly harder than plain boiled rice because it is cooked in less water. Quick cooling of the cooked rice while tossing it is the key to producing good, shiny sushi rice.

Pulses

Pulses are beans, lentils and chickpeas, all of which have excellent nutritional benefits and are valuable sources of protein. Pulses are economical ingredients and can be used to make a variety of salads.

Tinned, cooked pulses are liable to be more expensive than dried pulses, but are much easier to use as they do not require soaking. Pulses can be used as a main ingredient for salads.

CHEF'S TIP

Cooking pulses in a flavoured or spiced liquid can greatly enhance and complement the flavours of the dish.

CHEF'S TIP

There are many different salad items, such as lettuce, spinach, herbs, spicy greens, bitter leaves and microsalads. They can be used in different combinations to add a depth of flavour and varying textures.

SALADS

Salads are extremely versatile dishes and can consist of raw, cooked, cold or warm ingredients. Salads will usually be dressed and seasoned (unless requested otherwise by a customer), and can be served as an accompaniment, side dish or main course.

Many different contemporary styles of salad from around the world are used in modern menus. The main categories of salads are listed below:

■ *Simple salads* - the basis of a simple salad is the use of one main ingredient and an accompanying dressing or garnish. These salads can be either raw or cooked and can be made up of vegetables, fruits, meats, fish or shellfish, but they are always served cold and with a cold dressing such as vinaigrette. An example is a tomato salad.

- *Compound salads* – the aim of a **compound salad** is to combine multiple contrasting ingredients, differing in texture, flavour and colour, but still utilising items that are complementary to each other. A classic example is à la grecque (meaning cooking in a Greek style), which is cooked and served in a vinegar and oil solution with aromatic spices. Salad components can include meat, fish and vegetables.

- *Combination salads* – these are made up of several different types of ingredients which have been prepared separately but presented together on one plate. Crucially, the ingredients are not blended together. These are substantial salads and are usually featured on menus as main courses.

- *American salads* – originating in the USA, these salads are usually served as an accompaniment to a hot dish, such as roast turkey. In North America, salads are traditionally served during a banquet instead of sauces or cooked vegetables. An example is orange and watercress salad with a walnut vinaigrette, served to accompany roasted duck.

- *Salad tiède* - *tiède* means warm, therefore these salads will typically consist of a hot ingredient accompanied by cold items. **Salad tiède** is generally served as a starter or a main course.

When designing a salad, the chef garde manger must carefully consider the various factors that contribute to a salad's success:

- *Appearance* – the salad should not only be pleasing and colourful, but also be in keeping with the style of the menu.

- *Appropriateness* – this is quite a broad issue and often not fully considered. For example, it may not be appropriate to serve certain foods to people of specific religions or ethnic backgrounds or with particular medical conditions. Repeating ingredients used elsewhere in a menu will unbalance the eating experience.

- *Flavour* – if a food item lacks flavour it should not be considered; salads should always be appealing to the appetite. Salads are frequently used as palette cleansers or as a bridge in a menu between other foods or courses.

- *Texture* – variety and contrasts in texture add interest and value to most dishes.

- *Nutritional value* – customers are becoming increasingly concerned about health and nutrition. It is both good business and socially responsible to address this issue by making reasonable changes to ingredients or cooking methods where appropriate.

- *Portion size* – this is relative to the entire meal. Chefs should consider what is an appropriate quantity to serve. Salad ingredients should not be too large or too small to make a pleasing presentation.

- *Cost* – it is important to assess and evaluate the cost contribution and margin for profit for all salad and commodity items.

 CHEF'S TIP

Ensure that you prepare the cold element of a salad tiède in plenty of time before the hot ingredients are required so that the dish can be served at the correct temperature, giving the right balance of hot and cold temperatures on the plate.

 CHEF'S TIP

Do not dress a salad with a vinaigrette or dressing too early as this will break down the structure and texture of leaves and herbs.

A terrine presented alongside cold tuna and salmon

TERRINES

These meat, poultry, fish, vegetable or game products are named after the mould in which they are produced. Terrines can be produced in a variety of shapes and sizes, and can be presented as cold mousses, pâtés or parfaits, jellied and layered, or by cold pressing.

Terrines usually consist of more than one type of food product. The ingredients are used in varying proportions and are prepared in different ways, depending on the effect the chef garde manger wishes to create. The terrine mould will usually be lined with bacon, seaweed, vegetables or fat, which helps to hold the terrine together.

Lining a terrine with cling film

Lining a terrine with bacon

Lining a terrine with seaweed

VIDEO CLIP
Preparation of foie gras, artichoke and herb terrine

Placing vegetables into terrine

Brushing with aspic to set vegetables

Building next layer

PÂTÉS AND PARFAITS

These products can be made of offal, meat, poultry, fish, vegetables or game and are rich in flavour. Pâtés can be coarse textured or fine pastes, whereas parfaits have the consistency of whipped cream or butter.

There are two methods for preparing parfaits:

■ Prepared then cooked

■ Cooked then prepared.

The classical prepared then cooked method is to add cooked shallots, flambéed with alcohol, to melted clarified butter. Egg yolks and blended livers are added to the mixture and butter and cream are slowly mixed in. The mixture is then passed through a sieve, seasoned well and poured into a prepared terrine mould. It is then placed in a bain marie and cooked in an oven until the core temperature reaches 68°C.

CHEF'S TIP

Keep a container of hot water and a clean cloth when slicing products such as terrines and pâtés; a hot, clean knife will slice cleanly and produce neat slices.

PÂTÉS AND PARFAITS

Preparation of a pâté

Sautéing onions and herbs

Combining minced meat with onions and beating together

Adding eggs and cream to the base mixture

Blending in a food processor to a course mixture

Seasoning the pâté mixture

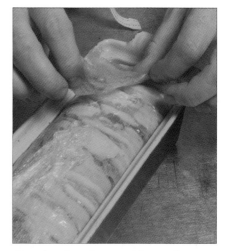

Covering the mixture with streaky bacon and plastic film

The second method varies in that the ingredients are cooked prior to preparation. Extra butter is used in this method to counteract the lack of protein structure and to achieve the same effect as the classical parfait. Shallots are cooked in butter with livers to a medium cooked point, alcohol is then added and flambéed. The shallots and livers are left to cool, then blended together with a small amount of cream until a smooth texture is achieved. The mixture is then passed through a sieve, and softened (but not clarified) butter is folded in. It is then seasoned and poured into the terrine mould and refrigerated until set.

MOUSSES

Mousses are lighter in texture than pâtés and are not as rich in flavour, which makes them a little more versatile.

A basic raw mousseline recipe for meat, poultry or fish uses 500g of fresh protein to approximately 900ml of chilled double cream, four egg yolks and two whole eggs. The protein needs to be **minced** twice and passed through a sieve, to break down the protein structure, and then chilled over ice. Using a blender, the protein is combined with the eggs and seasoning, which are added slowly until a smooth texture is achieved. The chilled double cream is incorporated into the mixture slowly to prevent the mousseline from splitting. The mousseline can then be poached, steamed or baked, or used in terrines that are to be cooked.

Cooked mousses differ by using a meat, fish, poultry or vegetable base that has already undergone cooking and gelatine or agar-agar is used to set the mixture. The base ingredient is blended until smooth while the gelatine or agar-agar is melted. The setting agent is then beaten into the base mixture, which is seasoned as required. Cream, lightly whipped to a soft peak, is gently folded into the mixture to form a light mousse, which can be **piped**, formed into **quenelles** or layered into a terrine mould, before being allowed to set in a refrigerator.

RECIPES

Gravadlax with beetroot dressing and chilli taco

INGREDIENTS	4 PORTIONS	10 PORTIONS
Salmon fillet (skin on, trimmed and pin boned)	300g	800g
Sugar	150g	425g
Good-quality salt	180g	500g
Orange juice and zest	1 each	3 each
Dill	½ bunch	1½ bunches
Plain flour	200g	500g
Lard	10g	25g
Good-quality salt	10g	25g
Saffron water	To soften	To soften
Ground chilli flakes	1tsp	1tbsp
Assorted leaves	50g	125g
Cooked baby beetroot	50g	125g
Olive oil	4tbsp	10tbsp

Method of work

1   Finely chop the dill. Mix the sugar, salt and chopped dill together. Slash the salmon skin and rub the salt mixture on both sides, then leave for at least 24 hours, wrapped in plastic film in a refrigerator.

2   Take the flour, lard and second amount of salt and mix well, then slowly add enough saffron water to form a soft paste (pasta dough consistency).

3   Sprinkle in the chilli and knead well, then wrap in plastic film and chill for at least 30 minutes.

4   Roll the paste using a pasta machine until the desired thickness is achieved.

5   Cut out desired shapes, lay onto a lightly oiled tray and bake at 50°C until dry.

6   Remove the salmon from the cure and wash off, pat dry and place onto a chopping board.

7   Slice the salmon, going from tail to head, into neat pieces then roll into rosettes.

8   To serve, lay a leaf on the plate, top with the rosette of salmon and garnish with a chilli taco.

9   Blend the beetroot with a little olive oil until a smooth dressing is achieved.

10 Drizzle the beetroot and oil mixture around.

Duck liver and orange quenelles, with caramelised oranges

INGREDIENTS	4 PORTIONS	10 PORTIONS
Shallots	60g	150g
Garlic	1–2 cloves	3–4 cloves
Duck livers (cleaned and trimmed)	200g	500g
Olive oil	30ml	80ml
Butter	80g	200g
Orange segments	12	30
Orange liquor (such as Grand Marnier)	60ml	150ml
Sugar	40g	100g
Good-quality salt and pepper	To taste	To taste
Cayenne taco (see recipe on p. 97)	4	10
Chives	8	20
Salad leaves	as required	as required

Method of work

1 Finely chop the shallots and garlic. In a frying pan, fry off in the olive oil until tender and without colour.
2 Melt the butter in a small saucepan.
3 In a separate hot pan, season and sear the duck livers. When rare, flambé with the orange liquor.
4 Place the shallots and duck livers in a blender and blend until a smooth paste. Slowly add the melted butter and the cream. Season as required.
5 Chill the mixture slightly until pliable then quenelle onto a lined tray. Cover and chill until required.
6 Boil the sugar with a little water until a light caramel is formed, add the orange segments, remove from the heat and allow to cool.
7 To serve, place three quenelles of parfait on the plate and garnish with a pluche of salad, caramelised orange, chives and cayenne taco.

Carpaccio of beef with rocket and horseradish cream

INGREDIENTS	4 PORTIONS	10 PORTIONS
Beef fillet	100g	250g
Olive oil	40ml	100ml
Horseradish cream	2tbsp	5tbsp
Double cream	50ml	125ml
Lemon juice and zest	½ lemon	1½ lemons
Rocket	60g	150g
Shaved Parmesan cheese	40g	100g
Reduced sherry vinegar	4tbsp	10tbsp
Good-quality salt and ground white pepper	To taste	To taste

Method of work

1 Heat a frying pan, add a little oil and roll the trimmed beef fillet until seared on the outside.
2 Season the fillet and then wrap in cling film.
3 Allow to cool, then freeze overnight.
4 Remove the beef, unwrap a little, then using a sharp knife or slicing machine shave thin slices and arrange on a plate.
5 Lightly whip the cream to soft peaks and fold in the horseradish, lemon juice and zest.
6 Spoon the cream around the plate.
7 Drizzle around the oil and drops of reduced sherry vinegar.
8 Finally, season the beef with salt and pepper and garnish with rocket and Parmesan cheese.

Warm crab cakes with tomato dressing

INGREDIENTS	4 PORTIONS	10 PORTIONS
White crab meat	100g	250g
Breadcrumbs	100g	250g
Mayonnaise	40ml	100ml
Finely chopped spring onion	1tbsp	3tbsp
Cayenne taco (see recipe on p. 97)	4 spirals	10 spirals
Assorted lettuce leaves	50g	125g
Tomato concassé	100g	250g
Finely chopped shallots	1tbsp	2½tbsp
Olive oil	3tbsp	8tbsp
Sugar	1tsp	3tsp
Red wine vinegar	1tbsp	2½tbsp
Good-quality salt and ground white pepper	To taste	To taste

Method of work

1 Mix the picked crab meat, mayonnaise, spring onion and half the breadcrumbs, season well, then mould into small cakes.
2 Roll the cakes in the remaining breadcrumbs until no crabmeat is showing.
3 Sweat the tomato, shallots, sugar and oil until very soft, then add the vinegar, season and blend until smooth.
4 Deep fry the crab cakes until a golden brown colour is achieved.
5 To serve, dress the leaves and arrange on the plate, add the crab cake and cayenne taco and spoon the tomato dressing around.

Rabbit terrine with plum chutney and garlic tomatoes

INGREDIENTS	4 PORTIONS	10 PORTIONS
Flesh from whole rabbit	½	1
Chicken breast	1	2
Pork trimmings	80g	200g
Brandy	½ measure	1 Measure
Thyme	4 sprigs	8 sprigs
Bay leaf	½	1
Double cream	100ml	250ml
Parma ham	8 slices	20 slices
Liver and kidney (from the rabbit)		
Chilled egg whites	1	2
Mace	Pinch	Pinch
Plum chutney (plums cooked in sugar, cinnamon, red wine, red chilli and redcurrant jelly, reduced to taste)	4 small spoons	10 small spoons
Good-quality salt and ground white pepper	To taste	To taste
Cherry tomato (heated in oil and garlic then cooled)	4	10
Thyme	2 sprigs	4 sprigs
Bay leaf	½	1
Mixed lettuce leaves	50g	125g
Cayenne taco (see recipe on p. 97)	4	10

Method of work

1 Marinate the rabbit, chicken and pork in brandy, thyme and bay leaf overnight.

2 Set aside the rabbit fillets. Mince the rabbit (including liver and kidneys), chicken and pork, once through a medium mincer and twice through a fine mincer. Then pass through a sieve. Blast chill to get very cold.

3 When the mince is cold, beat with the double cream in a robot coupe. Season with salt, pepper and mace and quickly add the chilled egg whites.

4 Poach a little to test for holding consistency and taste.

5 Line a small terrine mould with oil and two layers of cling film. Line with the Parma ham.

6 Place the rabbit mix in the terrine mould and layer in the slices of rabbit flesh from the fillet. Smooth down and fold over the Parma ham. Cover with foil.

7 Steam for 25–30 minutes at 100°C in a steamer.

8 Remove and chill until required.

9 To serve, slice the terrine carefully with a warm wet knife and position on the plate with the cayenne taco, add the garlic-infused cherry tomato, a plum chutney and some dressed mixed lettuce leaves.

Duck liver pâté with Belgian endive, herb oil and foie gras

INGREDIENTS	4 PORTIONS	10 PORTIONS
Duck livers	100g	250g
Port wine reduction	25ml	60ml
Shallots finely chopped	1	3
Garlic finely chopped	2 cloves	6 cloves
Pork fat finely diced	30g	75g
Fresh breadcrumbs	4tbsp	10tbsp
Liquid whole egg	20ml	50ml
Belgian endive	12 leaves	30 leaves
Foie gras fine dice	20g	50g
Chives	8	20
Cherry tomato	4	10
Herb oil	2tbsp	5tbsp
Ground white pepper	To taste	To taste
Good quality salt	To taste	To taste

Method of work

1 In a food processor blend the livers, egg, reduction, breadcrumbs, shallots and garlic until a course paste is formed.
2 Fold in the foie gras, season and taste raw. Place into a terrine mould lined with cling film.
3 Cover with foil and steam at 100°C for 25 to 30 minutes, until just set.
4 Remove and chill over night.
5 When required, quenelle onto a plate, garnish with Belgian endive, chives and cherry tomato.
6 Spoon around the herb oil.

Raw, lime marinated tuna with Dijon dressing and leaves

INGREDIENTS	4 PORTIONS	10 PORTIONS
Tuna loin	100g	250g
Lime juice	½ lime	1½ limes
Olive oil	50ml	125ml
Dijon mustard	1tbsp	2½tbsp
White wine vinegar	25ml	70ml
Saffron taco (see recipe on p. 97)	12 each	30 each
Mixed fine leaves	60g	160g
Sea salt	Pinch	Pinch
Chervil	Sprigs	Sprigs
Good-quality salt and ground white pepper	To taste	To taste

Method of work

1 Thinly slice the tuna then brush with lime juice and sea salt (this must be served within 4 minutes).

2 Prepare the Dijon dressing: combine the mustard with 1 part vinegar to 3 parts oil and season.

3 Dress the leaves with a little dressing.

4 Arrange the tuna on the plate, add the leaves, saffron tacos and chervil, then spoon a little Dijon dressing around the plate.

Smoked lamb's tongue with curly endive, blackened red peppers and red wine reduction

INGREDIENTS	4 PORTIONS	10 PORTIONS
Lamb's tongue	200g	500g
Tea bags (jasmine)	4	10
Long grain rice	80g	200g
Granulated sugar	50g	125g
Thyme	Sprigs	Sprigs
Curly endive	80g	200g
Red peppers	1	3
Olive oil	100ml	250ml
Red wine vinegar	50ml	125ml
Red wine	50ml	125ml
Redcurrant jelly	50g	125ml
Cherry tomatoes	4	10
Good-quality salt and ground white pepper	To taste	To taste

Method of work

1 Empty the contents of the tea bags into a roasting tray and add the sugar, rice and thyme. Place into an oven at 200°C until smoking.

2 Place a cooling rack onto the tray and lay on the tongue, cover with foil and return to the oven for 4 minutes.

3 Remove and allow to cool.

4 Brush the peppers with oil and hold over a naked flame until blackened.

5 Place the peppers into a bag, seal and wait 5 minutes.

6 Remove the peppers, peel and quarter, and remove the seeds.

7 Julienne the peppers and mix with a little seasoning and a splash of red wine vinegar.

8 Heat the red wine, remaining vinegar and redcurrant jelly until reduced by half, add the tomatoes and chill until ready to use.

9 Arrange the peppers, leaves, tomato and tongue on the plate, finish with a little reduction.

Asian pigeon breast with fine potato salad, oven dried tomatoes and lightly spiced yoghurt

INGREDIENTS	4 PORTIONS	10 PORTIONS
Pigeon breasts	4	10
Tandoori paste	2tbsp	5tbsp
Lime juice	½ lime	2 limes
New potatoes (blanched, peeled and diced)	80g	200g
Basic vinaigrette	2tbsp	5tbsp
Plum tomatoes (1/6 dried overnight in a cool oven)	4 pieces	10 pieces
Cherry tomatoes	4	10
Greek yoghurt	2tbsp	5tbsp
Ground cumin	1tsp	3tsp
Ground cayenne	1tsp	3tsp
Lemon juice	½ lemon	1½ lemons
Cayenne taco (see recipe on p. 97)	4	10
Good-quality salt and ground white pepper	To taste	To taste

Method of work

1 Marinate the pigeon in tandoori paste, lime juice and seasoning for 30 minutes.

2 Place the pigeon on a tray in a hot oven and bake for 8 minutes.

3 Take the potatoes, season and add vinaigrette.

4 Mix the yoghurt with lemon juice, cumin and cayenne

5 To assemble, spoon the potato salad onto the plate. Slice the pigeon around, add the tomatoes and spoon the yoghurt on to the plate.

6 Finish with the cayenne taco for added height.

Quail egg and kedgeree potato cake with wild leaves and citrus oil

INGREDIENTS	4 PORTIONS	10 PORTIONS
Quail eggs	6	15
Natural smoked haddock	80g	200g
Fresh milk	100ml	250ml
Clouté	½	1
Braised rice	50g	125g
Grated potato	100g	250g
Curry powder	To taste	To taste
Pasteurised egg	To bind	To bind
Fresh white breadcrumbs	2tbsp	5tbsp
Wild lettuce leaves	50g	125g
Lemons	½	1
Limes	½	1
Olive oil	50ml	125ml
Good-quality salt and ground white pepper	To taste	To taste

Method of work

1   Boil the quail eggs, refresh and peel.
2   Poach the haddock in milk infused with the clouté until just cooked.
3   Remove the haddock, flake into a bowl with the breadcrumbs, rice, potato, curry powder and enough egg to bind.
4   Form small cakes and pan fry until golden.
5   Place the lemon and the lime into the olive oil and bring to the boil. Simmer for 10 minutes, then pass and cool quickly.
6   Assemble by placing halved eggs around the plate, cakes in the middle, dressed leaves on top and citrus oil around.

Smoked salmon and king prawn terrine with a light cucumber, pepper and lemon salad

INGREDIENTS	4 PORTIONS	10 PORTIONS
Smoked salmon	300g	1 kg
King prawns (cooked)	8	20
Double cream	150ml	450ml
Horseradish cream	To taste	To taste
Lemon juice and zest	½ lemon	1½ lemons
Cayenne pepper	Pinch	Pinch
Gelatine	2 leaves dissolved	5 leaves dissolved
Diced cucumber	50g	125g
Diced yellow peppers	50g	125g
Microleaf salad	35g	85g
Sun-blushed tomatoes	8	20
Cayenne taco (see recipe on p. 97)	4	10
Good-quality salt and ground white pepper	To taste	To taste

Method of work

1 Line a small terrine mould with cling film, then lay in thin slices of smoked salmon and chill.

2 Blend the remaining salmon with the horseradish cream, half the lemon juice and zest and cayenne.

3 Remove and place into a cold bowl.

4 Whip the cream until soft peaks are formed then fold into the salmon.

5 Fold in the dissolved gelatine (ensuring it is at room temperature – no hotter).

6 Spoon a little salmon mousse into the mould, then add half the king prawns.

7 Top up with mousse. Slice the remaining king prawn and add to the terrine.

8 Finish with mousse and fold over the salmon.

9 Chill for at least 1 hour.

10 Remove from the mould and roll in extra cling film; this will help the terrine keep its shape when slicing.

11 To assemble, slice the terrine and lay on the plate, arrange the microleaves and sun-blushed tomatoes.

12 Combine the remaining lemon with the diced cucumber and pepper and arrange in a small spoon. Finish with a cayenne taco.

Oriental duck salad with apple, sesame and roasted cashews

INGREDIENTS	4 PORTIONS	10 PORTIONS
Duck breast	2	5
Honey	2tbsp	5tbsp
Soy sauce	1tsp	2½tsp
Hoi sin	1tsp	2½tsp
Julienne of apple	60g	150g
Toasted sesame seeds	1tsp	2½tsp
Coriander	20g	50g
Roasted cashew nuts	2tbsp	5tbsp
Oyster sauce	40ml	100ml
Water	40ml	100ml
Red chillies	1	2½
Spring onions	1	2½
Garlic chopped	2 cloves	5 cloves
Ginger grated	1tsp	2½tsp
Good-quality salt and ground white pepper	To taste	To taste

Method of work

1 Score the duck breasts and rub with honey, soy sauce and hoi sin. Leave to marinate for 2 hours.

2 Pan fry the duck until pink, then allow to cool slightly.

3 Mix the apple with the sesame seeds and coriander.

4 Boil the oyster sauce, water, chillies, spring onions, garlic and ginger for 1 minute, then pass and chill.

5 To assemble, slice the duck and lay on the plate with the apple salad and roasted cashews. Serve oyster sauce in a small spoon.

Assessment of knowledge and understanding

You have now learned about cold larder work; the range it can cover and the array of commodities and cooking techniques that can be used.

To test your level of knowledge and understanding, answer the following short questions. These will help to prepare you for your summative (final) assessment.

Quality identifications

1 Explain in detail why it is best to use produce that is in season.

_____

_____

2 Name the three main types of hors d'oeuvres and explain the differences between them.

i) _____   ii) _____

iii) _____

Preparation methods

1 Give three examples of different salads and explain what factors should be taken into consideration when preparing them.

i) _____   ii) _____

iii) _____

Cooking methods

1 List five presentation elements that need to be considered when creating salads.

i) _____   ii) _____

iii) _____   iv) _____

v) _____

2 Explain the safest way to ensure that terrines or pâtés are cooked through but will still have a pink colour inside.

_____

_____

Health and safety

1 Detail why larder items are at such high risk of cross-contamination.

_____

_____

2 Explain the importance of clear labelling and storage within the larder.

_____

_____

CHEF'S PROFILE

Name: **MARTYN NAIL**

Position: Executive chef

Establishment: Claridges

Main responsibilities: I oversee everything.

When did you realise that you wanted to pursue a career in the catering and hospitality industry?
I thought I liked cooking and so went on to college.

Training:
After finishing school, I attended Catering College at Highbury College of Technology. I passed my three year diploma in July 1986, achieving a distinction.

Experience:
I have only worked at Claridge's. It's a fascinating place, always throwing up new challenges. There's always something new to learn! In 2003 I was awarded a scholarship to Cornell University in New York. Whilst I was there I visited various restaurants and hotels (such as La Bernardin) which gave me new insights and was very inspiring. In January this year I also did a trip round New York, Las Vegas and San Francisco, exploring their restaurants. It was a great way to gain knowledge and understanding about America's dining concepts.

What do you find rewarding about your job?
Training, and seeing young people progress to be confident, capable chefs.

What do you find the most challenging about the job?
Ensuring that change is communicated well and clearly to achieve maximum buy-in.

What advice would you give to students just beginning their career?
Be patient even if you think what someone is trying to teach you is boring, one day it will be of use.

Who is your mentor or main inspiration?
Chef Jean-George Vongerichten. Not only is he incredibly talented, but is also a very nice man! He's just so approachable. Vong at The Berkeley hotel was an amazing place. It had amazing food and service.

What traits do you consider essential for anyone entering a career as a chef?
Passion, dedication and discipline.

Can you give one essential kitchen tip or technique that you use as a chef?
Treat all ingredients with respect. Cook them with the respect they deserve.

Claridge's grouse and foie gras pie with apricot and wild mushrooms

INGREDIENTS

Hot water pastry

Milk	400ml
Water	200ml
Lard	325g
Plain flour	1.300kg
Salt	2tsp
Egg wash	2 egg yolk equal amount of cold water

For filling

Grouse bones removed and flesh checked for shoot	5
Lobe of duck foie gras, pre-cooked	1
Mixed wild mushrooms	200g
Dried apricots	15
Leafs of gelatine	8
Ruby port	30ml
Madeira	15ml
Salt	10g
White pepper	
Thyme	2 sprigs

For lining the pie

Streaky bacon	500g
Consommé jelly	500ml
Chicken consommé	
Gelatine	10 leafs

Method of work

1 Heat the water, milk and lard to 85°C.

2 Put the flour and the salt in a well on a bench.

3 Gradually add the liquid to the flour and stir as you do it.

4 Work the ingredients lightly to form the pastry.

5 Wrap in cling film and chill.

6 Allow the pastry to come to room temperature then roll to 0.4cm.

7 Cut the pastry to desired shape to line mould, reserving some to form the lid.

8 Line the greased mould with pastry, being sure to overlap the edges and pressing tight in to the tin and leaving a 3cm border of pastry out of the edge of the tin.

9 Line the pastry with streaky bacon.

10 Add all the ingredients for the filling in a bowl and mix in the seasoning. Allow to stand for 1 hour.

11 Arrange the filling in the pie to form a mosaic.

12 Close over the bacon and bring up the overlapping pastry border.

13 Now prepare your lid and make one or two steam holes, egg wash and decorate.

14 Brush the top of the overlap with the egg wash and apply the lid to the pie.

15 Allow to rest for at least half an hour before cooking.

16 Cook at 210°C until golden (approximately 15 minutes) then cover with foil and continue to cook at 210°C until you get a core temperature of 55°C. Allow to rest at room temperature for 25–30 minutes then cool in a fridge for 1 hour until the pastry sets.

17 Soften the gelatine in cold water.

18 Bring the consommé to the boil, add the gelatine and allow to cool.

19 Pour the prepared jelly through the steam hole. Allow this to set in the fridge for 20 minutes before topping up with the jelly again. Repeat this until the jelly reaches the top of the steam hole.

20 Allow to rest for at least 24 hours before de-moulding and slicing.

9
Complex soups

LEARNING OBJECTIVES

The aim of this chapter is to enable you to develop skills and apply knowledge in the principles of producing a range of different types of soups. This will also include the use of resources, ingredients and associated equipment.

At the end of this chapter you will be able to:

- Identify each type of soup and how it is finished
- Understand the use of relative ingredients in various types of soups and their quality points
- State the quality points of soups
- Prepare and cook each type of soup
- Identify the storage and holding procedures of soups
- Identify the correct tools and equipment to utilise during the production of soups
- Recognise alternative healthy eating options in different soup recipes

INTRODUCTION

Historically, soup has been an important part of our nutrition. As time has passed, our nutritional requirements have not changed a great deal, but the sourcing and use of soups have evolved greatly. A soup can provide the main part of a light lunch, or it can be used as a small appetiser at the beginning of a dinner. Soups are used in large modern menus to stimulate the appetite and create a delicate introduction for meat and fish courses. The service has also changed, with soups sometimes being served in small shot glasses, or in demitasse cups with a light foam layered on top to give a frothy cappuccino effect.

Soup should be included on the menu to reflect seasonality. During the autumn and winter, hearty and robust soups accompanied with bread bring a warmth of hospitality that is welcoming on a menu. In the summer months, a chilled soup revives a palette and gives a sense of lightness.

 CHEF'S TIP

On the contemporary menu, a soup is usually served as a first course, where its purpose is to stimulate the appetite. Soups should have delicate flavour and a natural colour. Thick soups should not be too heavy in consistency.

Special requirements

Consideration should be given to the needs of the diner when preparing soups, for example:

■ Patients and the elderly require easily digestible soups that are light and nutritious, such as a chicken broth, and with few complex carbohydrates, such as beans

■ Many medical conditions or dietary restrictions require the use of alternative ingredients:

  – *Diabetes* – include as many complex carbohydrates as possible; use foods that are high on the glycaemic index, such as chickpeas, beans and wholemeal flour
  – *Coeliac disease* – use potatoes instead of gluten-rich flour to thicken soups
  – *Dairy intolerance* – use soya milk instead of dairy milk; make the soya milk into thin béchamel to use in place of cream
  – *Vegetarians and vegans* – ensure that the base stock is vegetarian and that any fats are vegetable oils and not butter; this seems an obvious point but it can be easily overlooked.

Most guests with specific dietary requirements will make their needs known in advance. However, any prior knowledge of these needs and how to successfully address them will allow the chef to be flexible with the menu and able to accommodate most requirements.

Healthy options

There are always ways to take to make a soup healthier; the addition of yoghurt or single cream instead of double cream and the use of unsaturated oils instead of butter will reduce the fat and cholesterol content. Generally, however, soups are a healthy part of our diet, especially lightly cooked broths, which are nutritious and easily digested.

A pureé soup

A cream soup

A broth

A consommé

A bisque

A chowder

SOUP CLASSIFICATION

Soups can be categorised as follows:

■ *Purée* – a soup named after or thickened by its main ingredient, such as mushroom, potato and leek or tomato.

■ *Cream* – a purée soup with the addition of cream, thin béchamel or crème frâiche. Cream of mushroom, cream of potato and leek, cream of tomato and cream of vegetable are all variations. It is essential that these soups have a smooth consistency and have been passed.

■ *Velouté* – a soup to which a liaison of cream and egg yolk has been added.

■ *Broth* – a soup that is composed of a strongly flavoured stock and a named garnish, such as mutton. This type of soup is not passed, and the vegetables are cut in varying shapes according to the recipe's requirement. Examples are mutton broth and Scotch broth. Potages also come under this type of soup.

■ Consommé – clear soups that are prepared from stock flavoured with various meats and vegetables. They are clarified and should be clear when finished. Bouillons also come under this category, but they are not clarified to the same level. Examples are consommé julienne, consommé Celestine and consommé royale.

■ *Bisque* – taken from the French term *bi cuit* (biscuit), bisque is a soup made from crustaceans and is traditionally served with water biscuits. It is thickened with rice and the shell of the crustacean used and finished with cream. Examples are lobster and prawn bisque.

■ *Chowder* – this is generally a seafood soup, usually based on molluscs but can have added smoked white fish. It is usually associated with New England, and the most popular version is clam chowder. The term may also describe a buttery, hearty soup made with corn and chicken. The term 'chowder' may derive from the French word for a large caldron, *chaudiere*, in which Breton fishermen threw their catch to make a communal fish stew. Examples are clam, cockle or chicken and sweetcorn chowder.

■ *Foreign* – also known as miscellaneous soups, these are all soups of a traditional, modern and national nature that do not fall into any other category. There are many examples, such as: the simple Jewish chicken soup; the gumbos made from okra, chicken, seafood or meat in the American south; India has many types of lentil soups; Middle Eastern Muslims break their Ramadan fast with harira, made from lentils, chickpeas and lamb; Japan is famous for soups based on miso (fermented soybean paste); Eastern Europe possesses goulash (a beef and paprika stew that started life as soup) and borsch (beetroot and meat soup); Spanish gazpacho is always in vogue; the Greeks have avgolemono, an egg and lemon soup; Italy has numerous bean and pasta soups, such as

VIDEO CLIP
Preparation of gazpacho

minestrone; and Scotland is renowned for cullen skink (smoked haddock soup) and Scotch broth (mutton and barley soup).

■ *Chilled* – nearly all soups that are served hot can also be served chilled. However, when chilled the intensity of flavour is reduced. They may therefore need a stronger base or a more intense seasoning.

The skills required to create an outstanding soup are the same as those needed to make a delicate sauce. The modern chef has a wide variety of ingredients at their disposal to meet the requirements of today's more perceptive customers. The balance of flavours, seasoning, consistency, texture and temperature needs to be understood to create a well-flavoured and satisfying soup.

VELOUTÉS

The quality points of this type of soup are that they should have a delicate flavour and have a velvety, smooth texture. This will be attributed in part to the use of well-flavoured stocks, careful simmering and the addition of a liaison of egg yolks and cream. Once the liaison is added the soup needs to be reheated very carefully and must never be allowed to reboil.

CHEF'S TIP

It is imperative that unblemished, fresh ingredients are used when making soups. Always check that the ingredients meet with the dish requirements by using correct mise en place methods and weighing each ingredient prior to preparation.

Basic velouté recipe

INGREDIENTS	MAKES 1 LITRE
Butter	60g
Flour	60g
White stock	1250ml
Egg yolks	2
Cream	100ml
Good-quality salt and white pepper	To taste

Method of work

1   Prepare a blond roux with the butter and the flour.

2   Mix in the boiling white stock gradually using a wooden spoon. Avoid lumps by adding a little at a time and bring to the boil whilst continuously stirring.

3   Bring back to the boil, skim and season and leave to simmer for 45 minutes.

4   Pass through a fine chinois into a clean pan and reboil.

5   Whisk together the egg yolks and cream and add one third of the soup, whisking quickly. Add to the remaining soup and continuously stir until the liaison is fully combined and has slightly thickened to velouté. Correct the seasoning and add any garnish before serving.

GARNISHES AND ACCOMPANIMENTS

Most soups are accompanied by bread, usually in the form of bread rolls or sliced baguettes. However, croûtons, sippets and toasted flutes may also be served at the table. Today, croûtons are often quite rustic is style, with large pieces of bread drizzled with olive oil and baked in the oven until crisp.

Croûtons, sippets and croûtes de flûte

- Croûtons – small cubes of white crustless bread (1cm × 1cm) that are pan fried in clarified butter. The butter is heated in a pan and the diced bread added; the pan is constantly shaken so that the croûtons colour evenly. The croûtons are spooned out onto kitchen paper and patted dry.
- *Sippets* – triangles of bread cut from the corners of pan loaves, thinly sliced and toasted in an oven. To add flavour, garlic can be rubbed onto the bread before turning over to toast the other side.
- *Croûtes de flûte* (toasted flutes) – slices taken from a thin baguette. They can either be toasted on both sides or brushed in melted butter and crisped in the oven.
- *Diablotins* – thin round slices of toasted bread, topped with grated cheese and browned in the oven. Can be coated with reduced béchamel.
- *Melba toast* – melba toast is toasted bread that is cut between the toasted surfaces whilst still hot. The uncooked side is rubbed on a service cloth to remove the rough bread and then also toasted.
- *Cheese straws* – puff pastry strips the have cheese added at the last turn. They are twisted and baked until crisp.

Brunoise

Vegetable garnishes

Used as a light garnish for consommés, broths or purée-based soups. Careful cutting into neat, even and standardised shapes is important to the finished result.

Julienne

- *Brunoise* – cut equal amounts of carrot, turnip, leek and celery into 2mm dice, for consommés and slightly larger for broths
- *Julienne* – cut equal amounts of carrot, turnip, leek and celery into thin strips up to 35mm in length
- *Paysanne* – cut equal amounts of turnips, carrots, swede, potato, leek and celery into 1cm squares.

Paysanne

SERVING TEMPERATURES AND QUANTITIES

Hot soups should be served very hot and any accompanying garnishes should be added when serving. The Food Hygiene (England) Regulations 2006 state that hot food needs to be kept at or above 63°C in order to control the growth of pathogenic micro-organisms and the formation of toxins. The soup should not be kept for service or on display for sale for a period of more than two hours.

Cold soups should be served chilled at below 8°C and not at room temperature.

When calculating the amount of soup required for a given number of portions, take into account the following points:

- Portion size is dependent on the size and style of the menu and the number of courses that follow
- The recipe method must be followed correctly
- Each ingredient must be accurately measured
- No more than 200–250ml per portion should be served.

RECIPES
Basic clear consommé

Clockwise: fish, game, chicken and beef consommé

 CHEF'S TIP

Make sure the raft of clarification stays floating. If it starts to sink, raise the temperature. This will help to combat cloudiness.

 **VIDEO CLIP**
Preparation of consommés Celestine

INGREDIENTS	4 PORTIONS	10 PORTIONS
Minced flesh (e.g. beef, fish, poultry, game)	200g	1kg
Carrot	40g	100g
Onion	40g	100g
Celery	40g	100g
Leek	40g	100g
Bay leaves	1	2
Thyme	1 sprig	2 sprig
Peppercorns	4	10
Good-quality salt	Pinch	5g
Cold stock (e.g. beef fish, poultry, game)	200ml	500ml
Hot stock (e.g. beef fish, poultry, game)	1 litre	2.5 litres
Egg whites	1	2–3

Method of work

1 Peel and chop all of the vegetables into a macédoine.

2 Thoroughly mix all of the minced flesh, vegetables, herbs, seasoning, egg whites and cold stock (this is called the clarification) together and allow to stand for 30 minutes.

3 Mix well with the hot stock and bring to the boil as quickly as possible. Keep the bottom of the pan clear by using a spatula, but avoid disturbing the clarif.

4 Allow to simmer gently for 2–3 hours.

5 Strain through a dampened muslin cloth and adjust the seasoning with salt only.

6 Serve in a warm consommé cup, plain or with a named garnish.

Tomato consommé _Consommé madrilène_

INGREDIENTS	4 PORTIONS	10 PORTIONS
Basic beef consommé clarification	4 portions	10 portions
Very ripe tomatoes	4	10
Tomato concassé	120g	300g
Extra celery	100g	250g
Shredded sorrel	1tbsp	1–3tbsp

CHEF'S TIP

Tomatoes are over 90 per cent water, therefore it important to squeeze as much out as possible. You can still use the juice in the consommé as long as it is clarified along with the stock.

Method of work

1 Squash the tomatoes and squeeze the water into the clarification.
2 Add the tomato flesh and celery to the clarification and proceed as for basic consommé.
3 Serve hot or cold, garnished with the evenly cut tomato concassé and shredded sorrel.

Consommé with poached quail's eggs _Consommé Colbert_

INGREDIENTS	4 PORTIONS	10 PORTIONS
Chicken consommé	1.25 litres	3 litres
Quail's eggs	12	30
Fine julienne of carrot celery, leek and turnip	160g	400g
Butter	20g	50g
Chives	To garnish	To garnish

CHEF'S TIP

Hen's eggs are the classical choice for this soup, but the easy availability of quail's eggs means they are now preferable.

Method of work

1 Cook the vegetables in the butter in a covered pan until just cooked and drain on dish paper.
2 Poach the eggs in a little of the consommé, taking care to keep the yolks runny. Refresh and keep for service.
3 Place the vegetable garnish and three eggs per portion in the bottom of the consommé cup.
4 Pour the very hot consommé onto the eggs and vegetables.
5 Allow to stand for 1 minute before service to allow the eggs to heat through.
6 Serve with some chopped chives.

Consommé with chicken quenelle

INGREDIENTS	4 PORTIONS	10 PORTIONS
Chicken consommé	1.25 litres	3 litres
Chicken breast meat	100g	250g
Double cream	40ml	100ml
Egg whites	1	2
Good-quality salt and white pepper	To taste	To taste
Chives	To garnish	To garnish

CHEF'S TIP

Do not return the cooking liquor from the quenelles to the consommé; it will make the consommé cloudy.

VIDEO CLIP
Preparation of chicken and herb quenelles

Method of work

1 Mince the chicken through a fine plate three times, making sure that the flesh is chilled between each mincing.
2 In a metal bowl over ice, beat in the cream to make a fine forcemeat of chicken.
3 Season and test a small piece in simmering stock. Adjust the seasoning if necessary.
4 Make small quenelles of chicken forcemeat and poach in a little of the consommé.
5 Serve the remaining consommé with chicken quenelles and garnish with chopped chives.

Petite marmite

INGREDIENTS	4 PORTIONS	10 PORTIONS
Basic consommé	1.5 litre	3.5 litre
Diced lean rump beef	80g	200g
Chicken wings	4	10
Carrots	80g	200g
Leek	80g	200g
Turnip	80g	200g
Celery	80g	200g
Savoy cabbage	50g	125g
Bone marrow	8 slices	20 slices
Baguettes	12 slices	30 slices

CHEF'S TIP

Petite marmite is named after the pot in which it is served:
marmite = pot,
petite marmite = small pot.

Method of work

1 Blanch and refresh the beef, add to the consommé and simmer very gently for 1 hour.
2 Trim the wings and blanch in boiling water, add to the consommé and simmer for 20 minutes.
3 Turn the carrots and cut the celery into diamonds, add to the consommé.
4 Add the shaped turnips, cut leeks and cabbage and continue to simmer.
5 Dip the slices of bread into the fat from the soup and toast in the oven.
6 Degrease the soup and correct the seasoning.
7 Add the sliced marrow to the soup and poach for 2–3 minutes.
8 Decant into either a single or individual earthenware dishes and serve accompanied by the toasted flutes.

Consommé with turned vegetables and flutes
Croûte au pot

CHEF'S TIP

Croûte au pot was originally served from a petit marmite. However, by today's tastes the vegetables would be considered to be overcooked.

INGREDIENTS	4 PORTIONS	10 PORTIONS
Consommé	1 litre	2.5 litres
Carrot, turnip, courgette	160g	400g
Flutes	¼ loaf (4 thin slices)	½ loaf (10 thin slices)
Goose/duck fat	20g	50g

Method of work

1 Shape the vegetables into small barrel shapes and cook in seasoned boiling water or stock.
2 Brush the flutes with melted fat, season and bake in the oven until crisp.
3 Serve the soup with the vegetables as a garnish and the baked flutes separately.

Chilled consommé and garnishes

CHEF'S TIP

Instead of using gelatine, the addition of an alternative setting gel such as agar-agar can be used.

INGREDIENTS	4 PORTIONS	10 PORTIONS
Consommé	1 litre	2.5 litres
Named garnish	200g	500g

Chilled consommés are normally placed in the refrigerator one or two hours before service. Their sometimes gelatinous appearance is due to the concentration of protein. The addition of 10g of leaf gelatine per litre of consommé will set it to the required consistency. Various flavours can be added to base consommés:

- *Consommé Madrilène en Gelée* – consommé flavoured with celery, tomato and pimentos, garnished with tomato julienne, shredded fresh sorrel and cooked vermicelli pasta
- *Consommé à l'essence d'estragon en Gelée* – chicken consommé infused with fresh tarragon leaves after the clarification process
- *Consommé Madeira en Gelée* – beef consommé flavoured with Madeira

Clear chicken soup with egg

INGREDIENTS	4 PORTIONS	10 PORTIONS
Dried shitake mushrooms	4	10
Chicken stock	1 litre	2.5 litre
Chopped onion	80g	200g
Poached eggs	4	10
Fresh chervil	4 pinches	10 pinches
Dark soy sauce	1tbsp	2tbsp
Chilli sauce	1tsp	1tbsp
Good-quality salt and pepper	To taste	To taste

Method of work

CHEF'S TIP

The onions are boiled to give a slightly acidic background to the flavours. The mushrooms can be left in to give a more rustic broth.

1 Boil the mushrooms in water for 5 minutes. Drain, remove the hard stalks and cut the caps into julienne. Reserve for garnish.

2 Simmer the chopped onions in the stock for 15 minutes, drain and discard the onions.

3 Add the soy sauce, chilli sauce and mushrooms.

4 Bring to the boil, correct the seasoning and strain through muslin cloth. Reboil.

5 Add the eggs and allow to simmer for 1 minute to poach them.

6 Serve with one egg per portion and the fresh chervil.

Chilled almond and garlic soup

INGREDIENTS	4 PORTIONS	10 PORTIONS
Crushed garlic	4 cloves	10 cloves
Ground almonds	80g	200g
Fresh breadcrumbs	50g	125g
Olive oil	80ml	200ml
White wine vinegar	20ml	50ml
Grape juice	500ml	1.25 litres
Skinned grapes	200g	500g
Water	200ml	500ml
Sliced toasted almonds	20g	50g
Good-quality salt and mill pepper	To taste	To taste

Method of work

1 Purée the almonds, garlic and breadcrumbs in a food processor.

2 Add the oil to make a paste.

3 Add the vinegar and then the grape juice and water.

4 Season to taste.

5 Quarter the grapes and mix with the chilled soup.

6 Serve with toasted almonds.

CHEF'S TIP

This is a traditional wedding soup of the city of Cordoba in Spain.

Bortsch

 CHEF'S TIP

The overriding flavour and colour of bortsch should be beetroot, whether it is a consommé or a more rustic purée.

INGREDIENTS	4 PORTIONS	10 PORTIONS
Duck stock	1.25 litres	3 litres
Minced duck meat	100g	250g
Minced shin of beef	100g	250g
Duck carcass	1	2–3
Egg whites	1	3
Parsley stalks	4	10
Celery	80g	200g
Fennel	40g	100g
Marjoram	1tsp	1tbsp
Grated beetroot	200g	500g
Carrot	80g	200g
Onion	80g	200g
Leek	80g	200g
Smoked duck	100g	250g
Diced rump beef	80g	200g
Beetroot julienne	40g	100g
Shortcrust pastry tartlet cases	4	10
Duck fine forcemeat	80g	200g
Double cream	100ml	250ml
Lemon juice	½ lemon	1 lemon

Method of work

1 Make a consommé using the vegetables, herbs, egg whites, minced beef and duck (see recipe for basic consommé on page 115).

2 Cook and purée the beetroot, add to the consommé and pass through a fine sieve.

3 Garnish with a julienne of cooked beef, smoked duck, beetroot and leek julienne

4 Serve with tartlets filled and baked with a fine forcemeat of duck and cream soured with the lemon juice.

Hot and sour soup

INGREDIENTS	4 PORTIONS	10 PORTIONS
Finely shredded pork or chicken	160g	400g
Grated fresh ginger	20g	50g
Minced garlic	40g	100g
Chopped spring onion	80g	200g
Sherry	40ml	100ml
Clear chicken bouillon	1 litre	2.5 litres
Drained straw mushrooms	200g	500g
Bamboo shoots	200g	500g
Diced firm tofu	200g	500g
Cider vinegar	40ml	100ml
White pepper	To taste	To taste
Dark soy sauce	To taste	To taste
Red chilli pepper	½	1
Eggs	1	2
Sesame oil	25ml	50ml

Method of work

1 Heat the sesame oil. Add the meat and sauté until cooked.
2 Drain and set aside.
3 Sweat the garlic and ginger, add the sherry and stock.
4 Add the bamboo shoots, mushrooms, onions and tofu and bring to the boil.
5 Flavour soup with the vinegar (which gives the sour taste) and the white pepper (which gives the hot taste).
6 Add enough of the soy sauce to give a brown colour, then season with salt.
7 Cut the chilli pepper into thin slices.
8 Bring the soup back to the boil and add in the sliced chilli pepper.
9 Simmer for 3 minutes.
10 Slowly and evenly pour in the lightly beaten eggs. Do not stir again until the egg comes to the surface.
11 Add a small amount of the sesame oil for extra flavour and colour.
12 Reheat and serve garnished with chives.

 CHEF'S TIP

Cayenne or hot chilli powder can also be used to create the hot flavour.

Japanese noodle soup

INGREDIENTS	4 PORTIONS	10 PORTIONS
Chicken consommé	1 litre	2.5 litres
Miso	40ml	100ml
Soba or egg noodles (cooked)	200g	500g
Sake	40ml	100ml
Rice vinegar	20ml	50ml
Japanese soy sauce	40ml	100ml
Sliced asparagus	120g	300g
Sliced shitake mushrooms	80g	200g
Julienne of carrot	80g	200g
Sliced spring onions	40g	100g
Chopped chilli	1	2–3
Good-quality salt and pepper	To taste	To taste

 CHEF'S TIP

Miso is made from fermented soya and comes in the form of a paste.

Method of work

1 Dissolve the **miso** in the boiling consommé.
2 Add the soy sauce, vinegar and sake and cook until the alcohol has evaporated.
3 Add the vegetables and simmer for 3 minutes. Correct the seasoning.
4 Divide the noodles and pour on the soup. Serve immediately.

Bisque

Bisques are named after the crustaceans used as the main ingredient. With lobster and crab, do not use the claws as they will not get passed through a chinois.

INGREDIENTS	4 PORTIONS	10 PORTIONS
Named crustacean, shells and flesh	300g	750g
Butter	60g	150g
Carrots	40g	100g
Onion	40g	100g
Celery	20g	50g
Leek	40g	100g
Bouquet garni	1 small	1 medium
Brandy	20ml	50ml
Fish stock	800ml	2 litres
Dry white wine	80ml	200ml
Tomato purée	20g	50g
Cayenne pepper (approx.)	Pinch	3g
Rice flour	60g	150g
Unsalted butter	40g	100g
Double cream	40ml	100ml

CHEF'S TIP

For large crustaceans, such as lobster, crawfish and crab, the use of a large mortar and pestle will produce a smoother paste than a food processor.

VIDEO CLIP
Preparation of lobster bisque

Method of work

1 Peel, wash, dice and sweat the vegetables in the butter.
2 Add the shells and flesh and cook at a higher temperature for 2–3 minutes.
3 Raise the heat and add the brandy. Shake the pan and flambé until the flames disappear (this burns off the alcohol).
4 Add the rice flour, tomato purée and cayenne pepper.
5 Add the stock and wine and simmer (skimming when necessary) for 20 minutes.
6 Remove the crustacea and cool slightly.
7 Remove the flesh and pound the shell using a pestle and mortar until smooth. Reserve some of the flesh for garnish.
8 Return the flesh and shell to the bisque and simmer for a further 20 minutes.
9 Purée the soup and pass through a chinois into a clean pan. Adjust the seasoning and consistency.
10 Reboil and add the unsalted butter and cream.
11 Serve with crushed water biscuits, and garnish with the reserved flesh.

Iced mussel soup

CHEF'S TIP

Sauté the mussel garnish in a little green herb oil just before service to give a warm and cold sensation for your guests.

INGREDIENTS	4 PORTIONS	10 PORTIONS
Mussels	1kg	2.5kg
White wine	80ml	200ml
Crushed garlic	1 clove	2–3 cloves
Red pepper	1	2–3
Cucumber (medium sized)	1	2–3
Sliced radish	100g	250g
Button mushrooms	200g	500g
Peeled broad beans	400g	1kg
Peeled tomatoes	300g	750g
Lemon juice	½ lemon	1 lemon
Tabasco sauce	To taste	To taste
Good-quality salt and mill pepper	To taste	To taste

Method of work

1 Steam the mussels in the wine and garlic.
2 Remove the flesh and keep the juices.
3 **Grill** the pepper to loosen the skin and deseed.
4 Peel and chop the cucumber, sprinkle with salt and allow to sit in a colander for 10 minutes.
5 Keep some red pepper, mussels and broad beans to one side for garnish.
6 Purée all the ingredients in a food processor, adding water to correct the consistency. Pass through a fine chinois.
7 Chill in the refrigerator for several hours.
8 Serve garnished with a dice of red pepper, mussels, beans and a fresh herb of your choice.

Chicken velouté with tongue and mushrooms
Velouté Agnes Sorel

INGREDIENTS	4 PORTIONS	10 PORTIONS
Chicken velouté (see recipe on p. 113)	1 litre	2.5 litres
Button mushrooms	80g	200g
Cooked ox tongue	80g	200g
Cooked chicken breast	80g	200g

Method of work

1 Cut the chicken, mushrooms and tongue into a fine julienne.
2 Sauté the mushroom and add the tongue and chicken to heat through.
3 Add to the soup just before service.

Pumpkin velouté with toasted pumpkin seeds

INGREDIENT	4 PORTIONS	10 PORTIONS
Pumpkin flesh	200g	500g
Onion	50g	250g
White of leek	50g	250g
Celery	50g	250g
Butter	40g	100g
White vegetable stock	1 litre	2.5 litres
Bouquet garni	Small	Medium
Double cream	40ml	100ml
Egg yolk	1	2–3
Good-quality salt and pepper	To taste	To taste

Method of work

1 Peel, de-seed and chop the pumpkin.
2 Sweat the vegetables in the butter with the chopped pumpkin.
3 Add the stock and bouquet garni. Simmer until all the ingredients are fully cooked.
4 Purée and pass through a fine chinois.
5 Adjust the seasoning and consistency.
6 Whisk the yolks and cream in a bowl until mixed.
7 Add a little of the soup and add the liaison back to the soup.
8 Serve with toasted pumpkin seeds.

 CHEF'S TIP

This soup can be made from other squashes, such as butternut, but still garnish with roasted pumpkin seeds.

Fish velouté with quenelles and mussels

INGREDIENTS	4 PORTIONS	10 PORTIONS
Fish velouté	1 litre	2.5 litres
Mussels	1kg	2.5kg
White wine	40ml	100ml
Fine fish forcemeat	80g	200g

Method of work

1 Steam the mussels in the wine.
2 Remove the mussel meat and strain the juices into a clean pan.
3 Make small quenelles with the forcemeat and poach in the mussel juices.
4 Add the quenelles and mussels to the soup just before service.

CHEF'S TIP

Reduce the mussel juice to enrich the soup, but take care not to over-reduce as the liquor can go from cooked to burnt in an instant. When prepared in smaller quantities there will not be enough mussel juice, so add fish stock and season well.

Chicken velouté with parsley and chicken dumplings

INGREDIENTS	4 PORTIONS	10 PORTIONS
Chicken velouté	1 litre	2.5 litres
Parsley purée	20g	50g
Double cream	20ml	100ml
Chicken stock	200ml	1 litre
Fine chicken forcemeat	80g	200g
Good-quality salt and pepper	To taste	To taste

Method of work

1 Mix the parsley purée and add to the double cream to make a loose purée and season well. Heat carefully in a small saucepan and keep hot for service.
2 Season the forcemeat well. Form quenelles using two teaspoons. Place each quenelle in simmering stock and poach until cooked.
3 Heat the velouté and serve with the parsley purée and chicken quenelles.

 CHEF'S TIP

This is a visually striking soup, but you can use other purées such as carrot or black bean.

Lettuce and asparagus velouté

INGREDIENTS	4 PORTIONS	10 PORTIONS
Asparagus	200g	500g
Iceberg lettuce	200g	500g
Onion	50g	250g
White of leek	50g	250g
Celery	50g	250g
Butter	40g	100g
Chicken stock	1 litre	2.5 litres
Flour	40g	100g
Bouquet garni	1 small	1 medium
Good-quality salt and pepper	To taste	To taste
Double cream	40ml	100ml
Egg yolk	1	2–3
Cooked asparagus tips	16	40
Finley sliced lettuce	100g	250g

Method of work

1 Sweat the vegetables in the butter.
2 Add the flour to make a roux.
3 Add the stock and bouquet garni. Simmer until all the ingredients are fully cooked.
4 Purée and pass through a fine chinois.
5 Adjust the seasoning and consistency.
6 Whisk the yolks and cream in a bowl until mixed.
7 Add a little of the soup and add the liaison back to the soup.
8 Garnish with the asparagus tips and sliced lettuce.
9 Serve with croutons.

 **CHEF'S TIP**

Iceberg lettuce when cooked has a very similar flavour to asparagus.

Assessment of knowledge and understanding

You have now learned about the use of the different varieties of soup and how to produce different soups applying an array of commodities and preparation techniques.

To test your level of knowledge and understanding, answer the following short questions. These will help to prepare you for your summative (final) assessment.

Quality identifications

1 List three examples of velouté.
  i)_____ ii) _____ iii)_____

2 List three examples of consommé.
  i)_____ ii) _____ iii)_____

3 List the two most important aspects to check before serving every soup.
  i)_____ ii) _____

Materials and storage

1 List three pieces of equipment that can be used to pass a soup.
  i)_____ ii) _____ iii)_____

2 Give two reasons why the weighing and measuring of ingredients is so important.
  i)_____ ii) _____

Preparation

1 Explain the term 'clarification' in relation to consommé.
_____

2 Describe the process of making a royale.
_____

3 List four different accompaniments for soup.
  i)_____ ii) _____
  iii)_____ iv) _____

Cooking

1 Explain why you should never boil a velouté soup.
_____

2 State three factors in relation to portion control which should be considered when preparing and serving soup.
  i)_____ ii) _____ iii)_____

Health and safety

1 List two safety points when passing a hot soup through a chinois.
  i)_____ ii) _____

2 State two healthy options when making soups.
  i)_____ ii) _____

CHEF'S PROFILE

Name: PAUL RANKIN

Current job role and main responsibilities: Paul Rankin runs a successful restaurant business, the Rankin Group.

When did you realise that you wanted to pursue a career in the catering and hospitality industry? Paul first became interested in cooking when he was travelling the globe in his twenties. It was on these travels that he met his Canadian wife Jeanne in Greece. The couple returned to Canada where Paul started working as a waiter and instantly fell in love with the excitement of the restaurant world.

Experience:

1 After travelling through India, Australia, Singapore, Malaysia, Thailand, Hong Kong and China, Paul and Jeanne returned to work for 3 years under the expert guidance of Albert Roux.

2 Following a period as Head Chef in a Californian Restaurant, Paul and Jeanne returned to Belfast in 1989 to open their first restaurant – Roscoff – and soon had been credited with Northern Ireland's first Michelin Star.

3 Almost two decades on since first opening Roscoff, Paul now boasts two of the best restaurants in the country with the new Roscoff and the funkier and more casual Cayenne. In addition, Paul runs a host of premium cafes and has trained a legacy of star chefs who are ensuring that Ireland continues to boast a world class reputation for cuisine.

Achievements:

- Paul's TV career took off soon after with three series of the popular 'Gourmet Ireland' - a showcase for Irish produce and the country's artisan producers.

- Paul's TV career is still flourishing and this summer he has been busy filming for numerous new shows about to hit the screens. From 'The People's Cookbook' with Anthony Worrell Thompson, a new series and new format of 'Ready Steady Cook' to 'Local Food Heroes' with Gary Rhodes. In addition, he has just appeared in 'Take on the Takeaway' and has been working on a brand new series called 'Food Poker' which starts on BBC2 this autumn.

- To date, Paul and Jeanne have written five books and contributed to countless others. *Gourmet Ireland I & II* accompanied the television series. *Hot Food* and *Ideal Home Cooking* followed with the fifth title, *New Irish Cookery*, a compendium of over 140 mouth-watering recipes with an authentic spirit that reflects their shared passion for cooking with fresh and tasty Irish ingredients. *The People's Cookbook* has also just been released following the very successful TV series.

Red lentil and ham soup

INGREDIENTS	SERVES 8
1 ham shank about 900g (about 2lb) or 500g piece of ham or bacon, or a ham bone	
Large onion, finely chopped	1
Stick celery, finely diced	1
Medium carrot, grated	1
Large potato, peeled and cut into 1cm dice	1
Red lentils, washed and drained	200g
Chopped fresh parsley to garnish	
Optional	
Serve with floury potatoes	

Method of work

1 Place the ham shanks in a large pot with about 3½ litres of cold water.

2 Bring to the boil, skim off any scum which rises to the surface. Simmer for 2½–3 hours or until the meat is very tender. (This will not take as long if you are using a piece of ham or bacon.)

3 45 minutes before the end of the cooking time, add the vegetables and the lentils. Skim the soup as it comes back to the boil. The soup is ready when the lentils are cooked, but it will taste much better if it is left to stand for 4–5 hours, or over night. Season to taste.

4 To serve, remove the ham and either save it for another use or chop, or flake the meat into small pieces and return to the soup. Ladle into warmed soup bowls and sprinkle with parsley. Serve the potatoes on the side.

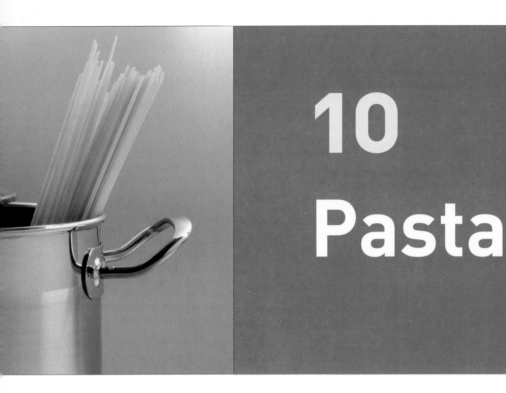

10 Pasta

LEARNING OBJECTIVES

The aim of this chapter is to enable you to develop skills and implement knowledge in the preparation and cookery principles of pasta. This will also include materials, ingredients and equipment.

At the end of this chapter you will be able to:

- Identify each pasta variety and finished dish
- Understand the use of relative ingredients in pasta cookery
- Prepare and cook each type of pasta variety
- Be competent at preparing and cooking a range of pasta-based dishes

PASTA COMPOSITION

Pasta is a generic term used to describe many products made from semolina and/or flour that has been milled from the hardest of all wheat, durum wheat. The name 'durum' comes from the Latin word *durus*, meaning 'hard'.

The key to creating a good pasta dough is to use the strongest flour, which has the highest gluten content. Gluten is essential for creating the elasticity required to form a pliable dough. The amount of water the dough can absorb depends on the quality of the protein and starch. The size of the semolina also plays a key role in this process: too small will result in sticky dough, too large and the dough will be dry, resulting in white spots in the finished product.

Durum wheat's hardness makes it the wheat of choice for producing pasta. When most wheat is milled, the heart of the wheat kernel (endosperm) breaks down into a fine, powdery flour, but the endosperm of durum is hard enough to hold together. The result is the granular product called semolina. Durum wheat kernels are amber-coloured and larger than those of other wheat varieties. Also unique to durum wheat is the fact that its endosperm is not creamy white but yellow, which gives pasta its distinctive colour.

OO flour is now used extensively within the catering trade for making pasta. It is an Italian wheat flour which has a very low extraction rate (this is the amount of whole wheat extracted from the grain during the milling process) and low ash content. Italian flours are classified by ash content, which measures the mineral content of flour.

> ### ASH
>
> The ash content of flour is determined by burning a given quantity of the flour under prescribed conditions and then measuring the residue. The mineral content varies, depending on many factors such as the variety of wheat, the terrain, the fertilisation and the climate. The greater portion of minerals found in a kernel of wheat is contained in the germ and in the husk (the bran), and the least amount is in the endosperm. As a consequence, if flour contains a greater number of bran particles, it will have an elevated ash content. The determination of the ash content serves to estimate the degree of the endosperm separation from the bran during milling, i.e. the grade of flour. Generally, flours thought to be of higher quality are more refined and produce less ash. OO flour also has a low protein content.

Wheat kernel

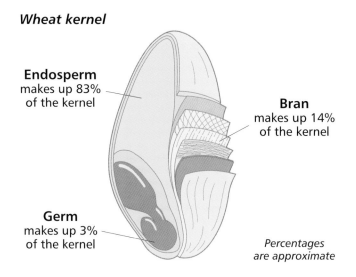

Endosperm
makes up 83%
of the kernel

Bran
makes up 14%
of the kernel

Germ
makes up 3%
of the kernel

*Percentages
are approximate*

Different flavoured pastas

Pasta being put through a pasta machine

Pasta hanging to dry

Pasta shapes and flavours

When making pasta dough you should use only the best and freshest ingredients; this will ensure the end product will be of the highest quality in both appearance and flavour.

The traditional way of making pasta dough is to prepare the mixture on a large unvarnished wooden table, which keeps the temperature and humidity constant. The method, still used in classical training, is to create a mound of flour with a well in the centre for the eggs, oil and salt, bring in the flour slowly to form the dough and then **knead**.

The modern method, now widely used, is to place all the ingredients into a food processor and blend for 10–20 seconds until a loose ball is formed.

Whichever method is used, the dough should feel just firm and not sticky. Depending on the size of the eggs used, extra flour may be required to bring the dough together. Knowing the correct feel to the dough will come with experience, and once mastered will allow you to produce perfect paste every time.

The finished dough should be wrapped in cling film and rested for a minimum of 30 minutes (overnight if possible), which will allow the gluten to relax and so prevent shrinkage when the dough is rolled out.

The dough can be rolled out with a rolling pin or using a pasta machine, with the latter allowing large quantities to be rolled out to exact thicknesses and at greater speed.

A–Z OF PASTAS

There are over 500 varieties of pasta, all with different designs and shapes. Here is a selection:

- *Angolotti* – small, crescent-shaped dumplings, usually stuffed with meat
- *Bucatini* – slightly thicker and hollow version of spaghetti
- *Cannelloni* – large, short tubes, stuffed with an appropriate filling and baked
- *Capellini* – 'angel hair', the thinnest of all pastas, like spaghetti
- *Cappelletti* – 'little hats', small peaked-hat shapes stuffed with chicken, pork, mortadella and cheese
- *Conchiglie* – small, round shells, either ridged or smooth, the cavity is ideal for stuffing or sauce
- *Farfalle* – small bow-tie shapes
- *Fettuccine* – like tagliatelle but a bit narrower and thicker
- *Fusilli* – spiral-shaped pasta twists
- *Lasagne* – the broadest pasta, around 5–8cm wide, either ridged or smooth
- *Linguini* – flat spaghetti

1. Linguini being made: roll out the dough until a number 2 thickness is achieved

2. Trim the pasta to achieve a neat edge

3. Put the trimmed pasta through the fine attachment

4. Finished linguini

- *Macaroni* – short hollow pasta, sometimes with an elbow to form an angle
- *Orecchiette* – 'little ears', small ear-shaped pasta
- *Pansotti* – triangular ravioli
- *Papardelle* – broad egg noodles, sometimes with wavy edges
- *Patina* – the term used to describe all the tiny pasta shapes used in soups
- *Penne* – tubular pasta, ridged or smooth, about 4–5cm long, cut on the angle
- *Ravioli* – flat stuffed pasta shapes

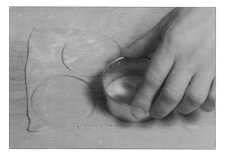

1. Ravioli being made: cut out neat circles of pasta dough

2. Spoon filling onto half of the discs, leaving the others to use as lids

3. Brush the base with water

4. Lay the lid over the filling

5. Squeeze the discs together and then cut a neat disc with a cutter

6. Finished ravioli

- ■ *Rigatoni* – ridged tubular macaroni, 5cm long
- ■ *Spaghetti* – thin, solid strings of pasta (vermicelli in southern Italy)
- ■ *Tagliatelle* – long, thin egg noodles, about 6mm wide

3 Finished tagliatelle

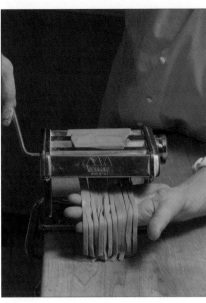

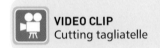

VIDEO CLIP
Cutting tagliatelle

1 Tagliatelle being made: roll out the dough until number 2 is achieved

2 Put the trimmed pasta through the medium attachment

- ■ *Tortelli/tortellini* – small, ring-shaped pasta dumplings, stuffed (tortellini are half the size of tortelli)

1 Tortellini being made: brush the pasta disc with water

2 Fold over and form a seal by squeezing the pasta together

3 Stand the pasta up and squeeze the tips together

4 Gently fold back the edges

5 Finished tortellini

VIDEO CLIP
Producing various tortellini

RECIPES

Egg pasta dough

INGREDIENTS	4 PORTIONS	10 PORTIONS
OO grade flour	110g	225g
Eggs	1	2
Egg yolks	1½	3
Olive oil	8ml	15ml

 CHEF'S TIP

When making fresh pasta dough, numerous flavours can be incorporated, such as pesto, tomato or spinach. Care must be taken to adjust the recipe to ensure the same firm consistency is achieved in the finished product.

Method of work

1 Place flour on to a clean work surface and make a well.
2 In a medium bowl beat the egg yolks and whole eggs together with the olive oil.
3 Slowly add the egg mixture to the flour, stirring in stages, until a paste is formed.
4 Knead the dough until a smooth texture is achieved.
5 Place the dough in a refrigerator to rest for at least 30 minutes before rolling out.

Sun-dried tomato pasta dough

INGREDIENTS	4 PORTIONS	10 PORTIONS
OO grade flour	110g	225g
Eggs	1	2
Egg yolks	1½	3
Olive oil	8ml	15ml
Sun-dried tomato paste	15g	30g

Method of work

1 Place the flour on to a clean work surface and make a well.
2 In a medium bowl beat the egg yolks and whole eggs together with the olive oil and tomato paste.
3 Slowly add the egg mixture to the flour, stirring in stages, until a paste is formed.
4 Knead the dough until a smooth texture is achieved.
5 Place the dough in a refrigerator to rest for at least 30 minutes before rolling out.

Saffron pasta dough

INGREDIENTS	4 PORTIONS	10 PORTIONS
OO grade flour	110g	225g
Eggs	1	2
Egg yolks	1½	3
Olive oil	8ml	15ml
Saffron strands	2g	5g

Method of work

1 Place the flour on to a clean work surface and make a well.
2 Warm the olive oil in a small saucepan and infuse the saffron strands, then leave to cool.
3 In a medium bowl beat the egg yolks and whole eggs together with the saffron-infused oil.
4 Slowly add the mixture to the flour, stirring in stages, until the mixture becomes a paste.
5 Knead the dough until the paste is a smooth texture and yellow in colour. If needed, infuse more oil and saffron then add, introducing more flour to dry the paste.
6 Place the dough in a refrigerator to rest for at least 30 minutes before rolling out.

Spinach pasta dough

INGREDIENTS	4 PORTIONS	10 PORTIONS
OO grade flour	110g	225g
Eggs	1	2
Egg yolks	1½	3
Olive oil	8ml	15ml
Spinach	70g	150g

Method of work

1 Place the flour on to a clean work surface and make a well.
2 Warm a small saucepan and wilt down the spinach with a small amount of water then allow to cool. Place the spinach into a blender and blend until a smooth paste is achieved.
3 Remove from the blender and spoon into a muslin cloth, then squeeze into a clean saucepan until all the chlorophyll has been extracted.
4 Reduce the liquid until it is a concentrate then chill.
5 In a medium bowl beat the egg yolks and whole eggs together with the chlorophyll.
6 Slowly add the mixture into the flour, stirring in stages, until a dough is achieved.
7 Knead the dough until a smooth texture is achieved and it is a subtle green colour. More flour can be added to the dough if it is too wet.
8 Place the dough in a refrigerator and allow to rest for at least 30 minutes before rolling out.

Squid ink pasta dough

INGREDIENTS	4 PORTIONS	10 PORTIONS
OO grade flour	110g	225g
Eggs	1	2
Egg yolks	1½	3
Olive oil	8ml	15ml
Squid ink	2tbsp	5tbsp

Method of work

1 Place flour on to a clean work surface and make a well.
2 In a medium bowl beat the egg yolks and whole eggs together with the olive oil.
3 Slowly add the mixture to the flour, stirring in stages, until a paste is formed.
4 Knead the dough with the squid ink (remember to wear gloves for this recipe) until a smooth texture is achieved and it is a subtle black colour.
5 Place the dough in a refrigerator to rest for at least 30 minutes before rolling out.

Tomato linguini with black pudding and roasted butternut squash with an olive oil infused with lemon thyme

INGREDIENTS	4 PORTIONS	10 PORTIONS
Tomato pasta dough	400g	1kg
Black pudding	100g	250g
Butternut squash	100g	250g
Extra virgin olive oil	50ml	125ml
Lemon thyme	¼ bunch	½ bunch
Chives	Sprigs	Sprigs
Good-quality salt and white pepper	To taste	To taste

Method of work

1 Roll out the pasta until thin then cut into thin strips (see making linguini, page 168).
2 Heat the oil with the lemon thyme and leave to infuse for a minimum of 20 minutes (best overnight).
3 Peel, deseed, dice and roast the squash until caramelised.
4 Cut the black pudding into dice and fry quickly in oil then mix with the butternut squash.
5 Blanch the pasta in boiling salted water until al dente, then drain and mix with the black pudding mix.
6 Place the pasta into a bowl, drizzle with the remaining oil and garnish with sprigs of chives.

CHEF'S TIP

Ensure there is at least double the amount of water to pasta when cooking as this prevents the pasta coagulating.

Ricotta and wild sorrel tortellini with a pistachio pesto and garlic foam

INGREDIENTS	4 PORTIONS	10 PORTIONS
Plain pasta dough	400g	1kg
Ricotta cheese	200g	500g
Pistachio nuts	50g	125g
Parmesan cheese	50g	125g
Olive oil	70ml	175ml
Basil leaves	¼ bunch	½ bunch
Wild sorrel	70g	175g
Garlic	4 cloves	10 cloves
Fresh full fat milk	50ml	125ml
Good-quality salt and white pepper	To taste	To taste

CHEF'S TIP

When rolling and storing pasta, use semolina and not flour to prevent it sticking together; this will ensure the strands or sheets are separate and prevent the cooking liquid becoming cloudy and thick with gluten.

Method of work

1 Mix the ricotta with the chopped blanched sorrel leaves, season well.
2 Roll out the pasta into thin sheets and cut out into circles approximately 5cm in diameter.
3 Brush the pasta circles with water and spoon the ricotta into the middle.
4 Fold the pasta over and pinch the points together (see making tortellini, page 170).
5 Make the pesto using half the oil, lightly toasted pistachios, basil and Parmesan by placing all the ingredients in a liquidiser and pulsing until almost smooth (the consistency should be slightly thicker than a sauce).
6 Blanch the garlic in boiling water for 2 minutes, place the garlic into the milk and bring to the boil; remove the pan from the heat and liquidise.
7 Blanch the pasta in boiling salted water, drain and mix in a bowl with the pesto.
8 Pulse the garlic mixture until a foam appears, spoon over the tortellini and serve.

Saffron papadelle with mussel and Pernod sauce, sautéed leeks and a selection of wild mushrooms

INGREDIENTS	4 PORTIONS	10 PORTIONS
Saffron pasta dough	400g	1kg
Mussels	200g	500g
Pernod	25ml	60ml
Double cream	150ml	375ml
Diced onion	75g	180g
Baby leeks	50g	125g
Assorted wild mushrooms	50g	125g
Mussel or fish stock (see recipe p. 103)	75ml	180ml
Good-quality salt and white pepper	To taste	To taste

Method of work

1 Roll pasta and cut into papadelle then cook in boiling salted water for 2 minutes, refresh in ice cold water and drain.

2 In a hot pan, sweat the onion then add the mussels and the Pernod, cover with a lid and cook for 1 minute.

3 Remove from the heat and pass the liquor.

4 Add the double cream, reduce and season.

5 Cut the leeks into diamonds then sauté with the trimmed wild mushrooms, season well.

6 Mix the sauce through the pasta and mussels and arrange in a bowl.

7 Finish with the leeks and wild mushrooms.

Open spinach lasagne of lobster with chervil, tomato and shellfish foam

INGREDIENTS	4 PORTIONS	10 PORTIONS
Spinach pasta dough	100g	250g
Whole cooked lobster	1	2½
Concassé of tomato	2tbsp	5tbsp
Chopped chervil	4tsp	10tsp
Wild garlic and red pepper vinaigrette	4tbsp	10tbsp
Shellfish shells	200g	500g
Brandy	30ml	75ml
Tomato purée	1tbsp	2½tbsp
Fish stock	100ml	250ml
Double cream	100ml	250ml
Butter	50g	125g
Good-quality salt and white pepper	To taste	To taste

Method of work

1 Sweat the shells in butter for 3 minutes.

2 Add the brandy and flambé.

3 Add the tomato purée and cook for 2 minutes.

4 Add the stock and allow to simmer for 25 minutes, until the liquor has reduced by half.

5 Add the cream and reduce until slightly thickened.

6 Pass, correct the seasoning and keep warm.

7 Roll the pasta dough into lasagne sheets and blanch in boiling salted water until al dente. Drain and pat dry.

8 Add to the shellfish sauce with half the lobster tail meat chopped, tomato concassé and chervil.

9 Arrange the mix into a bowl

10 Remove a little sauce and blend until a foam is achieved, then spoon over.

11 Finish with the red pepper dressing, remaining lobster tail and claw.

Spaghetti carbonara with a cep mushroom dressing, crispy streaky bacon and a Parmesan crisp

INGREDIENTS	4 PORTIONS	10 PORTIONS
Plain pasta dough	400g	1kg
Double cream	100g	250g
Fresh eggs	2	5
Parmesan cheese	100g	250g
Cep mushrooms (fresh or frozen)	100g	250g
Olive oil	50ml	125ml
Whole grain mustard	2tbsp	5tbsp
White wine vinegar	20ml	50ml
Streaky bacon	50g	125g
Grated Parmesan cheese	100g	250g
Good-quality salt and white pepper	To taste	To taste

Method of work

1 Roll out the pasta dough thinly and cut into spaghetti.
2 Cook in boiling salted water until al dente then refresh in ice water and drain.
3 Mix the egg, mustard, cream and cheese then slowly heat, stirring constantly until the sauce thickens.
4 Spread the grated Parmesan into circles on silicone paper about 7cm across then bake at 180°C for 7 minutes.
5 Once the cheese has slightly coloured, lay over a rolling pin and allow to bend.
6 Sauté the mushrooms in oil and add the vinegar, then season.
7 Mix the pasta with sauce then arrange in a bowl.
8 Finish with mushroom vinaigrette, crispy bacon and Parmesan crisp.

> **CHEF'S TIP**
>
> Pasta once cooked can be bland and requires careful seasoning; this, however, must be balanced with the addition of sauce and/or garnish.

Spinach tagliatelle with seared lemon sole and vine-ripened tomato coulis and aged balsamic vinegar

INGREDIENTS	4 PORTIONS	10 PORTIONS
Saffron pasta dough	400g	1kg
Lemon sole	280g	700g
Olive oil	50ml	125ml
Vine-ripened tomatoes	200g	500g
Basil	¼ bunch	½ bunch
Shallots	4	10
Aged balsamic vinegar	20ml	50ml
Curry powder	pinch	pinch
Good-quality salt and white pepper	To taste	To taste

Method of work

1 Mix the oil, chopped shallots, basil stalks and chopped tomatoes and place on the heat. Simmer for 1 hour, remove from the heat and liquidise.
2 Roll out the pasta dough until thin then cut into tagliatelle.
3 Reduce the balsamic vinegar in a pan over a fierce heat until tacky, then cool.
4 Dust the lemon sole with curry powder and sear gently on both sides.
5 Blanch the pasta in boiling salted water then drain, mix with tomato coulis and place in a hot bowl.
6 Lay slices of lemon sole over the pasta with tomato coulis, basil and drops of balsamic glaze.

> **CHEF'S TIP**
>
> Do not reboil the tomato coulis once cooked as it will split and unlike other sauces it will not emulsify again properly.

Chilli goat's cheese pansotti with tomato, lime and spring onion salsa

CHEF'S TIP

This dish works very well as a starter if made slightly smaller. The filling can be changed to mozzarella marinated in garlic, oil, lemon and sage.

INGREDIENTS	4 PORTIONS	10 PORTIONS
Fresh egg pasta squares (7cm × 7cm)	12	30
Goat's cheese (chevre)	175g	400g
Coriander	¼ bunch	½ bunch
Green chillies	½	1½
Garlic	2 cloves	5 cloves
Parmesan	50g	125g
Olive oil	1tbsp	2½tbsp
Butter	40g	100g
Plum tomatoes	400g	1kg
Limes	1	2½
Spring onions	¼ bunch	½ bunch
Castor sugar	1tbsp	2½tbsp
Ginger	1tsp	2½tsp
Herb oil	1tbsp	2½tbsp
Good-quality salt and white pepper	To taste	To taste

Method of work

1 Combine the goat's cheese with the chopped coriander, chopped green chilli, Parmesan and half of the chopped garlic.
2 Wet the edges of the pasta squares and divide the goat's cheese mix between them all, fold one corner over to form triangles then seal the edges.
3 Brush the bottoms of each pasta shape with olive oil then place onto a steamer tray and steam for 5 minutes.
4 Melt the butter and sweat down the chopped tomato concassé with the remaining chopped garlic, chopped ginger and lime juice and zest.
5 Add the sugar to taste and the thinly sliced spring onions.
6 Arrange the pasta in a bowl, top with the salsa and finish with herb oil.

Truffled spaghetti with asparagus

CHEF'S TIP

Soft poached quail's eggs work very well with this dish; they require a little more effort and practice.

INGREDIENTS	4 PORTIONS	10 PORTIONS
Fresh egg spaghetti	350g	875g
Asparagus	1 bunch	2½ bunches
Butter	50g	125g
White truffle oil	1tbsp	2½tbsp
Grated pecorino cheese	100g	250g
Black truffles	10g	25g
Rocket	100g	250g
Good-quality salt and white pepper	To taste	To taste

Method of work

1 Place the spaghetti into a large pan of boiling salted water and cook until al dente, refresh in ice water.
2 Peel the asparagus, quarter lengthways and cut into 4cm strips. Blanch in boiling salted water and refresh in ice water.
3 Reheat the spaghetti and asparagus in the butter then mix together with the rocket.
4 Arrange in a bowl, place the truffles and pecorino onto the pasta. Drizzle some truffle oil over and serve.

Assessment of knowledge and understanding

You have now learned about the use of the different types of pasta and how to produce a variety of them utilising an array of commodities and cooking techniques.

To test your level of knowledge and understanding, answer the following short questions. These will help to prepare you for your summative (final) assessment.

Quality identifications

1 Explain the importance of selecting the correct type, quality and quantity of pasta ingredients and other ingredients used when meeting dish requirements.

2 Give a brief description of durum wheat.

Materials and storage

1 State the correct temperature for storing fresh pasta.

2 Explain how dried pasta is stored and state what ingredient is usually missing from the dough to make it non-perishable.

Preparation

1 Explain why colour, texture and flavour are important when creating complex pasta dishes.

2 Explain why semolina is used when rolling out fresh pasta dough.

Cooking

1 Describe how and when fresh pasta should be cooked during service.

Health and safety

1 List three possible dangers associated with preparing, cooking and serving fresh pasta dishes.

   i) _____   ii) _____

   iii) _____

CHEF'S PROFILE

CHEF'S PROFILE

Name: ANGELA HARTNETT

Current job role and main responsibilities: I am Chef Patron of my own London restaurant and I oversee all the food and beverage operations.

When did you realise that you wanted to pursue a career in the catering and hospitality industry?
I always wanted to run my own restaurant from an early age. My grandparents owned a fish and chip shop.

Experience:
1   Midsummer House, Cambridge
2   Gordon Ramsay, Aubergine
3   Marcus Wareing, Petrus
4   Gordon Ramsay, Holdings

What do you find rewarding about your job?
I love teaching young cooks and get pleasure from seeing the customers when they have enjoyed dining with us.

What do you find the most challenging about the job?
Finding good staff and retaining them.

What advice would you give to students just beginning their career?
Choose a path you enjoy and are passionate about.

Who is your mentor or main inspiration?
My family and their love of food. Also Gordon Ramsay and Nadia Santini.

What traits do you consider essential for anyone entering a career as a chef?
•   Understanding the source of your produce
•   People management skills
•   Common sense
•   Organisation

A brief personal profile:
•   Chef de Partie, Aubergine
•   Sous Chef, Petrus Restaurant
•   Executive Chef, Hilton Creek Dubai
•   Chef Patron, Connaught Hotel
•   Won Hotel Restaurant of the Year
•   Won BMW Newcomer of the Year

Can you give one essential kitchen tip or technique that you use as a chef?
Taste everything.

Pumpkin tortelli

INGREDIENTS	4–6 PORTIONS
Fresh pumpkin (seeded and cut into wedges)	2kg
Freshly grated Parmesan	100g
Chopped mustard fruits	100g
Pasta dough	
Amaretti biscuits (crushed)	2–3
Good-quality salt and freshly ground black pepper	To taste
Sage butter	
Vegetable stock	200ml
Butter	100g
Fresh sage	12 leaves

Start this recipe the day before you want to eat it.

Method of work

1 Preheat an oven to 180°C.

2 Arrange the pumpkin wedges in a roasting tin and sprinkle with rock salt.

3 Cover the tin with foil and cook in the oven for 45–50 minutes or until tender when pierced with the point of a knife.

4 Remove from the oven. Leave until cool enough to handle, then scrape the pumpkin flesh from the skin.

5 Place the flesh in a muslin cloth or a fine sieve and hang overnight above a bowl in a cool place to drain off all the excess liquid.

6 Place the pumpkin in a food processor and blend until smooth. Add the Parmesan and mustard fruits and season. Pulse blend to combine.

7 Roll out and cut up the pasta dough. Place teaspoons of filling at 2cm intervals along each strip of pasta, then fold into parcels about 3cm square.

8 At this stage you can par-cook them to use later. Bring a large pan of salted water to the boil and blanch the tortelli for 30 seconds.

Drain and plunge immediately into iced water. Remove and place on a lightly oiled baking sheet. Drizzle with a little olive oil and then cover with plastic film. The tortelli can be refrigerated for up to 24 hours.

9 Place the stock and butter in a pan and bring to the boil over a medium heat, whisking vigorously to prevent the mixture from splitting. Add the sage leaves and a little seasoning just before serving.

10 Bring a large pan of salted water to the boil. Add the tortelli and cook for 3 minutes. Drain and serve, drizzled with the sage butter and with the amaretti crumbs sprinkled on top.

11
Fish and shellfish

3FP1 Prepare fish for complex dishes

3FC1 Cook and finish complex fish dishes

3FP2 Prepare shellfish for complex dishes

3FC2 Cook and finish complex shellfish dishes

LEARNING OBJECTIVES

The aim of this chapter is to enable you to develop skills and apply knowledge in the preparation and cookery principles of fish and shellfish. This will also include references to materials, ingredients and resources.

At the end of this chapter you will be able to:

- Identify fish varieties and the use of each variety
- Indicate the quality points of fish and shellfish
- Prepare and cook a range of fish and shellfish
- Identify the storage procedures for fish and shellfish
- Illustrate an understanding of the fishing methods used and how to purchase fish and shellfish efficiently
- Understand the importance of careful menu planning with regard to sustainable fish stocks and introducing variety

Chefs inspecting the day's catch at Newlyn, with a local fisherman and the project director from Seafood Cornwall

FISH

For the professional chef, fish has possibly become the most important ingredient on the menu. It is one of the most fulfilling foods to prepare and cook and there is a wide variety of fish and shellfish available to choose from, but the chef must reflect on the health aspects of fish, select carefully from the wide variety available and ensure that the menu choice helps to contribute positively to the issues of fish sustainability. When selecting fish for a menu, the chef should consider the quality, freshness, availability – due to weather conditions or seasonality – and suitability for different cooking techniques.

CHEF'S TIP

If there has been several days of bad weather, the choice of fresh seafood will be limited. Be guided by your fish supplier, and remember that there are fish that can be substituted, such as megrim instead of lemon sole and pollack or gurnard instead of cod.

FISH TYPES

Fish can be divided into two distinctive types:

■ *Pelagic* – fish that swim relatively close to the surface of the sea

■ *Demersal* – fish that are found on or near the seabed

Demersal fish can be further divided into subcategories:

■ Flat

■ Round

■ Oily

■ Non-bony

CHEF'S TIP

Stocks of skate have been depleted in certain regions, and in Cornwall almost all the fish landed and sold as skate are in fact ray. The two names are interchangeable, which is quite confusing for chefs and customers. The species of ray landed include: blonde rays, owl rays, star rays and thornback rays.

CATEGORIES OF FISH

Pelagic fish	Demersal fish			
	Flat fish	Round fish	Oily fish	Non-bony fish
Herring	Brill	Cod	Salmon	Monkfish
Mackerel	Dover sole	Conger eel	Trout	Ray (skate)
Sardine	Lemon sole	Grey mullet	Tuna	Shark
Sprat	Megrim sole	Hake		
	Turbot	Pollack		

The sea contains a wide variety of flat fish and round fish. The colour and pattern of their skin is used as camouflage to protect them from potential predators. Most fish have darker shades of skin on the top of the body, which makes them blend into the sea floor when viewed from above. When viewed from below, the pale undersides blend in with the light from above.

The percentage of weight loss should be taken into account when considering fish dishes for a menu. It is unusual to have more than 60 per cent of usable flesh when preparing filleted fish. If preparing round fish for grilling whole, there will be an approximate 5 per cent weight loss from the discarding of the trimmed fins and the gutting, with a further 10 per cent loss if the head is removed.

To estimate the weight loss of fish, the calculation below should be applied:

$$\frac{\text{Total waste weight}}{\text{Total original fish weight}} \times 100 = \% \text{ wastage}$$

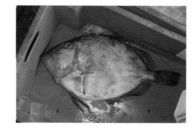

John Dory fish at market

FISH SEASONALITY

	Variety	Jan.	Feb.	March	April	May	June	July	Aug.	Sep.	Oct.	Nov.	Dec.
Round white	Bass												
	Bream												
	Cod												
	Gurnard												
	Haddock												
	Hake												
	Huss												
	John Dory												
	Ling												
	Monkfish												
	Pollack												
	Red mullet												
	Red snapper												
	Redfish												
	Sea bream												
	Whiting												
Flat fish	Brill												
	Dab												
	Dover sole												
	Halibut												
	Lemon sole												
	Megrim												
	Plaice												
	Skate												
	Turbot												
Oily fish	Eel												
	Herring												
	Mackeral												
	Salmon												
	Sardines												
	Trout												
	Tuna												
	Wild salmon												

Key:　in season　out of season

COMMERCIAL FISHING

The figures below illustrate the quantities of fish landed by UK vessels into the UK each year. In 2005, the five most popular species of fish landed were:

SPECIES	TONNES LANDED
Mackerel	120,600
Herring	76,400
Haddock	47,600
Blue whiting	28,800
Cod	13,800

Source: UK Sea Fisheries Statistics, DEFRA

The decline of the North Sea cod stocks is a serious problem for the UK. The pressures on fish stocks have made the UK seafood industry adapt, so that fish stocks are better managed in order to meet present needs without compromising the needs of the future. Consumers can, however, still eat fish, a fact that is recognised by leading environmental fisheries campaigners at the WWF (the global conservation organisation) and the Marine Conservation Society.

Chefs and consumers must be more inquisitive and taste a wider range of seafood in order to reduce the pressure on more traditional species – such as cod and skate. There are 21,000 species of fish and shellfish in the world, and at least 100 different varieties available in the UK.

Cod landed in the UK is caught within strict management regimes. The control measures already in place at a European level to help preserve stocks include, for example, the closure of certain fisheries during the spawning seasons, catch quotas and restrictions on the type of fishing gear that can be used. The quota system sets safe limits for catches agreed by fishermen, scientists and government. Cod is caught within these agreed limits so consumers can eat it without concern.

Fish is also traded on an international market. The UK's buyers, processors and retailers source imported supplies from sustainable sources to compensate for reduced landings from their own fleets while work is undertaken to recover stocks in the North Sea. Obviously, purchasing fish from further distances increases the carbon footprint of the ingredient, and it may also lead to concerns over quality and freshness. Currently almost 90 per cent of the cod eaten in the UK comes from waters outside the UK, such as Icelandic and Norwegian waters.

Over-fishing

Many once-common fish, such as cod and skate, are now quite rare, with cod close to commercial collapse. Due to over-fishing, the productivity of our seas

CHEF'S TIP

When selecting fish for menus try to use alternative under-utilised local varieties, such as pollack, coley or dab. All have great flavours and are not in short supply.

and rivers is becoming exhausted. The UN Food and Agriculture Organization reports that nearly 70 per cent of the world's fish stocks are now fully fished, over-fished or depleted. If a responsible attitude to fishing is not adopted and the public does not embrace changes to eating habits, the consequences on the world's fisheries will become disastrous. Consumers can contribute to the responsible management of fish stocks by demanding that the fish they eat is from sustainable, managed stocks and that the way in which it is caught or farmed causes minimum damage to the marine environment.

A small fishing boat, Cornwall

Fishing methods

Fishermen use a variety of methods to catch fish, but each is based on one of four basic techniques:

- Pulling an open net through a shoal of fish, either above the seabed or on the seabed itself; this captures the fish in the path of the net and is known as trawling or dredging
- Enclosing an area with a net and then advancing inward, trapping the fish within the encircled area; this is sometimes known as purse-seining or seining
- Snaring passing fish in set nets
- Attracting fish to either bait or bright lures, such as in lining or potting

VIDEO CLIP
Sea fishing

Trawling

There are three types of trawler:

- Beam
- Mid-water
- Bottom

A beam trawler has two nets (one on either side of the boat), each suspended from a metal beam. The nets have chains in the front edge, which will generally dig 3–8cm into the seabed to help gather the demersal fish – such as cod, monkfish and sole – into the net.

This type of fishing has attracted many critics because of the potential for damage to the seabed and because the nets pick up everything that gets in their way (including urchins and starfish, which are not used). Most skippers of these trawlers use technology such as sonar, echo sounders and computerised 3D maps to find the softer, sandy ground that is suited to this type of trawling. It would be counterproductive to trawl on rocky ground or over wrecks as this would damage the nets. Recent research has shown that 95 per cent of beam trawlers now use wheels on their beams to help increase fuel efficiency and reduce contact with the seabed.

Fisherman repairing a trawler net

Smaller inshore boats use the netting method

Handlining for mackerel on a small inshore boat

Netting

Static nets are fixed on the seabed (known as tangle nets), around wrecks or at sea (known as gill nets), and are left for several hours before being hauled in. This method tends to capture a broad range of species, such as monkfish, pollack, turbot, hake and spider crabs, although this will always depend on locality and location. Mesh sizes are controlled to avoid catching small and immature fish.

Handlining

This method is used by inshore and day boats, where baited hooks on lines are dropped into the sea. The number of hooks used per line depends on the species being caught. Handlining is used mostly for mackerel, sea bass, pollack and cod.

This is a preferred method because each fish can be marked and traced and is generally in very good condition. Small fish are rarely caught, but if caught they are returned alive immediately. Line fishing also has no unwanted by-catch. Chefs and customers will pay a higher price for fish caught by handlining.

Caring for the catch and inspection at the market

Catching fewer fish but ensuring that they are effectively cared for can result in increased freshness, quality and value in the fish caught. Seafish Quality Advisors, working mainly in Scotland, Northern Ireland, Cornwall and the Humber, provide free independent and unbiased assessment on catch quality for fishermen and their crews.

Fish are inspected at the market for standards of grading, size, gutting, washing, icing and presentation, and the quality advisors can advise on how to improve quality of preservation and presentation, thus increasing the value of the catch. A scored analysis report shows the quality of the fish compared with the average for a particular port.

Skippers on pelagic vessels are encouraged to track times of hauls and record the temperature of tanks and details of the frequency and type of cleaning carried out aboard. This information is forwarded to processors and customers.

Handline caught mackerel stored in a seawater slush

Quality advisors have also been working with skippers to show that if they weigh fish boxes at sea, and not over-fill them, the quality of the catch is improved. By restricting boxes to a stated weight, and labelling when and where caught, fish can achieve an increased value at market.

Small handline boats use large plastic tubs filled with a slush of ice and seawater (usually held at a temperature of 0°C). The fresh catch is put into the slush straight from the line to maintain its freshness and quality.

Seafood Cornwall and Seafood Scotland have employed former skippers as Seafood Quality Advisors. This is another significant quality control step to help ensure that fish suppliers and chefs receive the best possible standard of fish.

Tagging: the mark of quality

In 2001 the South West Handline Fishermen's Association (SWHFA) was among the first UK fisheries to gain accreditation from the Marine Stewardship Council (MSC), for its handline mackerel scheme. Mackerel carrying the MSC mark is guaranteed to have been caught in south-west waters using the traditional method of handline fishing. Recently, the SWHFA has introduced tagging schemes for handline caught sea bass and pollack, clearly identifying these fish as being caught in Cornish waters. Customers who purchase these species with tags can match the tag numbers with the fisherman and boat on a website (www.linecaught.org.uk).

This method has developed a new market, where small numbers of dedicated boats can sell directly to suppliers using this tag as a sign of quality and sustainability. The volume of fish caught is very small compared with what a trawler will catch in one day, but the fish is arguably better quality and there is no 'unwanted catch'. The fish will also have a smaller carbon footprint because the boats used are smaller and do not travel so far out to sea. Because sustainability of fish supplies is the major factor, the emphasis is on the quality rather than the quantity.

CHEF'S TIP

The first hour after the fish has been caught is the most crucial for maintaining its quality and freshness. Therefore, the correct storage and rapid chilling of fish as soon as it is caught significantly improves shelf life, appearance and keeping qualities.

Tagged line-caught sea bass

THE FISH MARKET

After fish has been landed, some is sold at the fish market in the port of landing and some is sent to other markets around the UK, such as Billingsgate in London. The quality of product and food safety issues are of utmost importance throughout this process. UK seafood markets are constantly taking steps to ensure that only the best quality product reaches the customer. There is constant investment in innovative procedures, such as temperature controlled fish halls and electronic auctions and/or remote bidding. Also, major new investments have been made in building new markets at some ports, such as Hull and Peterhead.

Newlyn fish market, Cornwall

What to look out for when purchasing fish

■ Fresh whole fish will have eyes that are bright and not sunken and the skin will have a shiny, moist and firm appearance. There will be a pleasant sea-fresh aroma if the fish is really fresh.

■ When buying fillets, look out for neat, trim fillets and a white translucent appearance.

■ Smoked fish should always appear glossy and have a fresh smoked aroma.

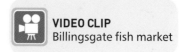

VIDEO CLIP
Billingsgate fish market

■ When purchasing frozen seafood, check that the fish is frozen solid with no signs of partial thawing. Ensure that the packaging is undamaged and there is no sign of freezer burn to the fish.

FISH FARMING

Aquaculture is an important industry in the UK, made up of an established shellfish sector and a rapidly developing fish sector. Many of the sheltered bays, estuaries and lochs around the UK coastline are suitable for farming a wide range of species. With the development of new equipment that can withstand more extreme weather conditions, opportunities to move to sites further offshore are likely to arise. The shellfish species that are currently produced in UK waters include:

■ Mussels

■ Oysters

■ Clams

■ Scallops

The main fish species being farmed at the moment are:

■ Salmon

■ Halibut

■ Turbot

The farming of haddock and Dover sole is still at the research or semi-commercial level. Farmed sea bass is also now starting to appear in UK supermarkets.

How fish are farmed

Young fish are produced in land-based hatcheries and then transferred to sea cages for growing on to market size. This is taking place in Scotland, where the infrastructure for producing salmon is well established, and some of the producers are diversifying into other species. Norway is another country where this is happening. Recirculation systems are gaining interest, especially in areas where there are no sheltered sites for the mooring of cages.

The selection of a suitable site is crucial to the success of any aquaculture business. Growth and survival of the stock, whether fish or shellfish, are influenced by a range of physical and biological factors, including seawater temperature, exposure of the site to the elements, dissolved oxygen and pollutants. Sites near large urban and industrial developments are generally unsuitable for cultivation because of potential pollutants in the water. More specifically for shellfish, growth and survival are also affected by water flow rates, food (phytoplankton) in the water, predators and fouling organisms. Starfish and crabs, abundant in estuaries and coastal waters, are probably the most damaging of all the shellfish predators.

ADVANCED PREPARATION TECHNIQUES

Preparation of a whole salmon

Clean the cavity of the salmon

Remove the scales

Remove the head with a heavy knife

Fillet by cutting along the backbone

Trim the side of salmon

Remove the belly, trimming the side of salmon

Remove pin bones from the side of salmon

Cut traditional supremes from the side of salmon

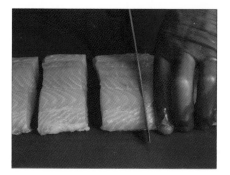
Cut modern style supremes from a side of salmon

Examples of the two styles of supreme

Preparation of a whole trout

Cut the trout along belly so the guts can be removed

Remove the guts from the cavity

Remove the blood line and wash thoroughly

Remove the fins

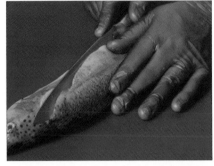

Fillet by cutting along the backbone

Continue to fillet as a double fillet

Remove double fillet from the bone

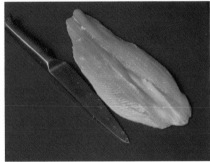

A double fillet of trout

Bone removal

Remove the head of the trout

Press down the backbone to loosen it from the flesh

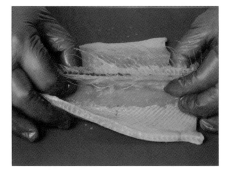

Remove all the pin bones and backbone

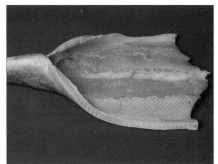

Trout with head and bones removed

Removing a double fillet (cross cutting) from a plaice

Make an incision for the removal of the double fillet from the plaice

Continue the process of removing the double fillet

Continue along the bones as closely as possible, ensuring no flesh left on the bones

Continue across the fish to remove the double fillet

Remove the roe from the double fillet

VIDEO CLIP
Preparing a délice and paupiette

FISH RECIPES

Pan fried fillet of red mullet with lemon thyme noodles, fine ratatouille sauce and crispy spring onion

INGREDIENTS	4 PORTIONS	10 PORTIONS
Red mullet fillets	4 × red mullet fillets	10 × red mullet fillets
Linguini noodles (cooked with cream and chopped thyme and lemon juice)	400g	1 kg
Courgette	40g	100g
Aubergine	40g	100g
White onion	40g	100g
Mixed peppers	40g	100g
Tomato coulis	8tbsp	20tbsp
Spring onions	1 bunch	2½ bunches
Butter	50g	125g
Olive oil	50ml	125ml
Black olives	2tbsp	5tbsp
Good-quality salt and white pepper	To taste	To taste

 CHEF'S TIP

The mullet should only be gently cooked to retain as much of its flavour and nutrients as possible. However, the dish requires a crispy skin so ensure the fish is skin-side down for at least 80 per cent of the cooking time.

Method of work

1 Prepare the fillets by cutting into a **butterfly**. In a frying pan heat a little oil until it just begins to smoke.

2 Season and lay the fish into the pan, skin-side down, and **shallow fry** until the skin just begins to crisp without burning.

3 Turn the fish over and allow to cook for a further 30 seconds.

4 Neatly dice the courgettes, aubergines, peppers and onions. Sweat in a little butter in a heavy-based saucepan until just cooked and season well. Reserve to one side.

5 Using a pestle and mortar, grind the black olives and remaining olive oil into a paste.

6 Slice the spring onions finely into julienne and dry them of any excess water. Place into hot oil (180°C) and deep fry until they are crisp. Reserve under hot lamps for service.

7 Ensure the linguini noodles are cooked and well seasoned then arrange in the centre of the plate. Lay the cooked fish on top.

8 Arrange the fine ratatouille vegetables around the edge and spoon the warmed tomato coulis around the plate, finish with drops of black olive purée and the crispy spring onion.

Poached Cornish pollack with Caerphilly mash, baby leek étuvé, langoustine and saffron beurre blanc

INGREDIENTS	4 PORTIONS	10 PORTIONS
Pollack fillets	4 × 160g	10 × 160g
Mashed potato	400g	1 kg
Caerphilly cheese	40g	100g
Baby leeks	12	30
Butter	50g	125g
Langoustines	12	30
Beurre blanc sauce	200ml	500ml
Saffron	pinch	2 pinches
Fish stock	300ml	750ml
Fresh dill	4tsp	10tsp
Good-quality salt and white pepper	Pinch	Pinch

 CHEF'S TIP

Ensure the langoustines are fresh, and alive where possible, before preparation; this will help to achieve a higher quality end product.

Method of work

1 Prepare and wash the langoustines. Poach in the fish stock, remove and allow to cool. Save the claws for decoration and carefully remove the flesh from each tail.

2 Put the langoustine tail shells into a little of the fish stock and slowly reduce to a glaze, extracting as much flavour from the shells as possible.

3 Pass the langoustine glaze and carefully whisk into the beurre blanc, add the saffron to infuse the flavour and colour.

4 Poach the pollack in the fish stock until the flesh is creamy and just set. A lightly buttered cartouche may be required to help with the cooking process.

5 Slice the baby leeks into lozenges and cook in a little stock and butter until tender, season well and reserve for service.

6 Heat the mashed potato in a heavy-based saucepan with a little butter and add the grated Caerphilly cheese. Check the seasoning, and while still hot pipe onto a warmed service plate. Top with the poached fish.

7 Finish with the baby leeks, langoustine tails and one set of claws for decoration. Serve with the beurre blanc and the fresh dill.

Smoked haddock brandade, soft poached egg, wilted spinach and chive cream sauce

INGREDIENTS	4 PORTIONS	10 PORTIONS
Home-smoked haddock	400g	1kg
Fresh milk	500ml	1250ml
Dry mashed potato (with chopped parsley)	400g	1kg
Lemon juice and zest	1 lemon	3 lemons
Free range eggs	4	10
Fresh baby spinach	100g	250g
Butter	50g	125g
Fish cream sauce	200ml	500ml
Chopped chives	6tsp	14tsp
Good-quality salt and white pepper	Pinch	Pinch

CHEF'S TIP

The eggs can be poached in advance and reheated to order; this will help to guarantee uniformity of shape and size and improve speed of service.

Method of work

1 Heat the milk in a large heavy-based saucepan and add the smoked haddock. Slowly poach until the flakes of the fish can easily be separated from the fillet.

2 Drain the fish and carefully flake the flesh. Mix the fish gently into the warmed mashed potato with the lemon juice and zest. Season well. Retain the mixture warm for service.

3 Wilt the washed and drained baby spinach in a little butter for a few seconds and place into the base of a bowl plate.

4 Top with the haddock brandade, shaped in a stainless steel moulding ring.

5 Poach the eggs until soft then arrange on top of the haddock.

6 Mix the chopped chives with the fish cream sauce and delicately nape over the poached egg.

Grilled swordfish with wild rice, mango, coconut, lime salsa and coriander foam

INGREDIENTS	4 PORTIONS	10 PORTIONS
Swordfish	4 × 160g	10 × 160g
Wild rice	50g	125g
Basmati rice	350g	875g
Fresh mango	¼	1 whole
Fresh coconut	¼	1 whole
Lime	1	3
Tomato concassé	4tbsp	10tbsp
Olive oil	50ml	125ml
Fresh coriander	8tsp	20tsp
Fish stock	100ml	250ml
Fresh milk	50ml	125ml
Good-quality salt and white pepper	To taste	To taste

CHEF'S TIP

If the swordfish is hard, has a rubbery texture and breaks easily it has been over cooked. It will have lost its moisture content and nutritional value.

Method of work

1   Boil the wild rice and basmati rice separately with salted water. Refresh and mix together.

2   Make a salsa using diced fresh mango, fine coconut shavings, coconut milk and the lime juice and zest. Add the tomato concassé. Drizzle in a little oil.

3   Reduce the fish stock by half. Add the milk and reduce by one-third, then add the coriander leaves. Blend to create a foam.

4   Grill the swordfish until pink in the centre and marked with a quadrillage.

5   Place the warmed rice on the service plate and arrange the swordfish on top.

6   Spoon the salsa around and finish with the coriander foam.

Char grilled tuna niçoise with a lemon and grain mustard emulsion

INGREDIENTS	4 PORTIONS	10 PORTIONS
Tuna	4 × 160g	10 × 160g
Fine green beans	100g	250g
Plum tomatoes (blanched, deseeded and cut into quarters)	4	10
Red onion (finely chopped)	½	1½
Black olives (halved)	2tbsp	5tbsp
New potatoes (boiled, peeled and sliced)	12	30
Curly endive lettuce	¼	1
Lemon juice and zest	1 lemon	2½ lemons
Grain mustard	2tbsp	5tbsp
Egg yolks	1	3
Olive oil	100ml	250ml
Sherry vinegar	100ml	250ml
Good-quality salt and white pepper	Pinch	Pinch

CHEF'S TIP

Use only the freshest tuna possible, and when cooking aim to serve it pink in the centre. The tuna can be marinated in lime, garlic and chillies then seared quickly.

CHEF'S TIP

When grilling fish, always brush the grill bars with oil to prevent the fish from sticking.

Method of work

1   Cut the green beans into 6cm lengths, blanch in boiling water and refresh in iced water. Split each bean lengthways.

2   Cut each tomato quarter in half on an angle and mix with the green beans, chopped red onion, black olives, curly endive and cooked potatoes. Season the salad well.

3   To create the emulsion, blend the egg yolk, grain mustard, lemon juice and zest and slowly add the olive oil in a blender. Season with salt and white pepper.

4   Use half of the emulsification to dress the salad.

5   Reduce the sherry vinegar until slightly thickened.

6   Bar mark the seasoned fresh tuna to a quadrillage style on a grill and cook until pink in the centre.

7   Arrange the salad on the service plate, place the tuna on top and brush with a little oil, drizzle the emulsion around, broken up with the vinegar reduction.

Seared sea bass with curry oil, yoghurt, onion bhaji and spiced plum chutney

INGREDIENTS	4 PORTIONS	10 PORTIONS
Sea bass	4 × 150g	10 × 150g
Diced potatoes	400g	1kg
Turmeric	2tsp	5tsp
Fresh baby spinach	200g	500g
Mustard seeds	1tsp	3tsp
Curry powder	2tbsp	5tbsp
Olive oil	200ml	450ml
Greek yoghurt	50ml	125ml
White onions sliced	2	5
Flour	100g	250g
Garam masala	2 tbspn	5 tbspn
Plums (stoned and chopped)	500g	1250g
Red chillies chopped	2	5
Brown sugar	6tbsp	15tbsp
Cinnamon stick	1	3
Red wine vinegar	50ml	125ml
Red onion chopped	2	5
Good-quality salt and white pepper	To taste	To taste

 CHEF'S TIP

There is very little connective tissue in fish, making it very fragile during cooking. All fish should be cooked as little as possible to maintain its shape and moisture content.

Method of work

1. Mix the plums, red chillies, sugar, cinnamon, red wine vinegar and chopped red onion together. Simmer for 4 hours until totally broken down and thickened, chill and store in an airtight container.

2. Mix the curry powder with a little olive oil to form a paste, then gradually add the remaining oil. Simmer for 1 hour until the spices are cooked through and the oil is brightly coloured and flavoured.

3. Thin the yoghurt with a little water or fresh milk until it resembles a sauce consistency.

4. Bring the washed potatoes to the boil with the turmeric, a little water to cover and the mustard seeds. When cooked, pour off any excess water and add the spinach over the heat, allow the mix to break down a little.

5. Mix the sliced onions with the garam masala, a little water and the flour and leave the paste aside for 1 hour.

6. Form small flat bhajis and deep fry until golden in colour.

7. Sear the seasoned sea bass in a shallow pan of oil, skin-side first, and finish cooking in a hot oven until just cooked.

8. Spoon the yoghurt on the plate and drizzle on the curry oil.

9. Position the potato mixture, with the sea bass on top, the plum chutney and then the onion bhaji to serve.

Monkfish and tiger prawn skewers with sweet potato sagaloo, Shishu cress and spiced pineapple compôte

INGREDIENTS	4 PORTIONS	10 PORTIONS
Monkfish	320g	800g
Peeled tiger prawns	320g	800g
Sweet potato	400g	1kg
Fresh spinach	100g	250g
Coconut milk	1 × 400g tin	2½ × 400g tins
Turmeric	2tbsp	5tbsp
Mustard seeds	2tsp	5tsp
Shishu cress	1 punnet	2½ punnets
Pineapple	¼	1 whole
Cinnamon stick	1	3
Stock syrup	100ml	250ml
Chilli flakes	pinch	2 pinches
Good-quality salt and white pepper	To taste	To taste

Method of work

1 Soak the bamboo skewers in water for 1 hour. Put the prawns and diced monkfish alternately onto the skewers (one portion should equal a total weight of 160g).

2 Dice the sweet potato and cook with turmeric, mustard seeds and coconut milk until tender. Add the torn spinach leaves and allow to wilt with the residual heat from the potato mixture.

3 Dice the fresh pineapple and simmer in the stock syrup with the cinnamon and chilli flakes until just tender. Cool down and refrigerate in an airtight container.

4 Shallow fry the fish skewers and finish in the oven if required. Use the excess syrup glaze to brush over as they cook in the oven.

5 Place the sweet potatoes on the centre of the serving plate with the skewers and pineapple compôte and garnish with Shishu cress.

CHEF'S TIP

To test if fish is correctly cooked, the flesh should feel tender to the touch and offer little resistance.

Roasted pavé of salmon, wilted pak choy, shitake mushrooms and a tomato butter sauce

INGREDIENTS	4 PORTIONS	10 PORTIONS
Salmon pavé	4 × 160g	10 × 160g
Pak choy	4	10
Shitake mushrooms (quartered)	200g	500g
Unsalted butter	100g	250g
Tomato fondue (passed and reduced)	50ml	125ml
Beurre blanc	100ml	250ml
Olive oil	50ml	125ml
Good-quality salt and white pepper	To taste	To taste
Lemon juice	To taste	To taste

CHEF'S TIP

When roasting fish, always constantly baste with olive oil or butter to help maintain the moisture and prevent it from burning in a dry heat.

Method of work

1 Preheat an oven to 200°C. Brush the salmon **pavé** with olive oil and season well. Place onto a roasting tray and roast until just slightly undercooked in the centre.

2 Cut the pak choy down the centre and wash well. Sweat in butter in a shallow pan and season.

3 Sauté the shitake mushrooms until tender and season with salt, pepper and a few drops of lemon juice.

4 Mix the tomato fondue with the beurre blanc and correct the seasoning and the consistency.

5 Carefully arrange the pak choy and the shitake mushrooms on the service plate and position the roasted salmon on top.

6 Spoon the sauce neatly around the plate and serve.

Poached paupiette of lemon sole with salmon and lemongrass mousseline, champagne and chervil fish cream sauce

INGREDIENTS	4 PORTIONS	10 PORTIONS
Lemon sole fillet	8 × 60g	20 × 60g
Salmon mousseline	240g	600g
Lemongrass	2 sticks	5 sticks
Carrot	100g	250g
Leek	100g	250g
Courgette	100g	250g
Mouli	100g	250g
Unsalted butter	100g	250g
Fish cream sauce	175ml	400ml
Champagne	50ml	125ml
Fresh chervil	¼ bunch	½ bunch
Fish stock	200ml	500ml
Good-quality salt and white pepper	To taste	To taste

 VIDEO CLIP
Shallow poach a délice and paupiette

Method of work

1 Lightly bat out the skinned fillets of lemon sole between plastic film.

2 Finely chop the lemongrass, quickly blanch in boiling water and refresh in iced water. Add to the salmon mousseline.

3 Pipe the mousseline onto one half of the sole fillet and fold the other half on the top. Retain in a refrigerator ready for cooking.

4 Cut the vegetables into long julienne strips and sweat in butter in a shallow pan. Season well and retain warm until needed for service.

5 Lightly poach the paupiette of sole in the fish stock with a cartouche until just cooked. Retain warm for service.

6 Chop half of the fresh chervil and add to the fish cream sauce with a little of the champagne. Bring to the boil and check the seasoning and consistency.

7 Place buttered vegetables on the bottom of the plate and rest the sole on the top. Nape with the fish cream sauce and garnish with a sprig of chervil.

Grilled gravadlax with crisp potatoes, oyster mushrooms, rocket and puy lentil cream

INGREDIENTS	4 PORTIONS	10 PORTIONS
Thin supreme of gravadlax	4 × 100g	10 × 100g
Diced Maris Piper potatoes	400g	1kg
Oyster mushrooms	100g	250g
Fresh rocket	200g	500g
Puy lentils (braised with brunoise of vegetables)	50g	125g
Fish cream sauce	100ml	250ml
Fresh dill	6tsp	15tsp
Good-quality salt and white pepper	To taste	To taste

Method of work

1   Thoroughly wash the gravadlax and dry well. Char grill, creating a quadrillage effect. Retain warm for service.

2   Wash the diced potatoes under running cold water for approximately 2 minutes to rinse off the starch. Drain well. Deep fry the potatoes in groundnut oil at 150°C, until blanched. Drain well and place onto a tray lined with absorbent paper. Chill in a refrigerator.

3   Sauté the mushrooms then mix with the fresh rocket.

4   Deep fry the potatoes at 190°C until golden brown. Drain the potatoes, season well and mix with the rocket and sautéed mushrooms.

5   Arrange the potato mix on the service plate with the gravadlax on top.

6   Chop half the fresh dill and mix with the lentils and fish cream sauce then spoon around the plate.

7   Finish with the remaining sprigs of fresh dill.

CHEF'S TIP

When deep frying fish or potatoes, try to use groundnut oil as this has a superior quality when cooking.

Seared hot-smoked halibut with treacle-cured bacon, chestnut mushrooms, wilted baby gem and pesto vinaigrette

INGREDIENTS	4 PORTIONS	10 PORTIONS
Hot-smoked halibut	4 × 160g	10 × 160g
Treacle-cured bacon	200g	500g
Chestnut mushrooms	200g	500g
Baby gem lettuce	2	5
Pesto dressing	50ml	150ml
White wine vinegar	50ml	50ml
Olive oil	150ml	150ml
Good-quality salt and white pepper	To taste	To taste

Method of work

1 Cut the treacle-cured bacon into lardons and the chestnut mushrooms into quarters. Ensure there is no dirt or grit in the mushrooms.
2 Wash the baby gem lettuce and cut lengthwise into eight pieces.
3 Sauté the treacle-cured bacon lardons and add the quartered chestnut mushrooms. Once cooked, add the baby gems and wilt in the residual heat.
4 Heat a shallow pan with a little olive oil. Sear the halibut for approximately 2 minutes on each side to colour and warm through.
5 Reduce the pesto to a slightly runnier consistency with the white wine vinegar and olive oil.
6 Set the bacon mixture in a stainless steel ring in the centre of a service plate, lay the halibut on top and spoon the dressing around.

Peppered mackerel with Thai vegetable salad and ginger crème fraîche

INGREDIENTS	4 PORTIONS	10 PORTIONS
Mackerel fillets	4 fillets	10 fillets
Chinese leaf lettuce	¼	1 whole
Fresh carrot	100g	250g
Fresh mouli	100g	250g
Red onion	100g	250g
Spring onions	4	10
Cucumber	½	1½
Red chillies (cut into fine brunoise)	2tbsp	5tbsp
Garlic (cut into brunoise)	2tbsp	5tbsp
Ginger (cut into brunoise)	2tbsp	5tbsp
Lemongrass (cut into brunoise)	2tbsp	5tbsp
Champagne vinegar	50ml	125ml
Olive oil	150ml	375ml
Crème fraîche	50ml	125ml
Finely grated fresh ginger	20g	50g
Crushed black peppercorns	2tbsp	5tbsp
Good-quality salt	To taste	To taste

Method of work

1 To make the Thai dressing, combine the chillies, ginger, garlic and lemongrass with the vinegar and olive oil. Leave to stand at room temperature for a minimum of 24 hours to infuse all the flavours.
2 Sprinkle the mackerel fillets with the crushed peppercorns and lightly oil before placing onto a tray and under a salamander until cooked through.
3 Dress the washed and shredded Chinese leaf, finely sliced red onion, julienne of carrot and mouli, shredded spring onion and julienne of cucumber with the Thai dressing and warm together in a saucepan.
4 Mix the grated fresh ginger with the crème fraîche and season.
5 Arrange the salad on the service plate and set the grilled mackerel on top with a quenelle of crème fraîche on the fish.

Deep fried ray in turmeric flour with chive pomme purée and a mussel, tomato and tarragon liquor sauce

INGREDIENTS	4 PORTIONS	10 PORTIONS
Ray wing (boned and cut into 4cm × 4cm pieces)	20 pieces	50 pieces
Flour	50g	125g
Turmeric	2tbsp	5tbsp
Pomme purée (with double cream and butter)	400g	1kg
Chopped fresh chives	0.25 bunch	1 bunch
Fresh live mussels	20	50
Chopped shallots	2	5
Dry white wine	100ml	250ml
Tomato concassé	50g	125g
Chopped fresh tarragon	4tsp	10tsp
Chilled unsalted butter (diced)	100g	250g
Good-quality salt and white pepper	To taste	To taste

Method of work

1   Prepare and wash the mussels, discarding any that are open. In a heavy-based saucepan, cook the cleaned mussels with the shallots and wine for 2 minutes with the lid firmly on.

2   Drain the mussels and pass the cooking liquor into a pan. The mussels should have all opened (discard any that remain closed). Pick the mussels and discard the shells.

3   Mix together the flour and the powdered turmeric and sieve together twice. Lightly flour the fresh ray wing pieces with the turmeric flour and deep fry at 190°C in groundnut oil until golden in colour.

4   Bring to the boil the retained mussel cooking liquor and reduce by one-third. Gradually add the chilled butter and blend in using a whisk over a heat. Add the mussels, tomato concassé and tarragon and correct the seasoning and consistency.

5   Heat the pomme purée with the chopped fresh chives and spoon into the base of the service dish.

6   Position the pieces of deep fried ray wing on top.

7   Spoon the sauce around the plate.

Tilapia cooked en papillote with Chinese spices and coconut egg noodles

INGREDIENTS	4 PORTIONS	10 PORTIONS
Tilapia fillets	4 × 160g	10 × 160g
Finely sliced red chilli	½ chilli	2 chillies
Grated fresh ginger	1tbsp	2½tbsp
Chinese five spice	½tsp	1tsp
Soy sauce	1tbsp	2½tbsp
Hoi sin sauce	1tbsp	2½tbsp
Finely chopped garlic	1tbsp	1tbsp
Fresh lemon thyme	4 sprigs	10 sprigs
Grated coconut	50g	125g
Coconut milk	½ × 200g tin	1½ × 200g tins
Egg noodles	300g	750g
Good-quality salt and white pepper	To taste	To taste

Method of work

1 Preheat an oven to 180°C.

2 Combine the red chilli peppers, fresh ginger, soy sauce, hoi sin sauce, finely chopped garlic, Chinese five spice and marinate the tilapia.

3 Create a pouch with greaseproof paper and place the fish inside with the lemon thyme and seal well. Wrap in tin foil for further protection and to trap the cooking vapours inside the pouch.

4 Bake for 15 minutes in the hot oven.

5 Bring the coconut milk to the boil and add the grated coconut. Blanch the egg noodles quickly and mix with the hot coconut mix.

6 Arrange noodles in a separate bowl. Serve with the tilapia en papillote at the table for the customer to open.

CHEF'S TIP

Cooking en papillote is the best way to retain the nutritional value of fish. All the juices, flavours and nutrients are held in the cooking pouch.

Whiting fillets steamed with coriander, seared oriental salmon with sesame and breaded sole with sauce vierge

INGREDIENTS	4 PORTIONS	10 PORTIONS
Whiting fillets	4 × 50g	10 × 50g
Coriander seeds crushed	1tsp	2½tsp
Salmon fillets skinned	4 × 50g	10 × 50g
Hoi sin sauce	4tbsp	10tbsp
Sesame seeds	2tsp	5tsp
Lemon sole fillets	4 × 50g	10 × 50g
Flour	4tbsp	10tbsp
Whole eggs	2	5
Breadcrumbs	8tbsp	20tbsp
Sauce vierge	4tbsp	10tbsp
Tomato coulis	4tbsp	10tbsp
Good-quality salt and white pepper	To taste	To taste

Method of work

 CHEF'S TIP

To increase the flavour of fish when steaming, place it on a bed of fresh herbs or aromatic vegetables or spices.

1 Prepare the whiting and fold into a delice. Season with salt and the crushed coriander, wrap in plastic film and steam in a steamer until just cooked.

2 Marinate the salmon in the hoi sin sauce and toasted sesame seeds. Shallow fry on both sides until the salmon is slightly underdone.

3 Roll the lemon sole into a spiral and pané à la Anglaise using seasoned flour, beaten egg and fine breadcrumbs. Deep fry in hot groundnut oil at 190°C.

4 Spoon a little warmed tomato coulis onto the service plate and rest the whiting on top.

5 Place a little of the warmed hoi sin sauce on the service plate and lay the salmon on top.

6 Spoon a little sauce vierge on the plate and set the deep fried lemon sole on top.

SHELLFISH

Shellfish is a collective term for crustacean, mollusc and cephalopod seafood. Using shellfish can be a rewarding experience, both in preparation and cooking. Each group of shellfish includes a range of species, each with its own method of preparation.

■ *Molluscs* Can have a single shell: univalves
Can have a pair of shells: bivalves
Can have no shell: cephalopods

■ *Crustaceans* Have an external skeleton

CLASSIFICATION OF SHELLFISH			
UNIVALVE	BIVALVE	CEPHALOPOD	CRUSTACEAN
Limpets	Cockles	Octopus	Lobsters
Whelks	Mussels	Cuttlefish	Crabs
Winkles	Razor shell clams	Squid	Crayfish
Tower shells	Scallops		Prawns
Tusk shells	Oysters		Shrimps
	Carpet shells		Langoustine
	Paddocks		
	Clams		

Shellfish generally live in, on or near the seabed, on the continental shelf, shelf slope and in very deep water. They can be obtained in two ways; by farming or by harvesting from the wild. There are good and bad points for each method.

Larger crustaceans, such as lobsters, crabs and crayfish, are often caught by small inshore fisheries, and prawns, shrimps and langoustine may be targeted by trawlers. Langoustine is fished extensively in the North Sea.

Univalve and bivalve molluscs, including scallops, oysters, mussels, clams, cockles, whelks and snails, can all be gathered by hand, trapped or dredged. Cephalopods (squid, cuttlefish and octopus) can be harvested using nets or hook and line.

The most common way to gather scallops is to dredge the seabed with a net This method can result in by-catch of undersized individuals or other species and can damage the shells. An alternative method is diving, where divers collect the scallops by hand from the seabed. This method is more selective, and dived scallops will sell at a higher price.

SUSTAINABILITY

The Sea Fish Industry Authority (Seafish) works across all sectors of the UK seafood industry to promote good-quality, sustainable seafood. Its research and projects are aimed at raising standards, improving efficiency and ensuring that the fishing industry develops in a practical and sustainable way. Established in 1981, it is the UK's only cross-industry seafood body working with fishermen, processors, wholesalers, seafood farmers, chefs, caterers, retailers and the import/export trade.

Seafish is helping the industry to become more sustainable through a variety of activities:

■ The Seafish Sustainable Fisheries Advisory Committee brings together fishermen and environmentalists from across all sectors of the seafood industry to consider the need for conservation and stability and to advise Seafish.

■ Seafish marine technologists work with fishermen to develop and test trawling gear designs that are more selective and less damaging to the seabed.

■ Guidelines have been produced for the use of square-mesh panels in prawn trawls, which reduce the by-catch of juvenile fish such as haddock and cod.

■ An international research project on scallop dredge design to reduce environmental damage is co-ordinated by Seafish.

■ A new trawl design with an escape hatch for dolphins is being developed.

Forthcoming projects include:

■ Developing a UK training course in responsible fishing

■ Co-ordinating a pilot project to develop a high-quality, low-volume sustainable pelagic fishery in Cornwall, and eventually a model which can be developed throughout the UK

■ Investigating new ways to use the waste products left over from the UK's processing industry

■ Leading an international project called Tracefish, developing a Europe-wide scheme which traces seafood from net to plate. This will help the seafood industry to deliver consistent, clear labelling for seafood so that consumers can make informed choices about what to purchase.

SHELLFISH PREPARATION

Bivalve molluscs

Scallops

Scallops are highly regarded and are expensive to purchase. The rounded, fan-shaped shells vary in size, from the smaller queen scallops about 7cm

across to the larger ones up to 18cm across. The edible parts are the round white muscle and the orange and white roe (coral). The frilly gills and mantle can be used for soup and stocks.

Scallops can be opened by separating the shells with a knife. This can be done relatively easily once the basic techniques have been mastered.

■ Hold the scallop shell firmly, with the flat shell uppermost.

■ Place a thick knife between the shells by the hinge and push up to break the connection.

■ Slide the knife along the inside of the flat shell, remove the flat shell and discard.

■ Work the knife under the skirt (frilly gills) then under the white and coral to separate from the shell.

■ Discard the skirt or save for making a stock.

■ Separate the white from the coral and gently wash both and store until required.

If the scallops are fresh, well prepared and in excellent condition, they can be used raw, simply marinated with an acidic dressing to gently denaturise the flesh.

Clams

Clams are well known for the classic dish clam chowder, which is mainly associated with the east coast of the United States.

Razor shell clams

Razor shells clams are shaped like cut-throat razors. They are caught by tipping salt onto the sand: the shells pop out of the ground and are carefully harvested.

Oysters

Many species and varieties of oyster are found around the world and so oysters come in a many shapes and sizes. The best British oysters are the 'native' or 'flat' oysters. Other British oysters include 'rock' oysters. Natives are available from September to April, though they are at their best from late October to late February when the sea is colder. Pacific oysters are available all year.

Oyster shells must be scrubbed well before opening and an oyster knife should always be used to open the shells.

■ Place the blade of the oyster knife between the shells by the hinge, and using gentle force carefully lift.

■ Lift the top shell, sever the muscle and discard the shell.

■ Slide the knife under the oyster to free it, check for any loose shell and discard, remove any foam residue.

It is important to use an oyster knife because a normal kitchen knife could break. An oyster knife also has a small guard near the handle to help prevent the hand from slipping and cutting against the sharp shell.

Any oysters that have an unusual smell should be discarded. Native oysters are best eaten raw, and as soon as possible after capture. Raw oysters are traditionally eaten with lemon and a little cayenne pepper. Cooked rock oysters are used to produce chowders and fish stews.

Mussels

Mussels

These molluscs, which have a distinctive oval blue-black shell, are often seen attached to rocks and wooden structures around coastlines worldwide. The vibrant orange-coloured meat inside is sweet and salty. Mussels should only be harvested from unpolluted waters between September and March; they should be left alone during the summer months. Cultivated mussels are also available.

Purchase smaller or medium-sized mussels, and always buy more than you need because there will always be some dead ones that will need to be discarded.

Univalve molluscs

Whelks

Whelks resemble pointed snails when fresh, and are usually sold ready-cooked. Only retain the good whelks and discard any that are damaged or smell strongly.

Winkles

Winkles, known as 'black sea snails', are served as appetisers. They are usually sold pre-cooked, and can be seasoned with fresh tarragon or parsley and a little white wine. They are quickly and easily removed from their shells using a pin when cooked.

Cephalopod molluscs

Squid

Squid

Squid varies in size, from small ones of about 7cm to larger ones of about 25cm. Squid is available most of the year, either fresh or frozen. It freezes very well, and preparing squid is relatively straightforward. If the ink sac can be recovered intact from inside the squid, it can be used to colour and flavour risottos, pastas and sauces. There is a transparent flexible cartilage within the squid, which must be removed. Cooking must be either very quick or very slow, otherwise the flesh will be tough to eat.

Crustaceans

Lobster

Lobsters are more expensive than their close relatives the crabs because of the superior flavour and texture of their meat. When alive, lobsters' shells are mottled with dark green, blue and brick red colours, but they turn to their distinctive bright red on cooking.

Lobsters can grow to 4.5kg, but are best eaten at about 500g to 1.4kg. The smaller lobsters are more tender. Cold-water lobsters from the northern seas are considered the finest: the males have denser, meatier flesh, and the females have a more subtle flavour and an orange roe, the 'coral', which can be used to colour sauces.

Most of the lobster is edible, except the transparent bag-like stomach and the dark intestines. These should be removed with a sharp knife point. Do not remove the creamy green-grey liver, known as the 'tomalley', which has an excellent flavour. It can also be used to flavour sauces and soups.

Purchase lobsters that feel heavy for their size, with both claws intact, and preferably buy them while they are still alive and cook them yourself. A 1.4kg lobster should be enough for two portions.

VIDEO CLIP
Deep poaching lobsters in court bouillon

Lobster is best cooked simply – boiled, steamed or grilled – and can be served either hot or cold. Serve with melted butter, lemon juice or mayonnaise. Crack the claws with a hammer or back of a large knife to extract the meat. The shells can be used for fish soup, the base for bisque or a lobster sauce.

The reason for cooking lobsters alive is that once killed their flesh starts to deteriorate very quickly. Fishmongers and wholesalers will only buy live lobsters to sell, and in turn chefs and cooks, when cooking fresh lobster, will always choose live specimens for freshness. Lobsters sold in supermarkets in this country are generally sold already cooked as the demand for live lobsters is not as great as it is abroad.

Methods of cooking lobster

- The standard way of cooking is to place the live lobster head first into a pan of boiling water – the lobster dies very quickly.
- Another method is to freeze the live lobster for approximately 30 minutes to desensitise it and then cook it in boiling water.
- A third method it to kill the lobster before cooking: in one sharp blow, pierce the live lobster between the eyes, which kills it instantly, then cook it in the usual way.

Method of preparing lobster

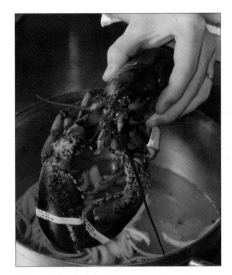

Plunge the lobster into court bouillon to cook

Remove the claws

Crack the claws with the back of a knife

Remove the claw flesh in one piece

Split the lobster in half lengthwise

Turn the lobster and continue to cut

Remove the white flesh and discard the dark flesh

VIDEO CLIP
Lobster Thermidor

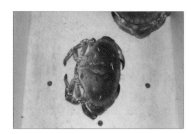

Crab

There are many varieties of crab and many regions throughout the world where crabs are abundant:

- *Europe* – the brown crab and the spider crab
- *Eastern USA* – the blue crab
- *Pacific coast of the USA* – the Dungeness crab

The soft brown flesh under the hard upper shell is strong and full-flavoured, this contrasts well with the sweet, delicate white flesh found in the claws and body. Male crabs often have larger claws and so more white flesh than females.

Purchase crabs that feel heavy for their size and smell fresh and sweet, whether alive or cooked. If there is a smell of ammonia, do not buy. Crabs are best bought alive and cooked fresh. You will need approximately 115g of meat per portion – for this you will need about 450g of whole crab (with shell intact).

The brown crab from Europe is available all year. It reaches 20–25cm across and has heavy front claws with almost-black pincers. Its shell is rusty-red or brown, and its legs are hairy and red but mottled with white.

VIDEO CLIP
Dressed crab

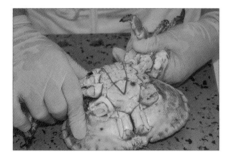

- Lay the crab on its back and remove the legs and claws by twisting.

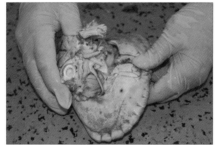

- Hold the belly of the crab near the eyes and pull, this will come off in one piece.

- Inside you will see the grey fingers and a sack – discard these.

- Scrape the meat from the shell and claws (keep the brown meat and white meat separate).

- The inside of the claws can be accessed by cracking the shell with the back of a knife and then carefully peeling.

Velvet crabs

Spider crabs

The velvet crab, sometimes known as the swimming crab, grows to 10–15cm. Its body is coated with short hairs, giving it a velvet-like appearance. It is one of the major crab species in UK waters, and is found in rocky areas near the shoreline and down to a depth of approximately 65 metres. Velvet crab fetches the highest price, especially abroad, such as in Spain, Portugal and France, where it is seen as a luxury food item.

The popularity of spider crab is increasing, and as the waters around the south-west coast of the UK begin warm up the population of these crabs is increasing. Tangle nets are the main fishing method used to capture spider crabs. Netting is less sustainable than potting; with potting there is no by-catch and undersized crabs can be returned to the sea alive. Avoid using immature crabs (the legal minimum landing size is 120mm maximum body width), egg-bearing crabs and fresh (not previously frozen) crabs caught during the spawning season (April to July).

Langoustine

Also known as Dublin Bay prawns, Norway lobster and scampi, these orange-pink shellfish from the north-east Atlantic and Mediterranean resemble small, slim lobsters. They are an expensive choice with little meat, but are delicious if freshly caught and cooked.

The best specimens can be bought from late spring to late autumn and are cooked in the same way as lobster. Because of their smaller size, they need less cooking. Usually only the tail is sold. In their shells, 200g should be enough per portion, however removed from their shells, half this quantity will be enough. They are available frozen all year round.

Prawns

There are many prawn species and they vary in size from 5cm to 18cm long. King prawns grow even larger at up to 23cm. They also come in many colours, from the familiar common pink prawns to the brown-blue tiger prawns.

Prawns are available all year round, though usually frozen in the UK. Fresh raw prawns are the tastiest. They should be firm and springy with bright shells. If they are limp, soft or have an ammonia smell then discard them. Ensure frozen prawns are properly defrosted before heating.

Prawns can be prepared in the same way as langoustine but do not require scissors to cut and peel as the shells are much softer.

TRANSPORTATION AND STORAGE

The best transportation and storage for live crustaceans is to use a seawater or freshwater tank. For shellfish to be transported in these conditions the following points should be observed:

- Controlled water temperature within the tanks
- Good aeration of the water
- Suitable water quality depending on the type of crustacean or mollusc
- Species should be separated into independent tanks

However, this method is costly and only catering establishments that specialise in serving shellfish will have this facility. Fish and shellfish suppliers will also have this facility on their own premises, but generally when being delivered crustaceans such as lobster, crabs and crayfish will be packed in cases (usually polystyrene), covered with wet cloths and kept in a refrigerated environment.

Follow these guidelines when storing fresh shellfish:

1 Keep the shellfish at a temperature of between 2°C and 8°C.
2 Keep shellfish in its packaging until preparation, this is to prevent moisture loss.
3 Ensure that all shellfish remain moist.
4 Molluscs should be kept in a container embedded in ice. The round side of the shell should face downwards to help collect and retain the natural juices.
5 Check regularly to make sure that they are still alive. Reject any dead or dying specimens.

SHELLFISH ALLERGY

Allergy to shellfish is quite common and people who are sensitive can react to a number of different types of shellfish, such as shrimps, prawns, lobsters and oysters. People who are allergic to one type of shellfish often react to others. Shellfish allergy can often cause severe reactions, and even the vapours from shellfish being cooked may be enough to trigger a reaction in some people.

Since November 2005, prepacked food sold in Europe must show clearly on the label if it contains crustaceans, including lobster, crab, prawns and langoustines. However, other groups of shellfish, such as molluscs (including mussels, scallops, oysters, and whelks), cephalopods (squid and octopus) or gastropods (snails) do not need to be labelled individually.

Shellfish is, however, recognised as being a healthy food which is low in cholesterol. It is important to support the UK's territorial fisherman and to utilise their skills in catching only what is required. This will help to increase the stock levels and generate a healthier UK economy.

SHELLFISH RECIPES

Deep fried oysters with a Thai salad

INGREDIENTS	4 PORTIONS	10 PORTIONS
Fresh oysters	12	30
White breadcrumbs	200g	500g
Lime juice and zest	1 lime	2 limes
Flour	100g	250g
Whole egg pasteurised	100ml	250ml
Chinese leaf lettuce (cut into chiffonade)	¼ lettuce	¾ lettuce
Assorted peppers (cut into julienne)	½ of each colour	1 of each colour
Red onion finely sliced	50g	125g
Baby gem lettuce (cut into chiffonade)	1	2
Julienne of carrot	80g	200g
Thai dressing	200ml	500ml
Good-quality salt and white pepper	To taste	To taste

Method of work

1. Carefully remove the fresh oysters from their shells and wash to remove any grit.
2. Marinate the oysters in the lime juice for 5 minutes.
3. Pané the oysters through the flour, then the beaten egg and finally the breadcrumbs with the finely grated lime zest mixed through.
4. Prepare the vegetables as required and dress with the Thai dressing.
5. Season well and arrange on a serving plate.
6. Quickly deep fry the oysters at 180°C until golden and serve on top of the salad.

Seared scallops with a sweet caper dressing and cauliflower purée

INGREDIENTS	4 PORTIONS	10 PORTIONS
Fresh scallops	12	30
Curry powder	5g	10g
Capers	80g	200g
Caster sugar	2tbsp	5tbsp
White wine vinegar	40ml	100ml
Vegetable stock	100ml	250ml
Cauliflower	¼	¾
Béchamel sauce	50ml	125ml
Olive oil	2tbsp	5tbsp
Fresh dill	4 sprigs	10 sprigs
Good-quality salt and white pepper	To taste	To taste

Method of work

1 Carefully remove the scallops from the shells and remove the corals.
2 Trim the scallops, wash, dry and dust lightly with the curry powder.
3 Drain and wash the capers, then blend with the vinegar, oil and sugar to form the dressing.
4 Cut the cauliflower into small florets and cook in the vegetable stock until tender. Drain and blend the cauliflower with the béchamel until smooth, pass through a sieve. Season to taste.
5 Quickly sear the scallops in a hot pan with a little oil for 1 minute on each side.
6 Spoon the purée and dressing onto a serving plate, arrange the scallops on top and finish with a sprig of fresh dill.

Tiger prawn and lemongrass cakes with chilli jam

INGREDIENTS	4 PORTIONS	10 PORTIONS
Minced tiger prawns (reserving one whole tail per portion)	16	40
Lemongrass brunoise	1tbsp	2½tbsp
Red chilli brunoise	2tbsp	5tbsp
Shallot brunoise	1tbsp	2½tbsp
Red wine vinegar	50ml	125ml
Caster sugar	100g	250g
Cornflour	50g	125g
Soy sauce	2tbsp	5tbsp
Fresh garlic (finely puréed)	1tsp	2½tsp
Ginger purée	1tsp	2½tsp
Mizuna	50g	125g
Good-quality salt and white pepper	To taste	To taste

Method of work

1 Preheat an oven to 180°C.
2 Mix the minced prawn meat with the lemongrass, garlic, ginger, cornflour, soy sauce and seasoning. Leave for 20 minutes.
3 Boil the vinegar and sugar until it becomes syrupy.
4 Add the chilli and shallots and simmer for a further 5 minutes. Cool down for service.
5 Divide the prawn paste into equal pieces, one per portion. Dust with a little cornflour and form into round shapes.
6 Fry until golden in a little heated oil, remove from the pan and bake in the preheated oven for 2 minutes.
7 Add the whole tails at the last minute to the pan and flash fry until just cooked.
8 Arrange a cake and tail with some jam and mizuna on the plate and serve.

Mussels cooked with a garlic cream sauce, sun-dried tomato bread and baby rocket salad

INGREDIENTS	4 PORTIONS	10 PORTIONS
Fresh mussels	400g	1kg
Garlic	1 clove	3 cloves
Dry white wine	50ml	125ml
Shallot brunoise	2tbsp	5tbsp
Double cream	150ml	375ml
Sun-dried tomato bread	4 slices	10 slices
Baby rocket	75g	180g
Lemon oil	2tbsp	5tbsp
Fish stock	100ml	250ml
Fresh coriander	4 sprigs	10 sprigs
Good-quality salt and white pepper	To taste	To taste

Method of work

1 Place the mussels, shallots, chopped garlic and white wine in a hot saucepan. Cover with a tight-fitting lid and cook for 2 minutes. The mussels should have all opened (discard any that remain closed).

2 Remove the mussels and keep warm, add the fish stock to the saucepan and reduce by half over a medium heat.

3 Add the double cream and reduce until the sauce thickens to the correct consistency.

4 Return the mussels to the sauce and warm through gently, check the seasoning.

5 Quickly toast the slices of bread and set into a serving bowl.

6 Add the mussels and the sauce.

7 Dress the rocket with lemon oil and arrange neatly to the side of the bowl and serve with the coriander.

CHEF'S TIP

Before cooking mussels always ensure that they are washed well under plenty of cold running water. Remove all beards and barnacles. Any mussels that are still open at this point should be discarded.

Fried medallions of lobster with coral pasta and a bisque foam

INGREDIENTS	4 PORTIONS	10 PORTIONS
Fresh lobster (hen)	1	3
Fresh egg pasta dough	200g	500g
Shellfish bisque	100ml	250ml
Fresh full fat milk	50ml	125ml
Double cream	50ml	125ml
Lemon thyme	Sprig	Sprig
Butter	100g	250g
Good-quality salt and white pepper	To taste	To taste

Method of work

1 Remove the coral from the hen lobster and add to the pasta dough during the initial process of mixing the ingredients.

2 Kill the lobster by plunging a knife through the cavity in the centre of its head.

3 Steam the lobster for 6 minutes and cool quickly.

4 Remove the tail meat and claws then reserve to one side.

5 Heat the bisque and separate into two, add double cream to one half and allow to reduce to form a sauce and season well.

6 Blanch the pasta in boiling salted water, drain and add to the sauce.

7 Slice the tail meat (2 slices per portion) and quickly fry in butter with the claws until golden and season.

8 Add the milk to the remaining bisque and blend using a handheld blender until a foam appears.

9 Lay the pasta neatly into a bowl, top with the lobster, spoon over the foam and finish with the lemon thyme.

CHEF'S TIP

European lobsters take five years to reach a size of just over 500g. They cast their complete shell to grow and can live to 15 years or more. Retain any leftover lobster or prawn shells for making bisques, sauces and shellfish stocks.

Crab and grain mustard beignets with an iced gazpacho

INGREDIENTS	4 PORTIONS	10 PORTIONS
White crab meat	200g	500g
Grain mustard	2tbsp	5tbsp
Choux paste	100g	250g
Pink peppercorns	1tsp	2½tsp
Fresh chopped parsley	2tbsp	5tbsp
Tomato juice	100ml	250ml
Cucumber brunoise	1tbsp	2½tbsp
Red wine vinegar	50ml	125ml
Olive oil	2tbsp	5tbsp
Finely chopped garlic	1tsp	2½tsp
Fresh basil	4 leaves	10 leaves
Shallot brunoise	1tbsp	2½tbsp
Good-quality salt and white pepper	To taste	To taste

Method of work

1 Combine the prepared tomato, cucumber, shallot, garlic, vinegar and oil together. Season well and place in the freezer until required for service (it is essential that it is not allowed to freeze completely).

2 Mix the choux pastry with the crab, ground peppercorns, fresh chopped parsley and grain mustard and season well.

3 Quenelle the choux mixture neatly, one quenelle per portion, and deep fry in groundnut oil at 190°C until golden in colour and completely cooked through.

4 Spoon the chilled gazpacho into a cold serving bowl and drizzle a little olive oil around.

5 Set the crab beignet on top and dress with the chiffonade of fresh basil.

Langoustines cooked in a sweet curry sauce with coconut rice

INGREDIENTS	4 PORTIONS	10 PORTIONS
Langoustines	20	50
Unsalted butter	100g	250g
Finely chopped onion	4tbsp	10tbsp
Long grain rice	200g	500g
Fish stock	400ml	1 litre
Fresh coconut	¼	1 whole
Flat leaf parsley	4 sprigs	10 sprigs
Sweet curry sauce	200ml	500ml
Lemon juice and zest	½ lemon	1 lemon
Finely chopped garlic	2tsp	5tsp
Finely chopped red chilli	1tsp	2tsp
Good-quality salt and white pepper	To taste	To taste

Method of work

1 Preheat an oven to 180°C.
2 Take half of the unsalted butter and melt in a heavy-based saucepan, add the chopped onion and sweat until translucent.
3 Add the rice and cook for a further 2 minutes allowing the grains to become coated in butter and completely mixed with the onion.
4 Add the hot fish stock and bring to the boil, cover with a buttered cartouche and braise in the preheated oven for 10 minutes or until the rice has just cooked.
5 Remove from the oven, fluff the rice over with a fork and fold in the coconut, seasoning and chopped parsley.
6 Marinate the peeled langoustine tails in garlic and lemon for 5 minutes before quickly frying in the remaining butter.
7 Carefully place the langoustines into the sauce and cook for 1 minute.
8 Arrange the rice neatly in a bowl, add the langoustines and garnish with red chilli.

Scampi fritters with a baby herb salad and vine tomato coulis

INGREDIENTS	4 PORTIONS	10 PORTIONS
Shelled cooked scampi	20	50
Olive oil	100ml	250ml
Lemon zest and juice	1 lemon	3 lemons
Cayenne pepper	Pinch	Pinch
Self raising flour	100g	250g
Finely chopped parsley	1tbsp	3tbsp
Baby herbs (tarragon and dill)	100g	250g
White wine vinegar	50ml	125ml
Dijon mustard	1tbsp	3tbsp
Vine tomato coulis	4tbsp	10tbsp
Good-quality salt and white pepper	To taste	To taste

Method of work

1   Marinate the scampi in lemon, cayenne and a little olive oil.
2   Mix the flour and parsley and enough water to form a light batter, season well (reserve a little flour to coat the scampi).
3   Dust the scampi with flour, dip into the batter and deep fry at 180°C until golden brown.
4   Produce a vinaigrette with the mustard, vinegar and olive oil then dress the baby herbs.
5   Arrange the herbs on a plate, add the scampi and spoon over the tomato coulis.

Individual crayfish mousse with a saffron foam

INGREDIENTS	4 PORTIONS	10 PORTIONS
Crayfish (peeled)	15	40
Egg yolks	2	5
White wine	50ml	125ml
Onion macédoine	1 tbspn	3 tbspn
Leek macédoine	1 tbspn	3 tbspn
Celery macédoine	1 tbspn	3 tbspn
Butter	100g	250g
Fresh lemon sole (minced)	200g	500g
Egg whites	2	5
Double cream	200ml	500ml
Fish velouté	100ml	250ml
Fresh full fat milk	50ml	125ml
Saffron	Pinch	Pinch
Fresh chervil	Sprigs	Sprigs
Good-quality salt and white pepper	To taste	To taste

Method of work

1   Sweat the vegetables in butter for 3 minutes without colour. Add the crayfish and wine, cover with a lid and cook for 3 minutes.
2   Mince the crayfish with the lemon sole and chill over ice for 10 minutes.
3   Add the egg yolks and cream very slowly while continuously beating over the ice, season well.
4   Whisk the egg whites to firm peaks then fold into the crayfish mixture.
5   Spoon the mixture into buttered dariole moulds and cook in a bain marie in the oven at 165°C for 20 minutes.
6   Heat the velouté with the saffron threads until a yellow colour is achieved, add the milk and reboil. Blend until a foam is achieved.
7   Turn out the crayfish mousse onto a service plate and spoon over the foam, finish with sprigs of fresh chervil.

Assessment of knowledge and understanding

You have now learned about the use of the different types of fish and shellfish and how to produce a variety of fish and shellfish dishes utilising an array of commodities and cooking techniques.

To test your level of knowledge and understanding, answer the following short questions. These will help to prepare you for your summative (final) assessment.

Fish preparation

1 Explain why the removal of fins is important during preparation of exotic fish.

2 Describe how the skinning of Dover sole is different from the skinning of other flat fish and explain the process.

Shellfish quality identifications

1 Explain when oysters should be bought and in what condition.

2 Explain the difference between crustaceans, molluscs and cephalopods.

Shellfish preparation

1 Describe the method for opening oysters.

2 Explain how langoustines should be prepared before cooking.

3 Identify which parts of lobsters and crabs should be discarded and why.

Materials and storage

1 Describe how shellfish should be transported.

Cooking

1 Describe the cooking of crab.

Health and safety

1 List the months during which raw oysters should not be eaten.

CHEF'S PROFILE

Name: DAVID CAVALIER

Position: Food Innovation Director

Establishment: Charlton House Catering Services Ltd

Current job role and main responsibilities: Food innovations, menu development and training. A large part of my role is to oversee 500 chefs within 140 different units on a day-to-day basis.

When did you realise that you wanted to pursue a career in the catering and hospitality industry? When I was 12 years old a French chef, who later became a great friend, was staying at our house. I was intrigued by the food he made for our family – it was very different to the meals my mother prepared.

Training:
I started working as a pot wash in the school holidays. I then got myself enrolled on a full-time catering course where I completed the City and Guilds qualification. From there I gained employment at top London hotels, such as the Dorchester, Grosvenor House and the Berkeley, while continuing with a one day a week course to achieve my City and Guilds 706/3.

Experience:
After working in the London hotels I went to America to work at the Stamford Court Hotel in San Francisco and the Belair Hotel in Los Angeles. I also spent two years in France, immersing myself in French culture and food while working at two Michelin-starred establishments. Upon my return to the UK, I opened my first small restaurant, Pebbles, in Aylesbury. From there I opened restaurant number two, Cavalier's, in London and then L'Escargot in Soho. I have consulted on many projects, from Chapter One to Regal Hotels to Pyrex cookware, spent some time as Executive Chef at Mosimann's, and in 2000 I gained another Michelin star for myself in just nine months. I am now concentrating on contract catering at Charlton House.

What do you find rewarding about your job?
Seeing customers' happy faces after they have experienced a wonderful meal. To me, this is the end result of hard work, being creative and mentoring chefs along the way.

What do you find most challenging about the job?
Always maintaining a consistently high level of food and service.

What advice would you give to students just beginning their career?
Catering is a long road, and it's not a job but a way of life. Once you have decided to follow this route, be passionate and fully committed. You will then find the area in which you excel.

Who is your mentor or main inspiration?
The young French chef who ignited my interest in food, François le Coz.

What traits do you consider essential for anyone entering a career as a chef?
Focus, natural flair, ability, talent, drive, enthusiasm and commitment.

Can you give one essential kitchen tip or technique that you use as a chef?
Never send out food that you are not 100 per cent happy with – keep your mistakes in the kitchen!

Roast scallops with wild mushroom ravioli

INGREDIENTS	4 PORTIONS
Scallops (cleaned with roe removed)	12
Sea salt and freshly milled black pepper	To taste
Asparagus	To garnish
Chervil	To garnish
Scallop mousse	
Scallop meat	300g
Egg yolks	2
Whipping cream	400ml
Sea salt and cayenne pepper	To taste
Ravioli	
Chopped shallots	20g
Crushed garlic	5g
Olive oil	
Mixed wild mushrooms	100g
Sea salt and freshly milled black pepper	To taste
Fresh thyme (blanched)	5g
Pasta dough	200g
Celeriac purée	
Celeriac (peeled and chopped into 3cm cubes)	1
Olive oil	
Double cream	150ml
Butter	15g
Sea salt and freshly milled black pepper	
Cappuccino sauce	
Diced raw celeriac	100g
Shallots	50g
Unsalted butter	120g
Cleaned beards and outer muscle of scallops	12
Fish stock	200ml
White wine	75ml
Dry vermouth	75ml
Garlic	5g
Whipped cream	100ml
Butter (for frothing the sauce)	40g
Cold full fat milk	50ml

Method of work

1 For the scallop mousse, blend the scallop meat to a paste, add the egg yolks and then blend again while slowly adding half the cream.

2 Pass through a chinois, then blend and add the remaining cream. Season with salt and cayenne pepper.

3 To make the ravioli, sweat the shallots and garlic in oil. Increase the heat and sauté the mushrooms. Season with salt, milled pepper and thyme. Leave to cool, then fold through 100g of the scallop mousse.

4 Roll out the pasta dough and cut to the required size. Fill the ravioli with the mushroom mixture and seal by pinching the edges. Blanch for two minutes in boiling salted water, then refresh in ice-cold water.

5 For the celeriac puree, put the celeriac on a foiled-lined ovenproof baking tray and drizzle with olive oil. Place another sheet of foil over the top and seal. Bake at 180ºC until it starts to soften (about 10 minutes).

6 Purée the celeriac in a blender and pass through a sieve. Put into a saucepan, add cream and butter, season with salt and pepper, and stir over a medium heat until smooth.

7 For the cappuccino sauce, sweat the celeriac and shallots in 20g butter, add scallop beards and outer muscle, fish stock, wine, vermouth, garlic and 80ml cream. Simmer until the celeriac is almost a purée. Blend well and pass through a strainer.

8 To assemble the dish, pan roast the scallops and season with salt and pepper. Reheat the ravioli for two minutes in salted boiling water. Reheat the celeriac purée.

9 To finish to cappuccino sauce, heat a small quantity of the strained liquid in a saucepan and add a spoonful of whipped cream and a small amount of butter and milk and combine to a light frothy foam by using a hand blender.

10 To serve, pipe the celeriac purée to one side of the plate. Place three roast scallops on top of the purée and the ravioli to the other side of the plate. Spoon over the cappuccino sauce and garnish with asparagus and chervil. Serve immediately.

12
Poultry

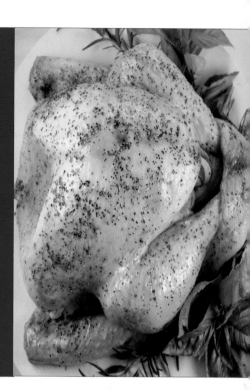

3FP4 Prepare poultry for complex dishes
3FC4 Cook and finish complex poultry dishes

LEARNING OBJECTIVES

This chapter describes how to prepare a variety of poultry dishes using some technically advanced skills and presentation expertise.

At the end of this chapter you will be able to:

■ Identify each type of poultry
■ Prepare poultry for complex dishes
■ State the quality points of poultry
■ Prepare each type of poultry
■ Identify specific storage systems

INTRODUCTION

When we refer to poultry we describe birds specifically reared for the table. This includes chicken, guinea fowl, turkey, goose and duck.

From left to right – battery, organic and maize red chicken

Chicken (*poulet*)

Chickens are descendants from the pheasant family and originate from northern India and southern China.

In the UK, more than 90 per cent of chickens are battery reared. Because of intensive husbandry, the birds achieve slaughter weight at 6 weeks. The birds grow very quickly and live relatively short lives, and the meat is bland and can have a grainy texture.

Free range and especially organic chickens are allowed to forage in the open and have space to develop muscle and a stronger bone structure. The term 'free range' only means that the birds have access to an outdoor pen. There are several labelling systems in use for these birds, such as the Soil Association scheme. One British company has developed a system of labelling and rearing chickens similar to the French *Label Rouge*. 'Label Anglaise' shows that the chicken has been produced by farmers who use older breeds, such as Cornish Red and White Rock, and free range/organic methods of rearing:

- The diet consists of 70 per cent cereals, including maize
- No antibiotics, hormones or growth stimulators are used
- Slaughter after 81 days old.

The label is featured on menus and assures the customer that the chicken has been well reared and is flavoursome.

Corn-fed chickens are fed on a diet of maize or containing a proportion of maize. This does not guarantee any kind of quality assurance. The distinctive yellow colouring of the skin is often gained by the introduction of a yellow dye into the feed and not by the natural colour of the maize itself.

QUALITY POINTS

When buying chickens we should be able to identify the quality points associated with them:

- Clear skin with no blemishes and unbroken; the colour varies from breed to breed, but the most common battery-reared breeds – the hybrids, Ross and Cobb – have a pale creamy colour
- Flesh should be firm and pliable
- Not too much fat; check the abdominal cavity for excess
- No bruising, blood clots, ammonia sores on the legs or cuts
- The breastbone should be pliable (this is for younger birds that are destined to be grilled, roasted or sautéed)

PURCHASE SPECIFICATIONS

In general, older and larger birds will have a more pronounced flavour.
However, organic poultry will ultimately have the best flavour, but it
will be more expensive to purchase.

TYPE	AGE	AVERAGE WEIGHT
Poussin	Up to 6 weeks	250–400g
Spring chicken	6–8 weeks	1–1.25kg
Chicken	12–20 weeks	1–2kg
French Label Rouge	11.5 weeks	1–1.6kg
Capon (castrated male)	Up to 32 weeks	2–4kg
Boiling fowl	Up to 40 weeks	2–4kg

Turkey (*dinde*)

Turkeys are members of the pheasant family and were first domesticated by
the Aztecs and Mexicans. They were introduced to Europe by the Spanish in
the sixteenth century via Asia and became popular because of the delicate
flavour of their meat. The term 'turkey' is thought to reflect the belief that
they were imported from Turkey, at that time part of the vast Ottoman
Empire.

Bronze turkey

The huge modern turkeys are mainly battery farmed. This practice originated
in the late 1920s in British Columbia, when a breeder developed an 18kg bird
with oversized leg muscles. This stock was used to perfect the more common
Broad-breasted Bronze.

Once again, it is well worth spending time sourcing organic and free range
birds, should budgets permit.

QUALITY POINTS

- Cock birds have a tendency to be drier and tougher than hens
- Bronze birds can have residual dark feather stubs; these can be removed with duck tweezers
- The flesh should be dry to the touch and without excess blemishes
- If the windpipe is still intact, it should be pliable and not rigid
- The breast should be plump in intensively reared birds and slightly leaner in the rarer organic varieties

Turkey is available in many weights, ranging from 4kg to 15kg. The Broad-
breasted White turkey is the most common in today's marketplace and has a

white, smooth and generally unblemished skin. Bronze turkeys are so called because of their distinctive plumage. Both Norfolk Black and Cambridge Bronze turkeys are worth looking out for as most of these birds are raised using traditional non-intensive farming methods. This means they take longer to mature, which contributes to a better overall flavour.

Duck (*canard*)

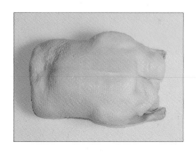

Norfolk duck

Duck is a web-footed water fowl, originally domesticated by the Chinese about 2000 years ago. It is highly appreciated for its rich moist meat. The common duck is the wild mallard, which is native to the northern hemisphere. The Barbary duck is a descendant of the Muscovy duck of Central and South America.

The type and breed of duck should be taken into account when purchasing. Barbary duck yields excellent suprême portions while Aylesbury is ideal for roasting. Gressingham duck has a good flavour due mainly to the fact that the birds are slaughtered at an older age. It is also smaller than the other ducks. Nantais duck is a traditional French breed that is becoming fewer in number.

Ducks are usually slaughtered from 6 to 16 weeks. Strictly speaking, the term 'duck' is applied to birds that are more than two months old; the younger birds are called 'ducklings'.

QUALITY POINTS

General

- Pale skinned and undamaged (except with wild varieties)
- Feet and bills should be brightly coloured
- Fresh pleasant smell
- Moist but not sticky
- Free from bruises, feathers and blemishes

Breeds

- Aylesbury – a small bird with white feathers and delicate flesh
- Gressingham – a cross between a domesticated duck and a mallard, a highly prized breed with a low fat content and rich flesh
- Norfolk – from the county of Norfolk, a domesticated fowl with similar attributes to Aylesbury
- Lincolnshire – as Norfolk, a common duck with similar attributes to Aylesbury
- Barbary – firm lean flesh with a strong flavour
- Nantais – small and slightly fatty with delicate flesh
- Rouennais – a larger duck than the Nantais, similar to the Aylesbury

Guinea fowl (*pintade*)

This is an excellent alternative to battery-farmed chicken in that the flesh is comparable to organic free range chicken. It can have a tendency to be dry so care must be taken when cooking. All recipes that apply to chicken also apply to guinea fowl. The meat has a more pronounced flavour and the birds are usually aged between 10 and 15 weeks before they are slaughtered.

Goose (*oie*)

Goose has a rich dark flesh with a copious covering of fat which means that it will very rarely dry out during cooking. They can weigh anything from 2.5kg to 12kg, depending on whether or not they were used for the production of foie gras. Goose should have the same quality points as duck. When not in season it can be purchased frozen. Geese are usually aged between 24 and 28 weeks at slaughter.

Poultry offal (giblets)

The giblets of poultry have many uses and can be essential in the preparation of many dishes. Although most poultry is purchased without giblets, they are still available from good suppliers. With correct storage and when used as fresh as possible they will enhance your repertoire of poultry dishes.

POULTRY OFFAL	USES
Livers	Garnishes, pâtés, terrines, stuffings, sautés; foie gras is the liver of specially fed ducks and geese
Cockscombs and kidneys	Classic garnishes such as favourite, Chevalière and Tivoli
Hearts	Stocks, consommés and salade Périgourdine
Necks	Stocks and consommés
Gizzards	Stocks, stews and pies
Winglets	Garnishes, boned and stuffed for braising

White meat and dark meat

The differences between white and dark meat are due to the work performed by the various muscles. Leg muscles contain more fat than breast meat, and even in intensive rearing they get used and exercised. The result is that they are more grainy and tougher in texture. The leg muscles use oxygen to burn fat to generate energy, and myoglobin – a reddish brown protein – stores the oxygen in the muscles. The extra myoglobin and fat in the legs accounts for the slightly stronger flavour and darker colour of the meat.

White meat from the breast and in battery-reared poultry is muscle that is seldom used. These muscles use glycogen – a form of sugar – as a source of energy. Glycogen does not need oxygen or fat, therefore there is a lack of myoglobin and very little fat in the breast meat.

THE STORAGE OF POULTRY

Poultry is a highly perishable commodity and so requires careful storage control. Fresh and chilled birds should be placed on clean trays in single layers, not stacked on top each other. The optimum storage temperature range is 1–5°C. Poultry should be used as quickly as possible, but at least within three days. Refrigeration leaves the poultry relatively unchanged from its fresh condition; both bacteria and meat enzymes become less active at lower temperatures thus slowing down spoilage.

The modern practice of vacuum packing butchered poultry and meat has the economic advantages of reduced storage space and a longer shelf life. It stores well because the raw protein does not have prolonged exposure to oxygen and therefore the fatty elements do not break down as quickly. Oxygen in the air and direct light will cause the flesh to become a dull colour and will slowly change the flavour.

The freezing of poultry greatly extends storage life because all biological processes are halted. Frozen poultry must be kept in a deep freeze until required and must be completely thawed before being cooked. Freezing immobilises the liquid/water content and therefore the meat will continue to be preserved so long as a temperature of −18°C is maintained. It is advised that 24 hours is allowed when defrosting poultry in a refrigerator. Wrapped poultry can be quickly defrosted in an iced water bath, which keeps the surface of the flesh safely cold.

HEALTH AND SAFETY

Salmonella and *E. coli* are always a cause for concern when dealing with poultry. All safety procedures must be adhered to, from the receiving of deliveries to the service of finished dishes.

Salmonella causes more serious food-borne diseases in Europe than any other microbe. It often has no effect on the animal carriers, but in humans it can be the cause of chronic infection and sickness. A particular strain of *E. coli*, named 0157:H7, can cause kidney failure, especially in children and the elderly.

To help prevent bacterial infection from poultry, it should always be assumed that all meat and poultry is infected with at least some bacteria. Measures must be taken to prevent cross-contamination; all hands, knives, chopping boards and workbenches used in preparation must be cleaned thoroughly with hot soapy water. *E. coli* is killed at 68°C. At this temperature the protein content in poultry and meat will denature and coagulate, any connective tissue will begin to dissolve and the flow of protein bound water (meat juices) will stop.

PREPARATION TECHNIQUES

It should be noted that the structures of the different types of poultry birds are very similar and therefore the various preparation techniques can be transferred between the different varieties.

Preparation of spatchcock and crapaudine

Spatchcock and crapaudine can be prepared from a single poussin, double poussin or a spring chicken. The cooking method used is grilling, which dictates the tenderness of the bird.

Spatchcock

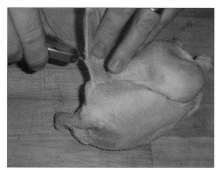

Pluck any remaining feathers

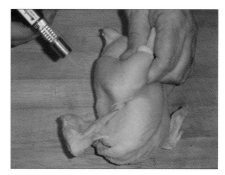

Singe using a flame

Remove the wishbone

Using a poultry scissors, cut either side of the backbone between the hip joints and the shoulder joints

Open the bird up and place in onto a board

Skewer across each end, between each wing and then between each drumstick

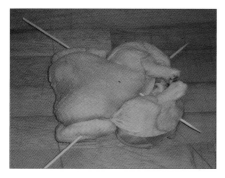

Alternatively, skewer diagonally across the bird

Crapaudine

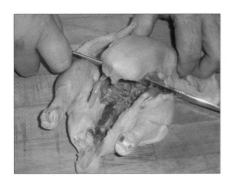

After plucking, singeing and removing the wishbone, cut under the breast but above the legs, almost to the neck of the bird

Pull open the bird and lay it onto a board

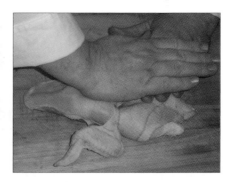

Press the bird onto the board

Force a skewer between each wing

Finally, force a skewer between each leg

VIDEO CLIP Removing the breast from guinea fowl

VIDEO CLIP Guinea fowl ballotine

VIDEO CLIP Removing legs from a guinea fowl

VIDEO CLIP Galentine of chicken

RECIPES

Spatchcock poussin Lyonnaise

INGREDIENTS	4 PORTIONS	10 PORTIONS
Poussin	4 × 300g	10 × 300g
Pommery grain mustard	150g	375g
Fresh breadcrumbs	400g	1kg
Unsalted butter	100g	250g
White chicken stock	100ml	250ml
Double cream	200ml	500ml
Tarragon	¼ bunch	½ bunch
Tomato concassé	50g	125g
Red onion	50g	125g
Good-quality salt and pepper	To taste	To taste

Method of work

1 Check that the poussin meets with quality standards. Spatchcock each poussin by splitting, flattening and securing with two skewers.

2 Season and **seal** in a hot pan.

3 Coat the poussin with half the mustard, leave for 30 minutes.

4 Melt the butter. Roll the poussin in breadcrumbs, sprinkle with the melted butter and grill until cooked.

5 Add the tarragon stalks to the stock and reduce by half. Add the double cream and remaining grain mustard then reduce by half again.

6 Pass through a chinois. Add chopped tarragon and correct the seasoning.

7 Mix the concassé with the finely chopped red onion, olive oil and seasoning and place on the chicken.

8 Serve sauce separately.

CHEF'S TIP

Care should be taken when grilling with breadcrumbs. Always ensure that the breadcrumbs are well soaked with butter to keep them moist. The majority of the butter will leave the breadcrumbs as they crisp up.

Royale of chicken purée

INGREDIENTS	4 PORTIONS	10 PORTIONS
White chicken meat	100g	250g
Béchamel sauce	50ml	125ml
Double cream	200ml	500ml
Egg yolks	6	15
White chicken stock	200ml	500ml
Tomato concassé	50g	125g
Chervil	¼ bunch	½ bunch
Tarragon	¼ bunch	½ bunch
Butter	50g	125g
Potato and parsley wafer	4	10
Good-quality salt and pepper	To taste	To taste

Method of work

1 Poach the white chicken meat then purée in a food processor.
2 Add the béchamel and half the double cream then pass through a drum sieve.
3 Bind with the yolks and season well. Place the mixture into buttered dariole moulds.
4 Place into a bain marie so the water comes half way up the sides of the dariole moulds and cook in the oven at 200°C for 15–20 minutes.
5 Reduce the chicken stock by half. Add the remainder of the cream and reduce by half again.
6 Pass the sauce and correct the seasoning. Add the tomato concassé, chopped tarragon and chervil.
7 Serve the royale on a heated plate with the sauce.
8 Arrange a potato and parsley wafer on top of the royale.

Chicken soufflé with thyme sauce

INGREDIENTS	4 PORTIONS	10 PORTIONS
Pot-roasted chicken	250g	625g
Thick chicken velouté	150ml	375ml
Egg yolks	3	8
Egg whites	3	8
Butter	100g	250g
Double cream	25ml	65ml
Light chicken jus	200ml	500ml
Chopped thyme	1tbsp	2½tbsp
Good-quality salt and pepper	To taste	To taste

Method of work

1 After pot roasting the chicken (with onion, carrot, celery, thyme and garlic with a splash of white wine at 180°C for 1 hour 15 minutes in a casserole with a tight-fitting lid), remove the chicken and strain the cooking liquor, which will be used to make the velouté.
2 Make a chicken velouté.
3 Remove the chicken skin and discard, remove all meat and place in a food processor until finely chopped.
4 Add the velouté and double cream, mixing well.
5 Add the yolks one by one and pass through a drum sieve using bowl scraper or wooden mushroom. Correct the seasoning.
6 Whisk the egg whites until stiff, then gently fold into the chicken mix.
7 Three-quarters fill buttered ramekins and bake in a hot oven, 200°C for 20 minutes.
8 Heat the chicken jus. Add the thyme and allow to infuse for 10-15 minutes. Remove the thyme.
9 Serve immediately with thyme chicken sauce.

Glazed duck breasts with sesame pak choy, crispy potato and enoki mushrooms

INGREDIENTS	4 PORTIONS	10 PORTIONS
Duck breasts	4 × 170g	10 × 170g
Honey	20ml	50ml
Soy sauce	4tbsp	10tbsp
Pak choy	400g	1kg
Sesame oil	2tbsp	5tbsp
Sesame seeds	1tbsp	3tbsp
Enoki mushrooms	100g	250g
Potatoes	400g	1kg
Good-quality salt and pepper	To taste	To taste

Method of work

1 Trim and score the duck breasts, sear skin-side down in a dry pan until coloured and the majority of fat has rendered down.

2 Pour away the fat, turn the duck over and drizzle with honey, place into a hot oven 180°C for 7 minutes, remove and rest.

3 Peel, grate and wash potatoes. Form into patties, season and deep fry until crisp.

4 Cut the pak choy into quarters and cook in sesame oil with the mushrooms, add the sesame seeds when nearly finished.

5 Arrange the pak choy and mushrooms on the plate and pour the liquid over.

6 Cut the duck in slices and lay on top, overlapping slightly.

7 Finish with crispy potatoes.

Stuffed chicken breast with sun-blushed tomatoes and olive mash

INGREDIENTS	4 PORTIONS	10 PORTIONS
Chicken suprêmes	4 × 170g	10 × 170g
Sun-blushed tomato	100g	250g
Parmesan	50g	125g
Mashed potato	400g	1kg
Black olives	3tbsp	7tbsp
Assorted peppers	½ of each	1 of each
Button onions	12	40
Baby asparagus	8	20
Baby fennel	4	10
Olive oil and tomato reduction	6tbsp	15tbsp
Good-quality salt and pepper	To taste	To taste

Method of work

1 Chop the sun-blushed tomatoes and mix with a little grated Parmesan then place the mixture under the skin of the chicken suprêmes.

2 Season the chicken and wrap in cling film to form cylindrical shapes then chill.

3 Warm the mashed potato and add chopped black olives and the remaining Parmesan.

4 Cut the peppers into diamonds and blanch, blanch the asparagus and cut into lozenges, peel and roast the button onions, trim the fennel and blanch.

5 Make a reduction by boiling a few sun-blushed tomatoes per person in olive oil until very soft then liquidise.

6 Cook the chicken in a saucepan of water for approximately 10 minutes. Remove from the cling film and fry in butter until golden.

7 Pipe the mashed potato onto the plate. Slice the stuffed chicken and arrange overlapping. Finish with the vegetables tossed in hot butter and the reduction.

Suprême of duck en croute with spinach

INGREDIENTS	4 PORTIONS	10 PORTIONS
Duck breasts	4 × 170g	10 × 170g
Puff pastry (10cm × 10cm)	5 sheets	13 sheets
Butter	100g	250g
Baby spinach	200g	500g
Fresh cranberries	50g	125g
Duck jus	200ml	500ml
Caster sugar	10g	25g
Red wine	50ml	125ml
Oranges	1	3
Eggs	1	3
Good-quality salt and pepper	To taste	To taste

Method of work

1 Trim the duck breasts and remove the fat, then seal in a hot pan all over. Chill and season.

2 Take three-quarters of the rolled out puff pastry and wrap thinly around the duck. Brush with beaten egg.

3 With the remainder of the puff pastry, form a trellis and wrap around the outside, brush again with beaten egg.

4 Chill for 30 minutes.

5 Bake the duck at 170°C for 25 minutes. Remove from the oven and rest for 5 minutes.

6 Heat the cranberries and add the zest of the oranges then add the sugar. Deglaze with red wine and orange juice, reduce then add the jus.

7 Wilt the spinach in butter and season.

8 Place the spinach on the plate, duck on top and cranberry jus around.

Confit of duck leg with baby aubergine and balsamic jus

INGREDIENTS	4 PORTIONS	10 PORTIONS
Duck legs	4	10
Sea salt	100g	250g
Cinnamon sticks	1	2
Oranges	1	2
Garlic	20g	50g
Duck fat	500g	1.25kg
Baby aubergines	8	20
Duck jus	200ml	500ml
Balsamic vinegar	1tbsp	2½tbsp
Puy lentils	100g	250g
Carrots	50g	125g
Celeriac	50g	125g
Onion	50g	125g
Butter	50g	125g
Vegetable stock	200ml	500ml
Good-quality salt and pepper	To taste	To taste

Method of work

1 Remove the thighbone from the duck legs and score the skin. Singe or pluck any remaining feathers and chop off the knuckle. Marinate for 24 hours in salt, crushed cinnamon sticks, chopped garlic and orange zest and juice.

2 Wash duck legs and place in duck fat heat in a pan then cover and place in the oven 150°C for 2–3 hours until very tender. Remove from the fat and drain over a wire rack.

3 Soak the Puy lentils for 1 hour in water. Cut the the carrot, onion and celeriac into brunoise and sweat in butter. Add the drained lentils, cover with vegetable stock and simmer until cooked, then season to taste.

4 Halve and char grill the aubergines then season.

5 Quickly boil the vinegar to reduce, and add to the jus.

6 Arrange the Puy lentils and aubergines on the plate and top with the duck. Spoon the sauce over the duck.

Breast of duck, duck faggot and confit with jasmine sauce

INGREDIENTS	4 PORTIONS	10 PORTIONS
Butter	50g	125g
Small ducklings (1kg)	2	5
Clear honey	2tbsp	5tbsp
Finely diced onion	100g	250g
Veal jus	125ml	300ml
Garlic, finely chopped	1 clove	2 cloves
Pearl barley	20g	50g
Fresh thyme	1 sprig	3 sprigs
Fresh parsley	1 small bunch	2 small bunches
Bay leaf	1	2
Duck livers	2	5
Duck hearts	2	5
Pig's caul	4 good pieces	10 good pieces
Veal stock	1000ml	2500ml
Finely diced carrots	50g	125g
Chopped shallots	50g	125g
Diced leeks	50g	125g
Red wine	100ml	250ml
Lime juice	¼ lime	½ lime
Blanched pistachio nuts	40g	100g
Sultanas marinated in jasmine tea	40g	100g
Sea salt and black pepper	To taste	To taste
Fondant potatoes	4	10
Red onion marmalade	40g	100g
Savoy cabbage parcels	4	10

 CHEF'S TIP

Add a little chicken forcemeat to the farce to bind it and make carving easier.

Method of work

1 Cook the pearl barley by bringing to the boil in salted water and cooking for 1 hour. Refresh immediately. Sweat the onions and garlic in some vegetable oil. Add the veal jus to cover the onions and garlic. Allow to reduce. Remove from the heat and allow to cool.

2 Mince the livers, hearts and thigh meat from the duck legs. Add to the reduction and incorporate the chopped fresh herbs. Season well. Fold in the cooked pearl barley. Wrap in pig's caul, creating one faggot per portion. Allow the faggots to rest in a refrigerator for at least 30 minutes before cooking. Colour the faggots in fat taken from the duck and then braise in the veal stock until just cooked.

3 Prepare the remaining legs into small ballotines. Stuff the legs with the pistachio nuts and sultanas that have been marinated in jasmine tea for 12 hours. Tie with string to keep the stuffing inside. These can now be braised and reserved in a warm place for service.

4 Remove the duck breasts from the carcasses and score the skin.

5 Fry the vegetables and the broken down duck carcasses. Drain off any excess fat. Place in a pan and cover with cold water. Add thyme, bay leaf and parsley stalks. Allow to simmer for 2 hours, strain, and bring back to the boil. Incorporate the braised faggot cooking liquor. Add the red wine.

6 Add the lime juice and bring back to boil. Adjust the consistency and the seasoning.

7 Season the duck breasts and fry with the skin side down until rendered and coloured. Brush warmed honey on the skin side and turn over to finish, cooking until golden brown and the breasts are still pink. Leave to rest in a warm place.

8 Carve each rested duck breast into thin slices and allow any juices to drain. Arrange on a plate with the red onion marmalade. Place the faggot on top of a cabbage parcel.

9 Take the ballotines and arrange on top of the fondant potato, check the seasoning and consistency of the sauce before serving.

Breast of duck with redcurrants and armagnac

INGREDIENTS	4 PORTIONS	10 PORTIONS
Butter	50g	120g
Duck breasts	4 × 200g	10 × 200g
Port wine	200ml	425ml
Redcurrant jelly	1tbsp	3tbsp
Fresh redcurrants	50g	125g
Jus lie	200ml	425ml
Lemon juice	A few drops	A few drops
Armagnac	2tbsp	5tbsp
Cocotte potatoes	12	30
Savoy cabbage parcel	4	10
Good-quality salt and pepper	To taste	To taste

Method of work

1 Heat the butter in a sauté pan. Season the duck breast well. Seal and colour the duck breasts on both sides in the hot butter and place into a hot oven, occasionally basting each breast with the fat. Cook for 8–9 minutes so that the breasts are cooked 'pink'. Remove from the oven, keep covered and warm and allow to rest.

2 Drain the fat from the pan. Add the port wine and reduce by three-quarters.

3 Add the redcurrant jelly and allow to melt. Add the Jus lie and bring slowly to the boil.

4 Adjust the consistency and seasoning and finish with lemon juice.

5 At the last moment add the redcurrants. Cover the sauce and keep warm for service.

6 Carve each duck breast into thin slices and allow any residual juices to drain. Arrange on a plate, overlapping slightly.

7 Add the Armagnac to the sauce, check the seasoning and consistency and spoon some over the duck. Serve with the cocotte potatoes and cabbage parcels.

Duckling with sherry vinegar sauce

INGREDIENTS	4 PORTIONS	10 PORTIONS
Ducklings	2	5
Vegetable oil	20ml	50ml
Chopped carrots	50g	100g
Chopped onions	50g	100g
Tomato concassé	40g	80g
Chopped celery	25g	50g
Garlic	2 cloves	4 cloves
Coriander seeds	½tsp	1tsp
Peppercorns (coarsely crushed)	½tsp	1tsp
Bouquet garni	1	1
Sherry vinegar	25 ml	50ml
Dry white wine	15ml	25ml
Chicken stock	1.25 litres	2.5 litres
Tomato purée	¼tsp	½tsp
Sea salt	1tsp	2tsp
Dijon mustard	½tsp	1tsp
Butter	40g	80g
Good-quality salt and pepper	To taste	To taste

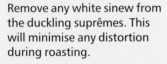 CHEF'S TIP

Remove any white sinew from the duckling suprêmes. This will minimise any distortion during roasting.

Method of work

1 Check the ducklings for quality. Remove the suprêmes and legs and keep refrigerated before use. Reserve the legs for later use. Chop the carcasses.

2 Heat the vegetable oil in a large casserole. Add the duck carcasses, wings and necks and brown over a moderate heat, stirring frequently. Cook for approximately 15 minutes. Lift the pieces of duck out of the casserole and remove all excess fat.

3 Place the pieces of duck back into the casserole with the carrot, onion, celery, tomato, garlic, coriander seeds, peppercorns and bouquet garni. Cook over a moderate heat for 3–4 minutes to soften the vegetables. Add the vinegar and wine and reduce.

4 Add the stock, tomato purée and salt. Bring to the boil and simmer for 35 minutes or until the stock has reduced by half.

5 Strain the stock into a bowl and reserve to one side. Skim off any fat that has risen to the top after 10 minutes. Whisk in the mustard and reserve for finishing.

6 Preheat an oven to 220°C. Season the suprêmes with salt and pepper. Place in a small roasting tin without any fat or oil and roast for 10 minutes.

7 Turn the suprêmes over and return to the oven and cook for 10 minutes further. Rest in a warm place for approximately 5 minutes.

8 Heat the reserved stock until warm and then whisk in the softened butter little by little to finish the sauce. Cover the sauce and keep warm for service.

9 Cut the suprêmes into thin slices. Dress each plate with the cooked duck and lightly dress with the prepared sauce. Serve the rest of the sauce separately.

Guinea fowl breast with mustard cream, pancetta and oyster mushrooms

INGREDIENTS	4 PORTIONS	10 PORTIONS
Guinea fowl suprêmes	4 × 170g	10 × 170g
White chicken stock	200ml	500ml
Double cream	200ml	500ml
English mustard	40g	100g
Mashed potato	300g	750g
Onions	200g	500g
Oyster mushrooms	100g	250g
Pancetta	40g	100g
Creamed horseradish	1tbsp	2tbsp
Butter	50g	125g
Olive oil	20ml	50ml
Flat leaf parsley	4 leaves	10 leaves
Good-quality salt and pepper	To taste	To taste

Method of work

1 Cut the pancetta into lardons. Season the suprêmes and pan fry with the pancetta. Place in the oven 180°C for 10–12 minutes.

2 Add the chicken stock and reduce by half. Add the double cream and reduce again by half, add the horseradish and mustard. Correct the seasoning, consistency and pass.

3 Remove from the oven and set the guinea fowl and lardons to one side to rest.

4 Sauté the oyster mushrooms in butter.

5 Finely dice the onions and sweat in olive oil until transparent. Mix with the mashed potato and, using a little flour, form small cakes. Shallow fry until golden.

6 Arrange a potato cake on the plate. Slice the guinea fowl and lay on top. Spoon sauce around and finish with lardons, mushrooms and flat leaf parsley.

 CHEF'S TIP

Vary the type of mushrooms used, e.g. chanterelle, shitake, cep or morel. The delicacy of guinea fowl is enhanced by wild mushrooms.

Roast goose with semolina dumplings

INGREDIENTS	4 PORTIONS	10 PORTIONS
Young oven-ready goose	1 × 2.5kg	3 × 2.5kg
Medium-sized dessert apple	1	3
Onion	1	3
Fresh tarragon	1 sprig	3 sprigs
Water	250ml	750ml
Brown chicken stock	400ml	1200ml
Butter	150g	450g
Eggs	4	12
Semolina	250g	750g
White bread	200g	600g
Soured cream	125ml	375ml
King Edward potatoes	450g	1350g
Sea salt	To taste	To taste
Freshly ground nutmeg	To taste	To taste
Dessert apples	4	12
Butter	40g	120g
Cranberries	2tbsp	6tbsp
Caster sugar	3tbsp	9tbsp
Lemon juice	½ lemon	1 lemon
White wine	2tbsp	6tbsp
Good-quality salt and pepper	To taste	To taste

Method of work

1   Rinse the goose, pat dry, cut off the fat by the vent and season inside with salt. Peel, halve and core the apple, stuff into the goose together with the whole onion and tarragon sprigs. Pour the water into a large roasting pan. Bring to the boil on top of the stove, then lower in the goose.

2   Roast for approximately 1½–2 hours in a preheated oven at 220°C. Baste frequently with the cooking juices. After an hour, remove the stuffing from the goose and place in the roasting pan. Return to the oven.

3   Beat the butter until light and creamy in texture. Add the eggs a little at a time, beating well between each addition. Then add the semolina. Leave the egg and semolina mixture to stand for 1 hour in a refrigerator.

4   Steep the diced bread in the soured cream to soften. Steam the potatoes until quite soft then peel, chop coarsely and lay out on a baking sheet. Place into the oven and lower the temperature to 200°C and dry out the potatoes for approximately 5 minutes. Push through a coarse sieve and season with salt and nutmeg, mixing thoroughly. Work this potato into the semolina dough.

5   Remove the goose from the roasting pan and keep warm. Add the stock to the pan, bring to the boil and pass through a fine sieve lined with muslin cloth. Skim off any excess fat and adjust the seasoning and consistency of the jus.

6   Form the dough into small dumplings and drop gently into boiling salted water. Cook for approximately 15 minutes.

7   Core the remaining apples and place in a buttered, ovenproof dish. Fill the cavities with the cranberries and sprinkle with sugar, dotting the remaining butter on top. Bake in an oven at the highest heat for 15–20 minutes. Add the lemon juice and wine and cook for a further 5 minutes until the juice has reduced.

8   Carve the goose into thin slices and allow any residual juices to drain. Arrange on a plate. Check the seasoning and consistency of the sauce and spoon some over the goose. Serve with two semolina dumplings per portion and one baked apple. Serve the rest of the sauce separately.

Seared chicken livers with a Madeira jus, saffron risotto and Parmesan crisp

INGREDIENTS	4 PORTIONS	10 PORTIONS
Chicken livers	12	30
Madeira	35ml	70ml
Brown chicken jus	50ml	145ml
Finely diced onion	40g	100g
Chopped flat leaf parsley	4tbsp	10tbsp
Butter	100g	250g
Arborio rice	100g	250g
Saffron white chicken stock	400ml	1 litre
Grated Parmesan cheese	100g	250g
Fresh chervil	¼ bunch	1 bunch
Good-quality salt and pepper	To taste	To taste

Method of work

1. Take half the Parmesan cheese and place onto a non-stick mat or silicone paper in a long rectangular shape, approximately 5cm wide by 20cm long.
2. Bake in the oven at 180°C until bubbling and very slightly golden.
3. Remove from the oven and trim back into shape with a knife (keep on the hot tray).
4. Wrap the cheese around a circular mould and press the two ends together to form a circle.
5. Allow to cool and set hard.
6. Sweat the onions in a little butter and oil, then add the rice and cook for a further 2 minutes. Add the hot stock and continue to cook the risotto until al dente. Finish with butter, Parmesan and flat leaf parsley.
7. Quickly fry the chicken livers in a hot pan until pink, then deglaze with Madeira and add the brown chicken jus.
8. Place the crisp in a bowl and fill with risotto, top with the livers and drizzle the sauce around, garnish with chervil.

Suprême of turkey wrapped in bacon with turkey ballotine

INGREDIENTS	4 PORTIONS	10 PORTIONS
Turkey suprême	1 × 600g	1 × 1.5kg
Streaky bacon	10 rashers	20 rashers
Turkey leg	1 small	1 large
Cumberland sausage meat	200g	500g
Dried cranberries	50g	125g
Fresh cranberries	80g	200g
Sugar	As required	As required
Turkey jus	120ml	300ml
Good-quality salt and pepper	To taste	To taste

Method of work

1 Lay the bacon **rashers** onto cling film. Season the turkey suprême with pepper and roll tightly.

2 Remove all bone, skin and sinew from the turkey leg. Mix the dried cranberries with the sausage meat and spread on top.

3 Roll the leg and tie at 2cm intervals. Wrap in cling film and then in foil.

4 Steam or poach the suprême for 40 minutes, remove to a roasting pan and remove the cling film. Roast for a further 40 minutes or until a core temperature of 70°C has been reached for 5 minutes.

5 Place the ballotine in an oven and bake for 1 hour.

6 Place the fresh cranberries in a pan with the sugar and heat for 2–3 minutes until the cranberries start to release their juices.

7 Add the jus and bring to the boil, simmer for 2–3 minutes.

8 Carve the suprême and ballotine and serve with seasonal potatoes and vegetables.

Medallions of turkey en papillote with lemon, sage and onion

INGREDIENTS	4 PORTIONS	10 PORTIONS
Turkey medallions	8 × 75g	20 × 75g
Lemon	1	3
Sage	¼ bunch	½ bunch
Onion (finely chopped)	1 medium	2½ medium
Butter	100g	250g
White wine	8tbsp	20tbsp
Fondant potatoes	4	10
Green beans tied with chive	4 bundles	10 bundles
Sea salt and white pepper	To taste	To taste

Method of work

1 Sauté the onion in a little oil until light golden brown.

2 Lay out a square of tin foil 15cm × 15cm, then place a piece of silicone paper on top.

3 Brush a little melted butter onto the paper and arrange the lightly browned onion, chopped sage (reserve a few sprigs) and thinly sliced lemon on top.

4 Bar mark the turkey medallions on one side to form a quadrillage effect.

5 Arrange the turkey on top of the mixture and drizzle with white wine, sea salt and ground white pepper.

6 Fold the paper and foil over the turkey, crimping the edges to form an airtight pouch. Leave to marinate for 30 minutes.

7 Place the pouch in a hot oven, 180°C for 10 minutes.

8 Arrange a fondant potato, a green bean bundle and a pouch on the plate.

9 Just before serving, cut the pouch open to expose the turkey.

10 Garnish with deep fried sage leaves.

Assessment of knowledge and understanding

You have now learned about the use of different types of poultry and how to prepare and cook a variety of poultry dishes using different commodities and preparation techniques.

To test your level of knowledge and understanding, answer the following short questions. These will help to prepare you for your summative (final) assessment.

Quality identifications

1 List three types of chicken.

i) _____ ii) _____

iii) _____

2 List three quality points you should look for when receiving poultry.

i) _____ ii) _____

iii) _____

3 Explain why free range and organic methods of rearing are so important when considering the quality of poultry.

_____

_____

Materials and storage

1 Explain why a heavy-bottomed sauté pan should be used when making sauté chicken dishes that have the sauce finished in the same pan.

_____

_____

Preparation

1 Explain the term 'sauté' in relation to cooking chicken.

_____

2 Explain the difference between white and dark meat in poultry.

_____

3 Describe the method of preparation for spatchcock.

_____

Cooking

1 Explain the reason for resting poultry prior to carving.

_____

Health and safety

1 State two healthy options when finishing poultry dishes.

i) _____

ii) _____

CHEF'S PROFILE

Name: **MARK ASKEW**

Position: Executive Chef

Establishment: Gordon Ramsay Holdings

Current job role and main responsibilities:
I liaise with all chefs and department heads to oversee current operations in all the kitchens within the group. I am also involved in ongoing and future restaurant openings and consultancy projects.

When did you realise that you wanted to pursue a career in the catering and hospitality industry?
I decided to pursue this career whilst working part-time when at school.

Training:
Craven College, Skipton, Yorkshire. I trained for two years to gain the 1961/2 City and Guilds.

Experience:
1   Savoy Grill
2   Pierre Koffman at Tante Claire
3   Michel Bourdin at the Connaught
4   Nico Ladenis at Nico's
5   Aubergine
6   Maison de Bricount
7   Gordon Ramsay Restaurant

What do you find rewarding about your job?
The sense of achievement, as well as helping to maintain the pride and passion of the group.

What do you find the most challenging about the job?
Providing consistency in the delivery of our product and standard of service.

What advice would you give to students just beginning their career?
To be 100 per cent committed; ambitious, enthusiastic and passionate.

Who is your mentor or main inspiration?
Gordon – we share the same ideals.

What traits do you consider essential for anyone entering a career as a chef?
Dedication, enthusiasm and passion.

Can you give one essential kitchen tip that you use as a chef?
To learn from others' mistakes, along with their achievements. Also, keep your eyes open!

Ballotine of English free-range chicken with foie gras and truffle

INGREDIENTS	4 PORTIONS
Chicken breast suprêmes (with skin on)	4 x 150g
Foie gras	100g
Sea salt and freshly ground black pepper	To taste
Double cream	50g
Black truffle (preferably from Perigold, finely diced)	20g
Knobs of butter	A few
Chicken jus	
Chicken bones	1kg
Oil	2tbsp
Carrot (chopped)	1
Leek (chopped)	1
Celery sticks (chopped)	2
Thyme	A few sprigs
Bay leaf	1
Garlic cloves (peeled)	3
Tomato purée	2 tbsp
Sea salt and freshly ground black pepper	To taste

Method of work

1 First, prepare the chicken jus. Preheat an oven to 200°C. Place the chicken bones on a roasting tray and roast for 20 minutes until browned. Heat the oil in a large stockpot and add the chopped vegetables. Stir over high heat for a few minutes until nicely browned. Add the herbs, garlic and tomato purée. Stir for another couple of minutes before adding the browned chicken bones. Cover with cold water, bring to the boil and skim off the froth and scum. Reduce the heat and simmer for 3 hours then pass through a chinois.

2 Boil the chicken stock in a clean, wide pan until reduced to the desired flavour and consistency. Season with salt and pepper.

3 Trim the chicken breast and leave the skin on. Remove the false fillets and purée them to a fine paste. Push the purée through a fine mesh (or drum) sieve to remove any sinew or large pieces. Chill the paste for an hour, then slowly incorporate the cream and return to the refrigerator.

4 Chop the foie gras into 1cm cubes. Heat a pan until hot, season the foie gras and lightly sauté until it is golden brown. Drain off the excess fat and transfer the foie gras to a plate and allow to cool completely. Chill the foie gras for at least 20 minutes then mix with the chicken purée along with the diced truffle. Season well. Spoon the mixture into a piping bag fitted with a large plain nozzle and chill again until ready to use.

5 Cut a 4cm-deep slit along the thicker side of the chicken breasts. Pipe the chicken purée into the slit, fold in the flaps and carefully stretch the skin of the chicken breasts to cover the purée. Wrap each stuffed breast tightly with cling film and secure both ends to achieve a neat cylindrical shape, about 12cm long. Chill for at least 1 hour.

6 When ready to serve, poach the chicken ballotine in boiling water for 6–7 minutes. The chicken should only be partially cooked but hold its shape. Remove from the pan, discard the cling film and pan fry with a few knobs of butter for 3–4 minutes each side until the skin is golden brown and the chicken is cooked through. Rest for a few minutes while you reheat the chicken jus for serving.

Serving suggestion

One of the most popular ways we have served this dish in the past is to arrange the diagonally cut chicken ballotine on buttered cabbage then surround it with braised baby carrots, onions, sautéed morels and light chicken jus.

13
Game

FP5 Prepare and cook game for complex dishes

LEARNING OBJECTIVES

The aim of this chapter is to enable you to develop skills and implement knowledge in the preparation and cookery principles of complex game dishes. This will also include materials, ingredients and equipment.

At the end of this chapter you will be able to:

- Identify each variety of both feathered and furred game and their finished dish
- Understand the use of relative ingredients in game preparation and cookery
- State the quality points of various game items and dishes
- Prepare and cook each type of game variety
- Identify the storage procedures of all types of game, both raw and cooked
- Be competent at preparing and cooking a range of basic game-based dishes

INTRODUCTION

The term 'game' encompasses all wild birds and animals that are hunted for sport and human consumption. Hunting is an age-old and worldwide tradition and is still a prominent part of life in many countries.

With domestic meat and poultry being comparatively predictable in flavour, this is where game comes into its own. The different grazing and eating habits of various types of game result in subtly different flavours, which can vary from region to region – such as wild rabbit from Provence in France where the diet consists chiefly of rosemary and thyme. The varying eating habits of game therefore create individual and delicately flavoured meats, before a chef adds further ingredients to a dish.

Game is a versatile product to prepare and to cook with as it is extremely flavoursome and of good texture in its natural cooked state. Is also very lean and low in cholesterol, which instantly makes it a healthier meat option.

There are two main classes of game:

- Feathered game – any wild bird
- Furred game – any wild ground animal

Furred game is also split into two sub-categories

- Small furred game
- Large furred game.

Game is seasonal, and the quality and flavour of meat is much better when the bird or animal is in season and at its prime. The only exceptions to this are rabbit and hare, which due to their breeding habits are readily available all year round.

QUALITY POINTS AND TYPES OF GAME

Feathered game

Wood pigeon   Inhabits woods, fields and gardens, feeding on grain crops and a variety of vegetable shoots. It is now viewed more as a common pest. Available all year round, although it is considered to be at its best from April to October.

 CHEF'S TIP

Research all local sources of game fully and compare their prices before buying to ensure you have the best possible produce at the keenest price.

 CHEF'S TIP

Specialist game suppliers will be able to provide the more unusual meats, such as those fed particular diets to achieve particular flavours.

 CHEF'S TIP

Due to its leanness, when cooking game ensure that you compensate for the lack of natural fats to prevent the meat from drying out.

 **VIDEO CLIP**
The UK Game Company

WOOD PIGEON PURCHASE CHART

Wood pigeon

Feet	Red to orange in colour, medium in length, scaled effect
Feathers	Both: Grey in colour with a white belly but can also be brown and cream in colour
Wings	Both: Large wings the same colour as the body with dark flecks to tips of wings
Beak	Both: Short and orange or grey in colour
Size/weight	Both: 600g Medium-sized birds
Cuts	2 legs, 2 wings, 2 breasts
Best used for:	Roasting (whole or crown), sautéing, grilling, braising/stewing, poaching, pot roasting

Pheasant   Inhabits woodland, hedgerows and open farmland, feeding on various types of vegetation and insects. It can be farm reared and then released into the wild. Considered to be at its best from October to early February.

PHEASANT PURCHASE CHART

Hen (top) and cock pheasants

Feet	Long, thick legs with chicken-like spurs on cocks, grey in colour
Feathers	Cocks: Rich chestnut or golden-brown with long tail, green head and red wattling on face Hens: Mottled pale brown and black
Wings	Both: Large and rounded Cocks: Same colour as body with some light blue depending on sub-species Hens: Same colour as body
Beak	Both: Large and pointed, off-white in colour
Size/weight	Cocks: 1.5kg Hens: 1.2kg Large birds
Cuts	2 legs, 2 wings, 2 breasts
Best used for:	Roasting (whole or crown), confit, braising/stewing, grilling sautéing, pot roasting

Woodcock Inhabits marshy inland areas and woodland areas. It is inclined to be nocturnal and feeds on surface insects and earthworms. Considered to be at its best in November and December.

WOODCOCK PURCHASE CHART

Feet	Short thin legs, yellow in colour
Feathers	Both: Mottled brown with flecks of black and beige, tiger stripe effect to the back of the head
Wings	Both: Same colour as body, short in size and slightly rounded in shape
Beak	Both: Medium pointed, off-white in colour
Size/weight	Cocks: 400g Hens: 325g Small birds
Cuts	Tends to be cooked whole due to small size but can get 2 legs, 2 wings, 2 breasts
Best used for:	Roasting (whole only due to small size), pot roasting, spatchcock, grilling, braising/stewing

Woodcock

Snipe Like woodcock, snipe inhabits marshy inland areas, but is not found in woodland areas. It feeds on small invertebrates, worms and inset larvae. Considered to be at its best in December and January.

SNIPE PURCHASE CHART

Feet	Very thin long legs, long toes, dark grey in colour
Feathers	Both: Dull brown and cream striped head, body speckled all over
Wings	Both: Same in colour as body, small and slightly pointed
Beak	Both: Long (only game bird other than woodcock that can be trussed using its own beak), creamy brown in colour
Size/weight	Cock: 125g Hen: 100g Very small birds
Cuts	Tends to be cooked whole due to small size but can get 2 legs, 2 wings, 2 breasts
Best used for:	Roasting (whole only due to small size), pot roasting, spatchcock, grilling, braising/stewing

Snipe

Teal drake

Teal Inhabits coastal and marshy areas, feeding on seeds and small invertebrates. Considered to be at its best in October and November.

TEAL PURCHASE SHEET

Feet	Webbed feet, the same as for mallard or other duck varieties
Feathers	Cocks: Head tends to be red and green in colour, body is grey/silver with an off-white tail Hens: Brown and grey
Wings	Cocks: Same as body generally, some light green flecks depending on sub-species Hens: Same as body Both: Large wings
Beak	Both: Short and pointed, off-white to grey in colour
Size/weight	Cocks: 500g Hens: 400g Large birds
Cuts	2 legs, 2 wings, 2 breasts
Best used for:	Roasting (whole or crown), confit, braising/stewing, grilling, sautéing, poaching

Grey-legged (top) and red-legged partridges

Red-legged partridge Inhabits dry, open countryside, feeding on crops and vegetable matter. Considered to be at its best in October and November.

RED-LEGGED PARTRIDGE PURCHASE CHART

Feet	Short and thin red legs with very small spurs on cocks
Feathers	Both: Grey with white throats, black, brown and grey flecks to body
Wings	Both: Grey in colour, small and rounded
Beak	Both: Small and pointed, red in colour
Size/weight	Cocks: 500g Hens: 400g Small birds
Cuts	2 legs, 2 wings, 2 breasts
Best used for:	Roasting (whole or crown), sautéing, grilling, braising/stewing, poaching, pot roasting

Grey-legged partridge   Similar to the red-legged partridge, it inhabits dry, open countryside and also feeds on crops and vegetable matter. Considered to be at its best in October and November.

GREY-LEGGED PARTRIDGE PURCHASE CHART

Feet	Short and thin legs, grey in colour
Feathers	Both: Orange/red head, red/brown heart shape to the middle of a grey breast
Wings	Both: Red/brown in colour with a mottled effect, small rounded wings
Beak	Both: Short, grey in colour
Size/weight	Cocks: 400g Hens: 350g Small birds
Cuts	2 legs, 2 wings, 2 breasts
Best used for:	Roasting (whole or crown), sautéing, grilling, braising/stewing, poaching, pot roasting

Squab   Squab is a young domesticated pigeon and therefore tends to inhabit built up areas. It is usually slaughtered when four weeks old and as its wings have not fully developed it is very tender. It will be fed regurgitated insects and domesticated food by its parent. Domesticated pigeon is considered a pest. It is available all year round, but is considered to be at its best during the summer months.

Squab pigeon

SQUAB PURCHASE CHART

Feet	Medium length and of scaled effect, red/orange in colour
Feathers	Both: Grey with white belly but can also be brown and cream
Wings	Both: Same as body in colour with dark flecks to tips, large
Beak	Short, orange or grey in colour
Size/weight	Both: 600g Medium-sized birds
Cuts	2 legs, 2 wings, 2 breasts
Best used for:	Roasting (whole or crown), sautéing, grilling, braising/stewing, poaching, pot roasting

Quail in feather

Quail Inhabits open grassland and cereal fields, feeding on grain crops and insects. Available and at its best all year round.

QUAIL PURCHASE CHART

Feet	Short and thin, grey in colour
Feathers	Both: Mottled brown in colour, grey/off-white underneath
Wings	Both: Same as body in colour, small and rounded, short in wingspan so do not fly
Beak	Both: Short and stumpy, grey in colour
Size/weight	Cocks: 170g Hens: 150g Very small birds
Cuts	2 legs, 2 wings, 2 breasts
Best used for:	Roasting (whole or crown), sautéing, grilling, braising/stewing, poaching, pot roasting, confit

Red grouse Inhabits moorland and is largely dependent for feeding on wild heather but will eat insects during the summer months. Red grouse is considered to be at its best from August to October.

RED GROUSE PURCHASE CHART

Feet	Short and thick legs, covered in feathers
Feathers	Cocks: Reddish brown, two scarlet combs above eyes Hens: Duller in colour with no combs above eyes
Wings	Both: Wings same as body in colour, large and rounded, very powerful
Beak	Boths: Small and pointed, black in colour
Size/weight	Cocks: 750g Hens: 650g Medium-sized birds
Cuts	2 legs, 2 wings, 2 breasts
Best used for:	Roasting (whole or crown), sautéing, grilling, braising/stewing, poaching, pot roasting

It is not easy to determine the age of any wild animal, but there are three main indicators that can give a good indication of an approximate age:

- *Spurs* – with cock (male) birds, the spurs get longer as the birds become older
- *Beaks* – the younger a bird, the more pliable the beak will be
- *Feet* – in younger birds with webbed feet, the webbing will tear more easily

When preparing game birds to be hung or for cooking, the following points should be taken into consideration and the bird thoroughly checked:

- Tears or breaks to the skin and broken limbs
- Bruising or shot damage
- Skin should not be slimy to the touch, smell pungent or have darkened patches
- Prominent breast and shape
- Not too dark meat, which could mean excess blood in the meat due to not being properly hung or being bruised
- Size of the bird

Small furred game

Wild rabbit   Inhabits farmland and woodland, feeding off pasture land and crops. Regarded as a pest, it is available all year round, but it is considered to be at its best between September and November. Domesticated rabbit differs greatly in flavour and texture as it does not benefit from the same varied diet as wild rabbit, nor will it have the same amount of exercise and therefore it will use its muscle tissues less.

Wild rabbit

WILD RABBIT PURCHASE CHART

Appearance	Both: Grey/brown in colour, long ears, short front legs, grey and white tail
Meat	Rosy pink in colour, quite strong in flavour compared with 'hutch' rabbit, which is lighter in colour and has a flavour similar to poultry
Joints	2 legs, 1 saddle*, 2 shoulders, 1 ribcage, 1 liver
Size/weight	Both: 1.5kg
Best used for:	Stewing/braising, grilling, poaching, confit, roasting, pot roasting, sautéing

* Saddle is cut as one joint for roasting but can be cut into two separate joints for other dishes.

Brown hare

Brown hare Inhabits exposed grassland and more open woodland areas, feeding on pasture land and crops. Baby hares, known as leverets, are much more tender than the fully grown hare. Brown hare is considered to be at its best between October and January.

BROWN HARE PURCHASE CHART

Appearance	Both: Coat colour can vary depending on age, either being light ginger/grey or a deep reddish brown. Long black ears, very long hind legs and a black and white tail
Meat	Dark red in colour, very strong in flavour
Joints	2 legs, 1 saddle, 2 shoulders, 1 ribcage, 1 liver, blood
Size/weight	Both (adult): 3kg Both (leveret): 2kg
Best used for:	Braising/stewing, roasting, pot roasting, confit

The best indicators of the age of small furred game animals are:

■ Teeth – in young rabbits and hares the two front teeth will be quite white, clean and not protrude from the mouth

■ Feet – in both rabbits and hares, the longer the claws, the older the animal

■ Ears – the ears on young rabbits and hares will tear more easily

When preparing small furred game to be hung or for cooking, the following points should be taken into consideration and the animal thoroughly checked:

■ Excess blood on fur

■ Tears or breaks to the skin and broken limbs

■ Shot damage and bruising

■ Pale pink meat with no dark spots

■ Fresh smell and not be tacky to the touch

■ Size of the animal

Large furred game

Red deer Typically thrives on open moorland and eats grasses and tree bark. Considered to be at its best in July and August for stags and December to February for hinds.

Red deer

RED DEER PURCHASE CHART

Appearance	Both: Dark reddish brown to grey in colour
Meat	Rich red in colour, very strong, very little fat
Joints	2 haunches or legs, 2 flanks, 1 saddle, 1 best end, 2 shoulders, 1 neck, 2 small fillets
Size/weight	Stags: 90–190kg Hinds: 63–120kg Large deer
Best used for:	Sautéing, grilling, stewing/braising, grilling, roasting, pot roasting

Fallow deer Tends to be more prominent on open pasture land and again will feed off pasture land and tree bark. Considered to be at its best in October and November for bucks and from December to February for does.

FALLOW DEER PURCHASE CHART

Appearance	Both: Light to darker brown in colour with white spots in the summer months
Meat	Rich red in colour, strong, very little fat
Joints	2 haunches or legs, 2 flanks, 1 saddle, 1 best end, 2 shoulders, 1 neck, 2 small fillets
Size/weight	Bucks: 46–94kg Does: 35–56kg Medium deer
Best used for:	Sautéing, grilling, stewing/braising, grilling, roasting, pot roasting, confit

Fallow deer

Two important factors should be taken into consideration when considering the purchase of large furred game:

■ *Time of year* – bucks or stags (male deer) are at their best just before the breeding season commences. This is because they have built up fat reserves to give them strength at this particular time of year. The same applies for does or hinds (female deer) as food will have been rich at this time of year which will have allowed them to prepare for the winter. This small amount of fat adds to the quality and flavour of the meat.

■ *Antlers* – It is advisable to steer clear of 'trophy animals', such as large adult deer with large antlers (bucks or stags in most species), as these will be older animals, and even though they would have a high meat yield it will be tough and if taken at the wrong time of year can be tainted by a strong musk flavour.

When preparing large furred game to be hung or for cooking, the following points should be taken into consideration and the animal thoroughly checked:

■ Shot damage, which tends to be more prominent in large game

■ Deep-red coloured meat, strong in smell but not too pungent

■ Excess fat and/or marbling

HANGING OF GAME

It is usual to hang game once it has been killed. Before hanging, the meat is often quite mild in flavour and is unrefined in taste and texture. Older animals will also tend to be quite tough after cooking if they have not been hung.

Hanging game for a few days in a cool place allows enzymes within the carcass to initiate a chemical reaction. This changes the tenderness of the meat by allowing the muscle to relax and helps to define some flavour compounds.

Terms used in the hanging of game are:

■ *Hanging* – the hanging of a game carcass in order to improve the flavour and/or texture of meat

■ *De-furring/feathering* – the removal of fur or feathers from the carcass

■ *Drawing/gutting* – the removal of the internal organs of the carcass

■ *Bleeding* – the draining of blood from the carcass

Feathered game is hung to mature the flavour of the bird; the flavour will not be at its best if the bird is eaten straight after being killed. Birds to be hung should be bled but left feathered and undrawn. A bird can be hung for between one and seven days, the exact length of time being dependent on the weather conditions, type of bird and taste preference. The modern tastes of the general public seem to prefer a shorter hanging time so that the full gaminess of the flavour does not develop.

Pheasant and woodcock should be hung for five to seven days; snipe should be hung for up to five days; grouse achieves its best potential when hung for three to four days; while wild duck should be hung for only two to three days. Farmed quail does not benefit from being hung and should therefore be frozen or cooked immediately after being killed.

Furred game is hung not only to improve and develop its flavour but also to tenderise the meat. Hare and wild rabbit should be hung and bled, but not skinned or drawn until the hanging time is complete. Venison is usually bled and gutted but not skinned before being hung.

 CHEF'S TIP

Ensure that all factors are taken into consideration when deciding how long to hang game: you do not want to waste produce by under or over 'ripening'.

Wild rabbit and hare only needs to be hung for one day to mature the meat fully, while venison is usually at its best after five days of hanging. Domesticated rabbit, if used, does not benefit from being hung, and like farmed quail should be frozen or cooked immediately after being killed.

To be suitable for hanging game, a room must be:

- Cool and dry
- Well ventilated
- Inaccessible to insects, vermin or other wild animals

In hot weather the meat will need to be stored in a refrigerated room at between 0°C and 5°C.

A carcass should be hung so that the air can circulate freely all around it. Feathered game should be hung by the neck and furred game by the hind legs. With both types, it should be ensured that the carcases are hung separately and do not touch one another otherwise the meat will bruise and putrefy, rendering it inedible.

> **CHEF'S TIP**
>
> Older game can be further tenderised by marinating for 24 hours.

PREPARATION TECHNIQUES

Basic preparation of feathered game

All birds are plucked and drawn using the same method. It is a tiresome process but one that requires attention at all times, especially when drawing. If it is not done properly it will not provide good results, and it will become messy and take longer to do.

Plucking

1 Always pluck in a draught-free area and ensure that a bag or box is close to hand into which feathers and down can be placed. Feathers should only be plucked a few at a time. It is easiest to start by plucking the breast of the bird and work around it, followed by the wings.

2 Lay the bird on its back and start plucking from the base of the breast. To pull the feathers away, hold the skin taught at the base of the feathers and pull firmly in a downwards motion. Once the breast has been plucked, complete the sides, back and legs.

3 To remove the wing feathers, with the bird still on its back, extend the wing fully by pulling away from the carcass in order to spread the feathers as far as possible. Pluck out the feathers, remembering to only go as far as the wing tip joints as the wing tips will be cut off. Repeat the process to the back of the wings.

4 Finally, remove the neck and tail feathers.

Plucking a bird in feather

Continue to pluck the feathers, exposing the flesh

Drawing

Once a bird has been fully plucked, it will need to have its innards removed. The only exceptions to this are snipe and woodcock, which after having the gizzard removed can be cooked whole. In addition to being drawn, ducks should have the oil glands at the base of their tails removed as if left these can give the meat a musky flavour.

1 Lay the plucked bird on its back. Cut off the hind and front toes and the wing tips. Singe any downy feathers that may still be on the bird.

2 Cut off the bird's head from the top of the neck, then using a sharp knife slit through the skin at the back of the neck, down to the shoulders. Peel back the flap of skin (leaving it intact) and sever the neck where it joins the body.

3 Feel into the neck cavity for the windpipe, gullet and crop and gently pull free. To remove the intestines and innards, make an incision by pinching the skin at the base of the breastbone, cutting away from the bird so as to not pierce the intestines. Create an opening from left to right just large enough to insert a finger.

4 Put a finger inside the bird and gently loosen the membranes that attach the innards to the muscle. Carefully remove the innards from the bird, using your forefinger and thumb. They should come out in one whole piece. Ensure the bird is checked thoroughly and all innards are removed.

5 To remove the two oil glands from a duck, use a sharp knife to cut out the tail section of the bird that contains the glands.

6 To remove the gizzard, use a sharp knife to make a slit in the abdomen, slightly right of the centre. Insert a trussing needle to locate the hard lump of the gizzard. Pull out gizzard and sever it from the remaining innards.

Singeing excess feathers from the body

Singeing hair from the legs

Stretching the neck away from the body before cutting away

Removing the head, leaving a flap of skin

Removing the internal organs

Drawing the gizzard from within the bird

Removing the wishbone

The wishbone can be removed once a bird has been plucked and drawn. This should be carried out before any type of portioning, preparation or carving.

1 Expose the wishbone. It is attached to the wing bones at both sides of the bird, runs either side of the cavity left by the crop and meets at the tip of the breastbone.

2 Slip a sharp knife behind the bone and cut in a downwards motion to release at the wing. Repeat the other side.

1   When the wishbone has been fully detached from the wings, carefully twist it three to four times until it is released from the tip of the breastbone.

Cutting down either side of the wishbone

Releasing the wishbone

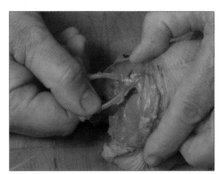

Removing the wishbone

Removing legs and breasts

Most game birds have very tough and sinewy legs, which if used in a dish will require a long cooking time to tenderise them. Their strong taste makes them ideal in stocks. The breast, however, can be cooked quickly and will only have one piece of sinew running along the inner fillet.

1 Pulling the leg away from the body, cut into the thigh muscle and around the oyster.

2 When removing the breast, cut along one side of the breastbone, starting at the neck and moving down to the vent. At the wing, cut through the second joint, leaving the bone on the breast. Repeat the process on the other side of the bird. The only bones in the cut breasts will be those from the wings.

3 Trim and remove any excess skin from the breasts. The bone and skin may be removed depending on how the breast is to be prepared.

4 The wing bones should be cleaned by scraping down the flesh and removing the ends.

Removing the wing at the second joint

Trussing whole birds for roasting

Cooking a game bird whole results in very even cooking and gives good moisture retention. It also creates a visually appealing and uniform dish. The wishbone should be removed before trussing.

1 Thread a trussing needle with butcher's twine.

2 Assuming the wing is intact, push the needle between the bones in the wing, just after the first joint from the tip, then through the fleshy part of the wing bone. Push the needle through the carcass, under the breast meat and out the other side, piercing the wing bone on the other side.

3 Pull the twine through, ensuring that enough extra line is left on the other side to tie-off.

4 Pull the legs back and place the needle under the bone at the first joint. Push the needle through the carcass and out the other side, making sure to hold the legs back. Pull the twine through and remove the needle.

5 Tie the twine in a butcher's slip knot, pull tight.

6 Tie a further knot to help hold the twine in place.

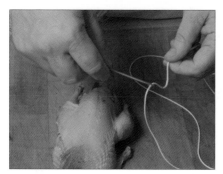

Threading the trussing needle

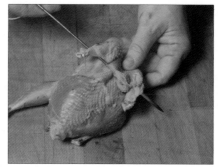

Pushing the trussing needle under the wing and through the back

Pulling the string through the bird

Pushing the needle through the thigh meat

Tying the string between the wing and the thigh

Tying a moveable knot on the side of the bird

Securing the bird in place

Splitting and flattening

This method is best used with small game birds that are to be grilled, barbecued or sautéed. Remove the wishbone before you start.

1   Using poultry scissors, split the bird lengthways by cutting down the backbone from the crop to the vent. Repeat to the other side and remove the backbone.

2   Turn the bird over. Use the palm of your hand to flatten the breast, pulling the legs around to either side of the breast.

3   Push a skewer under the leg bone at the first joint, go through the breast and out the other side. Repeat for the other leg. By doing this it will hold the legs and breast together and allow the bird to cook evenly.

VIDEO CLIP
Preparation of the breast of a small game bird for frying

Basic preparation of small furred game

After hanging, small furred game animals need to be skinned and drawn, with the same techniques generally applying to both rabbits and hares. The animals should be skinned before being drawn. Ensure a container is at hand to dispose of the fur and innards. During the hanging process, the blood will collect in the chest cavity and can be retained for use in certain dishes.

Skinning

1   Hang the animal by one hind leg so that the head and shoulder rest on the preparation table. Using a sharp knife, cut through the skin around the ankle joint.

2   From this incision cut lengthways down the inside of the leg and thigh to the base of the tail.

3   Grasping one paw, firmly but gently pull the skin away from the leg and thigh. Repeat the same process on the other leg.

VIDEO CLIP
Dissecting a hare

4   Slit the skin at the base of the tail, from the top of one hind leg to the other. Gently peel back the skin, turning it inside out and leaving the tail intact and attached to the body.

5   Slit the skin down the entire length of the belly, from the hind quarters, along the chest and to the neck.

6   Firmly hold the skin that has already been detached from the legs and gently pull the skin downwards until you reach the shoulders. (This should come away easily as the skin is only loosely attached to the animal.)

VIDEO CLIP
Preparation of a saddle of hare for roasting

7   Make a circular incision around the paw of the foreleg and up the inside of the leg to meet the cut at the shoulder. Repeat on the other side.

8   Using a chopping knife, remove all four feet.

9   Peel the remaining and full skin up the neck and over the head, cutting off the ears and leaving these as part of the skin. It is at this point the head can be removed if required, so as to create as little mess as possible.

Cutting around the ankle joint

Gently pulling the skin away from the leg

Pulling the skin down the entire body to chest and neck

Removing the feet

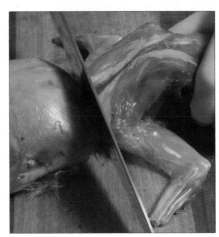

Removing the head

Drawing

Untie the animal and lay it on its back.

1 To remove the tail, lower intestine and anus, place a knife just under the tail bone at the base of the tail and cut upwards through the tail bone. Holding onto the tail, make a cut which will loosen the tail, lower intestine and anus away from the legs on either side. *Be careful not to cut into the lower intestine.*

2 Once the lower intestine has been loosened, pull carefully on the tail and the whole of what is left of the lower intestine and anus will come away easily.

3 Carefully pierce the diaphragm at the base of the chest and drain the blood. Slit along and through the ribcage then remove the remaining innards.

Removing the tail, lower intestines and anus

The liver of small furred game is edible and so you may wish to retain this for use, but do not forget to remove the gall bladder.

Jointing

1 Feel for the pelvic bone and make a cut around it, leaving the pelvis attached to the saddle.

2 After cutting around the top side of the rear leg, turn the carcase over and cut at the same angle on the inside of the leg. Once the meat has been cut away, pop the ball and socket joint to release the leg. When cutting around the hip bone, stay as close to the bone as possible. You will end up with a 'V' shape at the bottom of the saddle once both legs are removed.

3 There is a very small collar bone at the front of the front legs and this is the only bone that holds the legs in place. To remove the front legs, lift them slightly and cut straight through.

4 To remove the pelvis, place a knife on the inside of the bone and cut following the line of the bone. Repeat to the other side, then take hold of the pelvic bone and pull downward then upward to snap it off. Tidy if necessary.

5 Counting from tail to head, find the second rib bone and make a cut between the second and third rib bones, cutting outward and away from the loin. Turn the carcase around and carefully, in one sweeping cut, cut through the loin and stop at the backbone. Repeat to the other side and cut through the backbone.

6 To prepare the saddle, first cut away the two rib bones that are attached.

7 Turn the saddle over and using a knife carefully score along the edge of the loin, where the belly meets the meat. Be careful not to cut through the membrane, just score, and then pull it around the loin, unwrapping the meat and pulling the membrane back to the backbone. Repeat to the other side, then bring both sides of the membrane together and cut off along the backbone.

8 After removing this first membrane, you will see a second and thicker membrane around the loins. To remove this, start at one end and place the tip of a thin sharp filleting knife under the membrane. Keeping the knife as close as possible to the underside, push it up to the top. Once it emerges at the other end, angle it upwards and cut around the loin and then down. Repeat to the other side, then bring both sides of the membrane together and cut off along the backbone.

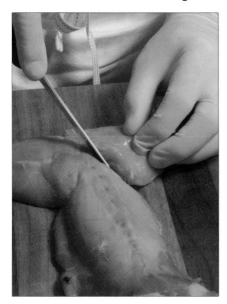

Cutting around the pelvic bone

Removing a rear leg

Making an incision between the second and third ribs

Scoring the membrane

The front end of the carcase is of no real value, apart from use in stocks or in competition work.

Basic preparation of large furred game: venison

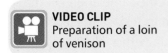

VIDEO CLIP
Preparation of a loin of venison

The skinning and gutting of large furred game is carried out in much the same way as it is for small furred game, but it will produce extra joints and obviously will be much larger in size. Large furred game will provide the following joints:

■ Haunch or leg (including rump)

■ Loin

■ Shoulder

■ Breast

■ Middle neck

■ Best end

■ Saddle with fillets

VIDEO CLIP
Boning, barding and tying a haunch of venison

Removing and preparing the best end

1 The best end should be cut with seven bones, one of which will be removed to produce a six-bone best end. Cut close to the last bone on the best end, all the way through to the backbone. Repeat on the other side, joining the cuts at the backbone.

2 Being careful not to damage the eye of meat on each loin, gently saw through the backbone to detach the saddle from the best end and middle neck.

3 From the bottom of the best end, count seven bones. Cut across to and through the backbone.

4 Keeping as close as possible to the bone, cut lengthways along the backbone to loosen the meat and down to the top of the rib bones. Repeat this on the other side.

5 Pull the eye meat away from the backbone and use a meat cleaver to cut through the base of the rib bones.

6 Remove any meat between the bones then scrape the rib bones clean with a small knife.

7 Clean the base of the eye meat and remove any unwanted sinew.

8 Remove the sinew from the outer side of the best end and cut out the last bone closest to the end, which will give a six-bone best end.

9 This can now be cut into cutlets or two three-bone portions for roasting whole.

Cutting through the best end to create two racks

Pulling back the fat from the rack

Removing the fat and sinew from the bones cleanly

Exposing the bones from the rack

Trimming away the sinew from the best end

Preparing venison cutlets

Preparing the saddle

The saddle can be left on the bone, with just the sinew removed, and roasted whole. The loins are removed in much the same way as the best end is removed, except there are no ribs and the meat is cut away from the bone. The fillets, which are usually quite small, should be removed.

1 Remove the sinew on the loins. Angle the knife upwards when cutting so as not to cut into the meat.

2 The loins can be left whole or cut into cannons, medallions or steaks. When preparing steaks, the loin can be wrapped in plastic film and chilled in a refrigerator for an hour or overnight to firm up to give a cleaner cut when portioning.

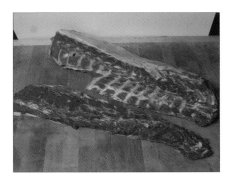

The loin removed from the saddle

Removing the second fillet

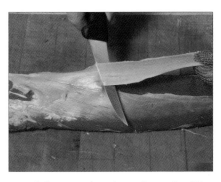

Carefully removing sinew from the fillet

Removing the sinew from the fillet

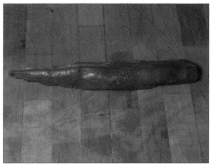
The finished prepared fillet

Rolling the fillet in cling film to ensure uniformity of size when cutting

Using the cling film to roll the fillet

Cutting through the cling film to give perfectly sized portions

STORAGE OF GAME

It is most convenient for kitchens to receive prepared game as the whole process of preparing game – hanging, bleeding, drawing and jointing – is very time consuming.

Once game has been hung for the correct amount of time it is quite safe to freeze the meat. All game that is to be frozen should be sealed in an airtight and water-impervious material, such as polythene bags. It must then be clearly labelled, stating the type of meat, the date of freezing and the date it should be used by. Feathered game can be safely frozen for six to nine months and furred game for up to six months. Once the meat is defrosted, it should be cooked immediately.

When refrigerating game, it should preferably be stored in a separate refrigerator to all other foods to minimise any possible risk of cross-contamination. As with other meats, game stored within the refrigerator should placed so that cooked items are at the top and raw items are at the bottom. Any raw or defrosting items should regularly be drained of excess blood or juices to ensure that the meat is not tainted. All items stored should be tightly wrapped and clearly labelled.

RECIPES
Pot-roasted snipe in stout with onion and rosemary dumplings

INGREDIENTS	4 PORTIONS	10 PORTIONS
Snipe (whole)	4	10
Stout	250ml	750ml
Game stock	250ml	750ml
Plain flour	50g	125g
Butter	50g	125g
Mirepoix of root vegetables	400g	900g
Carrot, celery, turnip, swede into macédoine	100g of each	220g of each
Soft flour	95g	230g
Baking powder	5g	20g
Water	100ml	250ml
Beef suet	50g	125g
Olive oil	1tbsp	2tbsp
Onion (finely chopped)	1	2
Fresh rosemary (finely chopped)	1tbsp	2tbsp
Peas	50g	125g
Curly kale	75g	180g
Good-quality salt and pepper	To taste	To taste

Method of work

1 Preheat an oven to 180°C.

2 Season and flour each whole snipe. Melt the butter in a large ovenproof casserole dish. Place the snipe into the dish and lightly colour on all sides.

3 Remove the snipe and leave to one side. In the same dish, brown the mirepoix of vegetables, season well and add the stout and game stock and bring to the boil. Return the snipe to the casserole dish, cover with a lid and cook in the preheated oven for 45 minutes.

4 In a small saucepan season and sweat down the onions with the olive oil and rosemary until tender. Remove from the heat and cool.

5 Once cooled, stir in the suet and sieve in the soft flour and baking powder. Slowly add the water until a dough is formed. Shape into medium size round balls, allowing one per portion.

6 In a pan of boiling salted water blanch and refresh the macédoine of vegetables and cook the dumplings until they float. Remove from the water and leave to cool slightly.

7 Once the snipe is cooked, remove from the sauce and leave to one side to rest. Pass the sauce through a strainer or chinois into a clean pan. Add the blanched macédoine of vegetables to the sauce and correct the seasoning and consistency.

8 Now return the snipe and dumplings to the sauce, adding the peas and curly kale. Place back in the oven at 180°C and cook for a further 15 minutes.

9 For service, allow one snipe and dumpling per portion with a serving of vegetables and sauce.

 CHEF'S TIP

Always remove excess flour from products before frying to stop the starch from burning and leaving a bitter taste in the final dish. This will also prevent lumps of raw flour appearing in a sauce.

Tandoori pigeon with sag aloo and a caramelised lemon and coriander dressing

INGREDIENTS	4 PORTIONS	10 PORTIONS
Squab pigeon breasts	4	10
Tandoori paste or spice mix	3tsp	8tsp
Olive oil	30ml	80ml
Maris piper potatoes (cut into macédoine)	500g	1.25kg
Baby spinach leaves	200g	500g
Ground cumin	1tsp	3tsp
Ground coriander	1tsp	3tsp
Ground turmeric	1tsp	3tsp
Garam masala	2tsp	5tsp
Vegetable stock	300ml	750ml
Lemons	2	5
Cardamom pods	6	15
Natural yoghurt	100g	250g
Fresh coriander	¼ bunch	½ bunch
Clear honey	1tsp	2½ tsp
Good-quality salt and pepper	To taste	To taste

Method of work

1 Place the tandoori paste and the pigeon breasts in a large bowl. Mix the breasts into the paste so that they are completely coated. Remove and place on a tray. Cover with plastic film and leave to marinate in a refrigerator for a minimum of one hour.

2 In a small sauté pan heat the olive oil then add the diced potatoes and sweat down without colour for a few minutes.

3 Season and add the ground cumin, turmeric and coriander. Continue to cook for a few minutes so that the spices have cooked out. Add the vegetable stock so that the potatoes are just covered. Season with salt and pepper and simmer until the potatoes are tender. Add the garam masala and the baby spinach.

4 Remove from the heat and allow the spinach to wilt into the potato mix. Stir well so that all the spices and the spinach are incorporated. Check the seasoning.

5 To prepare the dressing, peel and segment the lemons, chop the coriander roughly and open the cardamom pods, removing the seeds. In a shallow pan heat the honey, lemon segments and cardamom seeds until the honey starts to boil and caramelise. Remove from the heat and cool.

6 Once the honey and lemons has cooled, stir in the yoghurt and chopped fresh coriander.

7 Preheat the oven to 200°C. Place the marinated pigeon breasts onto a roasting tray and roast for approximately 10 minutes until the pigeon is cooked through. Remove from the oven and rest for a minimum of 5 minutes.

8 To serve, place the sag aloo into a ring in the centre of a plate, draining any excess liquid in the process. Arrange the breasts on top and pour the yoghurt sauce around the serving plate.

CHEF'S TIP

Experiment using other marinades, such as tikka or garlic and chilli. Pigeon is a strongly flavoured bird and this will come through even when other strong flavours are used.

Steamed roulade of woodcock with Jerusalem artichoke purée and braised baby gem lettuce

INGREDIENTS	4 PORTIONS	10 PORTIONS
Woodcock (whole)	4	10
Leaf spinach, washed and de-stalked	100g	250g
Sun-dried tomatoes	120g	300g
Jerusalem artichokes (peeled)	400g	1kg
Double cream	100ml	250ml
Baby gem lettuce	2	5
Butter	50g	125g
Orange zest and juice	1 orange	3 oranges
Vegetable stock	500ml	1.25 litres
Good-quality salt and pepper	To taste	To taste

Method of work

1 For each woodcock, using a sharp boning knife cut along the back of the bird, cutting the flesh away from the carcass. The bird should be left intact but with the main bone structure removed.

2 Once the bird is open, cut the wing and drumstick joints off so that the other wing bone and the thigh bone can be easily removed. Now the whole bird has been boned it can be stuffed.

3 Season with salt and pepper and lay the spinach leaves across the opened-out bird. Next, lay across the sun-dried tomatoes. Tightly roll up the bird – roll from side to side, not from tail to tip.

4 Tightly roll up in plastic film and tie at both ends, so that the roulade is sausage shaped.

5 In a medium sized saucepan place half the vegetable stock and the peeled artichokes with salt and pepper. Bring to the boil and simmer until the artichokes are tender.

6 Remove the artichokes from the stock and place into a blender with the cream. Blend to a smooth purée. Empty the purée into a small pan and dry the mixture slightly over the heat.

7 Remove the outer leaves of the baby gems, trim the bases and cut in half lengthways. Melt the butter in a sauté pan. Place the baby gems into the pan, flat side down, so that they start to fry.

8 Add the orange juice, zest and the remaining stock, bringing to the boil. Place a cartouche over the tops of the baby gems and simmer on the stove until soft and tender.

9 Place the roulades into a steamer and cook for 10–15 minutes until firm to the touch. Remove from the steamer and allow to rest for 5 minutes. Remove the plastic film.

10 To serve, carve the woodcock roulades into even slices. Pipe or quenelle the artichoke purée onto a plate and then lay the slices of woodcock over the purée. Cut the baby gems in half again lengthways and arrange around the outside.

CHEF'S TIP

When peeling Jerusalem artichokes, leave them in water with lemon juice or a touch of vinegar to prevent them oxidising.

Pheasant legs stuffed with a mousseline of duck liver and juniper, cep cream sauce and fondant potato

INGREDIENTS	4 PORTIONS	10 PORTIONS
Pheasant legs	4	10
Pheasant breast	2	5
Duck livers	250g	625g
Juniper berries (soaked in the gin below)	100g	250g
Gin	30ml	75ml
Double cream	300ml	750ml
Onion	1	2
Garlic	1 clove	2–3 cloves
Thyme	A few sprigs	A few sprigs
Butter	50g	125g
Brown chicken stock	150ml	400ml
Dried cep mushrooms	20g	50g
Pig's caul	80–100g	200–250g
Fondant potatoes	4	10
Fresh chopped chives and chervil	30g	80g
Good-quality salt and pepper	To taste	To taste

CHEF'S TIP

Dried wild mushrooms can be an economic commodity. As they are dried their flavour is much stronger. They are as good as fresh mushrooms for flavouring stocks, but only half the amount is required.

Method of work

1   Tunnel bone each pheasant leg to remove the thighbone. Neatly trim the drumstick flesh.

2   Season the duck livers. Over a high heat, quickly pan fry the livers and the soaked juniper berries in a shallow pan. Flambé with the gin. Remove from the heat and allow to cool.

3   In a food processor blend the pheasant breast and duck liver. Pass the mix through the back of a sieve to remove any sinew or large pieces.

4   Semi whip half the cream, ensuring the bowl used is freezing cold before use, then fold in the passed pheasant breast. Season, cover, place in a fridge and chill.

5   Once chilled, place the mixture into a piping bag with a plain tube and pipe into the legs. Carefully wrap the filled legs in the pig's caul before wrapping in plastic film and chilling further in the refrigerator.

6   Preheat an oven to 180°C.

7   Soak the cep mushrooms in a small pan of boiling water for 10 minutes. Remove the ceps and drain any excess water.

8   In a sauté pan gently sweat the garlic, onion and thyme in a little butter. Add the ceps, stock and a small amount of the water the ceps were soaked in and reduce by half. Add the remaining cream. Continue to cook for a further 5–10 minutes to infuse flavour into the sauce.

9   Using a hand blender or a food processor, blend the sauce ingredients together to maximise the cep flavour. Pass through a chinois. Adjust the consistency and seasoning before serving.

10 Season the stuffed legs. In a medium-hot pan with a small amount of oil seal the legs to give colour. Then place into a hot oven to cook for about 25 minutes. Remove from the oven and allow to rest.

11 To serve, lay the fondant potato on the plate and lean the ballotine against it. Warm the sauce, add the chopped chives and chervil at the last minute and spoon around the meat.

Roasted crown of partridge with butternut squash fondant and braised red cabbage and creamed Brussels sprouts

INGREDIENTS	4 PORTIONS	10 PORTIONS
Crown of partridge	2	5
Mirepoix	150g	400g
Unsalted butter	125g	250g
Butternut squash	1	3
Brown chicken stock	400ml	1 litre
Red cabbage	1	2
Sultanas	100g	250g
Grated dessert apples	100g	250g
Brown sugar	100g	250g
Raspberry vinegar	100ml	250ml
Game stock	200ml	500ml
Redcurrant jelly	50g	125g
Brussels sprouts	160g	400g
Double cream	100ml	250ml
Good-quality salt and pepper	To taste	To taste

Method of work

1 Preheat the oven to 180°C.

2 Soften 100/200g of the butter. Season the crown of partridge and coat the breasts with the butter. Place the crown on a tray with the mirepoix on the base. Roast in the oven for 15–20 minutes until golden brown and cooked all the way through. Use a digital thermometer to measure the temperature of the partridge inside. Remove from the oven, place on a cooling rack and rest.

3 Drain off any excess fat from the tray and then place on a stove and heat through. Add the game stock and deglaze the pan. Simmer for a few minutes then pass through a fine chinois into a clean pan. Warm the sauce. Add the redcurrant jelly and melt into the sauce. Correct the seasoning and consistency.

4 Warm the chicken stock in a small saucepan. Peel the butternut squash and cut into 4cm slices. Using a cutter cut out cylinder-shaped pieces, one per portion. Place the peeled and shaped butternut squash pieces in a small tray, brush with melted butter. Add stock so the squash pieces are two-thirds immersed, then place in the oven for 30–35 minutes until the squash is soft and lightly coloured on top. Remove from the stock and keep warm.

5 Put the raspberry vinegar, brown sugar, sultanas and grated apple into a heavy-based saucepan and bring to the boil. Shred the cabbage and add to the boiling vinegar mixture. Place a lid over the top and cook until the cabbage has become soft. Remove the lid and continue cooking until the liquid has reduced.

6 Prepare the Brussels sprouts by trimming the stalks and quartering. Heat a frying pan with a small amount of butter, fry the sprouts until softened and add the double cream.

7 Cook the cream until it has thickened slightly, season well and then remove from the pan and liquidise to a purée.

8 To serve, remove the breasts from the crown and arrange on the plate. Place a butternut fondant next to the breast and a spoonful of the cabbage. Spoon the creamed Brussels sprout next to the breast.

Quail and black pudding sausages with parsnip purée, étuvée of leeks and cider sauce

INGREDIENTS	4 PORTIONS	10 PORTIONS
Quail meat (leg and breast removed from the bone)	600g	1.5kg
Black pudding	200g	500g
Breadcrumbs	150g	375g
Double cream	100ml	250ml
Onions diced	50g	125g
Egg	1	3
Sausage skins (soaked in water and drained)	100g	250g
Parsnips	480g	1.2kg
Vegetable oil	40ml	90ml
Leeks	400g	1kg
Partridge or chicken stock (brown)	200ml	500ml
Cider	100ml	250ml
Unsalted butter	100g	250g
Double cream	250ml	600ml
Good-quality salt and pepper	To taste	To taste

CHEF'S TIP

Making sausages can be a good and cost-effective way of utilising leftover meats.

Method of work

1 Finely chop the black pudding and the quail meat and pass through a mincing machine. Soak the breadcrumbs in the smaller quantity of cream.

2 Preheat an oven to 180°C.

3 Fry the onions in a small amount of the butter in a frying pan until transparent but no colour. Allow to cool.

4 Mix the minced meat, egg and onions together to form a paste. Fold in the breadcrumbs and beat to a paste. Season well.

5 Fill a piping bag fitted with a plain tube with the sausage mix. Place the sausage skin over the end of the tube and fill the skin with the quail mixture. Pipe and twist the skin until enough length has been made to make one sausage per person. Place on a tray in a refrigerator to set.

6 Wash and peel the parsnips and remove the cores. Heat a roasting tray with a small amount of the butter, add the parsnips and season. Place in a preheated oven. Roast until soft and slightly caramelised. Remove from the oven and pass through a ricer. Beat in a little butter, seasoning and cream until a smooth purée consistency has been obtained.

7 Slice the leeks and wash them well. In a sauteuse, melt some butter and add the leeks to sweat down until softened. Season to taste.

8 In a saucepan reduce the cider and stock by half and add the 250/600ml of cream. Reduce the liquid until it coats the back of a spoon. Check the seasoning.

9 In a frying pan seal the sausages with the vegetable oil. Then place in a preheated oven at 200°C for 15–20 minutes until cooked all the way through and golden brown.

10 To serve, quenelle the mash. Slice the sausage at an angle and sit on top of the parsnips. Lay a little leek over the sausage and spoon the sauce around.

Sautéed saddle of rabbit with prune and Armagnac sauce

INGREDIENTS	4 PORTIONS	10 PORTIONS
Saddle of rabbit	4	10
Prunes	350g	875g
Armagnac	250ml	625ml
Chicken stock	250ml	625ml
Butter	125g	325g
Bouquet garni	1	1
Finely chopped parsley	30g	75g
Celeriac	75g	3
Desiree potatoes	150g	400g
Olive oil	30ml	75ml
Baby spinach	250g	700g
Salted butter	25g	60g
Nutmeg	10g	25g
Good-quality salt and pepper	To taste	To taste

Method of work

1 Preheat an oven to 180°C. Soak the prunes in the Armagnac for a minimum of 30 minutes. Remove half of the prunes from the Armagnac, chop and set aside.

2 Put the chicken stock and bouquet garni and the remaining liquor and prunes into a pan and reduce by half. Once reduced remove the bouquet garni, and using a hand blender blend the butter into the reduced liquor. Pass through a chinois.

3 Once amalgamated, stir in the chopped reserved prunes and chopped parsley. Season and keep warm to one side.

4 Season and pan fry the saddle of rabbit quickly for about 5 minutes. Place on trays in the preheated oven for approximately 15 minutes. Allow to rest for approximately 5 minutes. Carve the loins off the saddle and slice into thin strips across each loin.

5 Peel and grate the celeriac and potatoes into a bowl. Season and leave for 5 minutes. Remove from the bowl and squeeze so that any excess liquid is removed. Place a 6cm ring for each portion in a frying pan and heat on a stove. Add a touch of oil into each ring then place some of the potato and celeriac mixture into each ring. Fry on both sides until golden brown and cooked through. Remove from the rings and place on a cooling rack. Keep warm.

6 Put the salted butter in a shallow pan and heat on a stove. Wash and dry the spinach, then add to the butter and wilt. Sprinkle in the nutmeg and season. Remove from the pan and drain any excess water.

7 To serve, place the rosti of potato on the base then a layer of spinach. Arrange the rabbit around in a circle shape. Spoon the sauce over the rabbit.

 CHEF'S TIP

Try using different dried fruit with game dishes as the sweetness helps bring out the rich game flavour of the meat. Cranberries can give a nice sweet and sour effect.

Roasted loin of venison with baba ganoush and balsamic syrup

INGREDIENTS	4 PORTIONS	10 PORTIONS
Loin of venison	500g	1.2kg
Sumac spice	100g	250g
Aubergine	4	10
Tahini paste	1tsp	2.5tsp
Garlic	1 clove	3 cloves
Lemon juice and zest	1 lemon	3 lemon
Olive oil	100ml	250ml
Balsamic vinegar	200ml	500ml
Red peppers	3	8
Fresh coriander	¼ bunch	½ bunch
Reduced game stock	100ml	250ml
Demerara sugar	2tbsp	5tbsp
Good-quality salt and pepper	To taste	To taste

Method of work

1 Preheat an oven to 180°C.

2 Split the aubergine and roast in the preheated oven in a little olive oil. Cool until the outside is golden and crisp and the centre is soft and cooked through.

3 Cool the aubergine and remove the flesh. Pass through a course sieve. Purée the garlic and add to the aubergine along with the tahini, lemon juice and zest and the olive oil, season to taste.

4 Cut the peppers into quarters and remove the seeds, place onto a roasting tray and blister the skin under the salamander.

5 Remove from the heat and place the peppers into a plastic bag so that the peppers steam and the skin can easily be removed. Remove the skin and dice the flesh into a brunoise. Fold the peppers through the aubergine mixture.

6 Combine the balsamic vinegar, reduced game stock and sugar together in a saucepan and reduce to a coating consistency. Chop the coriander and stir into the sauce.

7 Season the loin of venison well with salt and pepper and the sumac spice. Seal in a very hot pan with a small amount of oil until golden all over. Place into the hot oven and roast for about 6–8 minutes until cooked to a medium pink stage. Remove from the pan and allow to rest for 5–10 minutes before carving.

8 To serve, slice the loin into thin slices, place a spoonful of the aubergine mix along the centre of the plate. Arrange the loin over the top of the aubergine mix so that the degree of cooking of the venison can be seen, run the sauce around the outside of the plate.

CHEF'S TIP

For venison, the longer the resting period, the more tender the meat becomes.

Assessment of knowledge and understanding

You have now learned about the different types of furred and feathered game. You will have gained an understanding of how to identify the different types of game and an awareness of their quality points. This will enable you to effectively recognise, assess and implement the knowledge gained in order to choose quality game products.

To test your level of knowledge and understanding, answer the following short questions. These will help to prepare you for your summative (final) assessment.

Quality points and types of game

1 Name four types of feathered game and a suitable dish for each.

i) _____ ii) _____

iii)_____ iv) _____

2 Name two types of small furred game and a suitable dish for each.

i) _____ ii) _____

Preparation techniques

1 List and detail the procedure to fully joint a wild rabbit.

_____

_____

2 Describe the process of trussing a whole game bird and give examples of two dishes suitable for a trussed bird.

_____

_____

Storage of game

1 Explain why it is best to drain raw or defrosting game regularly of excess blood and juices.

_____

_____

2 Discuss why it is best to store game in a separate refrigerator to other food items.

_____

_____

CHEF'S PROFILE

Name: ANDRE GARRETT MCA

Position: Head Chef

Establishment: Galvin at Windows

Current job role and main responsibilities: Ensuring high standards and pushing for culinary excellence. Also linking between Chris Galvin and the Hilton Hotel on Park Lane.

When did you realise that you wanted to pursue a career in the catering and hospitality industry? I was 14 years old and washing up in a local hotel in my home town of Bath. I caught the bug of the kitchen and decided to go to college, so they took me on as an apprentice chef.

Training:
I went to Bath College and did my City and Guilds 706/1 and 2 Food Preparation and Cookery. I had very good teachers – Mr Maslin was especially helpful to me. After college I started at Hunstrete House Hotel.

Experience:
After 2 years at Hunstrete House Hotel and my apprenticeship, I knew it was time to come to London. I came and knocked on the door of Nico Ladenis at Chez Nico and was lucky to get a job as Commis. I stayed with Nico for 5 years at a number of his establishments, but I finished as Chef de Partie at Nico at 90 Park Lane, where he gained three Michelin stars. Afterwards I spent time with Bruno Loubet and progressed to Sous chef at the Landmark Hotel fine dining restaurant. After this I met up with Chris Galvin at the Orrery and became his Sous chef. Later I was promoted to Head Chef and continued to run the Orrery for 3 more years.

What do you find rewarding about your job?
I like the fact people find pleasure in what I do and it is nice at the end of the day to know you've done a good job. I am now finding it interesting to train the next generation of chefs.

What do you find the most challenging about the job?
Getting up every day and striving to do better than before.

What advice would you give to students just beginning their career?
It is going to be hard for a long time but it is very rewarding. Be patient and learn. Ask lots of questions and make sure you work for someone who can teach you well.

Who is your mentor or main inspiration?
My mentor would be Chris Galvin; he has given me great opportunities and advice. I am inspired by every great chef and restaurateur.

What traits do you consider essential for anyone entering a career as a chef?
Patience, flexibility, motivation, determination and speed.

A brief personal profile:
- Travel and sport is what I like to do out of the kitchen.
- My job has been very good to me and I have also done very well in competitions. This is something that has motivated me and helped me to focus.
- Prix Pierre Tattinger, international finalist, 2000.
- Roux Scholor 2002.
- Bocuse dor 2007, 10th place.

Can you give one essential kitchen tip or technique that you use as a chef?
Be very organised and precise. Always cook with a timer.

14 Meat

LEARNING OBJECTIVES

The aim of this chapter is to enable you to develop skills and implement knowledge in the principles of preparing and cooking complex meat dishes. Generally the most expensive part of a meal is the protein element, whether it is meat, fish or poultry, therefore care should be taken to optimise its potential.

At the end of this chapter you will be able to:

- Demonstrate a range of skills related to the preparation of meat
- Demonstrate cookery skills using meat as the principal ingredient
- Identify quality points of beef, veal, lamb and pork
- List the health and safety regulations relating to the preparation, cooking and storage of meat and meat dishes
- Identify the different cuts of meat and relate appropriate cookery methods for them
- Identify healthy options with the preparation and cookery of meat dishes

INTRODUCTION

Meat can be defined as skeletal muscle of an animal reared for the table, the most common meats being beef, pork and lamb. Other types of meat include goat, mutton, veal and venison.

The proteins that make up the muscle are myosin and actin, which are found as long thin molecules in the muscle fibres. These molecules bind together to form complex molecules called acto-myosin. Approximately 15–20 per cent of lean meat is made up of protein, with the remainder of the bulk being 75 per cent water and 5–10 per cent fats and connective tissues. The quality of meat – its colour, texture and flavour – are determined by the arrangement of the muscle fibres, connective tissues and fat.

Connective tissues are those that physically bind all the tissues in the body – they literally connect individual tissues to each other. One of the main types of connective tissue is **collagen**, which breaks down into gelatin when cooked slowly over a long period of time. Muscles that undertake a lot of work (such as leg muscles) have dense fibres and a higher proportion of collagen. Muscles such as the loin have long slender fibres and less collagen. These meats can be cooked much more quickly.

Fat tissue is a form of connective tissue, where some of the cells take on the role of energy storage. Fat is found in three different areas of meat:

- Under the skin layer, to help provide insulation to the cold
- Around important organs, such as the kidney, for protection
- In connective tissues

Modern methods of farming tend to produce animals that have little fat. However, the intramuscular fat in meat (marbling) is important for achieving a soft texture. The fat renders (melts) and lubricates the muscle fibres during the cooking process, helping to give flavour and to tenderise the meat.

Meat obtains its colour from two sources:

- *Haemoglobin* – the red pigment in blood that transports oxygen around the body
- *Myoglobin* – a reddish brown protein that stores oxygen in the muscle

Myoglobin temporarily stores oxygen within the muscle in readiness for action or exercise. Age affects the amount of myoglobin present, which accounts for beef being darker than veal and mutton darker than lamb. Pork is pale because of the early slaughter weight of the animals and their lack of exercise.

When an animal is first slaughtered its blood will be oxygenated (oxymyoglobin) – if the meat is sliced shortly after slaughter the cut surface will be bright red. The blood will then become deoxygenated

CHEF'S TIP

Muscle fibres are the part of the muscle that moves. The basic texture of the meat is determined from the mass and thickness of these fibres, which produce the 'grain' of meat.

CHEF'S TIP

Rabbits, chickens and turkeys have predominantly white meat because they do not use their muscles as frequently as cattle or lamb. Their muscles therefore consist predominantly of white fibres, although their leg muscles are a mixture of half white and half red fibres.

VIDEO CLIP
Smithfield meat market

CHEF'S TIP

Well flavoured meat comes from animals that have led a full and active life. However, exercise increases the size and strength of the muscle fibres and so the meat will be tougher.

(metmyoglobin) and change to a burgundy colour. This reaction can take a very short time and it should be noted that it does not mean that the meat is bad. This effect can be prevented by creating a barrier using plastic film or a vacuum pouch.

ORGANIC PRODUCTION

Economics have forced modern suppliers to produce mild, tender meat, which has become the public's usual expectation. However, small producers are now rearing traditional breeds to produce more mature and flavoursome meat for customers who require a high-quality product. The rise of organic farming, with its greater emphasis on animal welfare, has improved distribution and supplies of better quality meat. Generally, organic meat is produced locally and is traceable - the full process it has gone through before it reaches the customer can be tracked. Certain standards must be met before meat can be labelled as organic:

- All meat must be produced to the Soil Association's standards
- All produce must be sourced either directly from the supplier's farms or from selected local organic producers who adhere to the same Soil Association standards
- The highest animal welfare standards must be observed at all times
- All meat must be butchered professionally, on site if possible
- All produce must be completely traceable
- Minimal transport of live animals, to reduce stress of animals before slaughter

Organic beef as an example

There can be huge differences in the amounts of time that non-organic cattle spend grazing. The most intensive systems involve keeping bull calves indoors or in yards. Bull calves are used because they grow quickly. They are fed on high levels of concentrated feeds and silage and are fattened up as quickly as possible. The animals are confined in large numbers, which can increase the risk of infectious diseases.

By contrast, less-intensive systems allow the calves – castrated bulls and heifers (female cows) – to remain with their mothers. The whole herd is allowed to graze for one or two summers and may be brought indoors during the winter.

All beef in the UK is either produced from herds that use specific beef breeds, such as Aberdeen Angus, South Devon or Hereford, or from dairy herds where a bull from a beef breed is crossed with the cows. Organic producers are encouraged to choose breeds that suit the conditions on their farms.

Black Aberdeen Angus

An organic beef system allows cows and their calves to graze in pasture for most of their lives. They can be finished in well-bedded spacious yards, provided this period does not exceed a fifth of their lifetime. Organic cattle do not have to be housed during the winter, but if they are kept outside, there must be shelter, food and water. At least 60 per cent of the diet must consist of grass, hay or silage. Intestinal worms are a common problem in all cattle. They can be avoided on organic farms by rotating the pastures (moving the cattle between fields) and also by allowing the calves to pick up natural immunity from their mothers.

The beef labelling scheme ensures that any information put onto packs of beef can be verified.

TRACEABILITY

Traceability is designed to give the chef and the customer the ultimate guarantee of safety and quality of food. Information can now be communicated through labelling that allows the customer to directly trace a piece of meat back to a particular country of origin, locality/area, farm, breed, abattoir and supplier; effectively giving the history from farm to plate. The label can also include further information, such as the date of slaughter, place of butchery, age and sex of the animal, production method (e.g. organic, grass-fed) and meat maturation time.

STORAGE AND PRESERVATION OF MEAT

Bacteria and moulds can multiply and grow very quickly on meat and so it will rot very quickly if it is not carefully stored. There are several methods of preservation that improve the storage life of meat.

- *Canning* – this was originally done by sealing a square tin can with solder and heating it until the meat was sterilised. Canning continues today but in a much refined form.
- *Dehydrating* – meat is cut into strips and hung to dry. This method is most popular in countries that have a dry climate.
- *Smoking* – meat and fish were originally hung in chimneys to dry. As well as having a drying effect, wood smoke contains compounds that have preserving and flavouring qualities.
- *Dry curing* – until the invention of canning, salting was the most important method of preservation. The meat would be smothered in salt for up to 2 months. It would then last for many more months.

- *Wet curing (picking)* – a heavy salt solution has the same effect as dry curing. The brine can be soaked into the flesh to speed the process and increase the water content.

- *Sealing* – meats have been sealed into containers for many hundreds of years. This has the effect of preventing air getting to the meat and so slows the growth of bacteria. Some meats are sealed in fats, such as confit of duck or potted tongue, which can then be cooked in the same fat. Even today, the vacuum pack system relies upon air being excluded. Care should be taken when using this method. Excluding the air affects bacteria that need air to flourish (aerobic) but it does not affect bacteria that do not need air (anaerobic). The smell of decomposing flesh is a safety marker – the smell tells you that the meat is not fit for consumption.

- *Refrigeration* – meat is kept covered at a temperature range of 1–4°C. This is a method of short-term preservation.

- *Freezing* – frozen meat is kept at a minimum of –18°C. When meat is frozen quickly the ice crystals that are formed will be much smaller, leading to less cell damage and less water forming during the defrosting process. Care should be taken when storing frozen meat. Freezer burn occurs if the food is not completely covered during the freezing process.

BEEF (*BOEUF*)

Beef is the edible meat of domestic cattle. Most beef comes from castrated males killed at 18 months of age. Heifers can also be used for beef if they are not required for breeding.

VIDEO CLIP
Preparation of beef sirloin

The carcases are allowed to cool naturally after slaughter and left to hang for up to 42 days. The hanging process (or ageing) creates a slow chemical change during which the meat becomes progressively more flavourful. Enzymes found in the muscle will generate flavour by breaking down other cells, turning large flavourless molecules into smaller well-flavoured deposits. Some chefs ask for longer ageing, but no appreciable difference is experienced after 28–30 days.

VIDEO CLIP
Preparation of beef fillet

BSE (bovine spongiform encephalitis), also known as mad cow disease, caused the death of millions of cattle. This was brought about by feeding cattle with by-products derived from sheep that had a brain disease called scrapie. A form of the disease known as variant CJD was also passed to humans. This disease has an extremely long incubation period and so it is not known how long it will take to eradicate. BSE appears to have been eliminated in the UK thanks to the culling of infected herds and changes in feeding practices.

QUALITY POINTS

- The muscle should be red with slight marbling. This is a clear indicator that the animal was well nourished

- The fat should be creamy in colour and brittle. If the fat on the outside of the meat (subcutaneous fat) is thin and soft to the touch the animal was probably force-fed or killed too young. There will be a resultant lack of flavour

- There should be a pleasant aroma that shows no signs of rancidity. Beef and its fat start to decay after a short period at ambient temperature, even after just a few hours, and gives off a characteristic rotting odour.

- The lean meat should not feel sticky to the touch. The surface of the meat is metabolised by bacteria and mould which causes discolouration and by-products that give a sticky feel to the flesh

Common breeds used in farming

- Aberdeen Angus
- Devon
- Herefordshire
- Holstein
- Cross breed of Limousin and Holstein

 Main beef-producing area

The main beef producing areas in Great Britain

Beef is almost always butchered into quarters and then broken down into primary cuts.

Beef hindquarter

Average weight 85–90kg

HINDQUARTER OF BEEF

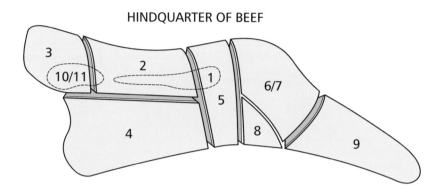

JOINT	FRENCH	USE	AVERAGE WEIGHT
1 Fillet	Le filet	This is the leanest and most tender piece of beef and lends itself to grilling, roasting, frying and pot roasting	3–3.5kg
2 Sirloin	L'aloyau	A lean piece of meat that is good for frying, roasting and grilling. Care should be taken to remove any sinew from the back prior to roasting and remove any piece of the rump that remains	12–14kg
3 Wing rib	Les côtes d'aloyau	There are three wing ribs on each side of beef. Can be roasted as a piece or chined and cut into cutlets	5–6kg
4 Thin flank	La bavette d'aloyau	Also known as skirt, this is coarse meat with about 50% fat. It is good for sausages or mincing	8–10kg
5 Rump	Culotte	Frying, roasting, braising. There are several muscles on this joint that give different textural experiences when eating	10kg
6 Topside	La tranche tendre	Braising, stewing, slow roasting at low temperatures. This piece is used in the sandwich industry and by upmarket delicatessens	9–10kg
7 Thick flank	Tranche graisse	A large piece of lean meat that lends itself to being braised as a piece as it can disintegrate if used in small pieces in stews	10–11kg
8 Silverside	Gîte à la noix	Silverside is very coarse and requires long slow cooking. Good for pickling and boiling	12–14kg
9 Shin	La jambe le jarret	Because of the amount of collagen present, the shin makes excellent consommé	6–7kg
10 Kidney	Rognon	Pies, puddings	1–2kg
11 Fat (suet)	Graisse de rognon	Suet pastry, rendering	5–6kg

Beef forequarter

Average weight 75–80kg

BREAKDOWN ON A FOREQUARTER OF BEEF

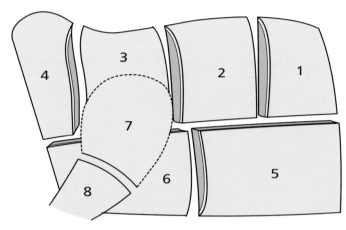

JOINT	FRENCH	USE	AVERAGE WEIGHT
1 Fore rib	Le côte première	The fore rib is the prime roasting joint from the side of beef. It has the best collagen to lean ratio, making it the most succulent. It can also be denuded of fat to give rib-eye steaks, suitable for grilling and frying	6.5kg
2 Middle rib	Le côte découverte	This is a flavoursome joint that can be used for braising in a single piece or for second-class roasting	8.5kg
3 Chuck rib	Le côte du collier	The high content of connective tissue in this joint means it benefits from stewing or braising. Be careful to remove all gristle and sinew	13kg
4 Sticking piece	Le collier-cou	Lean and high in flavour. Ideal for stewing and mincing	7kg
5 Plate	Le plat de côte	Remove all fat and use for stewing, mincing	8.5kg
6 Brisket	La poitrine	Brining and boiling brings out the best in brisket, although it can be boiled without brining	16kg
7 Leg of mutton cut (LMC beef)	L'épaule macreuse	When properly butchered, LMC beef is very lean and makes excellent braising steaks and paupiettes and is good for stewing and mincing	7-9kg
8 Shank	Jambe de devant	Very lean and high in collagen. Remove any gristle and mince for a consommé clarification mix	5kg

VEAL (*VEAU*)

Veal is the meat from beef calves, usually male calves from dairy herds. It has generally not been an important part of British cuisine, but it is very popular in Italy, Spain, France, Austria and Germany. There are moral arguments about the way that veal is reared.

Veal calves should be fed exclusively on milk – there should be a milky aroma from the kidneys and fat. The calves are slaughtered at between 2½ and 4 months. Because veal is very young it is low in myoglobin, which accounts for its pale colour.

The fat content is also minimal, and therefore the use of ingredients such as cream adds to the eating experience. Care should be taken not to over-cook veal, especially the parts that are grilled and roasted, as they can become dry and tough – they should be just cooked (**à point**) or slightly under-cooked.

VIDEO CLIP
Preparation of veal cushion

Side of veal

BREAKDOWN ON A SIDE OF VEAL

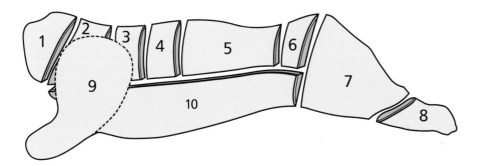

QUALITY POINTS

- The fat is white, pleasant to smell and with a faint hint of milk. The subcutaneous fat should only have any thickness around the rump. It should be dry and not greasy

- The muscles should not feel sticky to the touch. This is a sure sign of poor storage and the carcass being left at ambient temperature or poorly transported

- The flesh is very lean and a very pale pink colour, except when a rose colour is specifically ordered. There should be no marbling as the animal should not have had a long enough life to produce intramuscular fat

JOINT	FRENCH	USE	AVERAGE WEIGHT
1 Scrag	Le cou	A flavourless joint that makes excellent stock. Can also be used for mince to make porjarski or for blanquettes	1.25kg
2 Neck	Collet	The neck can be prepared for stews or fricassée. If minced it can be used for fine forcemeats	3kg
3 Neck end	Côte découverte	Used for stewing. Bone and remove sinew before cutting into 2.5cm cubes	2kg
4 Best end	Le carré	The best end is a prime cut that is suitable for roasting, pot roasting, cutlets and frying	2–3kg
5 Loin	La longe	This is a lean joint, good for roasting. It can be cut into chops or steaks, but its lack of marbling precludes successful grilling. Braising is a good option	4kg
6 Rump	Le quasi or cul de veau	Used for escalope of veal or for sauté dishes. The rump can be roasted or braised as steaks. The trimmings can be used for stewing	2kg
7 Leg	Cuisseau	The leg can be cut into the following joints: Cushion (noix) Under-cushion (sous-noix) Thick flank (noix pâtissière) Each can be used for pot roasting, frying or grilling. The cushion is the main joint from which escalopes are taken	6–8kg
8 Knuckle/ shank	Le jarret	Mince, stews, first-class stocks and osso bucco ('bone with a hole', an Italian dish of braised shank)	2kg
9 Shoulder	L'épaule	The shoulder can be stuffed and roasted or used for braised dishes	3–5kg
10 Breast	La poitrine	The breast can be removed and braised or stewed, but care should be taken not to over-cook the joint. Using a fatty stuffing or barding the joint helps to prevent it drying out when roasting	2–3kg

LAMB AND MUTTON (*AGNEAU* AND *MOUTON*)

Lamb is the meat from young sheep and has a characteristic and delicate flavour. The flavour develops, becoming much deeper, as the lamb develops. Mutton is the meat from the adult sheep.

- *Spring lamb* – lamb in its first 6 months, but usually slaughtered at 3–4 months
- *Lamb* – lamb up to 1 year old or when the lamb grows its first pair of permanent teeth
- *Hoggett* –1 to 2 years old; technically this is mutton but without the developed flavour
- *Mutton* – over 2 years old, and with a strong and well-developed flavour

In the UK, the sheep industry is located so that particular breeds occupy specific environments to which they are adapted. The sheep of these environments are connected by the movement of lambs and older animals from higher to lower ground.

The hills

Hardy hill and mountain sheep are largely kept as pure breeds. Lambs not required to maintain flock numbers are transferred to the lowlands as store lambs to be fattened.

VIDEO CLIP
Preparation of lamb best end

The uplands

In upland areas there are again specific breeds. These and older draft mountain ewes are crossed with the longwool breeds.

VIDEO CLIP
Preparation of lamb shoulder

The lowlands

In the lowlands, the sheep are crossed with lowland sires to produce lambs that can be fattened on summer grass. Slower growing lambs join those that have arrived from the hills and upland areas to be fattened on root crops over the autumn and winter months.

QUALITY POINTS

- The lean flesh should be a dull red colour with a close grain
- The fat should be evenly distributed, dry to the touch and flaky in texture. The amount of fat is determined by the age and feeding of the animal
- The smell of lamb is pleasing and characteristic to the animal. This can be lost if the very lean parts of the lamb are denuded of all connective tissue and fat
- Lamb bones should be porous, as they are yet to mature and become dense, and have a small degree of blood present

Main sheep areas

The main lowland sheep areas in Great Britain

It is important to keep lamb and mutton cold when cutting the meat as the fat becomes greasy and knife handles become slippery to use.

Side of lamb/mutton

Average weight 18–21kg

BREAKDOWN OF A SIDE OF LAMB/MUTTON

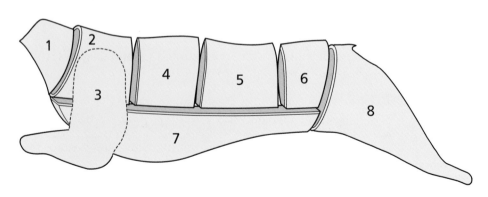

JOINT	FRENCH	USES	AVERAGE WEIGHT
1 Scrag	Le cou	Stewing and for broths This is the toughest part of the lamb and is traditionally cooked on the bone in Irish stew	1kg
2 Middle neck	Côte découverte	Stewing when the neck fillet is removed or grilling as uncovered cutlets. Be sure to remove all traces of elastin	2kg
3 Shoulder	L'épaule	Roasting, stuff with forcemeat and roast slowly. Can also be served as a half shoulder braised in a rich sauce, or diced for stewing	2 × 2.5kg
4 Best end	Le carré	The best end can be prepared into racks for roasting, or into cutlets, noisettes or rosettes for grilling and frying	2kg
5 Saddle	La selle	The saddle can be roasted on the bone or boned and stuffed. The loins can be removed and cut into rosettes and noisettes for frying and grilling. Fillet mignon also comes from the saddle, as do the cannons	3.5kg
6 Rump/chump	Le quasi	A rump of lamb will yield four pieces for braising or roasting	2kg
7 Breast	La poitrine	The breast can be boned and rolled for slow roasting, or steamed and pressed to make epigrams	2kg
8 Leg	Le gigot	The leg can be used for roasting and the shank can be used for braising. The leg can also be broken down into its various muscle groups for frying and grilling. Mutton leg can also be used for boiling	2 × 2.5kg

The preparation of lamb into cutlets

1 Prepare the lamb by sawing at the bottom of the ribs until the chine bone is released

2 Cut away the flesh from the chine bone to leave two pieces

3 Make an incision just above the lean eye of the meat. Remove the flesh making sure to stay close to the bone

4 Remove the bark

5 Scrape each bone and then push the flesh from each bone from the side.

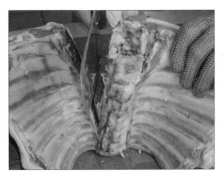
Removing the chine bone using a heavy knife

Cutting away the flesh at the top of the bones

Removing the bark

Scraping the bones

Pushing the flesh

Peeling the meat away from the bones

Trimming and removing the elastin

Cutting the cutlets

VIDEO CLIP
Preparation of pork loin for roasting

VIDEO CLIP
Preparation of pork belly

PORK (*PORC*)

Pork is the fresh meat of the domestic pig. Pigs are easy to breed and make slaughter weight in usually 6 months. Pork is widely used across the world, except within the Jewish and Muslim communities.

In the past it was recommended that pork should always be over-cooked to eliminate trichinosis (the larvae of a worm that can be passed to humans from under-cooked pork). However, with modern rearing, storage and preparation techniques, trichinosis has been practically eradicated, although care should be taken to cook the meat to 70–75°C. Pork is usually supplied butchered into sides.

New breeds of pig developed for the table have a high yield of flesh and a low proportion of fat, examples are Landrace and Duroc. Traditional breeds such as the Tamworth and Gloucester Old Spot have a greater covering of fat and much more tender flesh because they are generally reared free-range and are allowed to forage for food, especially acorns and apples.

Main pig production areas

The main pig production areas in Great Britain

QUALITY POINTS

■ Pale pink flesh with a fine texture. Marbling can occur with organic and free-range pork. A smaller portion of free-range pork will satisfy the appetite compared with battery-reared pork

■ Skin should be free of bristle and not wet to the touch. When the pig is slaughtered it is dipped and scalded, this loosens the hairs and allows them to be scraped off. Pork is the only meat where the skin is also eaten

■ There should be a covering of fat, but it should not be excessive. A layer of 1–2cm of subcutaneous fat is sufficient, although contemporary preferences are for a thinner layer

■ The bones should be small and pink. In older animals the bones are white and more dense

■ If you are purchasing a whole pig make sure that the tail is intact. If pigs become distressed they try to bite each others' tails. Some breeders will dock their young pigs' tails

Side of pork

Average weight (excluding head) 16–18kg

BREAKDOWN OF A SIDE OF PORK

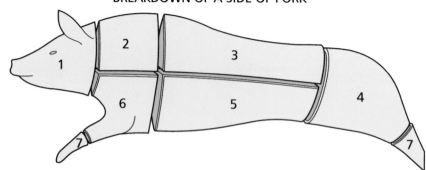

JOINT	FRENCH	USES	AVERAGE WEIGHT
1 Head	La tête	The head can be boned and stuffed, or it can be boiled and the flesh pressed for brawn. The cheeks can be braised. The head can also be boiled and presented with chaud-froid as a centrepiece for a buffet	4kg
2 Spare rib	L'échine	With the gristle removed, used for sausages, pork pies, slow roasting	2kg
3 Loin	La longe	Chops and cutlets are obtained from the loin, as is the fillet. All are suitable for frying and grilling. The loin can also be boned and rolled for roasting	5kg
4 Leg	Le cuissot	On or off the bone, pork leg is suitable for roasting. The legs can be dissected into individual muscles for cutting into steaks or stir frying. The leg can also be cured for ham, either a wet or dry cure can be used	4kg
5 Belly	La poitrine	Braised belly of pork is very popular. When boned and chopped it makes good emulsion sausages	3kg
6 Shoulder	L'épaule	With fat and gristle removed, the shoulder can be used to make sausages and forcemeats and can be diced for stews	3kg
7 Trotters	Le pied	The trotters should be blanched and then refreshed. They can be used to make gelatinous stock, stuffed and braised, or the meat can be picked off and added to brawn	0.5kg

BACON

Bacon is the cured side of a baconer pig (a pig that is allowed to grow bigger than a porker pig, usually a hybrid of Landrace and Tamworth). The meat is cured by either the wet cure or dry cure method. Dry cure is superior as it causes less shrinkage; the sides are strewn with salt and cured for 14 days. The pinkness comes from the addition of nitrate and the reaction of salt-tolerant bacteria. The cured bacon, referred to as green bacon, can be smoked or sold unsmoked.

QUALITY POINTS

- The lean muscle should be pink, firm and not sticky to the touch. Smoked bacon should feel dry to the touch

- The fat should be white and not excessive. With dry cured bacon the rind is usually left on and the fat should be dry to the touch. Vacuum packed bacon can be quite wet to the touch but can be dried with absorbent paper

- The rind must be free from wrinkles and not sticky. Wrinkles and stickiness indicate that the bacon has been poorly stored and is past its sell-by date

Bacon has been a staple of British society for many hundreds of years and was originally used as a way to store meat. Although the invention of refrigeration has made meat storage much easier, bacon continues to be produced because of its flavour. Bacon is still produced for the British market in many other parts of the world, the biggest producer being Denmark.

Side of bacon

Average weight 28–30kg

JOINT	USES	AVERAGE WEIGHT
1 Gammon	Boiled gammon is usually served cold, but it can be glazed, baked and served hot. Can also be sliced to make gammon steaks and grilled or fried	7–8kg
2 Back	Rashers of bacon and bacon steaks for grilling and frying	9–10kg
3 Collar	The collar can be tied for boiling or diced for pies and fricassées	4–5kg
4 Hock	The hock should always be boiled, but can also be roasted afterwards and served with mustard	4–5kg
5 Belly	Streaky bacon is taken from the belly and can be grilled or fried	4–5kg

BREAKDOWN OF A SIDE OF BACON

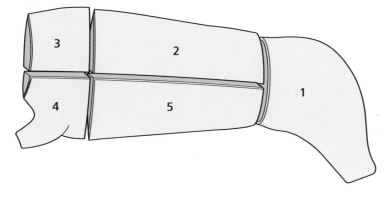

BEEF RECIPES
Beef Wellington

INGREDIENTS	4 PORTIONS	10 PORTIONS
Centre cut fillet of beef	600g	1.5kg
Vegetable oil	50g	100g
Chestnut mushrooms	300g	750g
Finely chopped shallots	50g	125g
Dry white wine	20ml	50ml
Butter	50g	125g
Foie gras	200g	500g
Puff pastry	500g	1kg
Egg whites	1	2-3
Chopped truffle trimmings	50g	100g
Madeira sauce	200ml	500ml
Good-quality salt and white pepper	To taste	To taste
Egg wash	1 egg	2 eggs
Herb pancakes		
Fresh eggs	4	8
Soft flour	150g	300g
Fresh milk	200ml	400ml
Chopped fresh chives and parsley	2tbsp	4tbsp
Vegetable oil for frying		

Method of work

1 Preheat an oven to 200°C.

2 Tie the fillet of beef to retain its shape, season well and seal in a hot pan with a little fat. Allow to cool completely. Reserve the pan juices. Lightly re-season the beef fillet and reserve in the refrigerator.

3 Finely chop or mince the mushrooms and cook with the shallots in the butter in a saucepan. Add the white wine and continue to cook until the wine has evaporated and the mixture is dry (**duxelle**). Season to taste and allow to cool completely.

4 To make the herb pancakes, beat the eggs and flour in a bowl until smooth. Slowly add the milk to create a thin consistency and then add the chopped herbs and seasoning.

5 Heat a little oil in a pancake pan and cook thin pancakes (one per portion) in the usual way.

6 Remove the beef fillet from the refrigerator and cut into the required portions. Cut away any remaining string.

7 Mix half of the truffles with the pâté and spread over each pancake, then add a layer of the duxelle. Place the sealed beef fillet on top and fold the pancake over to encase the fillet. Trim away any excess pancake. Wrap in plastic film and chill for 1 hour.

8 Roll out the puff pastry until it is large enough to wrap around the fillet of beef. Leave to rest for 15 minutes.

VIDEO CLIP
How to tie knots in butchery

🔖 **CHEF'S TIP**

Truffles are very expensive. A more economical method is to add a little truffle oil to the duxelle. Another cheaper alternative is to use chicken liver pâté in place of the foie gras. The beef is wrapped in herb pancakes to give extra protection from over-cooking the meat and to retaining the juices produced during the cooking process.

9 Discard the plastic film and place the pancake-wrapped beef fillet onto the pastry and roll the pastry around the beef, encasing it completely. Seal well to prevent any leakage during cooking.

10 Place on a baking sheet seam-side down and brush with egg wash.

11 Chill thoroughly for at least 1 hour and egg wash again. Score curved lines in the top of the pastry using the tip of a sharp knife.

12 Place in an oven for 20–25 minutes. Reduce the heat to 130°C until the required degree of cooking is achieved.

13 Allow to rest in a warm place for at least 5 minutes before serving.

14 Heat the pan juices and deglaze with some red wine. Add the Madeira sauce and strain through a fine chinois into a clean pan. Check the consistency and seasoning.

15 Add the remainder of the truffles and heat for 2–3 minutes.

16 Place each individual beef Wellington onto a serving plate and serve with the sauce.

Sealing the fillet

Portioning the fillet

Wrapping the fillet in the herb pancake

Tournedos Rossini

INGREDIENTS	4 PORTIONS	10 PORTIONS
Centre cut fillet of beef	600g	1.5kg
Foie gras	160g	400g
Thin slice of truffle (soaked in brandy)	4 slices	10 slices
Madeira sauce	200ml	500ml
Butter	40g	100g
Madeira wine	35ml	75ml
Thick sliced white bread (cut into a disc to the size of the fillet)	4 slices	10 slices
Fresh chervil	4 sprigs	10 sprigs
Good-quality salt and white pepper	To taste	To taste

Method of work

1 Completely remove any fat or connective tissue from the fillet and wrap tightly in plastic film. Place into a refrigerator and chill for a minimum of 3 hours. This allows the meat to set into a round shape.

2 Remove from the refrigerator and slice into the required tournedos steaks at approximately 150g per portion.

3 Remove the foie gras from the refrigerator for 5 minutes prior to slicing and cut into the required number of collops. Return to the refrigerator until required.

4 Heat the butter in a shallow pan until it starts to foam. Place the fillets into the pan and cook on both sides to the required core temperature.

5 Season the fillets, remove from the pan and keep warm.

6 Add the Madeira wine to the pan and deglaze with the cooked juices from the meat. Add the Madeira sauce and bring to the boil. Simmer for up to 4 minutes.

7 Strain the sauce into a clean pan, reheat and check the seasoning and consistency.

8 Sear the foie gras in a hot dry shallow pan until the collops are golden brown on each side. Place one on top of each fillet and keep warm.

9 Place the bread slices in the pan to fry quickly on both sides using the residue of the foie gras. Also warm through the truffle slices.

10 To serve, arrange the bread slice in the centre of each plate. Place the tournedos with the foie gras and sliced truffle on top with a cordon of Madeira sauce around it. Finish with a sprig of the fresh chervil.

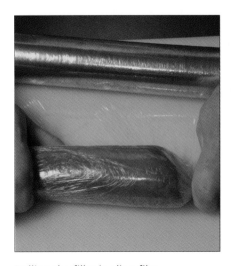

Rolling the fillet in cling film

Cutting the fillet into 150g steaks

Cooking fillet of beef

CHEF'S TIP

Tournedos are cut from the centre of the beef fillet and are usually sautéed in butter with a named garnish or sauce.

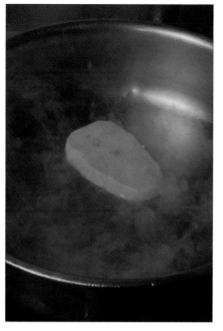

Cooking the foie gras

Arranging the dish

Garnishes for alternative tournedos dishes

NAME	GARNISH
Alsacienne	Toss lardons in hot fat with sauerkraut. Dress on a fried croûton with the garnish
Béarnaise	Serve with watercress and béarnaise sauce (see recipe on p. 73)
Choron	Serve with sauce choron (tomato flavoured sauce Béarnaise), garnished with artichoke bottoms filled with peas and noisette potatoes
Duroc	Coat with chasseur sauce and serve with tomato concassé and noisette potatoes
Forestière	Serve on a croûton with sautéed wild mushrooms and lardons accompanied by Parmentier potatoes. Can be served with a red wine sauce
Helder	Serve with sauce Béarnaise, piped on top with cooked tomato concassé in the centre with a jus lie and Parisienne potatoes
Rivoli	Set on Anna potatoes with truffle sauce

Steak and smoked oyster pudding

INGREDIENTS	4 PORTIONS	10 PORTIONS
Suet pastry		
Soft flour	290g	600g
Baking powder	10g	20g
Beef suet	150g	310g
Cold water	75ml	150ml
Good-quality salt	To taste	To taste
Filling		
Chuck steak	400g	800g
Tinned smoked oysters	125g	250g
Thinly sliced onion	70g	140g
Fresh thyme	6 sprigs	12 sprigs
Garlic	1 clove	2 cloves
Seasoned soft flour	4tbsp	8tbsp
Worcestershire sauce	To taste	To taste
Beaten egg yolk	1	2
Stout gravy		
Finely chopped shallots	100g	200g
Garlic	1 clove	2 cloves
Fresh thyme	1 sprig	2 sprigs
Bay leaf	½ leaf	1 leaf
Crushed black peppercorns	5	10
Stout beer	600ml	1.2 litres
Red wine	400ml	800ml
Beef stock	2 litres	4 litres
Good-quality salt and white pepper	To taste	To taste
Parsley purée		
Fresh flat leaf parsley sprigs	300g	600g
Double cream	150ml	300ml
Good-quality salt and white pepper	To taste	To taste

Method of work

1 To make the parsley purée, take the washed, picked flat leaf parsley and blanch in plenty of boiling water for 3 minutes. Drain immediately in a colander.

2 While the parsley is still hot, squeeze out as much water as possible. Place the drained parsley into a food processor and blend, gradually adding the double cream.

3 When the cream has been completely added, remove the purée as quickly as possible and place in an airtight plastic bag. Keep in the refrigerator until required.

4   To make the suet pastry, sieve the flour, salt and the baking powder together. Add the beef suet and mix in the cold water a little at a time. This pastry should not be too sticky, so there may be a little water left over depending on the quality of flour used. Knead until a smooth and elastic pastry is formed. Wrap in plastic film and refrigerate until required.

5   Cut the chuck steak into small (1.5cm) cubes and reserve any meat trimmings for the sauce. Mix the cubed beef in a bowl with the drained smoked oysters, onion, thyme, garlic and flour.

6   Line dariole moulds with plastic film, overhanging by a few centimetres. Pin out the suet paste and cut one 18cm disc and one 6cm disc per portion. Leave to rest in a refrigerator, covered, for 5 minutes.

7   Line each mould with the larger disc of pastry, pushing well into the base of the mould. Leave a 1cm overhang of pastry around the edge.

8   Divide the filling between the moulds and pour in some cold water, to come three-quarters of the way up the mould. Sprinkle with a few drops of the Worcestershire sauce.

9   Brush inside each pastry mould with the beaten egg yolk and place the smaller disc on top. Fold over the overhanging pastry and pinch inwards to seal the top. Wrap each mould tightly with plastic film twice.

10 Place the puddings into the steamer and steam for 2 hours.

11 To make the stout gravy, place the shallots, garlic, herbs, peppercorns and salt in a pan with the left over meat trimmings and carefully sweat for 10 minutes. Remove the lid and increase the heat to begin to caramelise the ingredients.

12 Add the red wine and reduce by three-quarters. Add the stout and reduce in the same way. Add the stock and reduce to the required consistency. Pass through a fine chinois and correct the seasoning.

13 To serve, unwrap the puddings and turn out onto serving plates. Take the required quantity of the parsley purée and heat as quickly as possible in a small, dry shallow pan, seasoning to taste. Serve the stout sauce around the pudding and drizzle a small amount over the pudding also. Using a dessert spoon, create a quenelle of the parsley purée to sit on the top of each pudding.

Slow cooked fillet of beef with braised red cabbage and a smoked onion soubise sauce

INGREDIENTS	4 PORTIONS	10 PORTIONS
Beef fillet (trimmed and cut from the centre)	1 × 750g	2 × 900g
Sunflower oil	50ml	100ml
Braised Red Cabbage		
Red cabbage (with the central stem removed)	½ cabbage	1 cabbage
Red wine vinegar	50ml	100ml
Balsamic vinegar	45ml	80ml
Red wine	300ml	600ml
Demerara sugar	300g	500g
Star anise	2	5
Bay leaves	4	10
Whole cloves	3	8
Black peppercorns	10	25
Cinnamon stick	½	1
Good-quality salt	For salting	For salting
Smoked onion soubise		
Onions	2	4
Garlic	½ clove	1 clove
Fresh thyme	1 sprig	2 sprigs
White vegetable stock	200ml	400ml
Double cream	100ml	200ml
Oak wood chips	75g	150g
Good-quality salt and white Pepper	To taste	To taste

Method of work

1 Preheat an oven to 56–59°C.

2 Take the centre-cut fillet of beef and quickly seal in the sunflower oil in a pan until lightly brown all over. Allow to cool.

3 Wrap well in plastic film to help maintain the shape of the beef fillet, place on a baking tray and place in the oven for a minimum of 1½ hours.

4 To finish the beef, remove from the oven and carefully cut away the plastic film. Heat some sunflower oil in a hot pan and brown for 2 minutes on all sides.

5 For the smoked onion soubise, cover the base of a baking tray with oak chips sprinkled with a little water and place a perforated tray or wire rack on top. Slice the onions and garlic thinly and arrange in a small tray, place the tray on top of the oak chips. Place on a medium heat until it begins to smoke, then cover with foil and leave on the heat for five minutes. Remove from the heat and allow to cool.

6 Sweat the smoked onion and garlic with the thyme until golden. Add the stock and reduce by half.

7 Add the cream and bring back to the boil. Pour the contents of the pan into a food blender to liquidise to a smooth consistency. Pass through a fine sieve into a saucepan and correct the seasoning. Set aside for service.

8 Salt the sliced red cabbage in a colander for 2–3 hours to help bring out the colour. Rinse in cold water and pat dry with a clean kitchen cloth.

9 Place the vinegars, wine and sugar in a pan and bring to the boil. Place the broken cinnamon stick, star anise, peppercorns, cloves and bay leaves in a small muslin cloth and tie into a little bag. Add the cabbage and the muslin bag and slowly braise, covering the pan with a lid until the cabbage has cooked completely.

10 Remove the muslin bag and strain the cabbage in a colander while still hot.

11 To serve, spoon the cabbage into the centre of a serving plate. Slice the beef fillet and arrange slices on top of the cabbage. Quickly blend and aerate the smoked onion soubise with a stick blender and spoon onto the plate to accompany the beef. Garnish as required. Accompaniments such as fondant potatoes and a red wine beef jus can also be served.

Daube of beef provençale with a garlic mash

INGREDIENTS	4 PORTIONS	10 PORTIONS
Daube of beef		
Chuck steak	4 × 150g	10 × 150g
White wine	50ml	125ml
Cognac	25ml	70ml
Crushed garlic	1 clove	2 cloves
Fresh parsley stalks	8	20
White flour	To dust	To dust
Sunflower oil	50ml	100ml
Pancetta lardons	100g	250g
Black olives	20	50
Carrot	100g	250g
Onion	2100g	50g
Bouquet garni	Small	Medium
Tomato concassé	200g	500g
Sliced chestnut mushrooms	100g	250g
Dried orange peel	10g	25g
Lemon juice	½ lemon	1 lemon
Good-quality salt and white pepper	To taste	To taste
Garlic mash		
Maris Piper potatoes	750g	1.5kg
Unsalted butter	125g	250g
Garlic	2 cloves	4 cloves
Fresh cream	60ml	120ml
Good-quality salt and white pepper	To taste	To taste

Method of work

1 Trim and slice the beef into neat steaks and marinate for 10 hours in the wine, cognac, crushed garlic and parsley stalks.

2 Remove the steaks from the marinade and pat dry with a clean kitchen cloth. Dust the meat with the flour and season with salt and pepper and gently beat it in with the back of a heavy knife. Preheat an oven to 180°C.

3 Season each steak and seal in hot oil, then transfer to a braising pan.

4 Add the cleaned, peeled and chopped vegetables and sauté quickly in the hot fat until golden, then transfer to the braising pot with the beef.

5 Deglaze the pan with the marinade and add to the braising pan.

6 Add the remaining ingredients to the pan. Cover with a tight-fitting lid and place in the oven for 2–2½ hours.

7 When the beef is cooked, remove the beef steaks and cover with plastic film and retain for service. Discard the bouquet garni and orange peel.

8 Reduce the sauce to the required consistency and correct the seasoning.

9 Wash, peel and rewash the potatoes. Cut into a rough dice and cook in boiling salted water until tender. Drain in a colander.

10 Finely chop the garlic and sweat in a little of the butter.

11 Purée the potatoes with the sweated garlic, remaining butter and cream. Season to taste.

12 On a serving plate, pipe the garlic mash and place the **daube** of beef next to it. Spoon the sauce over and garnish as required.

Slicing the chuck steaks

Marinating the steaks

Beating flour into the steaks

Braised oxtail with black pudding and champ potatoes

INGREDIENTS	4 PORTIONS	10 PORTIONS
Trimmed oxtail	2	5
Black pudding	350g	900g
Mirepoix of carrot, onion, celery and leek	200g	500g
Chopped tomatoes	200g	400g
Fresh thyme	1 sprig	3 sprigs
Fresh bay leaf	1	3
Red wine	400ml	800ml
Brown beef stock	600ml	1.2 litres
Beef dripping or oil for frying	50g	100g
Good-quality salt and white pepper	To taste	To taste
Champ potatoes		
Maris Piper potatoes	750g	1.5kg
Unsalted butter	125g	250g
Fresh cream	60ml	120ml
Spring onions	4	10
Good-quality salt and white pepper	To taste	To taste
Garnish		
Tomato concassé	100g	300g
Fresh chopped parsley	1tbsp	3tbsp
Finely diced and blanched mirepoix of carrot, leek, celery and onion	200g	600g

Method of work

1 Preheat an oven to 220°C.

2 Using boning knife, remove excess fat from the tails and bone out the oxtail. Keep the meat whole and retain the bones.

3 Remove the black pudding from the skins and mince it down. Lay it along the centre of the meat. Taper the pudding in the opposite direction to the meat to give an even shape.

4 Roll and carefully tie the tails to give a neat cylindrical shape.

5 Seal the oxtail in a hot pan with the beef dripping and add the mirepoix of vegetables, chopped tomato, thyme and bay leaf. Continue to cook until the mirepoix is golden brown.

6 Brown the bones in the oven and add to the oxtail.

7 Place all the ingredients in a large braising pan or casserole with the red wine and the beef stock and cook in the oven for approximately 3 hours.

8 Remove the oxtails when cooked and strain the sauce through a fine chinois into a clean pan and skim. Reduce the sauce and correct the seasoning and consistency.

9 Wash, peel and rewash the potatoes. Cut into a rough dice and cook in boiling salted water until tender. Drain in a colander.

10 Finely chop the spring onions and sweat in a little of the butter.

11 Purée the potatoes with the remaining butter and cream. Season to taste and add the spring onions.

12 Heat the sauce and add the mirepoix garnish and tomato concassé. Serve the oxtails sliced onto the champ potato on a serving plate, using slices from each end of the tail to give a correct ratio of meat to stuffing.

13 Serve with the finished sauce and the chopped parsley.

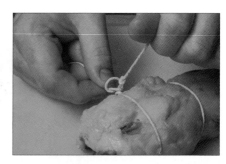

Trimming and boning the oxtail

Spreading the black pudding onto the open oxtail

Tying the oxtail before sealing

Hot smoked fillet of beef with rocket salad

INGREDIENTS	4 PORTIONS	10 PORTIONS
The cure	Makes 500g	Makes 500g
Good-quality salt	250g	250g
Dark brown sugar	200g	200g
White pepper	10g	10g
Allspice	10g	10g
Ground mace	10g	10g
Crushed juniper berries	10g	10g
Pink salt	10g	10g
The dish		
Centre cut fillet of beef	500g	1.25kg
Hickory wood chips	75g	150g
Fresh rocket leaves	100g	500g
Extra virgin olive oil	20ml	50ml
Grated horseradish	25g	50g
Crème fraîche	200g	500g
Chopped chives	1tsp	1tbsp
Good-quality salt and black pepper	To taste	To taste

CHEF'S TIP

This method can be used for preparing hot or cold beef. To preserve the beef, cure it for 24 hours and smoke to 70°C.

Method of work

1 Combine all the ingredients for the cure and mix together.

2 Trim the beef of all fat and connective tissue.

3 Place a layer of the cure mix on top of a sheet of plastic film, lay the beef on top and cover the beef with a generous layer of cure mix.

4 Roll the beef tightly in several layers of cling film.

5 Place the beef in a tray and lay another tray on top. Place a 1kg weight on top and leave in the refrigerator for 6–8 hours.

6 Remove from the refrigerator, unwrap and wash quickly in cold water. Pat dry with a paper towel and leave to stand in a well-ventilated room (this gives a sticky surface called a pellicle, which allows the smoke particles to attach to the surface of the meat).

7 Place the beef in a hot smoker set at 90°C for 1–2 hours until the core temperature of the beef reaches 65°C. Alternatively, preheat an oven to 90°C. Place the wood chips in the bottom of a roasting tray with a grill over the top. Heat the wood chips on a stove until they begin to smoke. Place the beef fillet on top and cover with foil before placing in the oven to cook.

8 Combine the olive oil, chopped fresh chives, grated horseradish and crème fraîche. Use half the dressing to dress the washed rocket leaves and season to taste.

9 Slice the beef very thinly and drizzle with the remaining dressing. Serve the beef with the rocket salad.

VEAL RECIPES

Braised cushion of veal *Fricandeau de veau*

INGREDIENTS	4 PORTIONS	10 PORTIONS
Cushion of veal	500g	1.5kg
Italian lardo (strips of fat)	200g	500g
Carrots	200g	500g
Button onions	200g	500g
Button mushrooms	200g	500g
Celery	200g	500g
White of leek	200g	500g
Bouquet garni	1 small	1 medium
Veal stock	1 litre	2.5 litres
Good-quality salt and white pepper	To taste	To taste
Noodle garnish		
Fettuccine	100g	250g
Olive oil	30ml	80ml
Fresh chopped parsley	1tbsp	3tbsp

Method of work

1 Preheat an oven to 170°C.

2 Lard the veal with the lardo by inserting strips of fat into the joint using a larding needle. Trim and tie the joint with string.

3 Wash, peel and cut the vegetables into equal sizes and lightly fry in some fat. Transfer into the bottom of a heavy braising pan.

4 Place the joint into the hot fat to seal on all sides before placing on top of the bed of vegetables.

5 Add the veal stock and bouquet garni and season well.

6 Bring to the boil, skim, cover with a tight-fitting lid and place in the oven.

7 Baste every 10 minutes until the veal is cooked through, approximately 1 hour.

8 Remove the lid from the braising pot and continue cooking for a further 30 minutes so that the liquid begins to reduce. Baste frequently so that the stock forms a glaze and coats the veal and vegetables.

9 Remove the veal from the braising pot and leave to rest for 5 minutes. Pass the sauce through a fine sieve and retain the vegetables to serve as part of the overall dish. Correct the seasoning and consistency of the sauce.

10 Cook the fettuccine in plenty of boiling salted water. Drain well in a colander and return to the pan with the olive oil and the chopped parsley, toss carefully until all the ingredients are well combined. Correct the seasoning as required.

11 Remove the string from the veal and carve against the grain. Serve coated with the sauce and accompanied by the vegetables and fettuccine.

Lardo, or strips of fat, to be larded

Larding the veal

Veal kidneys in a Dijon mustard and tarragon sauce

INGREDIENTS	4 PORTIONS	10 PORTIONS
Veal kidneys (skinned, trimmed and sliced in half)	400g	1kg
Vegetable oil for frying		
Chopped shallots	80g	200g
Butter	50g	130g
Brandy	30ml	80ml
Dry white wine	50ml	125ml
Double cream	250ml	700ml
Dijon mustard	3tbsp	8tbsp
Fresh chopped tarragon	4tsp	10tsp
Good-quality salt and white pepper	To taste	To taste

Method of work

1   Heat the oil in a shallow pan. Season the kidneys lightly and sauté for 3–4 minutes. The kidneys should be slightly coloured on the outside but still pink inside.

2   Tip the kidneys into a colander to drain.

3   Add the butter and the shallots and sweat for a few minutes without colour. Add the dry white wine and reduce by half. Add the brandy and reduce by half again.

4   Pour in the cream, bring back to the boil and reduce to a sauce consistency. Remove from the heat and stir in the mustard and fresh tarragon and season to taste.

5   Add the kidneys and carefully reheat the sauce without boiling.

6   Serve with braised rice.

Veal pojarskis with foie gras and Smitaine sauce

CHEF'S TIP

The bread and milk mixture is called 'bread panade' and is used as a binding agent in meat-based galettes.

INGREDIENTS	4 PORTIONS	10 PORTIONS
Minced lean veal	400g	1kg
Fresh milk	200ml	600ml
Unsalted butter	60g	125g
Double cream	100ml	250ml
White breadcrumbs	100g	250g
Grated nutmeg	To taste	To taste
Good-quality salt and white pepper	To taste	To taste
Smitaine sauce		
Finely chopped onion	50g	125g
Butter	25g	70g
Dry white wine	80ml	200ml
Lemon juice	¼ lemon	½ lemon
Soured cream	300ml	700ml
Garnish		
Foie gras	100g	250g
Baby spinach, washed and picked	400g	1kg
Fresh chervil	4 sprigs	10 sprigs
Veal jus	4tbsp	10tbsp

Method of work

1 Ensure that the minced veal has been passed through the mincer twice to break the protein down.

2 Soak the breadcrumbs in the milk for a few minutes and then squeeze out any surplus milk.

3 Add the breadcrumbs to the veal and mix well. Season with salt, pepper and nutmeg. Work in the cold double cream, a little at a time, using a spoon. Mix thoroughly and beat well.

4 Divide the mixture into equal portion sizes and mould into round discs about 3.5cm thick. Use some flour to help mould the shapes.

5 Heat the butter in a shallow pan and carefully place the pojarskis to shallow fry. Fry until golden brown on both sides and thoroughly cooked (up to 15 minutes approximately). To check, press the pojarskis gently – the juices should run out clear and with no sign of blood, indicating they are cooked through. Retain in a warm place for service.

6 To make the Smitaine sauce, place the chopped onion in a saucepan with the butter and sweat without colour. Drain off the excess fat and add the white wine, reduce by two-thirds.

7 Add the lemon juice and then the soured cream. Continue to reduce the sauce to a coating consistency. Season well and pass through a fine sieve. Keep hot.

8 In a separate shallow pan quickly seal and cook the foie gras on both sides, season and retain for service. Place the washed spinach in the same pan. Season well and cover with a lid, place on the side of the stove until the spinach is wilted. Drain any excess moisture in a colander.

9 To serve, spoon the spinach into a stainless steel ring placed in the centre of a serving plate. Remove the ring, position the pojarski on the spinach and place a slice of foie gras on top. Spoon over the veal jus and then the Smitaine sauce. Garnish with the chervil.

Osso bucco

INGREDIENTS	4 PORTIONS	10 PORTIONS
Slices of veal knuckle (shank) on the bone	4 × 300g	10 × 300g
Olive oil	40ml	100ml
Flour for dusting	30g	70g
Diced onion	100g	250g
Diced celery	75g	150g
Diced carrot	75g	150g
Chopped garlic	2 cloves	5 cloves
Tomato concassé	500g	1250g
Tomato purée	100g	250g
Dry white wine	400ml	1 litre
Veal stock	400ml	1 litre
Dried lemon skin	25g	60g
Dried orange skin	25g	60g
Good-quality salt and white pepper	To taste	To taste
Gremolata		
Chopped flat leaf parsley	1tbsp	2tbsp
Grated lemon zest	1 lemon	2 lemons
Lemon juice	½ lemon	1 lemon
Olive oil	25ml	70ml
Crushed garlic	1 clove	2 cloves
Good-quality salt and white pepper	To taste	To taste

Method of work

1. Preheat an oven to 180°C.
2. Dust the osso bucco veal slices with the flour and season well. Heat the olive oil in a shallow pan and add the veal slices, colouring on both sides.
3. Add the chopped onion, carrots, celery and garlic and continue to cook, with a lid placed firmly on the pan, for 3 minutes.
4. Drain any excess fat and add the white wine to deglaze the pan. Add the veal stock and the lemon and orange skin plus the tomato purée and bring to the boil.
5. Place the lid on the pan and place into the oven for 1½ hours to cook.
6. Add the tomato concassé and correct the seasoning. Return to the oven for a further 15 minutes.
7. Make the gremolata by combining all the ingredients together.
8. Correct the seasoning and consistency of the osso bucco and serve with a separate risotto and drizzled with the gremolata dressing.

CHEF'S TIP

Osso bucco is a classic dish from Milan that is served with risotto but it can also be served with plain boiled rice or a crisp green salad. It has many regional variations. The name 'osso bucco' means a bone with a hole, describing the veal marrow bone with the meat on the outside.

Braised veal cheeks with sweetbreads

INGREDIENTS	4 PORTIONS	10 PORTIONS
Veal cheeks		
Trimmed veal cheeks	4	10
Diced carrot	100g	200g
Diced onion	200g	400g
Chopped garlic	4 cloves	8 cloves
Chopped celery	80g	160g
Bay leaves	3	6
Fresh thyme	4 sprigs	10 sprigs
Veal stock	1 litre	2.5 litres
Black peppercorns	8	20
Good-quality salt	To taste	To taste
Veal sweetbreads		
Veal sweetbreads (trimmed, blanched and pressed)	400g	1kg
Vegetable oil	50ml	125ml
Chopped onion	50g	100g
Diced carrot	50g	100g
Veal stock	200ml	550ml
Good-quality salt and white pepper	To taste	To taste
Buttered savoy cabbage		
Savoy cabbage	½ cabbage	1 cabbage
Butter	75g	150g
Finely chopped onion	100g	220g
Lardons of bacon	50g	120g
Light chicken stock	75ml	150ml
Good-quality salt and white pepper	To taste	To taste

CHEF'S TIP

The veal cheeks can be braised the day before and simply reheated in veal stock to serve. This gives the cheeks time to set and so they will be easier to cut or carve.

Method of work

1   Preheat an oven to 180°C.

2   Trim, roll and tie the veal cheeks. Place all the ingredients into a pan with the veal cheeks. Slowly bring to the boil and cover with a lid. Pull to one side of the stove and slowly braise until the cheeks have cooked (approximately 3 hours).

3   For the veal sweetbreads, heat some of the oil in a shallow pan. Season the sweetbreads and quickly seal on both sides. Remove from the pan and add the carrots and onion to sweat for 2 minutes. Place the sweetbreads on top of the vegetables and add the veal stock. Cover with a buttered cartouche of silicone paper and place in the oven for approximately 40 minutes, basting occasionally with the cooking liquor.

4   Wash, trim, stalk and slice the cabbage into thin strips. Add the butter to a saucepan to melt before adding the cabbage and the chopped onion and bacon lardons. Sweat the cabbage and then add the stock and season with salt and white pepper. Continue to slowly cook on the stove until the stock has reduced.

5   Remove the veal cheeks and strain the cooking liquor into a saucepan. Reduce the liquid to a coating consistency, correct the seasoning and reserve. Remove the string and slice the veal cheeks.

6   Place the cabbage in the centre of a serving plate and set the veal cheek next to it. Remove the sweetbreads from the oven, carefully slice and arrange on the plate before finishing with the reduced veal jus.

14 MEAT

LAMB RECIPES

Roast rack of lamb with parsnip purée and garlic jus

INGREDIENTS	4 PORTIONS	10 PORTIONS
Best ends of lamb (prepared into racks)	2	3
Double cream	100g	250g
Butter	300g	800g
Romano potatoes	500g	1.25kg
Parsnips	500g	1.25kg
Garlic	8 cloves	20 cloves
Fresh thyme	8 sprigs	20 cloves
Chopped shallots	200g	500g
Brown lamb stock	2 litres	4.5 litres
Plum tomatoes	100g	250g
Olive oil	50ml	100ml
Fresh sage	2tsp	5tsp
Fresh chervil	4 sprigs	10 sprigs
Good-quality salt and white pepper	To taste	To taste

Method of work

1   Preheat an oven to 200°C.

2   Place the prepared racks of lamb into a pan and brush with olive oil. Chop half of the fresh thyme and sprinkle on the lamb, season well.

3   Place in the oven to roast for about 16–20 minutes until pink.

4   Cut the potato into discs 3.5cm in diameter and approximately 3cm thick. Slowly cook in two-thirds of the butter and sage and take out just before it is cooked. Make a hole all the way through the centre with an apple corer and keep warm to one side.

5   For the parsnip purée, peel, wash and cut the parsnips into quarters lengthways and discard the hard centres. Dice into cubes. Boil in salted water, and drain in a colander when cooked. Place on a baking tray and put into the oven to dry out. Pass through a sieve and finish with the remaining butter, double cream and seasoning. Reserve in a warm place.

6   Meanwhile make a provençale garnish by sweating off half the finely chopped shallot, two cloves of garlic and the remaining thyme. Add the de-skinned and de-seeded chopped plum tomatoes. Fill the centre of each piece of potato with this mixture.

7   Reheat the stuffed potato garnish in the oven.

8   For the garlic jus, reduce the lamb stock with the remaining cloves of crushed garlic. Correct the consistency and seasoning and reserve for service.

9   To serve, place the potato garnish slightly off centre, to the left of the plate. Pipe the purée lengthwise, adjacent to the garnish. Slice the lamb into two pieces and sit upright, garnish with the fresh chervil. Finish with the garlic jus.

Roast stuffed saddle of lamb with rosemary jus

INGREDIENTS	4 PORTIONS	10 PORTIONS
Saddle of lamb (boned)	1	2
Minced chicken	150g	300g
Chopped fresh tarragon	2tbsp	4tbsp
Egg whites	1	2
Double cream	75ml	150ml
Lamb or pig caul (crepinette)	1 sheet	2 sheets
Carrots	100g	250g
Onion	100g	250g
Celery	100g	250g
Leek	100g	250g
Brown lamb stock	1 litre	2.5 litres
Rosemary leaves	3tbsp	8tbsp
Balsamic vinegar	3tsp	7tsp
Red wine	80ml	200ml
Good-quality salt and white pepper	To taste	To taste

Stuffing the lamb saddle between the cannons

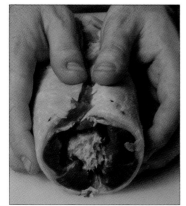

Folding over the flaps of the saddle to encase the stuffing

Method of work

1 Season the lamb well.

2 Mix the chopped tarragon with the minced chicken and place into a food blender. Add the egg whites while blending the ingredients then slowly add the cold double cream. Season well.

3 Place some of this stuffing in the centre of the two attached cannons in the saddle. Lay one of the detached fillets on top of the stuffing and cover the fillet with some more of the stuffing. Repeat with the second fillet and cover with the remaining stuffing.

4 Lift up one of the belly flaps and fold it over so that the cannons sandwich the fillets and stuffing in the middle. Repeat with the other side. Season well.

5 Rinse half the caul in cold water and then carefully lay on a board. Lay the saddle on the centre of the caul and bring the sides up to enclose it. Rinse the rest of the caul and lay it flat on the board. Position the saddle on the nearest edge of the caul and roll it up. Tuck in the flaps at each end. The saddle can be tied or roasted as it is.

6 Preheat an oven to 220°C.

7 Wash, peel and rewash the vegetables, chop and place into the bottom of a roasting pan.

8 Place the saddle to sear in a pan with some hot oil. Transfer to the roasting tray and roast in the oven for 30 minutes.

9 Remove the roasted saddle of lamb and allow to rest on a wire rack in a warm place.

10 Place the roasting pan on a hot stove and brown the vegetables further.

11 Add the vinegar, wine and the fresh rosemary to deglaze. Continue to cook on the stove for a further 3–4 minutes.

12 Add the stock to the roasting pan and deglaze.

13 Strain into a saucepan and reduce to the required consistency. Correct the seasoning.

14 Carve the lamb in thick slices and serve with the rosemary jus.

Rump of lamb with a wild mushroom sausage and Madeira jus

INGREDIENTS	4 PORTIONS	10 PORTIONS
Lamb rumps (off the bone, trimmed)	4 × 160g	10 × 160g
Boned shoulder of lamb	300g	750g
Fresh, cleaned wild mushrooms	50g	140g
Eggs	2	4
Double cream	100ml	230ml
Finely chopped shallots	50g	120g
Fresh chopped coriander	25g	60g
Fresh chopped parsley	25g	60g
Convenience sausage skins		
Good-quality salt and white pepper	To taste	To taste
Mint pesto dressing		
Toasted pine nuts	25g	60g
Olive oil	150ml	340ml
Fresh garlic cloves	2 small	4 small
Fresh mint	50g	100g
Fresh basil	25g	50g
Good-quality salt	To taste	To taste
Fig and onion marmalade		
Red onions, thinly sliced	125g	300g
Clear honey	25g	50g
Red wine vinegar	2tbsp	5tbsp
Red wine	3tbsp	6tbsp
Dried figs	25g	60g
Madiera jus		
Finely chopped shallots	50g	100g
Finely chopped garlic	1 clove	2 cloves
Fresh thyme	1 sprig	2 sprigs
Bay leaf	¼ leaf	½ leaf
Balsamic vinegar	1tbsp	2tbsp
Madeira wine	200ml	400ml
Strong brown lamb stock	400ml	800ml
Olive oil	1tbsp	3tbsp
Good-quality salt and white pepper	To taste	To taste

Method of work

1 Preheat an oven to 180°C.

2 Place a large shallow pan to heat on the stove and add a little oil.

3 Season the rumps of lamb and place into the hot fat, flat side down, to seal. Sear until golden brown on all sides. Place each lamb rump onto a roasting tray and place into the oven for 13 minutes.

4 For the wild mushroom sausage, place the diced shoulder of lamb, chopped shallots and seasoning into a food blender. Blend together until the meat resembles a farce. Add the eggs and blend further. Slowly pour in the cream while still blending. Add the chopped coriander and parsley and briefly blend together. Check the consistency and the seasoning of the sausage paste. Mix in the prepared, roughly chopped assorted wild mushrooms.

5 Pipe into the soaked sausage skins to create one sausage of approximately 100g per portion. Leave to rest for approximately 20 minutes in the refrigerator. To cook, place under a salamander, turning every few minutes until cooked through.

6 For the mint pesto, put the pine nuts, olive oil, garlic, fresh basil and fresh mint into a food processor and blend until a paste has been formed. Leave to one side and gently warm prior to service.

7 For the Madeira jus, heat the oil in a sauteuse and add the shallots, garlic, thyme and bay leaf and cook for about 4 minutes, stirring frequently. Add the vinegar and continue to cook until the liquid has evaporated, then deglaze the pan with the Madeira.

8 Cook rapidly to reduce by about three-quarters. Add the stock, reduce the heat and simmer for 15 minutes, removing any scum that appears. Pass twice through a muslin-lined sieve and correct the seasoning and consistency.

9 For the fig and onion marmalade, place the sliced onions, honey, vinegar and wine in a pan. Bring to the boil and gently simmer until the onions are soft. Add the figs and cook very slowly to a marmalade consistency. Reserve warm for service.

10 To serve, remove the rumps of lamb from the oven. Immediately wrap them individually in plastic film and rest for five minutes. Spoon the red onion marmalade in the centre of a serving plate. Remove the rumps of lamb from the plastic film and strain any collected juices into the Madeira sauce. Carve the lamb and arrange next to the marmalade. After having grilled the sausages, cut each one in half on a slant and place on top of the marmalade. Run the mint pesto over the sausage and the Madeira jus around the plate.

Roast shoulder of lamb with minted pea purée, celeriac boulangère and a bramble jus

INGREDIENTS	4 PORTIONS	10 PORTIONS
Boned shoulder of lamb	1 × 2kg	2 × 2kg
Olive oil	4tbsp	8tbsp
Fresh rosemary	8 sprigs	16 sprigs
Garlic	4 cloves	8 cloves
Chopped shallots	100g	200g
Chestnut mushrooms	140g	280g
Chopped flat leaf parsley	50g	100g
Brioche crumbs	100g	200g
Butter	50g	100g
Good-quality salt and white pepper	To taste	To taste
Minted pea purée		
Finely chopped shallots	50g	150g
Fresh mint	4 stalks	10 stalks
Double cream	75ml	300ml
Garden peas (fresh or frozen)	400g	1kg
Good-quality salt and white pepper	To taste	To taste
Celeriac boulangère		
Celeriac	1.3kg	3kg
Sliced onions	200g	500g
Lamb stock	400ml	1 litre
Butter	150g	400g
Good-quality salt and white pepper	To taste	To taste
Bramble jus		
Strong lamb stock	450ml	1.2 litres
Finely chopped shallots	75g	200g
Pink peppercorns	10	26
Crème de cassis	75ml	200g
Blackberries	20	50
Red wine	75ml	200g
Unsalted butter	50g	125g
Good-quality salt and white pepper	To taste	To taste

Method of work

1 Preheat an oven to 200°C.

2 Trim the shoulder of lamb and process the trimmings in a blender until smooth. Gently fold in the chopped parsley. Season well. Sweat the shallots with the chopped chestnut mushrooms and, when cooled, add to the parsley mixture. Mix together the brioche crumbs and the softened butter.

3 Stuff the shoulder with the mixture and tie up. Rub with a little salt, pepper and olive oil. Make eight incisions in the shoulder, cut each clove of garlic in half and insert half a clove and a sprig of rosemary into each incision.

4 Heat a large roasting tray on the stove with a little of the oil and seal the prepared joint until brown on all sides. Remove from the pan and set aside.

5 For the celeriac boulangère, melt half of the butter in a shallow pan, add the sliced onions and cook without colour. Leave aside to cool down.

6 Slice the washed and peeled celeriac and place flat side down in a lightly buttered and seasoned baking dish. Place a layer of the cooked onions on top.

7 Repeat this process with a final layer of celeriac on top. Pour in the stock to just cover the celeriac and onions. Place slices of the remaining amount of butter on top with a final seasoning.

8 Position the shoulder of lamb on top of a wire rack and place this on top of the baking dish with the prepared celeriac boulangère.

9 Place in the oven for 30 minutes and then reduce the oven temperature to 150°C.

10 Baste every 15 minutes using the juices that drip into the celeriac. The lamb should be cooked after another 1 hour and 20 minutes. Remove the lamb and allow the joint to rest.

11 Finish baking the celeriac boulangère by turning the oven temperature back up to 200°C if required.

12 For the pea purée, cook the peas with the mint stalks in a little boiling water until tender, and refresh quickly to retain the colour.

13 Sweat the finely chopped shallots, adding the cream and seasoning.

14 Remove the mint stalks. When cooled slightly add the chopped mint and purée until smooth. Pass the mixture and reserve warm for service.

15 For the bramble jus, sweat the shallots then add the pink peppercorns and deglaze with the red wine and the crème de cassis. Reduce by half.

16 Add the stock and reduce to the correct consistency. Strain and correct the seasoning.

17 Poach the blackberries in the sauce gently for two minutes and remove for garnish. Whisk the butter into the jus and reserve warm for service.

18 To serve, arrange the celeriac boulangère onto the centre of a service plate. Carve the lamb to lay the slices on top.

19 Spoon the pea purée next to the lamb and serve the bramble jus with the blackberries around the plate.

Grilled rosettes of lamb paloise with gratin potatoes

INGREDIENTS	4 PORTIONS	10 PORTIONS
Prepared rosettes of lamb	12	30
Olive oil	4tbsp	8tbsp
Béarnaise sauce (made using chopped fresh mint in place of tarragon; see recipe on p. 73)	300ml	800ml
Fresh chopped mint	2tbsp	5tbsp
French beans	200g	500g
Parma ham	12 strips	30 strips
Unsalted butter	50g	120g
Good-quality salt and white pepper	To taste	To taste
Gratin potatoes		
Desiree potatoes	4	10
Double cream	250ml	700ml
Garlic	2 cloves	5 cloves

Method of work

1. Brush each rosette with oil and season well.
2. Wash, peel and rewash the potatoes. Slice each potato into three even slices. Using a plain pastry cutter, cut out circles of potato the same size as the rosettes.
3. Put the cream and crushed garlic into a pan. Bring to the boil and season. Place the potato discs into the cream and gently cook until soft.
4. Carefully remove the potatoes from the cream and place onto a baking tray, spoon a little of the cream over each potato and reserve.
5. Blanch the French beans and refresh in iced water. Evenly divide the beans between the portions required. Create three small bundles of the beans per portion and wrap each one in a strip of the Parma ham. Lay the bundles onto a tray and reserve.
6. Grill the rosettes until golden brown on the both sides and slightly pink in the centre.
7. Place the gratin potatoes in a preheated oven at 180°C while the lamb is cooking. Cook for approximately 6 minutes until lightly golden.
8. Warm the French beans in a small pan of simmering water, remove and brush with the melted butter.
9. To serve, place three gratin potatoes in a line on a service plate and lay a rosette on top of each. Then place a bundle of French beans on each rosette. Mix together the minted béarnaise sauce with the freshly chopped mint and spoon over each rosette. Finish with some fresh chervil.

CHEF'S TIP

If required, remove the fat from the lamb rosette before grilling and slightly reduce the cooking time.

Cannon and faggot of lamb with Stilton dauphinoise

INGREDIENTS	4 PORTIONS	10 PORTIONS
Saddle of lamb	1 saddle	2½ saddles
Fresh rosemary	2 sprigs	5 sprigs
Sunflower oil	40ml	100ml
Lamb jus	300ml	850ml
Fresh thyme	2 sprigs	5 sprigs
Dry white wine	40ml	100ml
Lamb faggot		
Lamb liver	200g	600g
Lamb breast	100g	300g
Finely chopped onion	60g	180g
Butter	40g	80g
Fresh chopped parsley	2tbsp	6tbsp
Fresh chopped thyme	2tbsp	6tbsp
Garlic	1 clove	3 cloves
Whole egg	1 small egg	2 eggs
Wholemeal breadcrumbs	75g	225g
Pig's caul	4 sheets	10 sheets
Strong lamb stock	1 litre	2.5 litres
Good-quality salt and white pepper	To taste	To taste
Stilton dauphinoise		
Double cream	200ml	500ml
Fresh milk	100ml	275ml
Garlic	2 cloves	3 cloves
Desiree potatoes	3	6
Butter	25g	50g
Stilton cheese	100g	200g
Good-quality salt and white pepper	To taste	To taste

Method of work

1 For the lamb faggots, preheat an oven to 180°C. Finely chop the liver and breast of lamb and place in a saucepan with the chopped onion, garlic and the butter. Stew slowly for about 30 minutes with the lid on, do not colour the ingredients at this stage.

2 Strain off the fat and put the mixture into a bowl with the herbs and season well. Add the egg and combine all ingredients well.

3 Add enough breadcrumbs to make a mixture that will just hold together. Divide the faggot mixture into 60g pieces and wrap each in as little caul as possible to hold together. Shape into balls and put into an earthenware dish.

4 Pour the lamb stock over, enough to come half way up the faggots. Bake in the preheated oven for approximately 45 minutes until the faggots have a brown colouring. Reserve for service.

5 Remove the cannons from the saddle by cutting at the chine bone and following the bone with the knife until each cannon is released.

6 Carefully trim any silver membrane and fat. Remove the fillets and trim off any fat.

7 For the Stilton dauphinoise, place the cream, milk and garlic in a saucepan and bring to the boil. Remove from the heat and allow to cool.

8 Wash, peel and rewash the potatoes before slicing into 2mm thick slices. Butter an ovenproof dish and lightly season with the salt and pepper. Arrange the slices of potato over the base of the dish, slightly overlapping, and season each layer of potato.

9 Pour over the cream to cover the potatoes. Bake in an oven at 180°C for 30 minutes. Reduce the heat of the oven to 160°C and sprinkle the grated Stilton on top, cook for a further 15 minutes. Remove from the oven and set aside to rest.

10 Season and seal the cannons in hot oil in a shallow pan until browned on all sides. Place the cannons into the preheated oven for 6 minutes until the lamb is just pink inside, continually baste the cannon during the cooking process. Remove from the oven and allow the lamb to rest for 2–3 minutes.

11 Deglaze the shallow pan with the white wine and add the chopped fresh rosemary and thyme. Reduce by two-thirds and add the lamb jus. Bring back to the boil and adjust the consistency and seasoning, then pass through a fine chinois.

12 Cut the dauphinoise into rounds with a plain pastry cutter, one per portion, and set onto a service plate. Place a lamb faggot next the potato. Carve the cannons and place around the faggots. Serve with the rosemary jus.

CHEF'S TIP

Dauphinoise potatoes were not traditionally made with cheese, however Emmental cheese is now usually used to add flavour.

Removing the cannons from the saddle

Removing the silver membrane

The prepared cannons ready for cooking

Fillet of lamb tapenade, mini shepherd's pie and garlic roasted root vegetables

INGREDIENTS	4 PORTIONS	10 PORTIONS
Prepared lamb fillets	2 × 400g	5 × 400g
Olive oil	40ml	100ml
Black olives	200g	500g
Anchovy fillets	50g	125g
Garlic	2 cloves	5 cloves
Pig's caul	4 sheets	10 sheets
Mini shepherd's pie		
Finely chopped onion	75g	225g
Finely diced carrot	50g	150g
Olive oil	40ml	100ml
Minced lamb	200g	600g
Lamb stock	100ml	350ml
Peas	50g	150g
Medium sized baked jacket potatoes	4	10
Butter	25g	100g
Fresh thyme	4 sprigs	10 sprigs
Garlic roasted root vegetables		
Carrot	1 large	3 large
Turnip	1 medium	2 medium
Swede	1 small	3 small
Celeriac	1 small	3 small
Button onions	16	40
Garlic	8 cloves	20 cloves
Olive oil	50ml	145ml
Rosemary and redcurrant jus		
Strong lamb stock	400ml	1 litre
Port	75ml	200ml
Chopped shallots	50g	145g
Redcurrants	40g	120g
Fresh chopped rosemary	1tbsp	2tbsp
Good-quality salt and white pepper	To taste	To taste

CHEF'S TIP

Dried rosemary can be used for this dish, but the weight should be quartered to allow for the intensity of flavour of the dried herb.

Trimming the fillets

Method of work

1 Bone the fillets and trim from fat and sinew. Preheat an oven to 180°C.

2 For the tapenade, put all the black olives and garlic in a pan with a little olive oil and sweat for 2 minutes. Place in a blender with the anchovy fillet and blend together with the seasoning to make a thick paste. Take it out and keep until required.

3 To prepare the lamb, lay the caul on a clean working surface and spread the tapenade evenly on the caul according to the width of the lamb fillets. Lay the lamb fillets on the caul and roll the caul around each fillet so that the tapenade is all around the lamb. Wrap the fillets in cling film as tightly as possible and put into a refrigerator for about 15 minutes.

4 Cook the fillets in a preheated steamer for approximately 12 minutes.

5 For the shepherd's pies, sweat the onion and carrot in a little olive oil. Add the minced lamb and season well. Add the lamb stock and peas and simmer for 5 minutes.

6 Spoon the potato out of their jackets and mash with the butter, chopped fresh thyme, salt and pepper. Grease small stainless steel rings (one per portion) and half fill with the minced lamb. Pipe the mashed potato on top and place into the oven for 15 minutes.

7 For the garlic roasted root vegetables, cut all the vegetables (except the onions) into 2cm cubes. Blanch each vegetable separately in boiling salted water. Place the olive oil in a sauteuse and heat on the stove, adding the blanched vegetables, garlic cloves and seasoning. Toss the vegetables for a few minutes before placing in the oven to roast for 15 minutes.

8 To make the sauce, reduce the lamb stock by half with the rosemary and in a separate pan reduce the port, redcurrants (washed and stalks removed) and chopped shallots by half. Add the rosemary stock and reduce until the correct consistency has been obtained. Pass through a fine chinois and correct the seasoning.

9 To serve, turn out the shepherd's pie at the top of the service plate and arrange a selection of the roasted vegetables at the bottom. Slice each lamb fillet and place slices on top of the vegetables. Pour the sauce around the plate and serve.

PORK RECIPES

Honey glazed baked gammon with a peach compôte and piquant sauce

INGREDIENTS	4 PORTIONS	10 PORTIONS
Boned and rolled gammon joint	Allow 150g cooked gammon per portion	
Honey	100g	200g
Carrot	1 large	3 large
Onion	1 large	4 large
Bay leaves	3	6
Celery	2 large stalks	5 large stalks
White peppercorns	12	20
English mustard	20g	40g
Cloves	20	30
Peach compôte		
Fresh peaches (peeled and stone removed)	4	10
Sultanas	50g	100g
Ground cinnamon	½tsp	1tsp
Demerara sugar	50g	90g
Water	50ml	100ml
Piquant sauce		
Chopped shallots	25g	50g
White wine vinegar	40ml	75ml
White wine	40ml	75ml
Jus lie	400ml	800ml
Finely chopped gherkins	25g	50g
Finely chopped capers	15g	25g
Finely chopped fresh parsley	3tsp	1tbsp
Finely chopped fresh tarragon	1tsp	3tsp
Good-quality salt and white pepper	To taste	To taste

Method of work

1 Soak the prepared gammon joint for 24 hours in cold water in the refrigerator.

2 Preheat an oven to 185°C.

3 Remove the gammon joint and rinse in cold water. Place into a large saucepan and cover with cold water. Add the bay leaves, carrot, celery, white peppercorns and onion.

4 Bring to the boil and simmer. After 5 minutes skim the surface of impurities. Continue to simmer, allowing 1 hour per 1kg weight of meat plus an additional 30 minutes. To test if the gammon is cooked push a skewer or knife into the thickest part. There should be little resistance when the skewer is withdrawn.

5 Lift out the gammon and leave to cool for a few minutes.

6 Remove the rind and allow the joint to rest for 10 minutes, mix the mustard and honey and brush liberally over the gammon. Score the fat into diamonds using a sharp knife and push a clove into each diamond segment.

7 Place in a roasting dish and bake in the oven until deep golden brown. Baste the gammon with the pan juices from time to time.

8 For the peach compôte, cut the stoned and peeled peaches into large (3cm) dice and place in a saucepan with all the other ingredients. Slowly bring to the boil on a stove and turn the heat low to slowly cook the ingredients into a light compôte.

9 For the piquant sauce, place the shallots, white wine and vinegar into a small saucepan and reduce by two-thirds. Add the jus lie and reduce to a sauce consistency. Check the seasoning and add the gherkins, capers and herbs. Reserve for service.

10 Remove the gammon from the oven and dress on a platter for carving at the table, served with the sauce and compôte.

Fillet of pork with pea purée, herb noodles and sherry jus

INGREDIENTS	4 PORTIONS	10 PORTIONS
Butter	75g	150g
Trimmed pork fillet	2 × 300g	5 × 300g
Pea purée		
Finely chopped shallots	50g	150g
Fresh thyme	1 sprig	2 sprigs
Double cream	75ml	300ml
Garden peas (fresh or frozen)	400g	1kg
Good-quality salt and white pepper	To taste	To taste
Herb noodles		
Fresh noodle paste	350g	700g
Butter	50g	100g
Fresh chopped herbs (parsley, tarragon, chives and basil)	2tbsp	5tbsp
Sherry jus		
Olive oil	40ml	80ml
Finely chopped shallots	75g	150g
Chestnut mushrooms	75g	130g
Dry sherry	75ml	150ml
Madeira	50ml	100ml
Chicken stock	200ml	400ml
Veal jus	100ml	200ml

Method of work

1 Preheat an oven to 180°C.

2 Heat butter in a shallow pan, season the fillet and quickly brown on both sides. Place the pan into the oven to finish cooking for 15 minutes, basting the fillet continuously. Remove from the oven and rest for 5 minutes before finishing for service.

3 For the pea purée, cook the peas with thyme stalks in a little boiling water until tender. Refresh quickly to retain the colour.

4 Sweat the finely chopped shallots and add the cream and seasoning.

5 Purée the peas until smooth. Pass the mixture and reserve warm.

6 For the noodles, roll out the paste to a very thin rectangle using a pasta roller. Cut into 5mm wide strips and spread out onto a lightly floured tray and leave to dry for at least 30 minutes.

7 Place the noodles in a pan of boiling salted water and allow to simmer for 8 minutes. Drain in a colander. Melt the butter in a sauteuse, add the noodles and the herbs. Season well and toss until the herbs have fully mixed into the noodles. Reserve warm for service.

8 For the sherry jus, heat the oil in a saucepan and add the shallots and chestnut mushrooms and cook with a little colour. Add the sherry and Madeira and reduce by half. Add the chicken stock and veal jus and reduce by half again.

9 Pass through a fine chinois and correct the seasoning.

10 To serve, cut the fillet of pork on the slant into slices. Arrange slices on the plate, slightly overlapping each other. Garnish with the noodles placed to one side of the pork and the pea purée to the other. Spoon over the sherry jus.

Braised belly of pork with colcannon and cider sauce

INGREDIENTS	4 PORTIONS	10 PORTIONS
Pork belly	600g	1.5kg
Cider	320ml	800ml
Brown stock	160ml	400ml
Diced cooking apples	240g	600g
Demerara sugar	40g	100g
Butter	40g	100g
Diced onion	100g	250g
Mirepoix of carrot, celery and leek	200g	500g
Colcannon potatoes		
Maris Piper potatoes	250g	600g
Savoy cabbage	250g	600g
Leeks	100g	250g
Chives	2tbsp	4tbsp
Fresh milk	250ml	600ml
Butter	45g	100g
Good-quality salt and white pepper	To taste	To taste

Method of work

1 Remove the bone from the belly and singe any hairs with a flame.

2 Neatly trim the edges of the pork and then roll up the joint. Do not roll too tightly.

3 Starting in the centre, tie string around the joint. Repeat at 2.5cm intervals.

4 Preheat an oven to 180°C.

5 Season and sprinkle the belly of pork with the sugar. Heat a little oil in a hot pan (large enough to take the whole belly of pork) and place the belly of pork in the pan. Colour on each side until golden brown. Remove and set aside. Sweat the mirepoix and diced onion in the butter for 4 minutes without colour.

6 Place the mirepoix, diced cooking apples, pork, cider and stock in a covered pan and bring to the boil. Place in the oven and braise for 1½ hours. Check occasionally and add more stock or water as required.

7 Remove the lid and continue to cook for a further 1 hour, basting frequently.

8 Remove the pork and liquidise the cooking liquor. Pass through a fine chinois into a clean pan and correct the seasoning and consistency.

9 For the colcannon, shred the cabbage and cook quickly in boiling water. Drain in a colander. Cook and mash the potatoes. Slice the leeks and simmer in the milk until just cooked.

10 Mix in the potatoes, cabbage, chopped chives, butter and seasoning. Reserve for service.

11 Carve the pork belly, removing the string. Place slices onto a bed of colcannon potatoes and serve with a cordon of cider sauce.

Roast loin of pork with black pudding and apple, sage and onion foam

INGREDIENTS	4 PORTIONS	10 PORTIONS
Loin of pork joint	600g	1.5kg
Smoked pancetta	4 slices	10 slices
Butter	50g	100g
Braeburn apples	2	4
Chopped onion	50g	100g
Black pudding	200g	400g
Olive oil	25ml	50ml
Brown stock (beef, chicken or veal)	350ml	700ml
Good-quality salt and white pepper	To taste	To taste
Sage and onion foam		
Fresh sage leaves	1tbsp	2tbsp
Chopped onion	40g	80g
Garlic	1 clove	2 cloves
Chicken stock	200ml	400ml
Double cream	75ml	150ml

CHEF'S TIP

To achieve a successful crackling, ensure that there is a good layer of fat beneath the skin and that the skin has been evenly scored and well dried before roasting.

Method of work

1 Preheat an oven to 220°C.

2 Dry the pork skin with kitchen paper and leave to dry out for 20 minutes. Brush the skin lightly with the oil and season well with the salt and pepper.

3 Place into the preheated oven for 30 minutes and then reduce the temperature to 170°C. Occasionally baste the joint lightly. Allow 25 minutes per 500g of pork plus an extra 15 minutes cooking time.

4 For the sage and onion foam, sweat together the chopped onion, sage and garlic without colour. Add the chicken stock and reduce by half. Add the cream and bring back to the boil.

5 Place the mixture into a blender and liquidise until smooth. Pass through a fine sieve into a gas-charged canister and reserve at a temperature of 55°C. Charge the canister with the gas ready for service.

6 For the black pudding and apple, cut the apples into quarters and halve each quarter again. Discard the cores. Slice the black pudding into 5mm slices. Cut the pancetta into thin strips.

7 Warm the butter in a shallow pan until it begins to foam. Add the sliced black pudding and cook for 4 minutes. Remove the black pudding from the pan and reserve in a stainless steel bowl. Put the apple slices into the same pan and cook until a little colour has been achieved. Add the chopped onion and sliced pancetta and cook for a further 3 minutes. Finally, combine the black pudding with the apple mixture, season lightly and reserve warm for service.

8 When the pork is cooked, remove from the oven. Cover loosely with foil and rest for 20 minutes.

9 Allow the cooking juices and sediment from the pork to settle in the roasting tin, then drain off the fat without disturbing the sediment. Add the brown stock, bring to the boil and allow to simmer. Reduce to the correct consistency and season with a little salt if required. Pass through a fine chinois and skim off any remaining fat.

10 Using a sharp carving knife, remove the crackling from the loin of pork and cut the crackling into pieces. Carve the pork into slices. Serve each portion on a service plate with the crackling, black pudding and apple, sage and onion foam and the jus de rôti (roast gravy).

Pork and rabbit tourte with vegetable cream sauce

INGREDIENTS	4 PORTIONS	10 PORTIONS
Diced shoulder of pork	175g	350g
Skinned and boned rabbit	75g	150g
Smoked streaky bacon (rind removed)	25g	50g
Black pudding	50g	100g
Shredded suet	10g	20g
Brandy	50ml	100ml
Sherry	50ml	100ml
Fresh chopped thyme	½tbsp	1tbsp
Fresh chopped parsley	1tbsp	2tbsp
Fresh chopped sage	1tsp	2tsp
Puff pastry	250g	500g
Egg yolks (beaten for glaze with a drop of water)	1	2
Good-quality salt and white pepper	To taste	To taste
Vegetable cream sauce		
Carrot, leek, celery, red pepper cut into julienne	180g	350g
Fresh chopped chives	1tbsp	2tbsp
Dry white wine	50ml	100ml
Vegetable stock	125ml	250ml
Double cream	125ml	250ml
Good-quality salt and white pepper	To taste	To taste

Method of work

1 Cut the pork, rabbit, bacon and black pudding into small dice. Mix together in a plastic bowl with the suet. Add the brandy, sherry, herbs and seasoning. Cover with plastic film and leave to marinate in a refrigerator for 24 hours.

2 Drain off the marinade and place the ingredients into a blender. Blend into a farce or a finer texture. Test cook a small piece of the mixture in a frying pan to taste for seasoning.

3 Cut the puff pastry in half and pin out both pieces to approximately 3mm thick. Cut out 12cm discs (two per portion) and chill in a refrigerator for 1 hour.

4 Take approximately 100g of the meat mixture and roll to form a ball. Place in the centre of one puff pastry disc and brush around the edges with the beaten egg yolk. Cover with another disc of pastry and press the pastry discs together to form a seal. Trim the tourte with a 4cm plain cutter. Brush with the egg yolk mixture and chill in a refrigerator for 30 minutes. Brush once again with the egg glaze.

5 With the tip of a sharp knife, create curved shallow lines on the surface of the pastry. Preheat an oven to 180°c and bake the tourtes for 20–25 minutes, until the pastry is golden and well risen.

6 For the sauce, place the vegetable julienne into a saucepan with the white wine and slowly poach for a few minutes. Gradually reduce the wine before adding the stock. Reduce by half and add the cream. Bring to the boil and check the consistency and seasoning of the sauce. Add the chopped chives just before service.

7 Place a tourte into the centre of a service plate with the sauce spooned around.

Assessment of knowledge and understanding

You have now learned about the use of the different varieties of meat and how to prepare and cook different meat dishes.

To test your level of knowledge and understanding, answer the following short questions. These will help to prepare you for your summative (final) assessment.

Quality identifications

1 List three quality points you should check when receiving a veal delivery.

i) _____ ii) _____

iii) _____

2 State how marbling occurs in red meat and why it is important.

_____

3 State why it is important to consider the traceability of meat products purchased from suppliers.

_____

4 List four criteria for 'organic' products.

i) _____ ii) _____

iii) _____ iv) _____

Materials and storage

1 Explain the main benefit of hanging meat.

_____

Preparation

1 Describe the method of preparation for a stuffed shoulder of lamb.

_____

Cooking

1 Explain the reason for resting roasted meats prior to carving and serving.

_____

2 Explain why meat should be browned or caramelised before being put into a stew.

_____

Health and safety

1 List two safety points to observe when removing a heavy joint of meat from a hot roasting tray.

i) _____ ii) _____

2 Describe two safety procedures required when preparing a boned and rolled shoulder of pork.

i) _____ ii) _____

15
Vegetables

LEARNING OBJECTIVES

The aim of this chapter is to enable you to prepare and cook complex vegetable dishes. This chapter includes charts presenting information on varieties, usage, seasonality and quality points for the different varieties of vegetables.

By the end of this chapter you will be able to:

- Identify the different types of vegetarian diets
- State the quality points and types of different vegetables
- Manage the storage of vegetables
- Cook the various types of vegetables
- Display a range of advanced techniques in assessment situations
- Be competent to cook and finish complex vegetable dishes

291

VIDEO CLIP
Covent Garden
vegetable market

INTRODUCTION

The large number of different types and varieties of vegetables enables the chef to give great depth and variety to their menu and to the diet of the customer. A thorough understanding of the various qualities of each group of vegetables and the characteristics of each type within those groups enables the professional chef to create vegetable dishes that exploit those qualities to their own advantage. This understanding gives the diner a true gastronomic journey through a menu.

BRASSICAS (BRASSICAEA)

Brassicas, also known as flower heads, are part of the mustard and cabbage family. The main edible parts of these plants develop above the ground. Some varieties are grown for their roots (swede, turnip; see root vegetables).

VEGETABLE	CHARACTERISTICS	QUALITY POINTS	STORAGE	MAIN COOKERY METHODS
Broccoli	Varieties include calabrese (tight green flower heads) and spouting (longer stems and looser head)	Heads should be fresh and aromatic. Avoid wilted or yellowing heads	Refrigerate for 2–3 days	Boil, steam, stir fry
Brussels sprouts	Closely related to cabbage and named after is original place of cultivation. It has a nuttier flavour than cabbage and is most seasonal around the Christmas period	Tight heads with the leaves wrapped around and with no wilting. The cut end should not be overly discoloured	Refrigerate for 4–5 days	Boil, steam, sauté, stir fry
Cauliflower	Closely related to broccoli, it is characterised by its tight thick white flower	Look out for frost damage – looks almost black. The plant should feel heavier than it looks. The leaves should be tight to the flower	Keep in a cool place for 2–3 days	Boil, steam, stir fry, raw, pickle
Cabbage	There are several varieties in use: white, red, green, savoy, spring greens. The younger leaves at the centre of the head are usually used	White and red should be very firm with no obvious discolouration. Loose leaf varieties should have a large heart and no wilting of the outer leaves	White and red: up to 14 days in a refrigerator. Leafier varieties: in a cool place for 2–3 days	Steam, boil, stir fry, pickle, ferment

VEGETABLE	CHARACTERISTICS	QUALITY POINTS	STORAGE	MAIN COOKERY METHODS
Chinese leaves	Also known as Chinese cabbage, it has the same uses as pak choi. It gives a delicate flavour of cabbage	The leaves are pale green with no discolouration and are packed tightly together in a long cylindrical shape	Refrigerate for 4–5 days	Stir fry, salads
Kale/curly kale	A winter leaf that does not form a head. The leaves grow along a thick stem	Bright green leaves with no discolouration. Should feel firm to the touch and have no limp leaves	Refrigerate for 4–5 days	Boil, steam
Pak choi/bok choi	A common vegetable used in Chinese cuisine. It has a peppery flavour and lends itself to fast cooking	There should be no blemishes on the stalks and the leaves should be strong dark green colour	Refrigerate for 1–2 days	Stir fry, white can be braised

BULBS (ALLIUMS)

Bulbs are perennial bulbous plants that have a characteristic pungent flavour and aroma. In culinary terms they are the most important flavour enhancer next to salt and are used in the cuisines of almost every country worldwide. They vary in intensity from variety to variety. The pungency can be tempered with long slow cooking or through an understanding of the qualities of each variety.

VEGETABLE	CHARACTERISTICS	QUALITY POINTS	STORAGE	MAIN COOKERY METHODS
Garlic	Garlic is bulb that has its own unique flavour which changes if it is crushed or chopped. It benefits from cooking, but can be eaten raw when it has a pungent peppery flavour. The stalk can be eaten early in the season. Usually, the smaller the bulb, the more pungent the flavour	Papery skin, with the cloves tight together. There should be no sprouting and the should feel firm and heavy	In a cool, dry, dark place up to 2 weeks	fry, roast

VEGETABLE	CHARACTERISTICS	QUALITY POINTS	STORAGE	MAIN COOKERY METHODS
Leeks	The leek does not form a bulbous base. It has a long cylindrical shape with tightly wrapped leaf sheaths. It is used as used as ingredient, and in its own right as a main ingredient. The fibrous and tough green tops are usually used in stocks	The main part of the leek should be white or pale green with little dark green. Bend the leak to check that there is no woody centre (a sure sign that the vegetable had gone to seed, 'bolted'). Avoid buying if the leafy parts have started to yellow. Should feel firm and heavy	1 week in a cool dark place, but can be refrigerated	Braise, and as an ingredient in other dishes
Onions	There are many types of onion, almost all have a papery outer skin and a layered moist interior. The main types are red and white, which have a milder and more delicate flavour than the yellow. There is also the small button and pickling onions	Should feel firm and heavy, the skin should be dry and with no mould growing, and there should be no sprouting	Onions can be stored for many months in a dry dark place if they are hung on strings. If in bags store in a cool dark place	Braise, fry
Shallot	A small mildly flavoured onion that has a place of its own in the culinary world. Most commonly available varieties are banana, brown English and the pink shallot. They are mainly used as ingredients in other dishes and impart a mild onion flavour that does not overpower other flavours	Should feel firm and heavy, the skin should be dry and papery and with no mould growing, and there should be no sprouting	2–3 months in a cool dark and dry place. Avoid refrigeration if possible	Ingredient in other dishes
Spring onions	Also known as scallions (Ireland), gibbons (Wales) and cibies (Scotland), these are early-maturing varieties of onion that are harvested before the formation of a bulb. Some varieties do go on to form a small edible bulb	Colour ranging from white at the base to deep green at the top. They should feel firm to the touch, with no wilting or discolouration	Refrigerate for 1–2 days	Raw, stir fry

FUNGI/MUSHROOMS

Historically, fungi have been used as food in a variety of ways. Mushrooms are used in cookery, yeast is used in baking and mycelial fungi are used for making soy sauce and tempeh. Fungi have no green parts and do not need sunshine to grow, they digest their foods externally, absorbing nutrients into their cells.

Mushrooms are the above ground fruiting (spore producing) bodies of a fungus. There are both cultivated and wild varieties of mushroom. If you are buying wild mushrooms be sure that they are from a reputable source as there are many poisonous varieties that take an expert's eye to distinguish. In culinary terms, mushrooms add a huge variety of flavours and textures to any cuisine.

IMAGES COURTESY OF THINKVEGETABLES.CO.UK

VEGETABLE	CHARACTERISTICS	QUALITY POINTS	STORAGE	MAIN COOKERY METHODS
Cèpes	Known as porcini in Italy, cepes are highly prized, with a rich nutty flavour. Small cepes are held in high regard	Should be firm and feel heavy. Avoid slimy textures	Refrigerate in paper bags for 1–2 days. Can be dried or bottled for extended storage	Sauté
Chestnut mushrooms	Similar to a white mushroom but with a brown cap and a deeper flavour	No blemishes, firm and dry to the touch and feel heavy	Refrigerate in paper bags for 1–2 days.	Sauté and as an ingredient in other dishes
Chicken of the woods	A large meaty mushroom found on the side of woodland trees (mostly oak). It has a lemony chicken flavour	Use small and immature, or use the tender outer edges of the mushroom	Use within 1 day, or freeze	Any dish that applies to chicken
Giant puffball	A very large white fungus that has a white firm interior	The exterior should be white and firm. It should sound hollow when tapped and have a meaty aroma	Refrigerate for 1 day	Can be sliced and fried or used as white mushrooms
Morels	A highly prize mushroom that appears in the spring. It has a rough exterior with many nooks and crannies and a deep aromatic flavour. They can accompany rich dishes and still be detected.	Check for insects. Morels should be quite spongy with an intense aroma and not slimy	Refrigerate in paper bags for 1–2 days. Dry very well for extended storage	Stuffed, sauté

VEGETABLE	CHARACTERISTICS	QUALITY POINTS	STORAGE	MAIN COOKERY METHODS
Oyster mushrooms	Oyster mushrooms grow on trees but are easily cultivated. They have a pleasant deep flavour. Their texture when cooked is soft but this does not detract from the flavour	The mushroom has a pronounced cap and the gills and stem should be the same colour. Should feel heavy and not slimy	Refrigerate in paper bags for 1–2 days. Dry very well for extended storage	Stir fry, sauté
Shiitake	Shiitake are delicately textured mushrooms that are harvested from hardwood trees. They come in a range of colours and are quite meaty in flavour and have a slippery texture after cooking	Should not feel too slippery to the touch. Must be correctly delivered in paper-lined boxes with little sign of disturbance and no sign of bruising	Refrigerate for 1–2 days	Stir fry, sauté
White mushrooms	The most common of the cultivated mushrooms. They are sold as closed-cup and button mushrooms or as flat open mushrooms. Each type has a pleasant and delicate flavour that can carry and enhance the flavours of other ingredients	Button or closed-cup mushrooms should be white with no blemishes, firm to the touch and feel heavy. Flat mushrooms should have dark gills and a pinkish edge. They also should be firm and heavy	Refrigerate in paper bags for 1–2 days	Sauté, grill, deep and stir fry. Can also be used as a stuffing and as a vegetarian sauté dish, e.g. stroganoff

TUBERS

A tuber is a special type of root that acts as the plant's food store and is grown entirely underground. It is generally the only part of the plant used, indeed in the case of potatoes (which is a member of the tomato family) the fruit of the plant is poisonous.

Tubers are the staple food sources of many cultures. Their ease of cultivation, storage properties and versatility make them very important in the diets of these cultures. The potato in particular has many varieties and uses, which are listed in a separate usage chart.

VEGETABLE	CHARACTERISTICS	QUALITY POINTS	STORAGE	MAIN COOKERY METHODS
Jerusalem artichokes	Jerusalem artichokes are neither artichokes nor from Jerusalem. They are the tuberous roots of a plant from the sunflower family.	Firm to the touch, moist flesh, not too knobbly	In a dark cool place for 8–10 days	Boil
Potatoes	See potato chart on the next page.			
Sweet potatoes	Yellow to deep orange in colour (a source of carotene; vitamin A). Historically it was more important than the potato until the popularity of the potato came to the fore. It is the staple food of central America, the Caribbean and the tropical south.	Firm flesh, no sign of woodiness and free from blemishes	In a cool dark place for up to 3 weeks	Fry, boil, roast bake
Yams	All edible yams have to be cooked to destroy dioscorine, a bitter and toxic substance found in raw yams. They are the staple food of western Africa and the Pacific islands. The average size is that of a small marrow.	Should have a coarse brown skin, which should be firm and unbroken. The flesh should be moist and creamy	In a cool dark place for up to 4 weeks	Boil, fry, roast

Potatoes are available in many varieties, and most growers produce potatoes that they know will sell and which have distinctive uses.

The main categories of potato are:

■ *Early or second early* – which includes new potatoes. These potatoes are either grown to mature early in the season or are main crop potatoes that are picked before full maturity. These have the advantage of high nutritional values and require simple cookery methods that lend themselves to the delicate flavours. Their disadvantage is a comparatively short storage time

■ *Main crop* – these potatoes are allowed to come to full maturity and are robust enough for extended storage, which makes them such an important staple food for so many people

Each type of potato has a unique eating quality, which can be categorised into waxy or floury. This refers to the texture of the cooked potato. As a general rule, waxy potatoes are suitable for salads and boiling whole and floury potatoes are suitable for baking, for chips and for mashing.

POTATO VARIETY	WAXY	FLOURY	CHARACTERISTICS	EARLY	MAIN CROP	MAIN COOKERY METHODS
Anna		√	Uniform shape, white skin and flesh		√	Bake, boil, mash
Anya	√		A small variety, nutty flavour, pink skin	√2nd	√	Boil, salads
Avalanche		√	White skin, creamy flesh	√	√	Bake boil
Cara		√	White or pink skin, creamy moist flesh		√	All methods
Carlingford	√		White skin, oval, good new potato	√		Bake, boil, mash
Desiree		√	Pink skin, soft yellow flesh		√	All methods
Estima		√	White skin, moist white flesh	√2nd		All methods
Golden Wonder		√	Brown skin, white flesh, improves with storage	√		Crisps especially, and all other methods
Jersey Royal	√		Kidney shaped, pale yellow flesh, excellent new potato	√	√	Salads, boil
Kerr Pinks		√	Pink skin, white flesh	√	√	All methods
King Edward		√	White and pink skin, pale yellow flesh		√	All methods
Maris Bard	√		Creamy flesh, white skin	√		Not suitable for boiling but good for all other methods
Maris Piper		√	Cream skin and flesh, most popular in fish and chip shops	√	√	Chips especially, and all other methods
Pentland Dell	√	√	Pale skin and flesh, even sized	√	√	Bake, chip, roast
Picasso	√		Small, pale skin and flesh	√	√	Boil, salads

POTATO VARIETY	WAXY	FLOURY	CHARACTERISTICS	EARLY	MAIN CROP	MAIN COOKERY METHODS
Pink fir apple	√		Long knobbly, Excellent nutty flavour		√	Boil, salads. Best cooked in skin and peeled later
Record		√	White skin, creamy yellow flesh	√	√	All methods
Red Rooster		√	Red skin, creamy yellow flesh	√	√	All methods
Vitelotte	√		Also known as Truffe de Chine, a purple potato with dark knobbly skin	√		Boil, salads
Wilja		√	Oval shape, pale skin and flesh	√2nd		All methods

ROOTS

Edible root serve the same purpose of any other root in that they take up water and nutrients to nourish the plant. They may or may not be entirely covered with soil. For the chef, they provide flavour, texture, colour and valuable nutrition.

VEGETABLE	CHARACTERISTICS	QUALITY POINTS	STORAGE	MAIN COOKERY METHODS
Beetroot	A deep purple root that has a sweet earthy flavour. It is high in potassium. The leaves can be cooked like spinach	Firm to the touch. Even size and shape. The leaves should be intact and there should be a fresh earthy aroma	In a dark cool place for up to 4 weeks	Steam, boil, pickle, salad, roast, soups
Carrots	Carrots are the most popular vegetable after potatoes. They can lift a dish with a splash of colour and a sweetness of flavour	Main crop carrots should have no blemishes, cracks or heavy soil deposits. Young carrots should be thin and with fresh foliage	Refrigerate for 5–10 days	Buttered, glacé, Vichy, purée, baby, soup
Celeriac	Also known as turnip rooted celery. The plant is grown for its root rather than its stems. It has a faint aroma and taste of celery	Firm, should feel heavy, no blemishes other than the grooves on the skin	In a dark cool place for 10–14 days	Boil, buttered, creamed

VEGETABLE	CHARACTERISTICS	QUALITY POINTS	STORAGE	MAIN COOKERY METHODS
Horseradish	Horseradish is a root grown for its powerful flavour and is usually grated to mix with cream for sauces	Should feel heavy. The skin should not be too woody and the flesh should be slightly moist	In a dark cool place for 10–14 days	Grated
Mouli/daikon radish	A long white radish that has a mild flavour and is used extensively in Chinese cuisine	The leaves should be still intact and green, the skin should be smooth and free of blemishes	Refrigerate for 10–12 days	Mainly stir fry
Parsnips	A relation of carrots, parsnips have a very sweet flavour that is evocative of winter and Christmas	Choose medium-sized roots as the fully matured vegetable can be woody, unless it has been subjected to a frost. Should feel firm with no blemishes or shoots	10 days in a well-ventilated room	Boil, roast, creamed, fry, soups
Radishes	Radishes are pungent and peppery roots, usually a bright red colour that livens up summer salads	Should be free from blemishes	Refrigerate for 2–3 days	Grated
Salsify/ scorzonera	These roots are closely related; salsify is light in colour and scorzonera is much darker. Both have a white flesh that oxidises very quickly. They should be stored in acidulated water after peeling	Should be firm to the touch, have their tops intact and snap easily	Refrigerate for 7–10 days	Boil, deep and shallow fry
Swedes	Similar to turnips, the matured roots of a member of the cabbage family. Raw, the flavour is slightly peppery, and cooked a sweet flavour is produced	Not too large, should feel heavy and firm to the touch. Should not be split as this is a symptom of a poor watering regime in the summer months	In a cool dark place for 2–3 weeks	Boil, buttered, fry, glacé, purée, soups
Turnips	A root of the cabbage family. The flesh is white and the skin is white to purple. A mild peppery flavour. The leaves can be cooked as turnip tops	The leaves should be intact and the flesh should be firm and not spongy	In a cool dry place for up to 10 days	Boil, buttered, fry, roast, soups

LEAVES

These vegetables, as the name suggests, are mostly leaf and green in colour. They grow using photosynthesis, which is a process that uses water and sunlight to produce natural sugar and oxygen. Some varieties may also belong to other vegetable groups, such as cabbage.

VEGETABLE	CHARACTERISTICS	QUALITY POINTS	STORAGE	MAIN COOKERY METHODS
Chicory	Chicory can be either white or red. Because of its characteristic bitterness it is not always conducive to the northern European palate. If it is sweetened with honey or sugar it can be very pleasant	The leaves should be tight and blemish free. There should be no wilting	Refrigerate for 2-3 days	Raw for salad, braise
Cress	Delicate leaves with a faint peppery flavour	Fresh vibrant colour and no wilting of the stems	Refrigerate for 2 days	Salad
Lettuce	There are many types of lettuce. They are usually used in salads to give bulk and freshness. Some have a peppery taste, such as rocket or dandelion, and some have more delicate flavours, such as Iceberg, butterhead and frisee. It is up to the chef to mix varieties and use each type to their best advantage	The leaves should be vibrant, crisp and have no discolouration or wilting	Refrigerate for 2 days	Salad, braise
Pousse	This is a baby form of spinach. It has a light delicate flavour that is pleasing to the palate	The leaves should be crisp with a small stem	Refrigerate for 2–3 days	Boil, sauté, creamed, purée, salad
Spinach	A robust leaf that is the mainstay of many dishes. It should have the stem removed before cookery.	The leaves should be blemish free, crisp and deep green	Refrigerate for 2–3 days	Boil, sauté, creamed, purée
Swiss chard	Similar to spinach, this leaf should have the stem removed with a knife	The leaves should be blemish free, crisp and a deep green or mottled red	Refrigerate for 2–3 days	Sauté, boil
Watercress	A traditional garnish to roast meats in the English style. The peppery properties are an ideal accompaniment	Bright and deep green leaves with no bruising. Delivery should be in iced boxes	24 hrs in a cold refrigerator	Garnishes, soups

IMAGES COURTESY OF THINKVEGETABLES.CO.UK

STEMS

These vegetables are rooted and grow out of the ground. They can also have usable leaves but are generally grown for their stems.

VEGETABLE	CHARACTERISTICS	QUALITY POINTS	STORAGE	MAIN COOKERY METHODS
Asparagus	A very luxurious stem that comes in green and white varieties. Should be simply cooked to let its flavour come through	The tips should be compact, the stalks should not be limp or damaged. Avoid any woodiness	Refrigerate for 2–3 days	Poach, soups
Celery	Celery is at the heart of many dishes because of its distinct flavour and texture	The leaves should be fresh and bright, the stalks should be blemish free and firm	Refrigerate for 4–5 days	Braise, boil, raw and as ingredient in other dishes
Kohlrabi	A member of the cabbage family, there are two varieties: green and purple. The bulbous stem is eaten rather than the leaves	Look for small young vegetables with no blemishes and firm to the touch	In a cool place for 10–12 days	Boil
Sea kale	A rare vegetable that can be bitter if picked incorrectly. It should be buried with sand to keep the stalks white	Long slender stalks with fresh leaves at the top. Free from blemishes and firm to the touch	Refrigerate for 2–3 days	Boil, buttered, fry

VEGETABLE FRUITS AND SQUASHES

These vegetables are the fruits of the plants. They usually grow from a stem and have seeds, and can be dry or juicy on the inside.

VEGETABLE	CHARACTERISTICS	QUALITY POINTS	STORAGE	MAIN COOKERY METHODS
Aubergines	An aqueous vegetable that can be a little bitter and sponge-like when cooked. Salting for 30-40 minutes helps to remove this bitterness and reduces the amount of fat that is taken in	It should feel firm and have a fresh aroma and the skin should have a waxy feel	Refrigerate for 2–3 days	Fry, grill, bake, stuffed
Courgettes	A small variety of the marrow family. Best flavours are obtained from medium-sized courgettes during the summer months	Deep green or yellow in colour, firm to the touch. No wrinkles or blemishes	Refrigerate for 4–5 days	Fry, stuffed, provençale
Cucumbers	An aqueous vegetable that is light and delicate in flavour. It refreshes the palate and is very low in calories. The skin and seeds should be removed as they have a tendency to cause indigestion	Should not be too thick or knobbly, but should feel heavy and have a pleasing aroma. The flesh should be firm and very juicy.	Refrigerate for 3–5 days	Salads
Marrows	A large aqueous vegetable that can be rather bland but has a slightly sweet background flavour	Small vegetables with firm blemish-free skin, should feel heavier than looks	Refrigerate for 2–3 days	Fry, stuffed, provençale
Peppers	Members of the capsicum family, which includes the chilli peppers. The colour can indicate the sweetness: green and black are the sharpest while red, yellow and orange are sweetest	The skin should be shiny, waxy and not wrinkled. The flesh should be crisp	Refrigerate for 4–5 days	Grill, sauté, stuffed, soups, raw
Tomatoes	A red fleshed fruit that comes in many varieties. Tomatoes are at their best in the summer months. With modern production they are available all year round, but the flavour is best when they are in season. The stronger flavour and characteristic aroma of vine-ripened tomatoes come from the vine and not the tomato.	Firm red flesh with no blemishes or cracks in the skin. Break one open to see the flesh, which should be juicy and sweet	Refrigerate for 3–5 days	Grill, blanch, stuffed

PODS AND SEEDS

These are the seed-bearing pods and seeds of plants, especially those from the pea and bean family (legumes), usually grown as bushes and vines. They epitomise the summer, even though they are now available all year round.

VEGETABLE	CHARACTERISTICS	QUALITY POINTS	STORAGE	MAIN COOKERY METHODS
Broad beans	A large bean that is best eaten when just picked, or peeled and cooked if stored for short period of time	Should be as fresh as possible. The outer pod should feel strong and crisp. The beans should have a skin that is easily peeled	Refrigerate for 1–2 days after picking, after that frozen broad beans have a superior quality	Boil, stew, soups
Butter beans	A large bean that is best eaten when just picked	Should be as fresh as possible. The outer pod should feel strong and crisp	Refrigerate for 1–2 days after picking, after that frozen beans have a superior quality	Boil, stew, soups
French/dwarf bean	Long thin pods that are sweet to the taste	Bright green and sweet tasting, not limp	Use on day of purchase	Boil, buttered
Okra	This pod contains rows of seeds and becomes slimy when cooked. Popular with Cajun and Caribbean cuisines	Should be bright green and not fibrous and have no signs of bruising	Refrigerate for 2–3 days	Boil, fry, buttered, soups
Peas	Fresh peas are wonderful to eat. Unfortunately it is very difficult to get them fresh as they deteriorate very quickly after picking. Frozen peas are usually the only alternative	Fresh pods should be bright green. If they are shrivelled in any way, insist on a tasting. If they are not tender and sweet, resort to the frozen alternative	Use on the day of purchase. Peas freeze very well when just picked. Use frozen petit pois	Boil, buttered
Runner beans	Coarser than green beans, these are only really available in the summer. The pod is the main part that is eaten	Should not be too large and should snap easily	Refrigerate for 2–3 days. Freeze very well	Boil, buttered

IMAGES COURTESY OF THINKVEGETABLES.CO.UK

VEGETABLE	CHARACTERISTICS	QUALITY POINTS	STORAGE	MAIN COOKERY METHODS
Sugar snaps/ mange tout	Immature peas that are picked for their pods rather than the peas	Bright green and sweet tasting, not limp	Use on day of purchase	Boil, buttered
Sweetcorn	A variety of maize, which has been the staple food of the Americas for many hundreds of years. The plant is very easy to grow and harvest. Sweetcorn is grown chiefly for human consumption, but varieties are grown for animal consumption and flour production	Sweetcorn starts to deteriorate after picking: the sugars begin to turn to starch. Press a kernel: the juice should run clear. The outer leaves should be tight to the cob and the threadlike fronds should be a dark brown	Ideally use on the day of purchase but can be refrigerated for 2–3 days. Freezes and cans very well	Boil, fry, buttered, soups

RECIPES

Baby onion tart tatin

INGREDIENTS	4 PORTIONS	10 PORTIONS
Baby onions	200g	500g
Butter	80g	200g
Puff pastry	200g	500g
Good-quality salt and white pepper	To taste	To taste

Method of work

1 Cut the onions in half and caramelise in a pan with the butter.
2 Season to taste and allow to cool slightly.
3 Roll the pastry until it is larger than the pan.
4 Place the pastry on top of the onions and fold the edges between the sides of the pan and the onions.
5 Place the pan in a hot oven and bake until the pastry is thoroughly cooked.
6 Place a plate on top of the pan and turn the pan upside down so the tart falls onto the plate. Serve either individually or sliced.

 CHEF'S TIP

To reduce cholesterol, use sunflower oil flavoured with a little sesame seed oil.

 CHEF'S TIP

For individual portions use blini pans.

Cauliflower gratin

INGREDIENTS	4 PORTIONS	10 PORTIONS
Cauliflower	300g	750g
Butter	50g	125g
Mornay sauce	8tbsp	20tbsp
Grated Gruyère cheese	50g	125g
Good-quality salt and white pepper	To taste	To taste

Method of work

1 Remove the green leaves from the cauliflower and cut the florets away from the stem.
2 Boil the cauliflower in salted water until slightly under-done. Refresh under running water.
3 Drain well in a colander and then on absorbent paper.
4 Butter the inside of a gratin dish. Season the dish and the cauliflower.
5 Add the cauliflower to the dish, coat with the Mornay sauce and sprinkle the top with the grated cheese.
6 Bake in a hot oven until the top is thoroughly coloured.

 CHEF'S TIP

Mix the Gruyère with grated Parmesan to create a more intense flavour.

CHEF'S TIP

To reduce the fat, make the Mornay with semi-skimmed or skimmed milk.

Celeriac and potato croquette

INGREDIENTS	4 PORTIONS	10 PORTIONS
Celeriac	200g	500g
Potatoes	200g	200g
Egg yolks	2	5
Grated nutmeg	To taste	To taste
Butter	40g	75g
Good-quality salt and white pepper	To taste	To taste
Flour, egg wash, fresh breadcrumbs	To pané	To pané

 CHEF'S TIP

Use a dry variety of potato such as Desiree or Maris Piper to get a pleasant finish to the croquettes.

 CHEF'S TIP

Reduce or remove the butter content to lower the calories.

Method of work

1 Peel and boil the celeriac until almost tender. Cool and grate on the rough side of the grater.

2 Peel and boil the potatoes. Drain the water and allow residual water to evaporate. Pass the potatoes through a ricer.

3 Add the butter, egg yolk and seasonings.

4 Add the grated celeriac and form into croquettes, 5cm x 2cm.

5 Chill the croquettes and then pané.

6 Deep fry until golden brown, ensuring an internal temperature of 75°C.

Creamed broccoli Pithivier

INGREDIENTS	4 PORTIONS	10 PORTIONS
Broccoli florets	400g	1kg
Vegetable stock	100ml	250ml
Butter	50g	125g
Double cream	80ml	200ml
Puff pastry	200g	500g
Good-quality salt and white pepper	To taste	To taste
Egg wash		

 CHEF'S TIP

If the Pithivier browns too quickly reduce the oven temperature to 130°C and continue to cook.

 CHEF'S TIP

Cream sauce is used in this recipe because it has a neutral flavour and so allows the broccoli flavour to come through. However, a béchamel sauce will achieve a similar finish but with less fat.

Method of work

1 Blanch and refresh the broccoli, drain well.

2 Boil and reduce the stock by two-thirds, add the cream and reduce to a sauce consistency.

3 Add the butter and shake the pan until the sauce has thickened, adjust the seasoning and allow to cool.

4 Season the broccoli and mix in the now almost set sauce.

5 Roll the pastry and cut into two circles per portion, one slightly bigger than the other.

6 Divide the mixture evenly and place on the smaller of the pastry circles. Brush the pastry edges with water.

7 Place the larger pastry circles on top and crimp the edges. Brush with egg wash. Cut a spiral pattern in the top and bake in a hot oven until the pastry is fully cooked. Serve immediately.

Leek and wild mushroom ragout with toasted pine nuts

INGREDIENTS	4 PORTIONS	10 PORTIONS
Leeks	200g	500g
Wild mushroom	200g	500g
Shallots	50g	125g
Garlic	1 clove	2–3 cloves
Olive oil	50g	125g
Lemon juice and zest	1 lemon	2½ lemons
Cooked tomato concassé	100g	500g
Chopped fresh parsley	4tbsp	10tbsp
Pine nuts	50g	125g
Good-quality salt and mill pepper	To taste	To taste

Method of work

1 Wash and slice the leeks, chop the shallots and crush the garlic. Sweat in the olive oil and allow to stew until tender.
2 Remove the mixture and raise the heat in the pan. Sauté the mushrooms and season to taste.
3 Add the zest of the lemon and allow to cook for 1 minute.
4 Add the lemon juice to the mushrooms and allow the acid to evaporate.
5 Add the cooked leeks and tomato concassé. Bring to the boil, and season to taste.
6 Toast the pine nuts in a dry pan or grill under the salamander.
7 Serve the ragout sprinkled with the pine nuts and chopped parsley.

CHEF'S TIP

Most varieties of mushroom can be used in this dish, but avoid mushrooms with a very high water content.

CHEF'S TIP

Increase the nutritional value of this dish by adding cooked beans, such borlotti beans.

Mushroom soufflé

INGREDIENTS	4 PORTIONS	10 PORTIONS
Button mushrooms (fried and pureed)	200ml	500ml
Thick béchamel	100ml	500ml
Egg yolks	2	5
Egg whites	2	5
Butter	50g	125g
Good-quality salt and white pepper	To taste	To taste

Method of work

1 Combine the mushrooms and béchamel and correct the seasoning.
2 Mix in the egg yolks.
3 Whisk the whites to form stiff peaks.
4 Add three-quarters of the whites and mix into the mushrooms.
5 Fold in the remainder of the whites.
6 Grease the soufflé dishes and fill to two-thirds.
7 Bake at 180°C until well risen and the interior is still soft.
8 Serve immediately.

CHEF'S TIP

Dust the interior of the soufflé dish with flour to give a straighter rise.

Roasted vegetable ratatouille

CHEF'S TIP

Use over-ripe tomatoes to give a deep red colour, or alternatively add a little tomato purée.

CHEF'S TIP

Reduce the fat content by simply tossing all the vegetables in half the oil and roasting them together in the oven.

VIDEO CLIP
Ratatouille

INGREDIENTS	4 PORTIONS	10 PORTIONS
Aubergine macédoine	200g	500g
Courgette macédoine	200g	500g
Onion macédoine	200g	500g
Assorted pepper macédoine	200g	500g
White wine	50ml	125ml
Tomato concassé	200g	500g
Chopped onion	50g	125g
Crushed garlic	1 clove	2–3 cloves
Olive oil	50ml	125ml
Bay leaf	2	5
Thyme	2 sprigs	5 sprigs
Good-quality salt and mill pepper	To taste	To taste

Method of work

1 Heat the oil in a pan and add the chopped onion and garlic, allow to colour slightly.
2 Roast the pepper, onion, courgette and aubergine macédoine in a hot oven until golden brown at the edges and add to the onions.
3 Add the wine and allow to reduce.
4 Add the tomatoes then add the thyme and bay leaf tied together and season.
5 Simmer for 20 minutes, check the seasoning and serve.

Royale of carrots with garlic oil

CHEF'S TIP

Other root vegetables can be prepared as royals.

CHEF'S TIP

To reduce the fat content double the béchamel and remove the cream.

INGREDIENTS	4 PORTIONS	10 PORTIONS
Carrots	200g	500g
Sugar	Pinch	Pinch
Butter	50g	125g
Béchamel	50ml	125ml
Double cream	50ml	125ml
Egg yolks	4	10
Garlic oil	1tbsp	2½tbsp
Good-quality salt and mill pepper	To taste	To taste

Method of work

1 Cook the carrots in salted water with the butter and sugar.
2 Purée until smooth and combine with the cream, béchamel and egg yolks.
3 Season to taste and pour into buttered moulds.
4 Cook in the oven in a bain marie until set (approximately 20 minutes).
5 Serve drizzled with the garlic oil.

Sautéed Brussels sprouts with oak-smoked bacon and chestnuts

CHEF'S TIP

Lay the sprouts on a clean cloth after blanching to remove as much moisture as possible.

CHEF'S TIP

To reduce fat content use a julienne of lean bacon.

INGREDIENTS	4 PORTIONS	10 PORTIONS
Brussels sprouts	400g	1kg
Chopped onions	100g	250g
Oak-smoked bacon lardons	50g	125g
Chestnuts	50g	125g
Olive oil	50ml	125ml
Good-quality salt and mill pepper	To taste	To taste

Method of work

1 Prepare, blanch and refresh the Brussels sprouts.

2 Roast the chestnuts in a hot oven. Allow to cool and then peel.

3 Heat half the oil in a pan and sweat the onions. Add the bacon and cook without colour.

4 Heat the remainder of the oil in a separate pan and add the sprouts. Sauté on a high heat until the sprouts begin to colour, then add the chestnuts and the cooked onions and lardons and allow them to colour also.

5 Season to taste and serve.

Fried rice with oriental vegetables

INGREDIENTS	4 PORTIONS	10 PORTIONS
Boiled long grain rice	400g	1kg
Sliced red onions	80g	200g
Sliced spring onions	40g	100g
Grated ginger	20g	50g
Crushed garlic	1 clove	2–3 cloves
Julienne of mouli	80g	200g
Sliced pepper	80g	200g
Soy sauce	20ml	50ml
Sesame seed oil	10ml	25ml
Vegetable oil	20ml	50ml
Good-quality salt and pepper	To taste	To taste

Method of work

1 Heat the oils in a wok and add the garlic and ginger allow to cook for 1 minute.

2 Add the onions and peppers.

3 Add the mouli and spring onions and stir fry for 1 minute.

4 Add the rice and stir fry until hot.

5 Add the soy sauce, stir, season and serve.

CHEF'S TIP

For a different finish add a little oyster sauce.

Braised butternut squash with Quorn

INGREDIENTS	4 PORTIONS	10 PORTIONS
Butternut squash	400g	1kg
Chopped onion	100g	250g
Canned tomatoes	200g	500g
Crushed garlic	1 clove	2–3 cloves
Quorn mince	100g	250g
Olive oil	40ml	100ml
Vegetable stock	100ml	250ml
Good-quality salt and pepper	To taste	To taste

Method of work

1 Halve the squash, remove the seeds and scoop out the flesh.
2 Place the flesh of the squash in an ovenproof dish, add the stock, season and braise in the oven for 15–20 minutes.
3 Heat the oil and sweat the onion and garlic, add the Quorn and cook for 1 minute.
4 Add the tomatoes and season to taste.
5 Correct the consistency of the sauce with the cooking liquor from the braised squash.
6 Strain the squash, correct the seasoning and combine with the Quorn mixture. Serve immediately.

 CHEF'S TIP

If you find the tomatoes to be too acidic, add a small amount of sugar and vinegar reduced to a caramel (gastrique).

Spinach subric

INGREDIENTS	4 PORTIONS	10 PORTIONS
Spinach	200g	500g
Thick béchamel	50ml	125ml
Egg yolks	1	2–3
Double cream	1tsp	1tbsp
Nutmeg	To taste	To taste
Clarified butter	40g	80g
Good-quality salt and pepper	To taste	To taste

Method of work

1 Blanch and refresh the spinach.
2 Combine all the ingredients.
3 Allow to cool.
4 Divide into portions and fry in clarified butter until brown on each side.
5 Serve very hot.

 CHEF'S TIP

Other cooked vegetables can be used for this dish. Just keep the same ratio of ingredients.

 CHEF'S TIP

To reduce fat content use vegetable oil instead of butter

Bacon and cream cheese stuffed mushrooms

CHEF'S TIP

Mix the breadcrumbs with grated Parmesan for extra flavour.

CHEF'S TIP

Use low fat cream cheese and lean bacon for a healthier option.

INGREDIENTS	4 PORTIONS	10 PORTIONS
Flat mushrooms	4	10
Pancetta lardons	100g	250g
Chopped onion	80g	200g
Cream cheese	100g	150g
Breadcrumbs	50g	125g
Mill pepper	To taste	To taste

Method of work

1 Sauté the lardons to release the fat.
2 Sweat the onion and the chopped stems of the mushrooms in the bacon fat until tender. Drain off the excess fat.
3 Crumble the bacon, onion and mushroom stems and mix with softened cream cheese.
4 Stuff each mushroom and bake at 180°C for 10–15 minutes.
5 Sprinkle with fresh breadcrumbs and season with the milled pepper.
6 Finish under the salamander until tops are just golden.

Petit pois à la Française with pancetta crisps

CHEF'S TIP

If the sauce is too thin add some beurre manié to thicken.

CHEF'S TIP

To reduce the fat content use grilled back bacon that has been shredded.

INGREDIENTS	4 PORTIONS	10 PORTIONS
Fresh or frozen peas	400g	1kg
Button onions	100g	500g
Iceberg lettuce	100g	500g
Vegetable stock	1 litre	2.5 litres
Sliced pancetta	4 rashers	10 rashers
Flour	20g	50g
Lemon juice	½ lemon	1 lemon
Good-quality salt and pepper	To taste	To taste

Method of work

1 Blanch the button onions and shred the lettuce.
2 Cut the pancetta rashers in half at an angle. Press between two baking sheets and put in the oven to crisp.
3 Add the flour and lemon juice to the stock, mix thoroughly and bring to the boil.
4 Add the peas, onions and lettuce. Cook for 5 minutes.
5 Adjust the seasoning and consistency and serve topped with the pancetta crisps.

Rösti potatoes with a spinach stuffing

INGREDIENTS	4 PORTIONS	10 PORTIONS
Medium potatoes	4	10
Cooked spinach	100g	250g
Butter and oil	To fry	To fry
Grated nutmeg	To taste	To taste
Good-quality salt and pepper	To taste	To taste

Method of work

1 Peel the potatoes and boil for ten minutes (the time may vary depending on the size of the potatoes). The potatoes should remain hard; it is important not to boil them for too long.

2 Allow the potatoes to cool slightly then wrap in plastic film and refrigerate for at least 1 hour. Grate the potatoes (they should be quite sticky), season to taste and divide into individual balls.

3 Chop the spinach and season with salt, pepper and freshly grated nutmeg.

4 Press the spinach into the potatoes and form them into neat patties so that the spinach is completely enclosed.

5 Fry in the butter and oil for 5–10 minutes on each side or until golden brown.

CHEF'S TIP

Use a floury potato to give a white interior to the rösti.

CHEF'S TIP

Alternatively, brush the röstis with olive oil and bake them in a hot oven.

Pommes Anna with truffles

INGREDIENTS	4 PORTIONS	10 PORTIONS
Peeled potatoes	100g	250g
Truffle trimmings	40g	100g
Butter	80g	200g
Good-quality salt and mill pepper	To taste	To taste

Method of work

1 Slice the potatoes on a mandolin set at approximately 2mm. Do not place the slices in water.

2 Line the base of an Anna mould with silicone paper.

3 Heavily butter the sides of the mould and season the sides and base.

4 Arrange the potatoes in circles, adding a few pieces of truffle and seasoning to each layer, until the mould is full.

5 Cover with another disk of paper and bake at 170°C until the centre is cooked and the edges are golden brown.

6 Half way through the cooking time remove the paper lid.

7 Loosen the edges and turn out onto a dish for service.

CHEF'S TIP

This potato dish can be prepared using ramekin dishes for individual portions.

CHEF'S TIP

To reduce the cholesterol content replace the butter with olive oil.

Potato bake with sour cream

INGREDIENTS	4 PORTIONS	10 PORTIONS
Medium potatoes	8	20
Chopped celery	100g	250g
Chopped onion	100g	250g
Butter	80g	200g
Sour cream	80ml	200ml
Sugar	5g	25g
Rubbed thyme	1tbsp	2–3tbsp
Chopped basil	1tsp	1tbsp
Good-quality salt and pepper	To taste	To taste

 CHEF'S TIP

Grated cheese can be added to the main dish and sprinkled on prior to gratinating.

 CHEF'S TIP

Use thick béchamel to lower the fat content and omit the sugar to reduce the calories.

Method of work

1 Boil the potatoes in salted water until tender.
2 Sweat the onions and celery in half the butter.
3 Heat the sour cream and remaining butter.
4 Mash the potatoes and combine the vegetables, herbs, sugar and seasoning.
5 Place into an ovenproof dish or individual ravier dishes and bake at 175°C until browned. Serve immediately.

Saffron-infused potatoes with saffron cream

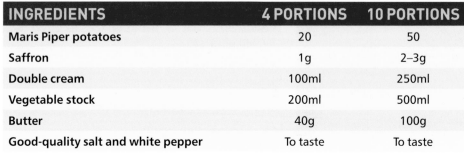

INGREDIENTS	4 PORTIONS	10 PORTIONS
Maris Piper potatoes	20	50
Saffron	1g	2–3g
Double cream	100ml	250ml
Vegetable stock	200ml	500ml
Butter	40g	100g
Good-quality salt and white pepper	To taste	To taste

 CHEF'S TIP

Deep fry the skins until crispy and serve with a sour cream dip as a bar snack.

 CHEF'S TIP

To lower the fat content use thin béchamel to replace the double cream and butter.

Method of work

1 Shape the potatoes with a turning knife until a neat barrel shape is formed (keep the peeled skins).
2 Place half the saffron into salted water. Add the potatoes and bring slowly to the boil, poach the potatoes until just done.
3 Meanwhile, boil and reduce the stock by three-quarters. Add the cream and saffron until a sauce consistency has been achieved. Monter au beurre the cream with the butter.
4 Very gently fold the potatoes into the cream and serve.

Spiced potatoes Kashmiri style

INGREDIENTS	4 PORTIONS	10 PORTIONS
Small Maris Piper potatoes (boiled)	600g	1.5kg
Clarified butter	40g	100g
Fennel seeds	1tsp	1tbsp
Mild curry powder	20g	50g
Thick natural yoghurt	160ml	400ml
Garam masala	¼tsp	½–¾tsp
Chopped coriander	1tsp	1tbsp
Green chilli	1	2–3
Good-quality salt	To taste	To taste

 CHEF'S TIP

The chillies are usually added at the end of cooking, but they can be omitted to give a less fiery finish.

 CHEF'S TIP

Use olive oil in place of butter to reduce the cholesterol content.

Method of work

1 Peel the potatoes and fry in the clarified butter until golden brown. When they are well coloured, remove with a perforated spoon and keep to one side.

2 Lower the heat and add the fennel seeds and curry powder. Allow the flavours to develop for 2 minutes.

3 Return the potatoes to the pan and add the yoghurt.

4 Add the garam masala, chopped coriander leaves and the chopped and deseeded chilli and season with salt.

5 Serve as an accompaniment to curried meats.

Baked potatoes with wild mushrooms

INGREDIENTS	4 PORTIONS	10 PORTIONS
Medium sized baking potatoes	4	10
Butter	100g	250g
Mixed wild mushrooms	100g	250g
Double cream	100ml	250ml
Noilly Prat	40ml	100ml
Chopped shallots	40g	100g
Chopped garlic	1 clove	2–3 cloves
Chopped tarragon	1tsp	1tbsp
Salt and pepper	To taste	To taste

 CHEF'S TIP

Use a floury potato such as Desiree or Maris Piper.

 CHEF'S TIP

Omit the alcohol and substitute thin béchamel or yoghurt for the cream to reduce the calories and cholesterol.

Method of work

1 Place the potatoes on a baking sheet with a layer of salt and cook until the centres are tender.

2 Meanwhile, sweat the shallots and garlic for a few minutes. Add the mushrooms and raise the heat to allow the mushrooms to sauté.

3 Add the Noilly Prat and flambé the mushrooms.

4 Add the cream and allow to come to the boil. Add the tarragon.

5 Season the mixture and serve with the baked potatoes.

Assessment of knowledge and understanding

You have now learned about the use of the different types of vegetables and how to prepare and cook different vegetable dishes.

To test your level of knowledge and understanding, answer the following short questions. These will help to prepare you for your summative (final) assessment.

Quality identifications

1 List four categories of vegetables.

i) _____   ii) _____

iii) _____   iv) _____

2 List two examples of each category.

i) _____   ii) _____

3 List two quality points you should look for when receiving each type.

I) _____   ii) _____

Materials and storage

1 Explain the recommended storage method for mushrooms.

_____

2 State three factors in relation to portion control that should be taken into consideration when cooking pommes Anna.

i) _____   ii) _____

iii) _____

Preparation

1 Explain the terms 'blanch' and 'refresh' in relation to cooking green vegetables.

_____

2 Describe the method of preparation for petit pois à la Française.

_____

Cooking

1 Explain what a 'subric' is.

_____

2 Explain the reason for not washing the starch from the potatoes in pommes Anna.

_____

Health and safety

1 State two healthy options when finishing vegetable dishes.

i) _____   ii) _____

2 State why it is important to consider using sunflower oil instead of butter when preparing vegetable dishes.

_____

CHEF'S PROFILE

Name: Paul Gayler

Position: Executive Chef de Cuisine

Establishment: The Lanesborough (London)

Current job role and main responsibilities: Responsible for all food and for ensuring exacting standards.

When did you realise that you wanted to pursue a career in the catering and hospitality industry?
At the age of 12. I began to help my parents with the running of an outside catering company and decided that was what I wanted to do as a career.

Training:
I did a two year course at Thurrock Tech, followed by work in France and in leading establishments in London.

Experience:
1   Crillon Paris
2   Royal Garden Hotel, London
3   Dorchester
4   Inigo Jones Restaurant
5   Halkin Hotel
6   Lanesborough

What do you find rewarding about your job?
Its diversity – no two days are the same. It also provides a chance to express yourself.

What do you find most challenging about the job?
Maintaining standards, 7 days a week, 24 hours a day, 52 weeks in a year – under constant pressure.

What advice would you give to students just beginning their career?
Keep focused on your objectives, know where you want to be and what you want to achieve as a goal. Set your target and go for it.

Who is your mentor or main inspiration?
The chefs I have worked with: Remy Fougere (Royal Garden), who is a great classical chef, and Anton Mosimann (Dorchester) for his insight into the modern cuisine of the 1980s.

What traits do you consider essential for anyone entering a career as a chef?
Do it because you want to – not because it sounds interesting and trendy! Long and unsociable hours and hard work are what to expect in a bustling hospitality business, but you can make it rewarding.

Can you give one essential kitchen tip that you use as a chef?
Keep your knives sharp and you will find the job easier! Blunt knives make things harder, and are far more dangerous as well.

Pan-fried potato and fruit terrine

This unusual terrine goes particularly well with slices of baked gammon or with game. It is best made a day or two before you need it – not only does this enhance the flavour but it also makes it easier to slice before frying.

INGREDIENTS	8–10 PORTIONS
Streaky bacon rashers (rind removed)	450g
Olive oil	4tbsp
Onion (finely chopped)	1
Waxy potatoes	675g
Mixed dried fruit, such as prunes, apples and apricots (cut into 2cm dice)	125g
Eggs	3
Double cream	100ml
Potato flour (or arrowroot)	2 tablespoons
Beaufort or Gruyère cheese (cut into 1cm cubes)	150g (5oz)
Freshly grated nutmeg	To taste
Unsalted butter	25g (1oz)
Salt and freshly-ground black pepper	To taste

Method of work

1 Preheat an oven to 180°C.

2 Stretch the bacon rashers by running the back of a knife along each one, then use then to line a 900g loaf tin or terrine dish. Overlap them slightly and let them overhang the top of the tin.

3 Heat the olive oil in a frying pan, add the onion and sauté until golden. Transfer to a plate and leave to cool.

4 Peel the potatoes and grate them coarsely. Put them in a tea towel and squeeze out excess liquid, then put them in a large bowl.

5 Add the onion, dried fruit, eggs, cream, potato flour and finally the cheese. Mix well and season with nutmeg, salt and pepper.

6 Pack the mixture into the bacon-lined tin and fold the overlapping bacon over the top.

7 Cover with a piece of lightly greased foil, place in the oven and cook for about 1½ hours, until soft when tested with a skewer. Leave to cool, then place in the refrigerator to set firm.

8 To serve, turn the terrine out and cut into slices 2cm thick. Fry in the butter until golden and slightly crisp.

16

Breads and doughs

3FPC4 Prepare, cook and finish complex bread and dough products

LEARNING OBJECTIVES

The aim of this chapter is to enable you to develop skills and implement knowledge in the bakery principles of producing a range of complex breads and dough products. This will also include information on materials, ingredients and equipment.

At the end of this chapter you will be able to:

- Identify the main methods of production for fermented dough products
- Identify each type of complex fermented dough and finished bread product
- Understand the use of enriching ingredients in bakery
- State the quality points of various complex dough products
- Prepare, bake and present each type of complex dough product
- Identify the storage procedures of fermented dough products
- Identify the correct tools and equipment used in the production of fermented dough products

VIDEO CLIP
A professional bakery at work

INTRODUCTION

To make good bread and fermented dough products it is important to understand the functions of the basic components (flour, salt, water and yeast) and how they can be controlled and the appropriate methods of making dough for different types of bread products.

FERMENTED DOUGH METHODS

There are four basic methods of producing fermented dough, each method has its own characteristics and applications:

- Bulk fermented dough
- 'No-time' dough
- Ferment and dough
- Sponge and dough

Bulk fermented dough (straight dough)

This is the process bakers and chefs use to make bread. It is a simple and effective method that is used in many recipes.

Flour and salt are blended together with water and yeast. These are mixed to a smooth, clear dough. The dough is then covered with a plastic sheet or damp kitchen cloth to prevent it drying out and forming a skin ('skinning'). It is given a 'bulk fermentation time' (BFT), allowing fermentation to occur over a set period of time. The next stage is carefully **knocking back** (de-gassing) the dough after the BFT and lightly **kneading** to encourage continued yeast activity, develop the gluten in the flour and ensure an even dough temperature.

The dough is rested for a few minutes, covered as before, then scaled off for shaping into the various products required by the baker or chef. The shaped dough products are then allowed to **prove** for a second time before baking. The total BFT can vary from 1 to 12 hours, depending on the recipe and the quantities of the ingredients, so it is important to always follow the recipe given.

'No-time' dough (activated dough development)

This method speeds up the fermentation through the addition of an improver. The improver contains chemicals and minerals that would normally be produced naturally during fermentation if allowed to continue over a longer time. This process is used by large-scale producers of packaged breads, such as supermarkets and large bakeries.

CHEF'S TIP

The fermentation process starts the development of flavour in the dough. Enzymes in the flour and yeast release simple sugars from the starch molecules in the flour.

Flour, salt, yeast, water and the improver are blended and mixed to a soft dough. An electric mixing machine is required as the mixing time is approximately double the normal time. The mixing speed is also higher to help develop the gluten quickly and to warm the dough to a specific temperature. Fermentation progresses quickly due to the effects of the improver on the other ingredients, so cutting down the time required to produce large quantities of fermented dough products. When this stage is complete the dough is ready for scaling off, moulding into the required shape and proving before baking.

Extra yeast is required in some recipes that use improvers as the normal growth rate of the yeast can not keep up with the speed of the fermentation. As this process does not allow time for the gluten to mellow, about 4 per cent extra water is usually added to the dough.

No-time dough is ideal for production systems with limited time, facilities and space. Improvers also assist prolonged quality maintenance, making these doughs suitable for retarding in a refrigeratered area. Improvers also help to make reasonable breads from weaker flours.

Ferment and dough

This process is intended for heavily enriched dough to allow yeast to become accustomed to high levels of fat and sugar, which slow yeast activity considerably.

The first stage is to produce a ferment; the yeast is blended to a thin batter and fermented with about 20 per cent of the recipe's flour and all of the water. Fermentation time depends on the yeast content, but it is ready when it begins to drop back (the ferment rises so much that it cannot support its own bulk and starts to drop back). It is best fermented in a proving cabinet as it needs to be sufficiently warm after dropping back to maintain the correct dough temperature.

The ferment is then blended with the remaining flour, salt, fat and other enrichening ingredients to form a dough. The dough is then bulk fermented for approximately the same time as the ferment and then scaled off. This method is sometimes known as a 'flying ferment'.

Sponge and dough

This method is used by many artisan bakeries and chefs who wish to create natural, full-flavoured and textured breads.

The 'sponge' is a thick batter which ferments slowly, helping to maximise the amount of flavour in the finished bread. It is made by combining equal amounts of liquid, flour and yeast and may contain some salt. It is then left

CHEF'S TIP

Retarding fermented dough means to slow down the fermentation process by placing the dough into refrigerated storage (1–4°C). This suppresses the activity of the yeast. Dough can therefore be produced the day before it is required and 'retarded' overnight before finishing and baking the next day.

CHEF'S TIP

Generally, the longer the fermentation time, the better the flavour developed within the dough. This is because the enzymes have more time to break down the starch molecules into sugars.

to ferment for between 6 and 24 hours, depending on the recipe and the amount of yeast used. This is sometimes referred to as a 'poolish'. It is then made into a soft dough with the addition of more liquid and flour. The dough can be used almost immediately as the yeast is fully activated.

This method will sometimes create a sour dough that is packed full of the natural flavours of the acids developed during the slow fermentation process.

Determining the water temperature for a dough.

Certain dough recipes specify a particular working temperature for the dough to ferment correctly. This represents the temperature the dough should be before fermentation begins. If the dough is too cold, fermentation will be slow. The following method is recommended for determining the temperature of the water for the dough:

1 Measure the temperature of the flour to be used

2 Subtract that value from twice the required dough temperature

3 The result will be the required water temperature

> The equation to find the correct water temperature for dough.
>
> $$\text{WATER TEMPERATURE} = (\text{REQUIRED DOUGH TEMPERATURE} \times 2) - \text{FLOUR TEMPERATURE}$$

CHEF'S TIP

The act of mixing dough in an electric mixing machine produces energy. This is transferred to the dough as heat and so will increase its temperature. If using this method of mixing, it is best to reduce the water temperature slightly.

EQUIPMENT

Small quantities of fermented dough can be kneaded by hand.

However, this takes time and most chefs will prefer to use an electric mixer with a dough hook attachment.

A proving cabinet (prover) is a standard piece of equipment in patisseries and bakeries. The first prove should be between 25°C and 28°C. The second prove must be warmer, but never hotter than 40°C. If you do not have a proving cabinet, wrap the bowl containing the dough in a plastic bag and leave it in an appropriately warm place.

Provided that the dough has been properly handled, you will not need a steam-injected oven. Preheat the oven to a temperature ranging from 180°C to 200°C. The larger the bread loaf or brioche, the lower the heat setting should be.

Non-stick loaf tins are best for producing a rich brioche Nanterre loaf

MAKING A FERMENT

Using a ferment will help to produce breads and yeast-based products with more flavour, improved crust colour and better texture. It will also allow the chef to reduce the yeast content and can increase the shelf life of the products.

Many top bakeries and kitchens maintain ferments from day to day for many months, ranging from basic recipes to natural starter-based recipes that contain little or no yeast at all. There are various methods of producing a ferment.

■ *Method 1* – retain a 200g piece of dough from the first batch of bread you make. This can be kept in the refrigerator or a cool room. Add this to the next batch of dough to enhance it. Retain another 200g from the new batch of dough to use the following day.

■ *Method 2* – an extension of the above method is to retain 200g of dough and leave it for 2 days at a temperature of 12–18°C in an airtight plastic container. Add the same amount of water (200g) and double its weight in flour (400g). Mix well until a dough is formed. This process is known as 'refreshing'. The dough will need to be refreshed every 5 days, or when some of the ferment is used to create a bread dough.

■ *Method 3* – the third method is to produce a natural starter using a good-quality stoneground organic flour with a high gluten content. A typical recipe for this method is:

– raisins, apples or sultanas	250g
– sugar	25g
– water (at 20°C)	250g
– fresh yeast	4g

Place the fruit in a clean plastic container. Cover the fruit with the water (a natural mineral water if possible) and add the sugar and the yeast. Leave for approximately 4–5 days, until the fruit can be seen to be fermenting. Press the fruit mixture through a sieve and measure the following ingredients:

– fermented fruit juice	250g
– strong organic stoneground flour	350g

Knead for 5 minutes at a low speed to create a firm dough and leave to rest in a warm place for a minimum of 4 hours. Refresh with ferment with the following ingredients:

– water	250g
– strong organic stoneground flour	375g

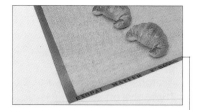

Non-stick baking mats reduce the expense of purchasing silicone paper and can be washed and re-used

A heavy-duty mixer with a dough hook can be invaluable when producing large quantities of fermented dough

Digital thermometers give a quick and clear reading of the core temperature of the dough

IMAGES COURTESY OF RUSSUMS.CO.UK

CHEF'S TIP

Many ferments can be fermented in a refrigerator. The longer, cooler fermentation process allows more flavour to develop. This is also known as 'retarding'; the yeast activity slows down but continues slowly.

CHEF'S TIP

Two varieties of bacteria are present in sour dough: *Acetobacter* and *Lactobacillus*. These give off acetic and lactic acids during fermentation, which help to impart the strong flavour required.

Knead for 5 minutes at a low speed. Leave to rest in a cool place or in a refrigerator and use after 24 hours. A starter dough can now be produced from this ferment by using the base recipe below. Alternatively, keep refreshing the ferment every day; for every 200g used, refresh with 100g flour and 100g water.

MAKING A STARTER (POOLISH)

To make a starter you will require the following ingredients:

–	water	300g
–	ferment	100g
–	strong organic stoneground flour	540g

Carefully place the ferment into the water and slowly add the flour. Combine the ingredients together to create a soft textured dough. Sprinkle some flour into the bottom of a bowl and place the starter into it. Set in a prover and leave for up to 5 hours (or until it has doubled in size). The fermentation time can vary. This starter can now be used for the country bread recipe on page 393.

ENRICHING INGREDIENTS

Bread and fermented goods are sometimes enriched with a variety of additional ingredients. These are included to help increase the food value, add to the flavour, produce a softer crumb and retard staling. Fermentation is slower in enriched dough.

Butter, eggs, spices, honey and milk

■ *Sugar* – this is an ingredient that requires careful usage in the presence of yeast. It should be used sparingly and should never come into direct contact with yeast because the yeast will be chemically broken down and become inactive. Sugar will help to increase the water retention of the dough, which will in turn enhance the softness of the crumb. However, sugar is used in fermented products to produce a sweet flavour, to give colour to the crust or to create a decorative effect on certain finished products (such as fondant and nibbed sugar).

■ *Milk* – as with water, milk will contribute to the moisture content of the product. Its fat content will also help to ensure that the dough will have a softer crumb. It also plays a role in helping to colour the crust and crumb during baking. Because of its natural sugar content, milk will have an important influence on the flavour of the fermented product. Generally, milk powder is usually used in the production of bread.

- *Egg* – an average fresh egg will weigh approximately 50g, of which nearly 60 per cent is egg white. The white has a high water concentration and contains minute traces of fat. The protein found within the white, albumin, has the ability to create a foam. Egg yolk has a high fat content and contains little water. It also contains the protein lecithin, which has the ability to emulsify fat-based and water-based ingredients. Egg yolk can be used in fermented goods to provide colour, additional liquid and fat content. It can also help to increase the shelf life of the product.

- *Butter* – the high fat content of butter means it is used primarily to create a softer texture to the baked dough. It will also add some colour and flavour to the overall finish. Butter contains approximately 16 per cent water, and in the case of fermented goods such as brioche it will considerably change the texture, colour and flavour of the finished product. Salt may have to be reduced when using salted butter or margarine (which contains approximately 2 per cent salt).

- *Spices, herbs, fruits, vegetables and flavourings* – these are all added to enhance the flavour and texture of the finished product. Because of their varying fat or sugar contents they will have an effect on the fermentation process and may slow it down considerably. During fermentation the chef or baker should always observe the physical reactions taking place in the dough to gauge the consequence of the added enriching agents.

BRIOCHE

Brioche is a very rich bread. There are four basic classes of brioche, describing the levels of richness:

- Surfine
- Fine
- Ordinaire
- Commune

The classes roughly correspond to the amounts of butter and egg used in the brioche and therefore how rich it is in taste, colour and texture. Commune contains the least amounts of egg and butter and so is the least rich.

Brioche is at its best within the first couple of hours of baking, once it has cooled, and should be eaten within a day. Brioche can be frozen, but it will lose its texture and will generally not be as pleasant.

There are two basic processes of making pâte à brioche. The first is a straight dough method (see recipe on p. 328), where all the ingredients are mixed together. The second uses a levain (a yeast sponge), which is added to the dough (see recipe on p. 329).

Types of brioche

Brioche comes in many shapes and sizes:

■ *Mousseline* – a round brioche. Can be baked in a cylindrical tin, buttered and lined with greaseproof paper. The dough is moulded into a ball, placed into the tin and proved until above the sides.

■ *À tête* – the brioche with the well-known head on top. Small brioches can weigh from 50g, large ones up to 1kg. Always baked in fluted moulds.

■ *Nanterre* or *Nantaise* – made in a straight-sided loaf tin, either in one piece or by laying balls of dough next to each other.

■ *Couronne* or *Pompe* (in Marseilles) – a large ring, snipped at intervals with scissors to produce a decorative effect. The ring is made by moulding a ball, making a hole in the centre and forming into a ring by gradually increasing the size of the hole.

■ *La tresse*– a plaited loaf that resembles the Jewish cholla breads.

Goods made from brioche

Croûtes:

■ *Aux fruits* – slices of brioche sprinkled with icing sugar, glazed, covered with a fruit compote mask with a kirsch-flavoured apricot sauce.

■ *Lyonnaise* – slices of brioche spread with a chestnut purée, coated with apricot glaze and sprinkled with roasted flaked almonds. Served dressed as a crown with the centre filled with marrons glacés.

■ *Madère* – slices of brioche formed into a crown with the centre filled with a macédoine of fruits, sultanas, currants and raisins and coated with Madeira-flavoured apricot sauce.

■ *Bostock* – stale Nantaise is cut into slices, imbibed with stock syrup, spread with crème d'amande, dusted with icing sugar and glazed in a hot oven.

■ *Goubaud* – produced by lining a flan ring with brioche paste. Another piece of paste is rolled into a rectangle, sprinkled all over with pieces of **glacé** fruit macerated in kirsch, rolled up and cut into 2cm slices. The slices are placed into the prepared ring, egg glazed, proved and baked. After cooling on a wire cooling rack it is finished with apricot glaze and a kirsch water icing.

Kitchen uses:

■ Coulibiac

■ Foie gras en croûte

■ Loaves for sandwiches, rolls and fingers

■ Crumbs (Chapelure) for coating suprême of chicken and similar dishes

RECIPES

Blinis

 CHEF'S TIP

Blinis can be used for canapés and hors d'oeuvre and are traditionally served with ice-cold caviar and soured cream. They are sometimes used as an accompaniment to smoked and cured fish.

Blinis pan

INGREDIENTS	15 INDIVIDUAL	30 INDIVIDUAL
Strong flour	110g	220g
Buckwheat flour	110g	220g
Fresh yeast	10g	20g
Warm milk (30°C)	280g	560g
Separated eggs	2	4
Good-quality salt	To taste	To taste
Finish		
Clarified butter	200g	400g

Method of work

1 Sieve the flours together. Mix the fresh yeast in with the warm milk.

2 Add the flour to the milk to create a light dough.

3 Cover the bowl with plastic film and leave to ferment for up to 1 hour.

4 Add the egg yolks and beat in well. Rest the mixture for a further 30 minutes.

5 Aerate the egg whites to soft peaks with a little salt added. Carefully fold into the fermented batter with a spatula.

6 Place small non-stick blinis pans onto a stove to heat and pour a small amount of the clarified butter into each one.

7 Ladle some of the blinis mixture into each pan and fry on both sides until just cooked; the blinis should be springy to the touch. Serve as soon as possible.

Brioche, using the straight method

Brioche à tête

INGREDIENTS	25 BRIOCHE À TÊTE OR 2 LOAVES	45 BRIOCHE À TÊTE OR 4 LOAVES
Strong flour	500g	1kg
Fresh yeast	25g	50g
Fresh milk	75ml	150ml
Good-quality salt	15g	30g
Caster sugar	50g	100g
Type of brioche		
Commune		
Eggs	4	8
Butter	125g	250g
Ordinaire		
Eggs	6	12
Butter	200g	400g
Fine		
Eggs	6	12
Butter	350g	700g
Surfine		
Eggs	8	16
Butter	500g	1kg

Method of work

1 Preheat an oven to 220°C.

2 Warm the milk to 30°C. Dissolve the yeast and sugar in the milk.

3 Sieve the flour and salt together. Add to the milk/yeast mixture with the eggs to form a smooth and elastic dough. It is easiest to use an electric mixer.

4 Carefully **cut in** the soft butter and mix in well. Place in a refrigerator to rest for at least 1 hour.

5 For brioche à tête, scale off 50g each and mould into 'boules'.

6 Create the 'heads' (têtes) by rolling the side of the hand one-third of the way up each boule to separate off a piece of dough for the head.

7 Place each boule into a prepared individual fluted tin and press the head firmly in the centre of the body. Glaze with an egg wash.

8 Bake in the preheated oven. The baking time will vary according to the size of the brioche so take care and inspect the brioches every five minutes during baking.

Creating the head for a brioche à tête

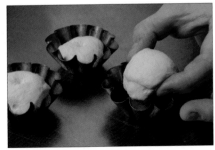

Placing boules into individual fluted moulds

Ensuring the heads are positioned correctly

Brioche, using the levain method

INGREDIENTS	1 LOAF OR 18 ROLLS	2 LOAVES OR 40 ROLLS
Levain ingredients		
Fresh milk	130ml	260ml
Slower acting fresh yeast (French hirondelle; if using British yeast then use only 20g and 40g)	25g	50g
Strong flour	250g	500g
Dough ingredients		
Strong flour	750g	1.5kg
Good-quality salt	20g	40g
Caster sugar	25g	50g
Size 4 fresh eggs	10	20
Unsalted butter (keep at a temperature which leaves it plastic and manageable; not cold and hard or too warm and soft)	700g	1.4kg
Egg wash glaze		
Whole egg	125g	200g
Caster sugar	25g	50g
Good-quality salt	Pinch	Pinch

Method of work

1 Preheat an oven to 220°C.

2 To make the levain, warm the milk to approximately 30°C. Dissolve the yeast in the milk. Combine the flour with the yeast/milk to obtain a stretchy and elastic dough. This will take 10 minutes by hand, less in a machine at medium speed.

3 Shape into a ball and stand in a bowl of tepid water (20–25°C). Leave to ferment and develop. When it is ready it will look like a large swollen sponge floating on the surface of the water.

4 When the levain is nearly ready make the dough. Combine the flour, salt and sugar. Make a well in the centre of the flour and pour in 10 lightly beaten eggs.

5 Work the eggs into the flour. Knead by hand for about 15 minutes.

6 Temper the butter by flattening it with your hand or a rolling pin. Take about a quarter of the dough and work it into the butter. Combine the butter with the rest of the dough and mix until smooth, either by hand or using a machine.

7 Incorporating the levain is a very delicate process. It is easiest to use an electric mixer and a dough hook. However, if you are working by hand lay the soft levain onto the slightly flattened dough and knead the two ingredients together.

8 Prove the dough until it is well risen.

9 Knock it back on the work surface. Fold it back into three, as though you were preparing puff pastry. Flatten it and again fold into three. Wrap the dough in plastic and chill for 2 hours.

10 To finish the brioche, lightly grease a bread tin. Unwrap the brioche dough and place in the tin. If making buns, scale into the required 50g weight and mould.

11 Prove the brioche at below 40°C. It should double in size. To test whether it is ready, lightly press the surface with a finger; the depression should spring back.

12 Brush the top of the brioche with the egg glaze, made by mixing the egg, sugar and salt together.

13 Bake in a preheated oven. The baking time will vary according to the size of the brioche, from a few minutes to 45 minutes. Remove when golden brown and cooked through.

Stöllen

INGREDIENTS	3 LOAVES	6 LOAVES
Ferment ingredients		
Warm water	150ml	300ml
Milk powder	15g	30g
Whole egg	100g	200g
Caster sugar	30g	60g
Fresh yeast	60g	120g
Strong flour	80g	160g
Dough ingredients		
Strong flour	600g	1.3kg
Good-quality salt	5g	10g
Caster sugar	80g	160g
Mixed spice	3g	5g
Unsalted butter	125g	250g
Fruit		
Currants	60g	120g
Sultanas or raisins	60g	120g
Mixed peel	100g	200g
Glacé cherries	50g	100g
Juice and finely grated lemon zest	½ lemon	1 lemon
Dark rum	25ml	50ml
Flaked almonds	50g	100g
Rope of marzipan	3 × 75g	6 × 75g

Method of work

1   Preheat an oven to 200°C.

2   Wash the currants and sultanas/raisins and drain. Place them into a stainless steel bowl with the mixed peel, cherries, flaked almonds and juice and zest of lemon and then add the dark rum. Leave to **macerate** for at least 1 hour.

3   To make the ferment, blend the yeast with the milk powder, egg, sugar, water and flour. Set the ferment at 26°C for 30 minutes. When it is ready it will begin to drop back.

4   Mix the dough ingredients together and incorporate the butter by **rubbing in**.

5   Blend the ferment with the flour mixture to form a soft dough. Blend in the fruit ingredients carefully; avoid breaking or bruising the fruit.

6   Bulk ferment for 1 hour.

7   Carefully knock back to release only some of the fermentation gasses. Scale off each loaf at 450g.

8   For each loaf, knead the dough into a rectangle slightly longer than the marzipan rope. Fold in the sides to prevent the marzipan from leaking.

9   Place the marzipan in the centre and then roll up. Set the stöllen onto a baking sheet lined with a silicone mat and prove for a further 45 minutes.

10 Bake in the preheated oven for approximately 40 minutes. Remove from the oven and while still hot brush well with melted butter. Leave to cool for five minutes and brush once more with melted butter then completely coat with sieved icing sugar.

11 Leave to cool on a wire cooling rack.

12 When cold wrap well in plastic film and store in a cool, dry area. To serve, simply slice and warm under a salamander with a little unsalted butter to spread.

Kneading the dough into a rectangle slightly longer than the marzipan rope

Folding in the sides to prevent the marzipan from leaking

Placing the marzipan before rolling up the stöllen

Ciabatta

INGREDIENTS	2 LOAVES	4 LOAVES
Ferment ingredients		
Strong flour	175g	350g
Fresh yeast	3g	5g
Water (at 20°C)	90g	180g
Dough ingredients		
Strong Italian flour	225g	450g
Good-quality salt	8g	15g
Fresh yeast	5g	10g
Water (at 28°C)	170g	340g
Olive oil	25g	50g
Finish		
Flour for dusting	50g	100g

Method of work

1 Mix the ingredients for the ferment together to form a soft dough. Place in a clean bowl and cover with plastic film then leave in a closed cupboard for 12–24 hours to slowly ferment.

2 Preheat an oven to 220°C.

3 For the dough, mix the yeast with the water and pour into the flour and mix in. Add the ferment and the remaining ingredients. Knead the dough well for at least five minutes.

4 Transfer to a lightly oiled surface and mould into a ball. Place the dough into a bowl, cover with a clean kitchen cloth and leave to rest for 1½ hours until risen.

5 Gently knock back the dough and divide it into equal quantities, according to how many ciabattas you wish to make.

6 Form each piece of dough into a rectangle and fold it in three (as if for laminating). Fold in half lengthways and seal the edges so that you have produced a long rectangle shape.

7 Leave to prove on well-floured tea towels for approximately 45 minutes.

8 Flour a baking tray. Pick up each ciabatta, turn it over, stretch it lengthways slightly and place onto the baking tray.

9 Spray the inside of the oven with a little water and quickly slide the ciabattas into the oven. Bake for approximately 20 minutes.

10 Remove from the oven and leave to cool on a wire cooling rack before serving.

Focaccia

INGREDIENTS	1 FLAT LOAF	2 FLAT LOAVES
Ferment ingredients		
Strong flour	150g	300g
Fresh yeast	7g	15g
Water (at 20°C)	200g	400g
Dough ingredients		
Strong Italian flour	375g	725g
Good-quality salt	10g	20g
Water (at 20°C)	150g	300g
Olive oil	20g	40g
Finish		
Fine sea-salt crystals	20g	45g
Fresh rosemary leaves	20 leaves	50 leaves
Olive oil	40ml	90ml

> **CHEF'S TIP**
>
> When working with a soft dough such as focaccia, it is important to keep the work surface and your hands clean and oiled with a little olive oil.

Method of work

1 Mix the ingredients for the ferment together to form a soft dough. Place in a clean bowl and cover with plastic film and leave in a closed cupboard at room temperature for 2 hours to slowly ferment.

2 Preheat an oven to 220°C.

3 To make the dough, mix the water and oil together and add the ferment. Combine the flour and salt and knead until soft.

4 Place in a clean bowl and leave to rest for 15 minutes.

5 Turn the dough out onto an oiled surface and fold and gently knead the dough for a few minutes. Leave to rest for 10 minutes and then repeat the process.

6 Lightly flatten the dough onto a baking tray rubbed with olive oil. Stretch the dough out until it reaches the corners of the tray, but ensure that it is at least 2cm thick.

7 Cover with a clean kitchen cloth and leave to prove for 25 minutes.

8 Sprinkle a little water, olive oil, sea salt and rosemary leaves on top. Press down onto the dough with your finger tips to create a dimpled effect.

9 Bake in the oven for 15 minutes then reduce the temperature to 180°C for a further 15 minutes. Remove from the oven and leave to cool on a wire cooling rack.

Croissants

INGREDIENTS	15 INDIVIDUAL	30 INDIVIDUAL
Strong flour	500g	1kg
Good-quality salt	10g	20g
Fresh yeast	25g	40g
Caster sugar	30g	60g
Fresh milk (at 20°C)	300ml	600ml
Butter	250g	500g
Finish		
Egg wash	100g	150g

Method of work

1 Sieve the flour, salt and sugar together. Mix the fresh yeast in with the milk.

2 Add the flour to the milk to create a soft dough.

3 Place in the prover to ferment at 28°C for 25 minutes.

4 Gently knock back the dough for 10 minutes. Roll out the dough into a rectangle to a thickness of 8mm.

5 Soften the butter and spread it over two-thirds of the surface of the dough. Fold the dough in three, turn a quarter of the way around and roll out again to 5mm thick.

6 Fold the dough into three again and wrap in plastic film and refrigerate for 1 hour. Repeat the rolling and folding process one more time and rest in the refrigerator for a further hour.

7 Roll out the dough to 5mm thick and cut into rectangular strips. Cut out triangles from the strips and roll up into a croissant shape.

8 Alternatively, cut into smaller rectangles, place a stick of chocolate in the centre of each and roll up.

9 Preheat an oven to 220°C.

10 Place all the croissants onto a baking tray set with silicone paper or a silicone baking mat. Lightly egg wash each croissant and prove at no warmer than 27°C for up to 2 hours or until they have doubled in size.

11 Place into the oven and bake for approximately 15 minutes. Cool on a wire cooling rack before serving slightly warm.

VIDEO CLIP
Croissants

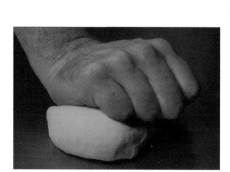

Knocking back the dough

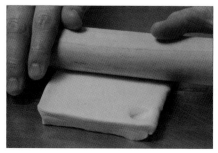

Rolling out the dough into an 8mm-thick rectangle

Folding the dough over the softened butter

Rolling out the dough to 5mm thick after turning a quarter of a turn

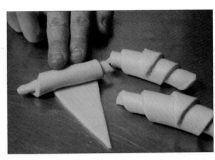

Rolling up the triangles of dough into croissant shapes

Alternatively, roll up smaller rectangles with a stick of chocolate in the centre

Croissants placed onto a baking tray set with silicone paper

Country bread

INGREDIENTS	3 LOAVES	6 LOAVES
Water	500g	1kg
Good-quality salt	20g	40g
Wheatgerm	10g	20g
Starter	350g	700g
Strong flour	700g	1.4kg
Rye flour	80g	160g
Finish		
Flour for dusting	As required	As required

Method of work

1 Preheat an oven to 230°C.

2 Place the starter in the water with the salt, wheatgerm, flour and the rye flour. Knead in a mixing machine at a low speed for 10 minutes.

3 Place into the prover to prove for 1 hour.

4 Scale off the dough at 500g per loaf. Rest the dough for 10 minutes under a sheet of plastic or a clean kitchen cloth.

5 Shape the dough into fat batons and place onto dusted linen cloths. Prove again for a minimum of 4 hours at 20°C, with a high humidity if possible.

6 Dust with flour and cut a decorative marking on the top of each bread. Bake for 45 minutes.

Danish pastries

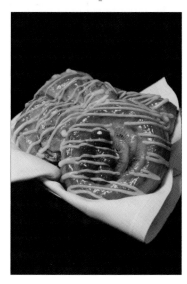

INGREDIENTS	15 INDIVIDUAL	30 INDIVIDUAL
Strong flour	450g	900g
Good-quality salt	5g	10g
Butter	25g	50g
Fresh yeast	15g	30g
Caster sugar	30g	60g
Fresh milk (at 20°C)	250ml	500ml
Whole egg	1	2
Butter	200g	400g
Finish		
As required		

Method of work

1 Preheat an oven to 220°C.

2 Sieve the flour into a warm stainless steel basin and rub the smaller quantity of butter into the flour.

3 Make a well in the centre of the mixture.

4 Mix half the milk with the yeast and the remainder of the milk with the salt, sugar and eggs.

5 Pour the solutions into the well and mix thoroughly. Knead the dough until it is an elastic consistency and free of any lumps.

6 Cover with plastic film and leave to rest for at least 20 minutes at room temperature. Carefully knock back the dough.

7 Roll out the dough to an 8-mm thick rectangle, as for the croissant recipe.

8 Soften the butter and spread over two-thirds of the surface of the dough. Fold the dough into three, turn a quarter of the way around and roll out again to 5mm thick.

9 Fold the dough into three again, wrap in plastic film and refrigerate for 1 hour. Repeat the rolling and folding process one more time and rest the dough in the refrigerator for a further hour.

10 Roll out and cut and shape as required and add any fillings. Place onto silicone baking mats and prove at 27°C for up to 2 hours or until they have doubled in size.

11 Bake in the oven for approximately 15 minutes. Cool on a wire cooling rack before serving slightly warm.

VIDEO CLIP
Technique for Danish pastries

CHEF'S TIP

It is preferable to make the paste a day before you need to use it.

Variations for finishing Danish pastries

Moulins à vent

Cut the rolled dough into equal squares (approximately 9cm × 9cm). Glaze the sides with egg wash. Pipe a small rosette of almond cream in the centre using a piping bag with a plain tube. Fold the four corners into the centre. Place a small disc of paste on top in the centre. Prove and bake. Glaze the pastries with a hot apricot glaze as soon as they are removed from the oven.

Tortillons

Roll out the dough sheet to 3mm thick. Cut out 6cm × 12cm rectangles and glaze with egg wash and sprinkle with granulated sugar. Then cut a slit in the centre and intertwine: pull one end through the cut slit and pull through to the other side. These can then be filled with almond cream if desired, and are baked and finished as above.

Apricot Danish pastry

Roll out the dough to 2mm thick. Cut out discs 10cm in diameter and place into the bottom of 8cm-diameter moulds. Fill with crème pâtissière and place an apricot half on top. Roll out a top sheet for the pastries, preferably using a marking device such as a perspex template to create a design. Garnish and leave to prove for 45 minutes at 28°C. Bake at 180°C for 15 minutes. Glaze with a hot apricot glaze and cool.

Pistachio and chocolate roulade

Roll out the dough to 2mm thick. Mix the crème pâtissière with the pistachio paste and spread onto the dough. Add a few chocolate drops and roll up to form a roulade. Cut into slices about 2cm thick (approximately 60g). Place the end of the roll underneath to prevent it from unfurling. Leave to prove for about 45 minutes and bake at 180°C for 15 minutes. Glaze with apricot glaze and sprinkle with chopped pistachio nuts.

Assessment of knowledge and understanding

You have now learned about the use of the different types of complex fermented dough and how to produce some bread varieties utilising an array of commodities and challenging techniques.

To test your level of knowledge and understanding, answer the following short questions. These will help to prepare you for your summative (final) assessment.

Quality identifications

1 Explain the importance of selecting the correct type, quality and quantity of ingredients when producing a natural starter.

Equipment and materials

1 State two advantages of using a prover, and what you would need to use if there is not one available.

i)

ii)

Preparation methods

1 Briefly describe how to retard dough.

2 Describe how you would laminate croissant dough.

3 If the required dough temperature is 38°C, and the flour temperature is 17°C, state what the water temperature should be.

Cooking methods

1 Explain the difference between a commune and surfine brioche.

2 Identify the critical quality points for the following baked products:

• Brioche

• Focaccia

• Danish pastry

CHEF'S PROFILE

Name: THIERRY DUMOUCHEL

Position: Director

Establishment: Boulangerie-Pâtisserie-Chocolatierie

Current job role and main responsibilities:
Boulanger, pâtissier, chocolatier.

When did you realise that you wanted to pursue a career in the catering and hospitality industry?
From a very young age. I was brought up on a farm around fresh produce and learned to love food.

Training:
Roven College de Boulangerie Pâtisserie

Experience:
1 Pelletier
2 Fauchon
3 Dallayau
4 Cordon Bleu
5 Alan Ducasse
6 Relais Chateau

After meeting and marrying my Leeds-born wife, I set up my own production unit in Garforth, Leeds, producing high-class breads, pastries, cakes and chocolate. I also have two successful shops in Garforth and Harrogate and now have a mobile outlet visiting local offices during the week and food fairs at weekends.

What do you find rewarding about your job?
Creativity!

What do you find the most challenging about the job?
Finding staff with the relevant skills.

What advice would you give to students just beginning their career?
Take every opportunity to learn. Get as much experience as possible. Go to demonstrations, read magazines, visit as many establishments as possible for work experience.

Who is your mentor or main inspiration?
My father. He taught me how to work hard. He is a farmer.

What traits do you consider essential for anyone entering a career as a chef?
To be fit, motivated and determined. To be able to observe and learn.

Can you give one essential kitchen tip that you use as a chef?
Reduce wastage as much as possible to keep costs down.

17

Pastes, tarts and pies

3FPC6 Prepare, cook and finish complex pastry products

LEARNING OBJECTIVES

This chapter describes how to prepare a variety of paste-based tarts, pies, puddings and desserts using some technically advanced skills and presentation expertise.

At the end of this chapter you will be able to:

■ Identify each variety of paste

■ Prepare different pastes for complex pâtisserie products

■ State the quality points of ingredients and various pastes

■ State the appropriate uses for convenience pastes

■ Identify important storage techniques

■ Display a range of advanced techniques in assessment situations

■ Be competent at presenting a range of complex pâtisserie products

VIDEO CLIP
French pâtisserie

Electric pastry break for rolling out puff pastry and dough

INTRODUCTION

The art of pastry making can be attributed to the Egyptians, who were the first to make basic yeast cakes. The ancient Greeks and Romans produced a variety of confections, made primarily from seeds, honey, almonds and flour. The introduction of sugar to Europe via Asia gave impetus to the first French pastry cooks, who were then called *oubloyers* after a type of waffle (oublies). Great innovations in pastry making were later introduced in other countries, notably Italy, Switzerland and Spain. However, the greatest innovator worked at the beginning of the nineteenth century was Marie-Antoine Carême (1784–1833), who took pâtisserie to new heights through his introduction of ornate designs and by perfecting the recipe for puff pastry.

New techniques are being developed all the time as the modern pastry kitchen is well equipped with innovative machinery and small equipment. These also help the chef to produce high-quality, standardised products that are well presented and economical.

Identifying the correct tools and equipment for each job is as important as reading recipes carefully. As mundane as this might sound, the careful identification of the correct ingredients, tools, equipment and production method is the first stage to creating success as a pastry chef.

INGREDIENTS USED IN PASTRY WORK
Fats

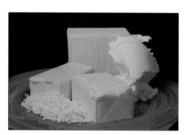

Different types of fat – butter, suet, margarine, lard and shortening

Fats are used in pastry making to add flavour and texture. Certain fats are referred to as 'shortenings' because they give a tender, crumbly texture to pastes by shortening the strands of gluten, preventing them from coming together and producing a tough finish to the pastry. Flakiness in a pastry is produced by creating layers of fat between layers of paste. When placed into an oven to bake, the fat melts and pockets of air expand from where the fat was present. This expansion separates the layers of paste which, after baking process is complete, will produce a flaky pastry. This is the basis of puff pastry.

There are two basic types of fats: unsaturated and saturated. The chart below shows the main differences:

UNSATURATED FATS	SATURATED FATS
Usually of vegetable origin Are soft or liquid at room temperature Monounsaturated fatty acids have double-bonded carbon atoms with one hydrogen atom attached. These can be found in both animal and vegetable fats and especially in olive oil Polyunsaturated fatty acids have more than one double bond. Good sources are walnut and sunflower oils	Usually of animal origin Are solid at room temperature Highly evident in butter, lard, coconut oil and cocoa butter Filled to capacity with hydrogen atoms; each carbon atom is bonded to two hydrogen atoms

Tenderness versus flakiness in pastry pastes

● Fat ▬▬▬ Paste

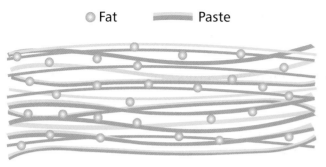

Tender paste with the fat more evenly distributed in smaller, finer pieces. The fat melts into the pastry paste creating tenderness by coating gluten strands but producing little flakiness.

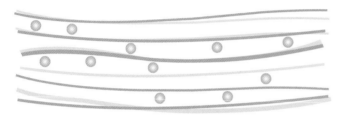

Flaky paste with fat in pea-sized pieces unevenly distributed in the pastry paste. The fat melts into the pastry paste creating spaces during baking which separates the layers producing flakiness.

Tender paste versus flaky pastes

Hydrogenated fats

Since the turn of the twentieth century, manufacturers have been making hydrogenated fats – solid pastry shortenings and margarines – from liquid seed-based oils. Hydrogenated fats are essentially unsaturated fatty acids that have been saturated with hydrogen. This gives the fat the desired texture for baking and also extends its shelf life. Most of these compound fats have no flavour and are free of salt.

Hydrogenated fats have excellent shortening capabilities and can be used in the production of convenience pastes, especially puff paste. When used with high-ratio flour for making cakes, high-ratio fat has the ability to absorb higher amounts of liquid than usual.

These fats are usually stored in coloured plastic wrapping otherwise light may destabilise the colour. They must be kept covered in a refrigerator. Do not store next to produce with strong odours, such as cheese.

Margarine

This product was developed in France in the nineteenth century as an inexpensive fat to supplement inadequate supplies of butter. Modern margarine is made from hydrogenated liquid vegetable oils and has a minimum of 80 per cent fat and a maximum of 16 per cent water. The water content is usually derived from a skimmed milk product, which helps to deliver flavour and colour. Salt may also be added; this type of margarine is sometimes known as 'stick' or 'table' margarine. Pastry margarine is formulated to produce a higher melting point and has a good plasticity to aid the production of certain pastes. Margarine is best stored covered in a refrigerator at 1–4°C.

Butter

This is the most widely used fat in the production of pastes. It is composed of milk fat, lactose, water and casein and can have salt added to improve flavour and shelf life. Unsalted butter is sometimes specified in recipes due to its intense creaminess. Because it is a saturated fat, butter is stable and is slower to become rancid than unsaturated fats. However, the storage criteria for butter are the same as for margarine.

Lard

This is a rendered fat derived from pork fat. It has no colour but it does have a distinct flavour. In paste recipes, such as pâte brisée, lard is usually combined with butter or margarine to create a shorter textured finish. Storage is the same as for margarine.

Suet

Commercial suet can be either beef fat obtained from around the kidneys or a vegetable fat that has been hydrogenated and mixed with a little flour to prevent the pieces sticking together. Suet is a hard fat and does not have creaming properties. Traditionally it is used for the production of suet paste and puddings. It should be stored in a refrigerator in an airtight container.

Eggs

Fresh eggs will keep for up to four weeks in a refrigerator. To determine the freshness of an egg, crack it onto a plate and check that the white is holding the yolk firmly in the centre and that the yolk is standing high rather than flat. Eggs keep best when stored away from foods with strong odours, such as cheese, onions or garlic, because the eggshell is porous and will allow air and moisture to enter the egg.

Eggs can be purchased frozen and pasteurised and also dried. Chefs will often use pasteurised eggs in the professional pastry kitchen because of their ease of use and also to help reduce the risk of salmonella. Always read the label on the packaging because other ingredients may also be present, products such as salt to aid shelf life and beta-carotene to simulate the colour of egg yolk.

THE USE OF CONVENIENCE PASTES

Being able to purchase ready-made and ready-to-use pastes has been both a revelation and a concern for many chefs in the industry. The issues of ease of production, use of human resources, cost and standardisation of the product suggest that the purchase of convenience commodities is inevitable in many high-turnover restaurants. In contrast, the issues of quality, freshness and flavour can discourage the purchase of such products, especially in the case of 'artisan' pâtisseries and restaurants.

Puff paste and filo paste

The popularity of filo paste is largely attributed to its success as an easy to use, convenient paste – it is no longer necessary to spend the time needed to make it from fresh. Other pastes that require skilled labour and are potentially time inefficient can also now be presented on a menu with relative ease, such as puff paste and strüdel paste.

Most pastes can be purchased as a convenience product in either a frozen or fresh variety. If using frozen paste it is important that the paste is correctly defrosted in a refrigerator and in the packaging in which it was first purchased (provided that it is hygienic and intact). The paste should then be stored as for fresh paste: wrapped in plastic film, refrigerated and accurately labelled.

The word 'convenience' simply refers to something that is easy to use. Another convenient way of using pastes is to prepare large batches of different pastes using your own recipes and techniques, thus ensuring quality, and then to freeze them individually for use at a later date.

LES PÂTES FRIABLE – SHORT PASTE VARIETIES

This family of tart and pie pastes comprises several different varieties, each one having its own method of preparation and use. All of the pastes are easy to prepare, but they do require careful handling and an understanding of their individual characteristics.

There are five different short pastes which come under the collective heading of *les pâtes friable*, all of them being short, crisp and friable (crumbly):

■ Shortcrust pastry – *la pâte brisée*

■ Lining paste – *la pâte à foncer*

■ Sweet paste – *la pâte sucrée*

■ Shortbread/sable paste – *la pâte sablée*

■ Linzer paste – *la pâte à linzer*

Two main methods are used to obtain the crispness characteristic of these pastes:

■ *Sablage* (rubbing in) – the aim of this method is to coat the particles of flour with a layer of fat to protect them from the liquid ingredients. This prevents the gluten from becoming activated, which would result in a tough paste with a hard crust.

■ *Creaming* – in this method the liquid ingredients are first combined with the butter and worked to a smooth cream. This mixture contains a high proportion of fat. The flour is added at the last stage and is not manipulated for as long as in the 'rubbing in' method and therefore the fat tends not to penetrate the flour particles.

BASIC RECIPES FOR SHORT PASTES

Shortcrust paste *Pâte brisée*

INGREDIENTS	MAKES APPROXIMATELY 400G
Soft flour	250g
Butter	160g
Whole egg	1
Good-quality salt	5g
Cold fresh milk or water	1tbsp

CHEF'S TIP

If using a forced-air convection oven to bake pastry it is often necessary to use a lower temperature than stated in the recipe. Follow the manufacturer's recommendations.

Method of work

1 Sift the flour onto a clean work surface or into a stainless steel bowl.
2 Cut the butter (at room temperature) into small pieces and rub into the flour with the salt.
3 When the butter has been rubbed into the flour, incorporate the cold liquid and the whole egg.
4 Gently amalgamate the ingredients, forming a light dough. Do not overwork this paste.
5 Wrap well in polythene or silicone paper and place in a refrigerator for 30 minutes before using.

Lining paste *Pâte à foncer*

INGREDIENTS	MAKES APPROXIMATELY 500G
Soft flour	250g
Softened butter	125g
Caster sugar	20g
Whole egg	60g
Cold water	40ml
Good-quality salt	5g

CHEF'S TIP

If the oven has too much bottom heat it will cause the underside of pastries to colour too quickly. Use two baking sheets, one on top of the other, to help insulate the paste on the bottom.

Method of work

1 Sift the flour onto a clean work surface or into a stainless steel bowl.

2 Cut the butter (at room temperature) into small pieces and rub into the flour with the sugar and the salt.

3 When the butter has been successfully rubbed into the flour, incorporate the cold water and the whole egg.

4 Gently amalgamate the ingredients, forming a light dough. Do not overwork this paste.

5 Wrap well in polythene or silicone paper and place in a refrigerator for 45 minutes before using.

Sweet paste *Pâte sucrée*

INGREDIENTS	MAKES APPROXIMATELY 530G
Soft flour	250g
Butter	100g
Caster sugar	80g
Whole egg	100g
Good-quality salt	5g
Vanilla pod or extract	Optional

Method of work

1 Place the flour onto a clean work surface or into a stainless steel bowl. Make a well in the centre.

2 Cut the butter (at room temperature) into small pieces and place in the centre of the well with the salt and sugar.

3 Work the butter and sugar with your finger tips until completely creamed together and pale in colour.

4 Slowly incorporate the whole egg, mixing well until the mixture is completely smooth and creamy. At this stage you can add a few drops of vanilla extract to help flavour the paste.

5 Gradually draw the flour into the creamed butter and when all ingredients are thoroughly mixed, lightly work the paste to a smooth texture. Do not overwork the paste at this point.

6 Wrap well in polythene or silicone paper and place in a refrigerator for 60 minutes before using.

CHEF'S TIP

When rolling out this paste into a thin sheet, rotate it frequently to prevent sticking and lift it off the work surface several times to check the elasticity. If the paste is too elastic, allow it to rest for a few minutes on the work surface and then resume rolling.

Shortbread paste *Pâte sablée*

INGREDIENTS	MAKES APPROXIMATELY 500G
Soft flour	250g
Ground almonds	30g
Unsalted butter	140g
Icing sugar	100g
Whole egg	60g
Good-quality salt	5g
Vanilla extract or zest of 1 lemon	optional

CHEF'S TIP

If at any point during the rolling the paste gets too soft or too warm, slip it onto a baking sheet lined with silicone, cover with plastic wrap and refrigerate until firm. Alternatively, you can continue to roll out the paste on the silicone-lined baking sheet and then cut it to the desired shape without having to move it again.

Method of work

1. Sift together the flour and ground almonds onto a clean work surface or into a stainless steel bowl.

2. Cut the softened butter into small pieces and place into the centre of the flour well with the sieved icing sugar.

3. Cream together the butter and sugar with the salt and then slowly incorporate the whole egg. Mix well and add any additional flavours (such as the vanilla or lemon) at this point.

4. Gently incorporate the flour with the other ingredients, forming a light dough. Do not overwork this paste.

5. Wrap well in polythene or silicone paper and place in a refrigerator for a minimum of 2 hours before using.

Preparation points for short pastes

It is important to be aware of the roles of the different ingredients. For instance, any increase in the fat content will shorten the paste by reacting with the gluten in the flour. It will also enhance the flavour the paste if the correct type of fat is used (butter).

■ *La pâte à foncer* – This paste is always prepared using the sablage technique. The use of water as the binding agent produces a very elastic paste that must be rested for 30 minutes before use. The paste must be rested again after the food items have been prepared.
 Baking temperature: 230°C

■ *La pâte sucrée* – This paste may be prepared using either the sablage or the creaming technique. The paste is soft and fragile, therefore it must be handled carefully. Flour should be used when rolling out the paste, but too much will produce a heavier texture to the finished item.
Baking temperature: 200°C

■ *La pâte sablée* – It is extremely short and difficult to use. This is due to the high fat and egg content. This should be used in small quantities and kept refrigerated at all times. Finished products should be kept in an airtight container otherwise they will quickly become soft; this is due to the hygroscopic properties of the product.

LE PÂTE FEUILLETAGE – PUFF PASTE

Uses of puff pastry

- Vol-au-vents
- Fleurons and various savoury decorations
- Tart shells for assorted large and individual tarts
- Chaussons aux pommes
- Pithiviers
- Mille feuilles

Characteristics of puff paste

Puff paste has a specific structure, consisting of numerous alternating layers of *détrempe* (the basic paste) and *beurrage* (the butter or fat used). This structure is obtained by repeatedly folding and rolling the paste; this is known as giving the paste a 'turn'.

The puff paste itself should always have a somewhat firm consistency and should be completely chilled to at least 5°C while laminating. The détrempe must not become too elastic during processing. It is therefore important not to overwork the ingredients while preparing the paste.

Five different methods for making puff paste

- *French method* – It is essential to work on marble, using the 'envelope' method to position the fat inside the paste. Fold and give three 'book' turns.
- *English method* – Roll the détrempe out to an oblong and place the beurrage on one-third of it. Give six single turns.
- *Scottish method* –Beurrage is incorporated to the détrempe in pieces. This is a fast method.
- *Reversed method* – This method reverses the positions of the two principal elements. The détrempe is assembled in the same manner as in a basic puff paste. The butter is softened, then mixed with flour. A simple blending of the two ingredients is sufficient.
- *Viennois* – This method is basically the same as the French method but with a subtle difference. Enriching ingredients are added to the détrempe to give better flavour and colour to the finished article, for example the addition of egg yolks.

CHEF'S TIP

A variety of puff pastry made with oil can be traced back to the ancient Greeks. In France, records show a type of puff pastry being made in the thirteenth century, and a charter written by Bishop Robert of Amiens in 1311 mentions desserts using puff pastry. The creation of *talmouses* (puff pastry wrapped around a savoury farce) popularised this pastry in the early fifteenth century. Carême, in his book *Le Pâtissier Royal*, honoured Feuillet by describing his pastries as beautiful and inspiring.

BASIC RECIPES FOR PUFF PASTES
Three-quarter puff pastry recipe with pastry margarine
Pâte feuilletée

INGREDIENTS	MAKES APPROXIMATELY 530G
Strong flour	1kg
Butter	150g
Pastry margarine	600g
Lemon juice	1tbsp
Salt	30g
Cold water	500ml (approx)

Method of work

1   Sift the flour into a bowl. Combine the salt, lemon juice and water.

2   Rub the butter into the flour.

3   Mix in the liquid to form a firm but elastic paste, depending on the flour used and the product to be made.

4   On a lightly floured marble top roll out the paste to form a rectangle twice as long as broad and about 20mm thick.

5   Take a square of pastry margarine (also 20mm thick) which will fit neatly on to one end of the rolled out paste.

6   Fold the paste over the fat to enclose it. Seal the edges well.

7   Roll out the paste to 15–20mm thick; it must be four times as long as it is broad and a precise rectangle.

8   Give one book turn (double turn). Cover with plastic film and rest in a refrigerator for 20 minutes.

9   Repeat this three more times. It is then ready to use.

Puff pastry with butter *Pâte feuilletée*

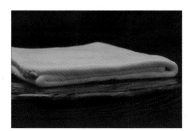

INGREDIENTS	MAKES APPROXIMATELY 530G
Strong flour	1kg
Butter	250g
Pastry (dry) butter	750g
Lemon juice	1tbsp
Salt	30g
Cold water	500ml (approx)

Method of work

1 Sift the flour into a bowl.
2 Combine the salt, lemon juice and water.
3 Rub the butter into the flour.
4 Mix in the liquid to form a firm but elastic paste, depending on the flour used and the product to be made.
5 On a lightly floured marble top, roll out the paste to form a rectangle twice as long as broad and about 20mm thick. (Alternatively, a large envelope can be produced; the French method.)
6 Take a square of pastry margarine (also 20mm thick) which will fit neatly on to one end of the rolled out paste.
7 Fold the paste over the fat to enclose it. Seal the edges well.
8 Roll out the paste to 15–20mm thick. It must be four times as long as it is broad and a precise rectangle.
9 Give one book turn (double turn). Cover the paste with plastic film and rest in a refrigerator for 20 minutes.
10 Repeat this three more times. It is then ready to use

Notes on puff pastry

■ *Flour* – use strong flour. Most white flour milled in the UK is no longer bleached and contains grey particles which look like ash. This will give a dull look to raw paste but will not affect the paste itself. Ensure the gluten content of the flour is high; it is this and not the overall protein content that is important.

■ *Salt* – any type of salt that is easily soluble can be used.

■ *Water* – cold tap water is adequate. The quantity required will vary according to the flour.

■ *Fat* – unsalted butter has a higher moisture content than pastry margarine. It is helpful to prepare it in a flat, plastic square about 20mm thick. Butter makes puff pastry more appetising and colourful, but pastry margarine is easier to work with. A little malt extract added to the paste can compensate for lack of colour.

- *Temperature* – it is possible to make puff paste in a warm kitchen, up to 22–25°C, but working with butter will become progressively more difficult.

- *Rolling* – always put the puff paste in the refrigerator, covered in plastic film, to rest before turns (although it may be unnecessary to refrigerate paste that contains pastry margarine).

- *Work surface* – marble is the best surface to use because it remains cool longer than stainless steel. It is also slightly porous, which makes rolling easier. Keep it cleaned at all times.

- *Single turn* – involves folding the sheet of puff paste into three.

- *Double turn* – also called a 'book turn', involves folding the paste sheet into four. The two sides are folded into the middle and then closed up like a book.

- *Rotating* - after each turn it is important to rotate the folded paste through 90 degrees before rolling it out again. Always roll out evenly, treating the paste with care.

- *Baking temperatures* – bake at 210°C to ensure the pastry cooks thoroughly before it colours too much.

PÂTE À CHOUX – CHOUX PASTE

Explanation of the method

During the first part of the production the chef is looking to dry out the mix of water, fat, flour, sugar and salt. This will denature and change the structure of the starch found in flour, resulting in a thick paste.

The second phase is the 're-moisturisation' of the paste through the addition of eggs in order to obtain a paste of piping consistency. This paste therefore contains a lot of moisture (that remaining from the first part of the process and that from the addition of the egg). During the baking the moisture will create steam, which acts as the raising agent for the paste.

- *Water* – the water can be half or totally replaced with milk. The resulting paste will be finer, more enriched and slightly softer in texture, but it may be a little heavier.

- *Fat* – the choice (butter or margarine) and quantity of fat will depend on the role required of the finished paste. The proportion can vary between 400g and 500g per litre of liquid. Salted butter is the preferred fat due to its colour and flavour-enhancing properties.

- *Salt* – this helps to improve the flavour. Use a fine salt, and ensure it is correctly weighed so as not to produce an over-salted taste.

- *Sugar* – the role of sugar is to produce a good colour during baking. Use a fine-grained sugar (caster). The quantity of sugar may be varied according to the temperature of the oven: for a higher oven temperature, a smaller quantity of sugar should be used.

CHEF'S TIP

The origin of choux paste dates back to the sixteenth century. Its invention is attributed to an Italian pastry chef named Popelini, who created a gâteau called *Le Popolin*. The gâteau was made from a paste dried out on the stove and which resembled a type of raw pasta dough. This paste was also know as *la pâte à chaud*.

- *Eggs* – the eggs should never be added to the panada when it has first been made as the temperature of the initial paste (approximately 82–88°C) will cook the egg protein. This will make the paste less elastic and less able to retain steam and so will limit its ability to rise. The eggs should always be added when the paste is warm to the touch as this will aid the general incorporation and mixing process. The protein value of eggs helps to give colour to the paste. Eggs also help to produce the blown texture of choux paste.

- *Flour* – strong flour should be used. The quantity of flour may vary between 500g and 800g per litre of liquid according to the recipe.

During baking, the heat from the oven will turn the moisture in the paste to steam. At the same time, the eggs and the starch from the flour begin to coagulate, forming a layer on the outside of the paste which retains the steam. The steam inflates the paste, which continues to coagulate and becomes solid as it has cooked. The result is the choux pastry's distinctive blown appearance.

BASIC RECIPE FOR CHOUX PASTE
Choux paste *Pâte à choux*

INGREDIENTS	20 ÉCLAIRS OR 40 PROFITEROLES
Water	150ml
Butter	60g
Strong white flour	90g
Sugar	5g
Salt	5g
Whole eggs	3

Method of work

1 Place the water and butter into a saucepan and bring to the boil.
2 Take off the heat and stir in the sieved flour, salt and sugar.
3 Return to the heat and cook out, continuously stirring until it leaves the sides of the pan clean.
4 Allow to partly cool.
5 Beat in the eggs a little at a time, making sure that they are well incorporated.

 **CHEF'S TIP**

The eggs should be beaten first and added gradually when the panada has cooled. This will aid the mixing process and ensure the eggs are totally integrated into the panada.

CHEF'S TIP

When drying out the panada, do so only until it leaves the side of the pan clean. Do not overcook the panada otherwise the fat content will separate.

VIDEO CLIP
Strüdel paste

STRÜDEL

Strüdel paste

The strüdel paste consists of flour, water, salt, sugar, eggs and oil. It is important to give as much elasticity to the paste as possible. To help create this elasticity, use a fine graded strong flour that is high in gluten. Once the paste has been made it is brushed with oil and allowed to rest for about 60 minutes.

The paste is then worked by hand, using fingertips which have been dipped in oil. It is gradually stretched from underneath until it is paper thin. This process should be carried out on a large, flour-dusted linen cloth.

Strüdel filling

The ingredients for strüdel filling vary from recipe to recipe. This may be due to regional preferences and traditions, or to individual chefs changing the components of a recipe at their own discretion. However, certain rules should always be followed in the make-up of a strüdel filling. The main one is that the recipe should have an equal balance of wet and dry ingredients: if the filling is too wet the strüdel may collapse, and if it is too dry it will not be pleasing to the palette.

Strüdel paste being pinned out on a floured cloth

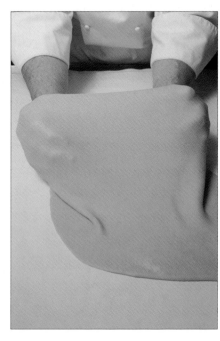
Strüdel paste being stretched gently by hand

RECIPE FOR STRÜDEL

Apple strüdel *Apfel strüdel*

CHEF'S TIP

You can replace the apples and add your own fruit of choice to create an alternative variety of strüdel, but you must always balance the water content of the fruit against the dry ingredients in the filling to prevent the strüdel from collapsing.

CHEF'S TIP

Make the strüdel paste the day before you need to use it. This will allow the paste to rest even longer, improving its flexibility.

VIDEO CLIP
Making apple strüdel

INGREDIENTS

Strüdel paste	**2 LARGE STRUDELS**
Strong graded flour	700g
Olive or vegetable oil	110g
Warm water (37°C)	180g
Whole eggs	3
Vinegar	3tsp
Salt	5g
Sugar	5g
Apple filling	**1 LARGE STRUDEL**
Bramley apples (sweet apples taste bland after cooking)	1.5kg
Lightly roasted ground almonds	150g
Brioche crumbs	150g
Cinnamon sugar	125g
Finely grated zest of lemon	1 lemon
Sultanas macerated in dark rum	200g
Melted butter	200g

Method of work

To prepare the paste
1 Place the flour, salt and sugar in a bowl and make a well in the centre.
2 Add the oil, eggs, water and vinegar. Using an electric mixer, mix until the paste is soft and comes away from the sides of the bowl. The paste should be elastic to the touch.
3 Transfer the paste to a lightly floured surface and knead well for approximately 15 minutes or until it is soft and pliable.
4 Depending on the number of strudels to make, divide the paste into two or three pieces. Using a pastry brush, lightly brush the pieces of paste with oil, cover with plastic film and leave to rest for a minimum of 60 minutes on the side of a table (not in a refrigerator).

To prepare the filling
1 Peel and slice the apples thinly and mix with a little cinnamon if desired.
2 Fry the brioche crumbs in a little melted butter until they turn a very light golden colour.

To prepare the strüdel
1 Spread a linen cloth, dusted with flour, over a table and initially pin out the paste.
2 Very carefully begin to stretch the paste using fingertips dipped in a little oil. The paste should eventually be stretched paper thin.

3   After stretching, trim the edges and brush the paste with the melted butter. Carefully build up layers of filling with each ingredient, apples first and then the remaining ingredients.

4   Fold in the ends of the paste and, using the cloth, roll it carefully to resemble a Swiss roll. Transfer onto a baking sheet and brush with melted butter.

5   Place in the oven at 225ºC and bake for approximately 35–45 minutes. Two-thirds of the way through baking, remove the strüdel from the oven and dredge with icing sugar. Replace to continue baking.

HOT WATER PASTE FOR SAVOURY PIES

VIDEO CLIP
Hot water paste

Hot water paste may be sweet or savoury. Savoury hot water paste is used for pork pies, veal and ham pies, game pies and a variety of terrines. The paste must be used while it is warm; if it is too hot it will be difficult to handle and if it is too cold it is liable to crack during handling.

Pork pies

To shape a pork pie case successfully, a block of approximately 10cm in diameter is required. Special wooden blocks are available for this purpose, but if one is not available a suitable alternative – such as a tin can or individual mousse ring mould – can be used.

The heel of the hand is used to form a cup shape, with the paste around the mould. The block is then rotated while pressing firmly to raise the paste up the side. The paste is then allowed to set and is removed from the block.

The meat filling is made into a ball and dropped into the case and then carefully pressed to remove any air spaces. The lid is made from the same pastry, which is rolled to a thickness of 3mm and cut with a plain cutter a little larger than the diameter of the pie. A hole is cut in the top of the lid to act as a steam vent. The top inside edge of the lid is washed with egg or water and the lid is then placed on the case. It is pressed firmly into the sides and pinched with fingers or crimpers to seal. The sides and top are washed with egg and decoration applied to the top, such as diamonds of paste or leaf shapes. It is essential that the meat is thoroughly cooked to help prevent the build up of food-poisoning bacteria.

RECIPE FOR HOT WATER PASTE
English pork pie using hot water paste

INGREDIENTS	
Hot water paste	MAKES APPROXIMATELY 900g
Lard	150g
Good-quality salt	10g
Soft white flour	500g
Water	250ml
Filling	MAKES APPROXIMATELY 400g
Shoulder of pork (boned)	300g
Fresh chopped thyme	10g
Fresh chopped sage	10g
Fresh chopped parsley	10g
Good-quality salt	10g
Chopped, sweated onion	75g
White veal or chicken stock	25ml
Powdered white pepper	5g
Stock	
Gelatine	

Method of work

To prepare the paste

1 Sift the flour and the salt together into a stainless steel bowl.
2 Boil the water and the lard together, ensuring that the lard has completely melted.
3 Pour the liquid into the flour and begin to mix carefully with a spoon.
4 Gently amalgamate the ingredients. When you are able to touch the paste by hand, begin to knead.
5 Use immediately. Keep the paste warm by placing an upturned stainless steel bowl over it on the work surface to keep in the heat and moisture.

To prepare the pie

1 Mince the pork shoulder coarsely and then combine with the rest of the filling ingredients.
2 Keeping a quarter of the paste warm, roll out the rest and carefully line a well-greased raised pie mould.
3 Add the filling and press down firmly. Roll the remaining paste out to create a lid.
4 Egg wash the edges of the pie and seal the edges, trimming off any surplus paste. Cut a 1cm-diameter hole in the centre of the pie lid. Decorate the lid as appropriate.

 CHEF'S TIP

If the pie colours too quickly during baking, cover with either silicone paper or foil and continue baking. An oiled silicone paper funnel can be inserted into the hole in the lid to keep the hole open, allowing steam to escape during cooking.

5   Egg wash and place into a preheated oven at 230°C for 20 minutes, then reduce the oven temperature to approximately 160°C and bake for a further hour.

6   Remove from the oven and leave to cool for 30 minutes. Fill with a hot stock containing dissolved gelatine to create an **aspic** inside the pie (approximately 400ml stock to 5 leaves of gelatine).

7   Cool and serve as desired.

RECIPES
Suet paste

CHEF'S TIP

Vegetable suet can be used to replace the beef suet if vegetarian products are required.

INGREDIENTS	MAKES APPROXIMATELY 500G
Soft flour	250g
Baking powder	5g
Beef suet	150g
Good-quality salt	3g
Cold water	125ml
Caster sugar (optional)	25g

Method of work

1   Sift together the flour, baking powder and salt into a stainless steel bowl. Add the suet and lightly mix in.

2   If using sugar as part of the recipe, add to the water to dissolve. Make a well in the centre of the flour mixture and add the water or sugar solution.

3   Mix lightly together to form a firm paste. Rest for 5 minutes in the bowl covered with plastic film before using.

CHEF'S TIP

Suet is a hard fat that surrounds beef kidneys (to protect them) and is grated and lightly floured for commercial use. It is creamy white in colour, should be dry to the touch and can be stored in a refrigerator for 2–4 weeks in a sealed container. Ensure suet does not come into close proximity to strongly flavoured ingredients as it easily absorbs aromas.

Leek and goat's cheese tartlette *Tartelette de fromage de chèvre et poireau*

INGREDIENTS	4 PORTIONS	10 PORTIONS
Shortcrust paste (pâte brisée, see recipe on p. 344)	200g	500g
Full-fat goat's cheese	100g	250g
Chopped fresh mixed herbs (basil, chives, parsley)	2tbsp	5tbsp
Leeks	1	2
Eggs	1	3
Single cream	150ml	400ml
Ground black pepper and good-quality salt	To taste	To taste

Method of work

1 Roll out the paste thinly. Line the tartlet tins and chill for 15 minutes in a refrigerator.

2 Preheat an oven to 200°C. Bake the cases blind for approximately 10 minutes. Reduce the oven temperature to 190°C.

3 Wash, slice and dry the leeks. Quickly sweat them off in a little butter to begin the cooking process. Put aside to cool.

4 Place the cheese, herbs and leeks in a bowl and mix until well blended. Add the egg, cream, salt and pepper and mix again.

5 Divide the mixture evenly into the pastry cases and return to the oven for 10–15 minutes, until the filling has just set.

6 Serve warm or cold.

Lemon tart *Tarte au citron*

INGREDIENTS	8 PORTIONS (1 × 30CM TART RING)	16 PORTIONS (2 × 30CM TART RING)
Sweet paste (pâte sucrée, see recipe on p. 345)	250g	500g
Lemons	4	8
Eggs	9	18
Castor sugar	380g	700g
Double cream	300ml	600ml
Icing sugar	50g	100g

Method of work

1 Preheat an oven to 200°C.

2 Butter a flan ring and carefully line with the paste. Leave to rest for 15 minutes in a refrigerator.

3 Blind bake in the preheated oven for approximately 20 minutes.

4 Lower the oven temperature 150°C.

5 Wash the lemons and finely grate the zests. Extract the juice and mix together.

6 Break the eggs into a bowl and lightly beat in the castor sugar. Add the cream and lemon and mix. Remove any froth from the top. Place in a refrigerator before use.

7 Pour the filling into the pastry case and bake for approximately 30 minutes or until the lemon filling has just set.

8 When cooked, carefully remove the flan ring.

9 Leave to cool at room temperature for at least 1 hour.

10 Portion the tart and dust the top of each slice with icing sugar before serving. The tart can be caramelised using a blowtorch or under a salamander.

Chocolate and banana tart with a coconut ice cream and a mango compôte

INGREDIENTS	4 INDIVIDUAL TARTLETTES	10 INDIVIDUAL TARTLETTES OR 1 × 20CM TART RING
Dark couverture chocolate (70 per cent)	80g	220g
Unsalted butter	50g	110g
Whole egg	55g	150g
Egg yolk	1	3
Caster sugar	30g	75g
Icing sugar	50g	100g
Banana (to slice and caramelise)	1	2
Sweet paste (pâte sucrée, see recipe on p. 345)	250g	550g
Ripe mango	1	2
Water	250ml	400ml
Caster sugar	75g	180g
Lemon juice and zest	½ lemon	1 lemon
Under-ripe banana	1	2
Light stock syrup	75ml	150ml

Method of work

1 Melt the dark chocolate couverture and butter together.
2 Whisk the eggs and sugar until thick in a food processor, fold together with the melted dark couverture and cool.
3 Line individual tartlette cases with the sweet paste and bake blind.
4 Cut the banana into small slices and sprinkle over with a little icing sugar. Quickly caramelise using a blowtorch or a hot salamander. Add three or four slices to the bottom of the blind-baked tartlette cases.
5 Pour the dark couverture mixture equally into each tartlette and bake at 150°C for 6–10 minutes. Leave to one side to keep warm.
6 For the mango compôte, cut and stone the mango, removing the skin, and cut into small dice.
7 Bring all the other compôte ingredients to the boil in a saucepan. Add the mango and cook over a low heat for 3–4 minutes until tender. Leave to one side to cool.
8 For the banana crisps, preheat an oven to 110°C. On a slicing machine, slice the bananas lengthwise as thinly as possible. Submerge each slice in a light stock syrup for two minutes. Place the slices on a silicon mat and dry in the oven for about 30 minutes. Form into desired shapes and cool.
9 Serve the tartlette either warm or at room temperature with ice cream and the compôte.

CHEF'S TIP

Use a good-quality high cocoa content dark chocolate for this recipe to obtain depth of flavour and consistency in the tartlettes. As an alternative to the basic sweet paste, substitute 25g of flour from the recipe with 25g of cocoa.

Red berry streusel tart *Tarte streusel aux fruits rouges*

INGREDIENTS	1 × 20CM TART	3 × 20CM TARTS
Lining paste (pâte à foncer, see recipe on p. 344)	175g	550g
Pistachio crème		
Melted butter	50g	125g
Icing sugar	50g	125g
Ground almonds	50g	125g
Whole eggs	40g	100g
Cornflour	5g	20g
Crème pâtissière	50g	100g
Pistachio paste	10g	40g
Kirsch	5g	20g
Cinnamon streusel		
Ground almonds	40g	100g
Butter	40g	100g
Soft flour	40g	100g
Caster sugar	40g	100g
Powdered cinnamon	1g	2g
Red berry garnish		
Cherries steeped in kirsch	30g	100g
Raspberries	30g	100g
Strawberries	30g	100g
Redcurrants	30g	100g

Method of work

1 Line a tart ring with lining paste. Cover in plastic film and leave to rest in a refrigerator until required.

2 To make the pistachio crème, mix together the melted butter, ground almonds, icing sugar, eggs and cornflour to a smooth paste.

3 Fold in the crème pâtissière and the pistachio paste. Mix well and finally add the kirsch.

4 Pipe this preparation into the base of the lined tart to about two-thirds of the way up.

5 Ensure all the fresh berries are well washed and prepared. If the strawberries are too large, cut them up so that all the berries are similar in size.

6 Mix the berries together with some of the juice/kirsch from the cherries. Place a layer of this fruit gently on top of the pistachio crème.

7 Bake in a preheated oven at 170°C for approximately 20 minutes.

8 To make the streusel, rub the ground almonds, butter, sugar and cinnamon into the flour, until a large crumb has been produced. Place this in a ring on top of the tart and place back into the oven for a further 10 minutes.

9 Decorate the centre with some fresh berries and dust with icing sugar for service.

 CHEF'S TIP

Use fresh fruit that is in season. This will produce a finer aroma and personality to this tart. Source fruits from a supplier as local as possible to help ensure it is fresh and in good condition.

Gâteau Basque

INGREDIENTS	8 INDIVIDUAL PORTIONS	16 INDIVIDUAL PORTIONS
Butter	125g	250g
Hazelnut tant pour tant (equal quantities of ground hazelnuts and icing sugar)	50g	100g
Caster sugar	125g	250g
Good-quality salt	3g	5g
Finely grated lemon zest	½ lemon	1 lemon
Egg yolks	2	4
Whole egg	½ egg	1 egg
Soft flour	250g	500g
Baking powder	5g	10g
Almond filling	MAKES APPROXIMATELY 500g OF FILLING	MAKES APPROXIMATELY 1kg OF FILLING
Full fat milk	175ml	350ml
Vanilla pod	½ pod split	1 pod split
Egg yolks	3	6
Caster sugar	40g	70g
Custard powder	10g	20g
Cornflour	5g	10g
Ground almonds	100g	200g
Dark rum	5ml	10ml
Fresh apricots poached in syrup or tinned	250g	500g

 CHEF'S TIP

With the tant pour tant, ensure that you pass both the icing sugar and the ground nut content through a sieve twice. This will help to aerate the composition of ingredients and aid creaming with the butter.

 CHEF'S TIP

Larger tarts can be presented rather than individual ones. You may have to bake this for about 10 minutes longer.

Method of work

1 To make pâte à Basque, cream the butter with the tant pour tant, caster sugar, salt and lemon zest.
2 Incorporate the egg yolks and whole egg gradually.
3 Sift the flour and baking powder together. Add the sifted flour and begin to knead the ingredients into a paste. Take care not to overwork the paste. Place in a refrigerator wrapped in plastic to rest for at least 1 hour.
4 Preheat an oven to 177°C.
5 To make the almond cream, bring to the boil the milk and vanilla pod.
6 Whisk together the egg yolks, caster sugar and custard powder and cornflour.
7 Combine the ingredients together and cook out, stirring constantly, to make a basic crème pâtissière.
8 Reserve to one side, adding a little melted butter to the surface of the crème to prevent a skin forming.
9 Incorporate the dark rum and ground almonds and reserve to one side.
10 To assemble the gateau, line individual flan rings with the pâte à Basque and pipe the base with the pastry cream mixed with the ground almonds.
11 Place the quartered apricots on top of the pastry cream and place a disc of the pâte à Basque on top of the flan. Glaze with egg wash.
12 Place in a fridge to rest for 30 minutes. Mark the top with a sharp knife.
13 Bake in an oven at 177ºC for approximately 30 minutes. Halfway through baking sprinkle a few flaked almonds and icing sugar on top.
14 De-mould and serve warm with a hot apricot sauce and an appropriate accompaniment such as vanilla ice cream.

Lemon meringue pie

INGREDIENTS	1 × 20CM PIE	2 × 20CM PIES
Lining paste (pâte à foncer, see recipe on p. 344)	200g	400g
Lemon filling		
Butter	125g	250g
Caster sugar	125g	250g
Eggs	4	8
Lemon zest and juice	2 lemons	4 lemons
Swiss meringue		
Egg white	250g	375g
Caster sugar	125g	180g
Icing sugar	125g	180g

CHEF'S TIP

To help to stabilise the Swiss meringue further, a pinch of cream of tartar can be added during the cooking stage. With constant whisking and the protective effects of sugar and the cream of tartar, you can heat this meringue mixture up to 78°C and still maintain a successful, although dense, foam.

Method of work

1 Line a 20 cm tart ring with the paste and bake blind with minimal colour.

2 To prepare the filling, combine the finely grated lemon zest and juice in a saucepan with the caster sugar and butter.

3 Bring the ingredients to the boil, ensuring that the butter has completely melted.

4 Gradually add the beaten eggs, constantly stirring vigorously with a whisk until all of the egg content is successfully incorporated and the mixture has cooked out to a thick and creamy consistency.

5 Pour this lemon cream into the blind-baked tart case and leave to cool and set.

6 To prepare the Swiss meringue, mix all the ingredients together in a stainless steel bowl and place into a bain marie over simmering water.

7 Whisking continuously to aerate the egg whites, heat the mixture to 60°C. Use a thermometer or digital probe to accurately gauge the temperature.

8 Immediately transfer the egg white mixture into a mixing machine with a whisk attachment and beat until cold. The meringue will now begin to completely aerate as it cools down.

9 Transfer the Swiss meringue to a piping bag with a plain tube and pipe onto the set lemon cream in a decorative manner.

10 Lightly dust the meringue with icing sugar and place into a hot oven at 180°C to colour the meringue. Serve either at room temperature or warm as desired.

Linzer torte

INGREDIENTS	1 × 20CM TORTE	2 × 20CM TORTE
Soft white flour	175g	350g
Ground hazelnuts	75g	150g
Icing sugar	60g	120g
Finely grated lemon zest	1 lemon	2 lemons
Grated nutmeg	Pinch	Pinch
Powdered cinnamon	5g	10g
Butter	120g	240g
Egg yolks	2	4
Raspberry jam	175g	350g
Lemon juice	¼ lemon	½ lemon

CHEF'S TIP

This is a traditional torte that takes its name from the Austrian town of Linz, where it is served in coffee houses as an afternoon pastry. It can be stored in a refrigerator for up to a day after production. Do not store next to strongly flavoured products such as cheese.

Method of work

1   Preheat an oven to 175°C.

2   Sift together the flour, ground hazelnuts, icing sugar, cinnamon and nutmeg. Repeat this process to consolidate the aeration and mixing of the ingredients.

3   Dice the butter and rub in with the lemon zest until the mixture reaches a crumbly texture. Add the egg yolk and carefully form into a paste.

4   Wrap the paste in plastic film and rest in a refrigerator for 30 minutes.

5   Cut the rested Linzer paste in half. Roll out one half and use it to line the flan ring. Using the **thumbing up** technique to ensure an evenly lined pastry case.

6   Mix the jam with the lemon juice and spoon it into the lined case.

7   Roll out the paste that was set aside and cut into a lattice pattern.

8   Drape over the top of the torte base and seal the edges well.

9   Place in the oven to bake for approximately 30 minutes.

10 To finish, dust with icing sugar and fill the centres of the squares with more jam if required. Serve warm or chilled with crème chantilly.

Tranche Saint Honoré

INGREDIENTS	10 PORTIONS	20 PORTIONS
Tranche		
Basic choux paste (see recipe on p. 351)	150g	300g
Basic puff paste trimmings	250g	500g
Egg wash (whole egg beaten with a pinch of salt)	1 egg	1 egg
Crème chiboust	APPROXIMATELY 800g OF CRÈME	APPROXIMATELY 1.5kg OF CRÈME
Fresh full fat milk	350ml	700ml
Vanilla pod	½ pod split	1 pod split
Egg yolks	6	12
Caster sugar	70g	120g
Custard powder	20g	40g
Cornflour	10g	20g
Granulated sugar	300g	500g
Water	80ml	150ml
Glucose	25g	45g
Egg whites	6	12

 **CHEF'S TIP**

The use of glucose in the Italian meringue is essential as it helps sugar crystals to form in the meringue. To create a firm meringue, more sugar per egg white (70g per egg white) is required; this should help the crème chiboust retain its stability.

 CHEF'S TIP

For the crème chiboust you can add 1½ sheets of gelatine to the crème pâtissière base to help set the cream. This will make it easier to serve. You can also enhance the flavour of this crème by adding finely grated orange zest to the boiling milk and some Grand Marnier at the final stage.

Method of work

1 On a floured surface, roll out the puff paste into a 35cm × 11cm rectangle. (Use puff paste trimmings rather than virgin paste to reduce the rise in this pastry.) Prick with a fork or pastry dock.

2 Using a piping bag with a 1.2cm plain nozzle, pipe the choux paste lengthways down each edge of the puff paste, leaving a gap of approximately 1cm from the edge.

3 Egg wash the puff paste and the choux paste. Leave to rest in a refrigerator for 30 minutes before baking.

4 Pipe small choux buns, about 1.5cm in diameter, onto a separate baking sheet. Brush with egg wash and press lightly with the back of a fork.

5 Bake at 220°C for about 10 minutes with the vents of the oven open (if you have this facility). Lower the temperature to 200°C and bake the small choux buns for a further ten minutes and the base for a further 20 minutes. Remove and cool on a wire rack when cooked.

6 To make the crème chiboust, bring to the boil the milk and vanilla pod.

7 Whisk together the egg yolks, caster sugar, custard powder and cornflour.

8 Combine the ingredients and cook out, stirring constantly, to make a basic crème pâtissière.

9 Reserve to one side, adding a little melted butter to the surface of the crème to prevent a skin forming.

10 To create an Italian meringue, carefully boil the granulated sugar, water and glucose to 121°C. Meanwhile, whisk the egg whites to soft peaks. Gently pour in the hot sugar solution in a thin stream while still whisking. Continue to beat at a low speed until the mixture is completely cold.

11 While the crème pâtissière is still slightly warm, using a whisk stir in one-third of the meringue. Next, using a spatula, fold in the remaining meringue until completed incorporated. Do not over mix or the crème will collapse.

12 To assemble the tranche, cut a small hole in the base of each profiterole with the point of a knife or a cream horn mould. Dip the tops into some caramelised sugar and place onto a baking sheet to cool.

13 When cool, fill the profiteroles with some of the crème chiboust.

14 Pipe the crème chiboust decoratively down the centre of the baked choux/puff pastry base.

15 Place the profiteroles down the sides of the tranche, using a little of the caramelised sugar to help adhere if you wish.

16 Leave the Saint Honoré in a refrigerator for approximately 2 hours before serving.

17 Garnish the dessert traditionally with a sugar veil, or for a more modern effect add some piped sugar.

Pear Bourdaloue tart *Poire flan Bourdaloue*

INGREDIENTS	1 × 20CM TART (8 PORTIONS)	2 × 20CM TARTS (16 PORTIONS)
Sweet paste (la pâte sucrée, see recipe on p. 345)	175g	350g
Crème pâtissière	75g	150g
Unsalted butter	100g	225g
Tant pour tant	225g	450g
Eggs	2	4
Soft white flour	30g	60g
Almond flavour or dark rum	30g	60g
Poached pear halves	8 halves	16 halves
Sieved apricot jam	50g	100g
Stock syrup	25g	50g
Chopped pistachio nuts or flaked almonds	25g	50g

Method of work

1 Preheat an oven to 180°C.

2 Cream together the tant pour tant and the unsalted butter.

3 Slowly beat in the eggs, flour and almond flavour or dark rum.

4 Mix the crème pâtissière into the almond preparation and set aside in a refrigerator. For a traditional Bourdaloue filling, create a mix using two parts crème d'amande to one part crème pâtissière.

5 Line a tart mould with the sweet paste and trim the edges.

6 Pipe the Bourdaloue preparation into the bottom of the lined tart case to just two-thirds full.

7 Slice each pear half thinly and arrange on top of the filling.

8 Place in the oven and bake for approximately 35 minutes.

9 Carefully remove from the oven and cool on a wire rack. In a small saucepan, bring the apricot jam and stock syrup to the boil, stirring constantly to produce an apricot glaze. Apply the hot apricot glaze carefully with a pastry brush and decorate with the chopped pistachio nuts or flaked almonds.

10 Serve warm or chilled.

 CHEF'S TIP

You can vary the type of fruit used, but it is best to use fruits such as apples, quinces and plums due to the baking time of the tart.

Strawberry club sandwich *Club sandwich aux fraises*

INGREDIENTS	4 PORTIONS	10 PORTIONS
Shortbread paste (pâte sablée, see recipe on p. 346)	200g	500g
Passion fruit purée	140ml	350g
Passion fruit (whole with seeds)	2	5
Fresh full fat milk	160ml	400g
Caster sugar	75g	180g
Cornflour	10g	25g
Soft white flour	15g	40g
Egg yolk	1	3
Whipping cream	200ml	500ml
Fresh strawberries	280g	700g
Earl grey tea (with sugar to taste)	150ml	375ml
Passion fruit purée	140ml	350g
Icing sugar for dusting	50g	100g

Method of work

1 Preheat an oven to 200°C.

2 Roll the pâte sablée to about 2mm thick and cut out sandwich triangles about 15cm along the longest edge. Each triangle should be of identical size. Three triangles per portion.

3 Pile them on top of each other and make a hole through the middle using a skewer. Transfer separately onto baking sheets lined with a silicone baking mat and rest in a refrigerator for 15 minutes.

4 Place in the oven to bake until set but without too much colour. Remove and cool on a wire rack.

5 To make the crème, aerate the whipping cream to soft peaks.

6 Combine half of the passion fruit (reserve the other half for the sauce), purée and milk and heat to simmering point.

7 Blend the sugar, egg yolk, cornflour and flour whisked with 2 tablespoons of cold milk.

8 Add to the simmering liquid and cook out, stirring continuously.

9 Cool the mixture quickly then carefully fold in the whipped cream.

10 To make the sauce and serve, mix the tea (which has been previously made with water and sweetened with a little sugar), the remaining passion fruit and purée together. Refrigerate in a covered bowl.

11 Place a teaspoon of the crème in the centre of a plate. Position a triangle of pastry on it.

12 Put a dessertspoon of the crème on top and arrange some strawberries on it.

13 Repeat the procedure, layering the club sandwich and finishing with a third pastry triangle on top.

14 Place a small strawberry on the end of a sugar or bamboo skewer and push the skewer through the holes in the pastry to hold the sandwich together.

15 Splash the jus around the sides of the plate and dust the top of the sandwich with icing sugar. Serve immediately.

CHEF'S TIP

Dip a whole small strawberry into caramelised sugar and let the sugar slowly drip and set to create a sugar spike; use this instead of the bamboo skewer.

Gâteau Paris Brest

INGREDIENTS	10 PORTIONS	20 PORTIONS
Basic choux paste (see recipe on p. 351)	300g	500g
Egg yolks	6	12
Caster sugar	125g	250g
Cornflour	20g	40g
Custard powder	20g	40g
Fresh full fat milk	500ml	500ml
Vanilla	Optional	Optional
Crushed praline	100g	200g
Selection of fresh fruits for decoration (e.g. raspberries, kiwi, apple and orange)	200g	400g
Caramel sauce		
Granulated sugar	50g	100g
Cold water	40ml	80ml
Double cream	250ml	500ml

Method of work

1   Fill a piping bag fitted with a large star nozzle with basic choux paste. Pipe individual choux rings onto a lightly greased baking sheet.

2   Sprinkle the top with some flaked almonds and egg wash the tops. Bake at 220°C for about 15 minutes. Cool on a wire rack.

3   To make the praline cream, whisk the egg yolks with the sugar and then mix in the cornflour and custard powder.

4   Bring the milk to the boil in a saucepan with the vanilla.

5   Add the boiled milk to the egg mixture and stir until smooth. Add the vanilla if required. Return to the saucepan and bring to the boil, stirring constantly. Make sure the cream is the correct consistency, then cool it by pouring onto a clean work surface, such as a marble slab. Keep turning it back on itself for 2–3 minutes using a palette knife.

6   When cooled, stir in the praline. Reserve to one side.

7   For the caramel sauce, using a heavy-based saucepan dissolve the sugar in the water and bring to boiling point over a medium heat.

8   Wash down the inside of the pan with a clean pastry brush and clean water to prevent any sugar crystals forming. Continue to cook the sugar solution to a deep amber colour.

9   Remove from the heat and carefully add the double cream.

10   Set back onto the heat and slowly bring back to the boil, stirring constantly with a wooden spoon. Simmer while stirring for 2 minutes.

11   Pass through a chinois and store until required for use. (This sauce can be used either hot or cold.)

12   To serve, cut each individual gâteau in half lengthways and pipe some of the praline cream inside.

13   Decoratively arrange the fresh fruit on top of the cream. Place the top of the choux ring back on top of the filling and arranged fruit.

14   Dust with a little icing sugar and place in the centre of the dessert plate.

15   Pour some caramel sauce around the gateau, decorate as desired and serve.

CHEF'S TIP

The traditional presentation of this gâteau is as a multi-portioned confection with just the praline cream. To create a lighter praline cream you can substitute the pastry cream base for a preparation of crème chantilly and fold the crushed praline into this. The finish for the gâteau is a light dusting of icing sugar.

Profiteroles with pistachio ice cream *Profiteroles aux glace de pistache*

INGREDIENTS	20 PORTIONS	40 PORTIONS
Profiteroles		
Basic choux paste (see recipe on p. 351)	150g	300g
Chopped pistachios	45g	70g
Nibbed sugar	25g	50g
Pistachio ice cream		
Fresh full fat milk	225ml	550ml
Skimmed milk powder	20g	40g
Double cream	35ml	70ml
Egg yolks	25g	50g
Caster sugar	50g	100g
Glucose syrup	15g	25g
Pistachio paste	35g	70g
Ice cream stabiliser	3 g	5g
Kirsch	5g	10g

Method of work

1 Fold two-thirds of the chopped pistachio nuts into the paste.

2 Using a piping bag with a large star nozzle pipe individual profiteroles onto a baking sheet.

3 Sprinkle the top with the remaining chopped pistachio nuts and the nibbed sugar crystals. Lightly dust with icing sugar. Bake at 190°C for about 20 minutes with the vents of the oven open (if the oven has this facility). Remove when cooked and cool on a wire rack.

4 To make the pistachio ice cream, bring to the boil the milk, cream, stabiliser, pistachio paste and **glucose** syrup.

5 Whisk together the egg yolks, caster sugar and milk powder.

6 Combine the ingredients and reheat to 85°C stirring constantly.

7 Reserve to one side. Add the kirsch and cool down to a minimum of 4°C within one hour.

8 Freeze in an ice cream machine and reserve in a freezer in piping bags with star tubes for use.

9 To serve, cut the profiteroles in half lengthways.

10 Pipe the pistachio ice cream into the bottom half of the profiteroles.

11 Place the tops back on and dust with icing sugar.

12 Serve approximately three profiteroles per portion and present with an appropriate garnish and a raspberry coulis.

 CHEF'S TIP

Alternative ice cream or sorbet preparations can be used in this recipe. However, in order to help accentuate the flavour of the ice cream and also to settle the fat content in the mixture it is advisable to leave the cooked mixture to mature for 24 hours in a refrigerator at 0–3°C.

Warm cherry samosas with Amaretto bavarois

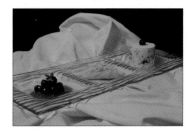

 CHEF'S TIP

The samosas can be deep fried instead of baked. This will help to achieve an all round golden colour, but it will also increase the fat levels to the palette when eating.

INGREDIENTS	4 PORTIONS	8 PORTIONS
Cherry samosas		
Melted butter	60g	120g
Filo paste sheets	4	8
Griottines soaked in kirsch	125g	200g
Cornflour	5g	10g
Icing sugar	60g	120g
Amaretto bavarois		
Fresh full fat milk	175ml	375ml
Amaretto	25ml	50ml
Egg yolks	2	3
Caster sugar	40g	60g
Whipping cream	175ml	375ml
Gelatine	2 leaves	4 leaves
Pre-crystallised white chocolate (see chapter 20)	200g	400g
Acetate strips (to line the mould)	4	8

Method of work

1 Gently heat the griottines in a saucepan. Mix the cornflour with a little cold water. Add the diluted cornflour and cook until the griottines and kirsch mixture has thickened. Retain some of this for the bavarois.

2 Take two sheets of the filo paste, brush one with the melted butter and place the other on top. Cut into strips and place the cooled griottine mixture in the centre. Fold into a samosa shape. Repeat this process for the required number of samosas.

3 Brush the samosas with the melted butter and dust well with the icing sugar. Bake on a lined baking sheet at 200°C until golden brown in colour.

4 Purée the remaining filling in a blender with a little Amaretto to create a coulis to use for decoration.

5 To prepare the bavarois, beat together the egg yolks and the caster sugar and soak the gelatine leaves in cold water to soften.

6 Bring the milk to the boil. Add the milk to the egg yolks, mix together and return to the pan. Stirring constantly, cook out the egg custard to approximately 82°C.

7 Add the softened gelatine, stir in well until melted, pass through a sieve and cool down the custard as quickly as possible.

8 Temper the white chocolate and spread over each acetate strip (see chapter 20). Carefully place each strip inside each mould to form a collar for the bavarois. Use any leftover chocolate for decoration to finish the dessert.

9 When the custard with the Amaretto is half set, whip the cream to the ribbon stage and gently fold into the custard.

10 Pipe bavarois mixture into each mould until half full. Spoon a teaspoon of the griottine mixture into the centre of each bavarois. Pipe in the rest of the bavarois mixture to retain the griottines in the centre. Level off the top and place in a refrigerator to set.

11 To serve, place the cherry samosas into the centre of the plate, with the amaretto bavarois to one side. Decorate as required and finish with the griottine coulis. Serve immediately.

Assessment of knowledge and understanding

You have now learned about the use of the different types of complex pastes and how to produce a variety of tarts, pies and confections utilising an array of commodities.

To test your level of knowledge and understanding, answer the following short questions. These will help to prepare you for your summative (final) assessment.

Quality identifications

1 Name four types of fat used in the production of pastes and state two uses of two of the fats mentioned.

i) _____ ii) _____

iii) _____ iv) _____

2 Explain the quality points to look for when producing puff paste.

3 Describe four causes of lack of volume in puff pastry products.

Equipment and materials

1 Explain why you would use a refrigerator to help rest paste before rolling out.

2 Explain why when producing strüdel paste is it necessary to use a linen cloth during the stretching of the paste and finishing of the strüdel.

Preparation methods

1 Describe the effect that gluten has on puff pastry.

2 Explain why it is important to shape hot water paste while it is still warm to the touch.

3 Describe how the fat and flour are incorporated into choux paste and why this technique is crucial to the overall success of the paste.

Cooking methods

1 Describe how you would test a choux bun to see if it is correctly baked.

2 Explain the process of lamination and why it is crucial to the success of puff paste.

Healthy options

1 Suggest what changes the chef can make to the recipe for a pear Bourdaloue tart to create a healthier option.

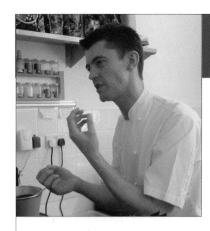

CHEF'S PROFILE

Name: WILLIAM CURLEY

Position: Pâtissier Chocolatier

Establishment: William Curley (Richmond upon Thames, soon to be Mayfair and Belgravia)

Current job role and main responsibilities: Owner of William Curley. We produce fresh (on the day) pâtisserie, handmade chocolates, ice cream and baked goods. We encourage and train young chefs to be future pâtissiers and chocolatiers.

When did you realise that you wanted to pursue a career in the catering and hospitality industry? I didn't grow-up dreaming of being a chef, although I did enjoy the odd cake. I left school with no qualifications and decided to enrol at a local college. It was on the spur of the moment that I went for a cooking class.

Training: I spent two years at Glenrothes College in Fife doing the 706/1 and 706/2 City and Guilds. I also went on to pass the 706/3 advanced pastry City and Guilds course. Although it was a job, I always regard working at Gleneagles under Ian Ironside (I arrived when I was 17 and stayed for three years) as very much part of my ground training.

Experience: I worked for Pierre Koffmann at La Tante Claire (three Michelin stars), Raymond Blanc at Le Manoir aux Quat Saisons (two Michelin stars) and Marco Pierre White at The Restaurant/Oak Room (three Michelin stars). I spent six years working for what I felt were the best restaurants in the country at the time. These experiences very much shaped me as a chef – they gave me focus, developed my skills and gave me a non-compromising attitude. From there, at the age of 27, I become Chef Pâtissier at The Savoy under Anton Edelmann; he gave me a huge opportunity. At times I must have driven him mad, but his support in a job where I was responsible for 21 chefs and for running the River Restaurant, private rooms, bakery, banquetting and afternoon teas was enormous. I also trained in Belgium at Maison du Bouche, Pierre Romeyer (three Michelin stars) for a season and I worked for Marc Meneau at L'Esperance (three Michelin stars) after winning the William Heptinstill Scholarship.

What do you find rewarding about your job?
Seeing how our shop has grown is very satisfying and knowing that the public will travel for miles to buy our pâtisserie and chocolates. Having my own shop is what I dreamt of for many years – to fulfil this dream is very rewarding.

What do you find the most challenging about the job?
To keep the standard that you believe in and not compromising on ingredients. Make an extra effort to create beautiful (not only look but taste) pâtisserie and chocolates!

What advice would you give to students just beginning their career?
Work in as many high-quality places as you can to get a solid foundation for your work. Our industry can be a bit of a marathon; a good base where you understand the basics will stand you well in the long run.

Who is your mentor or main inspiration?
The six chefs I worked and trained under – Raymond Blanc, Anton Edelmann, Ian Ironside, Pierre Koffmann, Marco Pierre White and Pierre Romeyer. When I was at Glasgow College of Food and Technology, my lecturer Willie Pike was a great inspiration – he is also very funny.

What traits do you consider essential for anyone entering a career as a chef?
To be a great, I believe you must truly enjoy cooking. Being determined and focused also helps.

Can you give one essential kitchen tip or technique that you use as a chef?
Never take shortcuts!

Seasonal fresh fruit tartlets

INGREDIENTS

Sweet pastry

Soft flour	480g
Unsalted butter	280g
Caster sugar	140g
Whole eggs	100g

Frangipane

Unsalted butter	250g
Icing sugar	250g
Whole eggs	250g
Ground almonds	250g
Plain flour	50g

Pastry cream

Milk	500g
Vanilla	1 pod
Egg yolks	120g
Caster sugar	100g
Flour	50g

Grand Mariner syrup

Water	450g
Sugar	375g
Grand Marnier	200g

Other ingredients

Neutral nappage	As required
Chocolate decorations	As required
Seasonal fruits: strawberry, raspberry, blackberry, blueberry, mango, kiwi fruits, grapes, plums, nectarines (cut into chunks and slices)	As required

Method of work

1. To make the pastry, chop the unsalted butter into cubes and sieve the soft flour.
2. Crumb together the soft flour and butter, until no lumps are left.
3. Add the caster sugar and salt and mix in.
4. Gradually add the eggs, mix until the mixture is smooth and a homogeneous mass.
5. Place the paste onto a floured tray, wrap with cling film and rest in the refrigerator for at least 1 hour before use.
6. Roll out the sweet pastry to 3–4mm thick. Line tartlet moulds and allow to rest for 30 minutes in the fridge.
7. To make the frangipane, sieve the flour and soften the unsalted butter.
8. Place the softened butter and icing sugar in a mixing bowl and cream together.
9. Beat the eggs and gradually add slowly.
10. Add the ground almonds. Once incorporated add the flour.
11. Pipe the frangipane into the tartlet cases to half full.
12. To bake the tartlets, preheat an oven to 180°C.
13. Bake for 15–20 minutes, then allow to cool on a wire cooling rack.
14. To make the pastry cream, boil together the milk and vanilla pods.
15. Simultaneously whisk together the egg yolks and caster sugar, whisk until the mixture thickens slightly and turns light in colour.
16. Sieve the flour and add into the mixture, whisk until smooth.
17. Add half of the milk to the base, whisk until there are no lumps.
18. Pass through a fine strainer, return the mixture to the pan (ensuring the vanilla pod is retuned to the pan).
19. Using a whisk, stir the mixture continuously. When it comes to the boil, reduce the temperature to a simmer. Continue to stir and cook out for 8–10 minutes.
20. Remove the pastry cream onto a shallow tray, wrap with cling film and cool rapidly.
21. To make the Grand Mariner syrup, boil together the water and sugar.
22. Allow to cool completely then add the Grand Marnier. Keep in an airtight container.
23. To Assemble, punch the tartlets with the Grand Marnier syrup.
24. Pipe a ring of pastry cream onto each tartlet.
25. Place fruits on the tartlet as required (you can support the fruits by surrounding with plastic).
26. Glaze the tart with nappage and decorate as required.

18
Desserts

3FPC14   Produce sauces, fillings and coatings for complex desserts

3FPC12   Prepare and cook complex hot desserts

3FPC13   Prepare and cook complex cold desserts

LEARNING OBJECTIVES

The aim of this chapter is to enable you to develop skills and implement knowledge in the principles of producing a range of complex hot, cold and iced desserts and their accompanying sauces and products. This will also include information on materials, ingredients and equipment.

At the end of this chapter you will be able to:

■ Identify the main methods of production for hot, cold and iced desserts

■ Identify each type of accompaniment, sauce and cream that may be served with desserts

■ Understand the use of the important ingredients in the development of complex desserts

■ State the quality points and critical control points of various complex products

- Prepare, cook and present each type of hot, cold and iced desserts
- Identify the storage procedures of finished hot, cold and iced desserts
- Identify the correct tools and equipment for use in the production of complex desserts

INTRODUCTION

The first desserts have consistently been attributed to the ancient Egyptians, who began harvesting honey from bees at around 5500 BC. A variety of fruits, nuts and cereals were also important ingredients, from which confections were created to show off great wealth during banquets and for use as gifts during religious festivals. Many of these ingredients (especially honey) were also used medicinally.

The European discovery of sugar in Asia in the twelfth century played a significant role in the development of more complex desserts. In the fifteenth century, the recently opened trade routes with Africa, Asia, East Asia and the Americas allowed spices and chocolate to be used as flavourings for desserts as well as for medicinal purposes, previously the main use of such extravagant commodities.

Eventually, these new ingredients became widely available and Europe was recognised as the focus of the development of more sophisticated recipes. The most famous chef of the early nineteenth century was Marie-Antoine Carême (1784–1833). His spectacular architectural constructions of sugar, meringue, pastries and desserts earned him great fame as the 'king of chefs and chef to kings'. Most of his career was spent in the service of nobility and royalty, such as the Prince Regent, Tsar Alexander I and Napoleon I. Throughout his career he dedicated his skills to the art of the pâtissier and generally changed the way menus were created and food was served. By the time of Carême, desserts were large, elaborate set pieces, often fashioned in great detail.

In the twentieth century, advances in technology such as refrigeration, sophisticated ovens and air transportation contributed immensely to the production of both simply designed and more complex desserts, and their popularity continues to grow. With the advent of a more diet-conscious public, desserts have had to adapt by using less sugar and fat commodities, but they retain their sense of decadence, art and flavour.

The skill of the pastry chef is to be able to create a dessert that is appealing to the eye, stimulates the palette through flavour, aroma, temperature and texture, and maintains a lightness that will not leave the customer feeling overindulged.

THE USE OF SPICES IN DESSERTS AND PÂTISSERIE

Spices offer the chef a wide range of rich flavours for use throughout the menu. Influences from China, India, Thailand and other countries can be used to create different fusions of cuisines and exciting new dishes.

Spices are the dried fruits, flowers, buds, seeds, roots or bark of plants. Sometimes more than one part of a plant is used, and the same plants (such as coriander) may also give us a herb. All spices are best used as fresh as possible because the oils which give the aroma and flavour will deteriorate with age. Both ground spices and whole spices must be stored in airtight, lightproof plastic containers.

Spices are used in dessert and pastry production to create added flavour and colour to a finished product. Some of the commonly used spices are detailed below.

Star anise

Anise

The distinctive aniseed flavour comes from the oils found within the seed. These oils are also found in unrelated plants, such as fennel and liquorice. This spice is used to flavour drinks, breads and pastries, but is also used as flavouring in crèmes and mousses.

Ground cardamom

Cardamom

Cardamom is best purchased as green pods, which contain the brown seeds packed full of flavour. Ground cardamom will rapidly lose its flavour. Cardamom is used in baking for pastries and in crèmes, sweet sauces and bavarois.

Cinnamon

Cinnamon is the dried bark of a tree found in Sri Lanka. It can be broken down into small pieces or ground to a powder. Cinnamon is used to flavour creams, syrups, apple tarts and sauces. It is one of the most commonly used spices in the pastry kitchen.

Cinnamon

Cloves

Cloves are the dried buds from a tropical tree found in Tanzania. Cloves are usually purchased whole, and are used as flavouring for steamed puddings, apple pies and mincemeat.

Ginger

Ginger is one of the most widely used spices across the world. It is the root of a plant usually found in East Asia. It has a strong flavour and can be used

Cloves

fresh, dried, powdered or candied. When preserved in sugar or powdered it is used in breads, biscuits, cakes, drinks and creams. Ginger can also be used with a combination of other spices to create alternative flavourings, such as 'mixed spice' and 'Chinese five-spice'.

Ginger

Nutmeg

This is the nut of an evergreen Indonesian tree. It is used grated or powdered to flavour cakes and various desserts and sauces. Ground nutmeg will lose its flavour if kept for too long. Mace is closely related to nutmeg; it is the dried 'cage' that separates the nutmeg from the outer fruit. It is more expensive than nutmeg and has a more delicate flavour.

Nutmeg

Saffron

Saffron is the most expensive spice in the world. It is the orange-red stigmas of a purple flowering crocus. To produce 500g of saffron, up to a quarter of a million flowers are harvested, by hand. It is produced in Spain, India, Asia and North Africa. It has also been cultivated in England, near the town of Saffron Walden in Essex. It is used to flavour crèmes, sauces, cakes and breads.

Saffron

Vanilla

There are approximately 75 different varieties of vanilla growing in the world's tropical regions. Initially discovered by the Aztecs and used to flavour cocoa-based drinks, vanilla is now produced predominantly in Madagascar, Indonesia, Réunion, Martinique, Tahiti and Guadalupe. Vanilla pods offer the best flavour and aroma for all desserts, crèmes, cakes and sauces. They should be split and infused in a liquid to impart as much flavour as possible. The pods can be reused two or three times. Dried pods can be stored in an airtight container with caster sugar so that the flavour of the vanilla permeates the sugar, creating vanilla sugar.

Vanilla

Genuine vanilla extract is an alternative to using pods. However, the labelling is not always clear and care must be taken to ensure that vanilla flavour is not substituted; this is a chemical-based vanilla flavouring that bears no resemblance to the aroma and flavour of real vanilla.

THE USE OF SALT

Salt (sodium chloride) is one of the most important ingredients in any recipe. It is a necessary part of the human diet and is present in many different types of natural food. All of the recipes mentioned in this book state that 'good-quality salt' is used. This is because the salt composition of human tissue is similar to that of seawater, and sea salt (such as large flake salt) provides one of the simplest ways of meeting our nutritional requirements. Good-quality

 CHEF'S TIP

Keep all spices, whole or ground, in containers that are airtight and lightproof. Keep in a cool and dry cupboard. Only purchase small quantities at a time to help establish regular stock rotation and so ensure freshness and maximum flavour.

Sea salt crystals

sea salt retains the valuable natural trace elements which are often removed during the processing of some table salts. The distinctive flavour of a good-quality salt means that less is required for flavouring and cooking. This is an advantage for those wishing to reduce salt intake in their diet.

The production of sea salt relies on favourable dry weather conditions. Seawater for processing is taken after a period of dry weather, when the salt content is at its maximum. The water is transferred to large holding tanks where it is allowed to pass through a filtration system and settle. After further filtering it is drawn off as required and used to fill saltpans, where the water is evaporated off.

The large stainless steel saltpans are mounted on a brick heating system designed to give the specific heating pattern required to evaporate the water. During the evaporation of the water, salt crystals begin to form on the surface. These crystals are known as *fleur de sel* and can be removed and used as a special high-quality salt. However, as the crystals become heavier they sink to the bottom of the saltpan. The pans are allowed to cool slowly and the salt is then harvested. The salt is put into shallow drainage bins before finally being transferred to the salt store for drying and packaging.

Salt is available in many different forms, such as table salt, iodised salt, flake salt, kosher salt, unrefined sea salt, fleur de sel and flavoured salts, such as celery or garlic salt.

Salt can be used as a preservative because it discourages the growth of bacteria in food. It also allows a harmless flavour-producing bacteria to grow and thus improves the flavour of the food while preserving it at the same time.

The addition of salt will enhance flavour in many recipes, whether sweet or savoury. Salt is now combined with alternative flavouring commodities to provide contrast in flavour and texture, such as caramel and sea salt combined to create an interesting filling for chocolate.

STABILISERS AND GELATINISATION

Various stabilisers, starches and emulsifiers are used throughout the kitchen to thicken or bind ingredients to create durable textures, different appearances and thickened liquids.

Starch

Starches are generally used to thicken sauces and creams and some fillings for gâteaux and tarts. Starch granules are made up of two types of molecule: *amylose*, which has a long, straight chemical chain of glucose sugars, and *amylopectin,* which has a branched chemical structure. These structures determine the different thickening properties. The amylose molecules require more liquid, higher temperature and longer cooking before the starch molecules are broken down; they then re-form on cooling.

Gelatinisation is the process that starch molecules undergo to thicken a liquid. There are three stages of gelatinisation using starch:

Cornflour, arrowroot and rice

THE THREE STAGES OF GELATINISATION	
1	Heating the starch – the starch is heated with the liquid to be thickened
2	Absorbing the liquid – as the temperature rises, the bonds within the molecules of starch begin to break down, which allows them to take on board and trap liquid, causing the molecules to expand
3	Thickening the liquid – once the starch molecules have absorbed the liquid they become soft and have a gel-like texture, and as more heat is applied the liquid becomes thicker

Factors that affect gelatinisation

There are several factors that can affect the gelatinisation of liquids:

■ *The amount of liquid used* – here must be an adequate balance of liquid to starch molecules to activate thickening

■ *Temperature* – different starches require different temperatures to thicken. Some starches, such as tapioca and potato starches, can be overheated, which can reverse the effects of gelatinisation and result in a thinner product

■ *Stirring* – overstirring can cause thinning of a mixture. The starch molecules are broken down and release any liquid that was absorbed

■ *Acids* – acids can break down starches, preventing them from swelling and thickening. If possible, acids should be added after gelatinisation has taken place. Alternatively, modified starches which are resistant to acid conditions can be used

■ *Egg yolks* – raw egg yolk contains an enzyme called alpha-amylase, which causes starches to break down. Pastry creams containing egg yolks should be brought to boiling point to destroy the alpha-amylase and so prevent it from breaking down the starch. Pastry creams that contain starch mixed with the egg yolk will not curdle when boiled due to the starch molecules protecting the yolks

■ *Sugar* – an excess of sugar can prevent gelatinisation by blocking the absorption of the liquid. When baking pastry, gelatinisation of starch is required to set the pastry. Pastry recipes with a high sugar content (such as pâte sablée) will therefore have a softer texture when cooked than recipes with lower sugar content. This is the basic principle for how sugars tenderise baked goods

■ *Time* – starches that have been stored for a long period of time may lose their ability to gelatinise and therefore a greater quantity of starch will be required to thicken a liquid

Leaf and granulated gelatine

Gelatine

Gelatine is a protein that is produced from the skin, connective tissue and bones of animals (primarily pork, veal and beef). These are soaked in an acid to break down the collagen and the gelatine molecules are then carefully extracted at low temperatures. Because the gelatine molecules are long and flexible, when they are warmed they disperse in liquids and will set the liquid into a gel. Gelatine will thicken and stabilise the consistency and texture of foods that cannot be further heated, such as ice cream.

Gelatine can be purchased in 2g sheets or in a granulated form. Gelatine sheets, which are also known as 'leaves', should be washed and bloomed in cold clean water to help remove any impurities and to soften the gelatine ready for the next stage of use. The liquid that is to be thickened must be heated, and the carefully drained gelatine sheets are then melted in the hot liquid.

When using granulated gelatine, the liquid to be thickened should be added cold to the required quantity of granules. The granules are then dissolved before the liquid is warmed over a bain marie. The granules will sometimes stick together, but constant warming and stirring will disperse them. The standard proportion advised by gelatine manufacturers is 7g granulated gelatine to 250ml liquid.

To set a dessert or ingredient after gelatine has been added it must be chilled in a refrigerator. The mixture can sometimes be set over an iced water bath while constantly stirring – this is a quicker method of setting.

Factors that affect gelatine

There are several factors that can affect gelatine:

- *The amount of gelatine used* – if too little gelatine is added to the liquid ingredients, insufficient gelling will occur. The amount required will vary between recipes, depending on the final texture desired, but a general rule is that six leaves of gelatine will set 480ml of liquid.

- *The amount of sugar added* – mixtures that contain a lot of sugar will take longer to gel, or may not even gel at all. More gelatine is added to compensate for this effect.

- *The amount of acid present* – acid can weaken the structure of gelatine and therefore more gelatine may be required to produce a set liquid.

- *Enzymes in fresh fruits* – the protease enzyme found in some fresh fruits, such as pineapple, kiwi fruit, melon, papaya and ginger, completely prevents gelatine from setting. This enzyme is inactivated or destroyed at 85°C, so canned or cooked fruit will not be affected.

- *The addition of salt* – salt reduces the strength of gelatine and so additional quantities may have to be added.

Other stabilisers

There are several other substances that work in a similar way to gelatine but which are derived from plants. Collectively referred to as 'gums', they are long chains of glucose sugars that are capable of absorbing large quantities of water:

- *Agar-agar* – derived from a seaweed, this has greater gelatinisation properties than gelatine so less is required for a recipe. It can be purchased in whole or powdered form and is suitable for vegetarian diets.
- *Carrageenan* – a similar substance to agar-agar and also a type of seaweed. Food manufacturers use this to thicken foods containing diary products, such as cottage cheese and ice cream.
- *Gum Arabic* – derived from the sap of an African tree, this has been used to stabilise icing, frostings, glazes and some fillings and creams.
- *Carob gum* – also derived from a tree (the carob tree), the seeds are used to make a gum that is used to stabilise ice creams and sorbets. An added benefit is that this substance will also improve a mixture's resistance to heat.
- *Pectin* – many fruits contain pectin, but fruits that are particularly high in pectin are apples, plums, cranberries and citrus fruits. Pectin is used to thicken glazes, jams, jellies and preserves.

BASIC DESSERT RECIPES

Crème diplomat

INGREDIENTS	MAKES 600G	MAKES 1.2KG
Fresh milk	250g	500g
Egg yolks	40g	80g
Caster sugar	70g	140g
Custard powder	20g	40g
Gelatine leaves	10 leaves	20 leaves
Kirsch	To taste	To taste
Whipped cream	310g	620g

Method of work

1. Bring the milk to the boil.
2. Mix together the egg yolks, caster sugar and custard powder. Add the boiled milk and return to the pan to cook out the mixture.
3. Strain through a fine chinois. Soften the leaves of gelatine in cold water.
4. Strain the gelatine sheets from any excess water and add to the hot, cooked custard. Stir until the gelatine has melted and been incorporated into the custard.
5. Cool the custard to 20°C then add the kirsch. Carefully fold in the whipped cream.
6. Use as required.

 CHEF'S TIP

Crème diplomat is a derivative of crème pâtissière and can be flavoured according to the requirements of the recipe by using a particular alcohol or a flavouring such as vanilla. Crème diplomat can be used as a filling in pastries, tarts, cakes and various desserts.

Crème mousseline

INGREDIENTS	MAKES 900G	MAKES 1.8KG
Fresh milk	500ml	1 litre
Egg yolks	6	12
Caster sugar	100g	200g
Flour	70g	140g
Vanilla	1 pod	2 pods
Unsalted butter	250g	500g

Method of work

1 Split the vanilla pod in half and remove the seeds. Add the pod to the milk and bring to the boil.
2 Mix together the egg yolks, caster sugar and the flour. Add the boiled milk and return to the pan to cook out the mixture.
3 Strain through a fine chinois.
4 Cut the butter into small pieces. Add one-third to the mixture while beating well and continue beating until it clears.
5 Cool the pastry cream to 20°C. Place the remaining butter in a mixing bowl and using a mixing machine beat until softened. On a medium speed add the pastry cream a little at a time. Ensure all the pastry cream is incorporated.
6 Beat a few minutes to produce a light and creamy finish.
7 Use as required.

CHEF'S TIP

Crème mousseline will keep in a covered plastic container in refrigerated conditions for up to 4 days. The crème can be flavoured with fruit purées, alcohol, chocolate or praline.

Chocolate sauce

INGREDIENTS	MAKES 1KG	MAKES 2KG
Water	710ml	1425ml
Caster sugar	400g	800g
Cocoa powder	60g	110g
Cornflour	20g	40g
Dark chocolate	125g	250g
Single cream	135ml	275ml

Method of work

1 Bring the water to the boil with the caster sugar.
2 Mix together the cocoa powder and the cornflour. Add the boiled sugar solution and return to the pan to cook out the mixture.
3 Chop the dark chocolate into small pieces and add to the mixture.
4 Stir continuously to melt the chocolate into the liquid. Ensure that the chocolate does not burn on the base of the saucepan.
5 Add the single cream and adjust the consistency.
6 Strain through a fine chinois.
7 Use as required.

CHEF'S TIP

This sauce can be stored in bulk in a refrigerator in a covered container. A little at a time can be taken to use either hot or cold.

Lemon cream

INGREDIENTS	MAKES 1KG	MAKES 2KG
Whole eggs	10	20
Caster sugar	360g	720g
Finely grated zest of lemon	5 lemons	10 lemons
Lemon juice	480g	960g
Caster sugar	300g	600g
Gelatine	5 leaves	10 leaves

Method of work

1 Bring to the boil the lemon juice, zest and the smaller quantity of caster sugar, stirring continuously. Meanwhile, soak the leaves of gelatine in cold water to soften.

2 Mix together the whole eggs and the larger quantity of caster sugar. Add this mixture to the boiled lemon mixture and place back onto the stove.

3 Cook out the lemon cream to 85°C, stirring constantly.

4 The lemon cream will thicken as it cooks out. Remove from the stove and add the softened gelatine (which has been squeezed to remove the excess water).

5 Strain through a fine chinois and chill in a refrigerator.

6 Use as required.

CHEF'S TIP

This recipe can be used as an alternative to lemon curd and as a preserve, a flavouring for creams or an accompaniment to a dessert.

Coconut foam

INGREDIENTS	6 PORTIONS	15 PORTIONS
Coconut milk (tinned)	250ml	500ml
Yoghurt	80ml	175ml
Whipping cream	30ml	60ml
Icing sugar	40g	75g
Desiccated coconut	30g	60g
Gelatine	1½ leaves	3 leaves

Method of work

1 Soften the gelatine leaves in cold water.

2 Add the desiccated coconut to the coconut milk and bring to the boil in a saucepan. Reduce the liquid by half. Add the gelatine and melt into the hot coconut milk.

3 Mix together the reduced coconut with the yoghurt, cream and icing sugar.

4 Pass the mixture into an aeration canister. Chill in a refrigerator.

5 Charge the canister with two gas cartridges and use as required.

CHEF'S TIP

The coconut elements can be replaced with a fruit purée and an alternative liquid, such as mint-flavoured syrup.

Pâte à bombe

INGREDIENTS	MAKES 180ML	MAKES 360ML
Granulated sugar	40g	80g
Water	75g	150g
Egg yolks	3	5

Method of work

1 Place the water into a heavy-based saucepan and add the sugar. Heat slowly until the sugar dissolves.

2 Increase the heat, and using a sugar thermometer boil the sugar solution to 121°C (hard ball stage).

3 Meanwhile, whisk the eggs in an electric mixing machine until they have reached a pale yellow colour.

4 With the machine still whisking the egg yolks very carefully pour the hot sugar solution in a thin but steady stream onto the yolks. Continue until all of the hot sugar has been added.

5 Continue whisking to increase the volume of the mixture and to cool it down. The mixture should stand to a peak when cold.

6 The pâte à bombe mixture should be kept covered in a refrigerator for up to 2 days.

CHEF'S TIP

This classical preparation is an important base for other recipes, such as mousses, parfaits and iced soufflés. It provides a stabilised foam of egg yolks and sugar to be flavoured accordingly and sustain the addition of whipped cream or aerated egg whites.

Chocolate glaze

INGREDIENTS	TO COVER 1 CAKE	TO COVER 3 CAKES
Water	275g	550g
Whipping cream	250g	500g
Cocoa powder	125g	250g
Caster sugar	275g	550g
Liquid glucose	125g	250g
Gelatine	7 leaves	14 leaves

Method of work

1 Place the water into a heavy-based saucepan and add the glucose, whipping cream, cocoa powder and caster sugar. Heat slowly until the dry ingredients dissolve.

2 Increase the heat, and using a sugar thermometer boil the cocoa solution to 104°C.

3 Meanwhile, soften the gelatine in cold water.

4 Add the softened gelatine to the cocoa solution and stir well to melt. Pass through a fine sieve and leave to cool covered with plastic film.

5 Use the glaze to coat tarts, cakes and gâteaux, but only use it at a temperature of 30–35°C, when it is fluid but ready to set.

6 This glaze can be kept in a refrigerator for up to 3 days and melted for use as required.

CHEF'S TIP

To melt the glaze place it in a microwave oven or on a bain marie. Try not to heat it above 40°C and always use it at the temperature stated in the recipe.

Muscat sabayon

INGREDIENTS	4 PORTIONS	10 PORTIONS
Egg yolks	3	8
Caster sugar	70g	170g
Water	50g	125g
Muscat (sweet white wine)	75g	200g
Vanilla	½ pod	1 pod

Method of work

1 Pour some water into a heavy-based saucepan large enough to hold a round-based mixing bowl on top. Heat the water on a stove to 45°C.

2 Combine the egg yolks, sugar, water, scrapped seeds from the vanilla pod and Muscat wine in the mixing bowl. Place onto the saucepan of heated water on a low heat.

3 Whisk continuously using a balloon whisk for about 12 minutes. Ensure that the water temperature for the bain marie does not exceed 90°C.

4 The mixture will aerate and a ribbon consistency should be obtained. The internal temperature of the sabayon should be 50°C with a smooth, aerated and light texture.

5 Use the sabayon while it is still warm. Serve as an accompaniment to a dessert such as a tart or as the main part of a dessert, in a wine glass with freshly picked strawberries and a biscuit à la cuillère.

 CHEF'S TIP

This sabayon can be served cold, but it would be best to stabilise the aeration by adding a leaf of softened gelatine. Alternative alcohols can be used to create different flavoured sabayons, such as Marsala and eaux de vie.

Fruit coulis

INGREDIENTS	4 PORTIONS	10 PORTIONS
Fresh fruit (such as raspberries, strawberries or redcurrants)	800g	1.7kg
Stock syrup	200ml	425ml
Lemon juice (optional)	1 lemon	2 lemons

Method of work

1 Carefully wash the fruit. Place into a food blender with the strained lemon juice and the stock syrup.

2 Purée the fruit mixture for approximately a minute until a smooth purée has been obtained.

3 Pass the purée through a fine chinois or muslin cloth and correct the consistency by adding more stock syrup or puréed raspberries.

4 The coulis is now ready for use, and will keep for 3–4 days in a refrigerator. Alternatively it can easily be frozen.

SOUFFLÉS

Soufflé is a French word derived from the verb *souffler*, which means to puff or to blow up. The soufflé was originally made in a croustade, which was a straight-sided pastry case into which the soufflé mixture was poured (but the croustade was never eaten). Modern practice it to use an ovenproof ramekin dish.

There are four main types of soufflé:

- *Hot soufflé* – this is a very fragile and delicate blend of eggs, flour, butter and egg whites and can be sweet or savoury. Hot soufflés must be served the moment they are released from the oven.
- *Pudding soufflé* – these are baked in a bain marie in a metal mould (dariole). They are turned out and always served with a sauce. Pudding soufflés are not as light in texture as a hot soufflé and are normally served for luncheon.
- *Cold soufflé* – a soft mixture of meringue, cream, egg yolks and sugar together with gelatine. The soufflés are set in prepared soufflé dishes or ramekins and served cold.
- *Iced soufflé* – this is prepared in a similar way to the cold soufflé but without the gelatine and is frozen like a parfait. A derivative of this type of soufflé is the omelette soufflé, which is produced directly onto a silver flat with a base of Génoise sponge, ice cream and fresh fruit, then decoratively covered with meringue and flash cooked under a grill or in a hot oven.

Ordinary hot sweet soufflés are served at the table in the dish that they were baked in. They are traditionally served without a sauce, but it is now commonplace to have a sorbet, ice cream or hot sauce as an accompaniment.

Soufflés are delicate and can be difficult to make. They are generally made using a base of crème pâtissière combined with a flavouring and aerated egg whites. The air trapped in the egg whites expands at cooking temperatures and the egg protein, along with the starch molecules found in the crème pâtissière base, will set the hot dessert. However, as the soufflé cools down the trapped air will escape and the soufflé will sink.

SOUFFLÉ RECIPES

Vanilla soufflé *Soufflé à la vanille*

INGREDIENTS	4 PORTIONS	8 PORTIONS
Fresh milk	250ml	500ml
Good-quality salt	3 g	5g
Caster sugar	40g	80g
Strong white flour	15g	30g
Cornflour	10g	20g
Egg yolks	3	6
Vanilla	1 pod	2 pods
Caster sugar	75g	150g
Egg whites	2	4
To coat the ramekin dishes		
Melted unsalted butter	50g	100g
Caster sugar	60g	120g

Method of work

1 Place the fresh milk, split vanilla pod (with the seeds removed) and salt in a saucepan and bring to the boil.

2 Sift together the flour and cornflour. Beat the egg yolks and the smaller quantity of caster sugar together and then mix in the sieved flour.

3 Slowly add the boiled milk to the egg mixture, whisking continuously to a smooth paste.

4 Return to the saucepan and back onto a medium heat. Stir until the mixture re-boils and the mixture is smooth and thickened.

5 Remove from the heat, transfer to a clean bowl, cover and cool.

6 Preheat an oven to 190°C. To prepare the soufflé dishes, brush the insides of the mould in vertical strokes with melted butter. Chill in a refrigerator until set. Brush a second layer of butter in the same way. Apply the sugar on the inside of the dish; rotate the dish to ensure that the inside is totally covered with the sugar.

7 Aerate the egg whites in a bowl until firm peaks are obtained and then gradually whisk in the remaining sugar.

8 Carefully fold in the meringue to the vanilla base and spoon equally into the prepared soufflé dishes. Level the tops with a palette knife.

9 Place on a baking tray and set in the preheated oven to bake for approximately 12–15 minutes. Remove from the oven and dust the tops immediately with icing sugar. Serve at once.

CHEF'S TIP

To create a chocolate version of this soufflé, replace some of the flour content with cocoa powder. Instead of coating the inside of the soufflé dish with caster sugar coat with grated chocolate.

Cold lemon soufflé with a lemongrass jelly and lemon tuille

INGREDIENTS	4 PORTIONS	10 PORTIONS
Cold lemon soufflé		
Gelatine	5 leaves	10 leaves
Egg yolks	3	6
Caster sugar	110g	260g
Lemon juice and finely grated zest	2 lemons	4 lemons
Egg whites	3	6
Whipping cream	200ml	500ml
Lemongrass jelly		
Sweet white wine	200g	400g
Caster sugar	15g	30g
Lemongrass	1 stick	2 sticks
Gelatine	3 leaves	6 leaves
Lemon tuille		
Finely grated lemon zest	1 lemon	2 lemons
Icing sugar	42 g	85g
Melted butter	34 g	67 g
Egg whites	38 g	78 g
Soft flour	42 g	85g
Additional ingredients		
Lemon cream (see recipe on p. 381)	75g	150g
Icing sugar	25g	50g
Caramel swirls	4	10
White chocolate acetate strips (1.5cm × 10cm; see recipe on p. 405)	4	10

Method of work

1 Prepare small ramekin dishes by attaching a strip of silicone paper to the outside of the dish so that it extends 2cm above the rim.
2 Soak the gelatine leaves in cold water.
3 Place the lemon zest and juice with the egg yolks and the sugar into a stainless steel mixing bowl.
4 Place the bowl over a bain marie of simmering water (not exceeding 90°C) and whisk continuously to thicken and aerate the mixture.
5 Add the gelatine and mix in until it has dissolved. Remove from the heat and continue to beat until cool.
6 Lightly whisk the whipping cream to the ribbon stage.
7 Stiffly aerate the egg whites.
8 Fold in the cream to the lemon mixture and then the egg whites.
9 Pour into prepared dishes and leave to set in a refrigerator for 1 hour.
10 To make the lemongrass jelly, select a small tray with 2cm sides. Warm a little of the wine with the sugar. Chop the lemongrass into small pieces and add. Infuse for 30 minutes.

11 Soften the gelatine in cold water and drain. Add to the warm lemongrass juice and melt. Strain this into the remaining wine and pour into the prepared container. Put in a refrigerator to set.

12 To make the lemon tuilles, mix the icing sugar and the egg whites. Add the lemon zest and soft flour. Finally, mix in the melted butter. Leave to rest in a cool place for 30 minutes.

13 Spread this mixture over a silicone baking sheet and place into a preheated oven at 200°C. Bake until the mixture turns light golden. Remove from the oven. Using a template cut rectangular strips of the tuille, one per portion (approximately 1.5cm × 10cm).

14 To serve, turn the lemongrass jelly out of the tray and cut into the same sized rectangles as the tuilles. Set the jelly on top of the tuille. Put the lemon cream in a piping bag with a small plain tube. Pipe small bulbs along the centre of the jelly and carefully position the white chocolate strip on top. Position this onto a rectangular plate and set the lemon soufflé next to it, with the paper removed, dusted with icing sugar and decorated with the caramel swirl.

HOT DESSERT RECIPES

Coffee and date pudding with a rum and raisin ice cream

INGREDIENTS	6 PORTIONS	12 PORTIONS
Medjool dates (stoned and chopped)	175g	350g
Water	300ml	600ml
Bicarbonate of soda	1tsp	2tsp
Unsalted butter	50g	100g
Caster sugar	175g	350g
Whole eggs	2	4
Soft white flour	165g	330g
Baking powder	10g	25g
Strong espresso coffee	6tsp	12tsp
Toffee sauce		
Double cream	300ml	600ml
Light muscovado sugar	50g	100g
Black treacle	2tsp	4tsp
Unsalted butter	30g	60g
Rum and raisin ice cream		
Pâte à bombe (see recipe on p.382)	180ml	360ml
Raisins	100g	200g
Dark rum	100g	200g
Water	30ml	60ml
Caster sugar	30g	60g
Fresh milk	120ml	250ml
Double cream	120ml	250ml

Method of work

1. Line a 22.5cm square baking tin with silicone paper and preheat an oven to 180°C.

2. Place the dates and the water into a heavy-based saucepan and bring to the boil. Continue to boil for 4 minutes then remove from the heat and add the bicarbonate of soda and coffee. Leave to stand.

3. Cream together the butter and sugar until light in colour and with a soft, fluffy texture. Gradually add the eggs, mixing continuously.

4. Combine the dates and water with the creamed butter mixture and fold in the flour and baking powder.

5. Pour the mixture into the prepared tin and bake for approximately 35 minutes or until the pudding is just firm to the touch.

6. To make the sauce, place the cream, sugar, treacle and butter into a saucepan and bring to the boil. Simmer for 3 minutes and pass through a chinois. Reserve warm.

7. To make the ice cream, wash the raisins in warm water and then place in a saucepan with the dark rum, sugar and water. Slowly bring to the boil and remove from the heat and cover with plastic film. Leave to cool and macerate for 24 hours before using.

8. Make the pâte à bombe and set aside. Place the milk and cream in a saucepan and bring to the boil, then leave to cool over a bain marie of iced water. Combine with the pâte à bombe and pour into an ice cream machine to churn. Halfway through the freezing process add the raisins and some of the dark rum liquor to taste. Continue to churn and freeze.

9. To serve, cut the pudding into portions and spoon the sauce over each pudding. Serve with a quenelle of the ice cream.

Chocolate fondant with spiced pears and vanilla ice cream

INGREDIENTS	4 PORTIONS	15 PORTIONS
Whole eggs	2	8
Egg yolks	2	8
Caster sugar	60g	220g
Dark chocolate	100g	400g
Unsalted butter	75g	300g
Soft flour	30g	120g
Vanilla	To taste	To taste
Spiced pears		
Williams pears	4	10
Unsalted butter	25g	75g
Caster sugar	25g	75g
Cinnamon (powdered)	1tsp	3tsp
Star anise	1	3
Clove	1	3
Vanilla ice cream		
Fresh full fat milk	570ml	1140ml
Double cream	160g	320g
Milk powder	40g	75g
Vanilla	1	2
Caster sugar	110g	220g
Glucose	40g	80g
Egg yolks	2	4

CHEF'S TIP

When making the vanilla ice cream, if possible cook the preparation 24 hours before churning and freezing. The vanilla pod should be kept in the preparation. The resultant flavour will be stronger with the texture of the finished ice cream much smoother.

Method of work

1 Preheat an oven to 175°C. Grease individual moulds well with melted butter.

2 Combine the eggs and sugar in a mixing bowl with the vanilla. Aerate until the volume has at least doubled.

3 Melt the chocolate and butter together in a microwave oven or in a bain marie and fold into the egg mixture.

4 Fold in the flour. Deposit the mixture into the prepared moulds to approximately half full.

5 Leave to rest in a refrigerator for 30 minutes.

6 Place into the oven to bake for 15 minutes. Remove from the oven and rest for 3 minutes then remove from the moulds.

7 For the spiced pears, wash, peel and cut the pears into brunoise. Place into a shallow pan with the butter, sugar and the spices and cook slowly. Half way through cooking place a cartouche of baking paper over the pan. Reserve warm for service.

8 For the vanilla ice cream, place the milk, cream, milk powder, half the quantity of sugar and split vanilla pod into a saucepan and slowly heat. At 45°C add the liquid glucose then bring to the boil.

9 Beat the remaining sugar and the egg yolks together and pour the boiled milk onto the yolks. Return to the pan and cook the mixture to 85°C, stirring continuously. Pass through a fine chinois into a bowl.

10 Chill quickly over a bain marie of iced water and then churn in an ice cream machine.

11 To serve, pack the spiced pears into a stainless steel ring in the centre of the service plate. Remove the ring. De-mould the chocolate fondant and place it carefully on top of the spiced pears. Spoon a quenelle of the vanilla ice cream on top of the fondant and decorate as required.

Apple and thyme crumble with mascarpone ice cream and salted caramel sauce

INGREDIENTS	4 PORTIONS	8 PORTIONS
Caster sugar	50g	100g
Butter	60g	120g
Ground almonds	55g	110g
Soft white flour	60g	125g
Bramley apples	3	6
Clear honey	25g	50g
Fresh thyme	1 sprig	2 sprigs
Unsalted butter	25g	50g
Sultanas	10g	20g
Salted caramel sauce		
Water	100g	200g
Granulated sugar	60g	120g
Double cream	50g	100g
Fleur de sel	2 g	4 g
Mascarpone ice cream		
Caster sugar	75g	150g
Egg yolks	3	6
Fresh full fat milk	250g	500g
Mascarpone	150g	300g

CHEF'S TIP

Always ensure that customers are aware of the nut content in the crumble topping for this recipe. Alternatively, the ground almond content can be replaced with flour and the butter content slightly increased.

Method of work

1 Preheat an oven to 180°C.

2 To make the crumble, mix the sugar with the butter. Incorporate the ground almonds and the flour and rub together to create a crumbly texture. Spread the mixture onto a baking sheet lined with a silicone baking mat and bake for 15 minutes. Remove from the oven and set aside.

3 Wash, peel and cut the apples into 1cm dice. In a shallow pan, cook the honey, butter and thyme to a light caramel. Add the sultanas and then add the apples. Place a cartouche of baking paper over the top and continue to cook until the apples are soft to the touch but still retain their shape.

4 Put the cooked apple mixture into the base of a 6cm stainless steel ring placed onto a silicone baking mat on a baking sheet. Place the crumble on top and return to the oven for 15 minutes to warm through and colour.

5 For the salted caramel sauce, place the water and sugar in a heavy-based saucepan and cook to a caramel. Deglaze carefully with the double cream and add the fleur de sel. Reboil and pass through a fine chinois. Reserve warm for service.

6 For the mascarpone ice cream, beat together the egg yolks and sugar. Meanwhile, place the milk and half of the mascarpone into a saucepan and bring to the boil. Add to the egg yolk mixture and mix well. Return to the saucepan and cook to 85°C, stirring continuously. Pass through a fine sieve and chill over a bain marie of iced water. Add the remaining mascarpone and freeze in an ice cream machine.

7 To serve, place the crumble onto the service plate and spoon the salted caramel sauce around it. Set a quenelle of the ice cream to the side and decorate accordingly.

Chocolate crêpe soufflé with orange and vanilla sauce

INGREDIENTS	4 PORTIONS	10 PORTIONS
Crêpes		
Soft white flour	100g	210g
Caster sugar	10g	30g
Cocoa powder	20g	40g
Good-quality salt	3 g	5g
Whole eggs	2	4
Fresh full fat milk	400ml	700ml
Orange and vanilla sauce		
Sweet white wine	300ml	650ml
Oranges	2	4
Vanilla	1 pod	2 pods
Caster sugar	50g	100g
Unsalted butter	70g	150g
Double cream	30ml	70ml
Chocolate soufflé centre		
Fresh milk	250ml	500ml
Dark chocolate (70% minimum cocoa content)	150g	320g
Caster sugar	40g	90g
Strong white flour	20g	40g
Cornflour	10g	20g
Egg yolks	3	6
Grand Marnier	4tbsp	10tbsp
Egg whites	3	6
Caster sugar	40g	80g

Method of work

1 Preheat an oven to 220°C.

2 To prepare the crêpes, combine the flour, cocoa powder, salt and sugar and slowly beat in the eggs. Stir in one-third of the milk and beat to a smooth paste. Add the rest of the milk and leave to rest in a refrigerator for 1 hour before using.

3 Stir the batter and pass through a chinois. Add a little sunflower oil to a crêpe pan and heat. Ladle a little of the batter and cook for approximately 1 minute on each side with very little colour. Place each cooked crêpe in between small sheets of silicone paper to retain the soft texture and refrigerate until needed.

4 To prepare the orange and vanilla sauce, add the wine, sugar and split vanilla pod to a saucepan and reduce by half. Segment the oranges and reserve to one side, retaining any juice with them. Add the double cream and cubed unsalted butter to the reduced liquor, whisk and cook until the fats emulsify into a sauce. Add the orange segments and reserve warm.

5 For the soufflé mixture, heat the milk in a saucepan until it just reaches boiling point. Meanwhile, sift the cornflour and flour together.

6 Beat the egg yolks and the first quantity of caster sugar together and then combine with the sieved flour. Melt the chocolate in a microwave or over a bowl of hot water.

7 Carefully pour the hot milk onto the egg yolk mixture, whisking continuously to prevent any lumps forming. Return to a clean saucepan.

8 Carefully heat up to simmering point, stirring constantly until the crème begins to thicken and the flour is cooked out. Transfer to a bowl and mix in the melted chocolate and Grand Marnier, cover with a buttered cartouche to prevent a skin from forming and leave to cool.

9 At the point of service, whisk the egg whites in a bowl while slowly adding the remaining caster sugar and aerate to a firm peak.

10 Carefully fold in the egg whites to the chocolate crème pâtissière and immediately pipe or spoon the mixture onto the middle of each crêpe. Fold each crêpe into quarters and pipe any remaining mixture into the cavities. Place onto a baking tray.

11 Bake in the preheated oven for approximately 5 minutes until well risen.

12 Serve immediately by dusting each crêpe soufflé with icing sugar and place into the centre of a plate. Spoon the orange and vanilla sauce with the segments around.

ICE CREAM

Ice cream is made by freezing a liquid mixture containing carefully balanced ingredients after it has been subjected to heat treatment. The conditions of the heat treatment are carefully governed by legal standards, and the process is subjected to regular scrutiny by local health officials.

Scrupulous cleanliness must be observed in every stage of ice cream making. The materials used can easily become contaminated and give rise to food poisoning bacteria. A special area should be reserved for the production of ice cream, appropriately equipped and kept solely for this purpose. Moreover, the equipment should be used solely for the making of ice cream. An abundant supply of hot and cold water for washing purposes is also essential.

The process of *pasteurisation* is essential to the production of ice cream. In 1864, while studying the fermentation of wines, vinegar, beers and milk, Louis Pasteur discovered that fermentation was caused by micro-organisms and realised that many infectious diseases derived from specific microbes. Pasteur ascertained that by boiling milk to over 100°C, all dangerous microbes could be destroyed. However, this heating also reduced the nutritional value of the milk itself. By carrying on his experimentation, Pasteur found out that heating milk to 65°C, keeping at this temperature it for 30 minutes, and then cooling it to 4°C destroyed all pathogenic microbes while leaving the main nutritional and structural characteristics of the milk unchanged.

It is important that all ingredients in the ice cream mix are subjected to heat treatment for the correct time periods and are then cooled down quickly. The treated ingredients must be kept covered to prevent any new contamination.

The Dairy Products (Hygiene) Regulations 1995 state that:

VIDEO CLIP
Ice cream

1 Pasteurised ice-cream shall be obtained by the mixture being heated—

(a) to a temperature of not less than 65.6°C and retained at that temperature for not less than 30 minutes;

(b) to a temperature of not less than 71.1°C and retained at that temperature for not less than 10 minutes; or

(c) to a temperature of not less than 79.4°C and retained at that temperature for not less than 15 seconds, and then reduced to a temperature of not more than 7.2°C within 1½ hours and kept at such temperature until the freezing process is begun.

2 If the temperature of ice-cream has risen above minus 2.2°C at any time since it was frozen it shall not be sold or offered for sale unless—

(a) it has again been subjected to the heat-treatment to which as a mixture it was required to be subjected under paragraph 1 above; and

(b) after having again been frozen, it has been kept at a temperature not exceeding minus 2.2°C.

It is also essential that all hygiene regulations are followed, including those that relate to:

■ Daily cleaning routines

■ Preparation of the mixture and the close monitoring of temperature control

■ The selling and dispensing of ice cream

■ Customer hygiene measures

■ Hygiene of specialist equipment, such as self-pasteurising machines

■ Storage of ice cream

Storage of ice cream

Ice cream should be stored at the lowest temperature possible, but in any event not higher than –20°C. However, at this temperature the ice cream is very hard and unsuitable for service. It should be brought out of storage prior to service and stored at a temperature of between –6°C and –12°C, according to the type of ice cream used and the consistency required for service.

Ice cream should not be sold unless it has been kept at a temperature of –1°C or below since it was frozen. If the mixture has risen above –1°C since freezing, it must be heat treated again and then re-frozen.

TYPES OF ICES	
Sorbet	Made from fruit purée or pulp and stock syrup
Water ice	Made from fruit juice and stock syrup
Spoom	A sorbet mixture with Italian meringue
Granita	Crystallised flavoured syrup or fruit purée
Pâte à bombe	A special preparation of ice cream
Pâte à biscuit glacées	As a pâte à bombe mixture but in a biscuit mould, sometimes lightened with meringue
Soufflé glacé	Iced soufflé
Ice cream	Contains egg, cream and usually milk
Omelette soufflé	Ice cream encased in a meringue preparation on a base of Génoise and fruit
Marquise	Granita with crème chantilly folded in before service

ICE CREAM RECIPES
Madagascan chocolate parfait

INGREDIENTS	4 PORTIONS	8 PORTIONS
Egg yolks	25g	50g
Caster sugar	30g	60g
Fresh full fat milk	45g	90g
Madagascan dark chocolate (66%)	65g	130g
Whipping cream	75g	150g
Caramelised hazelnuts		
Hazelnuts (toasted, skins removed and halved)	55g	110g
Demerara sugar	15g	30g
Good-quality salt	To taste	To taste
Warm water	A little	A little
Caramel salt and spice sauce		
Caster sugar	75g	150g
Liquid glucose	45g	90g
Double cream	350g	700g
Fleur de sel	2 g	4 g
Vanilla	1 pods	3 pods
Star anise	2	4
Cinnamon stick	½	1
Cardamom seeds	1g	3g
Decorative items		
Thin chocolate discs	4	8
Piped chocolate sticks	4	8
Vanilla ice cream	4 quenelles	8 quenelles
Decorative chocolate	4	8

Method of work

1   To prepare the chocolate parfait, place the milk into a heavy-based saucepan and bring to the boil. Meanwhile, beat together the egg yolks and sugar.

2   Pour the milk onto the egg yolks and mix well then return to the saucepan. Stirring constantly, cook the egg mixture to 85°C.

3   Melt the Madagascan chocolate and combine with the cooked out egg custard. Cool to 30°C in a refrigerator.

4   Carefully whisk the cream to aerate it to a ribbon stage. Gently fold in the cream to the chocolate mixture. Transfer the parfait mixture into individual savarin moulds (preferably flexible silicone moulds so it is easier to remove the frozen parfait) and freeze.

5   To make the caramelised hazelnuts, preheat an oven to 120°C. Toss the hazelnuts in a shallow pan with just enough warm water to make the nuts slightly sticky. Add the sugar and salt to taste and bring to the boil ensuring that the sugar coats the nuts. Turn the nuts out onto a baking sheet lined

CHEF'S TIP

Madagascan chocolate is generally renowned for its fruity character and dark bitter flavour, so it is an ideal single-origin chocolate to use for this recipe. However, it can be replaced by alternative dark chocolates, but they will need to have a strong, bitter flavour.

with silicone paper then place in the oven and bake for 30 minutes. Remove from the oven and cool. The hazelnuts should be totally dry and crunchy after cooling. If not, return to the oven and bake longer. Store tightly covered in an airtight plastic container ready for service.

6   To make the caramel salt and spice sauce, infuse the fleur de sel, split vanilla pods, star anise, cinnamon and cardamom seeds in the cream for at least 2 hours, covered in a refrigerator.

7   Place the sugar in a heavy-based saucepan and heat. When the sugar begins to melt add the glucose. Continue cooking until a caramel has been reached. Deglaze the caramel with the infused cream and spices.

8   Bring back to the boil, pass through a fine chinois and cool.

9   To serve, turn out the frozen chocolate parfait onto the prepared chocolate disc and position it onto the serving plate. Deposit some of the caramelised hazelnuts in the centre of the chocolate parfait and around the plate. Spoon the caramel sauce onto the plate and finish with the quenelle of vanilla ice cream and chocolate decorations.

Iced parfait of strawberries, lavender ice cream and champagne strawberry salad

INGREDIENTS	4 PORTIONS	8 PORTIONS
Strawberry parfait		
Caster sugar	150g	300g
Glucose	15g	30g
Strawberry purée	3tbsp	5tbsp
Egg whites	3	6
Egg yolks	3	6
Caster sugar	75g	150g
Strawberry purée	125g	250g
Whipped cream	175ml	350ml
Dacquoise biscuit	4 small discs	8 small discs
Lavender ice cream		
Lavender flowers or seeds (edible)	1tsp	2tsp
Caster sugar	60g	120g
Fresh full fat milk	230ml	460ml
Egg yolks	3	6
Double cream	50ml	100ml
Strawberry champagne salad		
Washed and hulled strawberries	125g	250g
Champagne	75g	150g

Method of work

1   To prepare the strawberry parfait, create an Italian meringue with the larger quantity of caster sugar, glucose, smaller quantity of the strawberry purée and the egg whites, cooking to 118°C (soft ball stage).

2   Over a bain marie at approximately 90°C, whisk the egg yolks and smaller quantity of sugar. Slowly add the larger quantity of strawberry purée and cook out. Remove from the heat and carry on whisking to cool and aerate the mixture. When cool fold in the whipped cream and then the meringue.

3   Prepare individual ring moulds with a small disc of dacquoise in the base. Pour the parfait into the moulds and freeze.

4   To prepare the lavender ice cream, grind the lavender into the sugar and beat with the egg yolks.

5   Bring the milk and cream to the boil. Pour the boiled milk onto the egg yolk mixture, stir well and return to the saucepan. Cook out to 85°C, stirring constantly.

6   Pass through a fine chinois and cool over a bain marie of iced water. Churn in an ice cream machine.

7   For the champagne strawberry salad, cut the strawberries into brunoise and carefully combine them with the Champagne at the last moment. Leave to one side for service.

8   To serve, create some red coloured 'bubble' sugar for decoration. Present the de-moulded parfait in the centre of the plate with a quenelle of the lavender ice cream on top. Spoon the compôte around the plate and place the bubble sugar on top of the overall dessert.

Almond ice cream

INGREDIENTS	4 PORTIONS	8 PORTIONS
Fresh full fat milk	570ml	1140ml
Double cream	160g	320g
Milk powder	40g	75g
Softened marzipan	50g	100g
Caster sugar	80g	160g
Glucose	40g	80g
Egg yolks	3	6
Amaretto (optional)	25ml	50ml
Roasted flaked almonds	50g	100g

Method of work

1   Place the milk, cream, milk powder and softened marzipan into a saucepan and slowly heat. At 45°C, add the liquid glucose and bring to the boil.

2   Beat the sugar and egg yolks together and pour the boiled milk onto the yolks. Return to the pan and cook the mixture, continuously stirring until 85°C has been reached. Pass through a fine chinois into a bowl.

3   Chill quickly over a bain marie of iced water. Add the Amaretto if required, then churn in an ice cream machine.

4   Serve in a chilled glass with some flaked almonds sprinkled over the top.

 CHEF'S TIP

Ice cream quickly absorbs the flavours of other ingredients stored alongside it. Ensure that a plastic container with a good seal is used for storage. Once ice cream has been made and frozen it is best to use it within a week.

Fromage frais sorbet

INGREDIENTS	4 PORTIONS	8 PORTIONS
Fromage frais	200g	400g
Lemon juice	18g	36g
Sorbet syrup	175g	350g
Sorbet syrup		
Water	2.1 litres	
Granulated sugar	2.25kg	
Glucose	270g	

Method of work

1　To make the sorbet syrup, place the water, sugar and glucose in a saucepan and bring to the boil. Simmer for 2 minutes and strain into a sterilised plastic container. Leave to cool and refrigerate for use.

2　Place the fromage frais, sorbet syrup and lemon juice together in a bowl and mix well together.

3　Pass through a fine chinois and churn in an ice cream machine.

 CHEF'S TIP

Use this sorbet syrup recipe as the base for all fruit sorbets. Use at a ratio of 1kg fruit purée to 550g sorbet syrup.

Apple and basil sorbet

INGREDIENTS	4 PORTIONS	8 PORTIONS
Green apple (such as Granny Smith)	140g	280g
Lemon juice	90g	190g
Caster sugar	110g	225g
Fresh basil leaves	5g	10g
Water	140g	280g
Milk powder	7g	14g

Method of work

1　Working quickly, cut the apples into pieces and place into a deep freezer (to prevent them turning brown).

2　Combine the water, sugar and milk powder together in a saucepan. Place on a medium heat and bring to the boil.

3　Pass the syrup through a fine chinois and chill to 4°C.

4　Chop the fresh basil and mix with the lemon juice.

5　Place the syrup and frozen apples into a blender and purée. Pass through a fine chinois then add the basil and lemon juice.

6　Place the mixture into an ice cream machine to freeze.

CHEF'S TIP

It is important that the apples are frozen as quickly as possible to prevent discolouration.
The citric acid found in lemon juice will also help to retain the natural colour of the apple. Always use the green skin of the apple to help with the flavour and colour of the sorbet.

Chocolate sorbet

INGREDIENTS	4 PORTIONS	8 PORTIONS
Whipping cream	250g	500g
Fresh milk	500ml	1 litre
Caster sugar	50g	100g
Cocoa powder	100g	200g
Dark chocolate (70%)	15g	30g

Method of work

1 Combine the cream and milk in a saucepan and place on a medium heat.
2 Add the sugar and cocoa powder. Stir in well and bring the liquid to the boil.
3 Remove from the heat and stir in the chopped chocolate. Pass through a fine chinois and leave to cool then freeze in an ice cream machine.

COLD DESSERT RECIPES

Vanilla brûlée with passion fruit cream and apple and basil sorbet

INGREDIENTS	4 PORTIONS	8 PORTIONS
Coconut crisp		
Egg whites	40g	80g
Caster sugar	60g	125g
Desiccated coconut	75g	130g
White rum	6g	12g
Zest of lime	1 lime	2 limes
Passion fruit cream		
Passion fruit pulp	30g	50g
Lime juice	3g	7g
Vanilla	½ pod	1 pod
Caster sugar	30g	60g
Whole egg	33g	65g
Unsalted butter	50g	100g
Vanilla brûlée		
Egg yolks	27g	55g
Full fat milk	35g	70g
Double cream	90g	180g
Caster sugar	23g	45g
Vanilla pod	½	1
Gelatine	2 leaves	4 leaves

INGREDIENTS	4 PORTIONS	8 PORTIONS
Basil and pineapple base		
Water	500ml	1 litre
Caster sugar	150g	300g
Fresh basil	11g	22g
Sliced pineapple with the core cut out (6cm × 3cm)	4 slices	8 slices
Assembling the dessert		
Dried pineapple crisp	4	8
Sugar stick	4	8
Apple and basil sorbet (see recipe on p. 397)	4 quenelles	8 quenelles
Sauce Anglaise	60ml	120ml

Method of work

1 Preheat an oven to 210°C.

2 To make the coconut crisps, mix the egg whites and sugar together and add the coconut, white rum and lime zest.

3 Place between two sheets of silicone paper and roll out as thinly as possible. Put into a freezer to set and then cut individual discs out of the sheet.

4 Place the discs onto a baking sheet lined with a silicone baking mat. Bake for 2 minutes then reduce the oven temperature to 170°C for a further 7 minutes.

5 To make the passion fruit cream, place the passion fruit pulp, lime juice and vanilla into a small saucepan and bring to the boil.

6 Mix together the eggs and sugar. Add the boiled passion fruit to the eggs and mix well. Return to the saucepan and cook out the mixture to 85°C as for a crème Anglaise. Immediately cool the passion fruit cream over a bain marie of iced water.

7 Slowly beat the softened butter into the passion fruit cream. An electric mixer will ensure that the butter emulsifies with the passion fruit cream. Reserve in a refrigerator for later use.

Add the boiled passion fruit to the eggs and mix into the butter

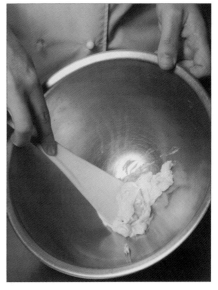

Slowly beat the softened butter into the passion fruit cream

Bake the brûlée for 60 minutes or until just set

8 To make the vanilla brûlée, preheat an oven to 90°C. Mix all the ingredients together except the gelatine. Pour this into an ovenproof dish and bake in the oven for 60 minutes or until the brûlée has just set.

9 Soften the gelatine in some cold water and drain. Remove the brûlée from the oven and place into a food blender immediately with the gelatine and process to a soft, cooked liquid. Pour the liquid into individual small savarin moulds (preferably flexible silicone moulds) and freeze.

10 When frozen, de-mould and leave to defrost on a tray in a refrigerator.

11 To make the basil and pineapple base, place the water, sugar and basil into a saucepan and bring the contents to the boil.

12 Place the slices of pineapple into a high-sided tray and pour over the basil syrup and cover with plastic film. After the syrup has cooled, put the pineapple into a refrigerator and leave to macerate for 24 hours.

13 To serve, set the coconut biscuit in the centre of the serving plate. Place the pineapple slice on top and pipe the passion fruit cream into the centre of the pineapple.

14 Position the savarin ring of vanilla brûlée on top of the pineapple with the quenelle of sorbet on top.

15 Finish with a dried pineapple crisp and sugar stick and spoon the sauce around the plate.

Pour the basil syrup over the pineapple slices

Position the savarin ring of vanilla brûlée on top of the pineapple

Almond cake with fig ice cream and a red fruit soup

INGREDIENTS	4 PORTIONS	8 PORTIONS
Almond cake		
Double cream	120g	240g
Raw almond paste	90g	180g
Egg yolks	60g	120g
Egg whites	90g	180g
Caster sugar	45g	90g
Fig ice cream		
Pâte à bombe (see recipe on p. 382)	180ml	360ml
Fresh figs	200g	400g
Dried figs	50g	100g
Raspberry purée	70ml	140ml
Double cream	120ml	250ml
Red fruit soup		
Red fruit berries (such as raspberries, blackberries, redcurrants and strawberries)	500g	1kg
Demerara sugar	25g	50g
Vanilla	1 pod	3 pods

Method of work

1. Prepare individual round stainless steel moulds by brushing with melted butter and lining with silicone paper. Ensure the silicone paper is 3cm higher than the ring. Brush butter onto the inside of the silicone paper. Place the moulds onto a baking sheet lined with a silicone baking mat. Preheat an oven to 180°C.
2. Place the double cream, raw almond paste and egg yolks into a food blender and mix the ingredients together for a few seconds. Remove from the blender and place the almond mixture in a mixing bowl.
3. Create a meringue with the egg whites and caster sugar.
4. Carefully fold in the meringue to the almond mixture a little at a time to maintain the aeration as much as possible.
5. Pour the almond batter into the moulds to two-thirds full and bake in the oven for 10 minutes.
6. To make the fig ice cream, place the fresh figs, dried figs and raspberry purée into a food blender and liquidise.
7. Combine the fig purée with the pâte à bombe and mix in the double cream.
8. Freeze in an ice cream machine.
9. To make the red fruit soup, place the fruit, sugar and split vanilla pods into a stainless steel bowl and cover tightly with plastic film.
10. Place the bowl onto a saucepan of simmering water and turn the heat down low. Maintain this for 2 hours; the heat generated will cause the fruit to shed its juices.
11. Put the fruit through a chinois without squeezing. Reserve the juice warm for service.
12. To serve, place the warm almond cake in the centre of a bowl and spoon the fruit soup around it. Finely chop a fresh fig and place into the soup. Set a quenelle of the fig ice cream on top of the almond cake and decorate as required.

Terrine of two chocolates

INGREDIENTS	1 TERRINE	2 TERRINES
White chocolate mousse		
White chocolate	200g	400g
Whipping cream	300ml	600ml
Gelatine	2 leaves	3 leaves
Grand Marnier	15ml	25ml
Dark chocolate mousse		
Dark chocolate	200g	400g
Whipping cream	300ml	600ml
Additional preparations		
Sheet of Japonaise (40cm × 20cm; see recipe on p. 423)	1 sheet	2 sheets
Crème Anglaise	400ml	750ml
Grand Marnier	To taste	To taste
Segmented oranges	3	6
Fresh mint	5g	10g
Caramel sticks for garnish	2 per portion	2 per portion

Method of work

1   Line a terrine mould with plastic film. Carefully cut four strips of Japonaise. Place one strip in the bottom of the terrine mould and one on each side so that the mould is lined.

2   Melt the white chocolate in a bain marie to no more than 45°C. Meanwhile, half whip the cream. Soften the gelatine in cold water and squeeze out. Melt the gelatine with the Grand Marnier.

3   Fold the white chocolate into the whipped cream to create a smooth mixture and add the melted gelatine.

4   Deposit the white chocolate mousse into the lined terrine mould half way up. Put in a refrigerator to set.

5   Melt the dark chocolate and whip the second quantity of whipping cream in the same way. Combine the two ingredients carefully to a smooth mousse and deposit on top of the set white chocolate mousse.

6   Set a final strip of the Japonaise on top of the terrine to totally encase the mousses. Place in a refrigerator to set for 2 hours.

7   Chop the fresh mint into julienne and mix with the segmented oranges. Any residual orange juice can be added to the crème Anglaise with the Grand Marnier.

8   To serve, remove the two chocolate terrine from the mould and using a large knife that has been warmed in hot water, slice a generous portion of the terrine and set on a serving plate. Garnish with the salad of mint and orange and serve with the Grand Marnier sauce.

Passion fruit mousse cake

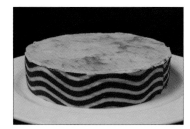

INGREDIENTS	1 MOUSSE CAKE	3 MOUSSE CAKES
Passion fruit purée	280ml	575ml
Caster sugar	15g	30g
Lemon juice	½ lemon	1 lemon
Gelatine	6 leaves	12 leaves
Egg whites	120g	240g
Caster sugar	150g	300g
Water	50g	100g
Whipping cream	280ml	575ml
Dacquoise disc (see recipe on p. 422)	1 × 16cm	3 × 16cm
Biscuit jaconde	1 strip	3 strips
Glaze		
Cocoa powder	20g	40g
Stock syrup	100ml	240ml
Gelatine	2 leaves	3 leaves

CHEF'S TIP

This recipe can be adapted to use other forms of fruit purées, such as banana, raspberry, cassis, mango and strawberry.

Method of work

1 Soften the gelatine in cold water and squeeze out the excess water once softened. Melt the gelatine in a bain marie.

2 Prepare a 22cm torten ring by lining the sides with the biscuit jaconde and placing the disc of dacquoise in the base.

3 Mix together the passion fruit purée, smaller quantity of sugar, lemon juice and melted gelatine. Leave to half set in a refrigerator.

4 Create an Italian meringue with the egg whites, larger quantity of sugar and water.

5 Softly aerate the whipping cream to a ribbon stage. Fold in the cream to the passion fruit purée and then gradually incorporate the meringue.

6 Set into the prepared torten ring and place in the refrigerator to set for 2 hours.

7 To make the glaze, soften the gelatine in cold water and warm up the stock syrup. Add the gelatine and allow to melt, then cool the syrup to 30°C. Lightly dust the top of the mousse cake with the cocoa powder and then quickly apply the glaze using a large palette knife. Return to the refrigerator to set. De-mould the ring when required for service.

Cappuccino crème brûlée

INGREDIENTS	4 BRÛLÉE	8 BRÛLÉE
Double cream	350ml	700ml
UHT milk	125ml	250ml
Strong espresso coffee	50ml	100ml
Tia Maria	2tbsp	4tbsp
Large egg yolks	6	12
Caster sugar	75g	150g
Demerara sugar	50g	100g
Vanilla foam		
Fresh full fat milk	120ml	240ml
Icing sugar	10g	20g
Vanilla	½ pod	1 pod
Powdered albumin	2g	4g

VIDEO CLIP
Brûlée

Method of work

1 Preheat an oven to 140°C.

2 Place the cream and milk into a heavy-based saucepan and bring to the boil. Add the espresso coffee and Tia Maria.

3 Beat together the egg yolks and sugar until pale. Pour the boiled mixture onto the egg yolks and mix well.

4 Pass the liquid through a fine chinois and pour into prepared coffee cups. Place the cups in a bain marie and bake in the preheated oven for approximately 50 minutes or until the brûlée is set. To test, the brûlée should be slightly wobbly and springy to the touch and the core temperature should read at least 80°C.

5 Remove from the oven and cool in a refrigerator.

6 To serve, sprinkle the demerara sugar on top and caramelise with a blowtorch.

7 For the foam, place the milk, sugar, vanilla seeds scraped from the pod and the dried albumin into a bowl. Using a hand blender, froth the milk quickly and spoon onto the top of the brûlée and serve immediately.

Garnishes and decorations: chocolate acetate collars

INGREDIENTS	20 COLLARS
Pre-crystallised chocolate	300g

Method of work

1 Cut acetate into a strip of the size required. Place on a clean, smooth surface.
2 Spread the chocolate thinly and evenly onto the acetate strip.
3 Leave to set slightly.
4 Form the acetate strip into a loop, or use it to line the inside of a mould, giving the collar shape. Allow for a 2cm overlap.
5 Leave to set and harden before carefully peeling away the acetate.

CHEF'S TIP

The acetate can only be used once. These collars can be used to contain desserts such as mousses, crèmes and cakes.

Garnishes and decorations: piped chocolate in sugar

INGREDIENTS	20 PIECES
Pre-crystallised chocolate	300g
Caster or demerara sugar	300g

Method of work

1 Evenly spread the sugar onto a tray.
2 Using a small piping bag, pipe the chocolate into your required design onto the sugar.
3 Leave to harden before removing and using as a decoration.

Garnishes and decorations: deep fried spaghetti sticks

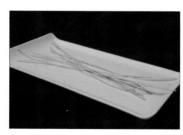

INGREDIENTS	10 STICKS
Spaghetti sticks (dried)	10
Cocoa powder	50g

Method of work

1 Preheat a deep fat fryer to 170°C.
2 Dust the spaghetti sticks lightly in cocoa powder.
3 Place the spaghetti into the deep fat fryer and cook until browned and brittle (this may take 2 minutes).
4 Drain and dry. Use as a garnish for a dessert.
5 An alternative is to blanch the spaghetti in water and then refresh in cold water. Pat dry and pane in cocoa powder before deep frying. The effect produced will be more of a nest of coca pasta.

Assessment of knowledge and understanding

You have now learned about the use of the different types of complex hot, cold and frozen desserts and how to produce some garnishes and sauces utilising an array of commodities and techniques.

To test your level of knowledge and understanding, answer the following short questions. These will help to prepare you for your summative (final) assessment.

Quality identifications

1 Explain the importance of selecting the correct type, quality and quantity of ingredients when producing an ice cream.

2 State the quality points to look for when producing a crepe soufflé.

Equipment and materials

1 State two advantages of using an electric mixer for producing a pâte à bombe.
   i) _____ ii) _____

2 Identify the difference between a Swiss and an Italian meringue.

Preparation methods

1 Briefly describe how to produce a vanilla ice cream.

2 Explain how pasteurisation plays an important part in ice cream making.

Cooking methods

1 State how a crème brûlée is tested in order to see if it is correctly cooked.

2 State the temperature for baking the following:
   (a) Chocolate fondant _____
   (b) Vanilla soufflé _____

3 Identify the critical quality points for the following products:
   (a) Chocolate sorbet

   (b) Iced parfait of strawberries

   (c) Crème mousseline

CHEF'S PROFILE

Name: TONY HOYLE

Position: Head Pastry Chef

Establishment: The Grove

Current job role and main responsibilities: Managing the pastry kitchen of a 230-room five-star hotel, with three restaurants and large conference and banqueting facilities. We have 13 chefs in the pastry kitchen and 90 chefs in all in the kitchens. We produce all the food in house, from our vienoisserie, chocolates, ice creams, breads, petits fours, plated desserts and buffet desserts to our artistic chocolate and sugar showpieces.

When did you realise that you wanted to pursue a career in the catering and hospitality industry?

I enjoyed cooking from an early age. My father was a chef. He prompted me to work with him for a while when I left school and it took off from there. I started my career in the hot kitchen but I was soon captivated by the creativity and artistry of the pastry kitchen. It was in large hotel kitchens and Michelin-starred restaurants that I did most of my training and discovered the world of French pâtisserie. So the next step was to work in France, which totally opened my eyes to how wide and diverse the field of pastry work is. I then spent the next few years learning all I could about all aspects of my profession. I have since been fortunate to be Pastry Chef in some of the most renowned hotels in London.

What do you find rewarding about your job?

My greatest pleasure in the kitchen has to be chocolate work. I am a bit of an obsessive about chocolate, unfortunately it is little understood as an ingredient and is not the single-flavour commodity that most people perceive it to be. At The Grove we use a number of different chocolates blended from some of the finest cocoa in the world.

What do you find the most challenging about the job?

For me the most interesting field of pastry work is running a large five-star hotel pastry kitchen. There is always so much going on; every day is different and brings new challenges. You get to work with people of the same mentality, who strive to produce the best they can for our guests and to make The Grove a special place to visit.

Who is your mentor or main inspiration?

I draw my inspiration from many different sources: books, travelling, looking at what our competitors are doing by eating out, trade magazines and sometimes by just taking ingredients and playing around with flavour and texture combinations. Most importantly, I talk to the members of my team for their ideas and menu suggestions.

What traits do you consider essential for anyone entering a career as a chef?

Be obsessive about food, work in the best establishments you can and listen to your chef. Watch how they work. Try and have an idea of where you want to be and set yourself goals. Too many people enter this profession as a last resort and have no idea what they want to do with their careers. Learn by your mistakes and don't take criticism personally. Get used to working when most people are out enjoying themselves.

Can you give one essential kitchen tip or technique that you use as a chef?

Always treat people with respect and as you would like to be treated yourself.

Whipped milk chocolate ganache, spice cake, vanilla jelly and honeycomb ice cream

INGREDIENTS

Milk chocolate ganache

Whipping cream	225g
Milk chocolate (40% pistoles)	350g
Invert sugar	50g
Whipping cream	500ml

Tuile mix

Flour	100g
Butter	100g
Sugar	100g
Egg white	100g

Spice cake

Water	450ml
Sugar	200g
Honey	450g
Strong flour	450g
Baking powder	2g
Ground mixed spice	5g
Bicarbonate of soda	25g
Grated lemon zest	1 lemon
Grated orange zest	1 orange
Clarified butter	280g

Vanilla jelly

Bottled still water	600ml
Agar-agar	5g
Sugar	30g
Leaf gelatine	1 leaf
Tahitian vanilla pods	2
Orange blossom honey	100g

Honeycomb

Sugar	200g
Golden syrup	75g
Glucose syrup	225g
Bicarbonate of soda	30g

INGREDIENTS

Honeycomb ice cream

Milk	500ml
Whipping cream	250ml
Egg yolk	120g
Sugar	70g
Invert sugar	25g
Malt extract	35g
Horlicks	100g
Glucose powder	25g
Milk powder	25g
Stabiliser	3g
Chopped honeycomb	40g

Method of Work

1 To make the ganache, boil the 225g of cream and the invert sugar.
2 Pour the hot liquid onto the chocolate pistoles.
3 Using a handheld blender, mix together to form a smooth emulsion.
4 Cool to 40°C and blend in the other amount of cream. Refrigerate overnight.
5 Whip on the KitchenAid mixer to the consistency of soft whipped cream.
6 To make the tuile, mix the dry ingredients together.
7 Whisk in the egg white then the melted butter, then rest in the fridge for 1 hour.
8 Take a little of the mixture and colour red with powder colour.
9 Cut a 10cm plastic tuile stencil.
10 Place the stencil on a silpat and spread the red mix inside the stencil.
11 On top of this, spread the plain mix so the two mixes have a marbled effect.
12 Bake in a deck oven at 160°C for approximately 10 minutes .

13 When baked, take off the mat and wrap round a 25mm tube until set.

14 Pipe the whipped ganache to fill the tube then dip each end in chopped peanut brittle. This must be done at the last minute to avoid the tuile going soft.

15 To make the spice cake, boil together the honey, water, zests, sugar and spice.

16 Mix together the dry ingredients, then pour on the liquid and whisk together.

17 Add the butter and rest in the refrigerator overnight.

18 Spread in a biscuit frame 5mm thick.

19 Bake at 180°C for approximately 20 minutes.

20 When cool, cut into rectangles 30mm x 105mm.

21 To make the jelly, split the vanilla pods and scrape out the seeds.

22 Boil the water, vanilla and honey and leave to infuse for 1 hour.

23 Mix the sugar and the agar-agar. Whisk into the liquid and bring back to the boil.

24 Pass through a fine sieve.

25 Spread 3mm thick onto a tray lined with acetate.

26 When set, cut into rectangles 105mm x 35mm.

27 To make the honeycomb, boil together the sugar, glucose and golden syrup to 145°C.

28 Sieve the bicarbonate of soda into the hot liquid.

29 Mix well then pour onto a tray lined with silicone paper to cool.

30 When cold, chop up into 3mm pieces.

31 To make the ice cream, mix the dry powders with the sugar.

32 Whisk the milk into the powders.

33 Add the cream, malt and invert sugar and bring to the boil.

34 Whisk some of the liquid onto the yolks.

35 Whisk this into the rest of the liquid and cook gently to 82°C to pasteurise the mixture.

36 Pass through a fine sieve and leave to cool in the refrigerator overnight.

37 Freeze in the ice cream machine then mix in the honeycomb pieces.

38 To assemble, place the vanilla jelly on the plate.

39 Onto this put the spice cake rectangle.

40 Onto this put the ganache-filled tube.

41 You can decorate this with a chocolate curl garnish and gold leaf.

42 Serve with a fresh raspberry sauce.

43 Scoop the ice cream and sit on almond streusel pieces.

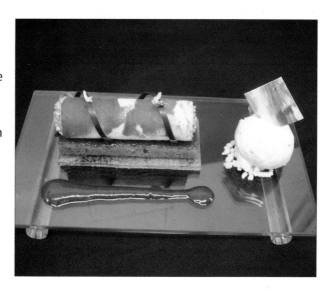

19
Cakes, biscuits and sponges

3FPC5 Prepare, cook and finish complex cakes, sponges, biscuits and scones

LEARNING OBJECTIVES

The aim of this chapter is to enable you to develop complex skills and implement knowledge in the bakery and confectionery principles of producing a range of cake, sponge, biscuit and scone products. This will also include information on materials, ingredients and equipment.

At the end of this chapter you will be able to:

■ Identify the main methods of production for cake, sponge, biscuit and scone products

■ Identify each type of complex preparation and finished product

■ Understand the use of the important ingredients in the development of complex cakes, biscuits and sponges

■ State the quality points of various complex products

■ Prepare, bake and present each type of complex cake, biscuit, sponge and scone product

■ Identify the storage procedures for finished cake, sponge and biscuit products

■ Identify the correct tools and equipment used in the production of cakes, sponges and biscuits

INTRODUCTION

Over the past few years, the production and presentation of cakes, gâteaux and torten within Europe and North America have changed significantly. For these types of pâtisserie the emphasis is now on producing individual portions, individually decorated with glazes and fruits or chocolate decorations. There is a trend towards lightness in texture and design of the dessert or cake – the use of biscuit jaconde, dacquoise and mousses seems to highlight this very well.

Unusual flavours and combinations are now being used in conjunction with sophisticated presentations, and influences from the Eastern and Indian regions and the Caribbean are now mixed with more traditional and classical European styles.

This chapter explains the various base components used in the production of modern-style and classical cakes, biscuits, sponges and scones.

USE OF FATS IN BAKERY AND CAKE MAKING

Fats that are solid at room temperature (e.g. butter) tend to be derived from animal sources. There are, however, a few exceptions, such as hydrogenated vegetable shortenings, cocoa butter and some tropical fats, which are derived from plants. Fats that are liquid at room temperature are referred to collectively as 'oils'. These tend to originate from plants, such as olives, maize, nuts and seeds. Oils can be chemically processed into solid form (hydrogenated), which will increase their shelf life.

Fats perform many different functions in baking, for example they provide flavour. They also create tenderness in the baked product by coating the strands of gluten present in batters and doughs. Fats add moisture and a rich quality that will help to increase the shelf life of many products. When creamed together with sugar, fats can also hold a great amount of air, and when used jointly with other leaveners (such as baking powder) this will help baked goods to rise.

Solid fats with a high melting point will help to provide flakiness to pastes and laminated dough products, such as croissants and puff pastry, by creating distinct fine layers of fat between sheets of dough. Fats can also impart flavour when used for frying, such as deep frying of doughnuts and beignets.

Choosing an appropriate fat to use for a particular recipe will make a big difference to the result. One of the main points of consideration is the fat's plasticity. The greater the plasticity of a fat (e.g. vegetable shortening), the

less pleasant it may be to eat because it will tend to leave a coating on the tongue. This is because highly plastic fats have a higher melting temperature. Butter is plastic at a cool room temperature, but once refrigerated it becomes harder and less plastic. Vegetable shortening will still have a good degree of plasticity even when refrigerated, which makes it easier to use in some laminated recipes.

Butter and vegetable shortening are both capable of holding air and are therefore good to use as creaming agents. When creaming, butter should always be soft enough to be beaten and therefore trap air. This happens best at temperatures between 19°C and 21°C. The flavour and colour of butter make it the most desirable fat for use in the production of cakes, biscuits and sponges. Vegetable shortening will hold more air than butter because it contains less water, but it has the drawbacks of a lack of colour and flavour and a slightly greasy feel on the tongue during eating.

Storage of fats

Solid fats absorb odours and strong flavours and therefore need to be stored correctly in the refrigerator, away from strongly flavoured ingredients. They can also be frozen for several weeks. Liquid fats will turn rancid more quickly and should be stored in airtight containers in a dark, cool and dry area. The longer a fat is stored, the greater the chance of it turning rancid. Liquid fats can be stored in a refrigerator; however, they can turn semi-solid at these cooler temperatures and must be brought back to room temperature before use.

USE OF EGGS IN BAKERY AND CAKE MAKING

Fresh shell eggs are undoubtedly best for most cuisine and bakery purposes. However, the time required for cracking the eggs, the inevitable waste, the mess caused by egg shells and the ever-present possibility of the inclusion of a stale egg in a mixing all highlight the benefits of using good brands of frozen pasteurised eggs.

Fresh eggs are made up of three main components:

- *Shell* – calcium carbonate — 12%
- *White* – protein: albumen — 58%
- *Yolk* – protein: lecithin — 30%

The average weight of an egg is 50 grams.

Eggs have various uses in cookery, especially in the pastry section:

- Eggs are used as moistening agents
- They absorb a large quantity of air when manipulated (whisked)

■ They act as enriching agents in food products, giving better structure, flavour and appearance

■ Egg yolk coagulates at 65–71°C

■ Egg white denatures at 60–65°C

Basic composition of eggs

Both egg white and egg yolk contain a large proportion of water, some protein, fats and minerals, but in slightly different quantities.

COMPOSITION OF EGGS: PER CENT

	EGG YOLK	EGG WHITE	WHOLE EGG
WATER	50–50.5	86–87	73–75
PROTEIN	16–16.5	12–12.5	12–14
FAT	31–32	0.25	10–12
MINERALS	0.8–1.5	0.5–0.6	0.8–1.5

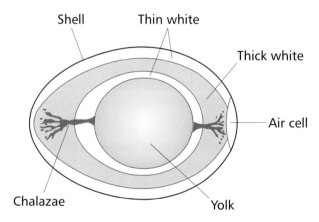

The structure of an egg

Storage of eggs

Fresh eggs should be stored in a cool but not too dry place, refrigeration at 2–3°C is ideal. Egg shells are porous and so eggs will absorb strong odours.

When an egg is stored, the thick white gradually absorbs moisture and therefore thins down. The yolk, in turn, absorbs moisture and begins to spread. Eventually the water will evaporate from the egg through its porous shell and is replaced by air. Since water is heavier than air, fresh eggs will be heavier than stale ones.

Frozen eggs

The use of frozen eggs is becoming more widespread due to fears of contamination of fresh eggs and the issue of wastage. There were initially problems with some imported frozen eggs, which were contaminated with *Salmonella* and other food poisoning bacteria. To overcome this, legislation was introduced in January 1964 stating that all eggs to be frozen must first be pasteurised.

Pasteurised frozen eggs must be defrosted gently before use. Immerse the can in cold running water until defrosted. When defrosted, remove the eggs from the can, thoroughly mix and then bring to room temperature. On no account should eggs be defrosted by the application of heat or the eggs will be denatured and lose their efficiency. Once defrosted, pasteurised eggs should be used without delay as, like all forms of egg, they are an extremely good medium for the growth of bacteria.

USE OF DRIED FRUIT IN BAKERY AND CAKE MAKING

Many types of fruit are available dried. Whereas fruit in its natural state is bursting with fresh, sweet juices, when dried it changes character completely. It becomes dense, concentrated in flavour and often not particularly attractive to look at, being wrinkled and leathery.

Dried fruit is an excellent source of dietary fibre, and although much of the moisture has been removed, most of the nutrients found in the fresh fruit are retained (apart from vitamin C). Dried fruit is higher in calories, volume for volume, than fresh fruit. When rehydrated, the nutritional value of the dried fruit approximates that of fresh fruit. Some fruits absorb larger volumes of liquid than otherS: tree fruits such as apples and pears increase by between three and five times their volume after soaking, vine fruits such as currants and raisins by about twice their volume.

Dried fruits also have the capacity to take on additional flavours when rehydrated, such as from fruit juices, alcohol, spices and tea. This is especially valuable when producing fruit cakes.

Not all dried fruit is soaked before use. Fruits such as dates, figs and raisins can be eaten as they are.

Before using dried fruits in cake recipes it is best to wash them then soak them in the required flavoured liquid. The fruit can be soaked for long periods of time, especially for rich fruit cakes for weddings and Christmas festivals, where the richness and moisture of the fruit will help to prolong the shelf life of the actual cake.

Dried fruits are often purchased in packs and can make very good winter fruit salads or compôtes.

AERATION PROCESSES IN CAKES AND SPONGES

There are four methods of aeration used in the preparation of cakes, biscuits and sponges. These are:

■ *Panary* – yeast

■ *Chemical* – baking powder

■ *Physical* – whisking and beating

■ *Combination*

Panary aeration

In 1859, the French scientist Louis Pasteur discovered that dough is aerated by living micro-organisms, which convert sugar into carbon dioxide (CO_2). This is the principle behind panary fermentation, which is brought about by the action of enzymes in yeast and flour. Fermentation in breads and doughs is dealt with in chapter 16, but it is also a prime concept in baked products such as pâte à savarin.

The initial gas production during panary fermentation comes from the breakdown of simple sugars present in the flour or in other added ingredients. Further glucose is made available by the conversion of other carbohydrates in the flour by specific enzymes. The gas is held within the structure of the gluten network, which gradually becomes more elastic during the fermentation process, and so the dough rises. Two by-products of this fermentation process are acids and alcohol, which make a contribution to the overall dough flavour.

When in the oven, gas production is accelerated until the yeast is killed by the heat, at which point activity ceases. The expansion of air and gas and the pressure of water vapour cause an increase in volume, which is maintained by the coagulation of all the proteins present as baking continues.

Chemical aeration

Historically, cakes originated from the practice of using up surplus ingredients – sugar (probably in the form of honey), fats or oils – by adding them to fermented dough. This produced a rich and pleasant range of finished goods.

This basic method continued to be used until the introduction of chemical aeration, when it was discovered that certain chemicals would give off gas when mixed with moist ingredients and then heated.

An examination of old recipe books shows that chemical aeration was known and in use many centuries ago. Certainly, bicarbonate of soda has been in use for over 200 years, and before that pearl ash, a pure form of potash obtained from deteriorating wood and vegetable matter, was used. It was

CHEF'S TIP

If too much baking powder is used in a recipe the flavour of the cake will become quite salty as the sodium residue builds up.

CHEF'S TIP

Over time the shelf life of baking powder is shortened because it absorbs moisture from the air, which weakens it. A quick test to determine whether baking powder is still active is to mix a little of it with some malt vinegar. If the powder is active it will quickly foam.

discovered that if potash was added to **gingerbread** dough it would become aerated during storage before baking. Potassium carbonate obtained from residues of beet sugar refining was another known aerating chemical.

Old recipe books also refer to muriatic acid, now known as hydrochloric acid. When mixed with bicarbonate of soda, the resulting reaction releases carbon dioxide and leaves a residue of sodium chloride (common salt).

A mixture of tartaric acid and bicarbonate of soda then came into favour, tartaric acid in turn being superseded by cream of tartar. Cream of tartar, however, was much more expensive than tartaric acid and more of it is necessary for a given amount of bicarbonate of soda. This mixture is known as baking powder.

Baking powder may be produced by combining one part bicarbonate of soda with two parts cream of tartar. Efficient baking powder should liberate the maximum amount of gas during baking. It must also be harmless and should not be unpleasant in taste or aroma.

Carbon dioxide generated by the chemical reaction becomes entangled in the gluten and albumin framework of a cake. This holds the gas and expands until the proteins coagulate, at which point the aerated structure becomes comparatively rigid.

The baking powder has a delayed action – only a small amount of carbon dioxide is given off when the liquid ingredients are added. The majority of the gas is released when the mixture is heated, therefore cake and pudding mixtures will not lose their ability to rise if they are not cooked immediately.

Hints on using baking powder:

■ Mix the baking powder thoroughly with the flour

■ Replace the lid tightly on the tin after use

■ Measure accurately

■ Do not slam the oven door in the early stages of cooking

■ Excess baking powder causes a cake to collapse in the middle and dumplings to break up

■ Insufficient baking powder results in a close, heavy texture

---

Physical aeration

Beating particular mixtures of ingredients will cause air to become incorporated into the mixture, resulting in a baked product with a light texture. This is known as physical aeration. Two principal bakery ingredients are capable of holding air when beaten: fats and eggs. It is probable that eggs were the first ingredient aerated in this way, but animal fats can also be made much lighter by beating, particularly when blended with other ingredients, such as sugar.

Beating eggs denatures the protein content by breaking it down into smaller fragments and allows air to be trapped. As the aeration of the egg continues, the denatured protein surrounds the air bubbles and locks in the air, preventing it from escaping. This process helps in the production of cakes and sponges by creating a lightness and leavens the cake (makes it rise) as it bakes.

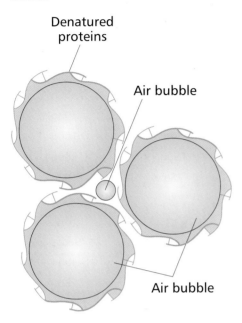

Aeration of albumin

When beaten, egg white can hold more air than either whole egg or egg yolk, and for this reason it is the ideal medium for meringues, soufflés and royal icing.

Short pastry is also lightened by physical aeration, but to a lesser extent. Air is introduced either when the fat is rubbed in to the flour or when the fat and sugar are beaten prior to mixing into the flour.

Combination method

A simple example of a combination method is that used for Danish pastry, when butter is laminated into fermented dough. This combines panary aeration with aeration by lamination.

The combination of physical and chemical aeration is quite common. A mixture of fat, sugar and eggs is beaten during the first stages of production. The aeration is then supplemented by the addition of baking powder during the later stages.

An example where panary and chemical aeration are combined is the fermented scone. This is made using a preliminary yeast fermentation which is then incorporated with other ingredients to which baking powder has been added.

RECIPES
Rich fruit cake

INGREDIENTS	1 × 20CM ROUND CAKE	1 × 30CM ROUND CAKE
Soft flour	180g	360g
Dark brown muscovado sugar	180g	360g
Unsalted butter	180g	360g
Washed currants	225g	450g
Washed sultanas	225g	450g
Seedless raisins	90g	200g
Glacé cherries	50g	100g
Mixed peel	150g	300g
Ground almonds	75g	150g
Eggs	3	6
Mixed spice	5g	10g
Nutmeg	2g	5g
Ground mace	2g	5g
Good-quality salt	2g	5g
Zest and juice of lemon	1 lemon	2 lemons
Brandy	75ml	150ml
Sherry	50ml	100ml

Method of work

1 First line your tin with a double layer of greaseproof parchment. Then clean and prepare the fruit, halve the cherries.

2 Mix all the fruit together with the lemon juice, zest and alcohol. This mixture can be left for about one week in advance of making the cake.

3 Sift the flour and spices together.

4 Beat the butter until soft and light. Add the sugar to create a good aeration. Gradually incorporate the egg.

5 Stir in the ground almonds and fold in the flour and spices.

6 Add the fruit with the liquid and mix well together. Transfer to the baking tin.

7 It is extremely important to follow the correct recipe balance. Preheat an oven to 140°C. Put a tray containing 1 pint of water into the oven; this will create steam within the oven and help the cake rise evenly. Remove the tray of water half way through the baking process. The cake should be cooked after 3½–4 hours.

8 Leave the cake in the tin for one day. Add a soaking mixture of rum and sherry every two days for one week. Wrap the cake in wax paper and place in an airtight container. The cake should be mature after three weeks.

 CHEF'S TIP

To calculate the size of cake required, eight portions are generally cut from each 450g of finished cake.

Decorating the cake

1. Select the correct sized board to present the cake. Trim the top of the cake to create a level surface.

2. Knead the marzipan (if required) and pin out so that it is at least 8cm larger than the actual cake. Brush some boiled apricot jam over the cake to completely seal it.

3. Carefully roll up the marzipan and lay it over the cake.

4. Manipulate the marzipan so it completely covers the cake and creates a protective skin.

5. Leave the marzipan to dry for at least 24 hours before attempting to cover with the cover paste (icing). Using the same method, cover the cake with the cover paste, but brush a little alcohol onto the marzipan to help the cover paste to adhere. Smooth out any creases using a special smoothing paddle or the palm of your hand.

6. Using a piping bag with a small (number one) plain tube, pipe small decorative sequences over the cake using royal icing.

7. Write the name of the person that the cake is for (or the message for the cake) onto some silicone paper. Carefully place this onto the top of the cake and using a small pin, prick the outline of the words directly onto the cake to form a guide to pipe over.

8. Pipe over the guide marks using royal icing.

9. Finish off with a pre-made decorative motif or flowers as desired.

Separated egg sponge

INGREDIENTS	1 SMALL BAKING SHEET	2 SMALL BAKING SHEETS
Fresh eggs	4	8
Soft flour	110g	220g
Caster sugar	110g	220g
Vanilla flavour	A few drops	A few drops

CHEF'S TIP

Replace one-third of the flour with potato flour to make the finished sponge soft and flexible for use as a Swiss roll.

Method of work

1   Line a baking sheet (35cm × 25cm × 2cm deep) with silicone paper or a silicone baking mat. Preheat an oven to 200°C.

2   Separate the eggs. Aerate the egg yolks with two-thirds of the caster sugar and the vanilla essence in a bowl until stiff and almost white in colour.

3   Meanwhile, aerate the egg whites with the remaining caster sugar to a stiff peak.

4   Mix in a little of the aerated egg whites to the yolk mixture.

5   Carefully fold in the sieved flour and then the remainder of the egg whites. At this stage you must fold in very carefully using a plastic spatula so as not to knock the air out of the preparation. Pipe the mixture onto the prepared baking sheet in fingers (biscuit à la cuillère) or spread onto the sheet and use as a base for gâteaux.

Flourless chocolate sponge

INGREDIENTS	2 × 20CM ROUND CAKE TINS	4 × 20CM ROUND CAKE TINS
Egg yolks	5	10
Cocoa powder	40g	80g
Caster sugar	55g	110g
Egg whites	5	10
Caster sugar	75g	150g
Vanilla flavour	A few drops	A few drops

 CHEF'S TIP

This sponge recipe can be used for desserts, gâteaux and cakes.

Method of work

1   Prepare the cake tins with silicone paper or line a baking sheet with silicone paper or a silicone baking mat. Preheat an oven to 200°C.

2   Whisk the egg yolks and the smaller quantity of caster sugar to a sabayon stage over a bain marie of warm water (softly aerated).

3   Create a meringue with the egg whites and the larger quantity of caster sugar.

4   Sieve the cocoa powder and carefully fold in to the egg yolk sabayon with some vanilla flavour.

5   Gently fold in the meringue mixture and then deposit onto the prepared baking sheet or cake tins.

6   Bake in the oven until the sponge contracts from the sides and it feels springy to the touch.

Biscuit jaconde

INGREDIENTS	2 LARGE BAKING SHEETS	4 LARGE BAKING SHEETS
Stencil paste		
Icing sugar	50g	100g
Unsalted butter	50g	100g
Egg whites	55g	105g
Soft flour	40g	80g
Cocoa powder	10g	20g
Biscuit		
Icing sugar	190g	375g
Ground almonds	190g	375g
Whole eggs	250g	500g
Soft flour	50g	100g
Melted butter	40g	75g
Egg whites	130g	260g
Caster sugar	25g	50g

 CHEF'S TIP

Biscuit jaconde is a flexible, highly moisturised biscuit designed to be used decoratively in association with cakes, torten, mousses, bavarois and other entremets.

 VIDEO CLIP
Using a silk screen to make a biscuit jaconde

 CHEF'S TIP

Other colours can be achieved in the stencil paste. Just replace the cocoa powder with 20g soft flour and add the appropriate coloured/ flavoured paste.

 CHEF'S TIP

A textured effect can be produced by liberally sprinkling chopped pistachio nuts, hazelnuts, poppy seeds or desiccated coconut over the silicone baking mat before carefully spreading on the biscuit mixture.

Method of work

1   Line a baking sheet (45cm × 35cm × 2cm deep) with a silicone baking mat. Preheat an oven to 240°C.

2   To make the stencil paste, beat the icing sugar and the softened butter. Add the egg whites and fold in the sieved flour and cocoa powder together. Mix to a smooth paste.

3   To make the biscuit, pass the icing sugar and ground almonds through a sieve twice.

4   Whisk the sieved mixture with the whole eggs to a ribbon stage on an electric mixing machine.

5   Sieve the flour.

6   Create a meringue with the egg whites and caster sugar.

7   Fold the sieved flour into the sabayon of eggs and almonds and then fold in the melted butter. Carefully fold in the meringue.

8   To create the frieze effect, spread the stencil paste using a decorative template or rake onto a baking sheet lined with a silicone baking mat. Freeze the baking sheet until the mixture is hard.

9   Thinly spread the biscuit mixture over the frozen stencil paste (about 5mm).

10   Bake at 240°C for about 5 minutes. The biscuit should be moist, springy to the touch and on no account dry.

11   Remove from the oven, cool, carefully remove from the silicone baking mat. Store wrapped in cling film in a refrigerator and use as required.

Dacquoise

INGREDIENTS	4 × 20CM DISCS	8 × 20CM DISCS
Egg whites	220g	440g
Caster sugar	80g	160g
Hazelnut tant pour tant	190g	380g
Almond tant pour tant	170g	340g

Method of work

1. Line a baking sheet with a silicone baking mat. Preheat an oven to 180°C.
2. Create a meringue with the egg whites and the caster sugar.
3. Carefully combine both tant pour tant preparations into the meringue using a plastic spatula to maintain as much aeration as possible.
4. Place into a disposable piping bag with a plain tube and pipe discs on to the baking sheet.
5. Bake in the oven for approximately 20 minutes.

Heavy Genoese sponge

INGREDIENTS	2 TRAYS	4 TRAYS
Butter or cake margarine	225g	450g
Caster sugar	225g	450g
Whole eggs	5	10
Soft flour	250g	500g
Cornflour	30g	60g
Baking powder	10g	20g
Vanilla	To taste	To taste
Good-quality salt	3g	5g

Method of work

1. First line the baking trays (15cm × 8cm × 5cm deep) with silicone paper. Preheat an oven to 180°C.
2. Beat the fat with the sugar to a light aerated consistency. Add the salt and vanilla.
3. Slowly add the eggs, clearing the mixture each time before adding another quantity.
4. Fold in the sieved flour, baking powder and cornflour.
5. Deposit into the moulds and place in the oven to bake for approximately 40 minutes.

Japonaise

INGREDIENTS	2 × 20CM DISCS	5 × 20CM DISCS
Egg whites	5	10
Caster sugar	150g	300g
Ground hazelnuts	150g	300g
Cornflour	25g	50g
Caster sugar	60g	120g

 CHEF'S TIP

Keep any excess Japonaise and reduce to crumbs. Keep in an airtight container and use for decorating various gâteaux (e.g. Gâteau Succés).

Method of work

1 Line a baking sheet with a silicone baking mat. Preheat an oven to 160°C.

2 Mix together the hazelnuts, cornflour and the smaller quantity of caster sugar.

3 Create a meringue with the larger quantity of caster sugar and the egg whites.

4 Carefully fold in the dry mix to the meringue and quickly pipe onto the prepared baking sheet.

5 Place in the oven to bake for approximately 15–20 minutes. Remove from the oven to cool. When nearly cooled cut out the required shapes or discs. When it is totally cooled down it will dry out like a meringue.

Schweizwein torten

INGREDIENTS	1 × 20CM TORTEN RING	2 × 20CM TORTEN RINGS
Sweet wine mousse		
Sweet white wine	250ml	500ml
Caster sugar	70g	140g
Egg yolks	4	8
Whipping cream	250ml	500ml
Orange zest	1 orange	2 oranges
Gelatine	5 leaves	10 leaves
Vanilla	½ pod	1 pod
Neutral glaze		
Light stock syrup	200ml	400ml
Gelatine	2 leaves	4 leaves
Additional ingredients		
Sweet paste (pâte sucrée; see recipe on p. 345)	100g	200g
Almond flavoured separated egg sponge (see recipe on p. 420)	1 × 16cm disc	2 × 16cm disc
Sieved raspberry jam	100g	200g
Mixed prepared fresh fruits (e.g. strawberry, kiwi, fig, orange segments)	250g	500g

Method of work

1 Cut out a 16cm diameter circle of the rolled out sweet paste. **Dock** the paste and lay onto a baking tray lined with silicone paper. Bake blind. Remove from the oven and leave to cool.

2 Soften the gelatine in cold water.

3 Spread the disc of sweet paste with the sieved jam and place in the base of the torten ring.

4 Place a circle of the almond flavoured sponge on top, then add the mixed fruit. At this stage you can place a collar of biscuit jaconde around the side of the torten if required.

5 Whisk the orange zest, caster sugar and egg yolks over a bain marie to create a light aeration. Meanwhile, warm the wine in a saucepan to 80°C. Slowly add to the egg yolk while whisking continuously to form a sabayon.

6 Add the softened gelatine and make sure it is dissolved completely into the sabayon.

7 Remove from the bain marie and slowly whisk until the mixture has cooled down. Place into the refrigerator to half set.

8 Whip the cream to a ribbon stage and carefully fold into the sabayon. Pour into the torten ring and set in a refrigerator for at least 2 hours.

9 Make the neutral glaze by warming the stock syrup and adding the softened leaves of gelatine. Ensure that the gelatine has completely melted, then cool down over a bain marie of cold water.

10 When the torten has completely set and the glaze has cooled sufficiently, glaze the top of the torten and refrigerate for another 15 minutes. Remove the torten from the ring and serve with a raspberry coulis.

Sacher torte

INGREDIENTS	1 × 20CM ROUND CAKE TIN	2 × 20CM ROUND CAKE TINS
Sponge		
Butter	105g	210g
Caster sugar	75g	150g
Egg yolks	3	6
Melted dark chocolate	40g	80g
Soft flour	100g	200g
Baking powder	5g	10g
Ground almonds	25g	50g
Cocoa powder	30g	30g
Egg whites	3	6
Caster sugar	30g	60g
Chocolate glaze		
Fresh milk	100g	210g
Double cream	75g	150g
Icing sugar	50g	100g
Water	50g	100g
Liquid glucose	50g	100g
Dark chocolate	375g	750g
Additional ingredients		
Apricot jam	100g	200g
Dark rum or kirsch	25ml	50ml

Method of work

1 Line the baking tins with silicone paper. Preheat an oven to 180°C.

2 To make the Sacher sponge, cream the butter and the larger quantity of caster sugar together to aerate. Slowly add the egg yolks and the melted dark chocolate.

3 Sift together the baking powder, flour, ground almonds and cocoa powder twice. Incorporate into the creamed chocolate butter preparation.

4 Create a meringue with the smaller quantity of caster sugar and the egg whites. Carefully fold this into the chocolate preparation. Deposit the mixture into the prepared tins and place into the oven to bake.

5 Remove from the oven when fully cooked and turn out onto a wire cooling rack.

6 To make the Sacher glaze, place the milk, water, icing sugar, cream and glucose into a saucepan and slowly bring to the boil.

7 Meanwhile, melt the chocolate in a bain marie.

8 Remove the boiled cream liquid from the stove and add the melted chocolate. Mix together to a silky smooth consistency. Pass through a fine sieve and leave to cool to 20°C.

9 To prepare the base, cut the chocolate sponge into three equal layers. Macerate each layer with the alcohol and brush the surface with some boiled apricot jam thinned with a little of the alcohol. Reassemble the layers and place onto a cake board. Brush the remaining apricot glaze over the Sacher sponge.

10 With the glaze at the correct temperature (nearly at setting point), ladle the glaze over to completely cover the sponge. Leave to set. Using a little of the chocolate glaze pipe the name 'Sacher' on top of the torte and decorate with a little chocolate.

Pear and chocolate mousse cake

INGREDIENTS	1 × 20CM ROUND CAKE TIN	2 × 20CM ROUND CAKE TINS
Pear compôte		
Poached pears	550g	1150g
Unsalted butter	50g	100g
Caster sugar	100g	200g
Vanilla	½ pod	1 pod
Pear liqueur	25g	50g
Nougatine		
Caster sugar	75g	150g
Pectin (optional)	1g	2g
Glucose	25g	50g
Butter	75g	125g
Flaked almonds	50g	100g
Dark chocolate mousse		
Melted dark chocolate	350g	550g
Whipping cream (half whipped)	480g	680g
Additional ingredients		
Flourless chocolate sponge (see recipe on p. 420)	2 discs	4 discs
Biscuit jaconde (3cm wide strip to fit the circumference of the torten ring; see recipe on p. 421)	1 strip	2 strips
Cocoa powder	50g	100g

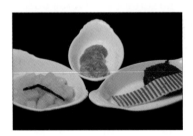

The different preparations required to assemble the mousse cake

Method of work

1   For the compôte, take the pears that have been poached in syrup and cut into 5mm dice. Melt the butter in a heavy-based pan then add the sugar and the split vanilla pod. Cook until a light caramel starts to appear and then add the pears and a little of the syrup. Cook for a further 3–4 minutes to evaporate most of the liquid. Add the alcohol and flambé then set aside to cool for later use.

2   For the nougatine, warm all the ingredients together in a saucepan and then roll the contents between two sheets of silicone paper. Remove the top sheet and bake in the oven until golden brown. Cut discs out of the nougatine when it has cooled a little.

3   For the dark chocolate mousse, melt the chocolate at 50°C. Combine with a little of the semi-whipped cream then mix together with the rest of the cream.

4   In a stainless steel torten ring, place the first disc of chocolate sponge in the base and moisten with a little extra liqueur. Place a disc of the nougatine on top. Wrap a strip of the biscuit jaconde around the inside of the ring. Half fill the torten with the chocolate mousse. Place the second chocolate sponge disc on top and spoon the compôte of pears over the disc. Finally fill the torten ring to the top with the chocolate mousse.

5   Leave to set in a refrigerator for at least 2 hours. Dust the top with the cocoa powder for decoration before removing the torten ring.

6   Serve with a crème chantilly.

Strawberry and lemon mousse cake

CHEF'S TIP

A classical pâte à bombe recipe is to beat cooked sugar (118°C) and egg yolks over a bain marie to a sabayon stage. This modern version for the lemon mousse recipe has the addition of water, glucose and milk powder to stabilise the egg yolk content. Cooking to 85°C will ensure that the eggs cook out completely without splitting the mixture.

INGREDIENTS	1 × 20CM TORTEN RING	3 × 20CM TORTEN RINGS
Lemon mousse		
Egg yolks	90g	180g
Water	90g	180g
Milk powder	30g	60g
Glucose	20g	40g
Lemon zest	3 lemons	6 lemons
Gelatine	10 leaves	20 leaves
Water	60g	120g
Lemon juice	180g	360g
Whipping cream (half whipped)	300g	600g
Italian meringue		
Egg whites	90g	180g
Caster sugar	90g	180g
Glucose	40g	80g
Water	40g	80g
Strawberry gel		
Strawberry purée	350ml	700ml
Gelatine	4 leaves	8 leaves
Water	25ml	50ml
Chopped fresh strawberries	100g	200g
Neutral glaze		
Stock syrup	320g	600g
Gelatine	4 leaves	8 leaves
Additional ingredients		
Dacquoise discs	1 × 18cm	3 × 18cm

Method of work

1 To prepare the lemon pâte à bombe base for the mousse, place the egg yolks, water, glucose, lemon zest and milk powder into a stainless steel saucepan and whisk while cooking out on the stove to 85°C.

2 Meanwhile, make the meringue to the Italian method by boiling the sugar, water and glucose to 121°C. Aerate the egg whites using an electric mixing machine until firm. Slowly stream the cooked sugar into the egg whites while beating on the machine. Continue to beat at a low speed until all the sugar has been incorporated and the meringue has cooled.

3 Fold the lemon pâte à bombe into the meringue. Melt the gelatine in a bain marie of hot water and add to the lemon mixture.

4 Carefully fold the lemon juice into the half whipped cream. Fold in all the ingredients together to create the lemon mousse.

5 Bring the strawberry purée to the boil. Soften the gelatine in the water and add to the hot purée. Strain onto the chopped strawberries and set in 150mm diameter rings.

6 Bring the stock syrup to the boil. Add the softened gelatine off the heat. Pass through a sieve and cool until required for glazing.

7 Lay the disc of dacquoise in the base of the torten ring. Add some of the lemon mousse to cover the base. Turn out the strawberry gel and place into the centre. Cover with the lemon mousse, filling to the top of the ring. Refrigerate for 2 hours.

8 Remove the torten ring and glaze. Set up in the refrigerator once again and decorate as desired.

Savarin

INGREDIENTS	12 INDIVIDUAL SAVARIN RINGS	24 INDIVIDUAL SAVARIN RINGS
Savarin		
Strong flour	200g	400g
Good-quality salt	5g	10g
Caster sugar	15g	30g
Fresh yeast	10g	20g
Eggs	2	4
Water (at 35°C)	100ml	200ml
Soft butter	50g	100g
Additional ingredients		
Crème chantilly	400ml	800ml
Mixed fruits	500g	1kg
Sugar decoration	12	24
Preserved vanilla stick	12	24

 CHEF'S TIP

For babas, prepare the raisins, checking them for stones, then rinse and drain them. The raisins are added to the dough at the last minute, just before moulding. Normally, raisins make up about 20–25% of the overall weight of the dough.

Baba and savarin doughs are prepared using the same method as for brioche. Always use a good-quality, high-gluten flour and simply cream or soften the butter. Baba and savarin doughs are softer than a brioche dough because the weight of the liquid ingredients is equal to that of the flour.

Method of work

1 Preheat an oven to 200°C.

2 Dissolve the yeast and sugar in the water.

3 Sift the flour and salt together. Add to the water/yeast with the eggs to form a smooth and elastic dough. It is easier to do this task using an electric mixing machine.

4 Carefully cut in the softened butter and mix in well. Place in a refrigerator to rest for at least 1 hour.

5 Take care when preparing the moulds. Wipe the moulds with a lightly oiled kitchen towel. Do not butter heavily unless you have previously experienced problems with baked savarins sticking to the moulds. Too much butter on the moulds can pit the surface of the savarin, giving an unattractive appearance and rendering them less able to absorb syrup.

6 Pipe the mixture into the prepared non-stick individual savarin moulds. Place in the prover until doubled in size.

7 Place into the oven to bake for approximately 20 minutes. Remove from the oven and leave to cool on a wire cooling rack.

8 To present, bring to the boil a large pan of stock syrup flavoured with dark rum, lemon zest, orange zest and cinnamon sticks. Set on a very low heat and add the savarins to soak up the syrup. The hotter the syrup, the quicker the savarins will absorb it.

9 Remove the savarins from the syrup and leave to drain and cool.

10 Decorate as required with fresh fruit and crème chantilly.

CHEF'S TIP

The rising times for babas and savarins are minimal. The temperature does not need to be so precisely controlled as with bread. Even though baba and savarin doughs are much softer than brioche dough, it is still important that the gluten is activated and that the dough has enough elasticity.

Warm water is used in this recipe for two main reasons;

1 It will penetrate the flour and reach the gluten more quickly than cold water, giving the dough maximum body and elasticity. This method can be used because the dough requires practically no rising time; 10 minutes maximum. Letting the dough rise too long can negatively affect the gluten in the dough; the heat and acidity generated by rapid fermentation cause the gluten to break down.

2 Warm water helps activate yeast. This is important because the rising time for babas and savarins is so short.

Babas and savarins should be baked in a moderate oven, 180–200°C, for individual sized cakes and a slightly slower oven, 170–180°C, for larger cakes. The cakes should be placed in the oven without being glazed. If oven vents are available, they should be left open during baking to enhance the drying and colouring of the dough. To check that they have been baked, the cakes should slip out of the moulds quite easily. They should be pale brown on the bottom and very dry.

The pâte à savarin can be used to make a range of products:

■ *Pomponette* – piped into tartlette moulds

■ *Marignan* – piped into barquette moulds

■ *Baba* – piped into baba moulds or dariole moulds

■ *Savarin* – piped into savarin moulds

Lemon tuilles

INGREDIENTS	25 TUILLES	50 TUILLES
Lemon zest	2 lemons	4 lemons
Icing sugar	85g	170g
Melted butter	60g	120g
Egg whites	70g	140g
Soft flour	85g	170g

Method of work

1 Preheat an oven to 220°C.

2 Beat together the icing sugar, egg whites, melted butter and the finely grated lemon zest.

3 Mix in the flour and place the tuille mixture into a refrigerator to chill and set up. This can take approximately 1 hour.

4 Using a template, spread the mixture onto a baking sheet lined with a silicone baking mat.

5 Place in the oven and bake until the tuille begins to colour to a golden brown.

6 Remove from the oven and manipulate over a rolling pin into the classical tuille shape.

VIDEO CLIP
Orange tuilles

CHEF'S TIP

Alternative flavours can be used, such as vanilla, cinnamon, orange, hazelnut and almond. Simply add the flavour to this basic recipe.

Classic tuilles

INGREDIENTS	25 TUILLES	50 TUILLES
Caster sugar	500g	1kg
Glucose	50g	100g
Melted butter	250g	500g
Flaked almonds	250g	500g
Water	200ml	400ml
Soft flour	150g	300g
Pistachio nuts	100g	200g

Method of work

1 Preheat an oven to 200°C.
2 Place the sugar, glucose, water, butter and almonds in a saucepan and bring to the boil, stirring constantly.
3 Remove from the heat and stir in the sieved flour. Ensure that the flour is incorporated thoroughly.
4 Put into a bowl and cool, then place in a refrigerator to chill down.
5 Place well-spaced piles of the mixture (approximately one teaspoon) on baking sheets lined with silicone paper. Flatten thoroughly.
6 Sprinkle with the pistachio nuts and place in the oven. Bake until golden brown.
7 Remove from the oven and cool for approximately 1 minute, then shape over a rolling pin and allow to cool.

Griddle scones

INGREDIENTS	12 SCONES	24 SCONES
Soft flour	225g	450g
Bicarbonate of soda	1tsp	2tsp
Cream of tartar	2tsp	4tsp
Butter	25g	50g
Caster sugar	25g	50g
Fresh milk	150ml	300ml

Method of work

1 Preheat a griddle or heavy-based frying pan and lightly oil the surface.
2 Sift the flour, bicarbonate of soda and cream of tartar into a bowl and rub in the butter.
3 Gradually stir in the sugar and the milk to form a soft paste.
4 Divide the paste in half and lightly knead on a lightly floured surface.
5 Roll each piece out to 1cm thick and cut out individual scone rounds. Place them onto the prepared griddle and cook for about 5 minutes per side, until the scones are evenly brown. Place onto a wire rack to cool.
6 Serve as quickly as possible with jam and cream accompaniments.

 CHEF'S TIP

Wholemeal flour can replace the white flour in this recipe, although a little extra milk will be required to balance the overall consistency of the finished paste.

Almond biscotti

INGREDIENTS	2 × 500G LOGS	4 × 500G LOGS
Unsalted butter	125g	250g
Caster sugar	225g	450g
Whole eggs	1	3
Aniseed	4g	8g
Lemon zest	½ lemon	1 lemon
Almond flour	To taste	To taste
Soft flour	850g	1.7kg
Good-quality salt	5g	10g
Baking powder	7 g	15g
Flaked almonds	85g	170g
Vanilla flavour	To taste	To taste

Method of work

1 Preheat an oven to 180°C.
2 Cream the butter and the caster sugar together. Add the egg to the creamed mixture and beat together. Add all the flavourings and mix well.
3 Sift the flour, salt and baking powder. Gradually combine with the creamed butter.
4 Fold in the almonds.
5 Scale off at 500g each and roll into thin baguette shapes.
6 Bake in the oven on a baking tray lined with silicone paper for 20 minutes. Remove from the oven and slice thinly while still slightly warm.
7 Place the slices back into the oven (or until they have reached a golden colour). Turn over and bake for a further 8 minutes.
8 Cool on a wire cooling rack and store in an airtight container.

Assessment of knowledge and understanding

You have now learned about the use of the different types of complex cakes, sponges, biscuits and scones and how to produce some varieties utilising an array of commodities and techniques.

To test your level of knowledge and understanding, answer the following short questions. These will help to prepare you for your summative (final) assessment.

Quality identifications

1 Explain the importance of selecting the correct type, quality and quantity of ingredients when producing a savarin.

2 State the quality points to look for when producing a separated egg sponge.

Equipment and materials

1 State two advantages of using an electric mixer for aeration and what you would need to use if there is not one available.
i) _____ ii) _____

2 State which two fats are ideal for aeration and creaming.
i) _____ ii) _____

3 Explain the term 'plasticity'.

Preparation methods

1 Briefly describe how to produce a separated egg sponge.

2 Explain how the aeration of egg helps to create a light texture in a sponge.

3 State three roles that fat plays in baking cakes.
i) _____ ii) _____
iii) _____

Cooking methods

1 Explain the difference between a savarin and a brioche.

2 Identify the critical quality points for the following baked products:
(a) Fermented scones

(b) Classic tuilles

(c) Dacquoise

20
Chocolate

LEARNING OBJECTIVES

This chapter describes how to prepare a variety of chocolates, small moulded show pieces and decorations using some technically advanced skills and presentation expertise. It also describes how to prepare, process and finish the chocolate items required for Level 3.

At the end of this chapter you will be able to:

- Understand how to pre-crystallise (temper) different couvertures
- State the quality points of couverture
- Understand the importance of temperature control for chocolate
- Identify the various skills required to prepare and present a range of truffles, pralines and chocolates
- Identify the important storage techniques
- Recognise a range of advanced techniques for presentation

COCOA

Cocoa tree

Cocoa flower

Cocoa pod

The cocoa tree grows in warm and humid climates around the equator. Plantations can be found in the tropical rainforests of Africa, Asia and Latin America. Africa produces the largest proportion of the world harvest today, providing up to 65 per cent of the world's cocoa. The tree itself is quite fragile and needs other tall-growing plants, such as palm trees or banana plants, to give it protection from strong winds and the burning sun.

There are three principal varieties of cocoa, although many hybrids have been produced by chocolate companies over the years.

VIDEO CLIP
Barry Callebaut Factory and Academy: types of chocolate

- *Criollo* – known as 'the king of cocoa' due to its exceptional flavour qualities, but is the most fragile variety.

- *Forastero* – this is a stronger type that is easier to cultivate and produces larger yields of cocoa. It has a stronger and more bitter flavour than the criollo and is usually blended with other varieties.

- *Trinitario* – this is a cross-breed of the criollo and forastero types and gives a strong but refined flavour.

Harvesting takes place twice a year and is always undertaken by hand because of the delicate nature of the process. After the pods have been gathered, the outer shell is opened and the pulp is removed. The cocoa beans are then extracted from the pulp and then left to ferment for up to seven days. Fermentation is important for developing colour and flavour in the beans. After the fermentation, the beans are spread out to dry naturally in the sun for up to seven days. They are turned regularly to stop the fermentation process.

Before the cocoa beans can be processed into chocolate, beans from various origins are blended according to the requirements of the recipe. The cocoa bean shells are removed and the beans are broken down into 'nibs', which are then roasted to increase the flavour of the cocoa.

Cocoa pulp

Cocoa beans fermenting

Fermented cocoa drying

The roasted cocoa nibs are then ground. The heat produced during this procedure melts the cocoa butter, which is removed by being pressed out. The cocoa solids will now be formed into a dry cake and used as the base ingredient in the production of chocolate or processed into a fine cocoa powder.

The next stage in chocolate making is conching, whereby the cocoa solids and cocoa butter are slowly mixed in tanks over a period of time. This develops the flavour of the chocolate and breaks down the particles into a smooth texture. Further ingredients are then added: cocoa butter, sugar, vanilla and soya lecithin. The chocolate is then tempered and set into blocks or drops, which are then packaged for storage and distribution.

Couverture is the term used for chocolate in which the fat content is pure cocoa butter. In family or bakers' chocolate the cocoa fat content is replaced by a vegetable-based fat. This has a detrimental effect on the texture and hardness of the chocolate but makes the product cheaper to purchase and easier to use. When used for making chocolates, decorations or moulded chocolates, couverture first has to go though a process of tempering called 'pre-crystallisation'.

MELTING CHOCOLATE

Melted dark couverture

Dark, milk and white couverture all contain cocoa butter. When the chocolate is warmed, the fat crystals in the cocoa butter melt and the chocolate becomes liquid. This starts to occur at 25°C, but cocoa butter contains a variety of fat crystals, some of which will not melt until a temperature of 37°C has been reached. To make sure that the mass of chocolate is totally melted it is common practice to heat the chocolate to 45°C. The following practices must be applied when melting chocolate:

■ Ensure that the chocolate does not come into direct contact with the heat source otherwise it may burn.

■ Use a dry bain marie or chocolate melting pot to prevent the chocolate coming into contact with moisture.

■ If storing melted chocolate for a long period of time, it is important to stir the chocolate regularly to prevent the cocoa butter rising to the surface.

VIDEO CLIP
Pre-crystallisation

PRE-CRYSTALLISING CHOCOLATE

If chocolate has been melted at 45°C then poured into a mould and left to set without further processing, the following will occur:

■ The chocolate will take a long time to harden

■ When the chocolate has eventually hardened it will have a grainy structure and a greyish colour

■ The chocolate will stick to the mould

The reason for this is that as the chocolate cools, crystals form in the cocoa butter, but these crystals are unstable. Cocoa butter actually contains six different forms of crystal, but only one is stable. It is this form of crystal that makes chocolate hard and shiny with a deep and even colouring. The chocolate will also turn out of the mould easily.

There are several different techniques used to pre-crystallise chocolate; crystals can be created in melted chocolate through manipulation and temperature control or by adding chocolate that already contains the stable crystal.

Tabletop pre-crystallising

It is preferable to use a marble or a granite worktop, which will retain heat better than stainless steel.

1 Melt the chocolate to 45°C

2 Stir well

3 Pour two-thirds of the chocolate onto the work surface. Leave the remaining chocolate in the bain marie.

4 Spread the chocolate over the work surface, moving it around with a palette knife and a scraper. This movement cools down the chocolate mass evenly. The chocolate will begin to thicken as it cools. This is an indication the stable crystals are forming

5 At 27°C the chocolate will be too thick to process and use. Return it to the bain marie and mix together well with the remaining warm chocolate

6 This will create the right amount of stable crystals throughout the chocolate, which is now ready to use as required

 CHEF'S TIP

Time, temperature and movement are the three essential factors in this method. If the chocolate is too thick after pre-crystallising, simply raise the temperature by 1°C to re-melt some of the stable crystals.

It is easy to focus on just the temperature when preparing chocolate. This will not guarantee that there are sufficient stable crystals present in the chocolate. Pre-crystallising is a form of 'tempering', in other words bringing the chocolate to a certain temperature. However, if the chocolate is just left to cool down to 32°C after melting, it will have been tempered but not pre-crystallised. Without the stirring and moving around of the chocolate required to form the crystals, the result will be a chocolate that hardens slowly, is dull and sticks in the mould.

The seeding method

This method uses ready-to-use pre-crystallised chocolate callets or small pieces of chopped chocolate block, which are added to the chocolate being processed.

1 Melt the chocolate to 45°C

2 Stir well

3 Add 15–20 per cent of callets or chopped chocolate block and stir well into the melted chocolate; these pieces contain the stable cocoa crystals. They will slowly melt and cool down the mass. When the chocolate reaches its correct processing temperature, stir well again; it will be completely pre-crystallised.

4 If all the crystals melt quickly before the correct temperature has been reached, just add a small extra quantity and stir in well until the correct temperature has been obtained.

 CHEF'S TIP

To test if the chocolate if ready, dip the tip of a palette knife into the melted chocolate. It should harden within five minutes and have a nice sheen. If you have too few crystals the chocolate will not harden. If you have too many crystals the chocolate will not have a sheen.

Couverture callets

Stirring the callets into the chocolate mass

The correctly pre-crystallised chocolate

TEMPERATURE CONTROL FOR CHOCOLATE

The ideal processing temperatures after melting and pre-crystallisation are different for the three different types of chocolate (dark, milk and white). This is attributed to their different compositions; for instance, the higher the quantity of milk fats (milk and white chocolate), the lower the processing temperature.

Irregular cooling can create a dull appearance and a soft structure in the finished chocolate. The ideal temperature to cool and harden chocolate is 10–15°C. A refrigerator with air circulation set to this temperature range is ideal for setting chocolate.

Dark chocolate: processing temperature is 31–32°C

Milk chocolate: processing temperature is 30–31°C

White chocolate: processing temperature is 28–29°C

SHELF LIFE AND STORAGE OF CHOCOLATES

The ideal temperature for storing chocolate is 12–20°C, and the temperature should not fluctuate. At higher temperatures the chocolate becomes soft and will lose its sheen, and at lower temperatures it may be affected by condensation. Chocolate that has been stored at a lower temperature should, when required for use, be left to acclimatise in its original packaging for a few hours until it reaches ambient temperature.

Chocolate is sensitive to humidity and easily absorbs smells and flavours. It is also liable to oxidisation if it is exposed to light, direct sunlight and air for too long. Therefore, chocolate should be stored in a cool, dry place, completely sealed from light and air. Always ensure that the packaging is resealed after using.

Finished products are also very sensitive to temperature, foreign smells, flavours, light, air and humidity and to the effects of time and transportation. Typical changes that can occur during storage of chocolate products include:

■ *Fat bloom* – a thin layer of fat crystals on the surface of the chocolate. The chocolate loses its sheen and a soft, milky white bloom appears on the surface, giving the finished chocolate an unattractive appearance. Fat bloom is caused when fats in the chocolate crystallise or when the fats in the ganache/filling migrate to the chocolate layer. The appearance of fat bloom can be delayed by storing the chocolate at a constant temperature of 10–15°C.

■ *Sugar bloom* – in contrast to fat bloom, sugar bloom creates a rough, coarse layer on top of the chocolate. Sugar bloom is mainly caused by condensation, which can form on the surface of chocolate if storage temperatures are too low or if the chocolate is left in a refrigerator for too long. This moisture will dissolve the sugar within the chocolate and when the moisture evaporates, the sugar re-crystallises on the surface. Avoid rapid changes of temperature to help prevent this occurrence.

If the storage time for chocolate can be kept short, the quality of the product will be much better. Each type of chocolate will have a different shelf life, which is measured from the initial production date and is shown on the packaging. Because of the milk fat solids present in white and milk chocolate, these have shorter shelf lives than dark chocolate. Chocolates that contain a filling need special consideration. Chocolates made with cream or butter fillings have a very short storage life (the recipes shown in this chapter have a shelf life of one week), provided they are stored in ideal conditions. The substitution of cream or butter with alternative ingredients (such as light sugar solutions) will help to increase shelf life.

RECIPES
Honey and cinnamon moulded chocolates

INGREDIENTS	40–50 CHOCOLATES
Dark chocolate (minimum 60% cocoa)	250g
Milk chocolate (minimum 32% cocoa)	250g
Double cream	250g
Clear honey	80g
Cinnamon	2 sticks or 20g powder
Pre-crystallised dark chocolate	50g
Pre-crystallised white chocolate for moulding	1kg

VIDEO CLIP
Moulding

Method of work

1 Place the double cream in a saucepan with the cinnamon and bring to the boil. Remove from the heat and leave to infuse for 15 minutes.

2 Melt the dark and milk chocolates together and add the cinnamon-infused cream. Blend well with a whisk.

3 Add the honey and allow the ganache to cool.

4 Prepare the chocolate moulds by polishing well with cotton wool to ensure there are no marks, dust or remaining chocolate.

5 Take a little pre-crystallised dark chocolate and using a plastic disposable glove, dip a finger into it. Rub some chocolate into each mould and leave to set.

6 If desired, at this stage a fine spray of coloured cocoa butter can be applied to build up a pronounced presentation of the finished chocolate. Leave to set.

7 Using the pre-crystallised white chocolate, fill the moulds. Shake out any air bubbles in the chocolate.

8 Pour out the excess chocolate and make sure all the edges and corners in the mould have been covered.

9 To leave a clean finish, remove any remaining chocolate from the top and the edges using a palette knife.

10 Invert the mould onto a wire rack or silicone paper for 4 minutes. Scrape off any remaining chocolate that has dripped down the mould and leave to harden for a few minutes.

11 Place the ganache into a disposable piping bag and pipe into the centre of each chocolate shell. Take care not to pipe too much ganache into the chocolate shell; it is best to leave a 2mm gap from the top. Make sure the ganache is not too warm otherwise it will melt the chocolate shell. Leave the filling to solidify.

12 To close the chocolates, put a small amount of the pre-crystallised white chocolate onto the mould and spread over each moulded ganache chocolate. Scrape off any excess chocolate and leave to set at 10°C for 30 minutes.

13 Tap the moulds gently onto a sheet of paper and carefully turn out the chocolates.

CHEF'S TIP

Wear gloves when removing chocolates from the mould to avoid fingerprints.

The ingredients required for the ganache

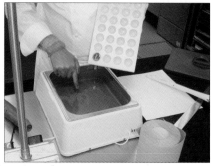

Rubbing pre-crystallised dark chocolate into each mould

The moulds sprayed with coloured cocoa butter

Filling the moulds with pre-crystallised white chocolate

Pouring out the excess white chocolate

Inverting the moulds onto a wire rack

Scraping off the excess chocolate

The chocolate shells filled with ganache

Scraping off excess chocolate after closing the moulds

Raspberry moulded chocolates

INGREDIENTS	40–50 CHOCOLATES
Dark chocolate (minimum 64% cocoa)	300g
Raspberry purée	150g
UHT cream	125g
Caster sugar	10g
Invert sugar	25g
Unsalted butter	60g
Alcohol (framboise or kirsch)	15g
Pre-crystallised dark chocolate (minimum 64% cocoa) for moulding	1kg

 CHEF'S TIP

Invert sugar is created by mixing basic sugar syrup with a small amount of acid, such as lemon juice or cream of tartar. This will break down the sugar (sucrose) into two simple sugars (fructose and glucose) and so reduce the size of the sugar crystals. Adding this to the chocolate filling recipe will help to create a smoother texture in the product.

Method of work

1 Melt the dark chocolate.
2 Place the raspberry purée, caster sugar and invert sugar into a saucepan and bring to the boil. Using a sugar thermometer, continue cooking the purée to 104°C.
3 Add the UHT cream carefully and stir in. Incorporate into the dark chocolate and add the alcohol. Leave to cool.
4 When cool, beat in the softened unsalted butter.
5 Follow the method for moulding the chocolates in the previous recipe, but using the dark chocolate.

Boiling the raspberry purée

Pouring the cooked raspberry cream onto the dark chocolate

Mixing the ingredients together well to form a stable emulsion

Filling the moulds with the pre-crystallised dark chocolate

Pouring out the excess chocolate, tapping the base of the moulds with the handle of the palette knife

Starting to remove the excess chocolate

Sliding the edge of the palette knife down to the bain marie to collect the excess chocolate

Carefully removing any remaining chocolate

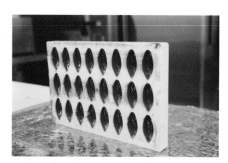

Letting the chocolate crystallise and harden before adding the filling

Vanilla chocolate truffles

INGREDIENTS	40–50 CHOCOLATES
Dark chocolate (minimum 70% cocoa)	400g
Whipping cream	325g
Milk chocolate (minimum 36% cocoa)	200g
Invert sugar	40g
Unsalted butter	50g
Vanilla	1 pod
Pre-crystallised dark chocolate (minimum 64% cocoa) for dipping	1kg
Cocoa powder	500g

Method of work

1 Melt the dark and milk chocolate together.
2 Bring the cream to the boil with the split vanilla pod. Remove from the heat and leave to infuse for 5 minutes.
3 Pour the infused cream onto the chocolate and add the invert sugar. Combine the ingredients well.
4 Beat in the softened unsalted butter when cold.
5 Fill a disposable piping bag with the truffle filling and pipe out small truffle shapes onto silicone paper. Leave to harden for at least 3 hours in a refrigerator.
6 Dip the individual truffles into the pre-crystallised dark chocolate. Shake off any excess chocolate.
7 Immediately place the truffles into a container filled with cocoa powder and roll until completely covered with a fine layer of the powder.

CHEF'S TIP

Alternatively, the truffles can be rolled in sieved icing sugar or small chocolate shavings for different effects.

Pralines

INGREDIENTS	40–50 CHOCOLATES
Milk chocolate (minimum 38% cocoa)	100g
Praline paste	220g
Pure hazelnut paste	50g
Unsalted butter	50g
Pre-crystallised milk chocolate (minimum 38% cocoa) for moulding	1kg

Method of work

1 Melt the milk chocolate to 40°C.
2 Add the praline paste and the hazelnut paste.
3 Blend together to form a smooth paste and beat in the softened butter.
4 Prepare the moulds using the pre-crystallised milk chocolate, as described previously (see page 440). An alternative is to marble with a little pre-crystallised white or dark chocolate to create an interesting design.
5 Pipe the praline filling into the prepared moulds and finish by topping off and leaving to set.

MOULDING HOLLOW FIGURES

Moulded hollow figures or Easter eggs can be made using one or more different types of chocolate. The chocolate first has to be pre-crystallised and is then poured into a mould and cooled down.

Most chocolatiers and chefs work with polycarbonate moulds because they are easy to maintain, are quite strong and will give a good end result. Metal moulds are also available, but are used less and less due to their price and weight. PVC moulds are also popular. They are flexible, allowing the chocolate shapes to be turned out quickly, and cheap, but they can scratch easily and will often break.

There are two basic forms of moulds:

- *Single moulds* – sometimes referred to as half moulds, the chocolate is poured into the mould, cooled and then removed from the mould. The chocolate halves are then joined together.
- *Double moulds* – these are made up of two half moulds linked together to form one mould. The chocolate is poured into the mould and cooled. The moulded shape is then removed by unfastening the two half moulds and prising them apart.

Before moulding figures, the moulds must be thoroughly cleaned and then polished with cotton wool, and they must be at room temperature. The chocolate must be pre-crystallised and the various pieces of equipment, such as palette knives, plastic spoons, stainless steel trays, silicone paper and wire cooling racks, should be prepared in advance.

The following method should be used to produce a small moulded figure:

1. Pour the pre-crystallised chocolate into the mould. Tap the back of the mould to remove any air bubbles and swirl the chocolate around to create an even layer of chocolate, then pour any excess out of the mould.

2. Scrape thesetting chocolate from the surface of the mould and place into a refrigerator at 12°C for at least 20 minutes.

3. After cooling, check to see if the chocolate figures are ready to come out of the moulds. If the chocolate has crystallised it should have contracted slightly away from the inside of the mould.

5. Lay two halves, with the open sides down, onto a warm stainless steel tray to melt the chocolate. Stick the halves together immediately. Press together and hold for a few seconds.

4. Tap the edges of the mould gently and remove the chocolate figure halves.

6. The finished figures can then be presented or wrapped in decorative packaging ready to be sold.

SMALL DISPLAY PIECES

Chocolate designs can be relatively simple and still be creative and eye-catching. Learning a few uncomplicated decorative techniques will equip the chef to be able to produce striking chocolate display pieces for banquets, festivals or dinners, or just for fun!

The moulding techniques explained in this chapter can easily be transferred to create Easter eggs, chocolate bars or other moulded pieces. However, the following techniques will further enhance any display, and can also be used in the decoration of desserts.

Acetate curls

1. Lay a sheet of acetate on a sheet of plastic film on a work surface. Pour some pre-crystallised chocolate onto the acetate and spread it over the surface evenly.

2. Leave the chocolate to begin to set. While the chocolate is still pliable and not fully hardened, quickly make curved cuts from the inside of the acetate to the edge, without cutting through the acetate.

3. Place a sheet of silicone paper over the acetate and quickly roll up the acetate before the chocolate sets. Leave to harden for approximately 15 minutes.

4. When the chocolate is set, carefully unravel the acetate sheet. The chocolate curls will break off where the cuts were made.

5. The finished curls ready for use.

VIDEO CLIP
Decorative acetate work

Flat cutting

This is a technique used to create different forms and shapes. The items produced can be used as decoration, as bases for decoration pieces or combined to create figures.

Display figure

The techniques discussed above have been utilised to create the small display piece shown here. The composition of the piece is a 22cm egg – that has been cut in half and re-sealed with chocolate – moulded mini bars of chocolate with a sprayed colour, acetate decorations and a flat cut base. The egg and the base have been assembled and then lightly sprayed with chocolate to give a soft matt finish.

Cut out the desired shape before the chocolate completely sets

1 Lay plastic sheet or silicone paper onto a board. Pour a layer of pre-crystallised chocolate and spread as evenly as possible to the required thickness. Lay another sheet of silicone paper on top and smooth it to remove any air bubbles that may have formed.

2 Before the chocolate completely sets, cut out the desired shape using a sharp craft knife. A template can be used for more detailed designs.

3 When set, peel off the paper and use as required.

A canister of confectioner's freeze spray is helpful when assembling the display piece; the spray will cool the melted chocolate used to glue the parts together and set it instantly. This saves time when working on large or multiple displays.

Preparation for the small display piece

To assemble the display figure:

1 Flat cut the base into triangles and join together with melted chocolate

2 Position and fix the egg in the centre of the base, maintaining the balance of the piece

3 Spray the piece with fluid chocolate if desired

4 Add the acetate curls around the base of the egg

5 Finish with a bar of chocolate on top of the piece.

VIDEO CLIP
Finishing a decorative display

The finished display piece

Assessment of knowledge and understanding

You have now learned about the use of chocolate and how to produce a variety of chocolates and decorations utilising an array of commodities and different chocolate types.

To test your level of knowledge and understanding, answer the following short questions. These will help to prepare you for your summative (final) assessment.

Quality identifications

1 Name the fat used in the production of couverture chocolate.

2 Identify the quality points to look for when using couverture.

3 Explain why we need to pre-crystallise couverture.

4 Identify and explain one technique for pre-crystallising (tempering) couverture.

Equipment and materials

1 Identify the difference between milk and white chocolate and why they have different processing temperatures.

2 State the ideal refrigeration temperature for setting chocolate.

3 Identify two pieces of essential equipment that may be used to make chocolates and describe their use.
   i) _____ ii) _____

Preparation methods

1 State the general melting temperature for chocolate.

2 Describe the effect that invert sugar has on ganache.

3 Explain the correct procedure for melting chocolate.

4 Describe the procedure for moulding hollow chocolate figures.

Storage

1 Describe how to store white chocolate to prevent it from losing colour and flavour.

2 State the factors that can affect the shelf life of chocolates after preparation.

CHEF'S PROFILE

Name: BEVERLEY DUNKLEY
Position: Head of UK Academy
Establishment: Barry Callebaut UK Ltd
Current job role and main responsibilities: To plan and organise all activity which takes place in the Barry Callebaut UK training Academy. This activity includes a variety of courses for chocolatiers, bakers, pâtissiers and pastry chefs plus bespoke customer training days.
When did you realise that you wanted to pursue a career in the catering and hospitality industry? From a very early age – I told my parents when I was 8 years old that I wanted to be a cook. At that age I was making cakes, and by the age of 11 I was cooking the family Sunday roast!

Training:
1 Peterborough Technical College: City and Guilds 706/1 and 2 Food Preparation and Cookery
2 Birmingham College of Food, Tourism and Creative Studies: City and Guilds 706/3, Parts 1 and 2 Advanced Pastry
3 Grantham College of Further Education: City and Guilds 730/7 Teacher's Certificate
4 University of Central Lancaster: City and Guilds Certificate of Education
5 Lancaster and Morecambe College: TDLB Training Assessor Awards D32/D33/D34/D36

Experience:
1 Barry Callebaut (UK) Ltd, Global Chocolate Manufacturer: Account Manager/Head of UK Academy
2 Lancaster and Morecambe College of Further Education: Lecturer of NVQ Patisserie levels 1, 2 and 3
3 Cooper Group, Bakery Supply of Ingredients and Equipment: Sales and Demonstrator
4 Oberweis, Relais Dessert in Luxembourg: Pastry chef for petits gâteaux
5 Edward Notters Sugar School, Zurich: School technician
6 Hambleton Hall, Relais Chateaux Hotel in Rutland: Head Pastry Chef

What do you find rewarding about your job?
Meeting new people. Watching people learn new skills and develop their careers and businesses. The commercial side of the business is also engaging; controlling the planning and budgeting of the Academy courses as well as actually promoting the desire to work with chocolate.

What do you find the most challenging about the job?
Making sure a specific course meets the expectations and needs of all attendees. After two successful years the challenge is to continually raise the standards and variety of the courses we run, and to increase the chocolate skills of chocolatiers, pastry chefs and bakers.

What advice would you give to students just beginning their career?
Just enjoy – absorb as much knowledge as you can from all sources, be that from lecturers, work colleagues, websites, books and exhibitions. This information is invaluable. Catering is a fantastic career that can diversify into so many other areas of industry. It is also a wonderful opportunity to travel and work all over the world.

Who is your mentor or main inspiration?
In the early years it would have been the Roux brothers, but with each stage of my career development I have been lucky enough to have a mentor figure to learn from and who has given me inspiration.

What traits do you consider essential for anyone entering a career as a chef?
Catering is all about passion. People work well beyond their paid hours to gain satisfaction from their work and are not driven by a nine-to-five job.
• Have the motivation to be a team player, work well under pressure and like challenges.
• Be respectful to others and learn from their experience and knowledge.
• Be prepared to relocate and relish the opportunity to travel in order to gain experience, whether in England or abroad.
• Have high values and do your best everyday.
• Be flexible and accept change within your job role. Never accept complacency and embellish the latest trends in the marketplace with new ingredients and techniques.

Can you give one essential kitchen tip or technique that you use as a chef?
Preparation is the key to success.

Raspberry and Saffron Ganache

INGREDIENTS

Whipping cream	100g
Raspberry coulis	100g
Saffron fibres	0.5g
Callebaut 823 chocolate	600g
Freeze dried raspberry pieces to decorate	

Method of work

1 Bring the cream, raspberry and saffron fibres to the boil.

2 Sieve onto the melted chocolate.

3 Blend together to make an emulsion.

4 Pour into a frame (1cm in thickness) and allow to crystalise over night.

5 Spread a thin layer of pre crystalised chocolate on one side of the Ganache.

6 Cut into desired shape.

7 Cut 2cm squares of clear stiff clear transfer sheet.

8 Dip the individual chocolates into pre crystalised Callebaut 823 Chocolate.

9 Whilst the chocolate is still wet sprinkle with a few pieces of freeze dried raspberry and then place a clear transfer sheet square directly on top of the dipped chocolate.

10 Allow to cool at least twenty minutes before the clear plastic is removed.

21
Sugar and confectionery

3FPC8 Prepare, process and finish marzipan, pastillage and sugar products

LEARNING OBJECTIVES

This chapter describes how to prepare a variety of marzipan, pastillage and small sugar decorative pieces and decorations using some technically advanced skills and presentation expertise. It will also describe how to prepare, process and finish marzipan, pastillage and sugar items required for Level 3.

At the end of this chapter you will be able to:

■ Understand how to cook sugar and isomalt

■ Understand how to prepare marzipan

■ Understand how to prepare pastillage

■ Understand the importance of temperature control for cooking sugar

■ Identify the various skills required to prepare and present a range of marzipan, pastillage and sugar confections

■ Identify the important storage techniques

■ Recognise a range of advanced techniques for presentation

INTRODUCTION

Sugar confectionery has a long and widespread history. Honey was the first source of sugar and was used to conserve fruits, herbs and grains. The ancient Chinese and Egyptians coated fruits, flowers, grains and plants with honey and served them as sweet treats. The Greeks and Romans also used honey to conserve raisins and other fruits. The Roman Empire, which influenced cookery techniques across in Europe, introduced the first confiture (or preserved fruit) recipes.

Sugar cane was first discovered in the south Pacific, where the sweet juice was extracted by pressing the juice from the cane. Sugar manufacturing began in the eastern Mediterranean as the trade routes between Asia and the Western regions slowly developed. The Arabs appear to have been the first to use sugar to create confections such as almond paste.

Sugar confections developed rapidly after they were first introduced to the Europeans. During the crusades, Europeans came in contact with many new ingredients, including various spices and sugar cane. The chefs to the noble courts and royalty began to experiment with sugar and candy making, and recipes for sugar bonbons had appeared by the sixteenth century. Candies were developed and given as precious gifts for weddings, birthdays and religious festivals. They were mainly reserved for the upper classes because sugar was so rare and expensive at this time.

The further development of sugar confections expanded when sugar became more available and the price began to fall due to the new large sugar plantations in Europe's colonies and to the later discovery of beet sugar. By the eighteenth century, bonbons were being made by many artisans in Europe. In France, the confiseurs were known as *marchands de plaisirs* (pleasures sellers) and their bonbons were made with flowers, essences, oils and spices.

Today, most sugar confections are made in factories, although modern candies have developed from the long tradition of artisan candy making. Confiseurs can still be found in well-structured pastry kitchens, where they provide a selection of bonbons and produce basic pastry ingredients such as marzipan, raw almond paste, pralines, fondants and nougatines.

SUGAR CONFECTIONERY BASES

Most of the bases made by confectioners are also available as finished products under a range of different brand names. Today, most hotels, restaurants, caterers and even pastry shops will purchase them to help save time and improve consistency of the final product. However, it is crucial for a professional chef to have the knowledge and the skills to produce them. Creating these bases will produce finished products that are fresher and more individual than products made with industrially produced bases.

VIDEO CLIP
A sugar artist at work

■ *Marzipan* (almond paste) – A paste made of ground almonds (or almonds mixed with other nuts) and cooked sugar. Trimoline and sorbitol (used as stabilisers) and flavourings can also be added. This is a primary ingredient that is widely used in any pastry kitchen. Marzipan is also used in a number of sugar confections.

■ *Raw almond paste* – A paste made of ground almonds and sugar. This is a primary ingredient in the production of various cakes, such as pound cakes, sponges and pain de gênes.

■ *Praline* – a paste made of caramelised sugar and roasted hazelnuts. Praline is a primary ingredient in various pastry products, used to flavour candies or as a filling in chocolates and cakes.

■ *Fondant* – A cooked sugar syrup that is re-crystallised by mechanical agitation. It can be flavoured and coloured as required. In the past fondant was used extensively in sugar confections. Today it is mainly used for glazing or covering pastries, sweets, cakes and choux pastries.

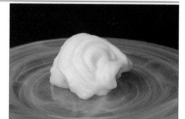

■ *Nougatine* – A mixture of caramelised sugar with glucose and nuts. Unsalted butter and fresh vanilla can be added to improve the flavour. To protect it against humidity, a drying agent, such as powdered pectin, can be added. In the pastry kitchen it is used in mousses, ice creams, croquembouche and many chocolate fillings.

■ *Caramelised nuts* – caramelised, sugar-coated roasted nuts are used for a few sugar confections, but mainly in industrially produced candies or candy bars. They are also used in mousses, cakes and ice creams and in chocolate making.

■ *Sugar syrups* – These have many different purposes in candy making, and may be used either as part of the recipe or in a finishing process (dipped, crystallised, powdered or glazed). The most important characteristic of sugar syrups is their sugar density. This can be determined using a saccharometer or a refractometer and is measured in degrees Baumé or degrees Brix. Measuring sugar density is very important in the production of sorbets and sauces to help control the freezing process and consistency of a sauce.

Lollipops

Caramels

Nougats

Dragées

SUGAR CONFECTION FAMILIES

Candies have been classified into groups based on a specific ingredient or a specific technique. Collectively they are called sugar confections or sugar candies (*bonbons de sucre*).

■ *Cooked sugars* – A sugar solution (often with the addition of glucose) is cooked until enough water evaporates to ensure the hard setting of the bonbon. These candies can be moulded, cut or pressed. Sugar and glucose syrups are both unflavoured and colourless, so the chef can be very creative in the choice of flavours and colours to be added. Examples of cooked sugars are lollipops and bonbons.

■ *Caramels* – These are composed of sugar, water, milk, glucose and butter. The sugar is usually caramelised with the liquid content and then re-cooked to the desired temperature and colour. They are produced from light brown to darker shades, depending on the strength of flavour being sought. After cooking and cooling, they are cut and wrapped. Nuts or other flavours can be added. Among the most famous found in Europe are caramels with salted butter from Brittany and toffees from the United Kingdom. Chewy caramels, hard caramels and toffees all belong in this family.

■ *Nougats* – The term 'nougat' is derived from the Latin word *nugatum* (of nuts), and there is a Roman recipe from Apicius made using nuts, honey and eggs. Nougat was first seen in Marseille and has became popular and famous throughout the south-eastern areas of France. There are four types of nougats in France:

–   Nougat de Montélimar: 28–30 per cent almond content

–   Honey nougat: minimum 20 per cent honey content

–   Nougat provençale: 25 per cent honey with almond, coriander, hazelnuts and aniseed

–   Black nougat: the same as provençale but not aerated or caramelised

The addition of egg whites or gelatine allows air to be incorporated to increase the volume and makes a difference in the texture between the nougats. Sugar and honey are cooked and then mixed with egg whites or gelatine. Roasted nuts, dried or candied fruits, and spices can be added and the nougats are cut when cold and set.

■ *Dragées* – These take their name from the popular almonds covered with honey favoured by the Greeks called *tragemata*. The first mention of dragées is found in the archives of the French town of Verdun (1220 AD). The technique used is to cover a whole nut or other filling in regular layers of sugar that are made hard and smooth. The centre can be made of whole nut, chocolate, nougat, marzipan or fondant. Dragées used to be made by hand, but today they are produced industrially in factories. The dragées are slowly covered with sugar syrup (maintained at a constant temperature) in a revolving pan until crystallisation takes place. They are traditionally used in Europe at celebrations of baptism and marriage.

■ *Gums* – Gums are centuries old, and in the past were used as medicines. They are made using gum Arabic, a natural vegetable substance. Purified, powdered and diluted in warm water, the gum is added to sugar syrup and glucose and then flavoured and coloured as required. Bonbons are then cast in starch moulds and when set are crystallised in sugar syrup before serving.

■ *Fruit jellies* – These delicacies are among the oldest candies and were introduced from the Far East along with candied fruits and the art of confiture. Fruit purées, sugar (a minimum of half the purée weight), glucose and pectin are cooked to the desired temperature. Pectin is added to help set the jellies and citric acid is mixed in prior to casting to ensure the setting of the pectin. Fruit jellies can be moulded and cut after cooling. They are usually covered with granulated sugar or crystallised in saturated sugar syrup.

■ *Liquorice* – Liquorice candies are made using a substance extracted from the root of the liquorice plant. This plant was valued in the Middle Ages as an aid in digestion, and at the end of the seventeenth century an Englishman was the first to use it to create a confection. The roots are cleaned and crushed before being heated in water. The solution is purified, filtered and concentrated to obtain the final flavouring. There are two kinds of liquorice: a hard type, made of liquorice, sugar syrup, glucose and gum Arabic, and a soft type, in which wheat flour and powdered sugar are added to liquorice flavouring and the candy is pushed through a machine to form strings or ribbons.

Liquorice

■ *Jams, marmalades and jellies* – Jams are made from whole or pieces of fresh fruits and are set with the aid of pectin. Marmalades are made from strained fruit purées such as Seville oranges. Jellies are made from strained fruit juice.

Jellies

■ *Candied fruit* – Fruit is dipped into a sulphur bath before being blanched in hot water and candied in a sugar solution. The sulphur lightens the original colour of the fruit and kills any bacteria that could later cause fermentation. Blanching is a crucial step. If the fruit is not blanched enough it may dry out and impart an unpleasant colour. If it is blanched too much, the fruit may become too soft and will result in a compôte texture being produced where the fruit structure breaks down. The fruit is soaked in a hot sugar solution, which rises slightly in density over time, to reach the centre of the fruit and so preserve it.

■ *Sugar-coated fruit* (*fruits déguisés*) – Fresh, dried or candied fruits or fruits shaped out of marzipan are covered in a protective shell of either crystallised sugar or cooked (coloured and flavoured) sugar.

■ *Fudge* – this is a soft caramelised sugar confection with added cream. It is usually cut into squares and served in many different flavour combinations, such as vanilla, chocolate, coffee or rum and raisin.

Fudge

MARZIPAN

Marzipan has been used for centuries by pastry chefs all over the world. It is a favoured delicacy in many European countries and can be used in baking, confectionery, biscuits, breads, gâteaux, torten and cakes. Marzipan is a sweet, pliable mixture of almonds and sugar. It is sometimes tinted with food colouring and modelled into a variety of decorative shapes.

Recent studies into the history of marzipan have shown that *marci panis* has had a long and complex journey. During the thirteenth century in such places as Venice, Naples, Sicily and Provence various spices and sweets were presented in thin wooden boxes. These boxes were called *mazaban* and eventually this word must have extended its meaning to cover its contents. In other languages this became *marzipan* (German), *marchpane* (English), *marzapane* (Italian) or *massepain* (French).

Marzipan is now known to have originated in Asia, where the delicate almond/sugar mixture was served at the sultan's table as the crowning of a meal. Through Arabian rule, marzipan reached Spain and Portugal, and during the crusades it spread through the rest of Europe via the largest trading port of the area, Venice.

Once in Europe, marzipan was produced in the early days by the apothecaries; it was well known as a remedy into the eighteenth century. In the fourteenth century, marzipan was used for artistic creations and figurines modelled by hand. Lübecker marzipan was first mentioned in the city's guild rolls in 1530. Lübeck's reputation as the City of Marzipan and its dominance in the production of marzipan was established after 1800. Much of this dominance was due to new production technology being introduced and the marzipan houses of the area being able to source the highest quality ingredients from around the world while still keeping to traditional recipes.

VIDEO CLIP
Moulding a marzipan rose

Lübecker marzipan

Lübecker marzipan has a great tradition and is world-renowned. Among the many companies that have set the standards for this type of marzipan, two stand out: Carstens and Niederegger. But what distinguishes Lübecker marzipan from other products?

The basic elements of marzipan are a marzipan paste and sugar. Marzipan paste is generally 75 per cent almonds and 25 per cent sugar, the almonds being roasted and blended together with the sugar. It is the relative proportions of marzipan paste and sugar that helps to determine the flavour and quality of Lübecker marzipan. A Lübeck Fine Marzipan contains up to 90 parts marzipan paste to 10 parts sugar.

Marzipan legislation

For a paste to be classified as a marzipan or almond paste it must not have less than 23.5 per cent dry almond content and not less than 75 per cent of the remaining content should be sugar. This standard does not, however, apply to items such as cake decorative figures and petit fours. With the high cost of almonds, other cake covering pastes are beginning to be used in place of traditional marzipan in some areas of confectionery. These have an almond content of less than 23.5 per cent and so cannot be called marzipan.

MARZIPAN RECIPES

Boiled marzipan

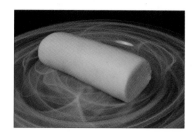

INGREDIENTS	900G MARZIPAN	2KG MARZIPAN
Caster sugar	400g	1kg
Water	240ml	600ml
Ground almonds	300g	750g
Egg white (lightly beaten)	1 egg	2½ eggs
Almond flavour (optional)	To taste	To taste
Icing sugar	100g (approximately)	225g (approximately)

Method of work

1 Place the sugar into a clean pan with the water and cook to 118°C (soft ball stage) and observe all the sugar boiling rules (see page 462).

2 Remove the pan from the heat and carefully add the almonds and flavour if required.

3 Add the lightly beaten egg white then return to the heat to cook for a further 2 minutes, stirring constantly.

4 Place the paste into an electric mixing machine with a paddle attachment and slowly beat, adding a little icing sugar, to create a smooth consistency to the paste.

5 Turn the paste out onto a marble work surface and knead until smooth and cool. Wrap the marzipan well in plastic film and store in a dry, cool area.

Raw marzipan *Pâte d'amande cru*

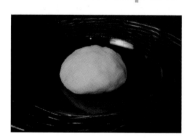

INGREDIENTS	700G MARZIPAN	1.6KG MARZIPAN
Icing sugar	450g	1kg
Ground almonds	250g	600g
Egg white (lightly beaten)	2 eggs	5 eggs
Additional icing sugar	50g (approximately)	100g (approximately)

Method of work

1 Sift the icing sugar and ground almonds together twice and place into a clean stainless steel bowl.

2 Make a well in the centre and add the lightly beaten egg white. Stir together to form a smooth paste.

3 Turn out onto a clean work surface and knead until smooth. Add the additional icing sugar if the paste is initially too wet. Wrap the marzipan well in plastic film and store in a cool area, such as a refrigerator.

Marzipan déguisés

INGREDIENTS	10 DEGUISES	20 DEGUISES
Cooked marzipan	50g	100g
Dried dates	10	20
Cointreau or kirsch (to flavour the marzipan)	To taste	To taste
Colour	As required	As required
Granulated sugar	250g	500g
Liquid glucose	30g	60g
Water	50g	100g

Method of work

1 Flavour and colour the marzipan as required.

2 Cut an incision lengthways into the date and remove the stone if still inside. Stuff the dates with small pieces of the marzipan and remould to their original shape. Leave to dry out for at least one hour.

3 Boil the sugar and water together, adding the glucose at 104°C. Cook the sugar solution further to 156°C and then immediately arrest the cooking by plunging the pan into a bowl of cold water for 10 seconds.

4 Carefully dip the dates into the hot sugar and leave to set on a lightly oiled marble worktop or a silicone baking mat.

5 Keep in a dry, airtight container until required.

Stuffing the dates with small pieces of marzipan

Plunging the pan into a bowl of cold water

Carefully dipping the dates into the hot sugar

Lemon and almond marzipan bonbons

INGREDIENTS	35 BONBONS	70 BONBONS
Granulated sugar	350g	700g
Liquid glucose	40g	80g
Water	100g	200g
Skinned whole almonds	350g	700g
Cooked marzipan	175g	325g
Sugar syrup (at 30B°)	100g	200g
Trimolene	30g	60g
Blanched lemon zest	1 lemon	2 lemons
Unsalted dry butter	60g	120g
Crystallisation syrup (saturated sugar solution)		
Granulated sugar	1375g	2725g
Water	500g	1000g

 CHEF'S TIP

Cover the candissoire with a paper that will absorb the humidity (not silicone paper), if you notice a delay in the crystallization process. The size of the crystals on the paper will be the size they are on the candies.

Method of work

1 Boil the sugar and the water, adding the liquid glucose at 104°C. Continue boiling until 119°C has been reached.

2 Grind the almonds to a powder using a food blender, then slowly pour in the hot sugar solution and blend for 30 seconds.

3 Add the marzipan, trimolene and the syrup at 30B° and continue mixing for another 5 minutes using an electric mixing machine with the paddle attachment.

4 Add the blanched lemon zest, and when the mixture is cold add the unsalted dry butter. Roll into small, evenly sized bonbons.

Method of finishing

Very clean equipment and utensils are needed for this task.

1 Place the sugar and the water into a clean saucepan and slowly bring to the boil, stirring to dissolve the sugar solids.

2 Skim the sugar syrup just before it comes to the boil to remove any impurities. When the sugar boils, clean the sides of the saucepan with a clean brush and clean water. Skim off any impurities as it boils.

3 Boil the syrup for 1 minute, then cover with plastic film and allow to cool down without stirring, to prevent any premature crystallisation.

4 Place the bonbons to be candied on a wire rack that fits in a shallow tray (candissoire). Ensure the bonbons do not touch each other so that they can be evenly coated. Pour the sugar syrup over the bonbons very slowly (to help obtain small crystals) until the syrup reaches the top of the bonbons.

5 Invert a rack over the bonbons if needed to keep them in place and leave them in the candissoire at room temperature until the syrup has cooled to about 40°C.

6 Cover the candissoire with baking parchment. Do not move the container in which the bonbons are crystallising otherwise the crystals will shift and start growing on other parts, rather than on the actual bonbons.

7 Let the bonbons crystallise for 17–20 hours, or more, depending on how dry the surrounding environment is. When the crystals reach the desired size, drain the bonbons on the bottom of the rack for 1 hour and remove them to a clean rack to dry until they are not sticky (this can take up to 6 hours). Keep the bonbons in an airtight container in the refrigerator at 5°C until required.

Bonbons to be candied placed on a wire rack that fits a shallow tray

Pouring the sugar syrup over the bonbons very slowly

Draining the bonbons on the bottom of the rack

PASTILLAGE

VIDEO CLIP
Pastillage

Pastillage is a flexible paste composed of icing sugar, cornflour, gum tragacanth or gelatine, water and lemon juice. Egg white and glucose may also be used in pastillage, but these are not strictly necessary. Pastillage is one of the easiest decorative mediums to work with in the pastry kitchen and can be moulded, coloured, cut, shaped and modelled. When allowed to dry it sets with a matt finish and a brittle, crisp hardness, and it can be brushed and smoothed to create a clean textured finish. Once set, pieces can be joined together with royal icing to form a display piece.

Pastillage is easy to handle and does not require specialist equipment or storage arrangements. The main ingredient is icing sugar to which a little cornflour is added to aid the drying process. The setting agent is either gum tragacanth or leaf gelatine (gelatine is often used as gum tragacanth can be difficult to incorporate), the egg white acts as a binding agent and also gives shine, and the lemon juice, if used, bleaches the sugar, giving it a high white definition.

Preparation of the paste

Cleanliness is essential. Dirt, dust, oil and grease and soiled and stained hands are to be avoided at all costs.

■ A marble slab or a clean wooden board can be used for preparing small quantities of paste; larger quantities may require an electric mixing machine
■ Use a stainless steel bowl; aluminium will discolour the paste during the mixing process
■ Use a dough hook so as not to aerate the mixture

Method of preparation

3. Strain the melted ingredients into the sieved dry ingredients and mix well until a fairly firm but not dry paste is formed. Knead this well to improve the consistency and whiteness of the paste.

1. Sift all the dry ingredients through a fine nylon sieve.

2. Soak the gelatine or gum tragacanth in the water. Add the glucose if used and melt over a bain marie.

Holding

Once the mass is ready to work with, it should be placed in a covered container to prevent it drying out. Use a clean damp cloth to cover the paste. If the paste is to be kept for prolonged periods it should be wrapped with several layers of plastic film and placed in the refrigerator, where it will last for up to 7 days. It must be kneaded prior to use.

Consistency

For general use the pastillage should feel like a lightly worked short paste. It should feel elastic and flexible in consistency. It should also be easy to roll out, but not so wet that it will stick to the working surface or so dry that it will crack when rolled out.

Adding colour

Food colours may be carefully added to obtain the required shade. Always remember to colour a sufficient amount of the mass to finish the project; trying to match the colour or shade will not be easy. Always try to use delicate or pastel shades. Harsh or deep colours do not always work well with this medium. Marbling effects may be achieved by carefully blending one or more colours, but do not overwork the paste.

The pastillage may be painted after it is dried, using edible water-based colour or standard food colour, to obtain stronger or more specific effects. If pastillage is to be painted it should be dried slowly to prevent the edges from curling. Before beginning to paint on the pastillage, lightly scrape its surface with the blade of a knife (or sometimes glasspaper) to make sure that it is perfectly smooth. Be sure to place the sheet of pastillage on several layers of kitchen towelling to prevent it from breaking. If the surface of the pastillage is to be painted with food colouring, rather than artist's paint, it should first be glazed in the oven with a coating of gelatine dissolved in water. This glazing creates an impermeable coating on the surface of the pastillage, otherwise the surface acts like a blotter and may cause the colours to bleed and run into each other.

If colour is to be applied to large flat surfaces it is often best to spray the colour using an airbrush connected to a compressor or gas canister. Always try out the colour on a small piece of pastillage to ensure that the correct shade and technique are being used.

Airbrushing a sheet of dried pastillage

Handling

It is best to estimate the amount required for the task at hand and to only use that amount; this will avoid drying out a large piece. The pastillage should preferably be worked on a wooden board to prevent rapid drying out, and the warmth of the hand can be used to render the pastillage soft and workable.

Rolling out

Pastillage is normally rolled out on a smooth flat surface that has been finely dusted with cornflour; this can be achieved using a 'dusting dolly'. Dusting with cornflour prevents the paste sticking. To ensure the smoothest surface, the paste can be rolled out on toughened glass, marble or polished slate.

A separate rolling pin should be reserved for this purpose as rolling pins generally have dents and scratches and so will not give a perfect finish. Textured and different finishes can be achieved by the use of specialised or shaped rollers.

> **CHEF'S TIP**
>
> A 'dusting dolly' is a square of muslin cloth into which an amount of cornflour has been placed; this is then tied at the top with string to form a loose bag to finely dust the cornflour.

Cutting

A clean, neat cut is essential to the finish of pastillage. A sharp blade should be used, such as a scalpel. Pastry cutters can be used, as well as pastry wheels or any other sharp object that will cut. A direct downward guillotine cut is best; the action of dragging the blade should be avoided as this can crease the pastillage. Always cut out more pieces than are required to allow for breakage.

Cutting pastillage carefully

Drying out

Pastillage cut-outs will dry naturally in a dry atmosphere in approximately one hour, but the drying process can be speeded up by the use of an oven with a low setting. Ultimately, the drying time will be governed by the thickness of the paste. The paste should not be handled until completely dry, but it will need to be turned over to ensure it will dry out effectively.

Decoration

Before assembling, any blemishes or rough edges can be sanded smooth with very fine grade glasspaper. The dried pastillage may be coloured, as previously described. Royal icing can be used as a decorative medium as well as a glue for joining the pastillage pieces; it can enhance the careful and fine work of the chef.

Avoid heaviness of decoration at all times; remember, *less is always better.*

PASTILLAGE RECIPE
Pastillage

INGREDIENTS	2KG PASTILLAGE	3.5KG PASTILLAGE
Icing sugar	1750g	3300g
Cornflour	100g	200g
Gelatine	6 leaves	12 leaves
Liquid glucose	60g	120g
Water	130g	260g
Lemon juice	¼ lemon	½ lemon

Method of work

1 Sift the icing sugar and cornflour together.
2 Soften the gelatine leaves in the water and melt in a warm bain marie together with the glucose and lemon juice.
3 Add the liquid to the dry ingredients and work together.
4 Knead on a clean surface until a soft paste has been achieved.
5 Wrap in a clean damp cloth and plastic film. Use as required.

SUGAR CONFECTIONERY

Sucrose, the main constituent of cane and beet sugar, is one of a number of natural sweeteners used in the professional kitchen. These sweeteners form part of a larger group of commodities known as carbohydrates. Carbohydrate molecules are made up from atoms of carbon, hydrogen and oxygen and are arranged as chains of simple sugars:

- *Monosaccharides* – a single sugar unit, such as glucose or fructose
- *Disaccharides* – are made up of two joined monosaccharides, for example sucrose, lactose or maltose
- *Polysaccharides* – these are long chains of monosaccharides and form starches

Sucrose is the most common sugar in our diet and consists of one molecule of glucose and one of fructose.

Glucose syrups are created by breaking down starch molecules found in wheat, maize and potatoes. The polysaccharides are broken down by heating the starch with an acid. When sugar (sucrose) is heated with an acid present (such as cream of tartar or lemon juice) a process called 'inversion' takes place. The sucrose is split evenly into fructose and glucose, which is termed 'invert sugar'. An invert sugar is sweeter than a sugar solution and will have a similarly small crystal size. Invert sugar inhibits crystal formation.

Cooking sugar

When boiling sugar it is important to observe the correct procedures and rules to prevent the sugar re-crystallising:

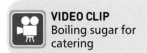
VIDEO CLIP
Boiling sugar for catering

1 Ensure cleanliness of the equipment and the ingredients at all stages of the boiling process. A copper pan should be cleaned with an acid (lemon juice) and scouring material (salt) and rinsed under cold water to ensure absolute cleanliness. All other equipment should be scrupulously cleaned. The sugar thermometer should be placed into cold water and brought to the boil on a stove.

2 Dissolve the sugar in the water completely over a low heat before boiling.

3 If scum forms on top of the sugar solution during boiling, remove it using a spoon or strainer (this could be the impurities from the actual sugar). Repeat until no more scum forms.

4 When the sugar solution begins to boil, brush the insides of the hot pan with a brush and clean cold water.

5 Add the glucose or invert sugar at 104°C.

6 Boil the sugar rapidly and continuously measure the temperature using a sugar thermometer.

7 Arrest the cooking once the desired temperature is obtained by dipping the base of the saucepan into some iced water for 8–10 seconds. Wipe the base of the saucepan dry.

Measuring the density of sugar solutions

Many different types of pâtisserie, dessert and confectionery goods require the use of a sugar solution, such as sorbets, ice creams and preserved fruits. The density of a sugar solution is measured using a saccharometer, and the units of measurement used are either degrees Baumé or degrees Brix.

Always ensure that the temperature of the sugar solution to be tested is 20°C. This is because the density changes with temperature. Put the sugar solution into a suitable container, a 500ml measuring jug is ideal, and place the saccharometer into the solution. Take the reading where the scale on the side of the saccharometer meets the surface of the solution. The density of the sugar solution can be adjusted as required: add a thicker syrup at the same temperature to increase the density or add water to decrease the density.

The following chart is designed to give the chef a working reference of the sugar to water ratios required to produce certain degrees of density. Although this book concentrates on degrees Baumé, the Brix measurements are also included:

WEIGHT OF SUGAR TO BE ADDED TO 450ML WATER	DENSITY REQUIRED	DENSITY REQUIRED
GRAMS	BAUMÉ: B°	BRIX: °Bx
51	5.6	10
74	7.8	14
100	10.0	18
144	13.3	24
204	17.0	31
255	20.0	36
317	22.5	41
480	28.0	51
742	33.5	62
1010	37.1	69
1083	40.0	75

During the sugar boiling process the water evaporates and so the solution becomes denser, which will result in the solution setting firm when cold. The thicker the sugar solution, the more the temperature increases, and it is by reading the changes in temperature that we can determine the physical change in the sugar solution. The chart below shows the changes that occur at different temperatures and the use of the sugar solution at each stage. The solution can be tested by dropping a small amount from a clean spoon into a bowl of very cold water and then quickly examining it or picking it up with the fingers to check the setting consistency.

TEMPERATURE: °C	NAME OF DEGREE	HOW TO TEST	USES
104	Boiling	Look for agitation of liquid surface	
107	Thread	At this relatively low temperature there is still a lot of water left in the syrup. Take a little of the solution between the thumb and finger and separate them to form an elastic thread of sugar	Stock syrup and some icings
110	Pearl	The thread formed by pulling the sugar solution may be stretched. When a spoon is dipped into the syrup and then raised, the syrup runs off in drops	Jelly, candies and some icings
113	Soufflé	The syrup spins a 5cm thread when dropped from a spoon	Delicate sugar candy and syrup
115	Feather	The film of sugar can be blown into feather-like pieces	Jams and confiture
118	Soft ball	A small amount of syrup dropped into chilled water forms a soft, flexible ball, but flattens after a few moments in the fingers	Fudge, fondant, pâte à bombe, Italian meringue and classic butter creams
121	Hard ball	The sugar concentration is much higher, which means less moisture in the sugar solution. Syrup dropped into chilled water may form into a ball that holds its shape on removal. The ball will be firm, but its shape can still be changed by squashing it.	Nougat, marshmallows
132–138	Soft crack	At this stage, the moisture content is low. Syrup dropped into chilled water separates into hard but pliable threads. They will bend slightly before breaking	Rock sugar
138–155	Hard crack	At these temperatures, there is almost no water left in the sugar solution. Syrup dropped into chilled water separates into hard, brittle threads that break when bent	Can be poured and pulled to make presentation displays
170	Light caramel	The sugar solution turns amber due to caramelisation. The sugar is beginning to break down and form many complex compounds that contribute to a rich flavour	Sauces and glazes
178–180	Dark caramel	A darker caramelisation has now occurred	Dessert decorations

SUGAR CONFECTIONERY RECIPES
Vanilla fudge

CHEF'S TIP

Derivatives of this recipe include:
Coffee – add diluted instant coffee to taste
Chocolate – add dark couverture (minimum 68 per cent cocoa solids) at the mixing stage. Do not add the chocolate earlier or it may burn.

INGREDIENTS	30–40 PIECES	80–100 PIECES
Granulated sugar	225g	450g
Soft brown sugar	225g	450g
Liquid glucose	110g	225g
Unsalted butter	110g	225g
Double cream	140ml	280ml
Vanilla extract	To taste	To taste

Method of work

1 Place all the ingredients into a large, clean saucepan and place on a medium heat. Boil steadily to 118°C. Remove from the heat.
2 Using a clean wooden spoon, stir constantly until the boiled mixture begins to grain.
3 Pour into a shallow tray that is lightly oiled (or lined with silicone paper) and allow to cool and set completely.
4 When set, cut into squares.

Pâte des fruits

INGREDIENTS	1 SMALL SLAB (18 × 18CM)	1 LARGE SLAB (36 × 36CM)
Raspberry purée	425g	850g
Apricot purée	250g	500g
Powdered pectin	20g	40g
Caster sugar	75g	150g
Granulated sugar	750g	1.5kg
Liquid glucose	175g	350g
Tartaric acid	5g	10g
Water	3g	5g

Method of work

1 Place the purées together in a clean heavy-based saucepan. Mix the powdered pectin with the caster sugar and whisk into the fruit purées. Bring to the boil.
2 Add the granulated sugar and the glucose. Stirring constantly, bring the temperature of the boiling mixture to 107°C.
3 Dissolve the tartaric acid in the water and add to the cooked fruit paste.
4 Line the bottom of a frame with silicone paper and pour the fruit paste into the frame. Leave to cool.
5 Remove from the frame, peel off the silicone paper carefully then cut the set fruit into 2.5cm squares and roll in granulated sugar.

Sugar candy lollipops

INGREDIENTS	10 LOLLIPOPS	20 LOLLIPOPS
Isomalt	100g	200g
Granulated sugar	350g	700g
Liquid glucose	150g	300g
Water	160g	340g
Yellow colour	As required	As required
Lemon flavouring	As required	As required

Method of work

1 Place the isomalt, granulated sugar, glucose and water in a heavy-based saucepan and boil to 140°C.

2 Add the colour and flavouring and continue boiling until 155°C has been reached. Arrest the cooking by plunging the base of the saucepan into cold water for a few seconds.

3 Pour the candy solution into lightly oiled individual stainless steel rings on a silicone baking mat and leave to cool slightly. Remove the rings and push lollipop sticks into each candy as required.

4 Leave to fully set and cool down. Remove from the silicone mat and store in an airtight container.

Mint chocolate caramels

INGREDIENTS	45 CARAMELS	90 CARAMELS
Double cream	350g	700g
Cubed sugar	200g	400g
Liquid glucose	200g	400g
Trimolene	50g	100g
Red colour	As required	As required
Dark couverture (minimum 64% cocoa solids)	120g	240g
Cocoa paste (100% cocoa solids)	60g	120g
Mint flavouring	To taste	To taste
Unsalted butter	40g	80g

Method of work

1 Boil together the cream, sugar, liquid glucose and trimolene in a heavy-based saucepan to 118°C.

2 Add the cocoa paste, couverture, colour, mint flavour and butter and stir in well off the heat.

3 Pour the mixture into a lightly oiled shallow stainless steel tray and leave to cool and set.

4 When it is cool enough, remove carefully from the tray and cut into 2.5cm slabs. Store in an airtight container prior to use.

Nougat Montélimar

INGREDIENTS	30 PIECES	60 PIECES
Granulated sugar	210g	420g
Clear honey	60g	120g
Water	50g	100g
Liquid glucose	60g	120g
Egg whites	25g	50g
Glacé cherries	30g	60g
Blanched pistachio nuts	30g	60g
Flaked almonds	20g	30g
Chopped hazelnuts	20g	30g

Method of work

1   Bring the sugar and water to the boil in a heavy-based saucepan. Add the honey and the liquid glucose at 107°C. Skim off any impurities that reach the surface of the boiling sugar solution.

2   Boil to 137°C. Meanwhile, aerate the egg whites to soft peaks and slowly pour in the hot syrup while still beating. Continue beating until the mixture becomes firm.

3   Warm the cherries and nuts in an oven for a few minutes and carefully combine into the cooked meringue mixture.

4   Pour the mixture into a shallow tray lined with rice paper. Place a further sheet of rice paper on the top of the nougat and weigh down with a flat board. Leave to set for 24 hours before turning out and cutting into small pieces.

5   Store in an airtight container if not required immediately.

Sugar-dipped fruit *Fruits glacés*

INGREDIENTS	20 DIPPED FRUITS	40 DIPPED FRUITS
Cube sugar	240g	480g
Liquid glucose	20g	40g
Water	70g	140g
Fruits to be dipped		
Grapes	As required	As required
Cherries	As required	As required
Mandarin orange	As required	As required
Strawberries	As required	As required

CHEF'S TIP

It is important to store these dipped fruits in a dry, airtight container. Sugar is hygroscopic and so will attract moisture in damp or cold environments. Dipped fruits are usually made at the last moment before being served.

Method of work

1 Prepare the fruit carefully, taking care not to bruise or cut the skins or membranes. Any leakage of liquid from the fruit will immediate begin to break down the sugar once the fruit has been dipped and will result in re-crystallisation. Cherries and grapes should be cut into pairs and kept on the stalk.

2 Place the fruit onto a wire rack and place on top of an oven or a warm place to dry their surfaces.

3 Bring the sugar and water to the boil in a heavy-based saucepan. At 104°C, add the liquid glucose. Continue boiling to 155°C (hard crack stage). Remove from the heat and arrest the cooking.

4 Dip the fruit into the sugar. Use a small set of tweezers to avoid burning the fingers. Ensure each fruit is fully dipped and that no part of the fruit is left without a covering of sugar.

5 Quickly transfer the dipped fruits onto a lightly oiled, clean marble slab or a silicone baking mat to set.

Vanilla macaroons

INGREDIENTS	40 MACAROONS	80 MACAROONS
Icing sugar	300g	600g
Ground almonds	75g	150g
Egg whites	90g	185g
Granulated sugar	85g	180g
Liquid glucose	45g	90g
Water	35g	70g
Egg whites	85g	180g
Vanilla	To taste	To taste

Method of work

1 Preheat an oven to 210°C.

2 Mix together the icing sugar, ground almonds and the larger quantity of egg whites to a paste.

3 Meanwhile, bring the sugar and the water to the boil in a heavy-based saucepan. Add the glucose at 104°C and continue boiling until 118°C has been reached.

4 Whisk the smaller quantity of egg whites to a soft peak. Slowly pour the boiled sugar syrup into the whisked egg white. Continue whisking until cold to create an Italian meringue.

5 Carefully fold in the meringue into the ground almond mixture. Add the vanilla at this stage. Place the mixture into a piping bag with a plain tube.

6 Pipe the macaroons onto a silicone baking mat and let them dry for 30 minutes at room temperature.

7 Place the macaroons into the oven. After 3 minutes reduce the heat to 170°C and bake for a further 6 minutes.

8 Remove the macaroons from the oven and place onto a wire rack to cool. Carefully remove the macaroons when they are cool. Pipe a little butter cream, ganache or apricot jam onto the underside of a macaroon and then stick two macaroons together.

CHEF'S TIP

It is simple to create different flavours to this recipe:
Lemon – add the finely grated zest of lemon
Orange – add the finely grated zest of orange
Pistachio – add some pistachio paste to taste
Raspberry – add raspberry flavour and colour

Florentines

INGREDIENTS	70 FLORENTINES	150 FLORENTINES
Unsalted butter	150g	300g
Caster sugar	200g	400g
Clear honey	50g	100g
Double cream	100g	200g
Mixed peel	100g	200g
Chopped walnuts	100g	200g
Flaked almonds	200g	400g
Pistachio nuts	100g	200g
Raisins	50g	100g
Tempered dark couverture	500g	1000g

Method of work

1 Preheat an oven to 200°C.

2 Place the butter, sugar and cream into a heavy-based saucepan and bring to the boil. Add the clear honey at 104°C and continue boiling to 115°C.

3 Remove from the heat and add all the nuts and fruit. Stir in well and pour the mixture onto a silicone baking mat. Place another mat on top and spread the mixture evenly between the two mats. Place in a freezer.

4 When the mixture has just frozen, cut out 2.5cm discs and place onto a baking tray lined with a silicone baking mat.

5 Place into the oven and bake for 12 minutes.

6 When the Florentines are baked they may spread a little. Let them cool before cutting them back to the required shape using a plain cutter.

7 Dip the base of each Florentine into the melted chocolate and set on an embossed plastic chocolate mat until the chocolate has set.

8 Reserve in an airtight container until service.

DECORATIVE SUGAR WORK

Health and safety issues

A chef must always be aware that boiling sugar can cause severe burns. The appropriate protective clothing should always be worn and oven cloths should be used at all times when pouring hot sugar. It is always wise to have a container of iced water nearby when working with sugar, in case a burn on the fingers or hands occurs. Quickly plunging the burned area into iced water will reduce the pain and stop the heat burning through the layers of skin.

Care should always be taken to prevent any accidents during the cooking of sugar. All pre-preparation should be undertaken before the actual cooking of the sugar takes place. This will ensure that you remain with the cooking sugar at all times to oversee the cooking process and tend to the sugar as it cooks.

PRE-PREPARATION FOR SUGAR WORK

The following equipment should be prepared and ready for use before any cooking of sugar takes place:

■ *Saucepans for boiling sugar* – Although it is commonly assumed that copper pans are essential for the boiling of sugar, this is not entirely true. The pan used must have a heavy base and be capable of being cleaned thoroughly; stainless steel, enamel and copper are all suitable. The pan should be thoroughly cleaned using a mild acid and an abrasive and rinsed thoroughly with cold water and left to drip dry before using.

Saucepans for boiling sugar

■ *Marble slab* – A marble slab or granite work top will be required for certain sugar work techniques. Before using, it should be washed with a light detergent, which will help prevent the sugar from sticking. It should then be rinsed, dried and very lightly oiled; any standard cooking oil is suitable for this purpose. Using too much oil used may result the sugar sticking to the marble.

■ *Cutting equipment* – A metal scraper and heavy knife (or a palette knife) is needed for turning sugar prior to pulling. A pair of scissors is also required for cutting the sugar after pulling.

Cutting equipment

■ *Clean pastry brushes* – A brush is required to clean the sides of the sugar pan with cold water during cooking. A separate brush should be kept for this purpose. Pastry brushes used for egg wash or general use are not suitable for this as they can contaminate the sugar.

Clean pastry brushes

■ *Leaf moulds* – These come in many shapes and sizes and are useful for producing sugar leaves efficiently.

■ *Heat lamp* – This is essential if no oven is available to keep the sugar warm. Suitable lamps can be obtained at most specialist culinary suppliers.

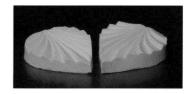

Leaf moulds

■ *Storage containers* – Containers should be airtight. Before use, silica gel or lime crystals should be placed in the bottom and they should be lined with foil. Containers are used to store sugar work until ready for use. Any leftover sugar can be vacuum packed and used at a later date.

Storage containers

ADDITIVES USED IN SUGAR WORK AND CONFECTIONERY

■ *Ascorbic acid* – Ascorbic acid (vitamin C) is an **antioxidant** and is used to conserve the colour of a product (for example, poached fruits).

■ *Tartaric acid* – This acid is found in many types of fruit, but it is always extracted industrially from grapes. The crystals are large and clear. One part of boiling water dissolves two parts of tartaric acid. Tartaric acid enhances flavours and brings tartness. It is also an antioxidant, so it improves colours and aromas. This is added to sugar to help prevent the sugar from crystallising.

■ *Citric acid* – Usually extracted from lemons, citric acid is used with cream of tartar in fondants or cooked sugar to make them softer and more pliable. It is also used to stabilise the albumin in whipped egg whites.

■ *Agar-agar* – Also called Japanese isinglass, agar-agar is derived from seaweeds found in the Pacific and Indian oceans. It expands in cold water but does not dissolve. It only dissolves in boiling water after a certain amount of cooking. Agar-agar is used in bonbons, jellies and even jams. The powdered form is the easiest to use.

■ *Pectins* – Pectin is a gelling agent found in fruits. It is usually extracted from crushed apples but is also derived from citric fruit rinds. Pectin is used in powder form in gums, fruit jellies and jams. It maintains the moisture in gum candies and fruit jellies. Adding an acid such as citric, lactic or tartaric to a recipe using pectin causes the pectin to set:

  – *Pectin NH* is used in fruit glazes and fruit fillings; its gelling effect is reversible by heating and it holds well on fruit

  – *Pectin (medium rapid set)* is especially well-suited for making fruit preserves and jellies; setting does not occur too rapidly, thereby increasing the time a product can be worked, for example casting fruit jellies in individual starch or Flexipan moulds

  – *Yellow pectin* is used in fruit jellies; its gelling effect is not reversible by heating. When using this pectin, it should be 1–2 per cent of the overall weight of the mix

■ *Gums* – These are neutral substances derived from trees. There are several varieties of gum of which three are used in sugar confections:

  – Gum Arabic

  – Gum tragacanth

  – Fruit-tree gum

Dissolved gums provide an elastic consistency. Gums dissolve slowly in cold water but quickly in boiling water. The alcohol contained in gums is forced to evaporate, making the product thicker and gummier, until it finally solidifies into a transparent mass that shows no traces of crystallisation.

 CHEF'S TIP

Sweetening power is a measure of how much (in percentage) a substance will increase the sweetness of the product that it is being added to.

- *Gelatine* – Colourless when pure, gelatine is extracted from the bones and cartilage of animals. It is used in sugar confections to set whipped pastes and jelly candies. Bringing gelatine to the boil will not destroy its gelling property, but boiling the gelatine for an extended amount of time will reduce it gelling power. Gelatine is bloomed (softened) in cold water and will absorb from five to ten times its weight in water.

- *Sorbitol* – This is used to stabilise moisture and prevent mould and bacterial growth and as a sweetener in low-sugar or sugarless desserts. Sorbitol prevents the drying of cakes, macaroons and sponges. It also helps to preserve freshness and flexibility in almond paste, ganache, praline paste and fruit jellies. Sorbitol has a solid content of 95 per cent and a sweetening power of 55 per cent.

- *Dextrose* – A form of pure glucose (99.5 per cent), supplied as a fine white powder. Dextrose is used as a stabiliser and as an anti-crystallising agent in ice cream and sorbets, and it has many uses in baking. It has a solid content of 95 per cent and its sweetening power is 70 per cent.

- *Glucose* – A monosaccharide sugar produced by the breaking down of starch found in potato, wheat or maize. It is used as an anti-crystallisation agent in the cooking of sugar.

- *Sodium bicarbonate* – Also known as baking soda, sodium bicarbonate is a salt that acts as a leavening agent and conserving agent. It is used to raise the boiling point of a liquid, and therefore speed up the boiling process.

SUGAR RECIPES

Fondant

INGREDIENTS	500G OF FONDANT	1KG OF FONDANT
Granulated sugar	480g	960g
Water	125ml	250ml
Cream of tartar	1tsp	2tsp

CHEF'S TIP

Convenience fondant is often used in the pastry kitchen because it is reliable, consistent and saves time. Fondant can be used for cooking in place of sugar – it has the advantage of already having undergone a degree of inversion.

Method of work

1 Bring the sugar and water to the boil in a heavy-based saucepan. Add the cream of tartar at 104°C.

2 Continue boiling until 115°C has been obtained.

3 Pour the sugar solution on a very lightly oiled marble slab.

4 Splash the surface of the sugar with a little cold water and let the temperature drop to 100°C. Agitate the sugar with a clean spatula. The mass will become thicker as it cools and as the agitation continues.

5 When the sugar solution has become stiff and hard to work, knead by hand into a smooth, plastic paste.

6 Cover with plastic film or polythene to prevent skinning and use as required.

Poured sugar *Sucre coulé*

INGREDIENTS	
Granulated or cubed sugar	750g
Liquid glucose	150g
Water	400g

Pre-preparation

1 If you require an opaque finish, mix chalk powder or titanium powder with an equal amount of water and blend to a paste.
2 Prepare the powder colour as required.
3 Prepare a few drops of tartaric acid.
4 Prepare any moulds (stainless steel moulds will need lightly oiling to prevent the sugar sticking).

Method of work

1 Place the sugar and water in a heavy-based saucepan and leave for 10 minutes. Bring to the boil and skim off any scum from the surface then add the glucose. Clean the sides of the pan with clean cold water and boil to 105°C, then remove from the heat, cover with plastic film and stand until required.
2 If the sugar solution is required immediately, continue to boil to 133°C (soft crack).
3 Add the chalk/titanium paste if required and boil to the final temperature of 155°C (hard crack). Add the colour just before the final temperature is reached and add two spots of tartaric acid as it reaches the temperature.
4 Arrest the cooking of the sugar. Pour into the prepared moulds in a continuous stream. Gently remove any air bubbles with a small gas blowtorch by running the flame carefully over the surface of the sugar. Leave to cool and set before carefully removing from the moulds ready for assembling.
5 Join the sugar pieces together using any left over molten sugar (cooked to hard crack stage) as glue. Ensure that no fingerprints are left on the surface of the sugar pieces and always protect the sugar from coming into contact with moisture.

CHEF'S TIP

While boiling the sugar, do not stir. Keep the sides of the saucepan and the thermometer continuously washed down with the cold clean water to re-dissolve any sugar crystals that have formed.

Pouring into the prepared moulds in a continuous stream

Gently removing any air bubbles with a small gas blowtorch

Joining the sugar pieces together

Temperatures for adding colour;

■ White and blue colour: 145°C

■ All other colours: 147°C

■ For clear and opaque sugar: 150°C .

Rock sugar *Sucre roché*

INGREDIENTS

Granulated or cubed sugar	480g
Royal icing	30g
Water	180g

Pre-preparation

1 If coloured rock sugar is required, colouring should be added to the royal icing.
2 Preheat an oven to 120°C.
3 Prepare the royal icing.
4 Prepare a suitable baking dish lined with foil.

Method of work

1 Place the sugar and water in a heavy-based saucepan and leave for 10 minutes. Bring to the boil and skim off any scum from the surface. Boil the sugar to 138°C and remove from the heat.
2 Dip the pan in cold water to arrest the cooking of the sugar.
3 Add the royal icing and mix in quickly. The sugar will now increase in volume.
4 Quickly pour into the prepared baking tray. Place into the preheated oven for 10 minutes to harden.
5 Remove from the oven and leave to cool and dry out for 12 hours.
6 Turn out the sugar and remove the tin foil before shaping as required, cutting with a small fretsaw or serrated knife. Sprayed colours can be added after the sugar has dried out.

CHEF'S TIP

Do not attempt to use the rock sugar too early after removing from the oven as it will still retain a little moisture. It must be allowed to dry out completely before carving/cutting in desired shapes. This type of sugar is used to give a rocky effect to an overall display.

Spun sugar *Sucre voilé*

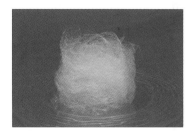

INGREDIENTS

Granulated or cubed sugar	1kg
Liquid glucose	200g
Water	330g

Pre-preparation

1 If coloured spun sugar is required, colouring should be prepared prior to the cooking of the sugar.
2 Prepare two wooden rods (rolling pins will do) by covering them in foil and positioning them so that they protrude over the edge of the work surface by about 10cm.
3 Place plenty of paper sheets on the floor directly underneath the wooden rods to catch any excess sugar.
4 Prepare an airtight, deep plastic container lined with silica gel for storing the spun sugar.

CHEF'S TIP

The colder the sugar solution when spun, the more wire-like the consistency of the set sugar will be and the longer the shape will hold.

Method of work

1 Place the sugar and water into a heavy-based saucepan and leave for 10 minutes. Bring to the boil on a medium heat and add the liquid glucose at 104°C. Add any colour at 145°C.

2 Increase the heat and boil the sugar solution to 155°C. Arrest the cooking of the sugar in a bowl of cold water for a few seconds.

3 Let the sugar solution stand for 2–3 minutes until it becomes slightly cooled.

4 Dip a whisk with the ends removed (to provide makeshift wire strands) into the sugar solution. Flick the sugar quickly, back and forth over the two prepared rods. Continue to spin the sugar until enough has been collected between the two rods.

5 Collect up all the spun sugar and store until required. The spun sugar will not last for more than 2 days in optimum storage conditions.

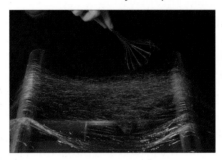

Flicking the sugar quickly back and forth over the two prepared rods

Collecting the spun sugar for storing

Dip a whisk with the ends removed into the sugar solution

Pulled sugar *Sucre tiré*

INGREDIENTS	
Granulated or cubed sugar	1kg
Liquid glucose	200g
Water	330g
Tartaric acid	10 drops

Pre-preparation

1 If coloured pulled sugar is required, colouring should be prepared prior to the cooking of the sugar.

2 Prepare a lightly oiled clean marble slab or a cleaned and dried silicone baking mat.

3 Have a sugar heat lamp or a preheated oven (to 150°C) to keep the pulled sugar warm.

4 Prepare an airtight, deep plastic container lined with silica gel for storing the pulled sugar.

5 Special plastic sugar gloves can be used when pulling the sugar if required.

Method of work

1   Place the sugar and water in a heavy-based saucepan and leave for 10 minutes. Bring to the boil and skim off any scum from the surface then add the glucose. Clean the sides of the pan with clean cold water and boil to 105°C, then remove from the heat, cover with plastic film and stand until required.

2   If the sugar solution is required immediately, continue to boil to 133°C (soft crack). Add the tartaric acid. Add the colour at the correct temperature, if required.

3   Boil to the final temperature of 155°C (hard crack) and add 2 spots of acid as it reaches the temperature. Arrest the cooking briefly.

4   Pour the sugar on the prepared work surface. Using a lightly oiled palette knife fold the edges of the poured sugar back into the centre. Ensure that no hard pieces of sugar are allowed to form. Continue to do this until the sugar mass stops spreading. The aim is to keep a uniform heat throughout the sugar mass and prevent any cool areas forming.

5   Handle the sugar mass by holding the sugar with one hand and pulling with the other. Fold it over and continue to use this technique until the sugar forms a shine and becomes smooth. Keep the sugar mass moving to maintain the temperature and to prevent it from setting. If the sugar begins to crack, it is ready.

6   Place the sugar mass on a silicone baking sheet under a sugar lamp or at the mouth of the preheated oven. The sugar must be turned over every so often to maintain an even heat throughout the mass.

7   Any pieces of pulled sugar not required for use can be cooled down, sealed in a vacuum bag and stored in an airtight plastic container with a little silica gel placed in the base.

8   Various shapes and designs can now be produced to create a centrepiece or decoration.

 CHEF'S TIP

If the sugar appears sticky during the pulling process this will be because too much glucose was added or the sugar was not cooked to the correct temperature. If the pulled sugar begins to grain (crystallise), this may be because it has been manipulated too much.

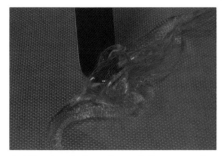

Folding back the edges of the poured sugar using a palette knife

Holding the sugar with one hand and pulling with the other

Continue folding the sugar until it forms a shine

Manipulating the pulled sugar into shape

Blown sugar *Sucre soufflé*

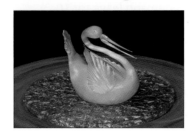

INGREDIENTS	
Granulated or cubed sugar	1kg
Liquid glucose	200g
Water	330g
Cream of tartar	1 small pinch

Pre-preparation

1   If coloured blown sugar is required, colouring should be prepared prior to the cooking of the sugar.

2   Prepare a lightly oiled clean marble slab or a cleaned and dried silicone baking mat.

3   Have a sugar heat lamp or a preheated oven (to 150°C) to keep the blown sugar warm.

4   Prepare an airtight, deep plastic container lined with silica gel for storage of the blown sugar and have a sugar pump ready.

5   Special plastic sugar gloves can be used when handling the sugar if required.

Method of work

1   Place the sugar and water into a heavy-based saucepan and leave for 10 minutes. Bring to the boil and skim off any scum from the surface, then add the glucose. Clean the sides of the pan with clean cold water and boil to 105°C, then remove from the heat, cover with plastic film and stand until required.

2   If the sugar solution is required immediately, continue to boil to 133°C (soft crack). Add the small pinch of cream of tartar. Add the colour at the correct temperature, if required. Boil to 151°C and arrest the cooking of the sugar immediately.

3   Follow the method for pulled sugar until you have a mass of sugar that is really to be blown.

4   Take a ball of pulled sugar that is elastic and uniform in temperature. Place a finger into the centre of the sugar ball and insert the tube of the sugar pump. Firmly press the edges of the sugar around the end of the tube so that it sticks.

5   Gently blow in the air so that the sugar ball begins to inflate. If the sugar is not uniformly warm, the warmer parts will expand more than the cooler parts. Constantly regulate the heat under a sugar lamp.

6   Use the fingers to manipulate and control the shape of the sugar while air is blown into it.

7   Once the desired shape has been achieved, blow cool air on the shape with a fan or hairdrier to set the shape quickly. Remove the tube using a hot knife or scissors.

Isomalt syrup

Isomalt is a natural sugar substitute derived from sugar beet. Isomalt is an odourless, white, crystalline substance containing about 5 per cent water. Isomalt is used in sugar sculptures and is preferred by some pastry chefs because it will not crystallise as quickly as cooked sugar. It will therefre maintain its shine and structure better in humid conditions than cooked sugar.

INGREDIENTS	
Isomalt	1kg
Water	100g

Pre-preparation

1 If coloured isomalt sugar is required, colouring should be prepared prior to the cooking of the sugar.

2 Prepare a lightly oiled clean marble slab or a cleaned and dried silicone baking mat.

3 Have a sugar heat lamp or a preheated oven (to 150°C) to keep the isomalt warm.

4 Prepare an airtight, deep plastic container lined with silica gel for storage of the isomalt.

Method of work

1 Place the isomalt and water into a heavy-based saucepan and leave for 10 minutes. Bring to the boil and clean the sides of the pan with clean cold water.

2 Continue to boil to 170°C. Add the colour at the correct temperature, if required.

3 Use the cooked isomalt in the same way as a normal cooked sugar solution. It can be poured or pulled as usual.

Troubleshooting

■ If the isomalt seems too brittle or too hard to work with, reduce the boiling time by reducing the water content or lower the cooking temperature to 160°C.

■ If the isomalt is too soft or sticky to work with, increase the boiling time to evaporate more of the water content.

■ If the isomalt is to be used for pouring and casting, cook it to 180°C.

Assessment of knowledge and understanding

You have now learned about the use of sugar in confectionery and how to produce a variety of sugar-based sweets and decorations utilising an array of commodities and different techniques.

To test your level of knowledge and understanding, answer the following short questions. These will help to prepare you for your summative (final) assessment.

Quality identifications

1 State how glucose is produced and why it is used.

2 State the temperature at which glucose is added to a sugar solution for cooking.

3 Identify the reason for pulled sugar being sticky during the pulling process.

Equipment and materials

1 Explain the importance of using a sugar thermometer.

2 Explain how a sugar pan should be cleaned prior to use.

Preparation methods

1 Describe the correct procedure for cooking a sugar solution for pulled sugar.

2 Explain how to prepare three pieces of equipment before pulling sugar.

3 State the procedure for preparing sugar for boiling.

Storage and safety

1 State how to store sugar decorations to prevent them from losing colour and absorbing moisture.

2 Name the agent which will help to keep the sugar decorations dry.

3 State two health and safety precautions when handling sugar.
   i)
   ii)

CHEF'S PROFILE

Name: JAVIER MERCADO

Position: Pastry Chef Lecturer

Establishment: Westminster Kingsway College

Current job role and main responsibilities: I am a tutor for a group of 16-year-old first year professional chefs (Diploma/NVQ). I also teach the pastry side of the foundation chef's degree course.

When did you realise that you wanted to pursue a career in the catering and hospitality industry? At the age of 19.

Training: Johnson E Wales University, Providence, Rhode Island, USA: AAS IBPI Applied Science Degree.

Experience:

1   R.D. Corporate Assistant Pastry Chef for Aibert Uster imports, Maryland, USA
2   Pastry Chef for the RitzCarlton Group, Virginia, USA
3   Pastry Chef for the Westin Hotel Group, St. Croix, US Virgin Islands

What do you find rewarding about your job?

The ability to create artistic impressions using my imagination and other inspirations.

What do you find the most challenging about the job?

The heat/rain, which acts as a reminder of what mediums I utilise to achieve a final end product.

What advice would you give to students just beginning their career?

Stay focused. Respect the instructors' advice, and if you work hard, always believe in yourself.

Who is your mentor or main inspiration?

Ewald Notter and Stephan Klein – I look up to them and they have given me the drive to push my skill level. Their works are simply awesome.

What traits do you consider essential for anyone entering a career as a chef?

The ability to remain practical and to never lose sight of their goals. If you are motivated, success will follow.

A personal profile:

My interests include airbrushing, sugar artistry and chocolate work.
*   Best Taste Award, World Chocolate Masters 2006
*   Most Creative Award, World Chocolate Masters 2004
*   Best in Class, Sugar Category, Hotelympia 2006
*   Best in Class, Sugar Category, Hotelympia 2004
*   Gold Award, Chocolate Category, Hotelympia 2004

Can you give one essential kitchen tip that you use as a chef?

Place a sheet of silicone paper on top of an induction hob, underneath the saucepan. If a product (liquid) spills, carefully remove the sheet and dispose. This leaves the hob always looking clean.

Yellow submarine: banana and cinnamon ganache

INGREDIENTS	YIELD
For the filling	
Whipping cream	180g
Ground cinnamon	2tsp
Cocoa Barry Blanc Satin couverture coins	684g
Liquid glucose	10g
Fresh banana, very ripe, chopped	135g
Salt	Pinch
For the coating	
Cocoa Barry Excellence 55% couverture coins	100g
Cocoa Barry Blanc Satin couverture coins	800g
Yellow cocoa butter	30g

Method of work

1 To make filling, bring whipping cream and cinnamon to boil. Add white chocolate and glucose and stir until melted. Add banana and salt. Puree mixture and cool to room temperature.

2 Wearing disposable gloves, rub a little tempered dark chocolate for coating, into the moulds in a swirl and leave it to set slightly then rub the yellow cocoa butter evenly over the entire surface of mould. Leave to set fully.

3 To coat the moulds, fill with white tempered chocolate. Scrape top level. Tap moulds to release any air bubbles. Drain out excess chocolate. Scrape the top again and then place mould – still inverted – onto a sheet of baking parchment and leave for a few minutes.

4 Lift moulds off baking parchment and scrape off excess chocolate. Chill them until set. Remove from fridge and leave for about 5 minutes before filling.

5 Warm ganache slightly until runny and fill squeezy bottle or piping bag. Pipe into cavities. Return moulds to fridge until ganache skins over.

6 Remove chocolates from fridge for at least 10 minutes to allow plastic moulds to warm slightly. Pour a thin layer of tempered white chocolate over tops and quickly scrape smooth. Return moulds to fridge until chocolates have set. Then remove from fridge and un-mould.

22

Prepare, cook and finish healthier dishes

2FPC13 Prepare, cook and finish healthier dishes

LEARNING OBJECTIVES

The aim of this chapter is to enable you to develop skills and implement knowledge in the preparation and cookery principles of healthy dishes and eating. This will also include materials, ingredients and equipment.

At the end of this chapter you will be able to:

■ Identify each variety of healthy eating dish and technique

■ Understand how to cook dishes to maintain their maximum nutritional value

■ State the quality points of various commodities and dishes

■ Prepare ingredients following a healthier concept and using appropriate skills

■ Have a concise knowledge of preparing and cooking a range of healthier derived dishes

ACHIEVING A BALANCED DIET

Food provides the essential fuel and raw materials that the body requires. The fuel is converted into energy to maintain body temperature, and the raw materials are used in growing tissues and in the repair of internal organs and systems. Our food composition is broadly made up from carbohydrates, proteins, fats, vitamins, mineral salts and fibre, and a balanced diet should contain all of these nutrients in the correct proportions. The lack of any of these foods in our diet can affect the body's overall performance and can lead to poor health, low energy levels, lack of growth in the early years and poor response to healing from wounds or illness.

The Balance of Good Health

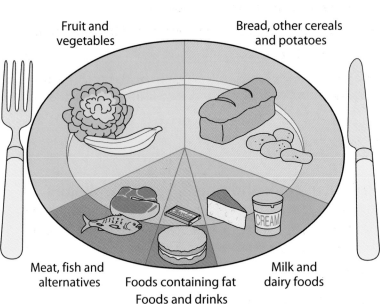

If certain foods are consumed in excess the body will build up layers of fat, leading to increased weight and imbalanced chemical levels within the body's system, such as increased levels of sugar or salt. This can lead to diabetes, high blood pressure or thyroid inactivity or overactivity.

The hospitality industry provides catering services for an overwhelming majority of the population through a variety of services:

- Restaurants
- Hotels, hostels
- Sporting and entertainment stadia
- Hospitals
- Care and residential homes
- Schools, colleges and universities
- Armed forces
- Workplace catering

GOVERNMENT GUIDELINES FOR HEALTHY EATING

Nutritional requirements vary depending on a person's age, gender and occupation. However, between the ages of 19 and 50 the dietary requirements do not vary a great deal. Recommended intakes of food are expressed in terms of DRVs (Dietary Reference Values), which are tailored to certain population groups. This term replaces RDA (Recommended Daily Allowance).

For a healthy diet, the Food Standards Agency suggests that we should aim to:

- Choose lean meat, and trim off the fat and any skin
- Eat more fish; try to eat fish at least twice a week
- Grill, bake, poach, boil, steam or microwave instead of frying or roasting
- Reduce the sugar in our diets
- Reduce the use of salt when cooking; do not add salt to cooked and served food at the table and be more aware of the salt content of ready-prepared foods
- Try to drink at least 6–8 cups of water a day, or more if you exercise

The Balance of Good Health

The *Balance of Good Health* (based on UK Government guidelines) divides foods into five food groups and shows how much of each group we should eat each day. It is a useful way of checking whether your diet is healthy and balanced. The five food groups are:

- Bread, cereals and potatoes – up to two servings per day

- Fruit and vegetables – five servings per day

■ Meat, fish and alternatives – up to two servings per day

■ Milk and dairy – up to three servings per day

■ Foods containing fat and foods containing sugar – one small serving per day

New recommendations about our diet are issued on a yearly basis, after the Government has produced a basic report on the public's health based on nutritional values and food trends.

PROTEIN

Proteins are active and sensitive substances that have many intrinsic uses and values. Chefs can take advantage of proteins by using various culinary techniques to change their structure (such as aerating egg whites).

Proteins are made up from chains of amino acids. Most amino acids can be produced by the body, but there are some that can not: these are referred to as 'essential amino acids' as they must be included in our diet. It is important that we understand what food types are protein based. The chart below indicates the types of protein sources available:

VIDEO CLIP
Using vegetable protein

PROTEIN COMMODITIES
Meat
Game
Poultry
Fish
Eggs
Milk, cream, cheese
Peas
Beans
Nuts
Seeds
Wheat flour

FATS

Fats provide the body with energy and certain important vitamins. They are also sources of essential fatty acids which the body cannot produce. Fats can be derived from both vegetable and animal sources.

It is recommended that lower fat alternatives should be used wherever possible, and that smaller quantities of foods containing saturated fats or trans fats should be eaten and replaced with foods high in unsaturated fats. Another recommendation is to increase the intake of omega 3 fatty acids, which are found in foods such as oily fish.

Animal fats are saturated fats. These fats can cause raised levels of cholesterol in the blood, increasing the likelihood of developing heart disease. Some animal fats also contain vitamins A and D. Examples of some commodities high in saturated fats are ready-prepared meat products, meat pies, sausages, hard cheeses, butter, lard, pastry, some cakes and shortbreads.

The effects of trans fats (partially hydrogenated fats) on our health are similar those of saturated fats, with emerging evidence suggesting that they may actually be worse. Some hydrogenated fats, such as some margarines (which are liquid oils turned into solid fats), also contain trans fats. This type of fat is increasingly found in ready-meals.

Unsaturated fats are a healthy alternative and provide the body with essential fatty acids. The unsaturated fats found in oily fish may further help to prevent heart disease. Products such as oily fish, avocados, nuts and seeds, sunflower oil, rapeseed oil, olive oil and vegetable oil all contain unsaturated fats.

CARBOHYDRATES

Carbohydrates are produced by all plants and animals for the purpose of storing chemical energy. Simple sugars and starch are energy stores, while pectin and cellulose are the plant's structural materials where carbohydrates can also be found.

Sugars are the simplest carbohydrates. Some sugars are small single molecules (monosaccharides), while others are made up of two or more simple sugar molecules joined together. Glucose and fructose are monosaccharides, while sucrose (normal table sugar) is a disaccharide made up of one glucose molecule and one fructose molecule. The following chart describes the characteristics of sugars commonly used in the kitchen:

Fructose is found in fruits and honey

SUGAR	CHARACTERISTICS
Glucose	Also known as dextrose. A simple sugar (monosaccharide) found in many fruits and honey. Pastry chefs may use this as corn syrup in the kitchen. Compared with sucrose, glucose is less sweet
Fructose	Also known as levulose. It is also found in fruits and honey. It is metabolised by the body more slowly than normal sugar and therefore is preferable for use for diabetics. It is the sweetest of all common sugars
Sucrose	This is common table sugar. It is extracted from sugar cane and from sugar beet. Sucrose can be broken down into two simple sugars (fructose and glucose) by heating it with some acid. This is known as inversion and the resulting mass is called an invert syrup. This syrup is useful in sugar work and candy making because it helps to limit the extent of sugar crystallisation
Lactose	This is found in milk. It is a disaccharide made up of glucose and galactose. It is much less sweet than sucrose
Maltose	This is found in wheat and flours and is much less sweet than sucrose

Lactose is found in milk

The body uses sugars as a source of energy to fuel the activity of cells and to provide the building blocks of growth. This is why we have taste receptors that register the presence of sugars and why our brains attach pleasure to a sweet taste sensation. Sweetness is a sign that a food is high in calories.

Polysaccharides are molecules made up of chains of simple sugars. By far the most important polysaccharide is starch. Starch is found in plants, including all cereals, such as rice, flour and grains, and also potatoes and pulses, such as lentils. Starch-based foods are rich in insoluble fibre and contain valuable nutrients. They form an important part of a healthy diet.

VITAMINS

Vitamins are chemical substances naturally found in food groups and are very important to the health of the body. Maintaining the correct balance of vitamins in the body is important to our overall health and growth. The main vitamin groups are:

▪ *Vitamin A* – found in dairy products, fish oil and green vegetables

▪ *Vitamin B* – found in yeast, meat and cereals

▪ *Vitamin C* – found in fresh fruit, green vegetables and potatoes

▪ *Vitamin D* – found in dairy produce and oily fish

MINERALS

Minerals such as iron and salt are required by the body to help maintain health. However, too much of any particular mineral may result in bad health, and this is reflected in the Government's guidelines for daily salt intake. Important minerals include:

▪ *Calcium* – found in dairy products, fish and bread

▪ *Iron* – found in meat, green vegetables and fish

▪ *Salt* – found naturally in meat, fish and eggs

ENSURING THE QUALITY OF INGREDIENTS

Labels on packaged food now contain a lot of information about the product purchased and its ingredients, such as:

▪ The name of the commodity

▪ Its weight or volume content

▪ An accurate list of ingredients used to produce the commodity in order of weight

▪ A 'use by' date for perishable food or a 'best before' date

▪ Allergy information

▪ Storage recommendations

▪ The name and contact details of the manufacturer

▪ A production code number for traceability purposes

▪ Nutrition information

The variety of commodities available to the modern chef is considerable. A factor affecting the purchase of some produce is the distance that it has travelled. Due to cheaper and increasingly quicker transportation, importing foods from far-away countries is now common practice. However, the length of the passage and the method of storage during transit can greatly affect the quality of the end product.

The best and sometimes the cheapest way of purchasing is to follow the seasonality of foods and to buy as locally as possible. This will help to ensure that commodities are purchased at their freshest and in optimum condition.

Correct storage of produce is important for maintaining its nutritional value; vitamins in particular can be lost if produce is not stored properly. Fruits and vegetables should be stored in cool, dark places or in refrigerated units. They will perish quicker if stored at higher temperatures and direct light will lead to wastage of vital vitamins and minerals.

THE HEALTHY PREPARATION OF INGREDIENTS

This section looks at how to prepare ingredients or dishes to maximise their health value.

Fresh ingredients that are prepared too far in advance of use will begin to lose vital vitamins and minerals. Flavour and moisture will also be lost. It is therefore important that ingredients are only prepared when they are required.

The fibre and starch content in dishes can be increased by simply using wholemeal flour in place of white flour in pastry recipes and using wholemeal pasta and brown rice. The addition of pulses in dishes will also help.

The reduction of salt in dishes is an important issue for health. Avoid the use of preserved ingredients that contain high levels of salt and continually check the labels of commodities that are used to add flavour or enrich specific dishes, such as soy sauce, butter, mustard and Worcester sauce. These commodities can contain high levels of salt and therefore the chef will be able to lower the overall salt content of a dish by omitting or significantly reducing the amount of salt added as seasoning.

Reducing saturated fats in dishes is an important aspect in maintaining a balanced diet. The use of olive, sunflower or seed-based oils in place of butter and margarine is effective. If using oil to fry with, always ensure that the oil is at the correct temperature; oil that is not hot enough will be absorbed into the protein being fried. Always drain on absorbent kitchen paper to remove as much excess fat as possible.

Reducing sugar in dishes is vital for diabetics and good for maintaining a balanced diet. Sugar substitutes have been successfully introduced to help with this aspect of dietary control. Other ways to reduce the sugar content of dishes include:

- Using fresh fruit juices when possible
- Reducing the amount of sugar used in the production of desserts
- Using low-sugar preserves
- Using natural sugars such as honey to sweeten desserts

USING THE HEALTHY OPTION

Ensuring that portion sizes are set at an appealing level and not too large will guarantee that a guest will not over-indulge.

Dishes that are grilled, poached, boiled, steamed or baked will not incorporate the oils or fats used to assist other methods of cooking and are therefore immediately healthier.

Lean meats, fresh fish and pulses have low levels of saturated fats and can increase the intake of fibre. They are naturally well-flavoured products so to complement them with additional herbs or spices will not compromise their quality or flavour in the finished dish.

To preserve their nutritional value, foods generally need to be cooked quickly and in some cases, such as vegetables, cooked slightly underdone (al dente).

VIDEO CLIP
Using pulses and grains

Assessment of knowledge and understanding

You have now learned about the benefits of healthy eating and an array of commodities and cooking techniques.

To test your level of knowledge and understanding, answer the following short questions. These will help to prepare you for your summative (final) assessment.

Quality identifications

1 List two ways of choosing quality ingredients when writing a menu.
   i) _____
   ii) _____

2 Name three of the five food groups needed to make up a balanced diet, explaining the benefits of each.
   i) _____
   ii) _____
   iii) _____

Cooking methods

1 Identify two ways you can reduce the amount of saturated fat in products when cooking.
   i) _____
   ii) _____

Research task

Below is a classical menu made up of three courses to cater for a banquet event. Using knowledge gained from this chapter, rewrite the menu using healthier ingredients and options. Reflect on and take into consideration all aspects of healthy eating in your answer and the allergies or food issues that can be resolved.

MENU STRUCTURE	HEALTHIER MENU STRUCTURE	REASON FOR CHOICE AND ALLERGY AWARENESS
Starter Prawn cocktail	Starter	
Main course Roast beef, Yorkshire pudding, roast potatoes, glazed carrots and cauliflower cheese	Main course	
Dessert Chocolate mousse	Dessert	

Glossary of terms

00 flour Speciality flour used in pasta making as it has a high gluten content

à la (French) 'In the style of', such as: à la Française (the style of the French)

à la bourgeoisie (French) The style of the family (family style)

à la broche (French) Cooked on a skewer

à la carte (French) Items on the menu that are priced individually and cooked to order

à la Florentine (French) 'In the style of Florence'. Generally refers to dishes served on a bed of spinach and gratinated with sauce Mornay

à la Française In a French style

à la minute (French) Cook food at the last minute

à la Provençal (French) Dishes prepared with garlic and olive oil

à la Russe (French) In the Russian style

à point (French) Food cooked just to the perfect point of doneness: when cooking beef steaks, 'à point' means that a steak is cooked medium

abats (French) Offal

acetic acid A natural organic acid present in vinegar and citrus juices

acidulate To give a dish or liquid a slightly acidic, tart or piquant taste by adding some lemon juice, vinegar, fruit juice. Also, one can acidulate fresh cream by adding lemon juice to get sour cream.

acidulated water Water to which a mild acid, usually lemon juice or vinegar, has been added to prevent sliced fruits (especially apples and pears) and peeled or cut up vegetables (such as artichokes and salsify) from turning dark during preparation

additives, food Substances added to food to maintain or improve nutritional quality, food quality and freshness. Additives are strictly regulated. Manufacturers must prove the additives they add to food are safe

agar-agar An extract of seaweed from the Indian and Pacific Oceans. When dissolved in water, it will set into a jelly on cooling. Often used as a vegetarian substitute for gelatine

ageing A term used to describe the holding of meats at a temperature of 1–4°C for a period of time to break down the tough connective tissues through the action of enzymes, thus increasing the tenderness

agneau (French) Lamb

al dente Italian for 'to the tooth': refers to the firm but tender consistency of a perfectly cooked piece of pasta

albumen The protein portion of the egg white, comprising about 70 per cent of the egg. Albumen is also found in animal blood, milk, plants and seeds

almond paste A confectionery preparation consisting of ground almonds mixed with a sugar solution to form a paste. Sometimes referred to as marzipan it can be a raw paste or a cooked paste

aloyau de boeuf Sirloin of beef

amandine (French) Prepared with or garnished with almonds

ambient temperature Room temperature

amuse bouche This is a pre-starter or mouth pleaser given as an opening for the coming menu

Anglaise (French) English style

antioxidants Substances that inhibit the oxidation of meat, vegetables and fruit. They help prevent food from becoming rancid or discoloured

Apicius Marcus Gavius Apicius, born around 25 AD, is credited with writing cookery books and devising recipes. His book *Cuisine in Ten Books* was used as a reference work for several centuries

appareil A mixture of different ingredients to be used in a recipe

aromates A mixture of herbs and spices used to increase or bring out flavours in a dish

arrowroot The starch extracted from the stems of certain tropical plants. A fine, white powder, it is used to thicken sauces and soups and certain desserts

ascorbic acid Vitamin C

aspic Clear savoury jelly

au blanc (French) Meaning 'in white'. Foods, usually meats, that are not coloured during cooking

au bleu 1. A term for the cooking method for trout: 'Truite au bleu. The fish is taken from a fish tank, killed, gutted, trussed and slid into boiling court bouillon. The fish skin is not washed. This gives a characteristic silver blue finish to the finished dish. 2. A steak cooked very rare

au four Baked in the oven

au gratin (French) Food topped with a sauce and cheese or breadcrumbs, then baked or glazed under a salamander

au jus (French) Served with natural juices

au lait (French) With milk

au naturel (French) Food that is cooked simply, with little or no interference in its natural appearance or flavour

au vin blanc (French) Cooked with white wine

bacteria Micro-organisms that can cause food poisoning

baguette A French bread that is formed into a long, narrow cylindrical loaf. It usually has a crisp brown crust and light, chewy interior

bain marie (French) Water bath used to cook or store food

bake To cook in an enclosed oven

baking powder A raising agent consisting of bicarbonate of soda and cream of tartar. It is commonly used in the baking of cakes

ballotine A prepared meat, poultry, game or fish dish where the flesh is boned out, rolled and tied before cooking whole; sometimes stuffed with a farce or mousseline

bard To wrap meat, poultry or game with bacon or pork fat. The bard will render during cooking and impart succulence and flavour

barquette Boat-shaped pastry case or mould

baste To pour drippings, fat, or stock over food while cooking

Baumé The Baumé scale is a hydrometer scale developed by French pharmacist Antoine Baumé in 1768 to measure density of various liquids. Notated variously as degrees Baumé, B°, Be°, Bé°, Baumé

bavarois A cold dessert made from a cooked egg custard set with gelatine and lightened with whipped cream

beard The common name for the hair-like filaments that shellfish such as oysters and mussels use to attach themselves to rocks. They must be trimmed before the shellfish are prepared

beat To introduce air into a mixture using a utensil such as a wooden spoon, fork or whisk, in order to achieve a lighter texture

beurre blanc A sauce made with reduced alcohol or vinegar and shallots into which butter is whisked

beurre fondue Melted butter

beurre manié A raw mixture of flour and butter in equal quantities used as a thickening agent

beurre noir Black butter; can be served with skate wings and brains

beurre noisette Nut-brown butter served with fish meunière

bicarbonate of soda An alkaline powder: used to soften water for cooking vegetables and is one of the main ingredients of baking powder

blanch To place foods in boiling water or oil briefly, either to partially cook them or to aid in the removal of the skin (e.g. nuts, tomatoes). Blanching also removes the bitterness from citrus zests

blend To mix together ingredients, usually of different consistencies, to a smooth and even texture, utilising a utensil such as a wooden spoon or blender

blind bake To bake pastry without a filling. Metal weights or dried beans are usually used to keep the pastry from rising

blinis Pancakes made from buckwheat flour and yeast

boil To bring a liquid to boiling temperature and to maintain it throughout the cooking time

boil rapidly Food is submerged into boiling liquid over a high heat and the bubbling state is maintained throughout the required cooking period. This method is also used to reduce sauces by boiling off the liquid and reducing it to a concentrated state

bouchee A small puff pastry case with high sides and a hollow middle

bouillon 1. Any broth made by cooking vegetables, poultry, meat or fish in water. The strained liquid is the bouillon, which can form the base for soups and sauces. 2. A salt paste used as a stock

bouquet garni A faggot of herbs and aromatic vegetables, usually parsley, thyme, bay leaf, carrot, leek and celery, tied together and usually dangled into a stockpot on a string. These herb bundles give the stew, soup or stock an aromatic seasoning. The bouquet garni is removed before serving

Braise A cooking method where food (usually meat) is first browned in oil and then cooked slowly in a liquid (wine, stock or water)

bresoala Beef cured in a wine-rich brine. It is then air dried and sliced very thinly for service

Brillat-Savarin Jean-Anthelme (1755–1826): French gastronome and author of the famous book *Physiologie du Goût*

brine A strong solution of water and salt used for pickling or preserving foods

Brix The Brix scale was originally developed by Adolph Brix. Degrees Brix (symbol °Bx) is a measurement of the mass ratio of dissolved sugar to water in a liquid. It is measured with a saccharometer, which shows the density of a liquid. It largely replaced the Baumé scale in the early 1960s

broil The American term for browning under the grill

brunoise 1 mm dice

buffet A buffet is a meal where guests serve themselves from a variety of dishes set out on a table or sideboard

butterfly To cut food (usually meat or seafood) leaving

one edge joined and then open it out like the wings of a butterfly

buttermilk Milk product that is left after the fat is removed from milk to make butter

calorie Unit of energy; 1 calorie = 3.968 btu = 4.1868 joules. The heat required to raise the temperature of 1g of water by 1°C

canapé A base of bread, pastry or porcelain onto which savoury food is placed as a pre-dinner snack or as a course at the end of a meal prior to dessert

caper The flower bud of a shrub that is native to eastern Asia and is widespread in hot regions of the world. Capers are pickled in vinegar or preserved in brine

caramelise To allow the surface sugars of food to caramelise, giving a characteristic colour and aroma

carbohydrate There are three major groups of carbohydrates which are found in fresh fruits, vegetables and cereals: sugars (e.g. sucrose, fructose, glucose), starches and cellulose

Carême Marie-Antoine (1784–1833): 'The king of chefs and chef of kings.' Commenced his career as a pastry chef and was a personal chef to Tallyrand, the future King George IV and Tsar Alexander I. Responsible for many ground-breaking changes in the preparation and presentation of food and classical cuisine. Author of many books, including *L'Art de la Cuisine*

Caroline A savoury mini éclair that can be served hot or cold with a filling on buffets

carpaccio Originally, paper thin slices of raw beef with a creamy sauce, invented at Harry's Bar in Venice. In recent years, the term has come to describe very thinly sliced vegetables, raw or smoked meats and fish

carte du jour Menu of the day

carving Slicing or cutting items, usually for customers or in front of customers

casserole To cook in a covered dish in the oven in liquid such as stock or wine

cassoulet A classic French dish from the Languedoc region consisting of white beans and various meats (such as sausages, pork and preserved duck or goose)

caul Also known as crepinette (lamb) or crepin (pork), it is a thin, fatty membrane that lines the stomach cavity of pigs or sheep. It resembles a lacy net and is used to wrap and protect foods such as pâtés, ballotines etc. The fatty membrane melts during cooking. It should be soaked in slightly salted water before use

chapelure Dried fresh breadcrumbs

charcuterie (French) cured or smoked meat items

chaud (French) Hot

chef (French) A culinary expert. The chief of the kitchen

chef de garde manger (French) The person in charge of the cold meat department

chef de partie (French) 'Chief of the section', a chef who leads a team of assistants in a section

chemiser To line or coat a mould with a substance (either sweet or savoury)

chiffonade (French) 'Made from rags'. A small chopped pile of thin strips of an ingredient, usually raw but sometimes sautéed

chine Removal of the backbone on a cut of meat such as a rack of pork

chinois A metal conical strainer used for straining

clamart Any dish that contains peas or pea purée

clarified butter Clarified by bringing to the boil until it foams and then skimming the solids from the top or straining through muslin before use

clarify To clear a cloudy liquid by removing the sediment

clouté An onion studded with cloves and bay leaf

coagulate To solidify protein with heat

coat To cover with a thin film of liquid, usually a sauce

coat the spoon When a substance is rendered thin/ thick enough so that when a wooden or metal spoon is inserted into it and taken out, the substance leaves a thin film 'coating the spoon'

cocotte A fireproof dish usually made from porcelain

coddling Cooking just below the boiling point, for example coddled eggs

collagen White connective tissue that gelatinises with long slow cookery

collop Small thin slices of meat, poultry or fish, but mainly refers to slices across the tail of lobster

commis chef de partie (French) A qualified chef who is an assistant to a chef de partie

compôte Stewed fruit

compound salad A salad with more than one main ingredient

concassé Coarsely chopped, e.g. tomato concassé

concassé a cuit A cooked small dice of peeled tomatoes

confit A method of preserving meat (usually goose, duck or pork) whereby it is lightly cured and slowly cooked in its own fat. The cooked meat is then packed into a crockpot and covered with its cooking fat, which acts as a seal and preservative. Confit can be stored in a refrigerator for up to 6 months.

consommé Clear soup

coquille (French) Shell

cordon A dish that is surrounded by a thin line of sauce

Cordon Bleu (French) 'Blue ribbon'. A term used to describe high quality household cookery

correct To adjust the seasoning and consistency of a soup or sauce

coulis Fine purée of fruit

coupe A rounded dish of varying size. Often used classically for presenting an ice cream based dessert with accompaniments such as fruit, salads and biscuits

court bouillon A cooking liquor made by cooking mirepoix in water for about 30 minutes then adding wine, lemon juice or vinegar. The broth is allowed to cool before the vegetables are removed

couverture A type of chocolate used for the preparation of cakes, confectionery and a variety of desserts; containing at least 35 per cent cocoa butter and a maximum of 50 per cent sugar

cream The process where sugar and softened butter are beaten together with a wooden spoon until the mixture
is light, pale and well blended. This process may also be carried out with a hand-held mixer or in a food processor

Crecy Any dish that contains carrots

crêpe (French) Pancake

crimp To seal the edges or two layers of dough using the fingertips or a fork

croquembouche A decorative cone-shaped presentation of choux buns glazed with caramel, usually placed on a base of nougatine and decorated with pulled sugar ribbons and flowers

cross-contamination The transfer of pathogens from contaminated food to uncontaminated food

croute A bread or pastry base that is used to hold sweet or savoury items

croûtons Shaped bread that is fried or toasted to accompany soups, entrées or as a base for canapés

crudites Raw vegetables, served with a dip

curdle When a liquid or food, such as eggs, divides into liquid and solids, usually due to the application of excess heat or the addition of an acid such as lemon juice

curing The preservation of food items, using acidic liquids, salt or marinating

cut in To incorporate fat into a dry ingredient, such as flour, by using a knife and making cutting movements in order to break the fat down

cutlet A cut of lamb or veal from the loin with the rib bone attached

dariole small mould used to cook individual portions of food, e.g. summer pudding

darne A cut of round fish on the bone

daube A slow-cooked stew, usually of beef in stock with vegetables and herbs. Traditionally cooked in a sealed daubiere

debone To remove bones from meat, fish or poultry

deep fry The process of cooking food by immersion in hot fat or oil in a deep pan or electric fryer to give a crisp, golden coating

deglaze To add liquid such as wine, stock, or water to the bottom of a pan to dissolve the caramelised drippings so that they may be added to a sauce, for added flavour

degrease Skim the fat from food, e.g. stock

demi glace A thick, intensely flavoured, glossy brown sauce that is served with meat

desalting The removal of salt from foods. Food is soaked in cold water or washed under running water to dissolve the salt. Some foods such as salt cod require long, overnight soaking

détrempe A mixture of flour and water for making a dough or a puff paste

diced Cut into cubes

disgorge To soak meat, poultry, game, offal in cold water to remove impurities

dock To prick or spike a raw pastry base using a metal pastry tool such as a fork or a specialised pastry docker

doria Food cooked with or garnished with cucumbers

dorure Glazing with an egg mixture on raw pastries and dough before baking to produce an attractive coloured finish

dredging To coat with dry ingredients, such as flour or breadcrumbs

drizzle To drip a liquid substance, such as a sauce or dressing, over food

dry butter European-style butter, with a fat content of 82 per cent or above, available in specialty pastry shops. It is used widely in the production of puff pastry and confectionery because it has reduced moisture content

drying off The removal of excess moisture from foods during cooking. Not to be confused with drying or reducing. An example of drying off is when potatoes are placed over a low heat after having been drained in order to dry them off before mashing

durian an oval fruit weighing up to 5kg. The flesh is cream coloured and textured and has a distinctive putrefying odour. It is found in Southeast Asia

dusting To sprinkle with sugar or flour.

duxelle Minced mushrooms and shallots cooked until dry

Ecossaise (French) Scottish

eggwash Beaten egg used to coat food as a glaze or as a binding agent

elastin Yellow connective tissue that does not break down during cooking

emincé (French) Cut fine, or sliced thinly

emulsify The blending of two liquids that would not naturally combine into each other without agitation. The classic examples are oil and water, French dressing and mayonnaise

en croute Cooked in pastry, e.g. beef Wellington

en papillote (French) Cooked in a folded greaseproof bag

enrober To completely cover a food item with a liquid

entrecôte A steak cut from the boned sirloin

entrée (French) A main course of meat or poultry that is not baked or roasted

entremet The sweet course. An entremet is usually a dessert of some distinction and can be presented with a showpiece (usually made from sugar or chocolate). Can be hot but are usually cold or iced and in the form of a layered gateau which is glazed to conceal its contents

escalope (French) A thinly sliced, boneless, round cut of meat that is batted until very thin

espagnole Basic brown sauce

étuvée French term to describe the slow stewing of a main ingredient (usually vegetable based)

farce (French) Forcemeat or stuffing

farci Stuffed

feuilletage Puff pastry

flake To separate segments naturally, e.g. cooked fish into slivers

flambé Ignite alcohol on a dish, e.g. crêpe Suzette or Christmas pudding

fleurons Crescent-shaped puff pastry used to garnish fish dishes

flute/fluting Used in pastry or biscuit making as a decoration. Pies and tarts are fluted around the edge by pinching the pastry between the forefinger and thumb to create v-shaped grooves

fold in To gently combine lighter mixtures with heavier ones usually using a metal spoon or spatula in a cutting or slicing 'J' movement whilst slightly lifting the utensil

forcemeat Ground meat or meats mixed with seasonings, used for stuffing

frangipane A pastry cream used in the preparation of various desserts, cakes and sweets. It is an almond based cream that was derived from the Italian Marquis Muzio Frangipani, who invented a perfume for scenting gloves based on bitter almonds. This inspired pastry chefs of the time to make an almond-flavoured cream, which was named 'frangipane'

freezer burn Food that is left uncovered in the freezer desiccates and becomes unusable

friand A small puff pastry case filled with sausage meat, minced meat, ham or cheese, baked in the oven and served as an hors d'oeuvre

friandise (French) A small delicacy, e.g. petit fours or small sweets

fricassée A white stew where the meat or poultry is cooked in the sauce

fritture Deep fat fryer

froid (French) Cold

fromage (French) Cheese

fume (French) Smoked

fumet A liquid obtained by reducing a stock or cooking liquid that can be added to a sauce to enhance the flavour

galantine A dish made from poultry, game, pork, veal or rabbit usually incorporating stuffings. The flesh is boned out and the whole meat (with the skin intact) is rolled and pressed into a symmetrical or sometimes a cylindrical shape. Galantines can also be made using fish

galette A flat round cake of variable size, can be sweet or savoury based

game Name given to wild feathered and furred animals hunted in certain seasons

ganache A flavoured chocolate-based cream used to decorate desserts, fill cakes and make petit fours

garnish To decorate. Also refers to food used as decoration

gastrique A reduced mixture of vinegar and sugar used in the preparation of sauces and dishes with a high degree of acidity. For example, tomato sauce

gastronomy The art of good eating and appreciation of fine food and drink

gelatine A colourless substance extracted from the bones and cartilage of animals. Supplied in powder or leaf form, it will dissolve into warm liquids and set the liquid when cooled. Widely used for making desserts

gingerbread A type of cake. British gingerbread is made using ginger and treacle and the French version, pain d'épiceuses, contains honey and a variety of spices

glacé Crystallised fruits in a syrup or liqueur

glaze To give a food a shiny appearance by coating it with a sauce or similar substance, such as aspic, sweet glazes or boiled apricot jam

glucose A clear simple sugar made by heating starch with an acid. Used in the production of jam and syrups, and also extensively used by the pastry chef in sugar work

goujons Small strips cut from a fillet of flat fish, often panéd or dipped in batter and then deep fried

gourmet (French) Food connoisseur

grate To reduce a food to very small particles by rubbing it against a sharp, rough surface, usually a grater or zester

grease To cover the inside surface of a dish or pan with a layer of fat, such as butter, margarine or oil, using a brush or kitchen paper

grill 1. To cook foods with radiated heat. 2. Cooking equipment that radiates heat from below, e.g. barbecue

hacher To cut very finely (often with a mincing machine).

hanging Hanging meat from a hook at a controlled temperature to facilitate ageing (see *ageing*)

hors d'oeuvres Small dishes served as the first course of the meal

hummus A Greek dish made from cooked chickpeas crushed with sesame oil; usually accompanies hors d'oeuvres

husk The tough outer casing of wheat, barley and rye. The French expression of *farine de gru* is used for wholemeal flour

icing A preparation of icing sugar used to coat cakes and confectionery

infusion The process of steeping an aromatic substance in a cool or warm liquid until the liquid has absorbed the flavour

iron An essential mineral that is found in food sources such as liver, red meat, spinach and egg yolks

jardiniere Batons of vegetables

jelly A cold dessert made of fruit juice, wine or liqueur to which sugar and gelatine have been added

julienne (French) A cut of meat, poultry or vegetables, which has the same dimensions as a match

jus (French) 'Juice', usually refers to the natural juice from meat

jus lie (French) Thickened gravy

knead A process where dough is made smoother, softer and more elastic by applying gentle pressing and stretching actions to it. One end of the dough is secured by the heel of one hand and stretched away then pulled back over the top. In bread making, two hands are used

knocking back To release pockets of gas in fermented dough before shaping and proving

lait (French) Milk

larding Larding is fat cut into strips and inserted into meat using a special needle. Used to add moisture to meat

lardons Bacon that is cut into small batons

levain (French) A dough that is used to make bread rise

legumes (French) Dried beans, peas, lentils etc.

liaison A binding agent made up of egg yolks and cream, used for enriching soups and sauces

Lyonnaise Refers to dishes accompanied by sautéed onions

macédoine A neat dice of mainly vegetables which measure 1/2cm square

macerate To soak a fruit in a liqueur or wine. This softens the fruit while releasing its juices and the fruit absorbs the macerating liquid's flavours

madeleine A small cake shaped like a rounded shell

marinade A mixture of wet and/or dry ingredients used to flavour or tenderise food prior to cooking

marinate To let food stand in a marinade (such as a liquid, dry cure or paste) before cooking. Some marinades add flavour, while those that contain acids or enzymes help to tenderise, e.g. made with fruits such as lemon, mangos papaya or kiwi fruits, or with wine, vinegar or yoghurt

marquise A chocolate dessert, a type of rich mousse that can be served chilled or iced

Melba toast Thin triangular pieces of crisp toast, classically served with pâté

menthe (French) Mint

minced Ground or chopped, usually refers to meat, fish or poultry

mirepoix A mixture of diced aromatic vegetables, e.g. carrots, onions, celery and leek

mise en place Basic preparation prior to cooking

miso A Japanese condiment of fermented soya

monosodium glutamate A type of salt used as a flavour enhancer

monte au beurre Addition of butter to create an emulsion of cooking liquor and butter

mousse A sweet or savoury preparation that has a very light consistency

nage An aromatic court bouillon in which shellfish are cooked. Dishes prepared in this way are often called 'à la nage'

nape To cover an item with either a hot or cold sauce

navarin A brown stew of mutton or lamb

noir (French) Black

noisette A cut from a boned loin of lamb

nori An edible scented seaweed used in Japanese cookery. Used as a powder, or pressed and dried for wrapping around sushi

nouilles (French) Noodles

nutrients The essential parts of food that are vital to health

oenology The study of wines

oeuf (French) Egg

offal The edible internal organs of an animal

open sandwich A sandwich that has a base only

organic farming A farming method which aims to maintain natural farming methods of growing crops or maintaining livestock without the use of chemicals

palatable Pleasant to the taste and edible

panache A selection of vegetables

panada A paste of various bases, either bread, flour or potato, used to thicken or bind products

pané à la Francaise Passed through seasoned milk and seasoned flour. Used as a coating for fried foods

pané à la Alglaise A coating of flour, eggwash and breadcrumbs

papillote (French) Cooked in foil or parchment paper to seal in flavour, then served and cut open at the table

parboil To cook partially by boiling for a short period of time

parfait (French) 'Perfect', a smooth pâté or iced dessert which can be sliced leaving an even and consistent appearance

pass Push liquids or solids through a sieve

pate (French) 'Paste'. 1. Pâté is either a smooth or coarse product made from meat, poultry, fish, vegetable, offal or game that has been blended and cooked with cream, butter and eggs. 2. Pate is different base pastry products: sweet, short, lining, puff, choux

pathogen Micro-organism that can cause food poisoning

pâtisserie Sweet or savoury pastries and cakes, generally baked in the oven

paupiette Rolled and/or stuffed fillet of flat fish

pavé A square or diamond-shaped piece of meat, poultry or fish, but can also be referred to pastry or cakes

paysanne Vegetables cut into thin slices

pectin A natural gelling agent found in plants and is abundant in certain fruits, such as apples, quinces, redcurrants and lemons. Pectin is an important ingredient when making jams and jellies

pesto Rustic Italian dressing made with basil, garlic, olive oil and pine nuts

petit (French) Small.

petit four A small biscuit, cake or item of confectionery, usually served after dinner with the coffee

petit pois (French) Small peas

pipe To shape or decorate food using a forcing bag or utensil fitted with a plain or decorated nozzle

piquante A dish or sauce that is sharp to the taste

pluche Small tips of salad leaves or herbs used as a garnish

poach To cook food in hot liquid over a gentle heat with the liquid slightly below boiling point

pressing To apply pressure to items to help shape or remove excess moisture, e.g. terrines to help them keep an even layering or sweatbreads to remove excess liquid

prove To allow yeast dough to rise

purée A smooth paste of a particular ingredient or a soup that is passed through a sieve

quenelle A poached dumpling, mousseline or cream presented in an oval shape. Classically made of veal or chicken

ragout A stew of meat or vegetables

ramekin Individual or small ceramic round baking dish.

rasher Thin slice of bacon

rechauffer Reheat food for service

reduce To concentrate the flavour of a liquid by boiling away the water content

refresh To plunge food into, or run under, cold or iced water after blanching to prevent further cooking.

roast To cook food in an oven or on a spit over a fire with the aid of fat

roux Fat and flour mixture used to thicken sauces and soups; can be cooked to white, blond and brown colours

rubbing in The incorporation of fat into flour. Butter is softened and cubed then gently rubbed into the flour between the thumb and forefinger, lifting the mixing at the same time. When the fat is fully incorporated the mixture resembles fine breadcrumbs

salad tiède A salad with the addition of warm or hot ingredients

salamander A small contact grill and poker used to brown or gratin foods, or a term to describe an overhead grill

salami An Italian charcuterie product made of ground pork or beef

sauté Cook quickly in shallow fat

savouries A small after-meal dish or item as an alternative to a dessert or cheese

savoury sorbet A flavoured water ice using savoury ingredients such as tomatoes

scald To heat a liquid, usually milk, until it is almost boiling, at which point very small bubbles begin to form around the edge of the pan

score To make shallow incisions with a small knife

seal To caramelise the outer surface of meat

sear To brown the surface of food in fat over a high heat before finishing cooking by another method, in order to add flavour

season to taste Usually refers to adding extra salt and pepper

sec (French) Dry

shallow fry To cook in oil or fat that covers the base of a shallow pan

shred To tear or cut food into thin strips

sift To pass a dry ingredient, such as flour, through a sieve to ensure it is lump free

simmer To maintain the temperature of a liquid at just below boiling

simple salad A salad with only one main ingredient, e.g. tomato salad

skim To remove impurities from the surface of a liquid, such as stock, during or after cooking

skin To remove the skin from meat, fish, poultry, fruit, nuts and vegetables

slice To cut food, such as bread, meat, fish or vegetables, into flat pieces of varying thickness

smoking Hot or cold method of curing and flavouring food using wood, herbs or spices

soak To immerse in a liquid to rehydrate or moisten a product

sorbet A smooth frozen ice made with flavoured liquid-based ingredients, such as fruit juices

sous chef (French) 'Under chief', second to the head chef

steam To cook food in steam, over rapidly boiling water or other liquid. The food is usually suspended above such liquid by means of a trivet or steaming basket, although in the case of puddings the basin actually sits in water

steep To soak food in a liquid such as alcohol or syrup until saturated.

stir fry To fry small pieces of food quickly in a large frying pan or wok, over a high heat, using very little fat and constantly moving the food around the pan throughout cooking, keeping it in contact with the hot wok

stock A cooked, flavoured liquid that is used as a cooking liquor or base for a sauce

sweat To cook gently in a little fat without colour

table d'hôte A set menu at a set price

terrine A dish used to cook and present pâté

thumbing up Producing an edge all the way around the top of a flan by pinching in with the thumb and forefinger

timbale A small high-sided mould

tronçon A cut of flat fish on the bone

truss To tie up meat or poultry with string before cooking

vegan Someone who will not eat any animal product

vegetarian Someone who will not eat meat or fish but will eat animal products such as milk, eggs and cheese

velouté (French) A sauce made with stock and a blond roux, finished with a liaison of cream and yolks

viande (French) Meat

whip To beat an item, such as cream or egg whites, to incorporate air

whisk To beat air into a mixture until soft and aerated

zester A hand-held tool with small, sharp-edged holes at the end of it, which cuts orange, lemon or grapefruit peel into fine shreds

Recipe Index

General Index